JAMES W. MARKHAM

A TEXAN by birth, James W. Markham received his B.J. and M.A. from the University of Texas. His journalism background includes reporting for both the Fort Worth *Press* and the Dallas *Journal* and advising the Texas Student Publications, University of Texas. He has taught journalism at Baylor University, the University of Missouri where he received his Ph.D., and Pennsylvania State University. In 1962 he joined the School of Journalism, University of Iowa, where he is currently head and professor in the Department of International Communication.

The author of several books, monographs, and professional and technical articles, Markham is a past recipient of the National Kappa Tau Alpha Award for the most distinguished research in the field of Journalism and Mass Communications.

He has served as chairman of both the International Liaison Committee and the International Communications Committee of the American Association for Education in Journalism. He organized the new International Communications Division of that organization and has served as its vice head.

Markham is national secretary of Kappa Tau Alpha, honorary scholarship society in journalism and mass communications, and editor of *ICB: International Communications Bulletin*.

In addition, he has lectured at the 1962 Annual Seminar, Inter-American Federation of Working Newspapermen's Organizations, Panama City, Panama, and is a member of the International Press Institute, and the Advisory Committee of the Center for International Studies, University of Iowa.

With VOICES OF THE RED GIANTS, Markham won the 1965 award by the Iowa State University Press for the most outstanding manuscript by an Iowa author.

VOICES OF THE

RED GIANTS

The Iowa State University Press, Ames, Iowa, U.S.A.

VOICES OF THE RED GIANTS

Communications in Russia and China

JAMES W. MARKHAM

JAMES WALTER MARKHAM, Professor and Head of International Communication Division of the School of Journalism, University of Iowa, has achieved success as a reporter, a teacher of journalism, and an author. His early experience in reporting began with student publications at the University of Texas and expanded with employment on the Fort Worth *Press* and the Dallas *Journal.* Professor Markham earned his B.J. and M.A. degrees at the University of Texas and his Ph.D. degree at the University of Missouri. Extensive travel in Europe and Central America has added to his background knowledge of international affairs.

Besides this book, he is author of *Bovard of the Post-Dispatch,* a number of monographs, and more than fifty professional and technical articles.

Before joining the School of Journalism at the University of Iowa, Professor Markham taught at Baylor University, the University of Missouri, and Pennsylvania State University. He is a member of the International Press Institute, the Advisory Committee of the Center for International Studies at the University of Iowa, and is active in other boards and committees related to the study of mass communications. He served as lecturer at the 1962 Annual Seminar, Inter-American Federation of Working Newspapermen's Organization at Panama City, Panama. Among his many citations and awards is the Kappa Tau Alpha National Award for most distinguished research in the field of journalism and mass communications.

Composed and printed by
The Iowa State University Press

FIRST EDITION, 1967
Revised Second Printing, 1970

International Standard Book Number: 0–8138–1085–X

Library of Congress Catalog Card Number: 67–12133

TO JAMES DAVID and SARA HOPE MARKHAM

FOREWORD

THESE CHAPTERS REPRESENT a persistent attempt over time to investigate Communist mass communication systems as exemplified by the Russian Soviet and Communist Chinese models. The primary objectives have been: (1) To probe deeply into how mass communications systems behave and function in the two largest Communist countries. (2) To investigate critically the world's most gigantic experiments in the use of public communications as instruments of political manipulation and social change. (3) To write an account that makes sense to the Western mind, describing analytically and systematically how such ideas of State communications were conceived, the nature of the societies that gave them birth and nourished them, and how they grow and change. (4) Finally, to evaluate critically by their own as well as Western standards the social function, behavior, and performance of the mass media in both countries as compared with each other, and in some degree, as compared with Western systems.

The totalitarian approach to formal mass communications systems resembles an approach that developed in Western Europe four centuries ago but soon died out as a dominant communications model. This is to say that exclusive State ownership, operation, and control of mass communications prevailed in Europe for a time soon after the rediscovery of printing in the West. The crown assisted by the church devised ways to monopolize the first printing presses and to guide the nature of their products. The early European presses, though owned or licensed by the political authority, differed from their twentieth-century Communist successors in that they were used more for censorship than for propaganda and persuasion. Imperial China's gazette press system during its almost two thousand years of activity was never conceived of as a vehicle for persuasion or even for mass enlightenment, being intended for the information of the court and the provincial princes. In Europe, as private ownership became the practice and as controls grew more difficult to enforce, royal monopolies over the printed work weakened. Libertarian theory of the seventeenth and eighteenth centuries ended State monopolies and fostered an independent, privately owned publishing system as "the fourth estate," a critic of government and arbiter between government and the governed. In the Russian part of Europe, however, such ideas were powerfully resisted by an absolutist monarchy which not only strengthened its controls over private printing but also developed an extensive, though not exclusive, state owned mass communication system. Such was tsarist policy practiced well into the first decade of the twentieth century. Something quite close to the Communist concept of the social role of mass communications was achieved in Germany in the prewar years after the opposition press was bought or adequately bludgeoned into submission by the Nazi regime. The monopolistic use of mass communications by the central political authority for the purposes of maintaining the single party in control of persuasion and agitation—all reinforced by informal person-to-person communication—was a new concept, though fashioned from elements of the past.

This new concept of mass communications sprang from a small group of Russian Marxists less than 70 years ago. Today almost one-third of the earth's peoples inhabiting nearly one-fifth of the globe's land surface live under communist systems and are exposed to Communist communications. Compared with absolutist communication systems known before, Communist systems appear to be the most extreme, the most grimly methodical, the most determined of purpose, and the most virulent. When compared with Western libertarian communications, Communist communications theory and practice appear to be so diametrically different that scholars tend to place them at opposite ends of an imaginary continuum drawn to illustrate the spectrum of world mass communication systems. Investigation of these differences leads to the conclusion that there is much in the Communist dogma, therefore, that is alien to Western thinking, and Westerners find little in their own experience to enable them to identify with it.

At the risk of appearing digressive in the introductory discussions for each country, the approach here may be described as "Gestaltian." That is, it has attempted to examine mass communications systems in their social setting. The "systems" approach to the study of social or political institutions within a given country at the national level has its origins in the psychological field theories of Kurt Lewin, Talcott Parsons, Harold Lasswell, and others who have built theory upon the conclusion of these and other writers. In these theories no specific stimulus is considered the "cause" of a certain event; rather all stimuli and all responses within the field are considered interactive and interdependent. Likewise no single factor or variable is considered to "trigger" or cause the rise, development, and present characteristics of a given set of institutions serving a given society, but rather all factors are considered interactive and interdependent. Wilbur Schramm writes in *Communications and Political Development* (Princeton University Press, 1964, pp. 30–31):

> When we refer to a system, we mean a boundary-maintaining set of interdependent particles. . . . By interdependent we mean a relationship of parts in which anything happening to one component of a system affects, no matter how slightly, the balance and relationship of the whole system. By boundary-maintaining we mean a state in which the components are so related that it is possible to tell where the system ends and its environment begins.

Thus there can be no single or simple explanation of why mass communication systems, both formal and informal, develop certain structural characteristics, perform certain social functions, and behave in a certain way. Rather, the mass communication system is a product of a society in which there is a reciprocal influence in operation among all the interacting social forces including the other systems of institutions that serve the society. As the mass communication system is acted upon by the various other institutional systems in a country, so it acts upon these other systems. How well a mass communications system serves its society is determined, then, not only by the nature of the system's capability but also by a whole host of other systems and facets of the society that both limit and expand that capability.

The purpose has been to focus on formal systems in each country and to examine mass communications as enormous yet sensitive, nationwide nerve networks subject always to push-button control from the central authority, yet not always responsive (at least in the direction expected) to the guiding strings. No mass communication system exists in a cultural vacuum. Functioning close to the heartbeat of society, it develops in relation to the other institutions of the society; it shapes and is shaped by the cultural heritage, the values, the ideals, the mind and the experience of a people bound together by a common tie of national existence and survival as a political entity. For this reason the method has been to examine the mass media systems as integral parts of their social systems and to consider them as products of their heritage. A special effort has been made to study values and value-systems, change and the process of change, but always with an understanding of values and change within the context of the past and in relation to the present social forces that impel them and determine their nature. Within this kind of historical and humanistic perspective, emphasis has been placed upon the evolution of the present-day communication media systems. Since communication is said to be the key ingredient in the political, economic, and social processes of growth and change that mark the developmental stages of mature industrial nations, this kind of approach should provide meaningful links to an understanding of the two countries as a whole.

After examining the evidence, an attempt has been made to interpret its meaning. This has usually taken the form of a critical evaluation of mass media performance and effect, not so much in terms of methodically stated Communist purposes and goals, but more in terms of responsible service in the cause of real mass enlightenment. People the world over, regardless of ideological commitments, look to their mass media for a reasonably accurate and adequate surveillance of their environment, for the stuff that makes for psychic mobility and contributes to the development of empathy. In substance, they expect of their media a knowledge of what is going on in the world, knowledge of what men are doing and thinking. They expect the media to transmit the cultural heritage to new generations. These functions provide the basic public knowledge necessary for the generation of public opinion. Mass communication systems are essentially professional, intellectual institutions, and even though politically manipulated, they must be judged not always in terms of the goals their manipulators set for them, but in terms of what their public and their society expect of them. Within the limitations, both implicit and explicit, which impede a project of this nature, these have been the guiding criteria of comparison and criticism.

Among the most obvious limitations inherent in virtually any study of closed societies is the relative unavailability of reliable source material. Chief primary sources have been the media themselves. Important secondary sources have been consulted; particularly studies by American scholars of Russia and the Soviet Union and of China, both ancient and modern. Especially helpful has been the research of institutes and area studies devoted to Chinese and Soviet scholarship.

Since the term "communication" has many meanings and may hold different connotations for different individuals, the reader may find helpful the following operational definitions of the concepts associated with the word as used in this book. The noun "communication" refers to the process of using language and symbols to transmit and receive meaning. By process is meant the step-by-step series of acts or events involved in conveying meaning from one person to another or others, as described by the various conceptual and theoretical models. Fundamentally the process of communication requires a sender, a message, and a receiver. The noun "communication" or its plural "communications" has also been employed here to refer to the message, the content, or the substance of what the media say. When referring to the process and not the message, the plural is not used.

The plural, "mass communications," refers to the mass media as organized systems of institutions, channels, or voices. It is an "umbrella" term convenient for encompassing the periodical print media such as newspapers, magazines, and topical books; film, motion pictures, and photography; and the new electronic media of radio and television. In this sense the word has been extended beyond its earlier usage to mean transport, highways, railways, bridges, telephone and telegraph lines. Under this umbrella term are now gathered the publishing, advertising, public relations, and broadcasting institutions; industries; equipment; apparatus; professional personnel and skills, etc., that function as a system within a given country. This conception constitutes the formal mass media system. The substantive "communications" may also refer to an informal, nonmediated, or interpersonal system that operates within a country, but when this kind of system is implied, the term is usually qualified by such adjectives as "informal," or "face-to-face." Perhaps because it sounds better, the *s* is dropped when communications is used as an adjective as in the phrase "mass communication media."

Space has precluded consideration of films as a part of mass communication systems. Although films and the screen are of unquestioned importance in the total mass communication scene, I have chosen here to concentrate on press and broadcasting because, for serving the uses of propaganda and agitation, they are the most immediate, sensitive, and versatile of all media. They are also the most commonly used media on a regular day-to-day basis by most people around the world, and the focus has been upon such raw materials of public opinion as news and information, discussion, ideas, and criticism, rather than upon drama.

The author is grateful to the publishers, publications, and authors listed below for kindly granting permission to reprint materials for which they hold the copyright. Copyrighted sources used in the book are identified by title and author in both footnotes and bibliography. Indebtedness is acknowledged to the following: George Allen and Unwin Ltd. (London); American Council of Learned Societies; American Marketing Association, publishers of the *Journal of Marketing;* Association for Education in Journalism, publishers of the *Journalism Quarterly;* Association for Professional Broadcasting Education, publishers of the *Journal of Broadcasting;* Helmut G. Callis; Central State College (Ohio), publishers of the *Journal of Human Relations;* The Clarendon Press (Oxford); Columbia University Press; Coward McCann, Inc.; Robert W. Desmond; Doubleday and Co., Inc.; Editor & Publisher Co., publishers of *Editor & Publisher;* Encyclopaedia Britannica, Inc.; Richard D. Irwin, Inc.; Free Europe Committee, Inc., publishers of *Free Europe;* Harcourt, Brace and World, Inc.; Harper and Row, Publishers, Inc.; Harper's Magazine, Inc.; Harvard University Graduate School of Business Administration, publishers of *Harvard Business Review;* Harvard University Press; Harvill Press Ltd. (London); William Heinemann Ltd. (London); Holt, Rinehart and Winston, Inc.;

Hong Kong University Press; Houghton Mifflin Co.; HRAF Press; International Press Institute (Zurich); International Publishers, Inc.; Institute for the Study of the USSR, publishers of *Studies on the Soviet Union;* Joint Committee on Slavic Studies, publishers of *The Current Digest of the Soviet Press;* The Macmillan Co. and the Free Press of Glencoe; Massachusetts Institute of Technology; McGraw-Hill Book Co., Inc.; McGraw-Hill, Inc., publishers of *Business Week;* David McKay Co., Inc.; The Board of Trustees of Michigan State University; The New American Library; The New York Times Co. and the following authors of *Times* articles: A. Doak Barnett, Deming Brown, Sripati Chandra-Sekhar, David Chipp, Peggy Durdin, Tobia Frankel, Mark Frankland, Allen Kassof, Michael Lindsay, Marya Mannes, Philip E. Mosely, Harrison E. Salisbury, Marshall Shulman, and Marc Slonim; W. W. Norton and Co., Inc.; Oxford University Press; Parade Publications, Inc.; Pantheon Books, Inc.; S. G. Phillips, Inc.; Frederick A. Praeger, Inc.; Princeton University Press; Printers' Ink, Inc., publishers of *Printers' Ink;* Public Affairs Press; Random House, Inc., and Alfred A. Knopf, Inc.; Henry Regnery Company; Harrison E. Salisbury; Charles Scribner's Sons; the Society of Nieman Fellows, publishers of *Nieman Reports;* Speech Association of America, publishers of *Quarterly Journal of Speech;* Stanford University Press; Syracuse University Press; Thames & Hudson Ltd. (London); Time, Inc.; University of Chicago Press; University of Illinois Press; University of Michigan Law School; University of Minnesota Press; University of Oklahoma Press; University of Oklahoma Press, publishers of *Books Abroad;* United States Information Agency, publishers of *Problems of Communism;* D. Van Nostrand Co., Inc.; The Viking Press, Inc.; and Yale University Press.

A work of this kind cannot be accomplished without incurring many personal obligations. I should like to acknowledge the help students, colleagues, and friends have contributed to the substance of this book. I owe special debts of gratitude to Professor Frederick R. Matson, Associate Dean for Research, College of the Liberal Arts, The Pennsylvania State University, for his support during the early phase of the research; to Professor Leslie G. Moeller of the School of Journalism at the University of Iowa, who provided staunch material and moral support of many kinds during the final stages and whose useful criticisms helped improve the manuscript; and to my friend Theodore T. H. Chiao of the Leo Burnett Company, Inc., Chicago, for his criticisms and suggestions. I am glad to acknowledge the indispensable aid of librarians, graduate and research assistants, and others who remain anonymous here, but who helped locate materials, collect and analyze data, and translate texts in Russian and Chinese. Acknowledgement is also due colleagues at the University of Iowa for their counsel. Finally, I want to acknowledge my indebtedness to my wife Myrtle for her advice and forbearance.

Iowa City, Iowa
March 1967

JAMES W. MARKHAM

CONTENTS

★ RUSSIA AND THE SOVIET UNION

★★ CHINA: CONFUCIAN AND COMMUNIST

ILLUSTRATIONS

TABLES AND MAPS

1

RUSSIA AND THE SOVIET UNION

N
ESTONIAN S.S.R.
LATVIAN S.S.R.
LITHUANIAN S.S.R.
Tallin
Riga
Vilnius
Minsk
BELORUSSIAN S.S.R.
MOLDAVIAN S.S.R.
Kishinev
Kiev
UKRAINIAN S.S.R.
MOSCOW
Volga
URAL MTS.
RUSSIAN
Kastroma
Irtysh
AZOV
CAUCASUS MTS.
GEORGIAN S.S.R.
Tbilisi
Yerevan
ARMENIAN S.S.R.
AZERBAIJAN S.S.R.
Baku
CASPIAN SEA
KAZAKH S.S.R.
Gurev
ARAL SEA
Balkhash
UZBEK S.S.R.
TURKMEN S.S.R.
Ashkhabad
Nukus
Tashkent
Frunze
Alma-Ata
KIRGIZ S.S.R.
Andizhan
TADZHIK S.S.R.
Stalinabad

UNION OF SOVIET SOCIALIST REPUBLICS

AREA: 8,650,140 sq. mi.
POPULATION: 227,687,000. Largest city and capital: Moscow.
CLIMATE: Varies widely; almost half the nation's land mass is covered by frozen soil.
ALTITUDES: Stalin Peak, Tadzhik, 24,590 ft. (highest); Caspian Sea, —92 ft. (lowest).

1

RUSSIAN SOCIETY AND PRESS: THE CULTURAL SETTING

IMPERIAL RUSSIA survived until 1917. The leaders and architects of the modern Soviet state grew up under the tsars. Even today's leaders can remember what life was like in the last years of the old empire. Although the USSR of today is different from the society of imperial Russia, its cultural roots extend deeply into the past. To look at the present-day communications system of the Soviet Union without seeing tsarist Russia in the background would make no more sense than to look at the American press without examining the censorship and repression of the Colonial period, the writings of Thomas Jefferson, and the reasons for the Constitutional guarantees of press freedom. To comprehend the development of Soviet mass communications, to assess their role in shaping Soviet society, to explore the role of the social system in shaping the mass media, we must see them in the context of history and approach them with a knowledge of the many other forces that have shaped the society. The Soviet Union was built out of the territory, people, and social structure inherited from tsarist Russia. To understand its development enough to gain insight into the growth of one of its institutions—the mass media system—one must also understand, if only in broad outline, the complex of forces out of which it sprang.

THE LAND AND THE PEOPLE

The vast land mass which today is the Soviet Union, an area largely consolidated by the Russian tsars, is three times the size of continental United States. A Russian proverb helps us to understand something of its vastness: " . . . the world's largest country is 'not a country, but a world.' " This world stretches from near the North Pole, farther north than any point in Alaska, southward to Iran and Afghanistan, its southernmost tip lying just north of San Francisco in latitude. Its east-west distance at the widest point is more than 6,000 miles.[1] When it is night in Moscow, it is daytime of the next day in Vladivostok on the Pacific. The area covers 8.65 million square miles, or almost one-sixth of the world's land surface.[2] Pictures show ice-covered wastelands contrasted with palm-lined beaches, snow-capped mountains against plains, forests, and deserts.

Somewhat comparable to its varied geography, the peoples of the Soviet Union include 115 different nationalities[3] of many different ethnic origins. For this reason, Gunther noted that it is not a country but "a patchwork." The range of population makeup extends from White Russians, tall blond Slavs like the Poles, to olive-skinned, dark-haired Armenians, to slant-eyed Tartars, to primitive Samoyeds living on the Arctic barrens. The majority of the non-whites are Mongolians. There are very few Negroes. The country includes approximately 25 million persons of Islamic faith and more than two million Jews. Traces of a civilization similar to that of the Greeks or Aegeans have been found on the Southern Steppes. Citizens of the Roman Empire colonized Rumania and spilled over into the Ukraine. The largest group today are the Slavs—which make up about three-fourths of the entire population—who migrated into Russia from the Balkan area between the Dnieper and Vistula rivers. The Scandinavians drove down from the north. The Avars from central Asia occupied Russia in the sixth and seventh centuries. The last and perhaps greatest invasion came in the thirteenth century when the waves of Khubla Khan's multitudes poured over Russia and washed up on the shores of central Europe.

As the Mongolian tide receded it left its traces deposited in varying degrees upon the cultures of south central Russia.

Population Trends, Transportation, and Resources

The Soviet Union ranks third among world states in population, its total of 218 million in mid-1960[4] places it well above that of the United States, at about half of India's 433 million, but at less than one-third of China's 669 million. The amount of land per person in the Soviet Union, about 22 acres, is meaningless because much of it is either cold wastelands or deserts. Siberia has the coldest temperatures outside Antarctica. Moscow's climate is similar to that of Minneapolis, but no other country has such extremes of heat and cold. For various reasons, the principal ones being climate and the short growing season, a good deal of the land is unsuited to cultivation. A more meaningful measure is the amount of arable land per person, about one hectare (2.47 acres)[5] as compared with about 2.5 acres in the United States and about one-half acre per person in China. Only about 9 per cent of the land is cultivated, but this is still more land than any other nation has planted to crops. The most fertile region is the agricultural triangle in south central Russia known as the "black earth" belt. Food production has been a perennial problem from earliest times to the present. Because of the large areas that will not support human life in appreciable quantity, the population, as it tends to do elsewhere in the world, has concentrated in more fertile areas.

About three out of every four persons in the population live west of the Ural Mountains in the European sector. The population ratio of West to East in 1939 was 76 to 24. In 1959 this ratio had changed to 70 to 30.[6] Migration eastward in the postwar years is a trend comparable to migration westward in the United States. The largest and most populous Soviet Republic is the Russian Soviet Federated Republic, and its European segment is the economic, political, and cultural hub of the Soviet Union. This large republic, which includes Siberia, contains more than half of the entire population of the country. A nationality problem inherited from the tsars was the fact that the Russians constituted only about 43 per cent of the total population. Although Russians now number well over 50 per cent, the subject minorities are still a problem for the Soviet government.

Another significant migration trend in the Soviet Union is the rural-urban movement; this ratio in 1939 was 67 to 33; twenty years later it was 52 to 48. The transition from an essentially agrarian economy to a more balanced agricultural-industrial economy is just about complete.[7] The population is young and growing rapidly. The average life expectancy in 1959 was estimated at 64 for males and 72 for females.[8] The effects of World War II resulted in a relatively young population, hampered the growth rate, and caused a disproportionate number of males, which are outnumbered by some 20 million females. According to Soviet statistics, 68 per cent of the population is classified as workers. In 1928, peasants comprised a majority of the population, but today only 31 per cent of the population is classified in this category. Approximately 80 different languages are spoken among the various population subgroups, although the Russian language is understood throughout the country and study of the language is required in the schools.

Transportation routes from earliest times followed rivers and lakes. Before the revolution, one-third of all transportation was by waterways, including the canals. Railroads were built in the populous West between Moscow and Leningrad in the 1880s and the Trans-Siberian Railway was completed in the 1890s. The Soviet government has added miles of railroads—including another track for the famous Trans-Siberian, the longest railroad in the world—and thousands of miles of airlines. No figures have been available since 1939 to indicate airways growth, but in that year transport planes carried 307,000 passengers, 1,500 tons of mail, and 39,654 tons of cargo over 137,000 miles of air route. Perhaps because of the absence of rock in much of the soil, highways have not been developed as much as other means of transportation. Distribution as well as production of goods is the joint responsibility of the state and the cooperative agencies.

In natural resources the Soviet Union ranks as one of the world's richest countries, despite the presence of huge areas of desert and frozen tundra. Timber, furs, and minerals are products of the arctic regions. Other parts of the country produce almost everything needed for modern industry excepting natural rubber, tin, and a few tropical products. Energy resources such as fuel (oil, gas, and coal) and water power have been estimated to be 23 per cent of the total world resources as compared with 29 per cent for the United States.[9] Soviet claims of 55 per cent of the world's oil and 28 per cent of the world's electric power must be discounted because they have not been substantiated by evidence. As for coal, which provides 94 per cent of the Soviet fuel reserves, the country has enough for generations to come. Water resources have not been developed for the production of hydroelectric power as much as they have been in other major industrial countries. Large dams are being built to correct this deficiency. Few authorities doubt that the Soviet Union has enough oil, timber, coal, iron, and sources of power to increase its industrial potential a great deal. One of the biggest problems in developing Soviet industry is created by the almost prohibitive distances between the location of natural resources and the sources of manpower and transportation. Parts of the country are thousands of miles from sea transportation. Although these handicaps have in some measure been reduced by the development of regional self-sufficiency, they have impeded industrial growth.

Geography endowed Russia with rich resources, but it failed to provide her with natural barriers against invasion and it frustrated her in the means of outside contact with Western Europe. Yet paradoxically throughout history Russia repeatedly has been subjected to overland attack by armies from both East and West. Russia is not favored with logistic advantages enjoyed by the United States with its friendly powers to the north and south and protective oceans on each side. Commerce with friendly nations has been difficult for landlocked Russia, barred from the open sea by lack of ice-free ports. The only year-round, ice-free port with direct access to the ocean is Vladivostok on the Pacific, thousands of miles from the industrial heartland. Murmansk on the Arctic Ocean, though ice free, has limited access, and Archangel is usable only a few months in the year. The Baltic seaports offer only one opening to the seas, the Skagerrak Straits—an opening which could be easily blocked in time of war. The big ice-free ports of the Black Sea are subject to limited control by Turkey, which has jurisdiction over the Dardanelles and the Bosporus, the only outlet to the Black Sea. Russians have battled Teutons, Swedes, and Poles over Baltic ports, and have clashed 13 times with the Turks over jurisdiction of the Black Sea and the Dardanelles.

Occupation, Fusion, Conquest, and Expansion

It is easy for the Westerner to assume as he often does that Russia was shaped by the same forces that made the West. This is a logical assumption because geographically Russia is a part of the

Russia in 1850 more than 75 per cent)[13] illiterate and living in impoverished personal bondage.

Autocracy and Social Change

The emperor was the supreme head of the Russian autocracy, ruling by divine right. In the tradition of the Byzantine potentate, whose successor the tsar believed himself to be, he felt responsible to God for his actions, for it was to God that he owed his position. This right and relationship with the divine were confirmed by statute. Since Ivan the Terrible had eliminated competition from the princes, it remained only for Peter the Great to remove the power of the two remaining institutions that might have any restraining influence on the monarchy: the *Boyar Duma* and the *Patriarchate,* which still paid homage to the mother church in Constantinople. He dissolved the Duma and made the Russian Church subject to the government.[14] The tsars who followed ruled from time to time through executive ministers or appointed councils of state, but had no prime minister or legislative body.[15] Since imperial Russia lacked both the institutions and the personnel either to form a viable government or to initiate and carry out the necessary domestic change that would have led to modernization,[16] reform depended primarily upon the autocratic power of the tsar. The nineteenth century in Russia was characterized by alternating periods of real progress and reaction.[17] As a result Russia in the 1850s was showing superficial signs of modernization and was even undergoing some early-stage phases of modern development.

The social and economic order of mid-nineteenth-century Russia revolved around the relationship between the crown, the nobility, and the serfs. It was founded upon a powerful paternalistic central government, a bureaucracy subject to the will of the crown, a strong military tradition, an agrarian economy based on wealth produced by slave labor, and a village and family structure.

From the time of Ivan the Terrible the crown's power had virtually gone unchallenged.[18] The society had not produced, as had Western European societies by this time, institutions strong enough to seize or dilute the sovereign's power. After 1800 the government was further centralized and made still more sensitive to the sovereign's will under Nicholas I. Jealous of ministerial and bureaucratic prerogatives and distrustful of public opinion, Nicholas expanded the authority of His Majesty's Own Chancery, a sort of personal cabinet assigned to augment the executive departments.[19] Of particular importance was the Third Section of the Chancery for it marked the beginning of the police state. It had charge of the state security police, much of whose work was secret. The need for the national police organization had been emphasized by the Decembrist plot in 1825 together with the increased activities of secret societies, all threatening the monarchy's position. The Third Section's powers expanded to include control, when it wished, of the lower echelons of local police, somewhat as if the Federal Bureau of Investigation and the Central Intelligence Agency were to take over the municipal and state police in the United States. Organized of course to combat subversion, the Third Section became a law unto its own and, according to one historian, an agency that investigated what the people were talking and thinking about.[20] With its two sets of agents, the gendarmery and the secret informers, headed by an aristocratic close friend of the tsar, the Third Section became a most oppressive and arrogant branch of the bureaucracy.[21]

The emperor stood at the top of a political system that fanned out and downward through provincial and local administration. Provincial governors and commandants (mayors) of the larger cities administered in their jurisdictions the decrees from the central ministries in St. Petersburg. The tsar ran the empire through a highly stratified bureaucracy which grew top heavy and expensive. Bureaucratic ranks included no less than 14 levels.[22] The top ranks were filled with the members of the nobility, the lower with a diverse group drawn from other social classes. One of these was "honorary citizen," a new social class created by Nicholas I. The honorary citizen was a lifetime rather than hereditary noble and unlike the lower classes, was exempt from the "soul tax," conscription, and corporal punishment. This class permitted lower born people with education to enter the government service. Despite such efforts to enlist qualified personnel, the bureaucracy never reached the high intellectual level nor the prestige attained by the ancient Chinese scholar-bureaucracy. In Russia, appointment to the government service seemed to beget arrogance,[23] money grubbing, and corruption. Still, corruption was not as insidious as some historians have claimed.[24]

But the emperor was not only the omnipotent political head to whom obedience was irresistibly due.[25] He ruled over his temporal kingdom as the head of the church and God's appointee on earth.

His image among the people took on the stature of a God-father. He became known as "Holy Tsar," and "Our Father." [26] Like the Chinese emperor, the person of the Russian tsar symbolized the enshrinement by his people of both political allegiance and religious fealty. The tsar exercised ecclesiastical authority far beyond that known to other European Christian rulers, except the Pope. Eventually in the minds of the people that which was God's and that which was Caesar's fused into one. The historian Sir Donald McKenzie Wallace wrote, "All who know the internal history of Russia are aware that the government does not draw a clear line of distinction between the temporal and spiritual, and that it occasionally uses the ecclesiastical organization for political purposes." [27]

As in imperial China, there was no provision in Russia for peaceful change of government. But unlike in China, there was no philosophy or precedent which recognized the right of the people to rebel when the empire fell upon troubled times and it was thought that the sovereign had lost favor with Heaven. In such a situation the antithesis to a thesis of total power could only be either peaceful change by voluntary concessions from the sovereign or the alternative, revolution. As Russia appeared more backward while other European nations forged further ahead, the pressures for change built up and focused upon the monarchy, the only source of possible relief. Russian history and thought throughout the nineteenth century was one of alternate periods of reform and reaction, punctuated by palace coups, peasant revolts, incipient anarchy, or revolution. From the reforms of Alexander I to the Revolution of 1905 and the Stolypin measures that followed, the story was one of concessions made, reforms attempted or promised. But from crisis to crisis the responses appeared to be too little and too late. While measures taken did not satisfy the revolutionary fervor, they more than served to demonstrate the autocracy's inefficacy and weakness. They served also to alienate the intelligentsia, the only other group that could have effectively aided the monarchy in achieving a peaceful revolution. But the division between the two became a dichotomous stalemate and the spirit of compromise was lacking.[28] After 1905 the monarchy was a self-confessed failure,[29] and the forces of revolution were gathering.

Constitutional government did not come into existence in Russia until the unsuccessful war with Japan in 1904 and the growing discontent that led to the student demonstrations, workers' strikes, peasant seizures of land, and occasional mutinies in the army and navy which constituted the revolutionary movement of 1905. This movement forced Nicholas II to proclaim a constitution which set up an elective body, the Duma, and recognized the legality of political parties. This concession did not stem the tide of revolution so much as it was weakened by disagreement among the revolutionary groups, and by 1907 the government was strong enough to change the election laws so that the conservative parties and the property-owning classes controlled the Duma. The liberal middle class which urged the tsar to accept the idea of parliamentary representative government had in mind the development of institutions like those of the British. But the establishment of the constitutional system ran 200 years behind the English revolution of 1688 and came 700 years after the Magna Charta. Representative government under a constitutional monarchy scarcely had a chance to become established. Thus, the transition from tsarist to Communist dictatorship could not in its essence be described as a drastic or radical change. The difference lay in the promises the Bolsheviks held out for the common people.

Social Classes and Economic Levels

Old Russian society was divided rigidly into specified classes ranging from the nobility down the ladder to the peasantry. Within the broad classifications there was elaborate stratification, exemplified for instance by subclasses of the nobility and peasantry. The nineteenth century saw important changes in the rigidity of the class structure. But from the time of Peter the Great, class distinctions had been a matter of privilege whereas before Peter, classes had been graded according to obligation to the state.[30] Peter established the role of each class and specified the kind of education needed.

In the nineteenth century the most important class continued to be the nobility. Qualification for membership in this class was by hereditary title, but the majority of the nobility at this time consisted of untitled persons some of whom had earned membership through military or civil service to the crown. The census of 1859 showed 1 noble for every 64 persons, or 887,000 nobles for 57 million persons in European Russia,[31] but only less than 1 out of 8 of these was counted as a serf owner. Distribution of ownership was not even, for only 1 per cent of the owners owned almost 30 per cent of the serfs, or about 4,500 serfs each. Two per cent owned another

15 per cent of the serfs, or approximately 1,300 serfs each. Three-fourths of the serf-owning nobility, however, owned 100 or less, and while the upper brackets of this group could live comfortably, they could not support a scale of living in the grand manner of the upper one-fourth. This exalted upper group constituted the large serf- and land-owning aristocracy which lived in great palaces on large estates, after the manner of the eighteenth-century European princes and kings. Each estate had its own chapel, orangerie, theatre, parks, and gardens; each supported its collection of writers, artists, musicians, and actors. This brilliant period for the high aristocracy reached its peak during Catherine the Great's reign. Beneath the veneer of wealth and beauty in this way of life lay the festering "rear courtyard" of serfdom. Western European university education and the Napoleonic wars exposed Russia's young nobles to Western ideas of liberty and progress and changed the aristocracy's role in the nineteenth century, first to political leadership and, that having failed, to service in the bureaucracy. The aristocratic intelligentsia brought its influence to bear upon the tsars for political and social reforms. They formed secret societies devoted to the ideals of liberty, equality, and fraternity. The early reform movement having ended in a period of reaction, the nobility sought rewards in military or civil service to the state. However, the wide gulf which separated the aristocracy from the larger numbers of the petty nobility continued. Between the two was the substantial middle group consisting largely of land overseers.

In the latter half of the century and the immediate prerevolutionary years, the nobility's position generally was one of decline. The class continued to occupy a role in local and national government. Its economic status and social influence gradually lessened as the land, from which status derived, passed into the hands of the peasants, merchants, and industrialists. The crop failures and low prices for agricultural produce further affected the noble's economic condition. Not all of the estates declined, however, but those which permitted their lands to be cultivated year after year in the same primitive manner did. Those which met the crises by improving agricultural techniques were able to hold their own. Also, ranks of the nobility were diminished as they contributed membership in the professional and commercial middle class and in the bureaucracy.

In turning to the peasant class it is, for the period before emancipation, important to distinguish between the peasants who were serfs and the others. The entire peasant population, including serfs, numbered more than 42 million and constituted approximately two-thirds of European Russia's entire population in 1859. A serf, unlike other peasants, was bonded to his landlord by ties of ownership. There were about 21.5 million serfs in European Russia, about 19 million peasants without landlords living on state lands, and some 2 million peasants on lands belonging to the imperial family.[32] It was the serfs and their condition that received the most attention, though they numbered slightly more than half of the peasant population. Although Russian and Soviet writings portray the condition of the serfs as miserable and depict all landlords as cruel, this picture is as distorted as the one of the opposite extreme, likening owner-serf relationships to those of a solicitous father with his children. Actually conditions were quite varied depending upon the kind of landlord a serf might chance to have and upon the nature of his rank. Good estate management obviously required keeping the peasant busy but not permitting him to become exhausted or physically handicapped. With the best landlords the peasant's lot was secure and prosperous; with the worst the extent of his misery was compounded. Personal conditions of work and existence were the worst among the 1.5 million household serfs. The others who worked for the nobility worked as either tenants who paid the landowner in money or goods or as laborers in the landlords's fields. The condition of the former was considerably better than that of the latter. Serfs who paid for the use of the land were relatively free to do as they pleased except achieve either physical or social mobility, as long as they met their payments. Those who worked in the landlord's fields were subject to the landlord's discretionary authority, which could be harsh and punitive. The Central Government expected the noble to see that the peasants provided army recruits and paid their taxes, and the landlord had wide powers over the individual in order to perform these functions. Conditions were especially harsh among the serfs belonging to the petty nobility. Cruel treatment resulted in uprisings, some of which had to be put down by the army, and there were instances of landlord murder by serfs.[33]

Conditions for the 19 million peasants living on State-owned lands were scarcely better before the Kiselev reforms. State lands were administered by the Finance Ministry which considered the peasants primarily as a source of revenue. Taxes and other obligations increased significantly in the nineteenth century, for the peasant not only paid to the central government his "soul" tax, the land tax, and his rent but also various taxes in money or labor to the commune. Such a situation kept the peasant poverty stricken, and when crop failure or other adversity struck, he defaulted on his taxes.

Efforts to improve the peasants' lot were effected at various times under the reigns of Alexander I, Nicholas I, and Alexander II. Nicholas I freed the state peasants from personal serfdom, and under his administrator Count Kiselev local communes were given a degree of autonomy in handling their own affairs. The Kiselev reform program aimed at providing education, medical care, and measures which would improve the peasant's economic status. It served as a model for the pattern of serf rehabilitation after emancipation.[34] Although emancipation freed the serf from the landlord's authority, he was still subjected to the authority of the *mir*—the communal village. In other ways, too, it was apparent that while the emancipation act was a giant step forward, it created some problems as it solved others. The freed serfs could with government assistance buy land from the owners. Most of them did this not individually, but through the collective agency of the commune. By the outbreak of World War I, one-third of the peasant class owned land, two-thirds had instead either remained on the land as tenants or had migrated to the cities to be employed in industry and trade. Sweatshop factory conditions, however, indicated that these peasants had only exchanged the hardships of the dirt farmer for the collective miseries of the underpaid, overworked plant laborer.

Other nineteenth-century social classes were much smaller than the peasant class. Among these were the clergy, the intelligentsia, and the members of the growing middle class of professionals, merchants, bankers, and industrialists. The intelligentsia grew on the foundations of the modern educational system and included the educated class as a whole (though this class cut across the aristocracy), the highest ranks of the military and civil service, the professional groups, and a few of the leading manufacturers. The rise of an intelligentsia in a country still culturally backward, still clinging to its obsolete despotic institutions, was somewhat anachronistic.[35] Unable to transplant many of their ideas gained from Western-style education, deprived of responsible political leadership, isolated from the masses by rigid class distinctions, the intelligentsia was a dissatisfied and frustrated class. Their wide knowledge of differences between life in Russia and life in other European countries, their great desire to improve conditions for the average Russian, yet the futility of combatting bureaucratic opposition and upper class indifference in the face of poverty and social injustice created a climate that nourished revolutionary thought. This intellectual class, then, contributed to the decay of the old order by providing the leadership and the thought for nihilistic and revolutionary political parties that arose in the latter half of the century.[36] This is not to say that most of the intellectual class were revolutionaries or that the revolutionary leaders came exclusively from this class. But the educated class was generally against the regime, and when it came to a matter of choice, sided with the revolutionary group in sympathy if not by action. Of this group, whom Tomkins labels the makers of the revolutionary state,[37] Seton-Watson writes, "It is essential to bear in mind the peculiar relationship of the intelligentsia to the government machine and to the people, the contrast between Russia and Europe, and the position of the intelligentsia with its head in the nineteenth or twentieth century and its feet in the seventeenth."[38]

The educated class contributed increasing numbers to a growing professional, skilled labor, and mercantile class which formed the nucleus of Russia's nearest approach to the middle class of Western societies. This class multiplied as the reforms after 1860 speeded industrialization and modernization. Russia entered the stage of transition from a feudal manor economy to the early stages of a modern capitalist society. This growing middle class was still too small in 1914 to be able to exert a stabilizing influence in public affairs. The absence from Russian society of a large, independent, and affluent middle or bourgeois class such as those which played a major role in the socioeconomic development and in political change in Europe and North America is one of the major points of contrast between Russia and the West.

So, as war came, Russian society was moving with great difficulty from feudalism and autocracy to modernization and the faint beginnings of democracy.

BASIC ETHOS AND VALUES

Attitudes Toward Authority and Law

The character and traditions of the Russian people—the beliefs and values that make Russian society different from other societies—were inherited from the accumulated collective experience of the past. Some of these characteristic traits were indigenous in origin, others borrowed from the West, still others attributable to Eastern influences. In the earlier periods of Russian history the major influences were the Church and Byzantine culture transplanted to a traditional society. Although such Christian beliefs as asceticism, the Golden Rule, and the brotherhood of man proliferated slowly in a pagan and superstitious culture, Christianity came to be generally accepted. The Byzantine world was a self-contained universe largely untouched by Western science and rational philosophy. Along with Orthodox Christianity, the Russians inherited the Byzantine concept of an absolutist central government.[39] From the Mongols they inherited the conception of the ruler as an absolute power, an overwhelming force to which obedience was irresistibly due.[40] As the church became the spiritual symbol of good, the place where men were equal before their God, and the protective refuge from evil, the tsar was identified with the church. Before Christianity the Russian peasant had learned to revere the soil and the motherland, from which he wrested a livelihood only with great effort. The harshness of the climate and the difficulty of survival taught him to find security in group life, motivated by the belief that by banding together men might conquer the forces of nature. As against the land and within collective security of the group, the individual usually counted for very little. The masses then learned obedience and subservience to the hierarchy of authorities above them from local commune officials on up to the nobility and the emperor. At the top towered the blessed trinity of powers: God, the motherland, and the tsar. The German historian Von Haxthausen observed:

> The people have shown invariable obedience to every government, even to that of the Mongols; they frequently indeed complain of the supposed wrongs, but there the matter ends. The common Russian entertains no slavish, but simply a childlike fear and veneration for the Czar; he loves him with a devoted tenderness. He becomes a soldier of vindictiveness for the coercion exercised upon him, and serves the Czar with utmost fidelity.[41]

More directly involved and closer to home than either the tsar or God were the primary objects of the Russian's allegiance: the family and the communal village, or mir. Both of these social units were operated on authoritarian principles under the household patriarch or the village elder, the *starosta,* chosen by the village leaders usually by virtue of age. Collective decisions were reached in mir councils by consensus rather than by vote. Minority or opposition views, though permitted expression, were not allowed to be registered. Decisions were unanimous. Dissenters were brought into the fold by group pressure. Those who violated group norms were ostracized or if their actions endangered group survival, punishment was severe. Thus justice was administered according to mir concepts. Up until modern times corporal punishment was legal. After a decision was sanctioned by the group, it took on an almost religious significance—it was always wise and right. The individual could leave the responsibility for it to the mir. His world was the mir. Although it might discipline him, it also provided safety and security. Church doctrine taught that men were essentially sinful and fallible, therefore they could not be expected to be wise enough either to control their emotions at all times or to manage their affairs without help. Hence the need to rely on the mir, the tsar, and the church. Because of the dependent, childlike quality of human nature as it was interpreted, violence and emotional conflict in human relations could be expected. For this reason the setting of limits and the exaction of discipline by community, church, or state were generally approved and supported. To the people these authoritarian seats of power represented the institutions for good and for order for dependent individuals in a hostile and dangerous world. Personal and collective order was valued as tantamount to survival; yet it was thought that individuals apart from society could never achieve it. In sum, official power over individual lives was considered by ruler and ruled alike to be a basic foundation stone for society's preservation and its transmission to posterity.

It was in essence a value-system that depended upon men and not upon laws. Despite public veneration of the monarchy, obedience to imperial decrees could not be expected to follow automatically. Consequently, the bureaucracy operated under a complex code of regulations based on decrees. There was little understanding of law as an arbiter between individual rights on the one hand and social values on the other. When the idea of statutory law, imported mainly from Germany, was applied to Russian needs, it was administered by the bureaucracy on a highly abstract, technical level unrelated to real human needs.[42] When the peasants ignored such laws or twisted them to suit their own advantage, they were made more complex, more strict, and more unrealistic.

Evasion was attributed to inability of the people to understand. So the insensitive bureaucracy tightened enforcement. Even today the Soviet bureaucracy often meets this kind of reaction.

Absence of Certain Western Belief Patterns

Two discernible antagonistic forces in Russian thought can be said to have prevailed in varying degrees since Peter the Great. One was the influence of the thinkers who admired Western civilization and sought to change Russia by importing foreign ways. Opposed to this was the view of the Slavophiles, who believed that Russian indigenous culture should develop independently without following any foreign pattern. Although the first wanted to adapt Western ways and the second wanted to stick to true Russian traditions, both sought change; and to a degree both sides were Utopian in outlook. The development of Russian ethos has veered between these two influences, native beliefs resisting Western influences successfully at times, but also succumbing to them at times.[43] Out of this dichotomy the Slavophiles eventually prevailed. Among Russians today there is an enduring faith in the basic values of the indigenous national culture, a belief that Russian society can stand on its own without the need to imitate other cultures.[44]

Middle-class values so potent in Western societies, for example, could not be expected to take root in a society which had no large middle class. Thus such virtues as thrift, pride of workmanship, industry and skill, respect and integrity in human relations, and business success which grew out of town life came to be regarded as hallmark values of Western advancement. Such business world standards meant little to the Russians who often sneered at German industry and thrift. Russians attributed Western superiority, not to the practice of such virtues, but to the happy circumstance by which Western societies were spared Asian barbarian invasions during the Middle Ages. Russians believed the West had time to develop such arts and crafts while Russia was being overrun. The development of technical skills was not equated in the Russian mind with the practice of Western virtues.

Another Western value alien to the Russians—indeed the whole foundation of Western value-systems—is a firm belief in the reliability and trustworthiness of facts. The scientific roots of Western knowledge and culture lie deeply embedded in this belief as the ultimate basis of reality. Although Westerners advance hypotheses to help explain facts, hypotheses unsupported by facts are usually rejected. Dogma, assumption, and premise are usually separated from fact and their validity tested by empirically derived fact. Yet this entire empirical approach to thought has been repudiated by Russians as self-defeating. In its place they have adopted an abstract, *a priori,* impressionistic, or conceptualized approach.[45] As Tompkins[46] notes, ". . . philosophical discussion turned less on the facts adduced by the participants than on the concepts from which they started." In 1890 a writer in the *Fortnightly Review* made an observation that rings strikingly familiar to students of the Soviet mind today: "They . . . lack that reverence for facts that lies at the root of Anglo-Saxon character," he said. "A Russian can no more bow to a fact, acknowledging it as final and decisive, than he can to a personal appreciation or to a mere opinion founded upon insufficient or no grounds; he is ever ready to act in open defiance of it."[47] Fifty years earlier the Marquis de Custine reported his impression of the Russian disregard of empirical truth, as follows: ". . . up to now I believed that man could no more do without truth for the spirit than air and sun for the body; my journey to Russia disabuses me. Here to lie is to protect the social order; to speak the truth is to destroy the state."[48] This characteristic devotion to abstractions without regard to factual support lies at the heart of Russian rigidity and inability to accept compromise.[49] It also helps explain much about Russian susceptibility and adherence to doctrine and dogma.

The tendency toward this kind of thinking is the corollary to a passion for extremes that seems to be characteristic of absolutist thought, and especially Russian intolerance. Some writers trace this concern with extremes, this dichotomy, to the absence of stable tradition in Russian history.[50] Tompkins concludes from his study of this phenomenon in the Russian thought process that this ". . . passion to seek virtues in the extreme has made violence and terror the chief arbiter of our times. Mass deportations, wholesale liquidations and purges, and . . . concentration camps are the logical outcome of a system that fixes its eye on the distant Utopia. . . . the modern believer in absolutes shrinks from no human cost in attaining his goal. . . ."[51]

Soviet Policy and the Value-System

The Soviet regime, in attempting to impose on the masses a system of Marxist-Leninist values and at the same time create a modern industrial society, has employed methods that draw on the

Russian cultural past. Basic prerevolutionary patterns of thought and traditional values are appealed to as fundamental strategy behind the use of persuasion, communication, and coercion. The regime has been moderately successful in changing values without seeming to depart from the venerated traditions of Holy Russia.[52] The leaders, however, are faced with the problem of grafting onto the society many values which conflict with those of the past. It is easier to replace one value with another than it is to completely blot one out, so the regime has attempted to substitute the State for religion in Russian culture. It has attempted by government fiat to substitute loyalty to the State for loyalty to the traditional institutions of family and mir.

In attacking all the rallying points of stability in prerevolutionary society—the tsar, the church, the family, and the peasant commune, the regime has to some extent undermined these values, but has not provided a complete substitute set of values that can maintain the degree of social orderliness that the old institutions provided.[53] It would seem also that satisfactory substitute values and loyalties have not always been provided by the regime in other areas. For example, the Soviet government has denied its people the present so that the glorious future may be achieved; it has denied individualistic human values, yet subscribes to the philosophy that man is sole master of his environment; it has rewarded the peasant with land, yet denied him the full proceeds from it. On the other hand the post-Stalin era has seen the development of greater incentives and rewards, a higher standard of living for the people, and a de-emphasis on coercion and fear as instruments of public policy. The rise of the Soviet Union as a leading world power and as a modern industrial nation and the country's achievements in science and space are substitute values that have stimulated nationalistic feelings to a high level.

If the regime is using more persuasion and less force in the present, like tsarist regimes before it, it has resorted to ruthless power at times in the past. It has done this in order to force the people to acept Communist values and goals as well as to increase industrial production. The sharing of values helps establish order in any society. Society must function according to established and therefore reasonably predictable norms. When the established order threatens to disintegrate, predictability disappears.[54] In resorting to force, the Soviet government, departing from tsarist tradition, has destroyed institutions and has punished not only the acts of individuals but also attacked private thoughts and feelings. By destroying the very fabric of the society, the regime was better able to maintain control, to rule by terror. But it neither restored the social order nor reestablished predictability. The regime several times has come close to the brink in its manipulation of values; and each time it has retreated and reasserted the old values traditionally associated with family and church. When this happens, the Soviet leaders resort to a variant of the old values themselves—they employ prerevolutionary scapegoatism. They never blame the regime for the situation they have created—this would undermine their own position. They assign guilt to a chosen culprit, and if he is within their reach, provide the indicated punishment. Of course such straw men as "capitalist warmongers" and "bourgeois exploiters of the working class" in foreign countries cannot be punished except by tongue-lashing in the mass media. Nevertheless they serve as scapegoats. While the regime since the *Thaw* * period has voluntarily limited the use of force, the threat of the return to its use to change values and achieve goals still lingers in the background.

Perhaps most important of all effects that accrue from this massive concerted drive to change the value-system of a whole nation is the effect on the individual. With all aspects of life under controls, with practically every detail of life arranged and managed from the cradle to the grave by the all-knowing, all-seeing bureaucracy, the individual human being tends to apathy and withdrawal from the realities. Or he may turn to religion or other forbidden activity in search of a consistent and reliable set of values. But this is just another form of escapism. From the regime's standpoint, the individual has surrendered. But personal responsibility has been weakened, and this, as we shall see, is a problem the regime has not satisfactorily solved.[55]

PRESS AND CENSORSHIP

Early Communication Forms

The first known Russian chronicles of contemporary events were written within twelfth-century monastery walls. They were current historical accounts of both church and village affairs re-

* This period, beginning about 1953, of compromise in ideologies is discussed more fully in Chapter 8.

corded on an irregular basis.[56] The forerunner of this kind of community journalism was the first Russian history, which had been written in the eleventh century by a monk of the Kiev monastery and based on records stored there and at Novgorod. This account, a Russian-type *Anglo-Saxon Chronicle,* described the glories of the past and stressed Russian cultural heritage, racial unity, and relationship to the Orthodox Christian world. The Kiev history led to the appearance of similar accounts in other principalities. In an effort to keep the record up to date, it became the custom to record contemporary events from time to time. Prince-bishops had their chroniclers to record events occurring in their domains. Although lay epics originated in the society of the military aristocracy (the *druzhina)* describing the military triumphs of heroes, most of these ancient Russian annals are saturated with religious overtones. They are said to reflect the struggle between Christian ethics and the evil forces within the human soul. Most famous of the epics is "Tale of the Host of Igor," a song of the heroic but unsuccessful campaign against the Cumans by Prince Igor in 1185, reminiscent of King Alfred's accounts of his men's valiant but vain struggle against the Danes.

Church literature also was the principal product of the first printing presses which are said to have been set up in Russia in the reign of Ivan IV (1530–1584). According to Vernadsky, the first printing plant in Moscow was established in 1553,[57] although the first printed Slavonic books had appeared in Cracow, Poland, in 1491; in Prague, Bohemia, in 1517; and in Vilna, Lithuania, in 1525.[58] The first presses were official and since there was not much the government wanted printed, the early books were ecclesiastical.[59] Before 1600 hardly a score of books had been published from the Moscow press. The earliest periodical appeared at the court in 1621, the year following the Pilgrim landing at Plymouth, but it was not printed. Entitled *Kuranty* (the Chimes), it was handwritten and its audience was the tsar and his courtiers.[60] Until the time of Peter the Great most writing was circulated in handwritten manuscript form.

Eighteenth-century Journalism and Its Literary Setting

The first newspapers appeared in the next century. Peter the Great first envisioned the potentiality of the press as a medium for the transmission of Western ideas to help "modernize" Russia. He made printing an instrument of propaganda and exploited the newspaper as the most rapid and sensitive communication channel.

In 1703 Peter founded the first Russian newspaper which he published from his official presses first at Moscow and later alternately at Moscow and St. Petersburg. The title was *Vedomosti Moskovskogo Gosudartsva* (Gazette of the Moscovite State). An alternative title appears to have been *Russkie Vedomosti,* but it was known primarily by its abbreviated title, *Vedomosti.* Published in the Slavonic language, it ran from two to seven pages and circulated about 1,000 copies. Peter himself read the German and other foreign papers, selected items for translation and republication, and sometimes personally read proof.[61] The paper advanced Western culture, fought parochialism, and kept the public informed of the tsar's decrees and of government activities. After Peter's death in 1725, the paper continued two more years before lapsing.[62] Only a year later, however, the Academy of Sciences began publishing the *Sankt Peterburgskie Vedomosti* (St. Petersburg Gazette) four times weekly. This paper became a daily in 1815.[63]

According to Rambaud, the first Russian review was *The Busy Bee* published by Sumarokof about 1750.[64] The historian Muller began editing for the Academy in 1754 what became a distinguished periodical under the title *Yezhemesyachnyye Sochineniya* (Monthly Publications). The forerunner of this magazine was *Primechaniya* (Notes), which was first issued as a supplement or appendix to the *Sankt Peterburgskie Vedomosti.* The oldest periodical of continuous publication appears to have been *Moskovskie Vedomosti* (Moscow Gazette) which was founded by the University of Moscow in 1756[65] and edited officially by the writer M. M. Kheraskov. The real editor and the moving power behind *Moskovskie Vedomosti* was M. V. Lomonosov, who founded Moscow University. It was an intellectual publication for scholars and gentry, continuing for almost 150 years, finally lapsing in 1894.

The reign of Catherine the Great (1762–1796) ushered in a period of growth for journalism and literature, though the period began with the suppression of two periodicals. Upperclass leisure inspired the appearance of a number of short-lived titles in the period beginning about 1760. Publication was possible only with the monarch's sanction, since permission was granted for printing on the official press. Likewise publication ceased with the monarch's disapproval. After 1764, Muller's *Monthly Publications* and Sankovskii's *Dobroe Namerenie* (Good Intentions) were suppressed, and by this time the others had disappeared, so for a period of five years only the official St. Petersburg and the Moscow *Vedomosti* held the field.

Beginning in 1769, however, a rash of some 16 popular satirical journals appeared under Catherine's encouragement and sponsorship.[66] Catherine admired French satire as a communication device for social criticism in the interests of reform.[67] She herself published and wrote for the satirical journal *Vsyakaya Vsyachina* (Miscellany).[68] This venture did not last long. With her right hand, the Empress seemed to encourage writers to attack public problems, but her left hand was ready to box their ears when they went too far.

In 1783 Catherine issued a *ukaze* permitting private printing presses and granting the owners a degree of freedom. Provincial governments and private citizens founded presses in a score or more cities. There followed an important era in periodical literature and journalism. The most significant result of this expansion in publishing activities was a series of publications at the University of Moscow, generally issued under the names of N. I. Novikov and Johann G. Schwartz. Both were active in the Masonic movement. Novikov organized the Society for the Friends of Learning at the University of Moscow where he leased the official press and took over publication of the *Vedomosti.* After the decree permitting the establishment of private presses, Novikov started two publishing houses and by 1784 he and Schwartz were associated with twelve other stockholders in the ownership of a large book publishing company known as the *Tipograficheskaya Kompaniya.* In addition Schwartz himself brought out four journals.[69] The Schwartz-Novikov combination exerted influence on public opinion and popularized reading.[70] After Schwartz died, Novikov's liberal views gradually fell out of favor with Catherine, and 416 Novikov books were seized and burned. His publishing house was liquidated. A 1787 decree granted the Synod exclusive rights to publish all eccesiastical books and required prepublication approval by a government commission for all others. Eventually Novikov was sent to prison.

The French Revolution roused the government's fear and brought further repressive measures.[71] A. N. Radishev's *Puteshestvie iz Peterburga v Moskvu* (Journey from St. Petersburg to Moscow), published in 1790, brought his arrest and trial. The court found the book "full of the most harmful arguments calculated to disturb the public peace, to destroy respect for authority, to raise among the people dissatisfaction with officials and the government and to lower the dignity and authority of the Sovereign . . . ." [72] Radishev was condemned to death, but the Empress commuted his sentence to Siberian exile. After her death both he and Novikov were released. A. Krylov's *Pochta Dukhov* (Courier of the Spirits), established in 1782, was noted for publishing Radishev's views, as was *Zritel* (The Spectator) ten years later.

While the upheaval in France stiffened Russian censorship, it increased the demand for information, and new periodicals appeared to fill the demand. N. M. Karamzin, historian and literary figure at the turn of the century, edited and published *Moskovsky Zhurnal* (Moscow Journal), founded in 1791, and founded *Vestnik Europy* (European Messenger) in 1802. Some other publications were *Rossiiskii Magazin* (The Russian Magazine) edited by Tumanskii; *Zerkalo Svyeta* (Mirror of the World); *Lekartsvo ot Skuki i Zabot* (The Cure for Boredom and Cares); and *Zhurnal s pokazaniem uchenykh i drugikh veshchei* (Journal to instruct the reader in learning and other things). In 1796 Catherine closed private presses and placed stricter censorship on imported books. Paul I increased the severity of the regulations, and as a result the number of periodicals was drastically reduced.

Growth in Communications

Alexander I brought a more relaxed government attitude, allowing restrictions to be lifted in 1801. The sovereign promised a free press, but prepublication censorship for books and periodicals was resumed shortly, although at the same time private presses were again permitted.[73] In the administration of censorship, the government's policy was a wavering one, so that, in the generally permissive atmosphere, the publishing business thrived again.

The most important Russian journal at the beginning of the century and later was Karamzin's *Vestnik Europy*, a bimonthly devoted to political discussion. This magazine had a brilliant career, publishing the best works of contemporary poets and authors. Both it and *Russkii Vestnik*, founded in 1808 by N. Glinka, continued publication till the end of the century. Other important titles were *Moskovsky Merkury*, 1802; *Severyn Vestnik* (The Northern Messenger), 1804; and *Zhurnal Rossiyskoy Slovestnosti* (Journal of Russian Literature), 1805.

The successful outcome of one of the great trials of Russian history—the defeat of Napoleon's invasion—was followed by a stronger nationalism and new Russian standing among European nations. Russia's greater involvement in European affairs, specifically the Napoleonic wars and the Congress of Vienna, stimulated an outburst of journals during the next decade, some devoted to patriotic themes. Among the new titles were *Genii Vremen* (Genius of the Times), 1807; *Syn Otechestva* (Sons of the Fatherland), 1812; *Moskovskii Zritel* (Moscow Observer), 1806; and *Dukh Zhurnalov* (Review of Reviews), 1815. *Otechestvennye Zapiski* (Notes of the Fatherland) founded in 1820[74] became a leading magazine of the century, and after 1865 an influential populist organ. The period saw suppressions, however. G. M. Yatsenkov's brilliant magazine *Dukh Zhurnalov* was suppressed in 1820 for advocating a constitution and press freedom for Russia. *Polyarnaya Zvezda* (The North Star) was suppressed for support of the Decembrists.

While the reign of Nicholas I was noted for its press restrictions, the rapid expansion of Russian literature and criticism and the outstanding role played by the newspapers and periodicals in social and literary life all were factors which made it a period of growth. Tompkins calls it ". . . one of the most remarkable [periods] in the history of Russian thought, and one in which the periodical and daily press overshadowed other publications . . . ."[75] For the first time, he said, ". . . Russian minds began to attain something like maturity and to move freely in the intellectual atmosphere of Western Europe." In the course of the half-century the number of journals increased considerably. In 1801 there were only ten periodicals in the country, but by 1841 to 1850 there were approximately 57.[76] In 1847 there were 55 privately owned publications which could be regarded as of more or less general interest, published by private individuals and societies. The number of political, social, and literary publications ran between 15 and 20.[77]

The playwright and journalist N. A. Polevoi founded a literary journal, *Telegraf,* in 1828 that soon had 2,000 subscribers. The progressive *Telescop* (1831–1836) was published by the professor and critic N. I. Nadezhdin. Polevoi sought to awaken in his readers an interest in Western European affairs and therefore was strongly opposed by the Slavophiles. Nadezhdin with his *Telescop* tried to make peace between the conflicting classical and romantic schools. *Otechestvennye Zapiski* in the 1840s attracted prominent authors and took up the cause Polevoi had left, becoming the organ of the

Utopian socialists or the Westerners. *Sovremennik* (Contemporary) was founded in 1836 by A. S. Pushkin, who was succeeded by N. A. Nekrasov in 1847. In the period 1845 to 1854, licenses were granted to 6 newspapers and 19 magazines.

In contrast to the privately owned journals, periodicals that might be classified as newspapers were subsidized or owned by the government. The Moscow *Vedomosti,* which had been founded at the University of Moscow and privately published by Novikov, became a government paper in 1806 and eventually returned to private ownership under Katkov in 1863. The St. Petersburg *Vedomosti* was official and began daily publication in 1815. In 1837 official papers were begun in the provinces. The *Guberninskiye Vedomosti* (Provincial News) was filled with both official and unofficial news. News of business and commerce was published by both *Syevernaya Pochta,* the Ministry of Interior's organ, and by the *Sankt Peterburgskie Kommercheskie Vedomosti* (The St. Petersburg Commercial News) 1802–1810, a government subsidized publication. *Russkii Invalid* (Russian Veteran) became the War Ministry's organ, reviewing the foreign press for international news, and later restricting its news to that obtained from official sources. There were government as well as private journals devoted to business, manufacturing, industry, mining, forestry, economic problems, and agriculture.

Official Thought Control and the Censorship Code

A detailed set of regulations for the guidance of censors known as the "Iron Code" of Admiral A. S. Shishkov, minister of public instruction, was adopted by Nicholas I in 1826. Too drastic to be workable, it was considerably modified two years later, but its philosophy of government control over public thought makes it significant. The code, based on the premise that people were to think what the government wished them to think, was a bold experiment aimed at making the press an instrument of state policy subjecting the content of all public media to the scrutiny of a large corps of censors under continuous instructions from the monarch. With this machinery it was believed that the government could at will direct the public opinion process in the desired direction.[78] Passages of doubtful or vague meaning were to be interpreted in a way unfavorable to the author instead of giving the author the benefit of the doubt. Nothing could be printed about the government without prior approval of the responsible official. Since it was a positive effort to inform and instruct the public along prescribed lines, censors were to decide whether books or periodicals were useful or meritorious. By 1828 the scheme was modified, the revised code stressing the negative aspects of censorship rather than the positive aspects of propaganda and mind conditioning. Instead of being designed to tell the public what it should believe, the new program instructed censors to decide whether material under review was harmful. It established central and local committees under a chief administration of censorship in the Ministry of Public Instruction. These modifications in the law, however, did not relieve the rigor, absurdity, and narrowness of its application. All forms of expression came under regular review of the authorities and the liberty of the press, already limited, was further encroached upon. While news of court functions and of the imperial family had received special restrictions, new edicts decreed prohibitions in other areas.

The infamous Section III of the Imperial Chancery (the secret police) was especially active in aiding censors, as it became customary for editors and authors to receive instructions from Count Alexander Benckendorff, Section III's director and significantly a member of the central administration, and his lieutenants. Benckendorff received copies of all periodicals, and regularly reviewed book lists. Not only were publications licensed, but the heavy hand of censorship extended to manuscripts. Yuri Samarin was imprisoned for circulating the manuscript of a critical study of official policy in the Baltic provinces, and Pushkin was caustically reprimanded by Benckendorff for reading his manuscript, *Boris Godunov,* in Moscow salons before it had been submitted to the tsar.[79] Polevoi's *Moskovskii Telegraf* was suspended in 1834 and Nadzhdin's *Teleskop* had to close in 1836 after publishing Peter Chaadayev's series of *Philosophical Letters.* What offended the authorities was Chaadayev's deprecatory references to the Orthodox Church[80] and his unfavorable comparison of Russia with Western Europe. Chaadayev was declared insane, the *Telescop* suspended, its editor exiled, and the censor who passed the articles dismissed. Chaadayev's persecution by the tsar, however, increased his popularity.

The best known case of thought persecution under Nicholas I was that of the Fourierist discussion group known as the Petrashevsky Group. M. V. Butashevich-Petrashevsky, a minor official in the Foreign Affairs Ministry, held Friday literary receptions that were popular with the intellectuals in his circle. After the European revolutions of 1848, Petrashevsky and his closer friends discussed the desirability of organizing a secret society for revolutionary propaganda, but they got no further than to discuss the ideal world pictured by Fourier. Fourier's depiction of the demise of cities and city life was later construed by the authorities who had Petrashevsky's meetings under surveillance as a plot to destroy the Russian capital. On April 22, 1849, 39 members of the group were arrested, 15 were sentenced to death, and 6 to forced labor or deportation to Siberia. Since "conspiracy of ideas" was all they could be charged with, and this did not violate the criminal code, a special military court handled the case. As the condemned were led to the scaffold blindfolded, their sentences were commuted to Siberian exile. Among the condemned were the poet A. N. Pleshchev and Fedor Dostoevsky, whose early novels had only recently appeared in print. Dostoevsky was sentenced to four years of hard labor and six years of army service with a Siberian detachment.

The Petrashevsky affair grimly highlighted the extremely broad interpretations the 1828 code was receiving under administrative fiat by the late 1840s. The code limited government powers to preventing what was harmful to the state. But in the hands of officials aided by the secret police, the limits of negative censorship were breached time and again. Especially after the outbreak of the 1848 revolutions that shook Europe, stricter precautions were taken by the Emperor ostensibly in the interests of the public safety —measures which admittedly censored material that did not violate existing law. The nefarious Secret Committee of April 2, 1848, was appointed by the tsar to examine censorship policy in the light of the February Paris uprisings.[81] While the committee was unofficial and its activities sub rosa, it was expected to cope with problems outside the purview of existing policy. Its main function was to censor foreign news to prevent exposure to the public of any reports that might incite unrest or subversion, but censorship of domestic news was tightened, too. Censors were ordered to redouble their vigilance against what had become a remarkably clever and effective device invented by writers to communicate what was desired without incurring censorship. This was the widespread use of "Aesopian language" to cover up what in less devious terms would clearly be a violation.

Aesopian language was an umbrella term meaning any kind

of circumlocution, between-the-lines implication, subtly disguised referent, allegorical and figurative speech, fictitious characters to represent real persons in reporting real events, thinly camouflaged labels for real organizations and institutions—all employed to satirize contemporary conditions and criticize the regime. Since prose studded with such devices could not literally be classified by the authorities as forbidden content, it had been skillfully used since the 1830s to frustrate the censorship process. Similar devices had been used by eighteenth-century English writers to evade Parliament's rule forbidding publication of its proceedings. The English writers served an eager public, and apparently so did the Russian. Ivan Aksakov summed it up as follows:

> . . . the writer, as if he were a thief, used any artifice to get his thought through to the public between the lines; the written work tore itself away from the censor's hands and entered God's world crumpled, ruffled, and mutilated, and was welcomed by the public as a token of victory or keenly relished as a forbidden, secret, and tempting fruit.[82]

Thus during the closing years of Nicholas I's reign the embattled writer struggled to outwit the censor. He made slim headway between 1848 and 1855, however. Contemporary writers dubbed this period the Reign of Terror.

It is curious that despite the unfavorable official climate, the period of Nicholas I (1825–1855) has earned the sobriquet, the "golden age of Russian letters." Besides the young Dostoevsky, there were such figures as Pushkin, Nicholas Gogol, Alexis Koltsov, and others whose works in the tradition of the new school of realism spearheaded the great flowering of Russian literature in the next half-century. With this intellectual activity reflected in the press there emerged a vocal public opinion that grew more critical of the government and its policies, and the demand for reform intensified. This was not a groundswell among the masses of the people, who largely remained outside the current of protest. It was an intellectual movement among a rising new class. As Vissarion Belinski described it:

> Our literature laid the basis for the internal *raprochement* of the orders, educated a kind of public opinion, and produced something in the way of a special class in society which is distinguished from the ordinary middle class by the fact that it consists not only of merchants and tradesmen but persons of all ranks drawn together by education, which with us is consecrated to love of literature.[83]

New newspapers and other periodicals appeared in the provincial capitals, under both private and government ownership. While this was a period of vigorous literary journalism, in which such leading literary figures as Pushkin, Belinski, and M. Lermontov edited and wrote for the leading prestige journals, there was also a group of less distinguished journalists who were laying the foundation for a popular mass-circulation press. Among the latter were N. I. Grech, V. G. Benediktov, N. Polevoi, O. I. Senkovskii, and F. V. Bulgarin. Bulgarin's *Severnaia Pchela* (Northern Bee), while currying favor with the Third Section and the other branches of government, was said to be the only private newspaper until the early 1860s that carried political news. Though disdained by the intellectuals for its bourgeois appeal, it was read abroad as an official publication, at the court, and in the cities. It and papers like it were envied by the highest class journals because of their popularity and financial success.

Yet surveying developments in journalism in Nicholas's closing years, Lemke concluded:

> This period is almost the darkest and most oppressive period in the whole history of Russian journalism. Aside from the ordinary official and very severe censorship . . . there hovered over the printed word still another censorship, secret and unofficial, in the hands of institutions endowed with the broadest powers and hampered in their operations in no way by the law . . . .[85]

Nevertheless there was continued growth in the number of periodicals and an increase in the variety of their content. Aside from the literary and popular press, there was a considerable expansion in the publication of trade, technical, scientific, economic, and educational journals. This kind of vertical growth was accompanied by a widening of the press horizontally.

2

THE PRESS GENERATES CHANGE, 1855-1917

THE ROLE OF THE PRESS and its relations with the government were crucial factors in the course of Russian society in the tempestuous half-century of political agitation and reform that followed Alexander II's accession in 1855.[1] Yet how the press was able to play a vital part in the face of the censorship, repression, and persecution that characterized tsarist policy most of the time has not been adequately explained. The role played by literature and the important literary figures in the swirling political currents sweeping through the society was also crucial. The streams of communication in the name of literature and journalism on the one hand and the movements of social change on the other were so intimately related that it is impossible to discern where one ends and another begins. To separate them in order to chart their courses individually and to determine the impact of each on the other is therefore unrealistic. A more fruitful approach is to study them together. Press performance provided a measure of the latitude of public expression permitted in the press, yet this performance could not be judged from the provisions of the censorship code at a given time.

More revealing was the changeable morass of public policy in applying the law to different cases. And the degree of severity with which the code was interpreted by the censorship officials fluctuated from time to time according to the changing government attitude.

FROM LIBERALITY BACK TO CONTROL

In contrast to the rigid controls under the "reign of terror," a period of relative freedom followed the accession of Alexander II. The impact of the Crimean War on Russian society had done much to discredit the existing order, and the new tsar was under public pressure to alleviate conditions. Sensitive to public opinion and to the people's needs, he committed his administration to a reform program. The new sovereign sought to build a government based on public confidence instead of force, fear, and suspicion. In this unusual atmosphere of comparative liberality the "Committee of April 2" was dissolved, and censorial activities were diminished. New titles appeared and the papers were filled with previously forbidden subjects. The press was responding to the public's need for information after the vacuum in news that had existed under Nicholas.[2] The periodical press flourished phenomenally during this honeymoon period. In 1830, according to Rambaud,[3] there had been only 73 periodicals of all kinds; but between 1855 and 1864 as many as 50 new newspapers and 135 new magazines, or reviews, were granted licenses.[4] In the 2-year period, 1858–1860, some 50 new titles appeared in St. Petersburg alone, 17 in Moscow, and 10 in the provinces.[5] Many of the periodicals that flourished at this time died in the more hostile political atmosphere of the 1870s. A notable characteristic of the period of growth was the development of the daily newspaper.

The Mass Journal Emerges

The development of the modern mass journal of general news or information appeal along Western lines was a phenomenon of the 1860s. These papers flourished on popular support from growing interest in public affairs and on such novel features as retail sales at newsstands and railroad stations and paid advertisements. These papers competed vigorously with the political opinion organs. Tabloids also enjoyed popularity, dealing in current news summaries, scandals, and occasional government criticism couched in camouflaged prose. Among the comic journals was *Iskra* (The Spark), founded in 1859 by Kurotchkin.[7] This periodical was a magazine of satire and humor noted for its clever cartoons, less famous today than another journal of the same name dedicated to more serious purposes published by Lenin at the turn of the century.

The leading daily newspapers in the final half-century of tsarist rule were the ones that flourished in the two large cities, St. Petersburg and Moscow. The city press led the provincial press in size, prestige, and influence. In St. Petersburg, the capital, the leading dailies[6] were the *Sankt-Peterburgsky Vedomosti,* which in 1863 had 8,000 circulation; the *Golos* (Voice) which had a larger circulation than the *Vedomosti; Novo Vremya* (The New Times), founded in 1868, a daily which was somewhat similar to the Paris *Figaro;* and Mikhail Katkov's St. Petersburg paper, *Ruskii Vestnik* (Russian Messenger), which the *Times* of London called the foremost organ in Russia. In Moscow the chief daily continued to be the ancient *Moskovski Vedomosti* now published also by Katkov. After Katkov's desertion of the liberals, this paper represented the pro-Western and nationalist viewpoint, and was very prosperous. In 1863 it had 12,000 subscribers. Some other leading newspapers founded later were *Grashdanin* (Citizen), 1872, a conservative paper; *Novosti* (News), a liberal and sensational Western-style newspaper; and *Russ,* a pan-Slav daily founded in 1880 by I. S. Aksakov, all in St. Petersburg.

Social Criticism and Ideological Ferment

Despite the increasing demands of the times for more information, the main contribution of the Russian periodical press lay in the areas of thought and social criticism. The writers were leading intellectuals, often literary figures, fired with a strong social conscience and a burning desire to change conditions as rapidly as possible by educating, influencing, and enlisting public opinion in the cause. There followed a dynamic period of crusading political journalism conducted brilliantly by these young idealists, most of whom came from the upper social classes.

The wave of conflicting ideas and ideologies that followed was an intellectual ferment of the first order. Its impulses came from the German philosophers, Hegel, Fichte, Kant, and Marx, and the French Socialists. It was stimulated by the backwash from the rising tide of democratic idealism that a decade earlier had swept throughout Western Europe culminating in the 1848 revolutions. In Russia the movements received further impetus from the government's reform program and the wide public interest the program aroused. Painfully aware of the backwardness of their country as compared with the stage of development they had observed in other European societies, the liberals saw in the periodical press a means of influencing the masses and speeding the course of change. They were the vanguard of the revolution, and the accession of the tsar of liberation gave them the opportunity to expose social conditions, to reveal the dark side of Russian autocracy, and to rally the nobleman to the cause of the peasant.

These revolutionary political philosophers, though of different persuasions, at first united in their support of Alexander II's reform proposals, but disagreement soon developed over the means to achieve the commonly desired ends. At first the moderates, trusting the Emperor's sincere desire to help his people, believed that the very best way to effect large-scale reform was through concessions from him within the existing form of government. The radical thinkers broke with Alexander II shortly after emancipation, convinced that accommodation would be impossible to achieve with the forces of autocracy. The majority of the moderates and indeed most of the intelligentsia in time came around to this way of thinking. Possible collaboration between the government and the intellectuals on the reform program failed because of the traditional belief that compromise is equated with weakness. Concession from the government therefore did not provoke respect but instead was viewed as a tactical defeat and a sign to increase demands. Tompkins has written:

> Actually the swing of the intelligentsia, which became markedly hostile to the government and the existing order, had its roots in the very character of the groups and in the nature of the intellectual life of Russia. An analogy is often drawn between the intelligentsia and the great crusading orders of the Middle Ages—both fired by a sense of devotion to a mission that made them see controversial issues not as something to be reduced to formal logic, but as challenges to their militant ardor.[8]

The prerevolutionary reform press consisted of three categories of periodicals: (1) the domestic, duly licensed "legal" journals, (2) the publications printed on presses located outside the country and smuggled across boundaries and circulated illegally by the thousands, and (3) the illegal underground papers printed from hidden presses inside Russia. From all three came the papers that were the spiritual forerunners of the modern Soviet press. The domestic and foreign illegal papers were of course considered the forerunners if not immediate forebears of the Bolshevist press.[9]

THE LEGAL AND REFORM PRESS

The principal legal magazines of the 1860s in the field of literary criticism and political thought were the radical *Sovremennik* (Contemporary) and the slightly liberal *Otechestvennye Zapiski* (Annals of the Fatherland). Ranking closely behind these in importance were Katkov's *Ruskii Vestnik,* nationalist or progovernment after Katkov left the liberal camp, and the radical *Ruskoe Slovo.* Then there were the rightist-leaning Slavophile journals including *Russkaya Beseda, Den', Moskva,* and *Moskvykh,* all of which disappeared after emancipation. Among the others were *Dyelo,* a radical periodical edited by Blagosvetlov, and *Vestnik Europy,* a Narodnik moderate left organ, and the conservative *Severnaya Pochta,* reestablished by the government in 1862 and edited by N. F. Pavlov. All of these journals, with the exception of *Sovremennik* supported reform, as did the daily newspapers.

Sovremennik, partly owned by Nekrasov and edited by Nikolai Chernyshevsky and N. A. Dobroliubov, was a literary, scientific, and political monthly. Chernyshevsky, a nihilist utopian socialist and revolutionary democrat, led the magazine to the radical left and to the forefront in opposing the government on the question of emancipation. Today, Chernyshevsky is regarded in the Soviet Union as the greatest of the "pre-Marxist" thinkers. Lenin credited him with first advocating the idea of a peasant revolution to overthrow the old powers of government.[10] Chernyshevsky's bitter attacks on the gentry, on tsarism, his demands for drastic remedies, and his advice to the tsar on how to effect liberation provoked Alexander II's first reprisal against the press. *Sovremennik* and another anti-government journal *Russkoe Slovo* were suppressed in 1862 for an 8-month period. Chernyshevsky's prosecution for criminal conspiracy ended in seven years of hard labor and permanent exile in Siberia. While in prison he wrote a novel *What Is To Be Done?*, which became a source of inspiration for the revolutionaries who followed him. Chernyshevsky's example, however, served to influence the revolutionary movement more than did his precepts.[11] The two journals were revived after the 8 months ban, Nekrasov in charge of *Sovremennik* and Dimitry Pisarev, a leading *nihilist,* was *Ruskoe Slovo's* chief contributor. But both journals were permanently stopped in 1866 in the government's tougher censorship policy. Nekrasov then took over *Otechestvennye Zapiski,* only to have it suppressed later. Pisarev was imprisoned.

Controls Return

Suppression and other government pressures on editors were indications that the period of comparative freedom was at an end. The 1865 censorship law had clarified policy and provided the courts and administration alike with an instrument that could be applied with some effectiveness to the situation. The Polish revolt and the attempt on the tsar's life indicated to the government that strong measures against the press were needed. While administrative censorship grew more severe, a series of committees drafted a new censorship law which became effective between 1863 and 1865.[12] The chief board of censors was abolished and responsibility for classes and kinds of publications left in the hands of an agency, the Chief Administration for Literary Affairs and Publishing, with the main responsibility resting in the Ministry of Interior. A basic provision was the apparent elimination of a preliminary or prepublication censorship, hated by the editors, in the cities of Moscow and St. Petersburg. This covered the great bulk of the press, but the organs of the provincial press, books, and some periodicals were still subject to preliminary censorship by the Central Government. In the cities, the courts had charge of postpublication offenses. However, the minister of interior could still harass periodicals where subversive utterances were at issue. He was empowered to issue warnings and to suppress publications on the third offense without resort to the courts. Such threats, of course, amounted to a form of preliminary censorship. Left to administrative interpretation were such problems as where to draw the line on political discussion, how to handle cases of libel and other abuses of press freedom, and how to deal with evasions of censorship such as trafficking in published literature from abroad, the dissemination of manuscript articles, and the sporadic circulation of underground issues from secret presses.

A Period of Reaction

In the seventies and eighties the mantle of conservatism and dullness seemed to have settled on the legal press. Katkov's death in 1886 brought the removal of *Russkii Vestnik* to Moscow. *Otechestvennye Zapiski,* much to Kravchinsky's regret, was suspended. He lamented, "Nobody can take a single step in the study of our domestic economy without referring for instruction and information to the back numbers . . . ."[13] This left the monthly *Vestnik Europy, Russkoe Bogatsvo,* and *Russkaya Mysl'* as the principal periodicals. *Vestnik Europy,* edited by the liberal Arsenyev, as Pares said, "with circumspection and dignity," was the only periodical that was able to give "any real reflection of public thought in this period." The principal newspapers were *Russkie Vedomosti* and *Novo Vremya.* The latter, described by Pares as "a miracle of astuteness and versatility," managed to survive the hazards. The venerable *Russkie Vedomosti* was suspended twice before and twice after 1900. It was decorated for its contribution to culture and political consciousness in 1914, changed its name during the war to *Svoboda Rossii* only to perish in the Bolshevik suppressions of 1918. If Russian editors did not interest their public, they lost readers but might escape the censor. If they printed material that attracted readers and sold newspapers, they risked persecution.

The Reign of Alexander III (1881–1894) marked a period of reaction and retrogression. Many of the gains of the reform period were undone. The law which had granted autonomy to the universities under Alexander II was replaced by another which took it away. The act of 1864 had provided that all secondary schools be open to all students "irrespective of faith and social status." Under Alexander III the country returned to the educational theories of the 1830s which provided that children should receive an education appropriate to their social class and that boys of the lower classes should be discouraged from attending secondary schools and universities. The courts fell more under administrative control and this trend took an element of justice out of the prosecution of the censorship laws. Four ministers of government might together forbid a person to practice journalism. The government had the power to bankrupt a paper by forbidding the printing of advertisements or its sale on streets.

The economy, on the other hand, was booming. The results of emancipation and other reforms were making themselves felt. While the government sought to keep things calm on the surface and the underground revolutionary movements continued quietly, economic development moved ahead. Peasant communes acquired more land. Peasants migrated to the cities to work in the factories, although 87 per cent of the population lived in rural areas and were untouched by the cultural advance. Extensive railway construction linked the larger cities, and the Trans-Siberian Railway crept across the continent. Iron and oil production tripled, and coal production increased more than seven times during Alexander III's reign. Foreign investments were coming into the country at a rapid rate, and import duties were increased to protect Russian industry. By 1891 industrial workers numbered more than two million.[14] Literacy, however, lagged, standing at only 21 per cent for the entire country, according to the 1897 census.[15] The level of literacy was larger in the European part of Russia and, of course, in the cities, but illiteracy still barred the potentially great leveling influence of the popular press.

THE EXPATRIATE AND ILLEGAL PRESS

The Russian press in exile consisted of the influential periodicals published from abroad and smuggled into the country in substantial numbers. Refugees from censorship and suppression, these papers could say what the domestic press dared not. The nature of their exposés that embarrassed and discredited the regime shocked the opinion leaders and the people at home. The underground illegal papers published from secret presses in Russia multiplied as the anti-regime spirit mounted. Beginning as organs of secret societies, they sought to arouse public opinion and to promote their viewpoint. The *émigré* and the underground periodical press, the forerunners of the Soviet press, not only played an important role in influencing the course of Russian history but also contributed to political thought and the spread of ideas.

КОЛОКОЛЪ

ПРИБАВОЧНЫЕ ЛИСТЫ КЪ ПОЛЯРНОЙ ЗВѢЗДѢ.

VIVOS VOCO!

№ 1.

1 Іюля 1857.

ПРЕДИСЛОВІЕ.

Fig. 2.1. The most famous and among the earliest of a long series of Russian expatriate journals devoted to social reform at home was **Kolokol** (The Bell). Its first issue (left) was published July 1, 1857, in London and smuggled into Russia. Founded and conducted by Alexander Herzen, philosopher of the pre-Narodnik period, the fortnightly **Kolokol** exerted a powerful influence on public opinion for almost a decade. Though Herzen was not a Marxist, Soviet leaders consider his paper a distinguished forerunner of the Russian revolutionary and present-day Soviet press. Page 1, Volume I, No. 1 began with a preface in poetry. The prose passages on this page set forth the prospectus of the new publishing venture.

Herzen and *Kolokol*

The greatest and among the first of the many expatriate journals was the fortnightly *Kolokol* (The Bell) founded in London in 1857 by Alexander Herzen, the wealthy, illegitimate son of a Russian nobleman (Fig. 2.1). Herzen was a socialist who had left Russia in 1847 never to return. According to Florinsky,[16] *Kolokol* was the most influential journal in Russian history. Sources high in the government provided Herzen in London with confidential information about corruption, abuses of freedom, bureaucratic ineptness, and other ills of absolutism. Published in London and circulated in Russia, where exposing such information was subject to severe penalties, Herzen's paper became the only public Russian source of information from secret government committees drafting measures to emancipate the serfs. Other state secrets were revealed. Names were printed of political prisoners confined in dungeons or working in Siberian mines. Even the numbers assigned to prisoners, supposedly known only to their keepers, were found out and published.[17] Kolokol was read by the Emperor, and its leadership doubtless influenced the provisions of the emancipation reform.[18] Herzen believed the important social and economic reforms he advocated might be achieved by the Crown, though after 1861 he reversed himself and branded emancipation a fraud. On July 1 1861, *The Bell* published an editorial entitled "What Do the

People Need?" The answer became one of Russia's revolutionary battle cries, "The people need land and freedom." Although *Kolokol's* circulation never surpassed 3,000, it was read by everyone of importance. But Herzen misjudged Russian public opinion and lost popular support. His espousal of the Polish cause fell into disrepute after the Polish revolt. Circulation of *Kolokol* dropped to 500, and publication was stopped in 1867. Herzen, however, was a forerunner of the early populists who became influential in the 1870s. Lenin, who hailed Herzen as a revolutionary leader and master of Hegelian dialectics, noted that Herzen had never embraced Marxian socialism. The historian Kornilov's opinion was that Herzen performed a great service by arousing public opinion.[19]

As Herzen's influence waned, other revolutionary thinkers in the 1860s and 1870s used the press to capture the imagination of the intelligentsia. *Nihilism,* a system of thought that denied all traditional values, conventional standards, or accepted beliefs as useful in solving Russia's plight, enjoyed a short period of popularity in the 1860s. The nihilists saw drastic action as the only possible answer. They had no patience with the slow processes of education. Nihilism was followed by and absorbed in a larger and longer-lasting movement known as *narodnichestvo,* hence adherents were known as *narodniks,* or populists. There were writers, journalists, and legal journals inside Russia which served these causes, the most prominent nihilists being Chernyshevsky and Pisarev. But, after 1866, political issues could not be discussed freely in the country; this forced into exile such leaders as Herzen who conducted or contributed to the expatriate journals which, though printed outside the censor's territorial jurisdiction, circulated profusely among the educated in Russia.

Three Narodnik Thinkers

Three other expatriate revolutionary thinkers whose foreign-published writings circulated in Russia in the 1870s were associated in the narodnik movement—M. A. Bakunin, P. L. Lavrov, and P. N. Tkachov. Bakunin, another son of the nobility, had been exiled in Siberia for his anarchistic leanings, but escaped to Geneva to write for a new periodical, *Narodnoyo Dyelo* (The People's Cause). In this paper he called for the people to free themselves from the binding traditions of religion, hereditary property, and family; advocated a utopian society based on a federation of free self-sufficient autonomous communities; and called on the people to take up arms against the authorities. Some of Bakunin's work appeared later in *Rabotnik* (The Worker), 1875–1876, and *Obschina* (The Land Commune), 1878–1879. Bakunin saw the intelligentsia as the general staff for the coming revolution and the peasants as the ranks of the army. As a member of a secret anarchist organization inside the First International (1864–1872) he waged a fierce struggle against Marx before being expelled.[20]

Lavrov, on the other hand, more constructively saw the revolution as a gradual process of social evolution in which reform is accomplished by education and persuasion. Like Bakunin he believed the revolution would have to be a mass movement. He, too, had escaped to Switzerland where from 1873 to 1876 he edited *Vpered* (Forward), issued from presses in Zurich and London. Whereas Bakunin was a romantic and active symbol around which impatient Russian radicals rallied, Lavrov was a theorist. Unlike Pisarev he did not commit himself to the view that Russia could bypass the stage of capitalism on its route to socialism. Like Pisarev, he stressed the moral and intellectual development of the individual. His ideas had important influences on the thinking of the revolutionary propagandists. A friend and admirer of Karl Marx, Lavrov fused in his thinking both the populist and the Marxist views of socialism.[21]

Peter N. Tkachev, Pisarev's friend and also a political refugee from a tsarist prison, had been a former contributor to *Russkoe Slovo*. In Switzerland he edited *Nabat* (The Alarm) from 1875 to 1881, a paper that was first printed in Geneva and then in London. Disagreeing with both Bakunin and Lavrov, Tkachev argued that revolutions can be made by small groups of determined men rather than by the masses. Tkachev, unlike Lavrov, felt that speed was of the essence. He advocated seizure and conversion rather than destruction of the existing government; then the use of propaganda to guide education in the principles of the new order.[22] His was a plan Lenin later used, and his ideas influenced other revolutionary leaders.

Illegal Sheets Inside Russia

A brief mention should be made of a few of the many illegal newspapers which sprang up inside the country only to be put down by the police. In some cases police interfered before the first issue could be printed. These were usually organs of secret societies or incipient political parties and workers' organizations. In 1878 the North Russian Workers' League attempted to publish *Rabochevo Zarya* (The Worker's Dawn) in St. Petersburg. But, seized on the eve of publication, it never saw the light of day. The revolutionary narodniks published *Zemlya i Volya* (Land and Freedom) in 1878–1879 also in St. Petersburg. After only five issues the organization split, and the moderates led by George Plekanov, a Marxist, founded their paper under the name of *Chorny Peredel* (The Total Reapportionment of Land). Associated in this venture were Plekhanov, P. Axelrod, Y. Stephanovich, and L. Deutch. But while the first issue was being printed, their plant in St. Petersburg was raided. Hence the first two issues were published abroad, and subsequent issues at Minsk. The more radical wing took the name *Narodnaya Volya* (The People's Will) and founded its organ of the same name. This party also published three issues of *Rabochaya Gazeta* (Worker's Gazette) in St. Petersburg. All of these short-lived illegal sheets were spawned between 1878 and 1881. The assassination of Alexander II in 1881 and its effect on the censorship apparatus ended the activities of those *narodnik papers* that remained. Plekhanov and associates exiled themselves to Switzerland.

The illegal expatriate publications were hazardous undertakings, doomed to persecution and short life. But they continued until the revolution and made a major contribution to revolutionary thought.

EARLY MARXIST POLITICAL JOURNALISM SPARKS THE BOLSHEVIK POWER OFFENSIVE

Among the more activist of the reform and what were later revolutionary media, both legal and illegal, both patriate and expatriate, were the Marxist journals, organs of the many Marxian socialist societies that sprang up in the 1880s and 1890s. This segment of the communications system is the real forerunner and predecessor of the present day Soviet Communist system, though the Soviet media also claim Herzen's *Kolokol* and Chernyshevsky's *Sovremenik* as their more remote forebears.

Russian Marxism as a political movement was born out of populism's bankruptcy. Terrorism, regicide, and rallying the public on behalf of the peasants had got the narodniks nowhere, it seemed.

Populist leaders too had lost faith in the ability of the peasant to understand what it was all about. The revolution the populists dreamed of was not noticeably nearer. In this situation a group of disillusioned populists resorted to Marxism because it seemed to offer a new approach. Among the first were George Plekhanov and P. B. Axelrod. They resigned from the Land and Freedom cause and in 1883 set up in Switzerland the first Russian social democratic organization under the name of *Osvobozhdenie Truda* (Liberation for Labor).[23] About the same time in Russia groups of Marxian socialists were forming among students and intellectuals. The movement, small and not yet militant, operated in the realm of ideas, and used the press as its principal communication medium.

In Switzerland also Axelrod and Plekhanov were the chief contributors to four volumes of their organization's publication called *Sotsial Demokrat* in the fields of Marxian philosophy and "scientific" socialism. The articles negated populist principles and advocated the creation of a strong working-class party that would lead a social revolution in Russia. By this time the works of Marx and Engels had been translated into Russian, and the intellectual leaders of the movement were able to study these writings and to apply the theories to practical conditions. The *Sotsial Demokrat* was published mainly for a small circle of Russian exiles living in Switzerland and elsewhere abroad.[24] Plekhanov, a brilliant thinker and versatile writer, also contributed to *Rabochy* (The Worker) which was brought out by one of the St. Petersburg Marxist societies.

Up until the middle 1890s the sporadic Marxist organizations in Russia were content to keep the movement largely at the verbal level, engaging in attacks on the populists and in arguing about Marxist theory. But in 1895, under the leadership of Vladimir Ilyich Lenin (Ulianov) and Jules Martov (Zederbaum) 20 organizations in the St. Petersburg region united to form a union dedicated to fight for working-class liberation. The union, *Soyuz Borby,* agitated among the proletariat, stressing the proposition that labor could advance its cause by organizing. Similar unions sprang up in Moscow and in other industrial centers. Worker grievances were exploited fully in the propaganda aimed at bringing about revolutionary changes. Publications issued from secret domestic presses and circulated in Russia from presses located abroad. In 1897 the organization acquired the monthly St. Petersburg *Novoe Slovo* (New Word), and began publishing the writings of Plekhanov, Lenin, Maxim Gorky, Peter Struve, and others. The federated Marxist unions organized a political party at Minsk in 1898, known as the Russian Social Democratic Labor Party.[25] Internecine dissent and police vigilance, culminating in the arrest of the Central Committee, prevented the party from developing a program of action. The organization, attracting members with broadly divergent viewpoints though bound together by a fierce devotion to their cause, was unable either to resolve its differences or to agree on policy. Lenin in his article "What Is To Be Done?" argued that to build a powerful organization that would stick together, the minority should submit to the majority after a decision was reached. He differed with Plekhanov on the question of collaboration with the non-Marxist bourgeoisie in the overthrow of capitalism and the tsarist government. Lenin felt that the socialist workers should not cooperate with the bourgeoisie but should exploit the situation to their own advantage. Plekhanov emphasized the advantages to be gained from working with the bourgeoisie. Where Plekhanov had no faith in depending on the peasant masses to assist in the cause, Lenin believed that the peasants led by the proletariat would provide potent support.[26]

Iskra Adds Its Voice

During an attempt to unify conflicting opinion the leaders decided to start a national political newspaper as a major means of developing a disciplined party machine. The paper should serve also as the party's central guiding organ.[27] Lenin pictured the paper as the "scaffolding" on which the party would be built:

> The newspaper would become part of an enormous pair of Smith's bellows that would blow every spark of class struggle and popular indignation into a general conflagration. Around what is in itself a very innocent . . . common cause, . . . an army of tried workers would systematically gather and receive their training. On the ladders and scaffolding of this . . . structure there would soon ascend . . . . [leaders] who would take their place at the head of the mobilized army and rouse the whole people to settle accounts with the shame and the curse of Russia. This is what we ought to be dreaming about.[28]

The paper entitled *Iskra* (The Spark) was established outside Russia, the first issue appearing in December, 1900, in Stuttgart, Germany (Fig. 2.2). Later it was transferred to Munich, then to London, and finally to Geneva. The front page carried the motto: "From the Spark—the conflagration." [29] Lenin was editor and mem-

РОССІЙСКАЯ СОЦІАЛЬ-ДЕМОКРАТИЧЕСКАЯ РАБОЧАЯ ПАРТІЯ

ИСКРА

№ 1. ДЕКАБРЬ 1900 ГОДА № 1.

НАСУЩНЫЯ ЗАДАЧИ НАШЕГО ДВИЖЕНІЯ.

ВИЛЬГЕЛЬМЪ ЛИБКНЕХТЪ

Fig. 2.2. Page one of the first issue of **Iskra** (The Spark) is dated December, 1900. The first article is headed "Urgent Problems of Our Movement." In the right-hand column is a biographical article about Wilhelm Liebknecht who died in August, 1900. Founded as a central guiding political organ of national scope by the Russian Social Democratic Workers' Party under the leadership of Lenin, Plekhanov, and Maxim Gorky, the expatriate **Iskra** was issued irregularly, first from Stuttgart, then from Munich, London, and Geneva. Its purpose was to build a strong fighting party organization. Though it failed to bring the two factions of the organization together, **Iskra's** motto "From the Spark is kindled the flame" did indeed prophesy a revolution.

ber of the editorial board consisting also of Plekhanov, Martov, Potresov, Zasulich, and Axelrod. The board's draft declaration set up these objectives:

> The journal should serve mainly for propaganda, the newspaper mainly for agitation. . . . the light of theory must be brought to bear upon every separate fact; propaganda on questions of political and party organization must be carried on among the broad masses of the working class. . . . the newspaper . . . . must periodically record workers' complaints, workers' strikes and other forms of proletarian struggle . . . and draw definite conclusions from . . . these facts.[30]

Because of the conditions in which the *émigré* press operated, there was to be no regular date of publication. According to a Lenin associate the paper was smuggled into Russia across the Prussian, Austrian, and Roumanian frontiers, by sea via Marseilles, Alexandria, and the Bulgarian ports, through Tavriz in Persia, through Archangel, and even through the Kola Peninsula, ". . . in spite of the vigilance of the police watchdogs." [31] *Iskra* sought to create a strong fighting party organization. Its pages were filled with philosophy, plans, strategy, and discussion of problems. It became the ideological and organizational rallying point for the party, but it did not bring the two factions together.

The rift between Lenin and Plekhanov grew too deep to be patched up. At the London congress in 1903 Plekhanov tried to compromise and keep the party together, but Lenin rejected efforts at accord. He was convinced the Marxists should oppose the bourgeoisie as vehemently as they did the regime. The basic point of disagreement was over means, not ends. Plekhanov enlarged the board to include members inclined as he was to maintain harmony. Lenin resigned in anger and left the paper in the hands of Plekhanov and the Mensheviks. Lenin's faction, the central organization of the party, followed him in exodus and became known as the Bolsheviks. For the new group Lenin founded a new organ, *Vperyed* (Forward) in 1904. *Iskra,* without Lenin's direction, was a different kind of paper after 1903. Lenin criticized its new policies, charging that the newspaper ". . . teaches the worldly wisdom of yielding and getting along with everyone . . . it goes in for petty scandal-mongering. . . . How they have disgraced our old Iskra." [32] The "old" fighting *Iskra,* as the Bolsheviks referred to the paper published before the split, was credited later by Stalin with having created, with the help of Lenin's writings, the theoretical foundation for the revolutionary movement. *Iskra* ceased publication in 1905.

The Social Revolutionaries and Constitutional Democrats Contend

Other principal combinations of splinter organizations besides the Social Democrats who followed G. W. F. Hegel and Marx, included on the one hand the Social Revolutionary Party whose thinking was shaped by Peter Lavrov, Auguste Compte, and Nicholas Mikhailovsky; and on the other a coalition of liberals known as the Constitutional Democrats, organized from among the Zemstvo organizations, the Union of Unions, the nobility, students and intellectuals, some of whom had disavowed Marx. The latter group advocated individualism, free democratic institutions, Christian morality, and social responsibility—ideas from John Stuart Mill, Herbert Spencer, and Vladimir Solov'ev. The former, the Social Revolutionary group, absorbed other groups to form a party dedicated to militant terroristic tactics and heavy propaganda in the struggle against the regime. The party's foreign branch published *Revolyutsionnaya Rossiya,* like *Iskra,* from foreign soil. It served as the party's popular agitation organ. At home its theoretical organ was *Vestnik Russkoi Revolutsii* (Messenger of the Russian Revolution). Equip-

withdraw their savings from banks—an effort to cripple government credit. The government closed all eight papers, among them a Menshevik paper called *Nachalo* (The Beginning). After this the two factions came together to publish jointly *Severny Golos* (The Voice of the North) in St. Petersburg, as the official organ of both parties.

Lenin had underestimated the climate of public opinion at the time of the elections for the First Duma. He was convinced that the country was on the verge of a widespread armed uprising and in the belief that participating in the elections would handicap the party in profiting from such an uprising, ordered the party to abstain from the elections. The Social Democrats elected a few deputies, but the majority went to the Kadets. Despite the fact that the Bolsheviks looked upon the Duma as a tool of the autocracy, they were represented in the succeeding Dumas, used them as a platform for agitation and for, as they said, "exposing Tsarism."[43] The next several years were periods of alternate cooperation and conflict between the two factions of the party. Both factions attended the Fourth Congress in 1906, but the central party paper, now called *Sotsial Demokrat,* fell into the hands of the Mensheviks. Once more the Bolsheviks began their own *Proletary,* this time in Finland, and Lenin contributed over 100 articles to this publication between 1906 and its demise in 1909.[44] During this period the Bolsheviks started two legal papers, *Volna* (The Wave) and *Ekho.* The Central Committee had published a number of organs for men in the armed forces between 1905 and 1906, including *Kazarma* (Barracks) in St. Petersburg, *Soldatskaya Zhizn* (Soldier's Life) in Moscow, *Soldat* in Sevastopol, *Golos Soldata* (The Soldier's Voice) in Riga, and *Zhizn Kazarmy* in Voronezh. This pattern of communications extending along vertical and horizontal lines was later adopted in the organization and structure of the Soviet press.

After legal party newspapers were suspended in 1907, Lenin was forced to flee the country and remained abroad until 1917. Other leaders of the two wings of the party were imprisoned or sent into exile. Party membership dropped from 8,000 to 3,000 in St. Petersburg alone. While Lenin contributed to *Proletary* from Finland and later Geneva where the paper was transferred, the Mensheviks, with Plekhanov contributing, brought out *Golos Sotsial-Demokrata* in Geneva. Intraparty warfare was resumed in Switzerland. Meantime the central party organ *Sotsial Demokrat* was revived in Russia, but its editors were arrested and it was moved abroad.

In Russia, Trotsky made an effort to harmonize the two factions and brought out the first periodical under the name of *Pravda* in 1908. Plekhanov supported his efforts.[45] In another attempt at unity in 1910, the Bolsheviks decided to stop publishing *Proletary,* the Mensheviks to close down *Golos Sotsial Demokrata,* and instead, the combined factions agreed to subsidize *Pravda,* though Lenin had at one time called its editor "Judas Trotsky." This shaky accord soon collapsed. The Mensheviks took *Pravda* and, in addition, created two legal journals in Russia, *Nasha Zarya* (Our Dawn) in St. Petersburg and *Vozrozhdeniya* (Renaissance) in Moscow, while the Bolsheviks founded a weekly newspaper in St. Petersburg in 1910 called *Zvezda.*[46]

Pravda Skirts the Tsarist Censorship

Early in 1912 the cleavage became final, the Bolsheviks expelling the Mensheviks and "other deviationists" from the party and replacing the weekly *Zvezda* with a legal daily newspaper directed to the masses of the workers. A gift to Lenin of 100,000 rubles covered publishing costs and again the name *Pravda* appeared on May 5, 1912, in St. Petersburg. Sources are not clear about the connection, if any, between Trotsky's *Pravda* and the Bolshevik *Pravda.* J. V. Stalin became this *Pravda's* first editor, but was soon arrested and sent into exile where he stayed until 1917. Lenin was its chief contributor from abroad, as was V. M. Molotov at home—that "incurable dumbbell," as Lenin called him. Lenin also was chief critic when the paper published articles that clearly were not in accord with policy. With daily publication and legal status as long as it could conceal its connection with the Bolsheviks, *Pravda* was now able to accomplish what *Iskra* had been forced to leave to pamphlets. It covered day-to-day developments among workers in factories and fields. A police report on the contents of *Pravda* said that it devoted much space to strikes and other overt actions because its editors knew worker-readers were more interested in their own plight than in revolutionary ideology.[47] *Pravda* appealed to the workers to elect deputies to the Duma who would support the party's program, which included land reapportionment and the 8-hour work day.

To survive at all *Pravda* pursued a perilous course. It was

Fig. 2.3. Collected above are different title lines from the early **Pravda**, 1912–1914, the daily mass journal first issued May 5, 1912, by the Bolsheviks in the heavily censored climate of St. Petersburg. When the authorities confiscated an issue under one title and arrested the "editor," the paper would promptly publish under a different one. Often only a word or two would be switched: thus, it was **Workers' Truth** which became **Northern Truth**, which became **The Truth of Labor**, then **In Search of Truth**, etc. (Reading top to bottom in the left column.)

under constant police surveillance. Its plant was raided. Issues were confiscated. Its editors were arrested, fined, and imprisoned. The censorship authorities used illegal subterfuge to keep the paper from reaching its subscribers. They attempted to destroy it from within by sabotage.[48] Through it all *Pravda* managed to survive because officials chose to operate within the literal framework of the law, because of police inefficiency, and because its editors were skillful in outwitting the authorities. When the paper under its first title was forced to close, it promptly appeared under a partially new name. This evasive tactic was used eight times before officials caught on and frustrated it (Fig. 2.3). The basic name *Pravda* was retained, but a qualifying adjective was added in small type above the large letters, P-r-a-v-d-a. Thus it became *Rabochaya Pravda* (Workers' Truth), *Put Pravda* (The Path of Truth), etc.[49]

Pravda's writers and editors again resorted to the use of Aesopian language, allegory, and other artifices—a practice that had proved useful to nineteenth-century writers. For example the phrase, "consistent and staunch labour democrats" was easily translated by readers as "Bolsheviks," but provided no legal grounds for the censors to seize upon. Moderately liberal papers got into occasional trouble with the censorship, and a revolutionary party organ like *Pravda* faced reprisal almost daily. One out of three of its 645 published issues was either confiscated or fined. Worker-readers made contributions to pay the fines, but when enough money could not be raised, editors were jailed. To prevent the loss of its talented editors who might languish in prison, *Pravda* hired "editors" among the illiterate, who did nothing but sign the controversial issues, as required by law, and sit out the sentences behind bars.[50] During its first year, police tried to confiscate 41 issues, editors were sued 36 times and spent a total of 4 years in prison, according to Lenin.[51]

The organizational, agitational, and propagandistic functions which are the foundation of Communist mass communication systems were fully in operation on the early *Pravda*. In addition to being the publishing center of the daily paper, the editorial offices were headquarters for party meetings where reports were heard and instructions from the central committee were handed down to party workers in mills and factories.[52] The activities connected with *Pravda,* the program of the party's deputies in the Duma, and the program of illegal subversion were all fused skillfully by party leaders so that the total effect was one of strength and unity. In December, 1912, Bolshevik deputies in the Duma raised the question of trade union persecution. *Pravda* and a party committee organized a mass campaign behind these charges, and *Pravda* published information to show that trade unions were being persecuted by the police. The committee published an illegal leaflet calling for a 1-day work stoppage to support the Duma. While speeches were being made before the Duma, workers walked out to show their support.[53]

On July 8, 1914, *Pravda* and a number of other periodicals were suspended, not to be revived until after the regime had fallen. Although the imminence of war was probably the reason for the government's decision to stop the paper outright, Bassow wondered why it hadn't happened sooner.

> When one examines the record of the struggle between the police and *Pravda,* it is impossible not to question the intentions of the police. Here was a numerous gendarmerie, properly officered and equipped, backed by the full force of the Russian state, trying to destroy a small, weak newspaper sustained only by its license, limited funds, and a small but loyal following. It was seemingly an unequal fight in which

> one would expect the police to win whenever they desired. However they appear to have been playing a game as long as *Pravda* was not considered an actual danger to the regime and to have given it the sporting chance that a cat gives a mouse it has trapped in a corner. The game lasted two years and two-and-a-half months, and ended with the paper's suppression. . . . This was not the end of the drama, for it was *Pravda* that had the last laugh. It reappeared on the streets of Petrograd five days after the March revolution had swept the tsarist government and the police into the limbo of history.[54]

Exactly a month after *Pravda's* closing, on August 8 (N. S.) all parties in the Duma except the Bolsheviks officially agreed to support the prosecution of the war. In November the party's five deputies in the Duma were arrested, tried with their accomplices on charges of subversion, found guilty, and sentenced to Eastern Siberia.

Pravda's chief competitor within the Social Democratic party in St. Petersburg was the Menshevik paper *Luch* (The Ray), which was publishing 10,000 copies by mid-1913, about one-fourth the number *Pravda* is said to have been publishing. Sources do not agree as to the financial solvency of the early *Pravda*. Though it had been endowed, a Tass article on the paper's 25th anniversary said it survived only through desperate struggles, lacking funds and equipment. Yet Popov and Bassow state that it was solvent when other papers, including *Luch*, were losing money.[55]

The paper was a potent influence, enabling the party to gain control of St. Petersburg labor and eventually of the revolutionary movement. It was by far the most important socialist organ among those that police had charged with spreading revolutionary ideas among the masses. *Pravda* devoted space to strikes, to national minorities, agrarian problems, government policy, and Marxist theory, all from the Bolshevik viewpoint. It fanned dissatisfaction among workers and aroused their anger toward their "exploiters," and contained instructions and signals for mass demonstrations. *The History of the All-Union Communist Party* states that,

> A whole generation of revolutionary proletariat, which later carried out the October socialist revolution grew up with *Pravda*. On *Pravda* were tried out most of the revolutionary methods, journalistic and otherwise, that later became standard Soviet mass communication theory and procedure. For example worker-peasant correspondents, or *rabsel'kor*, contributed to the early *Pravda*. Each issue contained dozens of items contributed by them, reporting instances of police or bureaucratic injustice, and harsh working conditions. In more than two years of publication, an estimated 17,000 items contributed from these amateur correspondents were published.[56]

Since Lenin sought to combine the cause of the peasant with that of the worker, he ran in the paper a special section called "Peasant Life" which included letters from peasants carrying themes similar to those touched upon in workers' reports published elsewhere in the paper.

During the period they were issuing *Pravda,* the Bolsheviks also published three legal magazines, *Prosveshcheniye* (Enlightenment), *Voprosy Strakhanovaniya* (Social Insurance), and *Robotnitsa* (The Working Woman), in addition to a number of trade union journals. Wartime revolutionary Russian newspapers continued to be published from abroad. *Sotsial Demokrat* and *The Communist* appeared irregularly in Geneva, and Plekhanov brought out a paper called *Zu Partu.* Trotsky, who had retired from the editorial board of *Luch* to publish the independent legal journal *Borba* along with Martov and others, supported *Nashe Slovo* (Our Word) published in Paris.[57] Within Russia, Bolshevik propaganda consisted mainly of leaflets, circulated by the thousands, especially among soldiers at the front. Seton-Watson states that the question of whether the Russian army was destoyed by military blows against it before the revolution, or by the defeatist agitator propaganda and organization at the front is a question that is still unanswered,[58] but each played a part.

The Bolsheviks Triumph

Shortly after the March, 1917, revolution, the Bolsheviks reappeared as a legal party and turned on the provisional government the same propaganda weapons they had used against the imperial government. *Pravda* was back on Petrograd streets by March 5, urging workers to carry the revolution on to its completion (Fig. 2.4). However, *Izvestia* had preceded it by a few days, having been started by the Mensheviks and the Social Revolutionaries on February 28, 1917. *Izvestia* attacked the Bolshevists, but supported the new government. The Bolshevik party in turn officially resolved not to cooperate with the new government. Stalin and Kamenev, however, returned to positions on *Pravda* and changed its policy to one of support and conciliation. This was changed again by Lenin upon his return in a sealed-train ride across Germany in mid-April. *Pravda* on April 20 published his "April Theses" calling for arousal of class consciousness, fraternization in front-line trenches, nonsupport of the provisional government, attack and exposure of its

ПРАВДА

Центральный Органъ Россійской Соціалъ-Демократической Рабочей Партіи.

ЕЖЕДНЕВНАЯ ГАЗЕТА

ЛИСТОКЪ „ПРАВДЫ“.

Fig. 2.4. The first number of the revived **Pravda** (left) appeared on Petrogard streets March 5, 1917, to urge workers to carry the revolution on to its completion. A one-page **Pravda** (right) bulletin-type "extra" was published July 16, 1917, during the Kornilov uprising. It was issued from an underground headquarters. **Pravda's** editorial offices had been destroyed July 5 by a band of noblemen. "Proletarians of all countries, unite," Lenin's slogan from the March 5, 1917, **Pravda** appears over the title line. Identified as the organ of the Russian Social Democratic Workers' Party, the paper contains "five theses of Lenin."

errors, nationalization of the land and banking system, adoption by the party of the name "Communist," and creation of the revolutionary international. Kamenev stated in *Pravda* that Lenin's position was unacceptable, and Plekhanov called him delirious. Kamenev and Trotsky eventually joined the Bolshevik party, but Lenin fled the country again in July after Kornilov led the demonstrations of workers and soldiers against the provisional government, and the party suffered other setbacks. The government suppressed *Pravda*, but in November it reappeared again after revolutionary detachments under Trotsky seized power for the Bolsheviks in the October revolution. This time it was an honored veteran of the revolution. The second All-Russian Congress of Soviets made *Izvestia* the organ of the party's Central Committee and of the Petrograd Soviet of Workers and Soldiers Deputies. Both newspapers published the party's decrees on land and peace, and other early Soviet government documents. Both papers moved to Moscow when the Soviet government relocated the capital.

Lenin signed a decree prohibiting the publication of all opposition newspapers only three days after the November 7, 1917, Bolshevik *coup d'etat*. Anticipating that the unusual nature of such a decree would provoke a torrent of outraged public opinion both at home and abroad, the framers made it appear to be a temporary measure, by attaching the following proviso:

> As soon as the new order becomes stabilized, all administrative restrictions on the press will be lifted and complete freedom of the press will be established, subject only to limitations of legal liability in accordance with the broadest and most progressive legislation on this problem.

The decree was never revoked, and it became the legal foundation for the reestablishment of Glavlit as the Soviet censorship agency, the only government agency that has functioned under the same name since tsarist days. It functioned under the Imperial Ministry of Internal Affairs from 1865 to 1917, to be revived by the new Soviet government on June 6, 1922. Under the supervision of joint deputy chiefs, one of which was to be a member of the security police, Glavlit was to exercise both prepublication and postpublication censorship.[59]

The Bolshevist newspaper is of a new type, says the *Bol'shaia Sovetskaia Entsiklopediia.* The bases of the Bolshevist newspaper are Party Spirit (Partiinost), Marxist-Leninist ideology, broad national and mass consciousness, irreconcilability with the enemies of the Communist party, and truthfulness.[60] On this kind of ideological foundation a new type of persuasive communication system was to be launched as a political arm of the state.

THE GENERAL PRESS IN THE FINAL DAYS OF EMPIRE

While Marxian socialist factions were experimenting in the use of the press as a weapon, the general domestic public press showed signs of further maturity during the last days of the empire. The period of unrest following the 1905 revolution when the government lost control of the press saw developments in the legal domestic press, chiefly in the founding of political organs. This was a period in which the press enjoyed its greatest freedom, due to the laxity of censorship. Three important journals should be mentioned: *Russkoye Slovo,* the same title as the earlier periodical censored in 1866, was a middle-class paper; *Golos Moskovy* (Voice of Muscovy) was moderately liberal; and *Byloe* was a historical journal concerned with the Russian revolutionary movement. These, of course, lent their voices to the other leading newspapers and periodicals founded in the nineteenth century and discussed above.

St. Petersburg and Moscow were the centers of a national press, publishing papers which were transported by rail to neighboring areas. Although efforts were made to establish a 1-kopeck press, 3 to 5 kopecks was the usual price for a paper, and this kept individual circulations at a low level, compared to those of the mass circulation press of New York and London. There was little emphasis in most of the press on especially local news, as the Western journalist defined it. The same was true of sensationalism. Russian editors rejected the idea of display headlines and bulletins as rude manifestations of Western-type yellow journalism. Along with sober reports of national and international news developments, the Russian reader seemed to prefer editorial articles and *feuilletons*.

In 1912 the number of newspapers in Russia totaled 1,131, located in 261 communities, and the number of magazines totaled 1,656.[61] These figures include 252 newspapers and 426 magazines that were published in foreign languages. The number of daily newspapers in 1913 was estimated at 50, one-fourth of which were published in the capital. Total combined circulation of newspapers (single-run totals) fell slightly below 3 million.

CHARACTERISTICS OF THE PRE-SOVIET RUSSIAN PRESS SYSTEM

Some characteristics of the Russian press as it evolved under the tsars find their echoes in present-day Soviet mass communications. Tompkins notes that the press reflected uniform lack of the critical faculty that is characteristic of the Russian educated mind which, though extensionally oriented in some respects, tends to be fascinated by the most irrational ideas, each compartmented and unrelated to the other.[62] This weakness in the Russian evaluation process together with the iron curtain of censorship led to the formation of unbalanced and unrealistic images among the Russian people of themselves, their country, and of other peoples. Such images were reflected in press content. Recurring themes stressed the superiority of Russians and Russian society over other less-fortunate peoples to an extent beyond that warranted by feelings of nationalistic pride. The popular media and even the scientific learned periodicals reflected a "condescending contempt" for the poor people of Western Europe, "crushed by the yoke of capitalism; . . . oppressed by militarism and religious intolerance." Only in Russia is all quiet and tranquil, they said. "Everything in the Tsar's empire is happy and contented. The Russian peasant is no proletarian, for he has land which he himself tills. The Russian Army is the strongest in the world . . . for it has no Jewish muskets." [63]

A supreme example of this sort of abstract assessment of situations without any basis in empirical fact or reality appears in the writings of Katkov, published in *Moskovskia Vedomosti* in 1886: In spite of the rigid government controls on the press at that time, Katkov was able to argue that "the press in Russia, and perhaps in Russia alone, is placed in a position approaching complete independence. We know of no organ of the foreign press that could be called independent in the true meaning of the term." In the "so-called constitutional states," according to Katkov, the press was not "an expression of public conscience but a tool of party interests." Russia had no political parties, hence the Russian press was basically independent. The state supervision of the press in Russia, he said, was not essentially different from any other measure for the protection of public order and safety. "What is not contrary to the law and institutions of the country, what does not offend public morality, what is not deceit and incitement to violence—can and is expressed in the press with complete independence." [64] This kind of rationale was used by Lenin 25 years later to support his argument that the Soviet Communist press was really free and independent.

Critics also have pointed to the lack of objectivity in the Russian press. Nagradow in 1894 wrote that the Western European periodicals were scrupulously painstaking in their efforts to get the pertinent facts and to report them accurately and truthfully, if for no other reason than because they would be exposed and humiliated by their competitors of opposing political views. In contrast, the Russian press, he said, resorts without hesitation to the ". . . most questionable methods—any methods other than objective presentation of facts, including sneering at the naïveté of anyone who doubts their statements or does not accept their argument, and casting suspicion on their opponents and their sources of information." [65] All controversial matters, it seems, were discussed on a partisan plane,

". . . so that the reader's doubts are swept away and he is left with the idea that there is only one side to the argument. This lends, in a discussion of all Russian questions, a certainty that is completely lacking in the discussion of great issues in the press of Western Europe." [66] These words in a slightly different context might have been spoken by a post-World War II diplomat, or any student of Soviet propaganda.

Although the imperial government did not try to own and control a press monopoly, there existed a substantial number of newspapers and magazines that were either owned and operated by the state or openly subsidized by the government. The former were the organs of the various ministries and the latter were publications in various languages disseminated to promote the government's position not only to the domestic minority populations under Russian rule, but also to foreigners. Moreover, the imperial government grew to be quite expert in using the press for its own purposes. For example, the close scrutiny maintained by the censors over information and views on foreign affairs imparted a uniformity and an authoritative air to the published information that made it appear official in all media. The public believed that all media reflected the official viewpoint.

The Russian press under the tsars managed to grow and develop as a capitalistic enterprise along with the economic system. In the face of alternating periods of rigid and relaxed government censorship, the private press flourished alongside a government-owned and subsidized press. In the last half of the nineteenth and the first decade of the twentieth centuries what had been largely a periodical press of literature, comment, and social criticism took two paths of development. The first was the evolution of a mass press of popular appeal after the manner of Western journals. The other was the evolution of a vigorous crusading and eventually revolutionary reform press, aimed first at the intelligentsia and later including the general public, dedicated to molding public opinion in the cause of social change. The effectiveness of the press in its efforts to change opinion was documented from time to time by the efforts of the censor. But the most telling proof of the effectiveness of its methods was written into Soviet history when in 1917 Lenin and the other Bolsheviks started to build a public communication system modeled after the propagandistic and agitational revolutionary press they had conducted.

Russian concepts of journalism also made their contribution

to Soviet concepts. Russian journalism generally was not objective and independent but frankly and sometimes even brutally partisan. In the Russian journalist's ethical code, if he had one, there was no dedication to the public weal, no feeling of responsibility to society, no respect for fair play or for standards of truth based on scientific empirical tests. The criterion of successful journalism depended upon whether the editor's views coincided with or opposed those of the administration which, in turn, depended upon the outcome of his bouts with the censor. Brilliant journalists became adept in circumventing the law by the use of Aesopian language and other devices. The battle between journalist and censor " . . . was never in the field of facts, but always . . . opinion, and not subject to any test other than that of conformity," Tompkins wrote. "It would seem that it was not a battle in which victory would go to the side which was most reasonable, but one in which the supreme arbiter was force . . . ." [67]

Although editors and writers fought for more freedom of the press and universally indicted prepublication censorship for themselves, they believed in the principle of suppression of opposition views whether expressed by government or political opponent. Therefore the Bolsheviks used to the fullest what freedom of the press they were allowed, but upon assuming power, monopolized press freedom for themselves by abolishing it for others.

3 ★

SOVIET MASS COMMUNICATIONS: GROWTH AND DEVELOPMENT

THE COMMUNIST REGIME IN RUSSIA, a coalition of Bolsheviks and Social Revolutionaries, set out to bypass the stage of capitalism altogether, and to establish a Communist system. A series of decrees established the principle of state ownership and control of the means of production, which included government seizure in the name of the workers of private lands and property, church lands and property, banks and credit, and the abolition of religion and private business.

PERSUASION BY COERCION

The constituent assembly was invited to disperse at machine-gun point, universal suffrage was abolished, and power theoretically transferred to councils (Soviets) elected by manual laborers. But the government faced hostility and disaster on every hand, and the first few years were ones of intense struggle literally to survive, then to centralize power and consolidate gains. Soviet armies still in the field put down rebellions and peasant uprisings, and battled foreign contingents. In foreign affairs, the regime negotiated postwar peace treaties with the European powers. The Bolshevik dictatorship lived and endured primarily by the use of brute terrorism on the one hand and persuasion on the other. Army officers were assassinated, massacres were conducted in prisons, peasant uprisings were crushed. Ordinary procedures of justice were modified by a code in which the most serious crime was opposition in word, deed, or thought to the Communist rulers or to Communism. Drawing upon their long experience in conspiracy against the Empire, the Bolshevik regime established its system of large-scale espionage which helped it anticipate and effectively deal with any incipient opposition.

While force and terror were being applied wherever needed, oral and written persuasion gushed forth unceasingly. Red army officers and men, the leaders and masses of the workers, every segment of society were bombarded with the products of an immense system of propaganda into which enormous ingenuity, enterprise, and money were poured.[1] Propaganda took precedence over the ordinary channels of education. Propaganda and agitation backed by force or the threat of force did more than anything else to break up powerful internal resistance in Russia. And the success of their propaganda methods exceeded even the regime's expectations.

Other potent factors accounted also for the Bolshevik success. Lenin's group was a strongly disciplined corps of fighting men, hardened by daily confrontation with near insurmountable obstacles. They were determined and stubbornly dedicated. To the most intelligent of the younger generation in Russia they were heroes symbolizing the end of tyranny and corruption, the end of the old regime, and the dawn of a new day for the common man. The prospect held out by the new regime released new opportunities which placed a premium on brains and courage. The regime sought and encouraged party participation and spearheaded the beginnings of political consciousness among masses of people many of whom never realized before that their contributions were important to the state.

However, the reaction to the sudden imposition of socialism resulted in near economic collapse. The country was already ravaged by the war. Lack of incentives closed businesses, slowed factory production, and dried up sources of credit. The international Communist movement had drastically curtailed foreign trade. Russia lived on its reserves for a time, barely avoiding collapse. Panic and famine ensued. When the regime claimed its share of excess farm produce, peasants produced only what they needed. Starvation and inflation depopulated the cities, causing huge migrations from urban centers. By 1921 conditions became so intolerable that Lenin was compelled to adopt a compromise with capitalism. The New Economic Policy stabilized the monetary system, revived old channels of domestic and foreign trade, and permitted limited private ownership. The state, however, retained control of heavy industry, banking, transportation, and foreign trade. While the country recovered, a bureaucratic communist dictatorship took shape.

State ownership and control of the press and its contents was ordained when private ownership was first abolished. By 1919, private publishing establishments, private newspapers and magazines, and the telegraphic news agencies had been taken over by the state for its use. With the advent of the New Economic Policy, no change was made in this arrangement. Thus practically from the first the principle of state monopoly of the channels of information and communication was established. With the small nucleus of party organs at the top, and the workers' journals below, the hierarchical press system was organized out of confiscated media facilities. As a pivotal party weapon the press was expected to grow rapidly in numbers and circulation. Theoretically the public communication channels were considered an integral segment of the whole society intimately linked with the arts, literature, music, and closely synchronized with the economy and all other institutions and systems of the Soviet state.

The Constitution of the Russian Soviet Federated Socialist Republic, adopted in 1918, guaranteed to the proletariat freedom of the press and access to communication facilities. The government's decree of December 29, 1917, authorized the development of a press system and the establishment of government publishing houses. The National Commissariat of Enlightenment, through its literary department, was authorized to organize a communications program, concentrating its efforts primarily on spreading among the masses all newspapers, magazines, and classical books of native and foreign literature, in Russian and other languages.[2] The education and indoctrination uses of the press mechanism were reiterated in the decisions of the party's Eighth Congress under the heading "On the Party and the Soviet Press." The decisions stressed the value of the press not only as a powerful propaganda weapon, but also as an instrument for organization and agitation—"an irreplaceable means of influencing the masses." The decree directed the party committees and government officials to shape and sharpen this weapon.

BARRIERS TO DEVELOPMENT

Administrative fiat could not provide the essential social and economic requisites for a modern mass communication system. Development of the public media depended on the regime's efforts, but it also depended on such factors as geography, literacy, language barriers, the development of an industrial technology, the rise of a consumer economy, and the degree of social and political participation among the people. Geography—Russia's vast distances alone—until the age of airborne cargoes, proved to be a major obstacle to the delivery of printed matter to the consumer. The postal service was slow. Transportation was chronically overtaxed because heavy industry took precedence over communication. The Khrushchev era had not solved the problem by 1965, for even then the transit system was being blamed for late delivery of periodicals. One might think the advent of the electronic media would make transportation less a problem, but the press has remained the main medium of public communication. Propaganda purposes are served best by media that are sensitive to change—media into which the regime might place a message and expect it to be delivered with all speed to the most remote potential consumer. For this reason the electronic media have advantages over the press—advantages which have not been fully realized.

Illiteracy also proved a formidable barrier. In 1928, 51 per cent of the population 15 years of age and older could not read or write. Moreover, literacy in one language means less in a multilingual state. Russian is the *lingua franca* of the country. But Russian was the native tongue of less than 50 per cent of the people at the beginning of the Soviet regime. Some 50 years later, Russian is the native language of slightly less than 60 per cent of the population. Each of the republics has its own official language, with approximately 80 languages said to be in use. Fourteen different languages have been found necessary to reach by radio the one million people of Dagestan; thus several tongues may be needed to communicate at once with only a small proportion of the populace. The popular education system has of course brought illiteracy down to a nominal level and is helping to break down language barriers, as children are required to learn to read and write in Russian whether or not it is their native speech. Nonetheless, the language problem is still one of the more important problems the mass media face.

Prime technological, engineering, and industrial resources were poured into heavy industry during the Stalin era. As a result communication facilities such as printing materials and machinery, radio broadcasting and receiving equipment, rural electricity, batteries, wire, and related needs were constantly in short supply or nonexistent. Presses and paper were pathologically scarce, and for decades the broadcasting branch of the media system had to mark time awaiting the production in quantity of tubes and other technical apparatus. Also aggravating the problem was the fact that the Soviet government in its drive to maturity placed severe restraints on production of goods for popular consumption, especially in such areas as agricultural food products, clothing, housing, and consumer durables. Individual income levels remained low, a condition that obviously limited the ability of the consumer to buy media. Since at first many of the periodicals were distributed free or for a nominal charge, consumer purchasing power was not then a major factor in mass media use. These, however, were some of the chief barriers to development of an effective communication system, barriers to building a state communication system that can provide immediate simultaneous exposure of a single message from a single source to the greatest possible number.

BUILDING A PRESS SYSTEM: FROM THE REVOLUTION TO WORLD WAR II

The formula for this new kind of newspaper which the communists hoped would appeal to the masses was a curious concoction of revolutionary journalism fitted into Marxist theory and adapted to nationwide scale to meet the political needs of a new regime. Perhaps because he realized only too well the danger to a regime that might come from wide discussion in the press of political theory, Lenin renounced the sensational, inflammatory type of polemics that had helped bring him to power. He also forbade what he saw as social deficiencies in the capitalist press, such as the evil influence of advertising, the overemphasis on the sensational for the sake of selling newspapers and advertising, and the widespread concern in the capitalist press with political matters and routine events. The press must be changed, he wrote, from an organ which "primarily reports the political news of the day into a serious organ for the economic education of the mass of the population." By this, Lenin said, he meant the press should deal with and report the practical everyday economic problems of the organized workers, not that the press should confine itself to theoretical economics and such "twaddle." [3] He urged on editors the slogan, "Less politics and more economics." How the press could abstain from politics, when by its very nature as a party and government organ it was a creature of politics, Lenin did not explain. It was clear that he wanted the press, in fulfilling its serious function, to avoid "wasting" space on such matters as entertainment or trivial happenings and matters of personal as opposed to social or collective interest. How the press was to fulfill this mission and still attract and hold its audience was a question Lenin left to the editors and writers. The party in April, 1921, officially adopted Lenin's formula and instructed the press accordingly.

The central press system was modeled along the lines of the revolutionary periodicals and the national models, *Pravda* and *Izvestia*. With variations suitable to type and purpose, the provincial and local press were cut from the same pattern. So were the magazines and technical journals. Replacing the tsarist regime as objects of attack were the vestiges of capitalism and resistance that remained, the "enemies of the state," "the imperialist powers," "rumor-mongers," "hoarders," "dissident elements," "sloth," and "inefficiency." Substitute scapegoats were found to aid in rationalization of the regime's failures, so that the regime could avoid taking the responsibility for such failures. The formula for the Soviet newspaper was relatively simple, the limits of its behavior and purpose prescribed and proscribed. Within these limits there was little room for innovation and change. Inkeles shows how the early formula for *Pravda* blueprinted by the Central Committee even to the number of lines and proportionate distribution of content among various categories of subject matter was still being followed almost thirty years later by the *Pravda* of the 1947–1948 period.[4]

The new government did not overlook the vital necessity of controlling the information stream. In 1917–1918 information and propaganda were being handled by two competing agencies, the Petrograd Telegraph Agency and the Press Bureau of the All-Russian Central Executive Committee of the Councils of Workers, Peasants, and Soldiers Deputies, located in Moscow.[5] Lenin merged the two agencies in the spring of 1918 under the title Russian Telegraph Agency, or Rosta. In July, 1925, after the creation of the Union of Socialist Soviet Republics, Rosta was relegated to the status of an agency for the Russian Republic, and the new Telegrafnoye Agentsvo Sovyetskoyo Soyouza, the Telegraph Agency of the Soviet

Union, was organized as the monopolistic state agency to handle official propaganda and information on national and international levels. Rosta disappeared in 1935.[6]

Early Soviet Periodicals

Among the leading periodicals[7] during the first decade were *Pravda* and *Izvestia; Krasnaya Zvezda* (Red Star), 1918, one of the several mass political magazines published in Moscow and other cities while the Bolshevik government was still fighting; *Red Army-Red Navy,* 1919, the armed forces organ, followed in 1938 by the present-day *Krasnaya Zvezda* and *Sovetskii Flot;* and *Trud* (Labor), the daily organ of the All-Union Central Council of Trade Unions, which first appeared on February 15, 1921.

The early magazines devoted to literature with a social consciousness were *Ogonyok* (Little Flame), edited by A. Lunacharskii from 1918 to 1920, to be succeeded by another magazine, a popular weekly, of the same name; *Dukh* (Genius) 1918–1922, edited by A. Serafimovich and others; *Krasnaya Rodina* (Red Soil), which was founded in 1921 with Maxim Gorky, novelist and dramatist, as editor. Gorky had started the short-lived *Letopia* in 1913, but after exile in Italy had returned to become a leading Soviet literary figure. The first issue of *Krasnaya Rodina* carried Lenin's essay, "About Tax in Kind." Later Gorky was identified in the publishing of an almanac, *Nashe Vremena* (Our Days), and after 1929, *S.S.S.R. Pyerestroikie* (USSR in Reconstruction), and *Nasha Prodvizhenia* (Our Progress). Socialist theoretical journals included another called *Proletary,* published in Moscow from 1919 to 1921, and *Bud-uschii* (The Future) published in Petrograd.

The Eleventh Congress of the party in 1921 created new publications, dissolved existing ones, and in April, 1922, the regime began its program of publishing specialized newspapers and magazines designed to reach and indoctrinate the population by class, age, special interest, place of residence, and language. The first youth publication was *Molodie Guardia* (Young Guards), begun in 1922 and discontinued in 1941. Currently a journal with a similar title *Molodaya Guardya* (Young Guard) is being published. *Krasnaya Molodoi* (Red Youth) appeared some years later. An evening daily newspaper, *Vecherniaia Moskva,* was founded on December 6, 1923, as the organ of the Moscow municipal committee of the All-Union Communist party and of the Moscow Soviet. *Sovetskaia*

Torgovlia (Soviet Trade), a magazine devoted to consumer problems, began publishing in 1926, stopped during the war in 1942, and resumed publication in 1953. Scientific, literary, and ideological journals previously published only in the Russian language began to appear in the more commonly spoken non-Russian tongues. Workers', peasants', and agricultural journals appeared. Three of the famous literary magazines of today date their origins in this period. *Oktyabr'* (October) appeared first in 1924 as the organ of the Moscow Association of Proletarian Writers and built a reputation on the literary works it published. A short time later *Zvezda* appeared first as a bimonthly, and later as a monthly, in Leningrad. *Novy Mir* (New World) began as a monthly literary and political magazine in 1925. *Krokodil* (Crocodile) the famous magazine of humor and satire, was founded in 1922, appearing as a supplement to a workers' newspaper. The late 1920s saw the emergence of a group of publications devoted to literary criticism, bibliography, and history.

The popular illustrated weekly *Ogonyok* (Flamelet or Little Flame) was started in 1923.[8] *Rabotnitsa* (Working Woman, or Woman Worker), taking its title from the previous publication of the same name, was also founded in 1923, to become the top circulation magazine in the postwar years. The Central Committee founded its theoretical organ *Bolshevik* in April, 1924, to explain Marxist-Leninist ideology on questions ranging from domestic economics to international politics. Forty-six technical and industrial magazines at the national level were being published in Moscow by 1927.

Although heavily concentrated in the two large cities, Moscow and Leningrad, the newspaper network spread out thinly into the various republics. As the model for the central papers took shape in Moscow, the pattern was duplicated horizontally at succeeding lower press levels.

The New Economic Policy ended and the first Five Year Plan for the economic development of the country was announced in 1928. Plans for press expansion were among the other long-range plans of this period. As the Communist regime consolidated and centralized its power, Stalin took steps to reorganize the media system, correct its ideological content, and to tighten Central controls over the entire apparatus. The Central Committee's decisions in 1931 concerning the work of publishing called for an overhaul of the press organization. Officials took note of the considerable amount of duplication and a tendency to scatter and dissipate the work of editorial cadres and authors. They deplored the generally poor quality of periodicals and the lack of aggressiveness and initiative shown not only in the content of the media but also by the editorial personnel. The document also scored excessive duplication and delays in publishing and delivery schedules. The Central Committee ordered these faults remedied. It urged that makeup, format, illustration, and ideological tone be improved, and urged party and press sectors in the future to assign each publication a specific role, and to distinguish carefully each periodical's role from every other.

Glavlit Oversees Communications

In the interests of national security and for more adequate central control of ideological content as well, the Chief Administration for Literary Affairs and Publishing (or Glavlit) which had been reestablished by decree in 1922 was placed under the Ministry of Education of the Russian Republic and its powers enlarged by a decree of June 6, 1931. Glavlit was empowered to supervise manuscripts, drawings, paintings, broadcasts, lectures, and exhibits. The agency was also given authority to prohibit publication and circulation of material deemed subversive or in opposition to the regime (and the dictatorship of the proletariat), pornographic matter, or material considered to reveal state secrets or foment racial or religious passions.[9] Under this decree Glavlit was also made the primary licensing authority. This agency was given the right to grant licenses permitting the opening of publishing houses, to allow the publication of newspapers and periodicals, to close any publishing house or any press establishment, to forbid or allow the importation or exportation of any literature, illustrations, etc., in accordance with existing regulations.[10] Ogiz, the party publishing house and its branches, was charged with the responsibility of improving the quality of published materials and assigned powers as a Glavlit representative to handle prepublication ideological censorship of periodicals. The practice of administrative preliminary censorship, without resort to the courts but with the aid of the secret police, was again in full force in Russia. Some publications were discontinued, others started. The general effect was a reduction in the number of publications, and from the regime's standpoint, an improvement in quality.

Among the central periodicals founded in the 1930s were

Znamya (Banner), a literary monthly begun in 1931; *Sovetskaya Pedegogy* (Soviet Education) in 1937, and a number of specialized periodicals devoted to medicine, science, agriculture, mathematics, and history. Publications for press workers included *Rabkor* (Worker Correspondent), 1924–1941; *Zhurnalist* (Journalist), 1922–1933; and *Bolshevistskaya Pechat* (Bolshevik Press), 1933–1941. *Rabkor* and *Pechat* were resumed after World War II with slightly different titles. The Central Committee's decisions on the press in 1940 required the leading newspapers and magazines to add permanent sections devoted to systematic critical reviews of literature and all branches of learning.

The Committee's decisions in 1931 and 1932 authorized the establishment of large numbers of district newspapers and magazines devoted to agriculture, and an expansion of the Lower Press, especially factory journals and wall newspapers. Their function was to stimulate fulfillment and overfulfillment of 5-year-plan production goals, to develop proper socialist attitudes toward work, and to further the Communist education of the masses. The number of newspapers operating at these levels was consistently increased during the years that followed. By 1940 the number of district papers totaled 3,753 with a more than 10-million single-issue press run circulation. The Lower Press category in the same year numbered 4,432 with total circulation of approximately 6 million copies.

The wall newspaper, hand or typewritten and posted on walls in clubs, plants, institutions, collective farms, etc., was a fundamental feature of the Soviet press early in the 1920s. The party's Thirteenth Congress in 1924, in its resolution on the press, said that "wall newspapers are acquiring an ever greater significance in our press system, as a means of influencing the masses and as a form of manifesting their activity." [11] This product of "creative" initiative and "amateur" participation developed simultaneously with the worker-peasant correspondent program. They are Communist devices for keeping the professional journals in touch with the masses and of utilizing and encouraging the help of amateurs in conducting the media.

Radio Is Introduced

Organized systematic radio broadcasting to the general public began in October, 1924, when the Sokolnicheslaya radio station operated by the Moscow Trade Union Council went on the air. The following year the first radio-diffusion transmitter with 50 wired speakers began its broadcasts in Moscow. By 1929 there were 20 transmitters and approximately 22,000 receivers in operation. Radio as a new communication medium was assigned the same role as the other mass media, the task of agitation, organization, and propaganda. After being for a time under the Commissariat of Posts and Telegraphs, the responsibility for radio broadcasting throughout the country was placed in the hands of the All-Union Radio Committee under the Council of the People's Commissars. Controlled by the Central Committee of the party and its Department of Propaganda and Agitation, the All-Union Radio Committee is assisted by local radio committees.[12]

At the close of the first Five Year Plan in 1933 the number of broadcasting stations had more than doubled, from approximately 20 to 57, and the number of speakers had passed the million mark. By 1940, 90 stations were broadcasting to almost 7,000,000 receivers. (See Table 3.1.)

In the prewar decades as at present Moscow was the center of the national publishing and broadcasting establishment. Central or All-Union periodicals in 1940 numbered 46 and published almost one-fourth of all circulations in the country. *Pravda* reported 2 million and *Izvestia* about 1.5 million.[13] In the same year the number

TABLE 3.1

THE GROWTH OF SOVIET BROADCASTING, 1925–1965 *†

Year	Radio (AM)		Television	
	Transmitters	Receivers	Transmitters	Receivers
		(thousands)		*(thousands)*
1925	1	0.2	...	...
1929	20	22	...	...
1933	57	1,360	...	...
1937	77	2,946	...	...
1940	90	6,976	1	0.4
1950	100	11,452	2	10
1955	130	25,641	12	823
1957	...	33,071	36	1,767
1958	250	36,500	57	3,000
1959	...	51,000	...	3,600
1960	...	57,800	75	5,000
1963	405	65,000	93	8,000
1965	...	78,000	116	14,000
1970 (est.)	...	...	...	42,000

* Sources: *National Economy of the USSR; Transport i Svyaz SSR;* press reports; *World Communications,* 3rd and 4th eds.; *Current Digest of the Soviet Press,* Vols. VIII–XVIII (1956–1966); F. Gayle Durham, *Radio and Television in the Soviet Union,* Cambridge, Mass., 1965.

† Totals are for the individual sets and wired speakers or viewers combined. Television transmitter data include transmitters (television centers), not major relay stations.

of nonnewspaper-type periodicals totaled 1,822 and circulated altogether 245 million annually. Most of this activity was centered in the capital. Because of its power, Radio Moscow dominated the air spectrum and most of the radio diffusion relays received Moscow originated signals.

Figures on growth of the Soviet press up to 1940 in comparison with figures from 1913, the last tsarist prewar year, showed an impressive increase both in numbers and circulation. In number of titles the increase was from 859 in 1913 (not counting foreign language papers) to 8,806 in 1940, while single-issue press run circulations increased from about 2.7 million to 38.4 million in the same period, as shown in Table 3.2. Yet in comparing growth during the decade

TABLE 3.2

NUMBER AND CIRCULATION OF SOVIET NEWSPAPERS*

Year[1]	Number[2]	Total One-time Circulation.[3]
		(millions)
1913 (Tsarist Russia)	859	2.7
1921	858	3.0
1922	803	2.7
1923	411	1.5
1926	613	7.6
1932	723	22.0
1938	8,850	37.5
1939	8,769	39.9
1940	8,806	38.4
1946	7,039	29.6
1950	7,831	36.0
1952	8,299	41.7
1954	7,108	46.9
1955	7,246	48.7
1956	7,537	53.5
1957	9,936	57.8
1958	10,463	59.3
1959	10,603	62.3
1960	11,463	66.7
1961	9,544	68.6
1962	6,692[4]	71.0
1965	6,595	90.0
1967	7,700	120.0

* Sources: Unclassified Intelligence Reports, Dept. of State, Washington, D.C.; Unesco, *World Communications*, 3rd ed., Paris, 1956, and 4th ed., New York, 1964; Unesco, *Statistics on Newspapers and Other Periodicals,* Paris, 1959; Alex Inkeles, *Public Opinion in Soviet Russia*, Cambridge, 1950; *Bolshaia Sovetskaya Entsiklopediia,* 2nd ed., Moscow, Vols. X and XVI *passim; Current Digest of the Soviet Press,* Washington, 1949–1965, especially Vols. VIII–XVIII *passim; The Soviet Press* Vol. V, No. 1 (Spring 1966).

[1] As of December 31 each year.

[2] Not including wall newspapers.

[3] Since most Soviet newspapers appear one to five times a week and not seven, the one-time circulation figures are much higher than average daily circulation. This is a crucial consideration when comparing data from different countries.

[4] The reason for the decline shown in 1960–1962 Unesco data is not clear. An assumption is that some of the figures for previous years have included the nonprinted collective farm and factory papers, numbering from 2,000 to 2,500 and that these have been dropped from the calculations.

of the 1920s with growth during the 1930s, two significant trends are indicated. The first is that there was a decline in number of periodicals between 1921 and 1932, while circulations, up at first, declined to an all-time low in 1923, but by 1932 had multiplied seven times. That is, during the adverse conditions of the early 1920s the number of newspapers declined from about 800 with an estimated 3 million circulation in 1921 to 411 with approximately 1.5 million in 1923. By 1932, however, the number had reached 723 with a tremendous increase to 22 million circulation. The second trend is that the regime in the 1930s broadened the base of the media system by adding a phenomenal number of different titles. From 1932 to 1940 the total number of newspapers had risen from 723 to 8,806, and circulation rose from 22 to 38.4 million. Data showing the publication of periodicals in as many as 50 to 86 languages indicate also that the regime had made efforts to provide some periodicals for the minority language groups in the Soviet Union.

GROWTH SINCE WORLD WAR II

The impact of World War II, with fighting on Russian soil, brought a sharp decline in the size and efficiency of the Soviet mass media system. Both the number of units in operation and the volume of total audience reached were adversely affected. During the period from 1940 to 1946 newspaper circulations fell approximately 9 million,[14] and the number of newspapers in operation decreased more than 1,500. The proportionate decline in nonnewspaper-type periodicals was greater, dropping about half, from 1,822 in 1940 to 960 in 1946. There was a corresponding decrease in annual circulation from 245 million to 102 million. Magazines, as opposed to other periodicals, fell off in numbers from 681 to 393. The attrition in the number of radio broadcasting stations was equally heavy, an estimated 50 per cent of the units on the air having been destroyed.

Recovery in most areas was slow. It was not until 1951 or 1952 that newspaper figures surpassed the totals of the prewar year, 1940. It was still later in the 1950 decade before periodicals caught up. Perhaps because of its value for immediate communication purposes and its cheaper transmission costs, broadcasting was reconstructed first. Soviet data showed that prewar levels in station numbers, power, and receiver numbers had been restored by the end of 1946.

But in the print media where plants and machinery had been demolished, full recovery came later. The loss of personnel had been critical and the paper shortage had restricted both page size and number of copies printed until well into the 1950s.

At the close of hostilities general media expansion was given a high priority and the party and government plans stressed the necessity of extending media reach. But still the shortage of technical facilities and supplies, hampered further by poor transport, consistently interfered with the attainment of goals, some of which were evidently set higher than the expected level of achievement. Nevertheless as rapidly as paper, type, presses, and broadcasting facilities became available, former publications were revived, new titles appeared, and the radio network gradually extended its perimeter.

The Printed Media Proliferate

Party discipline, which had been temporarily relaxed in wartime, was not long in reasserting itself. New themes associated with personal problems and human suffering born of the war and other nonsocialistic notes had crept into the media. A disquieting admiration of the United States, Great Britain, and their allies appeared in media content. The regime reminded editors once again that Soviet media are channels to be used in the education of Soviet peoples, especially youth, and that deviation from approved themes or ideologies would not be tolerated. A period of intense repression and persecution followed under the administration of Andrei Zhdanov. A new word, "responsibility," appeared in the official jargon at this time. Communications leaders were told they must accept more responsibility for guidance in politics and society—the vital foundations of the regime, it was said. For example, a resolution of the Central Committee, "On the Magazine *Znamya*," stated that the magazine press must "publicize the accomplishments, the truthfulness, and the glowing life reflected in the revolutionary movement, which revealed the superior quality of the Soviet Citizens—the builders of Communism." [15]

As a result of renewed stress on the political role of communications a score of new party journals was established, most of them counterparts at the lower levels of the central organs, *Pravda, Partinaya Zhizn, Kommunist,* and others. These were established largely outside the Russian Republic and in some cases were editions in non-Russian languages. The economic role of communications was stressed with the appearance of a large number of periodicals dealing with industrial, scientific, transportation, and agricultural problems. Scientific and technical journals published by the Academy of Science and its subdivisions and institutes broadened their scope to concentrate on specialized fields of learning, such as bibliography, the specializations in science, and specific phases of the national economy. For example there were such titles as *Sovetskaya Pedagogika Bibliografica Zhurnal, Sovetskaya Gesudartsvo i Pravo,* (Soviet State and Law); *Voprosy Filosofii* (Problems of Philosophy); *Voprosy Ekonomiki; Nauka i Zhizn* (Science and Life); and *Priroda* (Nature).

New popular illustrated political and public affairs magazines included *Sovetskii Soyuz* (Soviet Union) established in 1950 to replace Gorky's old journal *S.S.S.R. Pyorestroikie; Kolkhatnaya Molodoi* (Kolkhoz Youth), 1948; *Sovietskaya Zenschina* (Soviet Woman), 1945; *Sovetskii Soldat* (Soviet Soldier), 1947; *The New Times,* 1943, English language propaganda magazine; *Slaviane,* a pan-Slav organ, 1942; *Profsoyuz* (Trade Union) a successor to the former *Trade Union U.S.S.R.; U.S.S.R.,* an English language monthly established in 1956; and *Selskaya Zhizn* (Rural Life), established in 1960. In the immediate postwar period there were renewed efforts to publish journals in far-flung provinces and special organs for various linguistic-ethnic groups not formerly reached by media. This expansion was especially apparent in the case of the popular literary monthlies, the political and ideological periodicals, magazines devoted to children, sports and physical culture. Some of the titles listed have been replaced or changed.

The number of all kinds of periodicals dropped almost 50 per cent during the war years and the prewar high of 2,144 reported for 1932 was not regained until after 1955. (See Table 3.3.) The number increased rapidly after 1955 to reach a peak of 4,121 in 1962 and then dropped slightly to 3,833 in 1964. At the same time the total number of copies published annually increased almost four times between 1955 and 1964, from 361 million in the former year to 1,217 million in 1964.

Still individual magazine circulations, judged in terms of United States or British circulation records, could not be called commanding by the middle 1960s. *Krokodil's* circulation passed the million mark in 1957. In 1967 *Partinaya Zhizn, Kommunist,* and *Agitator* were printing 700–800 thousand each. *Molodoi*

TABLE 3.3

THE GROWTH OF SOVIET PERIODICALS AND MAGAZINES, 1927–1965*

Year	Number of Periodicals	Number of Magazines Proper	Annual Periodical Circulation
			(millions)
1927	1,645	...	229
1932	2,144	...	318
1940	1,822	681	245
1946	960	393	105
1950	1,408	410	181
1955	2,026	547	361
1957	3,007	650	418
1960	3,760	908	515
1962	4,121	1,000	872
1965	3,833	...	1,217

* Sources: *Sovetskaya Pechat; Bolshaia Sovetskaya Entsiklopediia,* 2nd ed., Moscow, Vols. X and XVI, *passim; Current Digest of the Soviet Press,* Washington, Vols. VIII–XVIII, *passim;* Unesco, *World Communications,* 3rd ed., Paris, 1965; 4th ed., New York, 1964; press reports.

Kommunist (Young Communist) was publishing about 300 thousand. *Krestyanka* (The Peasant Woman) numbered 3.5 million readers. The largest circulation magazine was the women's journal *Robotnitsa,* with 7.4 million readers. *Ogonyok,* the popular weekly, with almost 2 million, was still far behind *Life.* Among the literary monthlies *Oktyabr'* led with about 200,000. *Novy Mir, Neva,* a new literary monthly named after Leningrad's river, and *Znamya* were in the 100,000 to 150,000 bracket, while *Zvezda* reported less than 100,000. Totals for the other principal magazines fell below the 100,000 mark and ranged down to 4,000 for the monthly periodical *Vneshnyaya Torgovlya* (Foreign Trade).

Subject distribution of general magazines in 1956 showed 119 titles devoted to politics and economics; 113 to literature and art; 170 to technology, industry, transport, agriculture, and communications; 80 to the natural sciences and mathematics; and 61 to public health and medicine. In addition there was almost a score of publications devoted to military affairs, a larger number to culture and education, and some 50 or 60 children's magazines, and a like number of titles in the fields of physical culture, sports, and religion.

In the newspaper field the general pattern of postwar growth has been toward increasing the number of different individual titles by establishing more organs at each press level except the top, and toward increasing existing circulations as newsprint stocks rise. An exception is the Moscow *Pravda* published in 134 major cities from jet-flown matrics or radio and telephoto. *Izvestia* publishes similarly in 34 cities. The greatest increase in the number of newspapers occurred in the latter half of the 1950s when the Central Press increased from 18 to 24, and the newspapers at the republic level were multiplied from 148 to 176. The only decline during this period occurred in the number of newspapers serving cities and small political districts, a total that fell from 4,812 in 1954 to 4,606 in 1959. But this decline was offset considerably by the threefold increase in the number of collective farm papers in the period following mid-1956. In 1954 there were no more than 1,700 of these papers but by the end of 1959 their number had increased to 5,224. However, it is noteworthy that the number of newspapers being published did not regain and surpass their prewar level until 1957 (Table 3.2). Swelled by the thousands of new collective farm papers, the total number reported for 1957 amounted to 9,938 for newspapers of all kinds. By 1965 the number of different newspaper titles (ommitting the nonprinted collective farm papers) had declined slightly from the 1946 figure of 7,039 to the 1965 figure of 6,595. By 1966 the number had increased to 7,700.

Newspaper circulation totals showed a different pattern. Here increases were much more rapid and ground lost during the war was more than regained by 1952. Reported circulations for all one-time press runs increased from 29.6 million in 1946 to 88 million at the close of 1964, a gain of 191 per cent (Table 3.2). Periodicals of all kinds, including magazines, as shown in Table 3.3, increased in numbers about 4 times, from 960 in 1946 to 4,121 in 1962, then dropped to 3,833 in 1965. Annual combined periodical circulations rose from 105 million in 1946 to 1,217 million in 1965.[16] These figures should be read with the understanding that in their reported totals Soviet statistics group general and specialized magazines with bulletins, almanacs, and lesser publications such as annuals. The data thus far discussed apply to the entire press system, with the newspaper circulations given as totals of single-issue press runs, regardless of periodicity, and the magazine circulations grouped together to form annual totals. They also include daily newspapers.

The daily newspaper field has shown substantial growth since 1936 when approximately 135 newspapers appeared 6 days a week (*Pravda* is the only 7-day-a-week paper). Since the Soviet government counts papers appearing 4 to 7 times a week as dailies,[17] the number of dailies in 1956, or the number appearing 4 times a week or more, totaled 385 (382 morning and 3 afternoon papers). Total daily circulation for these was 21,475,000, or about 40 per cent of the 53.5 million total newspaper circulation reported for that year. By 1962 the number of daily newspapers had increased to 457 with a circulation of 39,355,000. These included 444 morning and 13 evening dailies and averaged about 18 copies of a daily for every 100 persons. Compare with the British ratio of about 50 for 100 persons.

In the mid-1960s Moscow was rivaling London and New York as one of the world's greatest centers of mass publishing. The soaring daily newspaper circulations accounted for a large share of the total, though copies of *Pravda* and *Izvestia* were being produced in different parts of the country. Circulation figures in single-issue press run totals for May, 1966, showed *Pravda* at 7 million; *Izvestia,* 7.1 million; *Pioneerskaya Pravda,* 7.4 million; *Komsomolskaya Pravda,* 6.9 million; *Selskaia Zhizn,* 6.7 million; *Sovetskaia Rossia,* 3.1 milion; *Trud,* 2.4 million; *Sovetskii Sport,* 1.6 million. Combined circulation of these 8 dailies was approximately 43 million.

Thus the Soviet Union was producing more newspapers and magazines in the 1964–1966 period than ever before in its history. In 1913, in the closing days of the Empire, the number of newspaper copies was estimated at one copy for every 50 persons. In 1964 there was published one copy of some kind of newspaper for every 3 persons. At the rate of 18 copies of a daily paper for each 100 in the population in 1962, more than 5 persons shared each copy of a daily. In 1913, 109 periodicals of all kinds were published in 29 different languages; by 1960–1962 the number of periodicals had increased to 4,121, appearing in 55 different languages. Multi-lingual magazines totaled 145.

Broadcasting Lengthens Its Nerve Network

Broadcasting, as has been shown, recovered rapidly from the effects of World War II. By 1946, with the initiation of the fourth Five Year Plan, the number and strength of stations was reported to have surpassed their prewar levels. By the end of 1949 the number had passed the hundred mark and receivers numbered more than 11 million. In 1962 the number of transmitters had multiplied to 405 and receivers had quadrupled to 44 million. (See Table 3.1.) Although the number of stations was not large in comparison with figures for other modern populous countries, the power of stations has been consistently stepped up. Since 1941, therefore, the ratio of power to number of stations in the Soviet Union has been considered high in comparison with that of other nations.[18]

While aerial broadcasting characterizes the central and republic-regional levels of the broadcasting system, the third, or lower level, consists of a system of radio-diffusion exchanges and wired speaker networks, which cannot in a technical sense be described as broadcasting. In 1947, approximately 82 per cent of all radio receiving equipment in the country was in the wired-speaker category. In that year the number of wired radio speakers reached 6 million, and the number of diffusion exchanges had been increased to 1,056, a figure that was far below the prewar level of 11 thousand. By 1954 the number of relay centers had increased to 27 thousand and that of wired speakers to almost 14 million. These data reflect the more than 1 million wired speakers that were installed in 1953 on collective farms where radio had not been previously introduced. By 1958 the number of wired speakers had grown to 27 million, a threefold increase since 1950, and about 70 per cent of all speakers produced were of this kind. The ratio of wired speakers to receiving sets was about three to one. From the middle to the late 1950s the principal development of wired-speaker systems has occurred in the rural areas. While some diffusion centers were able to originate their own local programs for their networks, most wired-speaker systems allowed listener reception of only one program. Late in the decade some thought was being given to the development of 2-program outlets in order to give the listener a choice, and by 1963 this was done.

Table 3.4 shows that only in recent years has the over-all developmental pattern in Soviet broadcasting changed from emphasis on wired to wireless reception. The trend over time has been toward an overwhelming predominance of the former, but from 1959 to 1965, more wireless than wired speakers have come into use each year. In 1958, wired speakers were almost three times the number of wave sets, but by 1965, the wireless sets outnumbered the wired by about 2 million. While AM transmission was reaching out into the hinterlands, FM was also expanding in Moscow and the more populous areas in the European segment of the USSR.

Compared with the rapid rise of television as a mass medium in the United States, that medium has developed slowly in the Soviet Union. Yet, invidious comparisons to the contrary, Soviet television has enjoyed a *rate* of development in its own country that generally has exceeded that of the other media for the same period

TABLE 3.4

SOVIET RADIO OUTLETS IN USE,
SETS AND WIRED SPEAKERS COMPARED, 1925–1965*

Year	Number of Radio Sets (Wireless)	Number of Wired Speakers
	(*thousands*)	(*thousands*)
1925	...	0.2
1929	...	2.9
1933	...	1,360
1937	...	2,946
1940	1,123	4,934
1945	...	5,000
1950	1,767	9,685
1955	6,097	19,544
1956	7,380	22,191
1957	8,380	24,691
1958	9,500	27,000
1959	20,200	29,000
1960	27,000	30,800
1963	32,000	33,000
1965	40,000	38,000

* Sources: *National Economy of the USSR; Transport i Svyaz SSSR;* Alex Inkeles, *Public Opinion in Soviet Russia; Current Digest of the Soviet Press; World Communications,* 3rd and 4th eds.

of time. This growth leadership has been held both in the rate of production and use of television sets and in rate of the extension of the telecasting network, attesting the regime's interest in developing it and the people's eagerness to watch. Recognizing television's obvious advantages over radio as a means of indoctrination, the regime has spent large sums and worked hard to extend its facilities with all possible speed.

In 1940 about 250 experimental television sets were reported to be in use in Moscow. Development, interrupted by the war, was resumed, and by 1950 approximately 10,000 sets were receiving a regular service transmission schedule that had been inaugurated in 1948. Telecasting to the general public was begun on a limited scale in 1953, and by the end of 1955 there were some 820,000 receivers in use, as compared with about 35 million in the United States in the same year. One-third of all sets were located in the Moscow *Oblast*. It was estimated that from 2 to 3 million persons in the Moscow environs and the city of Kalinin were viewing telecasts from the Moscow Television Center. Twelve stations were reported to be in separate and independent operation, although some were not broadcasting a full-time schedule. Plans in 1953 called for 51 stations tied to a relay system to be in operation by the end of 1958 and 75 stations with 25 million viewers by the end of 1960. Improvements were being made both in the construction of television sets and in stepping up the range of some stations. The original round screens were replaced by rectangular ones, commonly 12 inches in size. Some expensive sets featured 17-inch screens, and were equipped to receive 5 instead of the usual 3 channels. Large sets with screens over a yard wide were being introduced for use in clubs, institutions, and other types of viewing centers; wired screens connected with central reception points were being multiplied. (See Table 3.1.)

By the close of 1958 the officially announced number of television broadcasting studio centers had reached 57, exceeding the goal of 51; there were 80 relay stations in operation and approximately 3 million sets in use, although data do not indicate how many viewers there were per set. Relay stations served the double purpose of retransmitting telecasts from the centers both to the viewers in their own vicinities and to relay stations farther away from the centers. This means of transmission was still limited to short distances. Although only one coaxial cable was in use in 1950, the two primary systems, microwave and coaxial cable, were being developed by Soviet engineers. The goal of 75 television transmitting centers was reached in 1960, according to official announcements, but the audience reached was estimated at only 20 million, 5 million short of the goal. In addition to the centers, 100 relay stations served as connecting links between studios in the central cities and remote parts of the country.

Greater efforts have gone into widening public exposure to television than into improving its technical excellence or into the quality of its production. Technically Soviet television in 1961 appeared rather primitive. Moscow and Leningrad studios were small, their equipment appeared old, and procedures were relatively naïve when compared with more sophisticated Western ones. As in radio, emphasis has been placed on wired screens and diffusion networks as the best method of bringing television to a large number of people, but here too the trend is changing toward indvidual sets. As will be seen below, Soviet television is limited in the variety of its telecasts. Experimental telecasting in color was initiated in 1960 in Moscow, and is still in the early stages of development.

In the period from 1955 to 1962, the number of radio transmitters increased from 130 to 405, the number of television transmitters, not including relay stations, increased almost 8 times—from

12 to 93. (See Table 3.1.) Radio receivers multiplied from 25.6 million in 1956 to 78 million in 1965 while television receivers increased from 823,000 in 1955 to more than 7 million in 1962, and approximately 14 million in 1965. Television viewers were calculated at about four per receiver, making a total of 56 million viewers, though it was claimed that telecasting covered an area of 90 million people. While radio was becoming ever more ubiquitous, by the early 1960s television came to be no longer the exclusive privilege of residents living in the vicinity of the capital cities, and by late 1965 it was a medium rapidly growing in popularity and public demand.

Commercial Advertising: Harbinger of Economic Reform

Of significance to the mass media of communication is growth of commercial advertising, a postwar phenomenon that seems already to have established itself as a permanent characteristic of the Soviet economy. Although commercial advertising as we know it in the Western world has thrived most readily under a capitalist economy and a libertarian press system, for a long time it was forbidden in the Soviet Union. Marxist-Leninist dogma holds that commercial advertising is a bourgeois capitalistic device incompatible with socialism and is an artificial stimulant to the economy that forces people to buy what they do not need and cannot afford. The attitude was that advertising is a wasteful, parasitic form of activity because its cost is passed on to the consumer who must pay more than he otherwise might for the products he buys. Moreover, advertising as a marketing device was not needed in the Soviet Union where tight planning could be expected to cope adequately with problems of production and distribution.[19] Lenin's dictum abrogating a commercially based press system living on profits from advertising and dominated by the bourgeois class emphasized the profit motive as an evil influence on editorial policy. The Soviet press, he said, should be free from profit making in order to serve the state and to seek rewards in the form of effects on the public mind instead of in profits.[20]

But the official attitude was not the only factor that worked against advertising's usefulness to the regime and thus delayed its arrival on the Russian scene. Painful scarcity of consumer goods that negated altogether or restricted the range of the Soviet buyer's choice and the limited consumer purchasing power operated to make advertising superfluous. Absence of competition in manufacturing and the absence of brand-name commodities or other methods of product differentiation either among manufacturers or retailers also did nothing to create a demand for commercial advertising. Furthermore the mass media did not need advertising revenue.

Many of the conditions that worked against the use of advertising in the economy during the prewar years have changed since. The economy has shifted from one of scarcity to one of relative sufficiency and from a seller's market to a buyer's. Surpluses of goods accumulated in warehouses and distributors did not know what to do with them. The Khrushchev policy was to increase consumer purchasing power and to provide more consumer goods for the people. His successors have taken steps to change the basis of the production and distribution systems. Because product quality was low[21] due to lack of production incentives, product differentiation and competition among manufacturers and retailers was introduced. As an added aid in moving sluggish goods, the much derided capitalist devices, of credit plans and installment buying[22] were also provided. These changes testified to the new importance of the Soviet consuming public. The decentralization of industry in 1957 also changed and simplified the whole process of making a direct appeal to the Russian consumer. The use of advertising was the next logical step.

Production in the Soviet Union up until recent times was an exclusive state function; and distribution was a joint function of the state agencies and cooperatives.[23] The entire country might have been compared to a gigantic company town in which all the factories, commissaries (or retail outlets), and the organs of public information were owned and operated by a single management. It was a community in which ordinarily no competing voices vied for the consumer's patronage. The supply of most consumer goods was determined by the national economic planners who set 5-year or 7-year targets for each industry and major product. The selection, display, and pricing of all goods were centrally determined. The task of merchandising the output involved setting prices at a level that would clear the market and reduce the long queues awaiting buyers, and then distributing the State's merchandise equitably over the nation.[24] Since 1961 the entire economy has been undergoing revision toward a system based on supply and demand.

British firms bought a small volume of advertising in Soviet media as early as 1944.[25] But there appears to be no mention of domestic paid advertising aside from the usual theatre, entertainment, and sports events notices until after the end of World War II. Commercial radio announcements had been forbidden officially in 1935, but in May, 1947, Radio Moscow announced that it would accept commercials from "business and educational institutions," to be paid for according to the established "tariff." The dual purpose of this new policy was to provide market information and revenue for broadcasting's support. Radio Moscow began broadcasting on a regular schedule an 8-minute block of commercial announcements three times daily—morning, noon, and night. According to the report, Soviet citizens "listened happily and demanded more."

Paid advertising began to appear in Soviet newspapers probably about the same time.[26] By April, 1949, commercial advertising and other merchandising methods were being expanded steadily.[27] The largest advertisers were the State food trusts and the State insurance company, *Gosstrakh*. Advertising was placed regularly in outdoor, displays, magazines, and daily newspapers. These big organizations spent from an advertising budget. In addition, retail enterprises began to employ advertising to increase volume of turnover and to exceed 5-year plan norms. For example, advertisements carried by a Moscow evening daily in one 1949 issue included the following: a 2-column advertisement of the industrial Soya Trust for Soya cottage cheese; two 3-column advertisements for motion pictures; a 2-column display advertisement of the State Insurance Company; a column of theatre notices; an advertisement by a Moscow liquor plant seeking empty vodka bottles; two offers of state trusts to sell building materials; a notice of veteran's cooperative offering to buy, sell, and repair furniture; an advertisement by a trust wanting to buy asbestos and iron tubes; and an advertisement by a paint factory offering to sell paint. Although such advertising was bought, the motive for its use was not to make a profit. Aside from the purposes cited above for radio commercials, there was no official statement of function.

Former Senator William Benton observed in 1956 that advertising was used in the Soviet Union specifically to encourage the production of crops, to encourage savings in the state banks, and to promote the sale of nonessentials.[28] Since everything that is done officially or permitted to be done by the Soviet government is deemed to serve the political and social purposes of the Communist state, it was obvious that advertising was being used for a predetermined purpose to fill certain needs and to solve problems of adjustment in the economy.

Soviet advertising officials sought to learn from the marketing experience of the eastern European satellite countries. They read Western merchandising periodicals for "know-how." In 1957 east European delegates attended an international conference on advertising in Prague. The next year the first conference of workers in commercial advertising met in Moscow.[29] After the drastic reorganization of Soviet agriculture and industry in 1962, further stimulation of competition and the profit motive was undertaken. Bonus payments and a larger share of the profits were incentives proposed for industrial enterprises that overfulfilled their quotas.[30]

Although Russian economists have said there is no logical reason for advertising agencies in their country, advertising's growth has made them necessary. They are called "Advertising Bureaus." As early as 1949 a Moscow city agency handled bulletin board notices and outdoor advertising. *Kooptogreklam,* an agency known as the cooperative advertising office, opened for business in Moscow late in 1957. Several Soviet republics opened official advertising agencies between 1958 and 1960; and some cities and towns started their own agencies to serve local needs.[31] Commissions have been reported to run as high as 35 per cent. Recognizing the need to examine the whole advertising complex, the government late in 1960 decided to integrate its advertising interests under one authority.

New periodicals devoted to advertising of consumer goods and to merchandising made their appearance. *Novy Tovary* (New Products), which was started in 1957, is an organ devoted to reporting new consumer goods. Full of clothing and household advertising, the magazine came "under fire" because it carried ads of nonexisting articles soon to appear. *Advertising Bulletin,* a bimonthly, appeared first in June, 1958, as an organ of the Consumers' Cooperative. *Soviet Trade,* a well established periodical, and about 150 other trade journals accepted advertising. Ordinarily they published a greater volume of foreign than domestic commercial messages.[32]

The range of choice among the media available was not wide. In general, it was limited by the government's official policies, which may vary according to the social needs of the moment.[33] Newspaper advertising was limited by the type and field of interest of the particular newspaper—for example, whether a newspaper is national or local, or whether it is a collective farm daily or a labor union daily. Newspapers were chary with space, and chose advertisers according to the newspaper's special interests. The great national dailies, such as *Pravda* and *Izvestia,* limited their advertising to about one column, and were known to sacrifice advertising space for editorial needs. Advertising in these national papers consisted of lists of radio programs, theater and cinema notices, and literary announcements. Radio advertising in the form of brief announcements received 5- to 30-minute blocks of time. By late 1965 commercials had not yet invaded the television screen. The process of placing an advertisement was reported to be frustrating and time consuming. Both the censor and the editor had the right to reject an advertisement; and the latter had the right to restrict the amount of space devoted to advertising. The advertisement was required to be ideologically in line because both editor and censor were responsible to the Communist party. No exaggerated claims were allowed. Clearance by Moscow for foreign advertising has been known to take as long as six months.[34] However, newspaper advertising departments tried to facilitate matters by providing assistance and advice. Advertising rates seem to have little relationship to circulation. Rates indicated that a page in a large-circulation newspaper would cost $135, subject to reductions for contract arrangements. The same price was charged for a page advertisement in a magazine of 60,000 circulation.

Whether commercial advertising will continue to expand and take its place beside other official mass media and other marketing devices will depend more upon the decisions made regarding the economy in general than upon decisions made regarding advertising itself. So long as the government continues to encourage a buyer's market and to elevate the consumer's economic level, it will permit consumer desires to play a part in the regulatory process. While these conditions hold, commercial advertising probably will expand in volume and grow in importance. If the regime for any reason drastically changes the production and distribution patterns, or faces a period of austerity, advertising will be affected accordingly.

Skeptics who question the contributions made by advertising to any economy may take pause and reassess their premises in the light of these Soviet developments. First, the argument that advertising is superfluous waste and an unnecessary drain on the economic system is weakened by the historic fact that the USSR—the principal exponent of such an argument as the world's most advanced planned economy—adopts such a method to help solve its problems. Second, the establishment of differentiation as a means of stimulating improvements in product quality and in eliminating waste lends support to the value of the capitalist system for achieving such goals. "While product differentiation and advertising result in considerable waste, their elimination may also result in waste." [35] Third, the Soviet experience sheds light on the argument whether advertising causes or is the result of abundance. In the case of the Soviet Union, advertising would seem to have come as a result of abundance, although this conclusion must take into consideration the influence of government planning and control as motivating factors. Such a conclusion also finds support in the United States where studies indicate a positive relationship between prosperity cycles and expenditures for advertising. Actually, it seems whether it exists in a capitalist or communist system, advertising both causes and is the result of abundance. Finally, the premise that advertising flourishes only in a capitalistic, profit-motivated economy must be revised. Of course, the initiaton of advertising is just another in a long list of tried capitalist methods that have been adapted to Communist purposes, and apparently are becoming a part of Communist ways.

That advertising, installment buying, product differentiation, and competitive manufacturing are becoming a part of the Soviet picture is testimony to the fact that communist methods so far have been unable to provide the kinds of incentives and rewards the economic system needs in order to function most effectively. The reforms in the economic system as the new Five Year Plan went into effect in January, 1966, appeared to be heading in the direction of less centralized planning and more local initiative; more managerial autonomy; a new attack on chronic agricultural problems; greater incentives in production, marketing, and distribution (including competition and profits); and more emphasis on the need to increase consumer needs and welfare. The intention to give the Soviet people a larger share of what they produce is indicated in the forecasts of industrial production. Light industry is supposed to rise 22 per cent, while total industrial investment will increase only 5.2 per cent. This is not the first time that the exigencies of circumstance have forced the Soviet leaders to abandon or modify established dogma in order to pursue effectively the society's prescribed goals. Campbell concludes that what is happening to the Soviet economy today is

> . . . remarkable less for the fact that ideological positions on economic affairs are being subverted than for the fact that the offensive against ideology is now touching on doctrines that are more basic than any that have been involved before, and that it calls into question the fundamental institutions of the Soviet economic system as well as the authority of the party.[36]

Advertising has established itself in the modern advanced industrial communist societies as a necessity for both the consumer and the marketing and distribution process. With increasing volume of production for the consumer, advertising will grow, newspapers and periodicals using it will increase in size, and advertising revenue will become a regular contributor to the financial support of the mass media.

Estimates of Media Penetration

The indications are that, barring war or other calamity, the mass media system will continue to expand as population increases and as present levels of public education are maintained. Already the Soviet system, like advanced libertarian capitalist systems, is showing signs of leveling off in the number of different kinds of publications, with a corresponding trend toward larger circulations and audiences per unit. No trend has yet been set in decline in number of units, though. The regime will continue its prodding for greater production and consumption. Newsprint, presses, and electronic equipment are being manufactured in greater quantities. Communication channels are being systematically extended. The Soviet masses are persuaded with increasing crescendo to read, listen, and watch. As modernization progresses, media participation can be expected to increase. A 7-year plan begun in 1958 called for ambitious goals in publishing and broadcasting—goals that have been realized and exceeded. Newspaper circulations in 1965 reached the 90-million mark, almost a 75 per cent increase. Radio receivers were to be multiplied by one-third and television receivers multiplied three times. Figures for 1965 show that these goals were surpassed, indicating 78 million radio receivers and 14 million television receivers. (See Tables 3.1 and 3.2.)

Pressure was placed on radio and television networks to make available more multiprogram transmission, increase the amount of time per day on the air, and to extend broadcasting farther into remote rural areas. The regime rigorously undertook measures to step up per capita consumption rate of printed media and to multiply the size of broadcasting audiences, authorizing manufacturing priorities for newsprint and technical facilities. There were vigorous campaigns to improve media appeal, a step to be analyzed more fully in a subsequent chapter. If a consumer market in communications develops, a genuine Western-style circulation war would not be surprising, for efforts were intensified to raise the sale and circulation of newspapers and magazines.[37] In its drive for new subscriptions, the central press circulation office in Moscow adopted the slogan, "In every family—newspapers, magazines." The office published 650,000 copies of a catalog of Soviet periodicals. It advised local managers to use newspaper advertising and radio announcements in their sales campaigns. The Department of Advertising for Press Circulation, created in 1958, spent 11 million rubles ($2,750,000) for newspaper advertising in 1959. The campaign to stimulate attention to broadcast fare has been characterized by similar zeal. This effort has been handicapped by continued delays in mass production of cheap, high-quality sets, the difficulty of overcoming apathy toward listening and viewing centers for multifamily audiences. Installation of radio in rural areas has been impeded by the acute shortage of wire. Set operation is frequently interrupted by short supply of batteries in nonelectrified areas. Television has been delayed by shortage of picture tubes and repair parts. The campaign to expand broadcasting has hinged largely on overcoming production problems.

Qualifications must be made for any comparison of Soviet data with Western World data. Nevertheless a few comparisons will be attempted. The efforts to expand and the actual rates of growth achieved have been impressive, even by Western standards. But the figures on media production and consumption are more informative when considered in the perspective of domestic growth factors and comparative data from other modern countries. Rates of growth may become somewhat misleading for a country like Russia that started at very low levels. Individual circulations of Soviet magazines do not appear to be high when compared with those of the United Kingdom, Japan, and the United States. For example, a group of 25 of the principal magazines in 1959 whose circulations have been made public showed an average total annual circulation figure of 188,560 and a range of 4,000 to 1.5 million. Obviously the wide variety of different kinds of periodicals is spread out over relatively small individual groups of readers. Newspaper circulations, on the other hand, bulk considerably larger and penetrate much deeper into the social strata than do those of magazines; yet even these, except for the individual circulations of a few large dailies, are not as great as one might expect to find in a highly literate society when total volume is equated with periodicity. In 1962 almost one copy of a daily newspaper for every five persons was being published in Russia. In comparison the United States, which ranks seventh in the world in daily newspaper per capita production, prints 1 newspaper copy for every 3.5 persons. The United Kingdom publishes slightly more than 1 copy for every 2 persons; France, about 1 copy for every 4 persons. In a group of 29 countries with more than 80 per cent adult literacy (circum 1956) the Soviet Union ranked twenty-seventh in number of dailies per thousand inhabitants. Of 21 of these same countries whose nondaily per capita circulations were known, the Soviet Union ranked sixteenth in nondaily per capita usage. Although giant strides are being made, it is clear that the Soviet Union still has some distance to go before its ratio can compare favorably with that of other advanced countries.

Furthermore, data on broadcasting audiences, estimated on the basis of family units, indicated that about two-thirds of the total number of families had access to radio in 1960, either by private set or wired speaker. About one-tenth of the families had access to television. In comparison to those of the United States and western European countries, radio and television audiences in the Soviet Union were still relatively small at the beginning of 1960. On special occasions where interest has been great, broadcasting audiences have been considerably larger than these estimates; yet the same can be said of the comparative estimates of other countries.

Media penetration of ethnic-linguistic minorities in the Soviet Union has not been as extensive as the regime would like to have one believe. In all the media the Russian language continues to enjoy a predominance out of proportion to the ratio of Russian versus non-Russian speaking populations. This appears to be true in spite of the fact that newspapers are published in almost all of the languages. The regime has stressed the point that the number of newspapers published in non-Russian tongues is now more than 42 times as great as it was before 1918, while the number in the Russian language has increased only 7 times in the same period. But language groups are not represented by media in proportion to their numbers in the population. For example, in 1956 fully two-thirds of the individual newspapers and their aggregate circulations were published in the Russian language, but only 55 per cent of the population was Russian. Twenty-five per cent of all newspapers were in Ukrainian, while Ukrainians, who made up 18 per cent of the population, received only 13 per cent of the newspaper circulation. Magazines were more Russian than the newspapers. In 1957 fully 70 per cent of the magazines and 85 per cent of the total periodical circulation appeared in the Russian language. This was true in spite of the fact that magazines were said to be published in 55 languages, 14 foreign, and 41 domestic languages. Data are not available to indicate the proportion of Russian in broadcast content. The dominance of Russian is attributable to a number of causes. All of the Central papers, commanding the largest circulations, are printed in Russian. Russians have a higher literacy rate. Russian political and cultural influence has made itself felt over the country. It seems clear that the differences will have less significance in the future as more adult citizens come into the population with literacy in Russian.

4 ★

SOVIET MASS COMMUNICATIONS: FUNCTION, STRUCTURE, CONTROL

SOVIET COMMUNIST THEORY regarding the place, purpose, and function of communications media in society grew out of Marxist philosophy regarding the nature of man, the nature of society, and the relationship between the two. Marxist concepts were fused with authoritarian principles—principles which had been practiced since the beginning of history, but which, with respect to the press, had their European origins in the sixteenth century.

COMMUNICATIONS THEORY, DOCTRINE, AND LAW

Vested in the authoritarian position is control of the public communication channels of a national state by the central political authority, though such control may be maintained ostensibly in the name of the people. The kinds of authoritarian controls were many, but they rarely included monopoly ownership and exclusive use of the channels of communication by the political establishment.[1] The Communist position adds a new dimension to these: exclusive ownership by government and party of the communication channels. Authoritarian theory evolved from a trust in the superior wisdom of the ruling elite to govern and a belief in the relative inability of the average man either to participate in governance or to guide his own destiny without help. Libertarian theory challenged the validity of authoritarian assumptions and developed a system based on faith in the wisdom of people to govern themselves, the reasoning power and dignity of man, and man's inherent ability, indeed right, to self-determination. According to the libertarians, as stated by John Stuart Mill, society with its institutions exists to serve the needs and to better the welfare of mankind, and to help men work out their own destiny. The corollary of this was the belief that that society is best which serves man best. The libertarian philosophers believed that communications in the free society can serve man and benefit the state best by being free and independent of government so that the self-righting process of truth might operate in a free marketplace of ideas.[2]

While both libertarian and Marxist theory have similar goals—the development of the ideal society and the evolution of a superior man—they diametrically differ in the means of achieving those goals. Marxist theory holds that the improvement of society must come first; therefore, man and his institutions exist to produce in and create the good society; but only after this task is accomplished, or in the process of accomplishment, will man himself benefit accordingly. The all-consuming goal of Communism then is to improve man by first improving society.[3] So the total use of communications as an instrument for building the society is seen as a primary means of attaining that goal.

Among the basic principles of Marxist philosophy of importance to this discussion are unity of thought with its corollary, absolute rejection of contradictory thought. Other principles include a rigid, dogmatic interpretation of right and wrong; an attempt to explain all social change, including human behavior, in terms of the class struggle and economic motivation; the belief that man's entire way of living is determined by his material environment which provides his sense of values, his motivations, his means of economic survival; and finally, the belief in the eventual evolution of a classless, stateless society, accompanied by the somewhat contradictory idea of the supremacy of the working classes.

Marxist theory as applied to the development of twentieth-century Communist states, together with their communication systems, has been adapted and modified considerably to fit the individual cultures in which they were expected to grow, and to meet changing conditions. Marx himself scarcely mentions the press. It remained for V. I. Lenin and Joseph Stalin to adapt Marxist doctrine to the newly emerging Soviet society after the Bolsheviks came to power in 1917. As we have seen in the previous chapter, the national press system developed slowly, to a considerable extent by trial and error. Its ideology, when put into practice, was conditioned by both the reality of circumstance and the beliefs of the leaders. The public communication system, however, was developed not separately, but as an integral part of the social system.[4] The mass media are conceived of as only one instrument among many engaged in the same endeavor to educate and indoctrinate, to agitate, and to organize. In theory they work and speak in unison with the other agencies of party, government, and special groups somewhat as members of the same team.

The press's social role is stipulated in broad terms in Lenin's definition of a newspaper, a definition that became a slogan as the communication system took shape. "A newspaper is not only a collective propagandist and a collective agitator; it is also a collective organizer." [5] Lenin assigned this same role to other printed media, to film, to the popular arts, and other forms of expression. Since Lenin's time the same function has been given to the broadcast media. Thus the entire mass communication system, and especially the press, is seen as the primary vehicle for persuading, teaching, and indoctrinating: in essence, for mobilizing all human and material resources for building and improving Communist society. In the words of M. Strepukhov, in 1955 a member of the Central Committee's "Agitprop" Department, this means that the media are the "powerful instrument for mobilizing the masses to carry out party and government decisions." [6] The charge to the mass communication system required that it function in four areas: To expose beneath-the-surface manifestations, that is to make "revelations" in order to stimulate popular political awareness; to elucidate doctrine, especially for the leaders; to "inform" all levels of the population; and to promote unity of thought.

The communication system, therefore, has the responsibility to do everything within its power to facilitate attainment of the society's well-defined goals. Conversely it must do everything possible to diminish the effect of forces judged to impede the achievement of these ends. In practice its first purpose has become that of indoctrination, and its secondary purpose that of information and "education." The media are used as tools to inculcate the values of the socialist system into the thinking of the masses and to mobilize public opinion in favor of achieving its program. The media are motivated, according to theory, out of loyalty to the party which acts for the best interests of the people. Theoretically they find their reward, not in financial profit, but in successful achievement. The party is owner, publisher, licensee, and operator of the entire communication mechanism—a system dedicated to advancing the cause by informing, teaching, organizing, crusading, leading, persuading, scolding, exhorting, wheedling, coaxing, threatening, and agitating.

The great importance attached to the mass communication apparatus in Soviet values has been expressed by Stalin and Nikita S. Khrushchev. Stalin saw the press as a ". . . prime instrument through which the Party speaks daily, hourly, with the working class in its own indispensable language. No means such as this for weaving spiritual ties between Party and class, no other tool so flexible, is to be found in nature . . . ." [7] The press, according to Stalin, is "a vital transmission belt" between the Party and the masses. First Secretary Khrushchev in 1957 pointed to the press's position of prestige and its crucial role. "Just as the army cannot fight without arms," he said, "so the Party cannot carry out its ideological mission without that efficient and powerful weapon, the press . . . ." [8]

Communist and Libertarian Press Systems Compared

The use of the press by government to serve the interests of the central authority and the society it ruled, whether by persuasion or force, was not a novel concept. European monarchs, notably the Russian tsars, for a long time tried to harness communication because they recognized it as a powerful force for influencing opinion. Even Western democratic political systems, it will be recalled, visualized the press as a medium that must usefully serve their various cultures by spreading new ideas of the industrial revolution, of personal freedom, of capitalist enterprise, and by educating the masses in their newly acquired responsibilities as citizens. Political philosophers such as Mill, Lord Bryce, and Thomas Jefferson stressed the important role of the press in making democracy work, especially as a catalyst of public opinion. Exclusive ownership, control, and operation of the communications apparatus was practiced for a time by Crown and church in fifteenth-century Europe. Political and religious authorities published their own papers. Licensing and the granting of patents to private competitive owners was initiated soon afterwards. In the twentieth century, Fascist domination of communications in Italy and Nazi methods in Germany attempted and accomplished almost total control, but never gained monopoly ownership and operation. With the advent of broadcasting, a few State-owned and operated electronic monopolies appeared in the democracies but these could not claim exclusive control of all channels of communication.

The whole idea of an independent press was contrary to the Communist concept of unity. To the Soviet way of thinking, the press might best accomplish its assigned tasks as an instrument rather than as either an ally or as an independent critic of the sovereign power. To libertarian thought, the press is in a better position to promote the public welfare voluntarily and without coercion simply by virtue of its independent status as a privately owned competitive business enterprise. Soviet theory says that only the party is qualified to determine the needs of the people and to chart the future course of the nation: therefore, the channels of public information must be relegated to the party's use as an instrument of national policy for the best interests of all. Of course, the Communists explain away the State-party monopoly of the mass media system by saying that ownership and operation by these segments of the power structure are only a form of temporary custodianship in the name of the workers and the common people. At some indefinite time in the future, when Communist society has been perfected, the State will wither away, they say, and then the people will in reality assume full control of their press system. Parallel democratic theory maintains that the mass media as molders, leaders, and mirrors of sovereign public opinion, stand as independent free mediating agencies between government and the people. The government governs only as long as it has the consent of the governed, and the press often serves as a check on the actions and policies of the government. Soviet claims that its system frees the media of economic dependence on profits are true, for outside of fees, subscriptions, and advertising revenue, the media are supported out of the public treasury. Under libertarian, democratic philosophy the mass media must make a profit, first in order to survive in a competitive economy, and secondly so that they may maintain their editorial independence, free from either the threat of bankruptcy or accepting subsidy with its inevitable strings.

These two main differences—(1) economic support, ownership and operation, and (2) relationships with the sovereign power, which prescribes and proscribes the social function— appear to be the principal fundamental departures from traditional press theory to be found in communist communication systems. Thus it is clear that just as the Soviet media are not profit-making private enterprises, they are not primarily purveyors of information exercising surveillance of the environment. They are not in theory primarily outlets for the expression of opinion, other than the opinion of the party leaders. They are not mainly market places for commodities and ideas, and they are not intended to be a sounding board for public opinion—although a prime purpose is to mold and change public attitudes. They are not chiefly entertainment media, nor are they expected to serve as outlets for escape literature. Even films and broadcasting have propaganda, and not entertainment, as their primary official function. Unlike their Western counterparts, the Soviet media do not attempt to present a realistic picture of life as it is, but of life as the regime's leaders see it. Focusing on the serious purposes to which the media as government instruments are dedicated, the Soviet people have found little room in their media for Western-style crime and sensation, human interest, humor, or escapist content.

Concepts of Press Function

Plainly the Anglo-American concept of freedom of the press as freedom from prepublication control or interference by government could not exist in the communist world. How can a government agency function independently of its government and its owner? Lenin himself admitted that the press, as a tool of government, could not claim to be independent of it. In his article on "Party Organization and Party Literature," written in 1905, Lenin expressed his determination to establish what he considered a truly free press, despite his antithetical belief that no press can really be free of its social milieu. He wrote, "We want to create and shall create a free press, free not only from the police, but also free from capital, free from careerism. It will also be free from bourgeois-anarchistic individualism."[9] Whether his free press would also be free of government censorship, Lenin did not say; but twelve years later just before he was to take over the leadership of the country, he discussed freedom of the press again, and this time he made it plain that his type of "free" press would not enjoy freedom from censorship, but rather somehow seemed to conceive of censorship as an aid to freedom. Lenin wrote,

> The capitalists (and with them, wittingly or unwittingly, many Social Revolutionaries and Mensheviks) define as "freedom of the press" a state of affairs under which censorship is abolished and all parties freely publish all kinds of newspapers. In reality, this is not freedom of the press, but freedom to deceive the oppressed and exploited masses of the people by the rich, by the bourgeoisie.[10]

Could it have been that as Lenin felt himself nearer to the actual seat of power he could bear less and less the thought of a press operated by the political opposition?

With the founding of the new state, the press was entrusted the custody of the party which through its government agencies was to exercise both pre- and postpublication censorship to make sure that no other party could use the press and to "guarantee" that the channels of communication would be used for the greater good of the people. Ironically some inherent capitalistic evils feared most, and other noncapitalistic evils not foreseen by Lenin, have developed under Communist tutelage. Chief among these is the fact that the communications system has been abrogated to the exclusive use and control of a ruling oligarchy whose membership consists of about 10 per cent of the population. Consequently, one of the purposes the communications system inevitably serves is to help the oligarchy perpetuate itself in power because the sovereign power and the press are one and the same. In a real sense, however, the mass media system serves other purposes. While the mythical image of a "people's press" advanced by the regime is exaggerated, the public does, to a degree, use and have access to the channels of mass communication.

Another democratic concept of a free press is that the people—in theory all classes of society—may own and have access to the press. In communist theory, as we have seen, ownership and access to mass communications is restricted to the party, which in the name of the people serves as custodian of the media. A third meaning of press freedom as understood in some Western democracies is that it includes the right to criticize not only the government, but

Fig. 4.1. Cartoons from the Soviet satirical magazine **Krokodil** reflect the Soviet concept of the American free-press system. In Soviet thinking, press freedom means a kind of irresponsibility; hence in the cartoon entitled "The Slander Department" (left), the editor asks the reporter to write a piece exposing the Communist plots. "But I haven't any facts," says the reporter. "What of it? Haven't we a free press?" the editor responds.

Another Soviet stereotype of American mass communications as a bought tool of the wealthy class, is summed up in the cartoon illustrating a "Compromising Situation." One young bird in the nest atop the newspaper building complains: "Mother, why did you build our nest so close to the Hearst editorial office? Now everybody will say that our quills are for sale, too."

also to question all values, including the underlying philosophy of the society. Freedom in this sense is not tolerated in the Soviet Union. Lenin wrote the classic statement of the regime's attitude toward political criticism and the use of the press by the foes of socialism: "Why should a government which is doing what it believes to be right allow itself to be criticized? It would not allow opposition by lethal weapons, and ideas are much more fatal than guns."[11] In a pamphlet on the press published a year later in 1921 the Founder of the Soviet Union said, "Freedom of the press is freedom for the organization of the bourgeoisie and their agents. . . . To give these people such a weapon . . . would mean facilitating the task of the adversary, helping the enemy. We do not wish to find ourselves committing suicide, and for this reason we shall not introduce freedom of the press . . . ." [12]

Freedom of the press in democratic theory means the right of all to have access to knowledge—the right to learn and know. In libertarian systems the mass communication media are free to discover, gather, and transmit information. In the Soviet Union the media make sincere efforts to reach the people but they are not free to search out and report. They must disseminate the Communist view of the facts in the context of the current line.

In his statement renouncing Western-style freedom of the press for the Soviet Union, Lenin was using the term according to its Western meaning. He argued, as have interpreters of the Soviet system since, that their mass communications are free. Moreover, the constitution of the Soviet Union (Article 125) and the constitutions of each of the federated republics guarantee freedom of speech, freedom of the press, freedom of assembly, and freedom of street processions and demonstrations. The text of the article further states, "These civil rights are ensured by placing at the disposal of the working people and their organizations printing presses, stocks of paper, public buildings, streets, communications facilities, and other material requisites for the exercise of these rights." [13] However the exercise of these rights is strictly limited by a clause in the article itself which specifies that they may be exercised only "in conformance with the interests of the working people." When are such rights exercised in conformance with the people's interests? Who is to determine this difficult question? The Communist party, of course, in its capacity as the "leading core" of the workers. The text also makes the stipulation that the exercise of such rights must be used for "strengthening the socialist system," implying that freedom of the press may not be used against that system. Indeed, to do so is counted as a counterrevolutionary crime to which the provisions of the Criminal Code are applicable.[14] These limitations simply mean that the Soviet people are merely granted the right to uphold the established order, not to criticize it.[15] Moreover, the provision of the implementing article placing printing presses, stocks of papers, communications facilities and the like at the disposal of the working people was nullified by a law passed in 1932. This law states that printing offices of any kind, including the use of duplication machines, etc., may be maintained only by the government agencies, the cooperatives, and public organizations.[16] And even the government agencies must obtain licenses for the use of such equipment requiring supervision and accounting for materials used and the nature of such use.

The abstract concept of freedom, if the Soviet citizen chooses to ignore the limitations, is subject to different connotations, and for American and Soviet journalists, freedom of the press has widely different meanings.[17] Communists say they believe that freedom to communicate one's ideas is much more important than abstract freedom from government, and that the Soviet people do have such freedom within the latitude permitted and under state protection for the benefit of all the people, not just certain classes. Where the United States Constitution, for example, sets up certain safeguards against invasion or infringement of fundamental freedoms by Congress and by state governments, the Soviet view holds that liberty can exist and be safeguarded only within the protective keeping of the party and government, which can prevent freedom of the press from being unsurped and monopolized by affluent minorities and vested interests to the detriment of the common people. Indeed, Lenin's instrumental concept appears to be derived from his interpretation of the abuses, as he saw them, to which the press has been subjected in capitalist societies. He saw the bourgeois employing the press as an instrument of propaganda for the "reactionary ideology of capitalism," and further as a means of deceiving and misinforming the workers. "Capitalism has made the newspaper a capitalistic concern, a tool for the profit of the rich, for the information and amusement of them, an instrument to deceive and fool the mass of workers," he wrote.[18] The *Bolshaia Sovetskaya Entsiklopediia* enlarges upon this theme and uses the American newspaper as an extreme example, as follows:

> . . . Its character false and corrupt throughout, the bourgeois newspaper is one of the means with which the bourgeois attempt to prolong the existence of the capitalistic, exploitative order which is historically doomed to destruction. The anti-proletarian nature of every bourgeois newspaper shows that it is full of bitterness and hate for the camp of peace, democracy and socialism; that, at the same time it is a zealous propagandist for imperialistic war. The American newspapers of the monopolists, who use the press for their own aggressive, thieving purposes, are lucid examples of the nature of the bourgeois newspaper.[19]

In a real sense, though, the Soviet public uses and enjoys access to its press, for members of the public are invited to write letters to newspapers. Many thousands are received and published each year, although there is no indication that the press feels obliged to print them all. If a letter stating grievances is published, the writer has a chance to receive some kind of redress. Another device to bring the press closer to the people is the use of worker-peasant correspondents whose duty is to prepare local material expressing the viewpoints and interests of the average citizen. The use of these worker-peasant correspondents has declined since World War II, although a considerable proportion of the Soviet newspaper appears still to be devoted to material prepared by interested citizens.[20] Such material represents the work of worker-peasant correspondents, experts in various fields of knowledge, writers of letters to the editor, and in part, no doubt, the anonymous work of staff members. Thus the people participate in mass communication by contributing to media content. In theory the public owns and has full access to the media, while the party merely holds the media system in its custody. In practice the party owns and uses the media primarily to serve its own ends—ends which need not always conflict with those of the general public, of course.

While the Soviet system flatly denies freedom of expression to those who would use it against the state, the press is free within prescribed limits to engage in loyal criticism. In fact, the press and other mass media have the duty of criticism and of participating in the national activity of self-analysis known as *samokritika.* Press and people are expected to expose fault and inefficiency in the ongoing work of communism. Such freedom of criticism is granted only upon the condition that it must be "in conformity with the interests of the working people and in order to strengthen the socialist system." [21] It must be confined strictly to the execution of a plan, to the performance of the work, to the methods adopted. Criticism must never question the plan itself, the goals, the ideology, or basic philosophy of the social system. Since the party determines such matters, it makes the decisions regarding when and under what conditions a person may exercise this freedom to criticize. In order to protect the function of criticism, the Supreme Court of the Soviet Union ruled on June 14, 1935, that divulging the names of nonstaff correspondents, or *rabselkory,* is a crime falling under Articles 96 and 121 of the Criminal Code.[22] This kind of legal protection became necessary to prevent the sources of criticism from drying up. Correspondents had often been subjected to physical violence at the hands of officials whose actions or performance they had criticized. As a result the identity of these workers must remain anonymous and local officials are forbidden to reveal either their names or the nature of their correspondence.[23]

Criticism of the basic tenets of the system, writing or utterances advocating a modification of the system, or questioning of any decision or dogma are punishable as crimes. The Criminal Code, Article 58, states that disseminating anti-Soviet literature or engaging in anti-Soviet agitation is subject to six months' imprisonment for minor offenses, and, in the case of serious offenses, a 5- to 25-year sentence in a labor and reeducation camp.

Fourth, in the Soviet view, freedom of the press is now closely associated with the concept of responsibility, although this idea does not appear to have been a part of Lenin's conceptual model of the press's role. The mass communication media are assigned the important task of promoting the best interests of the working people and of strengthening the regime, of imparting to the people the ultimate "truth," as revealed in Marxist-Leninist-Stalinist doctrine as interpreted by the party. This is considered to be a grave mission, requiring dedicated men who carry out great responsibility. Responsibility of the press in Soviet thinking, therefore, is often stressed more than freedom.

The meaning of freedom of expression and its status in the Soviet Union, it is clear, differs widely from common Western conceptions. Communist theory sees the press and other mass communications agencies as powerful instruments for forging social change, for hastening evolution from the stage of bourgeois capitalism to the stage of socialism and on to the stage of pure communism. It holds the mass communication system in high esteem and places great value in its effectiveness, as compared with other instruments, in helping accomplish the goals of the society. It holds that the media can best do their work, not as independent agents free to criticize, but as faithful responsible servants—responsible to the established order, and through the established order, to the society, rather than to the people. Communist theory conceives of the state not only as the paternalistic, beneficent protector and guardian of all social values, including personal freedoms, but also as the source of truth and wisdom. This being so, the state tolerates no voices of opposition, and forbids the use of mass communication by those other than the party.

Under the Soviet Constitution and laws, how can freedom of the press be abused or violated—aside from the crime of using the press to oppose, subvert, weaken, or overthrow the Soviet system by propaganda and agitation? Some of the more important restrictions are as follows: (1) The publication of state or military secrets is forbidden. A list of categories of such secrets is published from time to time, and Glavlit is authorized to prohibit the issuance, publication, and circulation of material divulging public secrets. (2) The writing, storage, publication, and circulation of propaganda and agitation aimed at instigating "national or religious" hostility or discord is prohibited. (3) Publication of pretrial investigations and police examinations is punishable by a fine or imprisonment. (4) Article 182 of the Criminal Code provides for imprisonment of individuals and confiscation of materials for the fabrication, storage, circulation, advertising of and commerce in writings, illustrations, and materials of a pornographic character. (5) Violation of Soviet copyright laws is punishable by fine and sentencing to correctional labor. (6) Article 160 provides penalties for publishing insults. (7) Article 161 provides punishment for slander in the press, which is the Soviet phrase for defamation or libel. Slander is defined as making public a circumstance known by the author to be false and dishonoring another person. If the statement is false but does not dishonor, then the law does not apply. Report based on fact is not considered slander. Slander and insult must be carefully distinguished from *samokritika,* however, for calling officials to account in the name of socialist criticism is considered a public service. A person so criticized has no recourse at law even if charges are based entirely on falsehood. Cases of insult and slander may be brought before the courts only by the person offended, and such cases may be settled by reconciliation.

The communication system's agitation and propaganda function comes first. This embodies, in broadest terms, the Communist "education" of the masses, with careful attention to the promotion of government policy both at home and abroad. Under this heading also is included the work of continual campaigning to mobilize the people ever toward greater realization of the country's economic and political ambitions. Successful methods of production are depicted for socialist "emulation." The people are exhorted to put forth greater effort to increase the volume of production. The system's organizational function takes the form of devoting huge proportions of media space and time to the affairs of the party as well as to government decrees and pronouncements in order to stimulate public interest, participation, and approval. The system also functions as a critic in the spheres of social endeavor.

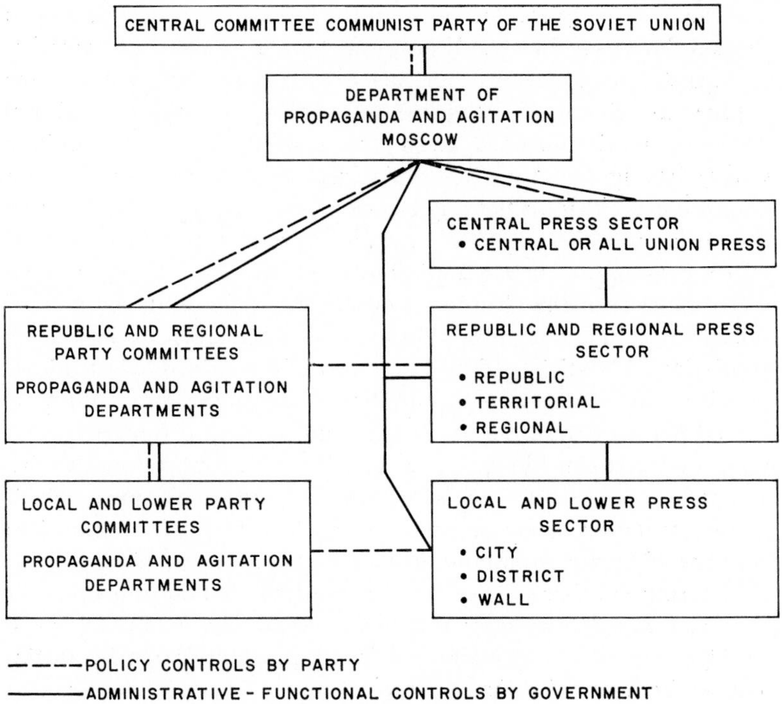

Fig. 4.2. Administrative and Functional Structure of the Soviet Press System. At the left is the party control mechanism and at the right the government's operational structure.

STRUCTURE OF THE PRESS SYSTEM

The Soviet press system has been carefully designed. It has developed in a direction best calculated to make it serve with maximum efficiency its instrumental purpose as organizer, propagandist, and agitator. This purpose is reflected throughout its organization and structure, from the largest to the smallest medium, from the national networks to the tiny wall newspaper. The organization pattern indicates that a serious attempt has been made to reach the masses of the workers and to consider the special interests of the society's various segments. The pattern has been shaped on the basis of what in the judgment of the regime's leadership will best serve the interests of the state, rather than on any systematic basis of audience desire and consumer sales. Because press and broadcasting differ somewhat in their structural outlines though they serve identical purposes we shall consider them separately.

The newspaper press as the oldest and largest of the media systems, has provided the basic organizational model for all print and electronic channels. The press is structured horizontally according to the geographical regions served, from the nationwide audience appeal media centering in the capital, to the local and "lower" media serving small villages, farms, or factories. Vertically the structure is designed to reach different occupation, age, or special interest groups, such as youth, labor, the military, sports, science, agriculture, and industry (Fig. 4.2). The result is that the majority of the newspapers are specialized in their content and appeal;[24] this contrasts with the press of democracies in which for the most part a press with general appeals has arisen to attract the greatest possible audience. More than half of the Soviet newspapers are agricultural papers, and additionally there is a large government and party press and a large press appealing to youth. The magazine press follows a similar pattern, with a few comparatively large circulation magazines on the one hand and a considerable number of highly specialized low circulation technical publications at the base. As might be expected, magazine and book publishing enterprises clustering as they do in Moscow have developed more along vertical than horizontal lines in order to serve the various segments of the population.

The Central Press

At the top of the structural pyramid one finds the large newspapers of national circulation. In 1961 the 25 newspapers in this category printed a single press run[25] total of 23,500,000 copies, more than one-third of the entire newspaper circulation of the country.[26] (See Table 4.1.) *Komsololskaya Pravda* on October 6, 1965, reported that the total combined circulation of the Central or All-Union Press, newspapers and magazines combined, (with the exception of supplements to *Izvestia* and *Sovetsky Sport)* had reached 35,241,600 in the month of September, 1965. In addition to *Pravda,* official organ of the Communist party, and *Izvestia,* official organ of the Supreme Soviet, other major party papers in the Central group include *Pionersakaya Pravda* (Young Pioneers' Truth) and *Komsomolskaya Pravda* (Young Communist League's Truth). These two youth papers, as well as some 30 more publications, are printed and disseminated from the Moscow plant of *Pravda. Partinaya Zhizn* (Party Life) and *Kommunist,* theoretical journals,

TABLE 4.1

TERRITORIAL DISTRIBUTION OF THE SOVIET NEWSPAPER PRESS IN 1961 *

Press Level	Type of Newspaper	Number Published	One-time Circulation
			(*thousands*)
Central	All-Union	25	23,500
Provincial	Republic Territorial Regional	581	26,300
Local sector	District City Lower	8,937	18,800
Totals		9,543	68,600

* Sources: *Sovetskaya Pechat; Current Digest of the Soviet Press,* Washington, Vol. XIV, 1962; *The Soviet Press in Translation,* Madison, 1961; press reports.

must also be counted prominently among the publications of the Central Press.

The leading government papers, aside from *Izvestia,* are *Krasnaya Zvesda* (Red Star), the daily newspaper of the Soviet Army; *Sovetsky Flot* (Soviet Fleet), official medium of the Navy; *Gudok* (Whistle), publication of the Transportation Ministry, and *Selskaya Zhizn* (Rural Life), published by the Ministry of Agriculture.

A third large branch of the Central, or All-Union Press consists of those newspapers and magazines published by "public" organizations and institutions such as the important trade unions and cooperatives. For example, *Trud* (Labor), the official organ of the Trade Union Council, is one of the most important papers in the country. The construction workers' organ is *Stroitel 'nyi Rabochii* (Construction Workers). Included in this same category are the well-known journals devoted to athletics, art, and literature. These include *Sovetskii Sport, Literaturnaya Gazeta* (Literary Gazette), *Kultura i Zhizn* (Culture and Life), the national magazine of sociopolitical satire, *Krokodil,* and some of the nationally circulated literary monthlies, which are organs of units of the Writers' and Artists' Union.

If we define a national daily press as one that emanates from a central location and attempts to reach a nationwide audience, we can see that the Soviet Union is one of the few great nations covering a wide expanse of territory that can claim a national press of any appreciable extent. The organs of the Central Press have great prestige over the country because of their authority. They set the example for the rest of the country, serving as models of practice, form, and content for similar types of publications in each of the political subdivisions. They are the first and final source of the latest "line" pronouncements from central party and government headquarters. Being close to the sources of Communist "truth," their voices provide among the mass media the only authoritative interpretations of Marxist-Leninist-Stalinist ideology.[27]

The Republic and Regional Press

This middle group of papers perform for their particular areas the same function that the Central papers perform for the nation as a whole. They serve the various geopolitical subdivisions such as the 15 socialist Soviet republics, the territories, and the regions. The range of subjects open to discussion and treatment permitted to this middle group is not as wide as that of the Central Press, but wider than that of the Local Press. Their focus is upon problems of their particular region instead of the whole nation. Some examples of party papers at this level are *Radyanska Ukraina* of Kiev (Soviet Ukraine) whose circulation reaches well over a half million; *Kommunist* and *Pravda Ukrainy* also of Kiev; *Pravda Vostoka* at Tashkent; *Leningradskaya Pravda;* and *Zvesda* of Minsk. Estimates for the regional press for 1961, given in Table 4.1, showed almost 581 papers at this level with a combined total one-time circulation of some 26,300,000.

Although the party papers make up a large part of the Regional and Local Press, there are many journals at these levels among the specialized press. Two examples, agriculture and military, suffice. *Sotsialisticheskoe Zemledelie* (Socialist Agriculture) and approximately 25 other agricultural publications are published at the Central and regional levels. Below these are about 3,000 district or local agricultural papers. At the bottom one finds several hundred papers serving State farms and farm machinery stations. Likewise the military press hierarchy below *Krasnaya Zvesda* consists of smaller papers serving military subdivisions. The same is true of the important industrial commissariats.

The Local and Lower Press

This group consists of the district (or county), the small city, and the "lower" press. The Local Press is required to concentrate almost exclusively on community problems, leaving the more general and complicated ideological matters to the larger papers. The term "lower press" characterizes that large group of small printed sheets and typewritten or handwritten "wall" newspapers. This group serves special projects, collective farms, schools, and industrial plants. Its mission is to promote better, faster production, to expedite decisions, and to transmit policy directives. The Local and Lower Press numbered 8,937 and circulated 18,800,000 in 1961. (See Table 4.1.) Although there are a few dailies in this group, most of them are weeklies or appear less frequently than once weekly.

The wall newspapers are ingenious devices for extending exposure penetration of important messages from the print media and for communicating special original messages to selected audiences. They attract some feedback from readers and thus prove of value as a measure of audience reaction. They are easy to change or revise; they are fast and cheap; they effectively communicate to surprisingly large numbers. Usually produced by a volunteer staff, their notices, suggestions, and discussions of immediate problems at the grass roots level are morale stimulators. There are too many wall newspapers to count, but they have been variously estimated as running to the hundreds of thousands.

The Administrative Machinery. An extensive, elaborate organization with its attendant bureaucracy is needed to carry on the task of planning, directing, conducting, and supervising the press structure outlined above. Let us examine briefly the hierarchy of party machinery that runs the press of the nation. The Central Committee of the Communist party has a Department of Propaganda and Agitation which is charged with final responsibility for all newspaper and periodical publishing. The department accomplishes its task by means of three press sectors assigned to operate at the three levels corresponding to the levels of the press structure.

For example, the Central Press Sector of the Department of Propaganda and Agitation has charge of the Central Press. The Provincial Press Sector administers the larger group of intermediate newspapers and periodicals, which we have called the Republic and Regional Press. The Local Press Sector is in charge of the Local and Lower Press. Just as the Central Press Sector is the operating arm of the Department of Propaganda and Agitation, which in turn is an agent of the Central Committee of the Communist party, so the Provincial and the Local Press Sectors are responsible immediately to their corresponding Party Committee Agitprop Departments. From the bottom the local media are held accountable directly to the Local Press Sector which in turn is responsible to branch Agitprop Departments created by the local party committees. The Republic-Regional papers are accountable directly to their Provincial Press Sector and indirectly to the Agitprop Departments of the Regional Party Committees. Thus through the party hierarchy the smallest press unit falls under the authority of the Central Committee in Moscow. At each level the departments see that directives from above are obeyed and deal on their own with specific problems in their areas, in addition to providing general supervision over papers at levels below theirs. The local papers are under the administration not only of the central organization in Moscow but also of the intermediate party departments at the next level above.

BROADCASTING

Since broadcasting postdates the founding of the Soviet Union, the leaders have been quick to realize its value as a mass propaganda-agitation instrument,[28] and have had the opportunity to shape this new medium to meet the party's needs and purposes. Yet progress toward full utilization of broadcasting's potentialities has been slow.

Like the press, the nation's broadcasting apparatus for both radio and television centers in the capital. Radio Moscow broadcasts on a 24-hour basis[29] four simultaneous programs in different languages throughout the country. Local broadcasting has centered in the capitals of the Soviet Republics and in the other territorial or administrative seats. The intermediate units serve as outlets for local programs as well as relays for national network programs. Reports for 1962 show that AM radio transmitters numbered 405, and the estimated number of receivers, both wired speakers and private sets, totaled 44 million, representing slightly more than 20 receivers per 100 persons.

Regular AM broadcasting has been supplemented with FM since World War II. In 1962 two FM transmitters were in operation in Moscow. FM has been utilized more because of its technical advantages which permit more perfect sound transmission for the high frequencies and offer relief from crowded AM broadcast bands. FM's development coincided with that of television because both could

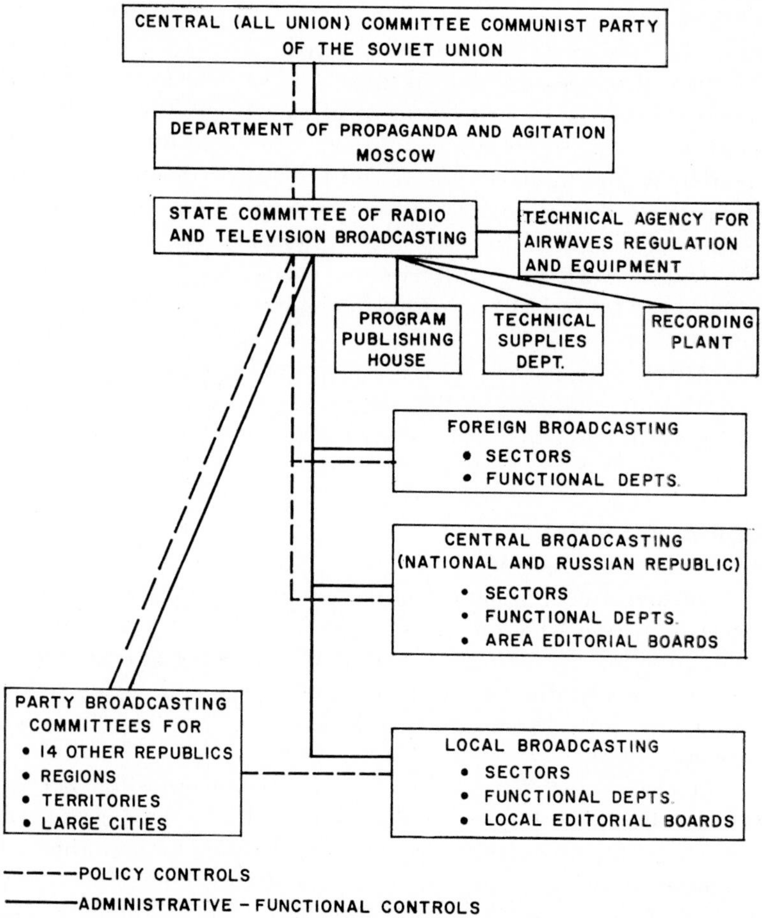

Fig. 4.3. Administrative and Functional Structure of Soviet Broadcasting.

use common transmitting antennae supports, and because television receivers came equipped with FM receivers.

Television stations are classified as either television centers, which have studio facilities to originate programs, or as relay (retranslation) stations, which transmit the signals from the television centers and have limited or no production facilities.[30] Data for 1962 show 93 television centers and 76 relay or auxiliary stations, and 7 million television receivers. By 1965 the number of centers had increased to 118 and sets had increased to 14 million. The Central studios are located in Moscow, the hub of a 20-station network of 9 centers and 11 relay stations. This is the network which serves most of European Russia. The main television centers and retransmission stations are augmented by the smaller relay or "booster" units some 75 to 90 miles away. Some academic institutions have their own television stations, and a number of mobile translation stations are in use. Stations use a 625-line definition, and 12-inch screens are common. While the main stations are at Moscow, Leningrad, and Kiev, there are stations at Odessa, Kharkov, Gorki, Stalingrad, Tomsk, and Sverdlovsk. New stations are being completed at Baku, Minsk, Murmansk, Riga, and other population centers.

The structure of radio broadcasting and receiving has been characterized by extensive use of group listening by means of radio-diffusion exchanges or redistribution centers, which relay by wire central broadcasts along with local announcements to millions of subscribers. Wired-speaker outlets are placed in homes, factories, farms, radio auditoriums, and other places where people congregate. The chief advantages offered by such systems are that they are cheaper than independent receiving units, each unit has a larger prospective audience than independent units placed in each home, and they permit maximum economical use of equipment. Networks or exchanges can originate local programs without going on the air. This advantage was especially valued during war time because it enabled officials to communicate with the people without being monitored by enemy aircraft. Another advantage was the fact that wired-speaker systems prevent the reception of foreign broadcasts. A disadvantage from the standpoint of the listener is the limited range of program selection permitted. Efforts were being made in the 1960's to remedy this objection.

Both private sets and wired speakers were growing, but the use of private individual sets was growing faster. For example, in 1958, the ratio was 9.5 million independent radio receivers to 27 million wired speakers. In 1963 the ratio was 32 million independent sets to 33 million wired-speaker outlets in use.

Though not as elaborate and complicated as the press administrative mechanism, broadcasting administration in the USSR is similarly organized. (See Fig. 4.3.) Like publishing, all broadcasting is operated under the party's supervision. The broadcasting agency of the Central Committee's Agitprop Department is the All-Union Radio Committee, now the State Committee of Radio and Television Broadcasting, attached to the Council of Ministers. This committee operates broadcasting through a number of subdivisions determined by function and geographical coverage.

Central Broadcasting has the responsibility for nationwide domestic broadcasting and for local broadcasting to the Russian Republic. At any one time Central Broadcasting may consist of a number of different units. For example there is the Propaganda and Agitation Sector, the Literary-Dramatic Sector, the Late News Sector, the Children's Broadcast Sector, and the Editorial Office of Defense. Each of these units is subdivided into functional departments.

Parallel to Central Broadcasting are the administration units for Local Broadcasting, Foreign Broadcasting, and Musical Broadcasting. To provide staff functions there is a Planning, Financial, and Accounting Sector which approves quarterly and annual plans for programs, collects fees, and finances the entire system. The All-Union Committee also operates a publishing house for program publications, a technical supplies department, and a recording plant. A technical agency assigns wave lengths, distributes sending and receiving equipment, and collaborates with the Ministry of Communications, which has charge of equipment and cable.

There are some 132 committees over the country: each of the fifteen other Republics has its own broadcasting committee appointed by its Council of Ministers, as do each of the territories, some of the regions, and a few of the larger cities. Each subdivision is by law an agent of the All-Union Committee which exercises control by directives, planning, and reporting. As it controls all other communications, the party controls broadcasting by means of criticism and instruction, by party decisions and directives, by assigning loyal party members to administrative positions, and by seeing that a large proportion of broadcasting workers are party members.

MANAGEMENT AND CONTROL METHODS

In Gruliow's words, the management system provides a means of continuous, overlapping supervision from Leningrad to Vladivostok and from the most modest wall newspaper to the mighty *Pravda*. This complex mechanism composes an interrelated web of party and government organization. The management system is a part of the bureaucratic system that oversees most phases of Soviet public life.

For convenient analysis the supervisory operation may be discussed under six general headings, as follows: (1) planning, (2) staffing, (3) making and administering policy, (4) supervising and evaluating, (5) controlling information, (6) regulating distribution, and (7) financing. Each phase of the operation will be considered in turn.

Planning

Since the entire Soviet social system is a planned system, press and broadcasting have been included in the successive 5-year plans. Plans for the communications apparatus have often, like those in other fields of endeavor, fallen short of their goals. Application of the plans to the actual situation resulted in many pragmatic adjustments and empirical adaptations because there were unforeseen handicaps.

Planning determines such matters as location, size, type of content, format, nature of audience, periodicity, power and frequency, area covered, and circulation size. With large-scale planning, officials discontinue functions no longer needed and meet new needs as changes occur in the population or as new political needs arise. Changes in media service may be dictated by a growth in literacy or by the successful completion of a government program whose special organ is thus made obsolete and is therefore discontinued.

Broadcasting service may be expanded in order to reach larger audiences in remote regions, or translated into additional dialects for minority groups. New organs may be launched to promote a program or campaign or to serve as a model for other media. *Krestianskaya Gazeta* was discontinued in 1939 after having reached some 300,000 in circulation. It had completed its task of campaigning for collectivization. *Sovietskaya Rossia,* a new daily founded in 1956, was established to serve the Russian Federated Republic, much as the other fifteen republics are served by their official party papers. *Economicheskaia Zhizn* (Economic Life) and *Za Industrializatsiu* (For Industrialization), former organs that were widely circulated, are now in limbo. World War II brought a large increase in its newsprint allowance to permit the army newspaper

Krasnaia Zvezda to expand. So the creation, rise, relative prominence, often the degree of popularity, the decline, and demise of media may be planned and decreed by party decisions. The power to create and dissolve mass media at will is obviously a fundamental one.

Systematic planning also determines on a regular basis all media content and format. Each department of newspaper and broadcasting units regularly submit advance plans (usually on a monthly basis) for the approval of next highest echelon of the directing hierarchy, although *Pravda* and some other high central organs are exempted from this requirement. Plans detail the subjects and themes of articles to be published and programs locally originated. Editors are guided by topics that may be suggested in the speeches, slogans announced on May Day and in October, the fortnightly *Agitators' Handbooks,* and by party briefings.[31] Plans are subject to change upon instruction from above and are usually revised from week to week. Planned articles may be withheld after being prepared for publication. The same kind of planning on the part of individual media is required also of wholesale agencies serving the media, such as the Tass Agency and the broadcasting networks.

Staffing

As owner and operator of the nation's communications system, the Communist party has exerted special effort to see that all media and their related institutions are staffed by persons who are, above all, loyal to the party. Employees must be well grounded in Marxist-Leninist ideology. Major editors and directors must be party members and, in addition to being well versed in ideology, must have "a fundamental Bolshevik firmness . . . the ability to organize aggressively the masses in the resolution of the basic tasks of socialist construction." [32] Journalists not only must be able to interpret the system faithfully and persuasively, but also be able to organize and agitate. In the training of communications personnel, education in Marxism and in the philosophy of the Communist state has taken precedence over the teaching of journalistic knowledge and professional skills.[33] To supplement formal education, however, training programs in the form of meetings, conferences, and special courses are conducted by party and media leaders.

Editors as well as other administrative personnel are appointed, according to the rules, by the media organization serving a particular territorial level. Appointments at each level are made with the appropriate superior party committee's approval. For example, the Central Committee appoints editors of the All-Union papers and approves the appointment of the editors of the Republic-Regional press. In the case of the government and union organs, the procedure is somewhat different; here the chief editor chooses his subordinates and the party ratifies his selection. Promotion and removal from office are handled in a similar manner.

It is noteworthy that his position automatically makes an editor a member of the party's executive committee and of the Agitprop bureau corresponding to his press level. These are the agencies which own and have the responsibility for publishing the newspaper. For example, the editor of a regional daily serves as ex officio member of the regional party committee and its Agitprop section.

Party secretary Khrushchev stated the position of communications workers while laying down the new party line for the creative and artistic professions in the de-Stalinized Soviet Russia of 1957 as: "We cannot put the press in unreliable hands. It must be in the hands of the most faithful, most trustworthy, most politically steadfast people devoted to our cause." [34]

The indoctrination system reasonably can be expected to provide the mass communication media with qualified, loyal personnel. The power over appointment and tenure assures continued competence and trust. Parallel posts of responsibility both on the medium and in the party's directing organization elevate the editor's prestige, and provide a direct line of communication from party to management.

Making and Administering Policy

In Centrally administered organizations, direction and supervision flow from the top down. Staff and "Line" below the top must be kept informed of party decisions, policy changes, or advised on unexpected situations not covered by standing regulations. During the earlier years directives were not always confined to policy matters, but were likely to cover almost any detail of publishing, such as the number of lines or amount of space to be devoted to a particular topic, or even price per copy. As experience has increased among communications workers, directives have tended to be confined more strictly to policy matters.

Directives are based on party decisions which are published at irregular intervals and circulated to the management. In general they concern the party's political position, the handling of official information, and the treatment of local coverage originating in editorial offices. Kremlin policy must be faithfully reproduced in the media in accordance with Central Committee's instructions. News of central government activities and of foreign affairs is scrutinized by top party officials before being distributed to the media by the Tass Agency. These two categories of information must be reproduced by the mass media without any alteration whatsoever. Khrushchev's speeches were required to be reproduced in full.

Correspondence and other content originating within the medium's territory and local office is treated according to the plan submitted in advance by the editorial staff or handled within the general limits prescribed by the directives. Local developments not foreseen in the plans and not specifically covered by directives, therefore, represent an area in which media editorial personnel must exercise responsible judgment and discretion.

An important function of administration is to censor and suppress. A classified list of subjects that must not be mentioned in the media is known as the *Perechen*. This body of directives bulked quite large during the 1930s. Interdicted subjects consist of reports of subversion or internal unrest, such as strikes, riots, student demonstrations, and agricultural worker agitation. Also forbidden was information about forced labor camps, unfavorable production figures, and similar matters. Central censorship and control of all news flowing into the country makes it unnecessary ordinarily to forbid categories of foreign intelligence, except on occasion when rumor may require official attention. Another important function of administration is the agitation function. Liaison officers assigned to the media make news by calling meetings which take some sort of action. This may stimulate a press campaign that may result in the issuance of a corrective decree.

The editorial decision-making process on *Pravda* is worth examining as an example of the execution of directives at the top level. As on most morning papers the working day begins early in the afternoon and continues until deadline. At 3 o'clock in the afternoon the editor and his chief subeditors assemble in a large conference room equipped with comfortable chairs for the daily editorial conference. As a member of the Central Committee and of the Agitation and Propaganda Department, *Pravda's* editor is in close communication with the high policy makers and thus can promulgate policy in his own organization. Pictures of finished editions are flashed on a screen for critical analysis. Long-range plans of the month or week are reviewed and plans for the next day's paper are made; space is allocated to various departments; and assignments are agreed upon. After the meeting each editor returns to his department and makes his assignments. The paper goes to press late in the evening and is on the streets in the small hours of the next morning.

The Soviet newspaper building has no counterpart for the large editorial room typical of most United States newspaper offices. Each writer and editor for *Pravda* has his own private office usually furnished with sofa, samovar, telephones, and typewriters. The chief editor's office boasts both radio and the common 12-inch-screen television receiver. Although typewriters are plentiful, writers have been reported to prepare copy in handwriting. Most assignments do not require "beat" coverage or even that the writer leave the building to cover events firsthand. He turns out his article, submits it to his immediate editor, who approves it and transmits it by tube to the chief editor's office. Here the chief editor's assistants read and approve it, then send it by tube to the composing room.

Pravda's departmental organization follows functional lines, consisting of such departments as Party Life, Propaganda, Agriculture, Economics, Foreign Affairs, Military Science, Literature and Art, etc. These departments have charge of content in their areas. The resulting newspaper product after printing and distribution, represents the ultimate execution of the directive and policy-making process.

Because it must operate within the considerable framework governed by top management, in comparison with the latitude of editorial discretion common in Western systems it would appear that the chief editors, with the possible exception of those at the highest levels, are left with only relatively narrow spheres in which they may exercise their own judgment. The latitude of discretion permitted subeditors is even more restricted.

How extensive are the directives? Contemporary directives are secret, but a collection appearing in 1940 numbered 220 pages, and a postwar edition numbered almost 700 pages.

Supervising and Evaluating

Planning, staffing, directing, and instructing are not enough. Without proper supervision, assessment of results, criticism of performance, and the fixing of responsibility—that is, without efficient follow-up—goals cannot be achieved.

Because of the nature of the system's functions the principal manager is inevitably the chief editor in press and broadcasting.[35] In addition to serving as the Central management authority in his own medium or network operation, he also aids the party mechanism in making policy within its own jurisdiction. The manager supervises line functions, controls personnel and budget, and deals with unions for technical services. A degree of national uniformity and centralization, however, characterizes government procedures regarding staff and budget functions, such as the mechanical, financial, and transportation operations for all media. There appears to be no Soviet business manager or advertising director who exercises authority on the same level or above that of the editor or director, or ranks above him in power. These other functions are considered line functions, thus subordinate in authority to the editor or program director.

To see that party guidance is diligently followed, an extensive system of reporting and accounting, criticism, and appraisal has grown up. First regular reports on performance from editors and the party agencies are required, then systematic samples of media content are examined and criticized. Public complaints are noted. Such data provide a basis for appraising performance. Those responsible are criticized, and the criticisms are presented to the medium concerned. Critical evaluation may be published in a Central party organ; or, when similar criticisms appear to have wide application, an important policy decision is made and a directive is issued.

Although the central function of assessment is to check ideological and political content for signs of deviation from the party line, many other areas of performance such as sins of omission or apathy receive attention. In the late 1950s, press content was being widely criticized for its dullness and lack of imagination.

Apart from the managerial processes, voluntary criticism in the media themselves often assists the party in its task of control. The prewar publication *Bolshevitskaya Pechat* (Bolshevik Press) evaluated press performance. Since the war the magazine *Kultura i Zhizn* (Culture and Life), organ of the Department of Propaganda and Agitation, has taken over this duty. *Sovetskaya Pechat,* the organ of the Union of Journalists, has been charged with the duty of improving the professional level of press content and performance.

Pravda not infrequently publishes press review material, but public criticism of *Pravda* occurs rarely.[36] The government organs criticize their counterparts at lower levels, as do the party organs. Criticisms of performance often appear under standing headings, such as "Review of the Press." An example of *Pravda's* criticism of *Udmurtskaia Pravda* is as follows:

> Unplanned and not always wise news items and correspondence appearing . . . in the "Party Life" column do not give an idea of the fullblooded life of the Party organizations in plants . . . collective farms. . . . How much the paper would gain from lively articles by party officials if they appeared more often! . . . The Udmurt Province Party Committee, of course, reads its paper. Why then do they tolerate the fact that *Udmurtskaia Pravda* stands aloof from the life of party organizations?[37]

Gruliow observed that at its own territorial-administrative level the newspaper is a house organ, subservient to those who own and publish it; for the press levels below it, the same newspaper becomes a watchdog and crusader for press excellence.

Controlling Information

As we have seen, the traditional methods of State thought control—those of censorship, suppression, and propaganda—are practiced in the Soviet Union. But the emphasis and approach are different from those of non-Communist societies. The term censorship, as it is generally understood, means that the censor and the censored are independent, perhaps antagonistic, forces working for different purposes. Such a concept could hardly apply in the Soviet Union because censor and censored are not independent and presumably are neither working at cross-purposes, nor motivated by divergent loyalties. Except in certain important areas the Soviet operation tends to stress affirmative agitation and positive propaganda-making rather than matters that are forbidden. The interdicted categories of intelligence, of course, are matters relating to national security, secret government information, and intelligence that, if released, might damage national (*e.g.* party or government) prestige both at home and abroad. The problem of control for the regime, however, becomes primarily one of tight, efficient management of its own operation. Viewed in this light, the control system takes on the guise of responsible self-discipline.

The formal censorship agency, Glavlit, was made operative in

1931, and charged with the responsibility for pre- and postpublication censorship of all public information matters relating to politico-economic-military security of the country. The act establishing Glavlit specifically prohibited the agency from engaging in ideological censorship over all party papers, *Izvestia,* and certain other government papers. Thus, a not inconsequential function of ideological censorship for a large sector of the communications apparatus was left to the editors themselves or to the party machinery. As a result Glavlit's general task, in addition to censoring other publications, has consisted largely of preventing the revelation of State secrets.[38] It has functioned also as a censor of correspondence prepared for transmission to foreign countries. It controls the export of Soviet publications, a duty that has grown in importance as the Soviet Union has systematically increased its volume of output in this field. It appears that the extent of Glavlit's authority and resulting activity fluctuates according to the relative degree of security felt by the regime at a given time, and according to the relative degree of confidence felt in the good judgment of editors.

Tass is the gatekeeper. The censorship functions of Glavlit are supplemented by those of the news agency Tass (Telegrafnoie Agenstvo Sovietskavo Soyuza). Its position as the gatekeeper of a large volume of information reaching the Soviet people makes it a significant arm of the control mechanism. Tass also sends a large proportion of officially approved information from the Soviet Union to the rest of the world. Tass ranks slightly below *Pravda* in its authority and prestige as an official spokesman of the regime. A national and world news and telegraphic agency, Tass possesses a newspaper service, a radio service, a mat and cut service, a photographic and feature syndicate, and a confidential information service distributed under seal to metropolitan editors and high State-party officials.

Its operations may be considered under four headings: (1) its domestic functions, (2) its function as gatekeeper of world news for Soviet consumption, (3) its function as reporter for the Soviet Union to the outside world,[39] and (4) its role as a major part of the confidential intelligence system.

Tass's internal services have two main functions: (1) To speed the duplication of daily lead articles from *Pravda* in the domestic press and broadcasting network. This is the daily political directive which lays down the line to be followed by local party organizations on important questions. Likewise Tass's channels carry all major government pronouncements having a bearing on national policy. (2) Tass serves as a central telegraphic agency for internal transmission of regional and local information prepared by its correspondents throughout the country. Correspondents prepare information originating in their own areas that is considered important by the local party organization and transmit it to Tass headquarters in Moscow where it is edited for rediffusion to the provincial press and broadcasting network, and to Tass offices abroad. Tass's provincial service also carries information from the national press and items carefully chosen from the incoming foreign news report. The domestic service is organized along functional lines[40] after the pattern of the average newspaper staff. There is a Party Life Department and a Propaganda Department. There are departments devoted to such specialities as youth, economics, culture, agriculture, sports, etc. Its staff members are either "operative" or "instructional." The operative staff consists of professional writers and subeditors, who are not necessarily party members. Instructors are party men whose function is nonjournalistic. In its domestic sphere Tass, as a matter of practice, shares its authority with party-government officials in determining what is selected at the local level for redistribution throughout the country, but some editing takes place in Moscow before transmission. The agency relies primarily on broadcasting for internal news dissemination. Tass distributes material within the Soviet Union on a subscription basis, with all of the news media required to subscribe to its services. This assures it of partial financial support and provides it with a complete channel of communication from the top down through the various levels of the press apparatus. Since its rates are low and some services are free, it is apparent that Tass's budget is underwritten by the regime.

For its news gathering abroad, Tass maintains correspondents in most foreign capitals. Only a fraction of the stream of information these journalists collect and send to the head office in Moscow appears in the Soviet press. Most of this information goes into the confidential file or mimeographed book intended to provide background for ministries, party members, and editors. As the gatekeeper of foreign news flowing into the country Tass is in a position to help determine what the Soviet people are told about world affairs. The agency's practice in handling foreign news well illustrates N. G. Palgunov's principle that some facts should not be reported. Other world news services contribute to the flow of foreign intelligence into Tass's Moscow headquarters, but this information is processed before relaying to subscribers. Tass maintains exchange agreements with Reuters, Agence France-Presse, the American Associated Press, and others. It has business relationships with the New China News Agency and with the news services of the Eastern European Communist countries. A considerable portion of the foreign news report as it goes to the media consists of quotations of foreign newspaper opinion presented in a context that makes it useful in lending support to the Soviet government's position, particularly foreign press opinion reflecting sympathy—or that which can be twisted to make it appear to reflect sympathy—with the Communist viewpoint. These quotations, aside from bearing the authority of foreign support, have the additional advantage of permitting dissemination of views which the Soviet official line is not in position to support and the media not in position to advocate, but which the regime feels should be exposed to the masses.[41]

Tass has been practically the sole exporter of Soviet information for foreign consumption, though this monopoly situation is changing. Its broadcasts are made in a number of different languages and dialects. Tass's overseas radio bulletin contains the daily *Pravda* leader and selected articles from the Soviet press representing a guide on world affairs for foreign Communist organization. It also carries cultural and economic information of propagandistic value selected from the Tass internal service. The number of subscribers to the bulletin in the Western world is small, however, being limited to a few Communist organs.

Tass's confidential file. The confidential file consists of material considered unsuitable for immediate publication. Unfavorable British comment on Soviet international policy declarations, for example, may be withheld from the wire and placed in the file. At the same time, Tass may widely disseminate information that those same policy declarations received front page attention in the British press—information which will be published and broadcast throughout the country. As a matter of practice the Soviet ambassador's remarks before the United Nations General Assembly are released in full to the domestic media, but arguments of the representatives of other countries against these Soviet viewpoints are dismissed with the statement that "several delegates crudely attacked the Soviet position."[42] The full report of such remarks is placed in the confidential file. Thus the Soviet people are shielded from exposure to reports of critical foreign reactions to their government's conduct. The confidential file is sent regularly to party, government, and communications leaders for their information. This immediate, comprehensive, and exclusive source of world information no doubt usefully supplements the flow from secret intelligence sources. It therefore contributes significantly to the Kremlin's foundation for policy decisions.

Tass's power grows. Tass's present position in the power structure of the country developed gradually. A forerunner, the Rosta Agency, was started in 1919, then on August 10, 1925, the Soviet government established Tass as a State-owned agency. At first, Tass competed with a special news agency handling economic information and a handful of local news agencies such as Ratau, the Ukrainian wire service. As Stalin slowly centralized political control in Moscow, Tass's monopoly was tightened and its power increased. In the early 1930s the economic news agency ceased to exist. The local agencies gradually lost their identity and autonomy as they were absorbed in the Tass organization.[43] Rosta disappeared in 1935. The way was prepared for the great purge of 1937–1938, which eliminated most of the Soviet foreign correspondents who worked for *Pravda* and *Izvestia*. Since World War II neither paper hastened to reestablish foreign correspondents who provided a regular comprehensive report, since both relied on Tass for this service. Outside of the country in the Soviet East European bloc, Tass also expanded at the expense of national agencies.

Since the early 1950s, however, Tass's monopoly position has changed. According to Kruglak, by 1962 its exclusive control over incoming and outgoing news had virtually disappeared.[44] *Pravda* and *Izvestia* have increased their staff correspondents abroad *Sovetskaya Rossia, Trud,* and Radio Moscow have established foreign correspondents. The news agencies of the eastern European Communist countries have broken their exclusive ties with Tass, and Tass is facing competition in the Communist world market from the New China News Agency. With both domestic and foreign clients, Tass's service is now supplemented by that of the new agency Novosti (APN) created in 1961 by the journalists' and writers' unions, *Pravda, Izvestia,* and other Soviet newspapers, the National Academy of Sciences, and other organizations interested in friendship and cultural relations with foreign countries. It appears that Novosti's purpose is to provide propaganda-colored feature material for foreign and domestic media in the interests of better international understanding,[45] leaving the reporting of hard news to Tass. This changed position does not mean that Tass's influence either as the principal international news agency or as a gatekeeper of information for the Soviet people has diminished, only that this function is no longer one to be exercised *exclusively* by Tass.

As a government agency, Tass is responsible to the Council of Ministers of the USSR. It coordinates its activities and policy with the Central Committee's Agitation and Propaganda Department. The Central Committee's presidium appoints its general director and major officers, and its performance is directed by the government and appraised by both party and government.

Some authorities say that Tass exercises limited editorial functions, and thus has very little power of selection for the information it collects and disseminates inside the country.[46] It is not clear how much control over the selection of content is exercised by Tass or how much by the government and party officials. This appears to be a moot point, for the agency as a creature of the government must do the government's will. It is apparent that simply by opening or closing the gate on the flow of information under its jurisdiction Tass has the power to manage the dissemination process from sources to media. What the media do with the carefully selected information they receive is up to the editors, the directors, the party and its Agitprop bureaus, and Glavlit.

Glavlit's functions. Where Tass's responsibility for transmitting information to the media leaves off, Glavlit's duties begin. First is the surveillance system which enables Glavlit to check on what the media say and do. Although statutory and traditional roles confine its censorship powers as far as the party press is concerned solely to matters of national security or to information involving the disclosure of state secrets, its legal range of authority is broad, and its powers subject to broad or limited interpretation as needs dictate. Thus its sphere of activity could, and apparently did at times in the past, extend to a wide range of discretion and power that might fluctuate in practice according to the degree of security felt by the rulers at a particular time, or according to the dependability felt in the communication apparatus.

It is known that Glavlit exerted considerable authority in the

Thus *Pravda,* which published 2,700,000 copies before World War II, was permitted to grow to 4,900,000 by 1955, to 6 million by 1960, and to 7 million by 1965. These earlier quotas did not relate as much to demand as the later ones. Editor Yuri Zhukov estimated in 1955 that *Pravda* could sell 10 million daily if it could get the paper allotment (and, he might have added, permission to expand). *Izvestia's* captive audience of government officials was not deemed sufficient cause at one time to secure for it enough paper to print one copy each for the 1.5 million Soviet deputies on its list of readers. However, paper is not the only factor that has operated to restrict the circulation of popular publications; shortage of technical facilities and supplies has played a part. Indeed, the nation's printing equipment appears to have been chronically overtaxed. As supplies and equipment become adequate, public demand may be permitted to play a more decisive role. Yet if an ample number of preferred copies became available, measures would doubtless have to be taken to move those titles that become a drug on the market.

There were indications in 1964 and 1965 that in the drive to boost retail sales and to build circulations, reader choice and desire were being given greater consideration by the planners in charge of allocating the increased resources of newsprint and other supplies. This is shown by the rapid increase in *Izvestia's* circulation to 8.3 million, 1.3 more than that of *Pravda*—the first time the government paper has been allowed to publish more copies than the party paper. The other Central media have also experienced large increases, and it appears that some restrictions on general availability of the Central or All-Union papers and magazines have been lifted. *Komsomolskaya Pravda* on October 6, 1965, announced that subscription lists to all Central newspapers and magazines had been opened to the public. Except for *Izvestia's* Sunday supplement, *Nedelia,* which was reported at 1 million, and the football supplement to *Sovetsky Sport,* total combined circulation of all Central newspapers and magazines for September, 1965, was estimated at 35,241,600.

Greater access to the Central media may not mean that subscribers frequently will receive their copies on time. This is still a problem aggravated by the impressive recent growth in the number of titles appearing and in the number of copies printed. In 1958, for example, one of the chief problems of distribution was late delivery in places most distant from the point of publication. *Sovetskaya Pechat* attributed this delay to four main causes:

(1) magazines and newspapers were published much too late ever to be delivered "on time";[57] (2) expansion of printing capacity had not kept pace with the rise in circulations; (3) post offices were slow in making delivery; and (4) publications were delayed en route at rail and air terminals. Indeed production delays explained fully half of the problem. Aleksei Romanov, one of *Sovetskaya Pechat's* editors, fumed about inexcusable sloth in the case of his own paper. "They [the production engineers] promise that my magazine will be on its way to the 10,000 Soviet journalists who subscribe to it within three days after copy is delivered. And then they take ten days to get it into the mails." Boris S. Borkov, chief of the new press agency, Novosti, agreed. "Just talk to any Soviet editor," Borkov said, "He will tell you that life is just one long fight with the production men." The party's Central Committee studied the problems of distribution and issued a directive to all agencies involved to improve transportation. It also ordered that retail sales be stimulated, and to this end, established 10,000 additional periodical stands and authorized 100 additional stores to sell publications.

Criticisms appearing in the press held the officials of *Soyuzpechat* accountable for much of the delay. Soviet citizens, it was said, were not always able to obtain subscriptions to the publications they wanted. While it was true that some journals were published and restricted to specified audiences under official quotas, it was charged that the distribution agency, in an effort to push the sale of less popular items, had imposed arbitrary quotas or required combination purchases of more than one item. Behind the usual charges of "lack of a sense of urgency in their work" against *Soyuzpechat* officials, bureaucratic mismanagement loomed. A part of the problem certainly could be blamed on the sluggish transportation facilities. And until these could be improved, *Soyuzpechat's* efficiency and zeal, should they be stepped up, could do little to improve the distribution of publications. Publication statistics, it was clear, do not always reflect the number of magazines and newspapers the population receives—or reads, of course.

Dissemination of word by air waves obviously need not depend upon transportation facilities. The spread of the broadcasting network, the low cost of receiving sets, the increased use of multiple language broadcasts, the extent of the diffusion networks, and other evidence points to the deliberate, planned endeavor of the authorities to increase broadcasting's penetration. As in the case of the press, neither popular demand nor location of advertising sources plays a major part in determining where, when, and on what frequency stations are to be operated or in deciding what audiences are to be reached. In general, the authorities plan and regulate the process to suit their needs as they see them.

Financing

The communications system is expected theoretically to be self-sustaining and even make a profit, although in practice profits are not insisted upon. Budgets of the communications media are a part of the public budget. The national treasury receives earnings and pays the deficits for the individual media units. Available information does not indicate to what extent the system has paid its own way. Inkeles reported that in 1941 radio services received a large sum from the national treasury.[58] A six-page edition of *Pravda* ordinarily sells three kopeks; larger editions for four or more kopeks. The paper's editor has said that it makes huge profits every year, clearing about two cents on every copy printed and sold. *Pravda* also makes a large profit from its other publishing enterprises, including a score or more of periodicals that are printed in *Pravda's* Moscow plant. *Izvestia* was reported in 1955 to have made 40 million rubles in profits. Other publications, doubtless, are not nearly so profitable, or even so fortunate as to find themselves able to break even.

Broadcasting is financed primarily by annual fees from set owners, although when fees fail to meet the expenses, the difference is paid by the State. Proceeds from the sale of published program guides contribute to a share of the cost. Since 1947 a limited amount of commercial advertising has been permitted on the air, and this contributes to the revenue earned by radio. The All-Union Radio Committee has charge of financial arrangements and the collection of fees. Press revenues, too, have been increasingly augmented by larger amounts of commercial advertising during the 1960s.

There appears to be no doubt that complete financial power in the hands of the managers of the system constitutes one of the primary control weapons. With it, the authorities are able to enforce their will with regard to all other aspects of management and control, from determining technical needs to planning, staffing, executing policy, and operating the entire apparatus.

SUMMARY

The Soviet system of public communication in its conception, organization, administration, and control has gone far beyond the traditional models of authoritarian press systems. It is the most intricate and complicated, yet comprehensive system in the modern world. Designed on a hitherto unheard-of scale to serve a big modern nation, it makes all forms of public communication a monopoly of the regime, owned and operated by the State and maintained for the exclusive use of the party and the State. The mass media system is not considered to be a separate and distinct social institution, but a part of the entire body of artistic expression in Soviet culture. Thus it is treated as means of communication in the same category with literature, art, and music. It functions as a unit in the vast party-State enterprise of building the socialist state—an enterprise noted for its campaigns, its 5-year plans, and its well-defined goals. As a tool of the society and as a responsible servant of the party, the mass communications system must do everything within its power to help achieve these goals. The system serves as an instrument of mobilization and mass persuasion. As the regime has the exclusive power to determine the goals, it also determines the methods to be used to achieve them. To this end, policy is determined at the top of the administrative hierarchy, from which all aspects of the media are directed. The system is staffed, financed, operated, and held accountable by its owners and managers. Its important position in Soviet society, as well as the emphasis and attention given to it by the regime, attest the regime's great interest in molding and controlling public opinion, and in indoctrinating a whole nation.

The control mechanism for the communications system, with final authority vested in the hands of the party, parallels the organizational structure and extends from the Central to the remotest organ. Although the formal censorship apparatus exists and has been used extensively in the past even with the aid of legal and police enforcement methods, the regime today appears to rely more upon positive methods of control through its prerogatives of monopoly ownership and management, rather than upon the usual negative ones of proscription and prohibition. This does not mean, however, that the control system is less efficient and vigilant today.

As is true of other aspects of Soviet life, the communications system appears to be overcontrolled and overcentralized. There appears to be little likelihood that centralization will be decreased within the foreseeable future. The entire system in its inception, its basic purposes, and its ultimate performance is predicated upon the necessity for centralized manipulation; otherwise, it could not adequately serve its instrumental function. Without direction from the top, the substructure would collapse.

5 ★

PROFESSIONAL CONCEPTS AND POLICIES

AGAINST A BACKGROUND OF GROWTH, theory, structure, and function, it is now time to consider the emerging body of professional principles and practices that underlie the operation and behavior of the Soviet mass media system. Considered here will be how policy and concept have evolved from the application of theory to practice and how, within the framework of its objectives and within the context of its evolution as a social instrument, the mass communications apparatus performs its assigned task.

NEWS AND INFORMATION—OBJECTIVITY

In spite of much talk directed toward Western ears by Soviet journalists about "fact" and "objectivity," it appears to be clear that a fact, as it is understood in the West, has little objective meaning separate and apart from the purpose behind that fact in the Soviet concept of news and information. When the Soviet journalist speaks of fact or truth he has in mind equating it with "socialist realism," which is something different from the criteria commonly used to determine fact in the United States and in western Europe. Factual news as it is generally defined and understood under libertarian press systems has little value or interest in the Soviet Union unless it can be made to serve the purposes of State propaganda, organization, and indoctrination.[1] In its single-minded determination to make the entire communications system a unified political weapon, the purpose of conveying information solely for its own sake, with no other motive than simply to enlighten the public, has been all but lost. "The purpose of information is not that of commercializing the news, but of educating the great mass of the workers, and organizing them under the exclusive direction of the Party according to clearly defined objectives . . . ." is a statement attributed to a Soviet press affairs specialist.[2] "Information is one of the instruments of the class war," he said, "not one of its reflections. As a result an objective concern with events prevents information from being used to its true purpose, namely to organize the workers."

Criteria of News Values

In the 1920s some Soviet editors classified news in two categories, "creative," and "factual." N. G. Palgunov, former Tass director in a series of lectures at Moscow University in 1954 denied that Soviet-style news could have a purely informative purpose or character, though he stressed the importance of facts.

> News must be organized; otherwise it is news of mere events and happening. . . . News should not be concerned with reporting such and such a fact or event: it must pursue a definite purpose. . . . News is agitation via facts. In selecting the subject, the author of the report must above all proceed from the realization that the press should not simply report all facts and just any events. . . . News must be didactic and instructive.[3]

This concept of news, by its very character and content, differs radically from that of libertarian press systems in several ways: It is not a current continuing historical record; it is not purely informative and therefore objective; it does not have the purpose of developing an informed public opinion or electorate; it does not purport to be a mirror of society; it does not consist of reports of accidents, disasters, daily court or legislative sessions, or other such mere "happenings." [4] Obviously, the Soviet media do not see their task as one of making a reasonably complete news report for a given period of time. The scope of media responsibility does not necessarily recognize the importance of entertainment or escape-type content. Spurned most of all by Soviet journalism is the Western policy of attracting attention and building audiences by means of sensationalism. The media contain factual information, not always devoid of sensational treatment, but information has a deliberate purpose and that purpose is usually without subtlety made apparent to the audience or reader. One example might be news of the market place, such as information about goods and services, a category of public information that has only recently come to be recognized officially as paid advertising.

Moreover news, as defined by Soviet editors and directors, does not need to be new or appealing to the readers. Timeliness also is one of those libertarian news values that make for "reader interest," and reader interest is a basic ingredient of news, Western variety. Information the public *wants* to know and information it *needs* to know are presented in a marketable package. On the contrary Soviet journalists find that news has value because it may contribute to the formation of the "right" ideas, inspire greater loyalty and effort, or develop a stronger belief in the political order. They give top priority to party propaganda themes, slogans, and campaigns. In brief, what the public needs to know (in the party's judgment)—not what it wants to know—is the major criterion by which news is judged and evaluated. Indeed, if Soviet editors were inclined to select and print articles solely on the basis of public interest criteria, they would be subject to dismissal.

Whether one sees this Soviet definition of news and news values as broad or narrow depends upon the point of view. In the Western conception, news is factual, truthful, reasonably balanced, and complete. It functions as a regular daily record of contemporary events. The transmission of news, particularly news of public affairs, in a context that produces understanding is in itself a professional goal of a high order because such a role serves the citizen of a free society. In the Soviet conception news is but one of several methods used in the conduct of propaganda, a role which is not a goal in itself, but a means to an end. Hence news is not conceived of as a continuous record of happenings, but a promotional chronicle of the unfolding drama of Soviet socialist construction. News in this view need not necessarily report the whole truth, nor be timely, nor strive for fairness, completeness, balance, or objectivity. In the Western view, news must be as accurate as it is humanly possible to make it. In the Soviet view, accuracy is secondary to usefulness to the regime in serving society responsibly.

Economic Versus Political News

What Lenin called a "new kind of newspaper" was the use of the newspaper as a medium for the economic education of the masses. In Western democracies the press exists primarily to report the political news of the day, he said. Instead, the Soviet press, unlike the "capitalist" press, should concern itself with every detail of the workers and the nation's economic life. Lenin probably had in mind here not only his view of the Western press of his day, but also his belief that because information about such things as trade secrets and the activities of private corporations is not always available to the capitalist press, it is not reported regularly. Actually, though business secrets are not exposed, the capitalist press, particularly that of the United States, carries more economic information than the Soviet press. Although economics is stressed systematically, Lenin's dream of substituting economics for politics in the Soviet press has not been realized. Paradoxically, industrial and trade secrets in the Soviet Union are State secrets, and information about them is no more available to the Soviet media than its counterpart is to the capitalist media. Capitalist enterprises, thriving on public knowledge of their products and operations, seek editorial space and buy advertising to keep the public informed as well as to sell. But in Russia the publication of much information of this nature is prohibited by Paragraph 58 of the Criminal Code, which prevents the reporting of certain classes of economic news quite as effectively as it does the full reporting of social and political information. During the Stalin regime the public was informed only of those facts and figures that supported official theory or opinion in vogue at the moment.[5] As in the case of political matters, economic material in the mass media must concern itself with methods and achievements rather than with fundamental philosophy.

Russian newspapers as well as periodical organs devoted to economics and finance[6] are filled with information, criticism, and exhortation about goals and records of achievement. These themes are repeated to the point of monotony, with no effort to make such material interesting to the average reader. Dissatisfaction with the press treatment was expressed by *Partinaya Zhizn* in 1961. "Unfortunately not all our newspapers and magazines deal thoughtfully, thoroughly or interestingly with economic problems," the paper said. The problems of socialist competition particularly with the West must be stressed more completely. Not very many meaningful articles on communist labor collectives appear in the newspapers, it charged. "Many articles on problems of industry and agriculture are purely informative and descriptive and fail to show the essentials . . . the major problems of developing productive forces."[7] Eschewing pure descriptive information as ineffective, the magazine suggested greater attention to what it called "problems" as a means of relieving monotony and attracting more readers.

The natural reluctance of editors, and party leaders as well, to expose problems in the press was understandable. Such problems ordinarily must be bared by the Central organs rather than those operating closer to the place where the problem arises. When more than a half million, or 8 per cent, of the livestock on Kirghiz collective and State farms perished of disease in 1960, the press was taken to task. Cried *Partinaya Zhizn,*

> Can Comrade Suvanberdiyev, editor of the republic newspaper *Sovettik Krysyzstan* and Comrade Denisyuk, editor of the republic paper *Sovetskaya Kirgizia,* or the editors of Osh and Tyan-Shan Province papers, say that they warned of this? . . . Or [have they] presented the question for consideration by Party and Soviet bodies? Or informed the central press about it? Not one of these questions can be answered in the affirmative. Of course, questions of animal husbandry were covered. . . . But this was done in weak, inexpressive articles that stirred no one and moved no one's spirit. The newspapers were very timid in touching on shortcomings and preferred to be altogether silent about instances of mismanagement and negligence.[8]

This sample of criticism is typical.

What the Media Say and Do Not Say

Besides economics, news subjects most likely to receive the greatest attention in the Soviet media are such matters as the anniversary observance of the Bolshevik revolution; international youth festivals; the convening of the Supreme Soviet; the periodic meetings of the Communist Party Congress; speeches, writings, and activities of Soviet leaders; achievements of the nation, such as the successful launching of a Sputnik, the construction of an atomic-powered icebreaker, or the flight of a cosemonaut; the important decisions of the government, *e.g.*, the reduction of the work day to seven hours; progress toward agricultural or industrial goals; international campaigns such as the "peace" offensive; and international events that threaten world peace or Soviet standing.

However, what the media contain is little more significant either to readers or to students of the Soviet press than what they do *not* contain. Editors and directors soon learn that it is just as necessary to know what is not news as it is to know what is news, and sometimes the former is more revealing. Although the shortcomings of individuals and government agencies are often exposed, party policies that fail of themselves are not reported. The Soviet public has never been informed of some news events judged of first importance by the media of other countries. Soviet media select and present those matters that can be reported in such a way that they project and preserve the image of steady progress in the building of the society or of the triumph of socialism over capitalism and "imperialism."

When events cannot be related "constructively" to the context of this unfolding story, or when the proper official "line" has not been decided, one of several alternative courses of action may be taken, as follows: (1) complete silence, (2) delay in publication until policy can be determined, (3) partisan or one-sided portrayal of the event, (4) falsification and distortion, and (5) various combinations of these procedures.

Examples of major world news developments that have been ignored, barely noticed, or falsely slanted are many. These are a few that have not been reported in the Soviet Union: The deportation of Baltic peoples in 1941 and again in 1949; the prison camp strikes of 1953; the liberation of political prisoners in 1955; the massive crop failure of Khrushchev's virgin lands program (the public being able, perhaps, to surmise such defeat from the absence in the media of claims of success); the trial of Hungary's freedom fighters, even though 600 were tried and 120 convicted; and the winning of the 1957 Nobel Prize by two Chinese scientists working in the United States.

High on the list of major news developments that have been delayed or slanted by treatment or emphasis are the coming to power of the Chinese Communists in 1948, despite the fact that they were winning victories for the cause of international communism. Although the Chinese Communist story was reported, it received scant attention—a curious circumstance, for news of such triumphs should have drawn big headlines and set off celebrations in the Soviet Union.[9] Silence was the treatment given the East Berlin revolt of June, 1953—silence for five days after it broke out. Then the uprising was reported as a "Fascist putsch prepared . . . by the agents of Wall Street," and treated in such a way that the public could not learn the truth that the East German workers had rebelled against the Communist regime. Similar treatment was accorded the Hungarian revolution of 1956. This event was portrayed as a movement of "hostile elements, counter-revolutionaries, and reactionaries" stimulated from abroad; an affair in which the Soviet army intervened at the request of the Hungarian working classes in order to save the country. Information about the receipt by Marshal Nikolai Bulganin in 1958 of a letter from President Dwight D. Eisenhower in reply to the former's suggestion of a summit meeting was withheld from the Soviet public for several days. Then a notice from Tass that there had been such a letter appeared on the inside pages. More than two weeks after the letter's delivery, *Izvestia* published the replies of the Western heads of state under a long front-page editorial discussing the "chief problem of international policy." The editorial noted that the replies to Bulganin contained nothing that could relax world tension. News of the introduction of communes in Red China was withheld from the Soviet people for a full month to permit time for the government to decide its stand on the question and to provide interpretations for public consumption.

Stressing Success; Ignoring Failure

The practice of the news media to stress success and ignore failure, especially with reference to the national interest, has been demonstrated frequently. A Soviet scientist explained why Sputnik launchings were not announced in advance. "It would make an unfavorable impression if the launchings failed. There is time enough to announce it when the Sputnik is in orbit," he observed. The same kind of reasoning applied to handling the news of Khrushchev's Chinese visit. It was secret until his mission was accomplished. In March and April of 1960 the Soviet media were filled with reports, amply illustrated, of the experiences of four young Soviet soldiers who were rescued by a United States Navy ship after spending 49 days adrift aboard a derelict landing craft in the Pacific. All media stressed the theme that the soldiers had been able to survive because of superior political knowledge, stamina, and discipline they had acquired as a result of their Soviet upbringing. It was not until five days after the soldiers were rescued that the party decided to exploit the story's propaganda potential. If the men had not survived, the probability is that nothing whatever would have appeared in the media about their fate. In any event, throughout the seven weeks they were lost at sea, the media did not report their disappearance. However, when it is deemed that the national interest will be served by public admission of fallacy, especially in the cases of deficiencies in the bureaucracy, failure to meet 5-year plan goals, or weaknesses and shortcomings among individuals or classes of workers, these matters are aired candidly in the media from one end of the country to the other.

Questions of Recency and Objectivity

Because Soviet communicators can manage and shape to suit themselves not only news and views but also many of the events about which news is written and reported, they are not pressed to report it accurately or faithfully as it happens or as rapidly as it happens. The official attitude toward timeliness in the news is explained by Inkeles. The great and continuing news story of all times, according to their viewpoint, is the story of the social process, and that process is going on all of the time, Inkeles said. Why stress late news when the process never gets out of date? Inkeles also notes,

> . . . It is this basic approach to news that enables editors . . . to make a detailed plan one month in advance, and to have 50 per cent of each current issue set in type and made up several days before the issue date.
>
> This is possible . . . because editors do not have to wait for a social process to happen. . . . This is also possible because those functions of Soviet newspapers which do not involve dealing with news at all bulk so large in the mandate of the Soviet press . . . .[10]

The unpredictability of the developing news scene requires Western editors to readjust minute by minute as the news breaks. *Pravda's* chief editor Pavel A. Satyukov is said to have stopped the presses only twice in six months! The relative unimportance of timeliness and the official practice of approving in advance material prepared for dissemination tends to discourage such widely used Western techniques as firsthand observation and on-the-spot reporting. Although Soviet newsmen claim they are free to probe deeply and enjoy full access to news sources, such privileges—if indeed they are enjoyed—seem of little value if what they write must be screened before it reaches the public. As William L. Jorden, head of the New York *Times*' Moscow Bureau, said, ". . . in a very real sense the Soviet press prints 'all the news the Communist Party sees fit to print'—and nothing more." News and information are what the party decides the people should be told.

There is no place in Soviet communications for the Anglo-American conception of news objectivity—the requirement that the news must be free of the newsman's bias or personal opinion and that opinions reported in the news columns must be quoted and their sources identified. Objective fact, or basic truth in Western societies is generalized as the *reality principle* or *consensual validation;* it is found by the Soviet communicator, not in the evidence of the senses, not in joint agreement of two or more observers, not in records and documents—but in the way the eyes of Soviet Communist dogma see reality. The Soviet newsman grasps and measures truth by squaring objective fact with the "universal truths" taught by Marxist-Leninist doctrine and applied at any given time by what is known as "the Line." Hence the newsman is a spokesman for the leaders and the Line. In speaking for the Line, the media sometimes find it difficult to keep abreast of the abrupt shifts and reversals that have become a type of behavior characteristic of Soviet policy. Such changes in the Line sometimes have been extreme, sometimes involving first the apotheosis and then the denigration of the same public official. Perhaps the most far-reaching shift was the campaign of de-Stalinization. Such extreme "abouts-face" appear to be the inevitable result of unquestioning acceptance of "unassailable" Marxian truth with its strong commitment to materialistic determinism. This behavior fosters a tendency among Soviet journalists to see everything as black or white, seldom recognizing the existence of variable shades of gray in between. Men, governments, programs, institutions—and yes, even events are seen as either entirely good or entirely bad. This method of reacting has been described as typical of the Russian character, and the political system encourages it. It means an inability or refusal either to compromise or to examine and reject old maxims with a skepticism born of new knowledge, or to recognize that two or more perfectly valid but opposing viewpoints can exist. This approach leads to behavior that on the surface appears to be a type of ambivalence that Schramm refers to as a double standard of truth.[11] On the one hand, Marxian teaching is considered immutable; yet in areas where ideology and dogma are not applicable, positions taken by Soviet media may shift as expediency dictates. It appears that Pavlovian strategy and tactics are deliberately employed to attain objectives.

Semantic exploitation of language to serve the purpose of deception both in communication with the Soviet people and with the outside world reinforces the dichotomy in this connection. Words to the Soviet communicator are powerful tools that are to be used to achieve desired effects. The use of Aesopian expressions is a cultivated art dating back to the nineteenth century and earlier. Thus "dictatorship of the proletariat" becomes "liberation," the "party" becomes the "people," and public talk of "cooperation, disarmament, and peace," is really a mask to cover up aims to spread world Communism by all expedient means. Capitalism is defined as a system in which a few property holders exercise absolute rights to make laws to suit themselves in order to increase profits and keep the masses in subjection. The Soviet viewpoint finds it convenient to ignore capitalism's obvious success and to speak of the system as all bad and beyond reform, to the end that the Communist mission can continue to be that of liberating the world from such evils.[12]

All this is the reverse of the kind of news objectivity libertarian journalists strive to achieve. Actually, like human liberty, objectivity does not exist in the absolute, but only as a precious ideal to be sought and achieved by varying degrees of success. Still, Western communicators believe it serves well the interests of making the reader's image of the real world coincide more closely with that real world. In principle this objectivity requires that (1) the news report be as free from the writer's bias or personal slant as it is humanly possible to make it; (2) when opinion, either of the writer or of others, is included in the news report, it should be clearly labeled as opinion and identified as to source; (3) the opinion and value judgment of the communication medium must be separated in time and space from the news and confined to the editorial section where it is clearly labeled; and (4) when opposing viewpoints are presented in the news they should receive fair treatment by the use of such devices as parallel columns or "equal" air time for political candidates.

Soviet logic on this matter of objectivity was elucidated by Lenin when he argued that the achievement of true objectivity is utterly impossible. He was no doubt interpreting objectivity as existing in the absolute. Complete objectivity, he maintained, cannot be attained because of the impossibility of separating fact from opinion. Any person who advances a fact cannot avoid becoming an advocate of that fact, however neutral it may be or however dispassionately he may advance it. Even if he should succeed in remaining absolutely impartial and unbiased, his hearers are likely to see him as an advocate of his own data, according to Lenin.[13] Thoughtful US newsmen would be inclined to agree with this argument, while at the same time upholding the indispensability of objectivity as a working principle. Soviet journalists instead make no effort toward achieving a degree of objectivity. "All dissertations on 'objective and complete' information are liberal hypocrisy," Lenin wrote. "The aim of information does not consist in commercializing the news, but in educating great masses. . . . This aim will not be attained by objective reports of events . . . ." [14] Or, he might have added, objective reports of views. Hence, why resist the inevitable? he asked. Since it is futile to attempt objectivity, the Soviet communicator makes no effort to keep bias out of the news report. He is even required to insert it. The partisan slant in which all reports must be cast is well understood—it is like one vast and continuing commercial in support of the regime. The only viewpoint in news and editorials is the approved one, the only prejudice permitted the Soviet journalist is the only "right" one. Communication specialists not only have been warned against the vice of objectivity but also have been criticized for falling into objective ways, much as an American reporter might be criticized for failing to be objective enough.

As the structure of libertarian communications rests upon a foundation of objective truth, the structure of Soviet communications rests upon impact or effect. These antithetical standards serve not only as purposes and methods, but also as criteria for judging performance. Western communicators do not overlook the value of effect but believe that effect will take care of itself as long as the real world is reported as it is. Likewise, Soviet communicators do not overlook the value of truth as long as truth serves their purpose. When a C. P. Scott of the *Manchester Guardian* declares that comment is free but facts are sacred, and charges the newspaper with seeing that the supply of news is not tainted, Soviet editors speak of loyalty or responsibility to the society and regime. When American media use such slogans as "Report the truth and an informed public will be able to make up its mind," or "Shed light and the people will find the way," Soviet media think in terms of results to be achieved by the society and the State. As Schramm observes, one system's creed is based on a faith in the abstract ideal of truth and reality; the other on a faith in the abstract inherent rightness of its fundamental social philosophy and national mission.

OPINION AND CRITICISM

Material just as didactic and persuasive as editorials is likely to appear in front-page, by-lined articles or mixed in anonymous factual reports. Although greater originality and depth has characterized press editorials since the communications reforms that came in the years after 1956, press opinion generally takes its cue from Moscow on all important issues domestic and foreign. *Pravda's* editorials continue to be widely reproduced and quoted. *Izvestia's* increased prestige attracts imitators and copyists. The system tends to discourage independence of viewpoint, the expression of new ideas, and even serious independent analysis of problems, except perhaps those at the provincial and local level. The prevailing habit is either to copy what comes from Moscow or to restate principles that have long been universally accepted and thus are unlikely to stir up controversy—especially to cause trouble for the editor. So the media from top to bottom hasten to adopt Moscow's interpretation. For example, the prosperity of West Germany is rationalized by picturing a great abundance of consumer goods manufactured for a population too poverty stricken to buy. To support this thesis, unemployment figures for the Western Zone, swelled weekly for a time by the daily influx of 2,000 East German refugees, were nevertheless extensively exaggerated. The heavy migration westward was conveniently ignored. The Suez War was pictured as a ruse of Western imperialist powers to colonize the Middle East. In a word, the aim of the regime through the media is to develop and maintain by the processes of persuasive communication a pliant public opinion which not only accepts the view of the world as the regime portrays it but also cooperates vigorously in the attainment of this national policy.

Self-criticism and the Role of Nonprofessionals

Closely related to the opinion function is the function of self-criticism, or *samokritika,* in which the continuous process of national self-examination is considered essential to the sound development of the Communist state as well as an informal means of mass control. In principle the function encourages the people to expose corruption, weaknesses, deficiencies, and errors in the work of building and perfecting the society. Ideologically this sort of criticism according to plan was to become a 2-way process of communication. It might flow from party and government leaders down to the common people, or it might flow from the lowliest ordinary citizen upward to the attention of the highest authorities. Such a process, it was felt, would enable the nation to see its mistakes and to learn from them. Moreover, it would provide an outlet of expression for the people, in the manner of the *"vox populi"* columns of Western newspapers. Public self-criticism flows into the communications media in the form of letters, interviews, personal testimonials, policy statements of leaders, and the writings of the nonprofessional correspondent.

The nonprofessional correspondent is a member of the extensive party organization known as the Worker-Peasant Correspondents' Group, or *Rabsel 'kor.* Each newspaper has its organization of nonprofessional workers, and membership in the organization may number into the thousands in the case of individual media.[15] Their assignment is to watch over, report, and criticize through mass or other channels all phases of performance at the workers' level. This responsibility commits them particularly to report signs of laziness, inefficiency, disloyalty, corruption, and over-zealous bureaucracy. Criticism is also constructive in that it includes mention of praiseworthy examples and extolls successful achievement. Beyond their critical function, however, worker-peasant correspondent organizations are expected to serve as means of popular participation in communications, politics, and public affairs. At the same time they are useful to the regime not only as a source of information about the progress of socialism but also as a sounding board for undercurrents of dissatisfaction and opposition. It must not be supposed from this that a citizen must be a worker-peasant correspondent to have access to the media. On the contrary, citizens in all walks of life are urged to write letters. Thus, theoretically at least, the mass media of communication are immediately available to all. In this sense the Soviet journalist can logically claim with some truth that access to the press is open to all the people, not just the party.

How does the process of self-criticism work out in practice? It is true that thousands of letters are received and made public each month by the larger newspaper and broadcasting establishments. Some of the letters have not been the spontaneous contributions they purport to be, for many that pledge higher production are known to have originated in *Pravda's* office. Some of the letters that appear to be voices of the common people are inspired or actually written by officials.[16] Although to the Western editor who has a relatively small number of correspondents on his list, the number of registered worker-peasant correspondents for each periodical seems large, estimates indicate that only about half or less of those registered have been active contributors. Analysis of published letters,[17] moreover, indicates that the range of content is quite limited, for it largely concerns minor, everyday matters. Ninety per cent of the letters reported the failure of individuals named to carry on their work properly. In no case were regime, policy, party, or party leaders brought under fire or even questioned. It was the analysts' conclusion that the letters system serves only as one more means of perpetuating control in the hands of the regime both by providing a source of information from below and a vocal escape mechanism for those growing restive under the pressures of the order. The free play of ideas in the Western sense being impossible, the letters in practice serve to bring disfavor upon the agents of policy rather than the determiners of policy. Since by means of the letters the people become informers, the system helps the mass media to perform that portion of their task which requires them to serve as eyes and ears for the party and to keep watch over all of Soviet life.

Range and Function of Permissible Criticism

In all areas of opinion and criticism, however, the range of permissive subjects for discussion, though widening in recent years, is narrow. Criticism within the party cannot threaten its basic unity or give aid and comfort to its enemies. Policy cannot be questioned, but the manner in which policy is carried out can be. There is no adverse criticism of Communist ideology and visible symbols of the Communist state such as party and leaders. Real criticism of significance that addresses itself to matters of major importance originates with party and government leaders. Criticism from other sources is mild—and understandably so, in view of the circumstances.

Restricted as it has been, self-criticism has been credited with improving party work, speeding the education of the masses, and

Fig. 5.1. Bumbling and stupidity in the Soviet State bureaucracy is a subject of frequent attack in the mass media. This kind of media behavior is approved as valuable self-criticism, or "samokritika." **Krokodil** impales a thickheaded bureaucrat, puts him in a desert, saying to vicious lion: "I don't care whether you snarl. Until you can prove to me in writing that you are a lion, I just won't believe it."

keeping bureaucracy in line. In more than one sense it has provided a means of communication and "one of the most vital links" between top party leadership and the mass of the Soviet people.[18] Undoubtedly it serves as an escape-valve function in that it provides an outlet for pent-up resentment. It fosters the impression that the people have a voice in their own affairs. It provides a channel for public expression. Admittedly the range of subjects open to this kind of expression of opinion has been narrow; there are indications that it is becoming more flexible, and has been widened considerably in the 1960s. In July, 1965, for example, *Komsomolskaya Pravda* accused Captain Alexei Solyanik, hero of whaling exploits and holder of the Order of Lenin, of overbearing treatment of his men by "rude suppression of criticism, inadmissable nepotism, and abuse of his high post. He killed the sentiments of justice, honor and dignity among his own men."[19] These kinds of attacks against suppression of individual rights and liberties together with thousands of letters of complaint were beginning to appear in the press in 1964 and 1965. It was a new experience for public officials to be required to answer charges at this level. Frequently editorials probed the principles and issues involved in the problems exposed—juvenile delinquency, hoarding, the farm-to-city migration, divorce, and bureaucratic mismanagement, etc. This was evidence of the broadening scope of public discussion. The operation of *samokritika* presents a convincing demonstration to help perpetuate the myth that the mass media really do belong to the people, despite the fact that discussion is cut off abruptly when it invades the sacrosanct realms of dogma. Nonetheless the function of public exposure and criticism as a principal agent of directed social change must not be underestimated; it is the chief means of correcting faults, profiting from mistakes, and overcoming obstacles. More important than this, when extended to its present form, it could mark the emergence for the first time of a process of genuine public debate which in turn could generate the growth of an independent expression and clash of opinion about important public issues. Whether this trend continues or not, when Soviet scholars assess the factors that have contributed most to their country's achievements over four decades in the face of heavy odds, the function of public criticism will surely rank prominently among them. And this function, of course, would not be possible without a smoothly working communications system, both formal and informal.

HUMAN INTEREST

In its treatment of human interest material the media system reflects the stress placed by the culture upon depersonalization of the individual. In the media, personalities and individual values are generally subordinated to group and national values. Exceptions are made to this rule in the case of public heroes, high-ranking public officials, and prominent figures in science, engineering, production, transportation, space, and the arts. Yet even here personal affairs and the family life of public figures are almost never reported in the public media. The existence of Khrushchev's college-age son became known publicly only after the leader's public appearances in England accompanied by the son. The Premier revealed to Mrs. Franklin D. Roosevelt—and thus, for the first time to the world—that he had a grandson in military school, the offspring of a son who was killed in the war. Not a word was published about an accident that befell Galina Ulanova, famous ballerina, during a performance.[20] Her collapse from a pulled tendon was the subject of much talk among those present at the ballet when it happened. Such an accident, of course, would have received full play in London or New York. A staff member of *Sovietskaya Kultura* explained why the story had gone unnoticed: it would have intruded upon her private life. The press was chastised for invading the privacy of Cosmonaut Yuri Gagarin after reporters had entered his home and brought away family pictures for publication.

Nevertheless human interest receives large quantities of space and time in the Soviet media. Contributions made by individuals to the society provide the opportunity for the media to glorify their achievements as symbolic of the Soviet way of life and as examples to be emulated. Since the organized campaign to improve the media got under way after 1956, human interest has received considerably more attention than before. Despite the post-Stalin campaign to downgrade hero worship and the "cult of personality," the political system tends to foster the apotheosis of the leader, and Khrushchev's personal image and prestige rapidly filled the place in the public mind formerly occupied by that of Stalin. But Khrushchev was not the only hero. The cosmonauts and space scientists have had their share of the headlines and pictures. *Pravda's* standing headline, "Heroes of Our Times," appears over sketches about "advanced personnel" and their accomplishments, a feature widely imitated by almost all provincial papers. Neither of Khrushchev's successors, Brezhnev and Kosygin, have projected the interesting kind of personality that earned for Khrushchev a human, real-life public image. In line with orthodox dogma, they have tended to discourage mass media efforts to build up their images—an attitude or policy that differs considerably from custom under Stalin, whose name filled headlines and each day dotted the gray pages in bold face.

Satire and social criticism are prominent in the feature writer's kit of techniques, although examples of what Westerners consider humor are hard to find. A news item from New York reporting that two men had been unable to obtain a fishing license because of their Communist associations stimulated *Sovetskaya Rossia* to satirize the situation under the heading "Rules and Statutes for Orderly and Well-Behaved Piscatorial Pursuits." [21]

The *feuilleton,* Soviet version, is a popular feature form. The *feuilleton,* a term borrowed from the French, is an exposé type story or critical article, written in a lively narrative style and filled with dialogue. Newspapers on the stands, folded so as to expose a *feuilleton,* are bought first because they signal a chatty, readable, gossipy piece. *Trud* carried an article on beggars—which according to standard propaganda do not exist in the Soviet Union. One beggar, according to the story, was a vagrant who had nine court convictions for theft before his thirtieth year. After this ninth conviction, he gave up stealing and embarked upon a career of alms-seeking. He married a woman of almost equal attainments (she had been in jail eight times) and the two worked together. He bandaged his eyes and she hobbled about on crutches. They averaged $35 a day. *Trud* confided that the couple took a brief respite from the busy workaday world by vacationing a month at the Black Sea.[22]

How features are to be written and human interest values exploited in communications copy are detailed in a hyperbolic parody dealing with the art of writing an effective human interest story. The article, appearing in the October 22, 1955, issue of *Literaturnaya Gazeta,* was titled "The Feature Writer's Handbook"; it was prepared by Natalya Ilyna for the "instruction" of newspaper and magazine feature writers. It reads, in part, as follows:

> We offer you a guide which will help you to write newspaper features without going anywhere and with only report figures for a district or even for a single collective farm. We shall try to enumerate the most common methods of turning report figures into a work of art for a newspaper.
>
> You should begin this way: "The train slowed down, its couplings squealing. We got out onto the platform. There was a trail of smoke from somewhere. 'Are you going to Dawn Collective Farm?' asked a stocky man, twisting his hat in his hands. A minute later a fat horse, briskly swishing its combed tail, was pulling us along a narrow road traversing the fields. Shoots of buckwheat, millet, wheat, oats, corn and potatoes (delete those which do not apply) showed green here and there."
>
> Now is the time to interpolate the report figures. We suggest the following presentations:
>
> Variant No. 1: Presenting the Report through the Driver. . . . [There follows a glowing description of the abundant life indicated on the farm with electricity everywhere, with high income from heavy crop production, increases over previous years, and goals reached—all brought out in conversation with the driver of the wagon.]
>
> Variant No. 2: Presenting the Report through a Meeting of Collective Farmers. . . .
>
> Variant No. 3: Presenting the Report through Interviews with Leading Workers. . . .
>
> As we were saying, "There was a look of abundance everywhere.
>
> "We found dairy maid Sitnikova as she was taking the daily 90 liters (4 per cent fat content) from the cow Zorka. 'Marya Savvishna, tell us how you obtained record milk yields.'
>
> " 'The people here are good and hardworking,' the dairy maid said excitedly, pushing a lock of blonde hair from her forehead (variant: twisting the ends of her kerchief). 'We're growing rich. Poultry farming alone gives the collective farm an income of a hundred thousand. There is abundance everywhere. We have a radio center, a

club, a library. Many people have bought radios, electric stoves, electric irons. It makes you want to roll up your sleeves and milk, milk, milk!' added Sitnikova, her eyes kindling.

"We found shepherd Peter Kozlov as his flock of coarse-wooled sheep was giving birth to another 141.2 lambs.*

" 'How did I achieve this?' Peter Ivanovich repeated our question. 'Have a seat and I'll tell you.'

"Drawing on his *mahorka* cigarette and toying with the buttons on his jacket, the shepherd said, 'The square-cluster method is increasing. . . .

(This is a good variant because it allows for changes of scene. We also advise you to introduce a love scene as this revives interest.)

"We found tractor-driver Fedya, a curly headed youth with a mischievous grin, as tractor-trailer operator Katya was decorating her beloved's cap with snowdrops, camomiles, cornflowers (delete those which do not apply). A mischievous breeze was playing with the girl's fluffy hair. . . .

"The forest looked blue in the distance. Owls hooted. The last rays of the setting sun . . . etc." [23]

If the "Handbook's" suggestions had been followed throughout the press, the resulting example of the application of bureaucratic methods to the clichés of Soviet journalism would not have been greatly different. The idea of such a mechanical model for writers reflects the sterility of imagination and lack of spontaneity which are the products of a system in which creativity is circumscribed. Human interest, in Russia as well as elsewhere, sells papers and attracts audiences. Soviet leaders are only beginning to realize this principle.

THE POSITION OF THE PROFESSIONAL WORKER

In view of the importance it attaches to mass communication, the regime has been somewhat slow in according status to the ranks of professional workers in communications, though the editor's standing ordinarily has been a relatively high one. Creative workers in other fields were organized in unions early in the history of the Soviet state, but creative workers in communications were not organized until 1956. Only recently has the Central authority made it possible for editors and broadcasters to earn distinction by competing for the Lenin prize and other types of awards. And these are

* The decimal in the figure represents an exact mean of total production reports for each collect farm. Copying it exactly into the text without questioning a fractional lamb illustrates the hazards of routine writing which slavishly follows a formula.

not usually available to rank-and-file communicators. Most media workers have been accustomed to serving with scant recognition.

On the other hand the editor traditionally has been a leader not only in journalism but in party and public life. His position in the party, as a member of the party committee and its corresponding government organization at his particular administrative level, has ordinarily carried considerable prestige and power. He is a member of the committee which publishes his newspaper, bears responsibility for the chief personnel of other media of the same level, and approves editorial plans and decisions. Reports go to the organization of the level above, and thence to the Central Committee in Moscow.[24] His position makes it possible for the editor to influence the course of public affairs and to stimulate active participation by citizens.

Professionals Versus Nonprofessionals

In a professional sense, though, the editor's position is not undiluted or monopolistic. He and his professional staff must share with a substantial body of nonprofessional workers the responsibility for the preparation of material for publication. Soviet communications policy dictates that as many nonprofessionals as possible be encouraged to make their contributions to the ultimate editorial product. As a result of this practice the size of the professional staff has been notably small and the ratio of content contributed by nonprofessionals to that contributed by professionals has frequently served as a criterion for judging performance. Media have been subjected to criticism when too much of their output is staff prepared. Historically, nonprofessional workers are of three kinds: (1) the expert or authority who writes about his specialty, (2) the nonspecialized worker and peasant correspondent, and (3) the "instructor." [25]

The first of these, the outside expert, makes it possible for the media to draw upon the broad sources of specialized knowledge, whose contributions, though frequently not newsworthy by Western terms, aid the press in fulfilling its mission to serve as a practical textbook and schoolroom for mass education in politics and economics. Although the specialist is fully employed in other occupations and is not ordinarily considered a staff member of the communications medium, he submits prepared material on a systematic basis to the editor who maintains an informal working relationship with all such sources in his area. His communications function resembles that of Western specialists who write letters or submit articles, voluntarily or by invitation, on subjects of their special competence, or that of the public relations representative.

The second type of nonprofessional, the worker and peasant correspondent, represents the organized movement of long standing which aims to "democratize" communications by placing their facilities at the disposal of workers and at the same time facilitating the process of self-criticism. Stalin euphemistically characterized correspondents as "the commanders of Proletarian public opinion." Although they are ultimately responsible to the Agitprop units, they are recruited, organized, trained, and assisted by the editor and his professional staff.

The third type of nonprofessional worker attached to media staffs is the "instructor" who is apparently a holdover from the cadre system of the Stalinist era. Unlike the first two, the "instructor" makes no editorial contribution and he is not a critic or a censor. He is presumably a party agitation expert whose work formerly consisted of being a sort of "catalyst" of public opinion. Hence his work is agitational rather than journalistic. He serves as liaison between party and press and some of his work consists of "making" news. He organizes meetings among groups of workers to bring out deficiencies. The meetings are followed by media campaigns properly timed to arouse public sentiment against the deficiency. At the proper stage the government steps in with a decree or other measures to remedy the situation. Final government action thus appears to be the result of popular demand, and the government is able with some truth to place responsibility on the public for a change it wanted to make all along. Instructors on a newspaper have been reported in some instances to outnumber the regular staff. However, this appears to be giving way to less circuitous methods. Instead, a battery of experts provides a mass of facts and figures to illuminate the problem and convince the people through both mediated and face-to-face communications channels. As a consequence the role of the instructor has become anomalous as agitation methods have changed, and his importance has correspondingly declined. Nonprofessional workers are, of course, a part of the party organization, and their function in connection with the media is considered a part of their obligation to the party rather than to the medium with which they are associated.

Standards of Education for Communications

As for professional workers, the type of orientation they received during the early stages of the Soviet regime was not calculated to enhance either their professional competence or status. From the first the party placed ideological above professional considerations in setting qualifications for editorial positions. To be able to understand abstract dogma requires a considerable amount of indoctrination. To be able to interpret such dogma in a way that will convince others requires a high degree of intellectual competence. So fundamental indoctrination came first because an editor must understand not only what he communicates but also how to communicate it effectively. Furthermore the editor has other organizational and agitational duties to perform—duties that have little to do with mass communication, although they are likely to fall within the sphere of communication. These noneditorial duties frequently interfere with his journalistic effectiveness. Still, some degree of professional competence is also a requisite, and the two qualifications together serve eventually to raise standards for the professional leaders in communications.

Such standards limit the number of qualified persons available and make formal training a necessity. At first the media apparatus was placed in the hands of loyal party members, whose professional competence was optional. Short courses and on-the-job training followed. Institutes for journalists were organized in the 1920s, the first having been established in Moscow in 1921.[26] These establishments trained cadres who in turn trained staff members and supervised the staff work. The extensive expansion of the media system during the next decade created a shortage of skilled workers and led to the establishment of the first schools and curricula in journalism.[27] After World War II, departments of journalism were established in connection with the faculties of philology at the University of Leningrad and a few other major universities. The largest center for basic and advanced training is at Lomonossov University in Moscow, which offers a 5-year course of study under its faculty of journalism. The average of 500 diplomas a year awarded by all higher education units between 1954 and 1958 did not fulfill the demand for educated communicators. Neither will the 3,220 regular and the 1,880 evening and correspondence students that were enrolled in 1958. In 1962, *Sovetskaya Pechat* reported that there were 8,000 graduates of journalism schools employed in the press.

In 1965, journalism schools in 18 universities were turning out 950 graduates a year.

Basic Marxist-Leninist philosophy continues to dominate the curriculum, although recently more attention has been given to training in mass persuasion techniques. Studies in Russian and Soviet history, language, and literature; Communist ideology and theory; and party history, including dialectical materialism and economic theory, are all required, as are courses in media management and history, theory and practice of persuasion, the organization of press and broadcasting, and the work of correspondents. According to E. L. Khudiakov, dean of the faculty of journalism at the University of Moscow, the purpose of education in communications is to produce creative workers who are able to understand social phenomena, the root causes of events in their own and other countries, and to explain them truthfully and honestly in order thus to contribute to international understanding and cooperation. "Whatever views a journalist may hold," Professor Khudiakov was quoted as saying, "his duty—if he esteems his profession and his status—is to present the facts objectively and truthfully, without concealing or distorting them." [28] He means Soviet nonobjective facts distilled according to Soviet concepts of truth, of course. Should the schools succeed in imparting a modicum of professional ideals based on truth (Western variety), the media themselves and the party organization would no doubt see that established practice remains unchanged. Despite the stated ideals of journalism schools the communications establishment with the party's help continues to play a major role in shaping the minds of media workers through its regular system of retraining and refresher courses in political and ideological indoctrination. The Union of Communications Workers with its organ also plays an increasing role in professional training.

The quality of journalistic education in the universities, according to a critical article by *Sovetskaya Pechat* in 1962, continues to fall short of desirable professional standards. The older theory that prevailed in the 1930s and 1940s continues to dominate the major portion of the curriculum; namely, that the journalist had first to know what to write about, not how to write; because if he knew the subject matter thoroughly, the writing would take care of itself. So *Sovetskaya Pechat* found that most of the journalism curricula were filled with studies that do not relate to journalistic techniques and practices. While the article did not object to the teaching of such things as Communist theory and doctrine, the history of party congresses, etc., it objected to the fact that schools of journalism were administered in departments of philology requiring so many philological lectures that no room was left for courses in practical journalism. An offshoot of this kind of arrangement to which *Sovetskaya Pechat* also objected was the fact that the members of the faculties in journalism rarely had journalistic experience. As for the students, their time during their five years of preparation was largely occupied with general education, while their main exposure to professional practice consisted of work during vacations in the editorial offices of the newspapers.[29] This kind of ratio of general studies to professional studies is roughly comparable to that which predominates in the United States, where the standard program for the 4-year baccalaureate degree is about one-fourth professional journalism courses to three-fourths general education and liberal arts courses. Furthermore *Sovetskaya Pechat* complained that the comparatively low status of journalism as a profession gave it a disadvantage in attracting the best qualified students, noting that most students came to journalism after their applications for study in other fields had been turned down. The journalism schools, it said, needing new recruits, often accepted such students without examining their qualifications.

The rewards offered by a career in journalism and mass communications should make it a more attractive field for study in the universities. An examination of the economic status of communications workers shows that it is relatively high in comparison with that of other intellectual workers, and especially in comparison with that of the millions of Soviet workers in general. In 1959, assistant editors and correspondents in Moscow received 147 rubles ($375) a month base, plus an average of $250 more in space rates. Local correspondents outside Moscow receive less than this, and the average for all communications workers below the executive level was $160 to $180 per month. In 1962, the editor of *Pravda,* Mr. Satyukov, was paid an annual salary of $7,200 and the American correspondent Boris Strelnikov received $6,000 yearly. Department heads were paid 500 rubles a month ($450). In addition to salary, the communicator may receive benefits in the form of bonuses and permission to sell articles to other media. As a member of the journalist's union he receives special rates for items he purchases, and for expenses incurred for a Black Sea vacation or weekend retreats near Moscow. Senior reporters, editors, and directors are paid higher salaries than these.

The Soviet Editor's Role and Its Difficulties

The Soviet editor's affluence and social position in relation to the nature of his duties, which in a controlled system appear on the surface to be limited to carrying out orders, give the impression that his lot is an enviable one. Typical of this oversimplified view is the judgment of *Scholastic Magazine:* "One of the softest jobs in the world is being an editor in Soviet Russia. He doesn't have to break his head to interpret the news. He doesn't have to think up what to say in his editorials. He doesn't even have to think—period. It's done for him." Such is not the case. The editor's position is far from easy and his responsibilities often get him into difficult, awkward situations. And his duties are far from simple. To keep his job an editor must be able to perform not only as an editor but also as an expert on doctrine, as a teacher, and as an organizer. In all of these spheres of performance he must exercise the utmost skill as a tactician and diplomat, if not as a tight rope walker. He is expected to perform successfully and produce results often without being delegated the requisite authority or power of control to achieve such ends. As a bureaucrat he is taught to believe that by virtue of his position he has policy-making powers within specified limits at his own level. So he has, but he is supervised and directed at each step. He must keep up with the cumulative party decisions on the press and with the flow of directives from above. If he slips, the penalty for his mistake can be severe. After his paper has been published, its pages are subject to critical scrutiny in several quarters: his local Agitprop bureau, the party committee, readers, and the party hierarchy of each of the echelons above his level, and finally the Central organs in Moscow. Editors at the regional or middle levels seem to stand at the most vulnerable spot.[30] They are too far removed from the capital to keep closely attuned to subtle policy shifts, yet they are held much more responsible for ideological interpretation than media at lower levels. Members of this group of editors are torn between pressures from above and below, and they usually serve as scapegoats when a scapegoat is needed.

The editor's chief problem is related to his ability to interpret correctly the announcements of changes in the party line and in the press directives that deal with these changes. An interpretation may be critical in the ideological sphere where meanings are frequently abstract or ephemeral and where change may be sudden and extreme. An example of these unpredictable reversals was Khrushchev's bitter attack on Stalin at the Twentieth Party Congress in February, 1956. The new Line became one which asserted that the late dictator and hero had made unforgivable mistakes and warned of the dangers of the "cult of personality" concept symbolized by the Stalinist era. It was almost a year later, on January 19, 1957, that Soviet editors and the general public received the first official indication that their leaders now thought Stalin had been a good man after all. Although he had committed serious errors, he had done so for a good reason, to safeguard the gains of the revolution, it was explained. How was the first inkling of this surprising counterreversal allowed to seep out to the public and to the world? The first suggestion that the new official Line might be modified was presaged by *Jin-min Jih-pao* of Peking when it published a lengthy statement eulogizing Stalin. Peking disagreed with Moscow. The statement appeared two days later in the Soviet press. The following day, Mr. Khrushchev at a New Year's Eve Party at the Kremlin avowed that "all of us are Stalinists" when it comes to opposing the enemies of Communism. This hint—an attempt at compromise between the opposing viewpoints—was published without delay, but it was more than two weeks before the press carried the full report of Khrushchev's remarks on another occasion,[31] praising the late master of the Soviet state as a good example of a Communist. President Tito of Jugoslavia underwent a similar metamorphosis in the official view—a hero one day, a traitorous enemy the next; and then accepted later as a loyal Communist again. Editors waited more than four years for the official Line to return to its 1956 posture with the events of November, 1961, when at the Twenty-second Party Congress, Stalin's body was removed from its place beside Lenin and further steps were taken to erase his memory from the annals of the great. Editors must indeed keep alert to be able to interpret such reversals accurately and to make them sound convincing to the public.

A second common problem, particularly acute in the case of regional and provincial editors, has hinged upon their ability to maintain a proper balance between outside and locally originated material. If the editor takes refuge from criticism by publishing a large proportion of what he considers relatively "safe" content received from Tass or copied from the Central Press, he runs the risk of criticism for evading his reponsibility to his local constituency. Yet if he slights the word from Moscow and shows initiative in developing original material, he not only risks being accused of dereliction of duty to the Central Party but also of possible deviation from approved dogma.

In the third place, an editor is often torn by divided duties in the service of the party on the one hand and of the press on the other. This problem has been the subject of editorial complaints. For example during an important campaign an editor may be drafted by the party to leave his editorial work and engage for a time in organization work. As a result he cannot give proper attention to his editorial duties, but still may be held responsible for them.[32] Finally editorial shortage of tenure has also provoked complaints. "Can editors of the district and city papers improve and grow in their jobs . . . if 43 per cent . . . were shifted in 1953 and 61 per cent in 1954?" *Partinaya Zhizn* asked in an article discussing the problem.

Effects Inherent in the System

The system tends to make of editors sycophants and dilettantes, if not outright copyists. According to E. A. Lazebnik, who vigorously attacked sloth and lack of initiative on the part of communications personnel, the editorial staffs of local newspapers "are in the habit of passing over in silence all new problems until the papers of the capital have pronounced on them. There is a tendency to repetition and to restate truths that have long been known." [33] Moreover journalists often deal superficially with important problems when they get around to it, Lazebnik said. It is hard to find a journalist who is capable of producing a serious article on social or economic affairs, though they are all ready to discuss anything, even those subjects they know nothing about. Even so, if "a journalist shows signs of independence and tries to write an article which . . . stands out against other articles, the editor-in-chief usually disapproves of it and advises him to rewrite it according to the established pattern," Lazebnik said.[34] Choosing editors primarily on the basis of their qualifications as loyal Communists it seems, has not generally produced able, authoritative critics and analysts of distinction or popular esteem. There are a few exceptions, however. The result may be partially attributable to the fact that many of those holding responsible positions in the mass media are bureaucrats who have little talent for writing or other creative work. This sort of attitude on the part of the professional worker, an attitude induced by the system, is in part responsible for the lack of popular appeal in the media. In 1955 the magazine *Sovetskaya Pechat* noted that the public's obvious dissatisfaction with the communications media was causing concern among journalists and concluded that the problem of ennui in the media was caused by editors' disregard of reader interests. It seems that editors and program directors are motivated more by the desire to please their superiors than by incentives which lead them to any real study of audience needs or wants.

Vigorous efforts to improve this condition have met with only moderate success, partly because they are due to habit-ingrained forces and partly because they stem from conditions that are the logical byproducts of the system itself. It is doubtful whether those conditions that appear to be the concomitant outgrowth of bureaucracy and centralized control can ever be entirely eliminated. A civilization based on collective values provides poor soil for the growth of individual initiative. Creative talents flourish weakly in a vacuum; they grow best in the open atmosphere. In a sense, then, authoritarianism defeats itself. But there are compensations. To the degree that communications leaders are better trained and disciplined, to the degree that they gain experience, they can be expected to become more trustworthy and reliable. As this process continues, the regime can afford to relax its vigilance and place more responsibility on the professional worker—thus neatly resolving the problem of constantly exerted direct control and close supervision.

Soviet leaders over the years have come to realize they can never achieve their aims without a body of professional communications knowledge and a large class of trained, skilled workers in mass communications industries. At first, practice was trial and error, hit and miss, in the massive effort to fit practice to theory. There was only a small group of professional workers managed by a large group of faithful party hacks who knew nothing about journalism. As the country has passed through the unstable transitional stage to maturity there has emerged a body of professional communications practices, techniques, and knowledge. With it has emerged a large corps of professional communicators—but one not large enough to meet the demand.

6 ★

HOW THE MEDIA PERFORM: NEWS, ADVERTISING, BROADCASTING

NEWSPAPERS, MAGAZINES, ADVERTISING, AND BROADCASTING respond more readily to manipulation than books, films, plays, and other less rapidly produced communications forms. They are the most sensitive of all propaganda instruments—with the single exception of face-to-face methods—at the command of Soviet leaders. These more versatile and popular media can put a new party dictum into the information channels and expose it most immediately to the greatest possible number of people. Because of this versatility and sensitivity, they reflect most vividly the multitudinous forces of mass persuasion that surge through changing Soviet society.

This chapter goes to the central wellsprings of power in the communications network of the nation to examine the messages from what may be termed information managers for the whole country and indeed for most of the communist world. These are the prestigious leading central organs, *Pravda* and *Izvestia,* and their energetic comrade and collaborator, the Tass agency. Also reviewed here is the content of other media: advertising messages and radio/television fare. In Chapter 7 the focus will be on kinds of messages to be found in selected specialized central newspapers and magazines that have special functions.

To assess how the media system performs and behaves it will be useful to examine what the media say and how effectively they say it. It might seem that instruments so sensitive to change would find it relatively easy to vary their fare, but this is not generally the case. Although trends since 1955 reflect concerted efforts to improve presentation techniques, the pedestrian tone of media content and its uniformity have been widely criticized both at home and abroad. John Gunther declared, ". . . of all dull things in the USSR the dullest are the great newspapers."[1] Yet close inspection shows that underneath the general impression of sameness, important differences exist among both individual media and groups of media at various levels. When media have different commissions and different audiences, their appearance and content reflect these dissimilar appeals and objectives. Still the familiar messages under various guises seep through, tediously ever-present, it seems, in all media.

THE SUPREME POPULAR VOICES:

Pravda, Izvestia, and Tass.

At one end of the newspaper continuum stands the powerful *Pravda,* conservative in tone, authoritative, heavy in rhetoric, serious, and solemn. It is the dignified paragon of journalism (if a paragon can be permitted to stoop to invective) and spokesman of the party. At the other extremity stand the light popular appeal evening papers which are exemplified in *Vechernaia Moskva* and in *Komsomolskaya Pravda.* Close to these two in popular appeal are the relatively new *Sovetskaya Rossia* (started on July 1, 1956) which is a general daily printed in eight cities of the Russian Republic, and *Sovetsky Sport,* the daily of the sport fans. In between these there is nothing in the Soviet press, however, that resembles the degree of sensationalism in writing and play that characterizes, for example, the popular press of Britain. In between the two extremes of appeal the various organs take their places, managing to disseminate information on a broad range of topics. Indeed, the ideological spectrum reflected in the papers is not nearly as wide as the variety of subjects treated. No Soviet newspaper is considered large in size by United States standards, most of them running 6 to 8 pages though some may on occasion increase this up to 14 and 16 pages. Only *Pravda* appears 7 days a week, the others customarily issuing 6 days a week, omitting Monday.

Magazines vary according to appeals and fields of specialization. The light, popular *Ogonyok,* the film magazines, the women's magazines, and the satirical magazine *Krokodil* serve the most popular fare and their appearance reveals their attempt to reach a broad cross section of the populace. On the other hand, the periodicals devoted to literature, pedagogy, the arts, culture, and the specialized journals in science and technology are likely to be thick, poorly illustrated tomes of nonglossy paper. Obviously these depend more upon what they are saying to attract interest and hold attention than upon the way it is said. For the most part magazines issue on a monthly or fortnightly basis, except for the popular weeklies.

Pravda: Communism's Olympian Oracle

In May of 1962, the mighty *Pravda* celebrated its fiftieth anniversary as the world's largest circulation newspaper (with 6.3 million readers), the foremost prestige daily of the communist world, and perhaps the world's most significant and influential paper. The first *Pravda* sold for two kopecks a copy and fifty years later a 4-page issue was still selling for two kopecks. As the official organ of the Central Committee of the Communist Party, *Pravda* is the authoritative voice of the power elite to the Soviet population, to party members, to communist parties and organs around the world, and to the East European communist countries. Leaders of the Western world and those of Communist China eagerly search *Pravda's* contents for clues to the changing direction of Soviet policy. *Pravda* is read to verify rumor, and its omissions are as important as its inclusions. When in 1953 the name of Lavrenti Beria, the former head of the secret police, was conspicuously missing from a list of Soviet leaders in *Pravda,* a Western ambassador told his government that Beria probably had been arrested. His assumption proved correct. The popular Russian jest that there is no truth in *The News (Izvestia)* and no news in *The Truth (Pravda)* is hyperbole, for *Pravda,* as do other Soviet papers, prints the news as it really is some of the time, just as some of the time it prints the truth as others see it. Even when it is not printing the truth *Pravda* reliably and faithfully prints or indicates what the Soviet leaders think is true and how they react. Through the years *Pravda* has come to be a useful index to Soviet behavior for the rest of the world—an index that has grown in importance in direct proportion to the growth in importance of the Soviet Union in world affairs.

Pravda's real meaning is not always plainly expressed; sometimes it is subtle, vague, devious, obscure. To decipher and interpret *Pravda's* real messages requires an expert well versed in Soviet history, behavior, and Communist ideology. The first four of its usual six pages are devoted to editorials, theoretical articles, propagandized reports on industry, economics, agriculture, or education. The spot news events published are often lacking in timeliness. The last two pages, which are often the only pages in the paper read by the millions of persons who are not politically interested or motivated, carry foreign news, theatre announcements and reviews, sports, and miscellaneous items.

Alongside its title, *Pravda* displays the two drawings of the Order of Lenin Award, the highest award in the Soviet Union. Underneath, the paper identifies itself as the organ of the Central Committee of the Communist Party of the Soviet Union and as the newspaper founded on May 5, 1912, by V. I. Lenin. *Pravda* usually appears as a 4-page issue, but frequently it has 6 pages, and special editions may run 8 or more pages.

The 6-page issue, of October 6, 1965, leads off with a 4-column spread filling the top half of the page devoted to information about the harvest under the heading LABOR WATCH OF MILLIONS. (See Fig. 6.1.) The story stresses the all-out effort being made not only by farmers to reap the harvest, but by miners and workers in transportation and construction who are going on emergency duty to raise production. Socialist emulation is expanding to honor the Twenty-third Congress of the Communist Party, the report says. One of the accompanying photographs shows the face of S. P. Simonov, a top producer in a tractor plant, and the other photograph shows a pair of tractors working the fields in the Voroneshkoi region. A dispatch from a *Pravda* correspondent at Minsk reports that the new BelAZ *(sic)* tractors have been successful in meeting government acceptance tests. An item describes the success of the Ukrainian and Buryat republics in fulfilling their production quotas of agricultural products. Most of the space below the fold is devoted to news and to a group photograph covering state visits to the Soviet Union by delegations from Sudan and Mali. Activities of the African delegations include conferences at the Kremlin (the picture shows the group seated around a conference table with Soviet leaders), a visit to Lenin's mausoleum, and to a Moscow automobile plant. The Kremlin meeting is the only story on the front page dealing with news of the Central Government.

Пролетарии всех стран, соединяйтесь!

ПРАВДА

Орган Центрального Комитета Коммунистической партии Советского Союза

ТРУДОВАЯ ВАХТА МИЛЛИОНОВ

УСПЕШНО ЗАВЕРШИТЬ РАБОТЫ НА ПОЛЯХ

УКРАИНСКАЯ ССР ВЫПОЛНИЛА ПЛАНЫ ПРОДАЖИ ГОСУДАРСТВУ ЗЕРНА, МОЛОКА, ЯИЦ И ШЕРСТИ

ИСПЫТАНИЯ ВЫДЕРЖАНЫ

ВКЛАД БУРЯТСКИХ ЗЕМЛЕДЕЛЬЦЕВ

В ОБСТАНОВКЕ ДРУЖБЫ И ВЗАИМОПОНИМАНИЯ

Переговоры в Кремле

Модибо Кейта у московских автомобилестроителей

НАЛЕТЧИКИ НЕСУТ ПОТЕРИ

Посещение Мавзолея В. И. Ленина

Пролетарии всех стран, соединяйтесь!

ПРАВДА

Орган Центрального Комитета Коммунистической партии Советского Союза

ВЫШЕ УРОВЕНЬ РАБОТЫ СЕЛЬСКИХ РАЙКОМОВ ПАРТИИ

День нашей Родины

ПРЕДОКТЯБРЬСКОЕ СОРЕВНОВАНИЕ МЕТАЛЛУРГОВ

На работу в деревню

НА ПОЛЯХ СТРАНЫ

Fig. 6.1. Comparison of page 1 of **Pravda** for October 6, 1965 (left), with the **Pravda** of the same day 12 years earlier at the end of the Stalin period indicates only minor changes in appearance. The later **Pravda** has two Orders of Lenin displayed in the title instead of one. There is little difference in the amount of space devoted to photographs. Both carry the day's editorial in the two left-hand columns. Page makeup in the more recent edition tends toward horizontal lines rather than vertical. Even fewer differences can be found in the general nature of the content. The words form different messages, but they are set to the same music and are interlaced with the same refrains.

Two left-hand columns on page one are set aside for the day's editorial, this one headed SUCCESSFULLY TO COMPLETE WORK IN THE FIELDS calls on the people to put into effect those measures to favor the increased effectiveness of all public production, including the rural economy—measures that were outlined by the September Plenum of the Central Committee and more concretely in the March Plenum for further growth of collective and State farm production. "Millions of village toilers, like all Soviet people," the editorial says, "greeted with great satisfaction the decisions of the September Plenum . . . . In them they see concrete manifestations of the anxiety of the Communist Party for the continued progress of the socialist economy and for further improvement of the people's welfare."

At the bottom of the page a brief story reports American raids on the "Democratic Republic of Vietnam." Since August 5, 1964, the report says, 639 American aircraft have been shot down over the Democratic Republic of Vietnam's territory. "Troops of the army of liberation" ambushed a 12-man American patrol 15 miles northeast of Saigon, and captured or killed its members. Among the other short items is one reporting the return stopover in Moscow of a Hungarian party-government delegation from a visit to Mongolia, and another with news that shipments of cement from plants in the Volsk (Saratovskaya region) are being supplied to many construction projects.

Pages two and three are normally devoted to domestic news, and the letters from readers appear on page two. Page two of this issue carries a 4-column photograph of steel workers who have exceeded their quota in cast-iron production. Almost one-third of the space on this page is occupied by the decisions of the September Plenum of the Central Committee of the Communist Party of the Soviet Union. The main headline reads: FAITH IN THE PARTY INSPIRES. Other news items on this page tell us that the Lipetskaya region fulfilled its plan in sales of milk, eggs, and wool to the State; two awards of the Order of the Red Banner of Labor were reported; and a story with a picture saluted a young woman graduate student in agriculture. The letters include one from a geologist who writes about the need to regulate "exploitation" of mineral resources; one from a museum director who describes the offerings of his museum in the Kaluzhskaya region; and three letters from republic and city officials under the heading TO PRAVDA THEY REPLY: MEASURES TAKEN. The three officials have replied to letters of criticism published earlier in *Pravda,* and have agreed to rectify mistakes that have been pointed out.

More domestic news and features occupy the top half of page three. Here are reports from three cities detailing new enterprises undertaken, new production quotas reached. A human interest story NATIVE PEOPLE fills one-fourth of the page with the usual moralistic patter. Here is a 3-column photograph of a refinery and adjoining it is a short item which says "Luna-7 photographed." There is a report from a *kolkhoz* chairman about "first totals," on completing the harvest season. The bottom half of this page is a rather factual review of Soviet foreign policy in the years since the end of World War II, and the story is broken over to fill the bottom half of page four under horizontal display headlines. Both sections of the article are spread across the entire page width. Thus by exposure, criticism, example, praise, and self-justification the "creative" rather than the "factographic" values in the news are selected and displayed to perform their appointed tasks.

Only slightly less moralistic in tone, world news appears on pages four and five. Newspapers around the world have expressed opinions regarding the accomplishments of the September Plenum of the Central Committee, and such press opinion that reinforces the ideology or testifies to the wisdom of the party leaders is selected and republished. A favorite technique of Communist journalism, as of other persuasive communication, is to capitalize on the testimony of others, a subtle way of saying "I told you so" while avoiding the onus of having preached too much. The consensus of these points of view was favorable as expressed by the headline: CREATIVE APPROACH AND EFFICIENCY; PRESS OF BROTHER COUNTRIES ABOUT PLENUM, CC, CPSU. A Tass dispatch from Prague adjoins a 1-column photograph showing rail workers using heavy equipment. The Prague dispatch describes the Soviet-Czechoslovakian agreement on commodity payments for 1966–1970. Another Tass story reports the Moscow observance of the sixteenth anniversary of the founding of the German Democratic Republic. One also learns from this page of a conference of historians of socialist nations to discuss plans to observe in 1967 the fiftieth anniversary of the October Revolution, of an exchange of telegrams between the Soviet government and Cyprus, and of the arrival in Moscow of the ambassador of the "Central African Republic."

Wire stories on page five carry Tass datelines from Ankara, Warsaw, Jakarta, Bonn, Helsinki, Copenhagen, Saigon, and other world news centers. A feature story RIO, OCTOBER, 1965 was dispatched from Brazil by *Pravda's* correspondent V. Levin. There is an announcement of the first issue of *Hranma,* newspaper of the Cuban Communists, which the headline says is to join the ranks "in the Struggle against Imperialism." Finland's Communist Party's Central Committee has held a Plenum, there are continued incidents on the India-Pakistan border, and an American fighter plane is destroyed, smaller items say.

Features, entertainment notices, literary items, and sports are the principal kinds of information on page six. A standing headline THROUGH THE MOTHER COUNTRY, over a daily roundup of stories and a photograph or so, brings nostalgic images of the Russian landscape, cities, and villages. Main illustration on this page is a pictorial woodland photograph showing "Golden Autumn below Leningrad." Sergei Smirnov's poem "October Lines" goes well with the photograph. There is also a short story by Dmitri Blinski about a Russian family. A brief dispatch from Kiev describes the effectiveness of direct telephone dialing from there to Moscow. Almost in the manner of her Western counterparts, *Pravda* has one story from the police court, which reports that plunderers have been arrested and charged. The sports news, consisting entirely of two chess match reports, appears on page six. Here also is OUR INFORMATION DEPARTMENT, a catalogue of theatre, radio, and television programs, motion picture announcements, and the weather report.

Because *Pravda's* editorials, reports, and major articles are read daily over radio, and many of them are reprinted widely throughout the Soviet Union and at times in China and in Eastern Europe, it is easy to conclude that, having sampled *Pravda,* one has sampled the entire Communist Press. It is true, of course, that the dominant, characteristic pattern of content is like the *Pravda* model. Variations occur within this general framework.

Izvestia: Innovative Voice of the Government

The traditional position of *Pravda* as top paper in the press hierarchy has occasionally been subjected to assaults from the paper just below it, *Izvestia,* which has on occasions dared to take issue with *Pravda.* Under the editorship of Alexei Adzhubei from 1959 to 1964, *Izvestia* outdid *Pravda* in the movement to make the press livelier, more readable and flexible (Fig. 6.2). He introduced a degree of cautious criticism and even some mild sensationalism such as reporting the activities of the Abominable Snowman. In 1960 *Izvestia* changed to afternoon publication and introduced its 32-page Sunday supplement, *Nedelia* (The Week). These measures attracted more readers, and Adzhubei, being Premier Khrushchev's son-in-law, apparently had the political power to wangle more newsprint from the government. As a result for the first time in its history, *Izvestia's* circulation of 8.3 million reported in May of 1965 was well ahead of *Pravda's* 7 million. Still *Izvestia's* achievements have not really threatened *Pravda,* whose pages also have been made more interesting, but not to the extent that dignity is sacrificed for liveliness. Adzhubei did succeed in making the official government organ the "most talked about newspaper in the Soviet Union." One of his countrymen called him "The Khrushchev of journalism—a fresh wind blowing through the pages of our press." [2] *Izvestia* under

Пролетарии всех стран, соединяйтесь!
Коммунистическая партия Советского Союза
ПРАВДА
Орган Центрального Комитета Коммунистической партии Советского Союза
Газета основана 5 мая 1912 года В. И. ЛЕНИНЫМ
№ 264 (16485) Суббота, 21 сентября 1963 года Цена 2 коп.
ЗАЯВЛЕНИЕ СОВЕТСКО

ИЗВЕСТИЯ
СОВЕТОВ ДЕПУТАТОВ ТРУДЯЩИХСЯ СССР
№ 225 (14388) Год издания 47-й
Суббота, 21 сентября 1963 г. Цена 2 коп.
ЗАЯВЛЕНИЕ СОВЕТСКО

Пролетарии всех стран, соединяйтесь!
Коммунистическая партия Советского Союза
ПРАВДА
Орган Центрального Комитета Коммунистической партии Советского Союза
Газета основана 5 мая 1912 года В. И. ЛЕНИНЫМ
№ 265 (16486) Воскресенье, 22 сентября 1963 года Цена 3 коп.
ЗАЯВЛЕНИЕ СОВЕТСКО
III.

ИЗВЕСТИЯ
СОВЕТОВ ДЕПУТАТОВ ТРУДЯЩИХСЯ СССР
№ 226 (14389) Год издания 47-й
Воскресный выпуск
22 сентября 1963 г. Цена 3 коп.
БЛИЗ
УСПЕХ ЗЕМЛЕДЕЛЬЦЕ
ЗАЯВЛЕНИЕ СОВЕТСКО
III.

Fig. 6.2. An upper left section taken from **Pravda** and **Izvestia** for the same day, September 21, 1963 (left), illustrate the occasional presentation and display of identical material in exactly the same way under the same headings in each newspaper. The United States and the Soviet Union had signed the Nuclear Test Ban Treaty in the summer of 1963, and Red China had attacked the Soviet government for this action. Here is the official government statement in reply to Peking's attack. The official statement continued in the next day's issues, September 22 (right), of both papers and was displayed under the same headings. This time **Izvestia** used slightly smaller type in the headline.

Adzhubei republished articles from Western writers critical of the Soviet government. As was to be expected, he was fired as editor in 1964 when his famous father-in-law was dismissed and replaced.

Izvestia's brighter makeup, interest-catching headlines, and use of illustrations set it apart from *Pravda,* although its general plan is similar. Sometimes the lead stories on the front pages of these two top dailies look alike and carry identical headlines. As it is the spokesman of the Central Government and the organ of the Presidium, about half of the content of *Izvestia* may be identical to that of *Pravda,* but the two papers differ in their specialized interests and in the fact that they are written for different audiences. For example *Izvestia's* foreign news coverage stresses the official viewpoints of foreign governments. Instead, *Pravda* reports internal affairs of foreign countries as seen through the eyes of the Communist Party.

Essentially *Izvestia* favors news about governmental matters while *Pravda* favors news about Party matters. *Izvestia* finds its readers largely among the government workers from the Central Government in the capital down to the bureaucracy of the local subdivisions. In contrast, *Pravda's* readers are the party members, overlapping to include some government officials who are also readers of *Izvestia*. The overpowering shadow of *Pravda,* however, does not dwarf *Izvestia's* monumental task, a task which includes reporting, analyzing, and criticizing the whole of a government whose activities cover almost the total life of the people.

To *Izvestia* was given the honor of reporting the on-the-scene account of man's first flight into space on April 12, 1961, from a rocket base at an undisclosed location in the country. The *Izvestia* reporter was present when Major Yuri Gagarin made his 108-minute spin, monitored his radiocasts from space, and described his return. The *Izvestia* report was released by Tass, and the following day *Pravda* carried an interview with Gagarin who described his experience of weightlessness and told how the Soviet Premier's paternal concern for his welfare moved him to tears.

Information in the title line explains that *Izvestia* is news of "Councils of Workers' Deputies of the USSR." Into the "I" of the word Izvestia is set the insignia of the Order of the Red Banner, a Soviet award of distinction second only to that of the Order of Lenin. The slogan "Workers of the World, Unite!" also appears here in 15 languages. *Izvestia's* price, like *Pravda's,* is two kopecks for four pages and three for six. Unlike the *Pravda* of the same date, *Izvestia* of October 6, 1965, (Fig. 6.3) has an index of "events of the Day" at the top of the page calling attention to important stores by location in the issue; for example, "Page 2 Dangerous Agreement of Thailand Authorities with USA."

Issues of *Izvestia* and *Pravda* for the same day carry some duplication of news, but the presentation differs. At the top right of the former's page one the headline says NATIONAL APPROVAL, and the major story below it presents a summary of "feedback" from reader assessments of the Central Committee's September Plenum. The story began as follows: "These days the editorial mail continues to bring scores and hundreds of comments from our readers on the decisions of the September Plenum, CC, CPSU, and laws adopted by the Supreme Soviet, USSR. In the letters are warm words of gratitude and approval from the heart, deep thoughts about how to use more quickly and more effectively the new opportunities for further

СТОЛИЦА ПОЛЬШИ ГОТОВИТСЯ К МЕЖДУНАРОДНОМУ ПРОФСОЮЗНОМУ ФОРУМУ

ОПАСНЫЙ СГОВОР ТАИЛАНДСКИХ ВЛАСТЕЙ С США

ПЕНТАГОН ПЕРЕБРАСЫВАЕТ В ЗАПАДНУЮ ЕВРОПУ ВОЕННЫЕ САМОЛЕТЫ

ИЗВЕСТИЯ

СОВЕТОВ ДЕПУТАТОВ ТРУДЯЩИХСЯ СССР

ВСЕНАРОДНОЕ ОДОБРЕНИЕ

ЕДИНСТВО УПРАВЛЕНИЯ ОТРАСЛЬЮ

ОТВЕЧАЮТ ТРУДОМ

КРЕПНУТ СВЯЗИ МЕЖДУ СССР и МАЛИ

НАЧАЛИСЬ ПЕРЕГОВОРЫ

ПРОТИВ ЗАКОНА СИЛЫ

ВАРШАВА ПЕРЕД КОНГРЕССОМ

ВАРВАРСТВО АГРЕССОРОВ

В СЕРДЕЧНОЙ ОБСТАНОВКЕ

ПО ЗАКАЗУ США

ПРЕЗИДЕНТ ПЕРЕИЗБРАН

ПЕРЕМИРИЕ НАРУШАЕТСЯ

ВЕНГЕРСКИЕ ДРУЗЬЯ ОТБЫЛИ НА РОДИНУ

ИЗВЕСТИЯ СОВЕТОВ ДЕПУТАТОВ ТРУДЯЩИХСЯ СССР

Поднять зябь под весь яровой клин

По Советскому Союзу

Предприятия увеличивают выпуск машин для сельского хозяйства

На заводах Белоруссии

У харьковских машиностроителей

Ленинградцы—в помощь колхозам

Трудовые успехи горняков

Fig. 6.3. The front page of **Izvestia** for October 6, 1965 (left), compared with one for the same date 12 years earlier. Comparative analyses of Soviet newspapers over time tend to indicate little change in format, content, or relative distribution of the content categories, but in this comparison some differences over the Thaw period and the influence of Alexei Adzhubei's editorship can be observed. **Izvestia** has shown more change than **Pravda** (see Fig 6.1). The page has been brightened by typographical variations and stylistic devices such as type face contrasts, the use of boxes, and horizontal rather than vertical display. More use of picture space and picture cropping for close-ups are apparent. The 1965 issue devotes more space to international news than does the earlier one. The writing in the more recent issue is livelier, indicating an effort to make the same themes more palatable. However, the location of the index and editorial matter has remained approximately the same.

development of industrial production, and concrete proposals and plans for the future." A writer from Erevan is quoted next, "We workers are assured that the new system of industrial management and the material stimulus of workers will remarkably raise the productivity of labor."

Izvestia's editors seem to differ from *Pravda's* in that they are not afraid to use big picture spreads; one—a close-up face shot of three workers wearing safety helmets—extending across three-fourths of the page is tied in with the Plenum story. The cutline reads "Builders of Gorlovskov nitrate mineral fertilizer factory answer the work call of the September Plenum and are using more effectively the means allotted by the state to develop our industry and to put new productive capacities into service more quickly . . . ." The editorial to the left is also a part of that Plenum theme already treated by picture and news story, discussing the new industrial management system established by the Central Committee.

In covering one other piece of news duplicated in *Pravda, Izvestia* also seems to cast the story about the Moscow visit of Sudan and Mali officials in an atmosphere of warmth and brotherly goodwill. "Ties between USSR and Mali grow stronger" and "Negotiations have begun in cordial surroundings," the story says. The same picture showing First Secretary Leonid Breshnev and other Soviet officials at the conference table with the African delegations appears in approximately the same relative position near the bottom of the page.

A "roundup" of international news briefs from *Izvestia* and Tass correspondents displayed attractively in two columns on the lower right side of the page is a distinguishing mark of this *Izvestia*. *Pravda* does not have it. In this section we read about such things as what Warsaw is like on the eve of the Congress of Professional Trade Unions; a stand against USA actions in Latin America by a Mexican Constitutional-Revolutionary Party official; firing of more than 20 rockets into a Vietnamese school by a USA F-105 fighter jet (barbarians of aggressors, the story says); a "victory" won after 19 days of a strike by Boeing factory workers (story with New York dateline); what dispatches from both New Delhi and Karachi say—that the India-Pakistan truce has been broken; and the "success" of progressive forces "in a remote Okinawa election."

Page two of this 4-page edition is the international page, we are told by a page-wide logotype at the top, "Through Countries and Continents: Reports, Statements, Commentaries." Here is a brief sample: charges from Hanoi that the United States is converting Thailand into a military base; from Havana that Castro has called to rally forces of revolution; from Ulan-Bator a "firm resolution" of solidarity between Hungary and Mongolia; from a United States newspaper, an INTERNATIONAL COMMENTARY: EXPLOSIONS IN THE SOUTH; also "Alabama's Governor George Wallace pushes his candidacy for President in 1968." This story is illustrated with a satirical cartoon called "Racist in White Heat" showing a 2-gun blusterer on a black stage horse bearing slogans, "Only for Whites," "Supremacy of the White Race," and "To the White House!"

There also are Paris and London dispatches on events in Indonesia; an item announces that the Soviet embassy in Peking has seen a motion picture consecrating the sixteenth anniversary of the founding of the Chinese People's Republic; from Prague there is a report on shortening the working day; from Venezuela, a report on the activity of partisans; and from the United Nations, a story summarizing the talks of foreign affairs ministers. Other stories concern NATO preparations with US jet aircraft; a "tragedy" in which South Koreans are killed and injured in mob panic; and a Rome dateline story reporting the "smashing success" of the USSR State Academic Russian Choir at a performance at La Scala in Milan. A New York report concerning Pope Paul's visit shows considerable straight Western-type factual reporting with perspective: "Pope Paul VI yesterday made a brief one-day visit to UN headquarters, marking the first time in history the appearance of the head of the Catholic Church inside the walls of the international organization and on the American Continent. The visit of Paul VI was at the invitation of UN Secretary General U Thant. The Pope met with U.S. President Johnson, served a 'message of peace' before 90,000 American Catholics in Yankee Stadium . . . ." The MIRROR OF THE WORLD PRESS department contains a Tass survey of unheaded items, covering worldwide reports on the Luna-7 rocket. Elsewhere appear Warsaw, Prague, and Sofia comments on the Comintern Congress, Chinese press opinion on aid to Pakistan, world opinion on NATO and arms for West Germany and on the Vietnam War.

Turning to domestic affairs on page three we are returned to the subject of the Central Committee's September Plenum. Here the top half of the page is filled with reactions from near and far to the Plenum's decisions. The only illustrations are two informal portraits of workers on the job. There are two by-line contributions on this page. One is called WAY TO PROFITABLENESS, by N. Bybuzenko, director of a heavy engineering industrial plant, and the other is CREATIVE CONCERN, by V. Berezin, director of a chemical plant. The bottom half of the page presents a bit of satire reprinted from *Krokodil;* three formal decrees of the Presidium of the Supreme Soviet naming two awards of the Order of the Red Banner of Labor and one People's Artist of the USSR award; and a lengthy story written by Victor Maamyagi, academician of the Estonian Academy of Science, reviewing Estonian advances under Soviet leadership.

The last page of this issue (4) is a miscellany like the final page of *Pravda*. There is a department called NEWS, REPORTS, PHOTO-INFORMATION, presenting items of interest both local and foreign—an example is a photograph of a new bridge across the Don at Rostov. A "wrap-up" of sports news covers chess matches, hockey games, and volleyball games. A considerable amount of space is devoted to letters from readers. One tells about "my book shelf," another "Treasures of nature and careless masters," and a third says "you just check into this," and starts with this sentence, "If there's a possibility that you'll publish this letter, I ask you to change my name . . . ." There are weather reports and radio program schedules, and one obituary.

Going back almost four years, let us briefly examine *Izvestia's* July 22, 1962, issue of six pages. Its first page is devoted primarily to the Soviet Union's image in international affairs and to some internal matters. Dominating the page is a 4-column group picture of members of Soviet and other Communist state delegations currently attending the All-World Youth and Student Festival in Helsinki. The article, by an *Izvestia* correspondent reporting from Helsinki, speaks of the "reactionary western youth" among the representatives who spread lies and half-truths about the festival, and stresses, "Their favorite comment seems to be 'Don't fall for Communist propaganda.' " The piece, however, devotes some space to factual information, reporting that 140 countries are to be represented at the Helsinki meeting by 1,400 delegates.

The lead article, SPEED AND HIGH QUALITY—MOTTO FOR THE HARVEST, reports the "usually successful" yields of wheat, beans, corn, and beets, praising some regions for record-breaking speed in completing the harvesting work, while berating others for being too slow. Delays were invariably attributed to "Poor organization, inability to appreciate and copy those techniques which enable the leading farms to forge ahead." This rationalizing is followed by an expository discourse on the proper procedures for sowing, ploughing, and harvesting, together with a sanguine prediction that more grain will be harvested this year than in previous years.

The editorial on this page deals with the problem of nuclear testing, publishing in full the official policy statement of the Soviet government announcing and rationalizing its decision to resume nuclear testing in the air. The statement attacks the USA government for its resumption of nuclear tests on Johnston and Christmas Islands, and argues that this action forces the Soviet Union to respond in like manner, as Khrushchev's warning to Kennedy on

March 3, 1962, had indicated. "The United States," the article says, "does not hide the fact that it began a new series of testings especially in space, in order to try to achieve military supremacy over the USSR. The Soviet Union would not have shown concern for its peoples and the future of its government, had it not drawn the necessary conclusions. The Soviet government, remembering the Hitler attack in 1941, cannot afford to be unprepared. Therefore orders for new Soviet testings have been called for. The Soviet tests are merely retaliatory measures." A call for deliverance of mankind from the threat of nuclear devastation leaves the reader to speculate who will deliver mankind from this fate.

Other items on page one include the following: Two short notices about the commander of an atomic submarine who was presented with the Lenin and Golden Star awards, and the title "Hero of the Soviet Union" for the "successful fulfillment of a special government assignment"; a report of Khrushchev's visit to the Northern Navy where he made the awards; a report on the Geneva Conference on Laos by a Tass special correspondent featuring Foreign Minister Gromyko's speech to the conference, and noting that "other foreign ministers made speeches"; and short items from Cairo, Paris, and New York.

Page two is given entirely to information of the outside world. Leading items recount at length the success and achievements of the United Arab Republic and the fury of the Japanese over American military installations, epitomized by the slogan "Yankee, free our land." The article on the Arab Republic says that with the help of the USSR and other socialist governments, the UAR withstood the imperialists' economic blockade aimed at bringing the country to its knees. According to the story, the UAR refused to join the aggressive Baghdad pact and rejected the "Eisenhower Doctrine." Much attention is paid to stressing the friendship between the two countries, the help freely given by the Soviet people to the people of the UAR in developing their national economy. The article goes on to express the opinion that the people of the UAR value deeply the help they have received from the people of the Soviet Union, and hope that friendship between the two countries will grow and strengthen.

This page is balanced by two illustrations. A cartoon on the Berlin situation and a map of Greece showing prisons and concentration camps in which the patriot-fighters for peace and democracy are incarcerated. The map is accompanied by a story which says that out of 8 million Greeks, 300 thousand are entirely unemployed. The report depicts the low standard of living in Greece and compares it to that of Salazar's Portugal and Franco's Spain as among the lowest of Western European countries. The blame for such conditions is placed on the reactionary government of Greece. Another article discusses why General Norstadt resigned as head of NATO armed forces, suggesting that he was too unyielding. General Lemnitzer, a general-diplomat, is a more pliable figure, it observed.

Page three of this issue is dedicated mainly to the achievements of the Soviet Union in the fields of science, city planning, and socialist construction. A long article discusses Moscow's growth rate, traces the history of that growth, and nostalgically recounts the changes that have taken place since the war. The page reports the number of houses built during 1961, and compares this figure with similar figures for the United States, England, and France. Two right-hand columns, set off by a box, are filled with letters from the people. One letter complains of the unnecessarily large number of meetings by the chairmen of sovkhoz and kolkhoz during the summer when each hour counts, thus wasting an endless amount of time on meetings.

Page four is divided chiefly among three kinds of material, human interest stories, satirical criticism of internal affairs, and a department called LETTERS ABOUT GOOD PEOPLE. One article describes the achievements of a Soviet woman geologist and her work with a soil builder, vermiculite. The other entitled MAN OUT OF A LEGEND, describes the plight and rehabilitation of one Anton Toporkow, who had been a partisan in a far Eastern Civil War and was assumed to be dead. The satire under the heading AMAZING STORIES, deals with the construction business. It attacks bureaucratic mistakes and waste, and undeserved grabbing of medals by supervisors and directors at the expense of architects, engineers, and others who do the real work.

Page five features achievements and shortcomings of foreign countries. An article saluting Poland's 18 years of freedom from the Nazi yoke is typical. Another describes the construction by Soviet engineers of a huge athletic stadium in Jakarta at the invitation of the Indonesian government, on ground that was jungle two years before. Another, under the headline LONELINESS—GLOOMY CONFESSION OF AN ENGLISH JOURNALIST, deals with the problem of the capitalist society where "indifference to the fate of a human being is one of the most terrible aspects of the system." This article quotes from the London *Sunday Times* a sociological analysis of the prevalence of mental illness and maladjustments of British society leading 15 persons daily to commit suicide. About one-third of this page is dedicated to the late American poet Ernest Hemingway on the first anniversary of his death.

Page six, like the final page of *Pravda,* is a mixture of sports, entertainment notices, and odds and ends of news. Among the subjects discussed is work of Soviet scientists who are melting glaciers for a source of water, headlined PURER THAN A TEAR; another reports the sentencing to death before a firing squad of the heads of a knitting factory and other "chief organizers" for stealing government property, speculation in currency, and bribery. All in all, the *Izvestia* of 1965 differs little from the one of three years earlier.

We have seen enough from the foregoing to acquire a notion of the typical treatment of news and opinion in the two leading Soviet dailies. A close associate of these two in building and modifying the images the Soviet citizen may possess of the communist as well as the outside world is the Tass news agency. Kruglak analyzed news from the Tass World Service with results that supplement and reinforce documented analysis of the mass media in this and the following chapter.

Tass Focuses on the World Scene

It should be remembered that with the exception of reports from the special foreign correspondents of *Pravda* and *Izvestia,* the Tass agency is the main source of world information for the Soviet people. Kruglak found that while almost 98 per cent of the material about the United States transmitted by Tass to Moscow fell into three categories—politics, foreign relations, and economics—there was an utter void in the coverage of American culture, science, and education.[3] He concluded that the image of the United States conveyed by Tass was distorted because of this disproportionate interest, not necessarily through misrepresentation or deliberate falsehood. This incomplete picture of the United States in information transmitted to Moscow was further distorted by editorial changes made in Moscow before the reports appeared in the Soviet media for exposure to the general public. The biased viewpoint that emerges from Tass reports reaching Soviet readers and listeners is that the United States receives attention mostly when its actions coincide with those of the Soviet Union.[4] Stories are slanted to provide the Soviet Union with political advantage in the dichotomy of Cold War strategy.

It is difficult to determine what kind of image of the Sino-Indian border war in the fall of 1962 seeped through to the Soviet reader. The customary 5-day delay ensued between the first announcement of the conflict by New Delhi and Peking and the first notice in *Pravda* and *Izvestia,* which consisted of the complete text of the Chinese government's statement, announcing that hostilities had erupted and proposing a truce. The reader was left to ponder what caused the clashes, where the clashes had occurred, and what was the nature of the Indian public's response. The editorials in both papers of the same day supported the Chinese truce proposal at "the line of defacto control," (a phrase which enabled them to avoid mentioning the advances of Chinese troops into Indian territory), and vaguely attributed the conflict to the instigation of "imperialist circles in the West." [5] No mention of the conflict appeared in other Soviet papers on that day. After this notice on October 26, 1962, the Soviet press plunged again into a full two weeks of silence while fighting in the Himalayas continued. The only news from India appearing during the period was a small item reporting the transfer of Krishna Menon from the Ministry of Defense to the Ministry of Defense Industry. Then *Pravda* again ignored the news, but published an editorial calling for a truce. This was the extent of contemporary coverage in the Soviet press for more than a month of hostilities, at the end of which the entire Soviet press reported the cease-fire and the settlement. One can only speculate upon the probable explanation for such behavior. Perhaps this policy was adopted because the regime did not feel that nonpartisan coverage of both sides of the conflict was possible, and therefore avoided reporting it at all, and because a show of partisanship might endanger already tenuous Sino-Soviet relations. Whatever the reasons, the Soviet public was not informed.

The Cuban affair provided a world crisis situation that the Soviet media could not easily ignore. But the Soviet reader's picture of what actually happened could not be described as either realistic, balanced, or even consistent. It must have left the Soviet public with at best a confused, disconnected, and distorted view. The American quarantine against long-range missiles, nuclear warheads, and jet bombers was an "illegal military blockade around heroic little Cuba," which at first was pictured as designed to "strangle"

Cuba's women and children by cutting off supplies, but which nevertheless plunged the world to the edge of nuclear war. The Soviet Union did send "arms" to the "Island of Freedom," but these were only defensive weapons to protect Cuba from the invasion planned by the Pentagon and the Central Intelligence Agency. The "offensive weapons" to which President Kennedy objected were not identified in the Soviet press until their existence was admitted by Premier Khrushchev. This came after three days of full press coverage of the Soviet demonstrations against the quarantine with the slogan "We Are With You, Cuba," repeated time and again. Meanwhile the Soviet public read that their government called the American aggressors to account before the United Nations Security Council. Its representative Valerian A. Zorin exposed the machinations of the imperialists while the USA delegate Adlai Stevenson could not produce a single bit of convincing evidence in defense of the American aggression.

That the weapons were placed in Cuba by the Soviet government, that they were indeed formidable, broke suddenly upon a Soviet press in the midst of its campaign of protest and vituperation. The Soviet leader himself on October 28 admitted as much in his message to President Kennedy. This switch in the official attitude caught *Izvestia* off guard. It found itself denouncing on an inside page the "unclean consciences" of those persons in the USA who propose giving up some American bases near Soviet territory in exchange for depriving Cuba of the means of repelling an American aggression, while on page one appeared Mr. Khrushchev's note to President Kennedy offering to remove from Cuba "what you regard as offensive weapons." Soviet newspaper readers and radio listeners were not informed that Soviet vessels and those of other nationalities carrying peaceful cargoes had been passed by the quarantine and that others had voluntarily turned back. They were not told that work on Soviet missile bases had been stopped; they were not told of the argument over inspection or of the differences between Cuba and the Soviet government over this point. The press never tried to explain the big switch in attitude. "One day it was rolling out a chorus of indignation, a few days later it was chorusing 'peace' and 'triumph of reason.' "[6] The outcome? According to the Soviet press version, the Soviet government, guided by its Leninist policy of peaceful coexistence, made fresh moves to save the world from catastrophe. In a letter to the American President, Savior-of-the-Peace Khrushchev offered to withdraw those weapons and in return the USA pledged not to invade Cuba. This generous proposal by the Soviet government was warmly welcomed by the entire world. The planet was pulled back from the brink of nuclear war. As a result the tense situation was eased and the United States suffered a great moral and political defeat. The wisdom and firmness of Soviet policy produced a great victory for the cause of peace.

The picture the Tass World Service presents of the Soviet Union and its behavior is like this view of the great leader among nations which seeks only to influence the world in the paths of virtue and peace. Furthermore the Soviet Union's world leadership extends also into areas of technological, scientific, cultural, and economic progress. But Tass chooses to ignore these very same areas of progress in the United States.[7] The Soviet Union is pictured as a country where more housing units are being built than in the United States, where power stations are popping up like radishes in a hothouse, and where agricultural quotas and production records are being broken year after year. So that this vision of success will not be marred, Tass ignored the problems of consumer goods shortages, crop failures, and existence of hoodlums in Soviet society.[8]

Kruglak found this same image of wisdom, tranquility, and harmony extended to the entire Soviet Bloc countries and Communist China in late 1959 before the idyllic picture was shattered by the Sino-Soviet quarrel. The impression that one gained of East-West tensions from an examination of the Tass World Service was one of "the good guys versus the bad guys." All was unity among Communist countries, neutral countries were friendly toward the USSR, while all was discord and strife in the West.

An examination of the New York *Times* world report for the same period of time revealed nothing resembling this Tass view of world behavior.[9]

ADVERTISING'S MILD MESSAGES

Leninist dogma to the contrary, advertising in its various forms has from the beginning been used as a means of communication and persuasion in the Soviet Union. Signs, billboards, exhibits, directories, window displays, and similar forms have been used by the State production and distribution monopolies to direct consumers to merchandise. The print media have published without charge as a part of their duty such matters as notices about meetings and

Вкусно,
сытно,
аппетитно!
Хрустящие
хлебцы
1

Министерство торговли СССР
Главмясорыбторг
Покупайте
сухой
молочный
омлет!
Состав омлета:
2

Министерство торговли РСФСР
Росбакалея
Пейте кофе
натуральный!
Тот, кто кофе утром пьет,
целый день не устает
3

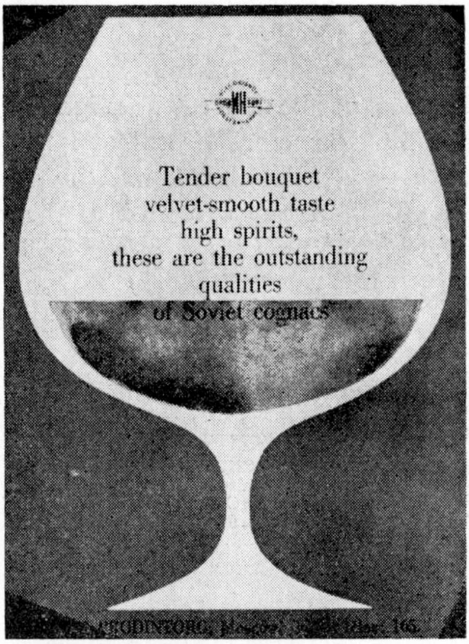
Tender bouquet
velvet-smooth taste
high spirits,
these are the outstanding
qualities
of Soviet cognacs
4

Не забудьте
индекс и номер
Москва К-31
ул. Жданова д. 7 кв. 54
Гришину С.И.
5

events, theatre and cinema announcements, and radio and television schedules. The party and the government traditionally employ advertising forms to promote nationwide political campaigns, and their slogans have become familiar benchmarks of the 5-year-plan drives. Classified advertisements have been used by those trading in secondhand goods. However, commercial advertising, a form of communication that has thrived most readily in capitalist economies, is compartively new but growing rapidly, as we have seen in an earlier chapter.

Since Soviet news, opinion, and even entertainment and art forms are heavily persuasive, it is surprising to find advertising matter generally the opposite—quiet and restrained (Fig. 6.4). Apparently advertising devoted to motion pictures, soaps, tobacco, staples, and insurance is not too greatly different from that of West-

6

7

Fig. 6.4. Soviet commercial advertising of the earlier period from about 1958 to 1963 was naive by Madison Avenue standards. Recently advertising messages have acquired more sophistication. Earlier advertisements are (1) biscuit ad in **Evening Moscow;** text: "Tasty, Filling, Appetizing." (2) Ad for packaged omelet in same paper reads: "Tasty, nourishing, easily digestible—Sold in all grocery stores." (3) A billboard ad for coffee advises that "He who drinks coffee in the morning does not get tired all day." More recent advertisements include: (4) ad in English for Soviet cognacs; (5) fountain pen ad saying, "Don't forget the index and number: use your fountain pen to write it down; (6) Volga automobiles; and (7) coffee "au naturale."

ern countries.[10] Unlike in the United States, however, State lotteries and winners are advertised. The most frequently used "formula" of advertising consists of the product brand, an illustration of the product, and a list of outlets where the product may be purchased. When more than a single product is to be promoted—if indeed such "mild" advertising can be called promotion—stores buy space to call attention in general terms to the variety of merchandise they carry.

Advertising copy does not possess vigor and emphasis. There are occasional messages in the form of jingles, the Soviet counterpart of the singing commercial and a cultural softener for brash commercialism. Here is one example:

> For breakfast and on the march
> Or as a snack for dinner
> Buy some processed cheese
> It's always a winner . . . .[11]

Messages also lack "hard-sell" characteristics. A biscuit advertisement in *Vechernaya Moskva* (Evening Moscow) reads, "Tasty, filling, appetizing"; another, for a packaged omelet, describes the product as "tasty, nourishing, easily digestible, and sold in all grocery stores"; still another reminds the customer that she can "select prints and solid color materials for any season." Typical are such messages as, "Mother is happy when she owns baby furniture"; or one reminding mothers, "It is very comfortable to ride in a baby carriage. No jerking, no shaking." [12] A coffee ad advises, "He who drinks coffee in the morning does not get tired all day." Another for Caspian herring declares that "the quality of this herring is in no way inferior to other brands of herring." [13] More than half the advertising space in local newspapers is given over to public notices consisting simply of announcements either that goods are available for purchase or that a buyer wants something; also to service advertising, such as the cards of cleaners, shoe repairmen, and schools. Divorce declarations, required by law, often are held over until space is available.

If the messages and themes are sober and simple, so also are the physical forms in which they are cast. Mass media advertisements are short, tiny, and unostentatious. Like a timid guest at a party who sits tucked away in a corner and tries hard not to attract attention, advertisements tend to be crowded together and are limited in most newspapers to less than one column. All newspapers are small by USA standards, usually running four pages and seldom more than eight.

In the promotion of political and social programs, matchbox covers, road signs, and even such small surface items as postage stamps carry reminders of 7-year-plan goals and messages about current campaigns.[14] It is not clear whether this kind of State advertising could be classified as commercial. Patriotic themes depicting the country's achievements such as "Laika, the first traveler in the cosmos," are favorite subjects. Such themes appear everywhere and decorate unexpected surfaces, often without regard for the fitness of the message for the audience reached. It is difficult to see what the city dweller who smokes can do about fattening the nation's pigs or about guaranteeing a fruit orchard to every collective farm; yet some matchboxes urge him to do these things. Other common slogans are: "Corn—a Valuable Feed Crop"; "Organize Cattle Fattening"; "Glorify Soviet Science"; and "More Honey and Wax for the Nation." This barrage of indoctrination messages constitutes one grand national commercial[15] of which the American counterpart is the avalanche of product commercials that crowd the airwaves and squeeze editorial matter up to a few inches from the top of inside pages. In comparison with the volume of what might be called institutional advertising in the Soviet Union, that in the United States dealing with the sale of government bonds, the promotion of patriotic drives, etc., is small. No field of advertising in the Soviet Union shows as much continuity, follow-up, and campaign planning as do these campaigns devoted to building the socialist state. Billboards too appear to be a favorite medium for this sort of promotion.

Judged by United States or British advertising volume, the amount of advertising in the USSR appeared to be comparatively small. Mass media advertising volume was so small that there was little chance it would compete seriously with editorial matter for space and time. Advertisers, of course, were not permitted either to sponsor programs on the air or influence their formation and content. The newspaper press in 1963 was still devoting relatively little space to advertising. Evening papers tended to carry more than the great national dailies *Pravda* and *Izvestia,* both of which limited their advertising space to about one column a day, and none of it purely product advertising. Magazine advertisements, except for those in trade publications, occupied minute proportions of space, and this was true even of such a likely medium as the weekly

Ogonyok. Radio commercials were confined to 5- to 30-minute blocks of time once or twice a day. Television commercials consumed limited though increasing quantities of time. In the face of this apathetic attitude, demand for outlets both by domestic and foreign advertisers seeking to reach the large Soviet market was increasing.

The government has attempted to do something about the unaggressive qualities in Soviet copy, but without too much success. "Zestless, uninformative advertisements" have drawn the scorn of the Soviet Ministry of Culture.[16] In response, the Soviet Union Conference of Workers in Commercial Advertising forthwith decided that the Russian people should have more art and news in their advertising copy. This newly organized group urged that Soviet copywriters make their advertising copy more aesthetic in appeal and attractive to the eye. The Ministry of Culture also chided advertising men for turning out deceptive copy. Goods not available had been advertised, and other examples of misleading copy were cited. Since the advertising bureaus are themselves government agencies, this incident might be roughly comparable to a situation in the United States in which the Secretary of Health, Education, and Welfare scolds the Secretary of Commerce for running deceptive advertising.

There were several interpretations of what role advertising is to play in the Soviet Union. One was its function as a marketing device simply to move sluggish goods or introduce new products. Now that commercial advertising had become an accepted practice the prevailing view was to rationalize Communist advertising as "pure and different" from capitalist advertising, arguing that socialist planners have the people's welfare at heart while capitalist advertising is ignorant of people's interests and "is concerned exclusively with the enrichment of individual entrepreneurs." [17] Professor Istvan Varga of Karl Marx University of Economics in Budapest claimed that honest distinction can be drawn between the function of socialist and capitalist advertising.[18] Capitalist advertising, he wrote, serves the interests of a particular private company while socialist advertising serves the interests of the community as a whole. "Socialist advertising is therefore not competitive in character but helps fulfill the economic plan by exerting an active influence on demand," he added. At the same time Professor Varga did not explain why the demand created by socialist advertising is necessarily more wholesome than that created by capitalist advertising.

Although becoming more unpopular, the view has persisted that advertising, whether capitalistic or communist, is equivalent to economic waste. Fears have been voiced that Soviet advertising might fall into the "wicked ways" of its Western counterpart. Housewives have complained that advertising makes products sound more attractive than they actually are. For example, the pitfalls of capitalistic advertising were pictured in a satire on America by Ilya Ilf and Yevgeni Petrov in part as follows: "The American does not have to think about anything; the huge commercial concerns think for him. . . . Drink Coca-Cola . . . Coca-Cola is good for the manufacturer and the country! Capitalist advertising, persistent, sensational, capable of deafening the consumer, seeks only to sell goods, to force them on the buyer by any means. Soviet commercial advertising pursues entirely different aims." [19]

Although the regime has made it plain that one of its current goals is to improve the living conditions of the average man (which means, among other things, an increased supply of consumer goods and more purchasing power), it has not taken into full account the power of advertising in stimulating demand. Advertising could be used in such a way that it might play a major role in increasing the Gross National Product, aiding the government substantially in its efforts to improve living conditions. Obviously the government thinks that advertising can be made useful in helping attain socialist goals. For this reason it has sought to make advertising appear respectable and therefore acceptable to Soviet citizens. This idea appears to be the basis of an emerging policy on advertising—a policy whose immediate objectives are the practical ones of helping to solve the economic problems that lately have beset the planners.

Official statements have stressed advertising as an "educator of public taste." The magazine *Sovetskaya Kultura* (Soviet Culture) announced the following as purposes of Soviet advertising: (1) to educate public taste, (2) to develop demand, (3) to help consumers quickly find what they want to buy, (4) to help them buy it easily, and (5) to tell them the price.[20]

However the development of commercial advertising may eventually affect the Soviet economy or communications media economy, it will continue to be useful as a medium of mass communication.

RADIO AND TELEVISION FARE

Broadcasting in the Soviet Union is regarded primarily as another means of popular cultural education and political indoctrination. Policy governing what goes on the air, therefore, has been largely determined on the basis of the extent to which it fulfills these functions.[21] Because the airwaves, like the printing presses, are manipulated by the state and not by the people, what is broadcast suits the manipulators' idea of what the people need or will tolerate. Although one of the objectives of radio was to provide a "constructive means of relaxation," the value of entertainment as a basic function of the broadcast media—a fundamental function in Western eyes—has only recently received some recognition in the Soviet Union. Mannes reported in 1961 that ". . . the set is a governess or a professor 90 per cent of the time, and an entertainer or a palliative 10 per cent—an almost exact inversion of our [United States'] programming." [22] This is not to say that such a ratio represents the undiluted will of the planners.

As a matter of fact the broadcasting administration has been charged officially as much with the responsibility of improving program quality as of paying attention to public wants. As in the case of the press, the public makes its feelings known by means of voluminous letter writing. Complaint and criticism from both the authorities and the public keep broadcasting constantly under review, at least theoretically (Fig. 6.5). In addition, broadcasting has its conferences of listeners and viewers which provide further means of modifying fare according to audience wishes. Letters from the audience provide the broadcasting administration's primary source of information about audience reaction. It has been estimated that daily mail to the Moscow Television Studio averages 10 thousand letters, and All-Union Radio's mail in 1958 reached 403 thousand letters. Studies of the time budgets of workers reveal information about time spent watching television and listening to radio. Out of 100 persons interviewed, 67 watched television during the course of a week. Regarding content, letters object to dull fare, repetition, long tedious official reports, and the like. However, since public opnion is not the ultimate authority, it seldom brings about more than minor changes in programming. Hence polling, so far as is known in the West, has not been employed on an extensive scale and there are few audience ratings to aid in the determination of program content. Watching and listening are officially

Fig. 6.5. A 1952 cartoon in **Krokodil** attacks Radio Free Europe.
Tiny bird to large grackle: "How did you get so dirty?"
Grackle: "I accidentally got tangled with the waves of Radio Free Europe."

sanctioned as approved social behavior, and in line with this policy, concessions are made to public taste and interest. Ultimately, though, program content and structure are controlled. Moreover the regime continuously appraises, apparently without the aid of polls, for its own satisfaction the effectiveness of both content and performance.

In the middle 1960s Radio Moscow was broadcasting throughout the country three simultaneous domestic programs in 70 languages. The first program consisted of political and economic talks, regular relays from Eastern Europe, and general music. The second and third programs offered fares of a generally higher intellectual caliber. Approximately 60 per cent of the air time (which in the Moscow area totaled almost 24 hours a day) was devoted to music. The ratio of serious to popular music on the Central network programs ran about four to one. Other kinds of programming consisted of relays from theatre and opera, educational and scientific material for specialized groups in agriculture, industry, and the professions, and for housewives and children. More than 50 per cent of broadcasting time for both radio and television has been consistently allocated to cultural subjects because broadcasting's education-indoctrination mission includes the duty of stimulating cultural advancement and elevating public taste. In this connection a distinguishing characteristic of Soviet programming has been the use of readings from great works of literature, with some emphasis for didactic purposes upon political polemics. However, almost any kind of literary selection is subject to interpretive slanting in the service of the familiar themes. Children's programs from the first have received special attention and the importance attached to them is indicated by the large blocks of air time allocated to them.

In 1961, telecasting centers in both Moscow and Leningrad provided two simultaneous channels that were on the air about 9 hours daily and about 13 hours on Sunday. In 1965 the Moscow Center was beaming three channels some 25 hours a day. There was one local, one national, and a third channel used for educational purposes. A new production center was scheduled to open in 1965 to serve the three stations, and construction had begun again on what will be the world's highest reinforced concrete television tower, a 1,250-foot tower topped by a 450-foot steel antenna. Color programming for the general public is scheduled to start in 1967. *Molniya I,* the Russian counterpart of communications satellites Telstar and Relay, was orbited in May 1965 and designed to bring television to remote areas. The relatively few hours of total air time in an average day and television's relegation largely to evening hours are decisions that have been prompted by an awareness of the distractive, time-consuming requirements of the medium. Officials and communications executives have taken care to see that television does not interfere with work routines. Television in the home during daytime hours must not lure housewives away from productive work with unproductive viewing. Anyway, most housewives work at regular jobs during the daytime hours.

Back in 1954, television time on the air was still more limited than it is today. A typical viewing evening in Moscow then might begin at 7 o'clock with a program announcement. A movie short, probably a travelogue, would follow to fill up the 30-minute period. At 7:30 the cameras might switch from the studio to the Maly Theatre where a production of *Ivan the Terrible* by Leo Tolstoy was to be presented. When the curtain parted, the television cameras focused on the stage. The performance became visible to the television audience exactly as it appeared to the theatre audience. Between acts the television audience was returned to the studio where a woman announced the 15-minute intermission, then the screen rested with camera focused on closed curtains until the next act began. The studio went off the air immediately after the close of the final act.

In the years since, air time has been extended and the scope of television's repertoire has shown more variety. Communications specialists have been comparatively slow to recognize the medium's potential for original productions, being content to transmit live pristine versions of sports events, opera, cinema, or concert hall entertainment directly from arena, stage, or film to viewer. Innovation in the direction of originality came primarily by moving the camera into hitherto uninvaded segments of society to give audiences a look. Style shows, lectures, factory production routines with blended background music, and sports events, specially prepared, poured out of sets. Courses in physical culture, designed for telecasting, were among the first original productions. Special events entered the field next. The annual November parade on Red Square, the air shows, and water carnivals flashed across screens. A special event of 1961, that of the traditional trooping of the color ceremony, in which Queen Elizabeth II on her birthday takes the salute of the Scots Guards amid British royal pomp, was viewed simultaneously in Moscow and in the United Kingdom, just as it happened. This unusual foray in international communication was made available to Soviet citizens, it was said, because nothing could give them a better idea of their own "democratic" way of life than this view of the Queen surrounded by some of the world's most gallant troops. It was the first time a live telecast had been sent from Britain to the Soviet Union and the result of an exchange arrangement with the British Broadcasting Corporation in response to Soviet cooperation permitting British viewers to see live the May Day parade in Moscow.

The year 1961 was also the year in which Russian viewers could receive programs from the eastern European Communist countries through Intervidenie (Intervision), and in 1963 through a link with the European international network Eurovision, the Soviet government transmitted the Telstar broadcast of President John F. Kennedy's funeral. In a new arrangement between Intervision and Eurovision signed in late 1965, news items were to be exchanged daily on a regular basis.

Perhaps the general availability to the television screen of a relatively large volume of up-to-date live material, particularly in the urban centers, has worked to discourage the proliferation of original productions. Because the theatre, the opera, ballet, the art galleries, motion picture houses, and sports arenas are all owned by the government, there are no legal impediments to restrict or delay telecasting their attractions. Box-office receipts or other economic considerations do not dictate that first-run motion pictures be shown for a period of time in theatres before being released for air presentation. Hence a new cinema production can be shown on television within two weeks after its premiere at a motion picture house. The same is true of the latest plays, Moscow games in Dynamid Stadium, and a multitude of other attractions which stand ready to feed television's voracious appetite. Theatre managers have protested against this competition from television because they are expected to make a profit, but their protests have been in vain.

Whether broadcast live or staged especially for television, approximately 430 talks a year dealing with such matters as popular science, recent agricultural methods, public health and medicine, and practical economics are predominantly educational in tone, yet often have their political slant. The lacklustre quality of such programs has come under domestic fire. For example, the experience of one Volgagrad studio with a series of lectures on education in economics was examined. According to A. Barinov, such a project could have been made interesting because it was designed to answer questions by giving concrete examples from economic life.

> How does industry gain from the installation of new techniques? How does the development of production affect the well-being of the people? How does one familiarize oneself with the investments of the seven-years plan? Undoubtedly live talk on such subjects would have aroused great interest. However it did not come about. In the studio they erected a platform from which the lecturer started to pronounce generally known, hackneyed truisms in a rapid patter (as you know, the time is limited). And that was all! But in such a manner any project can be ruined. The television screen is in itself a rostrum. Why then should another one, a wooden one, be dragged onto it? Who needs dry references to computations? Obviously the absence of professional television experience, the inability to make use of the golden opportunity of the screen, the habit of "rubber-stamping"—all this ruined the attractively conceived program on economics.[23]

Such lectures and talks are a part of public affairs information programming that occupies regularly a considerable proportion of air time on both radio and television networks. News and political propaganda programs are usually prepared from press content, mainly devoid of human interest or timely reportage.[24] Such programs frequently consist of lengthy reading of editorials clipped from *Pravda* and *Izvestia* or pedestrian statistical reports on production. Although programs of this nature, whether in news and opinion or in specialized fields, are almost always cast on an unemotional key, they are seldom without their political bent. The first program from the Moscow Television Center to 23 regions in 1962 featured the "latest news" three times a day in 10- to 20-minute telecasts. In addition there were regularly scheduled twice-a-week analyses of foreign and domestic political problems called "Foreign TV Chronicle" and "Through Our Country." Other regular weekly events are "Replies to Workers' Questions" and "Sporting Sunday." On special occasions the "latest news" department goes on the air more frequently with the latest information, as it did during the flight of the Soviet space ship. The second program, seen only by Muscovites, specialized in news of the capital. The news analyst or commentator, Western style, is only a recent development in Soviet telecasting of public affairs. In 1965, Moscow viewers were accustomed to 19 (13 female and 6 male) "diktors," staff announcers or newscasters, who read verbatim reports from Tass. Sometimes an editor appears to give his or her organ's interpretation of what is going on in the world.

Although emotional overtones are generally absent, distorted views of the facts tinged with anti-Western diatribes are frequent. Feature films are accompanied by propaganda that perpetuates the Line. The Soviet version of the Hungarian revolt, telecast some two months afterward, was depicted as it was in the press, as a reactionary counterrevolutionary uprising fomented by the United States and its capitalist allies. Khrushchev's personal appearances at the United Nations were carefully edited to show only his speaking appearances and the applause of the East European Communist bloc. The Soviet viewer did not see the delegates of some 80 nations sitting on their hands, nor did he see his leader pounding the table or waving a shoe. Western speeches are always cut to the bone, except those of Castro. As Mannes stated, the news the Soviet citizen gets to see is "that footage which redounds to the virtue and glory of the [Soviet] state . . . and only those dispatches which disparage the Western democracies and exalt the Communist or neutralist blocs." [25] Mannes concluded that dogma throttles the airwaves as it blights the printed page and the spoken word. Much of this is subtle or indirect, however, for Tuber measured only direct political propaganda of a controversial nature on Moscow television for a 6-months period in 1960 and found the maximum amount of air time devoted to this kind of propaganda to be 14 per cent for the First Program service (seen on full facilities of Central CST networks) and 9 per cent for the Second (limited to Moscow and environs). Of the news and public affairs, special events, and young adult programs, however, at least half were in categories devoted to propaganda.[26]

Propaganda opportunities offered by the new East-West agreement for the exchange of television news programs between Intervision and Eurovision were not lost on Soviet communications experts. Eurovision offers worldwide items, and events in Western Europe, but withholds nothing. In return the West is supplied with news briefs on Communist cooperation among East European countries, tours of State-operated farms and factories, Communist Party congresses, and visits from Westerners who are sympathetic with the communist way of life. As a result, the West accepts only a very few offerings from the East, and the communists accept a far larger per cent. In September, 1965, the West used only 12 out of 96 items offered. On the other hand the Soviet Union eagerly throws on its television screens such offerings as civil rights incidents in the United States, including a clip of Martin Luther King being struck in a southern hotel, and American student protests against the Vietnamese War. The absence of censorship in the West, of course, means that Communist governments can show viewers selected items portraying the West in the worst light, and the West cannot do likewise. An official of the European Broadcasting Union, the nonpolitical controlling body of Eurovision with headquarters in Geneva, said, however, "While we are not too happy about the range and quality of offerings from the East, [the agreement] is still a great step forward."

Perhaps the one single area of programming that remains relatively free of all but the subtlest propaganda touches is that area given over to children's programs. Among the most popular types of juvenile programming occupying prime evening time are the animated cartoons, the fairy tales, and the puppet shows. The latter borrow from the techniques of the famous Russian puppet theatre and rank among the best of such entertainment anywhere.

When Mannes asked Soviet television directors what they considered to be the main function of the medium, the answer came with conviction: "To make better people, to develop their tastes." But how, Mannes asked, can television become an art form so long as there are constant limitations on freedom of expression without which creative impetus cannot exist? N. A. Sakontikov, chief editor of Moscow programming, answered the question. "In time," he said, "the machinery of the state will wither away and television will become a social function." At the same time, he insisted, the foreign observer must not think of the State as apart from or superior to the broadcasters. "We are the state, and what we broadcast is what the people want." [27] Sakontikov's naïve belief in the eventual withering away of the State serves as a case in point to illustrate that much of the dogma on the Soviet airwaves possesses an escapist quality which isolates the recipient from reality. Speaking of Soviet films, some of which constitute a part of television fare, Leo Paladina of *Soviet Survey* writes, "With a few praiseworthy exceptions, soviet films . . . fall into two categories dedicated to two equally misleading myths: historical costume films . . . and films allegedly depicting 'modern life' and showing a nonexisting world of the *kolkhoz* with dancing and harvest girls and workers who spend their free time enthusiastically discussing how to increase the production of cast iron. Both categories are an escape from reality." As Mannes observes, when doctrine is served in this guise it matters not whether the fundamental aim is public entertainment as in the United States, or mass indoctrination as in the Soviet Union, the end result is the same—the use of the medium as a palliative and a soporific. What does matter depends upon the extent to which escapism is misleading in both intent and content.

Aside from the stream of dogma that flows through most media content, the materials carried on television vary in quality from the uncut original performances to programming designed for television as an art and communication form. The former represents the best to be had in television fare; the latter are generally not up to Western standards of technological and professional sophistication. Films shown are often the most recent and best cinema available. Original productions of the Bolshoi Theatre and the Russian Ballet telecast live exactly as presented are among the world's great attractions, and therefore make television fare that is as good as the original. Staple fare consists of these cultural programs which occupy a majority of time on the air—newscasts, economic reports, folk dancing, science programs, a weekly half-hour of discussion of international affairs, a current events quiz, movies, but few continuing-characters programs like those in the United States. Thus while Americans are seeing the Cartwrights in "Bonanza" or "Dr. Kildare" during prime time, Muscovites may be watching a 5-year-old German detective movie. There are no shows dubbed "Young Dr. Ivanov" or "I Love Tatiana," but there is a version of the "Ed Sullivan Show," called "Na Ogonyok" (The Blue Flame). There are no television stars, as yet; the only television personalities are the *diktors,* the staff announcers and newscasters. Except for a few cartoons promoting tomato juice and a national airline, television had been by 1965 free of commercial advertising. Commercials, however, will probably become a part of standard television fare within the next few years. Such is the emphasis that is being placed upon advertising by the regime, *Pravda* having in 1965 argued for the expansion of advertising in the Soviet economy and incidentally for an improvement in its quality. On the other hand the specially produced materials tend to be heavy, tedious, awkward, and lacking in imagination. As a general rule discussion materials and routine announcements feature people reading from notes. Spontaneous exchanges are rare. An occasional program devoted to public criticism consists of the reading of letters, some of which complain about unpopular fare. Television officials admit shortcomings and say they are striving to eliminate them. Television style is scored occasionally by *Krokodil* as stodgy and awkward. A cartoon deplores classical symphony concerts because they are long and tiresome. Another satirizes interview programs, depicting one in which an interviewer monopolizes the conversation leaving barely enough time for the distinguished authority to squeeze a word in edgewise. Another lampoons "how-to-do-it" pieces as boring and quiz shows as inane. While as yet television criticism is not a specialized field in journalism and no television critics have appeared, television is subjected to the same kind of criticism in the media and by the higher echelons of the broadcasting party and government hierarchy that the press receives. Recently a journalist was assigned the job of watching television for a whole week and writing a critical report. His conclusions described the content as "stultifying." The same thing could have happened in the United States of America.

All in all it can be said that Soviet broadcasters have succeeded in their efforts to elevate public taste, if one is to judge this by the large volume of high-level cultural content. The maintenance of such standards has tended to elevate the general character and reputation of Soviet broadcasting. The value to Soviet leaders of television as a propaganda instrument as compared to that of the press and radio remains relatively untested. As yet they tend to appraise its performance with more caution and less confidence than they do the older media, perhaps because they have not yet learned to use it skillfully for their singular purposes. The official goal of television in the Soviet Union has been set forth in a manual for broadcasters. "It should be the chief goal of telecasting," the guide states, "to propagandize party decisions. . . . it should throw light on the program of fulfilling the seven-year plan, should popularize and educate the Soviet people in Communist morality, collectivism, and industriousness." [42]

7 ★

HOW THE MEDIA PERFORM: THE SPECIALIZED JOURNALS

DESPITE THEIR ASSIGNED FUNCTIONS, *Pravda* and *Izvestia* may be classified as national information organs of general appeal cutting across classes and cultures and special interests. The Soviet communication system also makes sure that the communist education of the masses accomplishes its task with media whose function and purpose aim them vertically toward various groups, interests, strata, and segments of the society at all levels. Here will be examined and analyzed the content disseminated under selected titles from the leading specialized newspapers and magazines—voices of labor, youth, young adults, writers and artists, women's interests, cinema, party magazines, and the literary journals. The only magazines discussed here that are intended for broad general appeal are the Soviet picture magazine, *Ogonyok,* and the magazine of satire, *Krokodil.*

Trud: Respected Organ of Labor

Trud (Labor), is the influential, respected organ of the All-Union Central Council of Professional Unions. Founded in 1921, it had a daily circulation of approximately 2 million in 1965. The 4-page edition sells for two kopecks. In general appearance and makeup *Trud* resembles party and government dailies. Its contents are devoted mainly to the laboring man. The editorial fills the two left-hand columns of the first page of the September 8, 1965 issue (Fig. 7.1). The title is "Work Book," and the essay discusses the importance of keeping records of a worker's career and particularly of keeping those records accurately. "The laborer's work book," the editorial begins. "In its pages with miserly words are imprinted our life, our labor. One glances at some of them and is glad for their owners; one experiences a feeling of joy, pride—what a clear, straight road!" The editorial next cites the example of Vero Pavolvna Vorobova's workbook. Her work route began in a vocational school in the stormy days of the war. In 1944 she entered the Kemerovski coke chemical plant and worked there as a technician for 21 years. Of this kind of record, one can be proud, the editorial says, and goes on to point out the need and importance of such records. Yet many persons regard the document carelessly. "Readers of *Trud* obviously remember this newspaper's performance in defense of Khabarovsk worker F. N. Spesivtsev, who from confusion and mistakes in his work book almost lost his right to a favorable pension." The rest of the discussion concerns the problems caused by inefficient and inadequate work records. Too many workers do not find time to look at their workbooks and remember them only when retirement time comes and evidence to justify a pension must be presented. Hundreds of thousands of cases whose trials occupy retirement boards and all sorts of pension misunderstandings have as their origins mistakes in the workbook.

The top right of the front page displays two photographs about a new state farm threshing floor. One picture shows the floor and the other shows metal worker V. Siropin on duty at the threshing floor's control panel. Underneath the photographs is a collection of NEWS FROM THE FIELDS. We read here that 94.2 million hectares of grain have been reaped, that there has been a massive harvest of potatoes and vegetables, that the rice crop has ripened, that the combines are in the beet fields, and that autumn sowing is in full swing. Up above the title line, three important stories are printed; the first two say that the tempo of field work has increased and that a rare metal has been discovered in Dublin; the third is a narrative of the great deeds of the Red proletariat. There is elsewhere on the page a Tass story which describes how a Roumanian delegation is

ДЕНЬ РОДИНЫ

● ТЕМПЫ ПОЛЕВЫХ РАБОТ НАРАСТАЮТ
● БОЛЬШИЕ ДЕЛА КРАСНОПРОЛЕТАРЦЕВ
● В ДУБНЕ ПОЛУЧЕН СВЕРХЧИСТЫЙ ФРАНЦИЙ

ПРОЛЕТАРИИ ВСЕХ СТРАН, СОЕДИНЯЙТЕСЬ!

ТРУД

ТРУДОВАЯ КНИЖКА

С БЕРЕГОВ ВОЛГИ — В ГОРОД НА НЕВЕ

ВЕСТИ С ПОЛЕЙ

СТАРТ БУМАГОДЕЛАТЕЛЬНОГО ГИГАНТА

АТОМ РОЖДАЕТ РЕДКИЙ ЭЛЕМЕНТ

Дворец культуры профсоюзов в Рязани

ГОРОД ДВАДЦАТИ ОЗЕР

ПО ПРИГЛАШЕНИЮ ДРУЗЕЙ

ЗООПАРК НА ИРТЫШЕ

Путь начинается отсюда...

ПРЕБЫВАНИЕ В МОСКВЕ А. НОВОТНОГО

ТРУД

Трудовой день нашей Родины

НЕУКОСНИТЕЛЬНО ВЫПОЛНЯТЬ ЗАКОНЫ О ТРУДЕ

В восемь раз быстрее, втрое дешевле

Казанский порт строится

Fig. 7.1. **Trud,** Soviet labor's daily organ of the All-Union Central Council of Professional Unions, has also undergone considerable revamping of its front page. The issue of September 8, 1965 (left), is compared with that of October 6, 1953. The multitude and variety of typographical devices, the use of boxes, and horizontal rather than vertical display are apparent.

touring the country ". . . from the shores of the Volga to the city on the Neva." On September 7, the story says, the party visited the shrine honoring the heroes of the Battle of Stalingrad. A government story reports a meeting of Premier A. N. Kosygin with the Pakistan ambassador. The rest of the page is concerned with domestic news, mostly constructive reports about a new paper mill, the creation of artificial lakes, praise for workers in the Red proletariat machine tool factory, and a story which says "professional unions and youth are true fighters for peace."

Pages two and three of this issue of *Trud* present inspirational and ideological copy. An article tells about construction workers building a new electric power station and a photograph shows workers assembling turbines. There is a letter to the editor pointing to the need to centralize the shipping of bricks.

International news summaries appear on page four. There are

stories from world news centers by *Trud* correspondents, and condensed summaries of what the newspapers of the world are saying: a dispatch from London reports a meeting of the Congress of British Trade Unions; from Cairo the headline says CONSPIRATORS RENDERED HARMLESS; CRUSHED BY NASSER; from New York a message states that United Nations Secretary General U Thant has left for Pakistan and India to attempt to settle the dispute between the two nations; also from New York the Associated Press report of the Labor Day weekend automobile traffic death toll is quoted, showing 538 dead in holiday accidents. A lengthy analytical story with illustrations from both sides of the 38th Parallel in Korea presents this viewpoint: "Twenty years ago U.S. troops settled down in the South Korean peninsula, taking the place of the Japanese. After the Japanese occupation came the American occupation. Since that time not for one day has the South Korean people's struggle for their liberation ceased. The people seek liberation from their 'liberators' from across the ocean, and reunification of Korea on a peaceful and democratic basis." Elsewhere a Tass statement concerns itself with the India-Pakistan affair, concluding that the tendency toward further expansion of the India-Pakistan conflict is more and more aggravated by the tense situation in South and Southeast Asia created by the aggression of the USA against the Vietnamese people. "The prospect of armed conflict between India and Pakistan stirs serious anxiety in the Soviet Union which always holds dear the business of maintaining the peace . . . ."

Komsomolskaya Pravda: Youth's Watchdog and Journalistic Pace-Setter

This well-illustrated paper for the younger set is the organ of the Young Communist League, whose members are in the 15–28 age bracket. *Komsomolskaya Pravda* (Young Communist League's Truth) customarily employs a brisker, simpler style and a livelier makeup than most of the other dailies (Fig. 7.2). It differs also in the amount of human interest material it carries, treating of such themes as student ethics and morality, sex and romance, and various other youth problems. In 1965 its circulation was reported at 5.2 million.

Throughout the latter half of the 1950s, hardly a week passed without some major discussion in *Komsomolskaya Pravda,* or other youth publications, reflecting consternation over apathy, rebellion,

ПРОЛЕТАРИИ ВСЕХ СТРАН, СОЕДИНЯЙТЕСЬ!

Комсомольская правда

Орган Центрального Комитета ВЛКСМ

И ДАРИТ ТУНДРА ТЕПЛО

В ОБСТАНОВКЕ БРАТСКОЙ ДРУЖБЫ

НОВОСТИ

ТОРЖЕСТВЕННЫЙ ВЕЧЕР

ОТРЯДЫ ДЕРЖАТ КУРС НА БРЕСТ

Комсомольская правда

Орган Центрального Комитета ВЛКСМ

ДЕНЬ НАШЕЙ РОДИНЫ

СТРОЙКИ ОДНОГО КОЛХОЗА

ЗАВОДЫ — СЕЛУ

ПОСТОЯННО СНИЖАТЬ СЕБЕСТОИМОСТЬ УГЛЯ

Fig. 7.2. Possibly no other Soviet newspaper has undergone greater changes in appearance in the post-Stalin era than **Komsomolskaya Pravda**, the daily organ of the Young Communist League. The first page of the September 5, 1965, issue (left) employs the ultimate in border contrasts, pictures, typographical and other display devices, to place its messages in the most attractive settings. There are examples of human interest in the material. It can be compared with the relatively dull appearance of an earlier issue going back to the immediate post-Stalin period of 1953 (right).

and nonconformity among the rising generation. This admission is a puzzling paradox to the Kremlin's boast that the flights of its young astronauts prove the "superiority" of the "New Soviet Man" over the product of other societies. When undesirable attitudes result in frequent cases of delinquency, *Komsomolskaya Pravda* officially blames two main causes: The disruptions of home and family wrought by the war, and the influence of "capitalist encirclement" which injects "foreign poisons" into the consciousness of some Soviet young people, confusing their true values and "trivializing" their aspirations.[1] The paper's efforts to remedy or alleviate the situation were no more successful than those it made to overcome apathy toward joining the Young Communist League. Nevertheless, the public campaign in *Komsomolskaya Pravda* against youthful crimes, drunkenness, sexual delinquency, and drug addiction continues despite the fact that scandals rarely make news in the Soviet Union.

Komsomolskaya Pravda published on May 19, 1960, the results of the first Soviet public opinion poll conducted by the newly organized Public Opinion Institute as an affiliate of the paper. The poll addressed three questions to a representative sample of 1,000 persons living in ten localities of an area chosen because it had firsthand experience of war. The first question asked whether in the opinion of the respondent mankind can successfully prevent war, and the two other questions were, "On what do you base your conclusion?" and "What must be done first of all to strengthen peace?" It is not surprising that 96.8 per cent of the respondents expressed their belief that war could be prevented. There were many suggestions on how to prevent war, and the Institute did not fail to stress the similarity between these suggestions and party policies, implying that the party knows what the people want.[2] Later polls asked the people's views about their present living standards as compared with those of the recent past, questioned readers of *Komsomolskaya Pravda* about what they thought about their generation, and inquired about the high divorce rate in the Soviet Union.

The Public Opinion Institute of *Komsomolskaya Pravda* has become the major agency in the Soviet Union engaged in gauging the mood of various strata of the population, and the polls have become an accepted means of gathering information that can be used to support the over-all Agitprop effort. Opinions collected can be used as examples of correct or incorrect attitudes and thus document with actual cases various indoctrination lessons. By sampling public opinion the regime demonstrates that it is interested in learning what the people think so that it can act upon the findings, thereby encouraging public participation and helping overcome indifference. Dr. George Gallup of the American Institute of Public Opinion reported in 1965 that Russia had aproximately 200 polling organizations, but as yet no nationwide poll. The studies are conducted in research institutes and are generally confined to local areas, he said. Although they include market surveys to help solve production and distribution problems, Gallup found no evidence that polls had been taken on political issues.

The October 6, 1965, issue of *Komsomolskaya Pravda* shows very little differentiation in general appearance from the other newspapers, except that the faces in the photographs are of younger people. The top of the front page of this issue is devoted to some 28 column inches of world news and comment gleaned from Tass, Agence France-Presse, Reuters, the *Arbeiterbladet, La Prensa,* and *Siglo.* Much of the international news is the same as that we have already read in *Pravda* and *Izvestia* of this date. To the right side of the page, however, we find something new—an article describing the problems of a kolkhoz which is seeking to build a sports stadium and a culture center. Inadequate existing facilities for athletics and the performing arts are noted, as is the fact that the kolkhoz has the necessary funds to build. But, the story says, certain officials had decided to spend some of the money to build spare pigsties. Then, however, they grudgingly allocated some funds and building materials to the stadium-culture center project. Now a new problem has arisen—that of getting the construction trust to begin work. The writer bases his plea for new facilities on the ground that this is not simply a favor to be granted from surplus funds, but that such an investment will be repaid in increased productivity as a result of improved morale. A large illustrated story concerning mining operations by the Viktor Tikhomirov komsomol youth brigade rates a 3-column spread at the top, while another illustrated display at the bottom details army enlistment procedures, picturing a young soldier in uniform describing the attractions of military service to four potential recruits. The WE CONGRATULATE section hails the naming of Vartan Mkrtichevich as Peoples Artist of the USSR.

Domestic and local affairs on page two are dominated by a 6-column-wide grouping of pictures—portraits of a young man and a young woman flanking an oil refinery photograph. A student fills 37 column inches writing about the timber industry at Bratsck. A correspondent in another item hails the leadership of master commissars in vocational training. One full column on page three serves as a tribute to a komsomol soldier-poet killed in 1942, the short account accompanied by three of his poems. The rest of this page exploits the international news for didactic purposes in teaching youth. Slightly more than one-fourth of the page deals with social problems in Washington, an article written by Gary Frimen, who is identified as "an American publicist." Part of the story reads like this: "Washington is the capital of a government, but it's different from the majority of other great capitals, let's say Moscow, London, Paris, or Rome. In this city there is no industrial enterprise and the spiritual life is quite poor. A sharp contrast between rich and poor is characteristic of all big cities of the United States. But in none of them is there such a striking contrast between the pompous life of the minority and the vegetative life of the majority as in Washington." With this story is a photograph of Negroes praying on the church steps, not in Washington but in Americus, Georgia, as whites block their entrance to the church.

A good example of lively writing appears under COMMENTARY OF THE DAY and the heading NINETY MINUTES OF "FREEDOM." The story stresses anticolonialism: "Two days the South Arabian town of Aden lived in a state of siege. With the approach of dusk, residents, under fear of cruel punishment, were afraid to leave home. Through deserted streets passed only patrols of English soldiers armed to the teeth. Saturday night the state of siege was lifted. And in the first minutes, despite the late hour, onto the steets poured crowds of people scanning slogans: 'Down with colonialism!' 'Englishmen, go home!' " Short items from scattered points around the world are included: A hat made of dollar bills worn by Mrs. Ivy Baker Stevens provides the opportunity for a jibe about her candidacy for treasurer of California. ONE-ARMED BANDITS describes the spread of slot machines in Belguim. A lengthy WORD ABOUT NILS BOR written by academician L. Landau commemorates the eightieth birthday of the Danish scientist.

Almost one-third of page four, called AFTER THE VERDICT, is filled with the notes of a lawyer. An interview by a Tass correspondent with K. N. Postnov, deputy chief of the Central Board for the Dissemination of the Press, Ministry of Communication, reveals that subscriptions to all Central newspapers and magazines except *Nedelia, Izvestia's* supplement, and *Football,* the *Sovetsky Sport* supplement, are being promoted without restriction, and total single-issue subscription sales for Central newspapers and magazines was 35,241,600. A substantial section is devoted to readers' letters. Sports news includes a picture of two fishermen, accounts of the Olympic Council meeting in Italy, shooting matches, tourneys, and championships. Radio and television program guides and the weather forecast fill out the page.

Pioneerskaya Pravda: Russia's "Scouting" Daily

Pioneerskya Pravda (Young Pioneers' Truth) is the world's largest circulation youth daily, with totals for September, 1965, of 7.5 million copies (Fig. 7.3). It is the tabloid-sized organ of the All-Union Leninist Communist Youth's League and of the Central

Пролетарии всех стран, соединяйтесь!

Орган Центрального комитета ВЛКСМ и Центрального совета Всесоюзной пионерской организации имени В. И. Ленина

Ко всем пионерам страны!

Сияйте ленинские звезды!

Пионерский марш мира и дружбы

Малая олимпиада пяти колец

Поход боевой славы

Вахта труда

Fig. 7.3. Pages 1 (right) and 4 of a four-page issue of the largest circulation children's daily newspaper in the world. The organ of the Central Council of the All-Union Pioneer Organization, **Pioneerskaya Pravda's** September 7, 1965, issue can be opened up as one sheet to form a poster for display in classrooms and Pioneer dens. The usual black and white of adult newspaper pages is relieved here by bright inks. The campfire near the center is in red and yellow, with background shrubs in green. However, the stock used allows an excessive amount of "show through," clearly evident in the above reproduction. The pages are filled with stories, games, and puzzles featuring Lenin and Soviet slogans, emblems, and themes, all tempered with the usual moralistic exhortation.

Council of the All-Union Pioneers' Organization in the Name of V. I. Lenin. The slogan enjoining the workers of the world to unite appears in the title line of *Pioneerskaya Pravda* and with it another slogan reads "Be Prepared for the Struggle in the Cause of the Communist Party." The September 7, 1965, issue can be opened up to form a poster to advertise the Young Pioneers' Organization. Directions say, "Open it, children, and you will see that the first and fourth pages of this newspaper are a POSTER. You are invited to post it in classrooms, Pioneer dens, and other appropriate places." The poster shows a big red-and-yellow campfire in a setting of green grass and shrubs. Around the fire are groups of children engaged in various forms of recreation or listening to youth leaders, one of whom is a Soviet soldier in uniform. Most of the youths wear the red neckerchief of the Pioneers. A Pioneer emblem with the head of Lenin against a star and banner also are printed in red.

Articles in *Pioneerskaya Pravda* are neither as long nor as complex as those of the adult papers. Still the content is, of course, similar. The ideological and educational-moralistic overtones are always present. Most of the hard news of the day is not included. At the top of page one is this address and greeting from the Central Council of the All-Union Pioneers' Organization in the Name of V. I. Lenin: "To all Pioneers of the Country: Young Pioneers! In two years our beloved motherland—the Union of Soviet Socialist Republics—will solemnly mark the 50th anniversary of the Great October [Revolution]. In honor of the 50th anniversary of the Great October an All-Union review of the work of Pioneer detachments of the country has begun. To the credit of the Soviet Pioneer one finds many good and fine works for the use of the Motherland. To you workers and builders we say thanks for hundreds of tons of scrap metal . . . ." The address acknowledges contributions of the Young Pioneers and suggests other areas in which they can serve, including gift contributions for children in "embattled Vietnam and heroic Cuba." Another article, providing inspiration for the "Labor Watch," notes that this year the Soviet people completed the 7-year plan, during which time many new electric power stations and mines, factories and plants, schools and houses were built—and the "clincher" avers that "in everything Leninist youth helped their elders." The story ends with the reminder that the symbol of the labor watch is the Sickle and Hammer—and the symbol is printed in red ink at the end.

On pages two and three there are several features more simply written but much like those appearing in the adult press. An educational travelogue-type story on Bulgaria says that September 9 is the Day of Freedom and a national holiday for the Bulgarian people. It describes a scene like this: "The road winds through the Rodopsky Mountains. Suddenly the machine turns sharply. The driver announces, 'The old road is already under water.' From the crossing everything is spread before the eyes. In the rays of the mountain sun gleams the reservoir of the hydroelectric station . . . ." A photograph shows two girls at work in a Sofia plant making quartz lamps and we read that scores of countries use Bulgarian-made motors, transformers, and medical equipment. Another photograph illustrates a story about a pioneer hike in the Southwest Pamir Mountains with Geologist Yudnim.

A science worker in melon and potato culture, I. V. Skvortsov of the Uzbek Republic writes as follows: "Luxurious autumnal Uzbek bazaars; figs, peaches, scores of varieties of grapes. But the brightest decoration of all is the melon. Whole piles of golden delicate green, satiny yellow fruit. The generosity of our earth. But what is its generosity without human industry and talent . . . ." Another writer tells about the formative experiences of his childhood; another contributes a fictional narrative of children's conversation; and V. Odintsov, a graduate student at the Institute of Russian Language, USSR Academy of Science, discusses language usage errors in a "Journey into the Land of the Dictionary." A poem by I. Kholin "Who Lives on Mars?" speculates on the probability of Martians with three legs and eight eyes, and asks could there also be bears. "It would be nice to see!"

SHINE, LENIN'S STAR! emblazoned in red ink heads the last page. The story, accompanied by a picture of a group of happy waving children, says that the All-Union Pioneer Organization wears the name of Vladimir Ilyich Lenin and on the Pioneer banner appears the Order of Lenin, making the point that each Pioneer must know well how Lenin lived and fought for the happiness of people. Other items on this page include articles about Pioneer Olympic games, the "Little Olympiad Five Rings," and a story called "The Campaign of Battle Glory" explaining the symbolism of the Soviet Army's Red Star.

Literaturnaya Gazeta: Organ of Literary Politics

Literaturnaya Gazeta (The Literary Newspaper) is another variation from the standard pattern and perhaps in a class by itself. This is the thrice-weekly, 6- to 8-page organ of the Writers' and Artists' Union. As the main literary newspaper of the country, it should deal primarily with literary affairs. However, because it is read by the leading intellectuals who in turn communicate to the masses through their creative works, it has become a direct outlet for the most important phases of official propaganda, and consistently beats the drum for party and for country. Propaganda themes in the form of attacks, charges, cartoons, and polemics invade the various departments, subtly infusing the literary discussions, the play, and motion picture reviews, the feature stories, the notes on "works in progress," or "plans for the future," the section on queries, and even meeting reports. The paper campaigned from 1950 to 1954 against segregation of the sexes in the public schools, a project that appeared to be a bold challenge to official policy, but may have received authoritative approval for advocating a change the party had decided to make anyway. The campaign was successful and segregation ended in 1954. Its bravery—if it was such—in ostensibly flaunting authority by conducting the campaign was at that time a rare occurrence in Soviet communications. During the same year, 1954, *Literaturnaya Gazeta* reviewed favorably Vera Panova's *The Seasons of the Year* while *Pravda* denounced the book. Whereupon *Literaturnaya Gazeta* quickly reversed its position, abrogating its previous assessment of the work.

Literaturnaya Gazeta ranks high in the press hierarchy as a strategic instrument through whose pages the party communicates to those who pass the word along by means of their creative output. It serves a twofold purpose and has a multiple effect, for it indoctrinates the public directly by its own printed material and indirectly through the works of Soviet writers and artists for whom it provides guidance.[3] True to its role as the regime's official voice on all matters relating to literature and art, *Literaturnaya Gazeta* repeatedly reflected the party's guiding counsel in the ferment of liberal dissent and discussion that characterized first the "Thaw" and later the "New Wave."

This small sample of what the leading national newspapers are like is sufficient to provide an impression of the kind of persuasive information the Soviet press presents to its readers. The attitudes portrayed are typical. Because of the influence over the whole country exerted by the Central Press, this sample is perhaps fairly representative. It does not, however, reflect either the wide range of the different kinds of specialized newspaper organs or the number and variety of the provincial daily and weekly press.

Having examined briefly some of the national newspapers, let us now look at the magazines.

Krokodil Bares His Teeth and Wields His Pitchfork

The magazine *Krokodil* (Crocodile) is a unique national journal in the field of humor, satire, and criticism. Although not always

Fig. 7.4. Two issues of **Krokodil** illustrate varying uses of the cover. On the left a cover cartoon aims its barb at irresponsibility of Soviet youth. The young parents dash down the hospital steps abandoning their infant with a casual suggestion to the nurse, "Give the child a good public education!" The cover on the right carries a serious social theme, celebrating a goal achievement in electric power production. Text reads: "One More World Record: 2,500,000 kilowatts."

light in touch, *Krokodil* provides a welcome relief from the usual press fare. It is meant to fulfill a function similar to that of the *New Yorker* of the United States and *Punch* of Great Britain. But it differs rather widely from these two eminent parallels. Founded in 1922 as a picture supplement to *Robochy* (Worker), *Krokodil* was publishing only about 150,000 copies in 1948 when it received instructions from the Central Committee to broaden its appeal. At the same time the Committee gave *Krokodil* a new mission, leadership in the development of indigenous Russian satire (Figs. 7.4 and 7.5). The magazine's popularity has gradually increased until in 1965, its 3-times-a-month issues were reaching 2.9 million readers. It runs 14 to 18 pages of pulp paper filled with cartoons, poems, letters from readers, jokes, *feuilletons,* and fiction stories. *Krokodil* sells for 12 kopecks. Modeled after *Krokodil,* approximately 20 other satiric periodicals appear under such tites as *Nettle, Thistle, Wasp,* and *Hornet* in the minority languages of the country. *Krokodil's* symbol or "trademark" is a somewhat stylized figure of a crocodile standing upright baring its teeth and wielding a pitchfork in a stance suggesting its ready usefulness either to plunge into the hide of obnoxious social evils or pick them up and toss them out.

Although an occasional page may be printed in black only, color is generally used throughout with cartoons and line art, in headlines, as tint block backgrounds, and for cartoons. The editors sometimes indulge in imaginative treatment of story titles and credits, turning a title on its side or standing an artist's or author's name on end, using a second color for some letters within a title, reversing a title and illustration against a solid, and other attention getters. Full-page cartoons in full color or with spot color generally appear on front and back covers, but at times a single cartoon will be replaced with a group of several smaller ones. Frequently the front cover will feature satirical cartoon commentaries on contemporary Soviet life while the back cover attacks American "Imperialism."

Fig. 7.5. Art, plumbing, and of course the United States are among the many topics satirized by **Krokodil** cartoonists. (1) A comment on the notorious incompetence of the Soviet building trade is captioned "Does your apartment also have small imperfections?" (2) Modern art comes in for its share of lampooning. The text says simply "Who's doing the aping?" Savage cartoons on the United States include (3) "The View From the Sea," with the lower panel captioned "Closeup," and (4) a comment on U.S. militarism in the Vietnamese war. The coffinlike entrance is labeled "Induction Center." The stunned American youth drops his draft notice as the skeleton in uniform laconically says "Next! Please!"

1

2

ВИД С МОРЯ...
И БЛИЖЕ
Цена номера 12 коп.

3

ПРИЗЫВНОЙ ПУНКТ
US
ПОВЕСТКА

4

A typical issue of *Krokodil* will have front and back covers in color and will contain 12 or 15 cartoons interlaced with approximately the same number of essays, fact, and fiction articles. Much of the content is drawn from reader contests like the one conducted for accounts of "the funniest thing that ever happened to me," for short stories, and for cartoon ideas. The staff uses tips and suggestions from the approximately 100,000 letters it receives each year. Editors and writers travel extensively to investigate actual conditions they plan to expose and criticize. The magazine also has some 65 free-lance artist contributors.

Eschewing vulgarity, *Krokodil* pitches its general tone on a relatively sophisticated level, though in accord with its title, it can be cruel, vicious, and deceitful. Criticism of life at home in the Soviet Union is seldom as cutting as of that in foreign countries, in the field of Soviet foreign policy, aspects of international relations, and world problems. Favorite domestic targets of *Krokodil's* pitchfork are the negative, dark sides of the ongoing work of building the socialist state. Its brilliant staff of artists and writers under editor-in-chief Manuil G. Semyonov needles slipshod individuals who fail in their duty, factories and farms that fall short of quotas, dogmatism that is carried to ridiculous extremes, and the ever-present bumbling bureaucracy with its red tape. Caricatures jibe at such things as hoarding, house planning, plumbing, television antennas marring the landscape, shoddy apartment construction, the shoe industry, the typical Soviet man or woman caught up in the vise of heavy-handed planning.

Krokodil for November 20, 1965, ran a full-page front cover cartoon showing a pair of young moderns dashing down the steps of a maternity home and waving farewell to a nurse who is standing in the doorway holding an infant. Glad to be relieved of the responsibility of parenthood, they are saying to the nurse, "And give the child a public education." On the back cover is a coffin standing upended under a red, white, and blue shield over a banner which reads "Induction Center." From inside the coffin, which serves as a sort of doorway, a steel-helmeted, cigar-smoking skeleton in United States Army uniform holds open the coffin door and ceremoniously grunts, "Next, please!"

Inside, short sketches are intermixed with cartoons and poetry. Few pieces run as much as a full page, although installments of longer works may be continued over several issues. On page three appears a typical half-page cartoon showing two men carrying a shower stall and fixtures toward an apartment building still under construction. One of them looks toward a third man carrying a steam radiator and sink, and asks, "Does your apartment also have small imperfections?" This page carries four poems in a box under the logotype: IN POETICAL COMPETITION. One of the poems called "Obscure Genius," reads as follows:

"While I live," said the poet,
"I won't achieve glory,
When I depart the wide world
They will realize I was great."

Deeds are needed, and not words,
You see the truth is bitter:
From the cow that's dead,
There will be no milk.

Cartoons lampooning domestic affairs in this issue include one on page four showing a bureaucrat in his automobile parked in a boat being rowed down a flooded highway. Leaning out the window of his car he holds a notice, "Road Maintenance Completed." The caption says "From a Report to the Center." Another on page five concerns a pair of bureaucrats and the architect looking over a model of a new school to be built. One of them asks, "Why are there no windows?" The architect responds, "This will be a night school." Another half-page cartoon on page 11 pictures a youth leading two of his friends into the house to meet his doting parents. The friends blow clouds of smoke from their cigarettes, and the youth says to his friends, "Don't be afraid of my parents. We'll smoke them out!" In a series of eight cartoons using a circus theme, one pictures a newspaper reporter seated on a reclining lion with the animal trainer. The reporter is saying, "Tell me about your dangerous profession." Typical of the treatment of the United States is a cartoon on page seven in which a pith-helmeted white colonial type leeringly pulls a string which holds up the corner of a hollow box-like prison structure in the manner of a rabbit snare. The bait inside is a golden dollar. The title says, "Trap of the Colonialists." Other favorite emblems or symbols of the United States are Uncle Sam, the fat cigar-smoking capitalist with dollar marks all over his suit, the hooded Ku Klux Klan figure, and the Statue of Liberty in various poses. Figure 7.5 (3) shows a close-up sectional view as if through a telescope of the spikes around the head of the Statue of Liberty. The close-up shows that each spike is really a hooded klansman.

Krokodil customarily saves its big guns for the "external enemies" of the Soviet Union. Here the Line closely follows the very points currently stressed in official propaganda. Favorite foils are the United States, the United Kingdom, West Germany, and France, although Jugoslavia, Albania, and Hungary have come in for their share at appropriate times. A cartoon depicts a fat, cigar-smoking American doctor standing at the bedside of his emaciated patient and saying, "Your money or your life." Common stereotypes depict Americans as dollar mad, gangster ridden, and deprived of civil liberties by bought elections or by race prejudice. Under the rubric "A Weighty Argument" an American judge is pictured asking the prisoner at the bar, "Have you anything to add to your defense?" The prisoner says, "Another thousand dollars, your honor, and not a cent more!" [4] Many of the most cruel cartoons are gross distortions or outright fabrications.

Repetition of the same theme and idea is intended to arouse a specified emotion or to plant and cultivate the growth of an attitude. Soviet agitation, according to Lenin, appeals primarily to the emotion, while propaganda appeals to the mind.

> The agitator . . . will pick out one more or less familiar and concrete aspect of the entire problem. Let us say the death of an unemployed worker as a result of starvation. His efforts will be concentrated on this fact, to impart to the masses a single idea—the idea of the senseless contradictions between the growth of wealth and the growth of poverty. He will strive to evoke among the masses discontent and revolt against this great injustice and will leave the full explanation for this contradiction to the propagandists.[5]

By this definition, *Krokodil* is more agitation than propaganda. *Time* magazine once remarked, ". . . to dedicated Reds, *Krokodil's* snappish humor may seem funny; to most of the West it is a reminder that a crocodile never laughs without baring its teeth."

Ogonyok: Popular Mass Weekly

Second only to *Rabotnitsa* in circulation, *Ogonyok* (The Flamelet or Little Flame) is the popular weekly of the Soviet Union, dating back to 1923. It is the Soviet counterpart of the *Saturday Evening Post* combined with news-picture type of content such as

Fig. 7.6. The illustrated weekly **Ogonyok** varies its cover illustrations, but all strive for popular appeal. The two covers below are typical, since they show the faces of busy citizens or children in various life roles. The unusual cover on the August issue at left above is self-explanatory.

that found in *Life, Look,* the British *London Illustrated News,* or *Paris Match,* the main difference being the absence of advertising in *Ogonyok.* The magazine directs its sociopolitical, literary-artistic contents to the general urban reading public and to the rural intelligentsia, an audience of 2 million. Its material is necessarily varied to meet the needs of a wide circle of readers and at the same time to fulfill its propaganda purposes. Its relatively wide audience makes it, like *Krokodil,* a sensitive vehicle for the uses of propaganda. The color cover week after week features individual prototypes selected from a cross section of Soviet workers in various fields of endeavor (Fig. 7.6). They invariably show faces that are smiling and contented—the faces of busy citizens, each chosen to represent the particular project being promoted at the moment by officials. There are construction workers on a Volga-Don project, laborers in the steelworks, miners, engineers, farmers, teachers, soldiers, and occasionally members of minority Soviet racial or linguistic groups, or citizens of other Communist countries. The inside front cover displays with the aid of photographs and cartoons the basic promotion message of the week, a message that must be gotten across to readers, a message that must persuade and convince. The remainder of the magazine is apportioned among condensations of popular fiction, articles interpreting the country's achievements in terms of the average man, travelogues, theatrical and sports news, and an occasional page of interest to women. Reading matter is illustrated with drawings and photographs in both color and black and white.

An issue of August 22, 1965, for example, featured a story in pictures about a football (soccer) championship match. Shorter picture-story layouts concern the mystery of the lunar seas, socialist Roumania, and "our dear guests" from the Republic of the Congo. IN A KURSK MARKET LAST SUNDAY, a 2-page spread, describes agricultural programs to increase production as a result of party decisions put into practice by collective farms. Two photographs illustrate a personal experience narrative, WITH THE PARTISANS IN ANGOLA. There is a full-page, 4-color painting reproduction showing a young farm woman spreading fertilizer over the fields from a helicopter. Two other drawings in color are a landscape "After the Storm" and another of two pretty young peasant girls under the caption "Girlfriends." There are four full-color photograph pages accompanying a feature story on Kiev. A 2-page picture story (Fig. 7.7) tells of "Revolt in the City of Angels" (the Watts riots in Los Angeles). Regular features include a column of QUESTIONS, PROB-

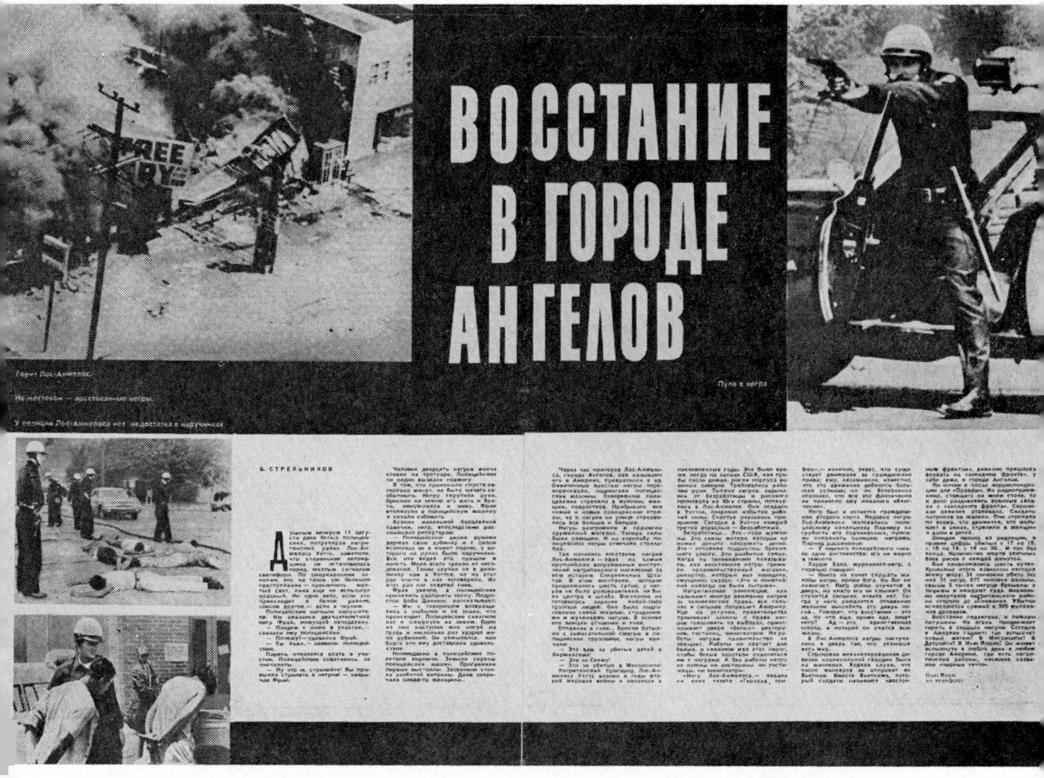

Fig. 7.7. An inside spread in the August, 1965, issue of **Ogonyok** reports the race riots in the Watts section of Los Angeles. The headline reads "Revolt in the City of the Angels." The picture at the right is captioned, "Bullets at Negroes"; top left, "Los Angeles burns"; center left, "On the Pavement." The bottom left picture shows Negroes under arrest.

LEMS, DISCOVERIES, FACTS; cartoons; AMUSING LITTLE THINGS; brief work—photo odds and ends, some contributed by readers; and a crossword puzzle. *Ogonyok* publishes a supplement of the collected works of Leo Tolstoy, Ivan Turgenev, Anton Chekhov, Nikolai Gogol, Alexander Pushkin, Honoré de Balzac, Theodore Dreiser, Émile Zola, Stendhal, Miguel de Cervantes, and Jack London. It also publishes a little library which is a collection of the best stories, plays, novels, and sketches that currently appear in Soviet magazines.

Sovetski Ekran Piously Promotes Soviet Films

A good example of the Soviet regime's concession to popular demand in mass communications is the fortnightly screen magazine,

Sovetski Ekran (Soviet Screen), circulation 200,000. A far cry from its Western counterparts, this magazine's careful selection of material also illustrates the somewhat prim and pious, almost Puritan, tenor of the ideology. It sticks strictly, even stodgily to its assigned task of promoting current cinema productions and announcing forthcoming attractions, both foreign and domestic. In doing this *Sovetski Ekran* does not engage in gossip or chitchat about the personal, private lives of the film stars. It avoids scandal, leaving exposure of the shady side of life in the movie colony to *Sovetskaya Kultura* (Soviet Culture). It also leaves the criticism of cinema productions to its sister publication, *Iskustvo Kino* (Film Art), with only 14,000 circulation. As a propaganda medium to increase the spread of propaganda in films by enticing readers to attend the productions it describes with full-page color prints and plot summaries, the magazine appears to lean over backwards to avoid suggesting objectionable precedents in social behavior. For example, it is careful to explain that Inna Makarova, a young brunette actress who appeared in a current movie with her hair a striking blonde, in life really "is against cosmetic contrivances," [6] lest too many young readers become tempted to dye their hair. *Sovetski Ekran's* habitual accent on the positive side and its avoidance of mentioning the negative assure that the image it presents of motion pictures is always favorable, enthusiastic, and optimistic.

The Women's Magazine, *Rabotnitsa*

The leading women's magazine, *Rabotnitsa* (woman worker) boasts the largest circulation of any magazine in the Soviet Union, is one of the oldest periodicals, having been founded on Lenin's initiative in 1914. It did not appear regularly, however, until 1922, and is now a monthly with about 7.4 million subscribers. While the magazine attempts to cover national and international affairs, it deals primarily with women's day-to-day activities and stresses domestic problems. It also espouses the causes of the "women's movement." Although it is filled with articles on medical advice, child upbringing by educators, and the usual material on housekeeping, fashions, beauty aids, needlework, and the like, it does not neglect the fields of fiction and poetry. Each issue contains reviews of theatre and cinema, and reports of late scientific-technological developments. The magazine is illustrated, its color reproductions including photographs as well as paintings by leading artists.

Kommunist, Prime Theoretical Journal

This theoretical organ of the Central Committee is designed for both home and foreign consumption, publishing 18 issues a year of 650 thousand each. Its plain, severe cover attests its intellectual appeal. It brings its readers a world view of international affairs as seen through Soviet eyes. It pictures, according to its own language, "the struggle of the peoples of the world for peace, national independence, social justice, humanism, and progress—for those great ideals which are so dear to people everywhere, whatever their political, philosophical, religious views or their nationality or color." The magazine analyzes Marxist-Leninist theory and discusses new developments in the progress of Communism in the Soviet State. It does not neglect the new developments in "imperialist" countries and the struggle of countries for freedom from "colonialism."

Party Affairs Discussion Magazine

Partinaia Zhizn (Party Life), the leading Central Party magazine is a bi-monthly published since 1919, dealing primarily with high-level questions of Communist Party policy and ideology and the relationship of such matters to the Soviet government. Its pages reflect the various current stages of party work and the activities of party organizations in the several spheres of economic, social, and cultural life of the nation. It is filled with articles, interviews, talks, advice, answers to readers' questions, fiction, essays, press and radio reviews, and bibliographical notes. Its contributors include prominent and typical public figures such as party leaders and government officials, journalists, collective farmers, and industrial leaders. The magazine claims that it provides a wide outlet for discussion of urgent party problems. It has about the same number of readers as *Kommunist.*

Teen-Agers' Companions: *Molodoi Kommunist* and *Molodoi Kolkhoznik*

These two leading monthly magazines devoted to youth are spiced with illustrations, cartoons, and photographs. The first title, which means "The Young Communist," identifies the magazine as a party organ. The second, meaning "The Young Collective Farmer," aims at rural young people. Both magazines attempt to present Marxist-Leninist dogma in simple, clear, convincing terms, thus serving their function which is the Communist education of youth. *Molodoi Kommunist* differs from its country cousin in that it is primarily a nonfiction magazine of affairs, though it does print summarized novels of special appeal to youth. It carries articles and sketches of young people's activities and stresses the work of the Young Communist League. Leading figures in Soviet life express their views in by-lined articles. The magazine reports teen-age life in other countries. *Molodoi Kolkhoznik,* a sociopolitical-literary magazine, seems to specialize in fiction by the best Soviet writers. It also publishes poetry and science-fiction material. Articles depict young people working on State and collective farms, such as agricultural machine operators, rural intellectuals, and students. Both magazines report teen-age life in other countries, stories of adventure, achievement, legends, and heroic feats from history. Both magazines use a substantial amount of original work by young artists, writers, and photographers.

THE LITERARY MAGAZINES:

Novy Mir, Oktyabr', Znamya, and Zvezda

The leading monthly miscellanies are predominantly devoted to literature and literary matters (Fig. 7.8). Yet they, too, are not without their political and ideological slant. Occasionally space is devoted to such matters as FOR PEACE, FOR DEMOCRACY, a heading used over a series of anti-Western articles. Their main fare, however, consists of the better novels, which they publish in serial form, poetry, plays, translations from foreign languages, reviews and criticism, and scholarly analyses of a wide range of subjects. The following summarizes the principal characteristics of the literary periodicals.[7]

Fig. 7.8. As popular channels for the country's leading poets, novelists, writers, and intellectuals, the literary journals of the Soviet Union have few counterparts in the Western world. Three of the four major literary monthlies on the opposite page are published in Moscow. Top left is the magazine **Oktyabr'** (October). Top right is the famous liberal journal **Novy Mir** (New World), which has been in the vanguard of the Thaw movement among writers for greater truth and honesty in expression. Bottom left is **Neva,** the only one of the four published in Leningrad, and named after Leningrad's river. At bottom right is **Znamya** (Banner). These voices are important leaders of thought and opinion.

oto by Don Woolley

Novy Mir's Liberal Voice

Novy Mir (The New World) is perhaps the most distinguished and certainly the most in demand of all the literary monthlies. Alexander Tvardovsky's brilliant editorship has placed *Novy Mir* in the forefront of the ideological conflict over freedom of expression for intellectuals that has been raging in the Soviet Union since the time of the Thaw. He has made it the chief forum of liberal thought in the country.[8] Its circulation, probably kept small for political reasons, is no indication of its great influence, for its copies are in great demand and cannot be bought on the newsstands. Dennis Brown describes how his Moscow friend could not buy a copy of the November, 1962, issue containing Solzhenitsyn's *One Day in the Life of Ivan Denisovich,* and how he finally was able to borrow a copy one evening with the promise of returning it the next morning. He and his family with the neighbors gathered in his small apartment and read the novel aloud in relays all night. This example is exceptional, but it may be taken as typical of the way the magazine is received when it publishes important literary works advancing ideas to which Soviet readers have rarely been exposed.

Novy Mir's pastel blue cover and conservative format which have changed hardly at all in 20 years misrepresent its liberal content, which Brown characterizes as "the most constructively disruptive force in Soviet intellectual life." [9] The monthly averages 288 pages, carries no illustrations, and has 127,600 subscribers. Approximately two-thirds of the magazine is devoted to fiction, poetry, and criticism; the remaining one-third to travelogues, foreign and domestic developments, memoirs, and finally party material accompanied by the usual editorials in support of the national program. *Novy Mir* is in the tradition of the nineteenth-century Russian "thick journals," as are a number of its competitors such as *Oktyabr'* and *Znamya.* But it differs from the others in its daring liberalism which it has been able to advance without serious penalty, possibly because of its editor's adroit leadership. Like its nineteenth-century predecessors, *Novy Mir* publishes the fiction and poetry of Russian writers who, again in the nineteenth-century tradition, employ allegory, metaphor, symbolism, satire, and Aesopian language to spread ideas, to describe social conditions, or political attitudes that, expressed in other forms, would incur the regime's wrath, and hence would be too dangerous to write about. The only other Soviet magazine that goes as far as *Novy Mir* in the liberal direction is

Yunost, an attractively edited journal for rebellious and questioning teen-agers and young adults. *Yunost* publishes the works of the younger writers and enjoys a circulation of 1.48 million, some ten times that of *Novy Mir.* Obviously the lusty group supporting *Yunost* commands a higher degree of suasion with that branch of bureaucracy in charge of newsprint and paper supplies than does the eager group of intellectuals who read *Novy Mir.*

Founded in 1925, *Novy Mir* celebrated its fortieth anniversary in 1965 as the country's leading voice in the fight to replace the fear, frustration, and falsification of the Stalin era with free discussion as the only way to search out the truth and expose the shams of Soviet society. In the 1920s and 1930s, the magazine published the works of the leading writers including Boris Pasternak, Mikhail Sholoknov, Alexei Tolstoy, Isaac Babel, Maxim Gorky, Alexander Fadeyev, Ilya Ehrenburg, and others. In the purges of 1937, *Novy Mir* was also a victim. Its editors and writers being under arrest, it shared the fate of diminished activity along with other magazines during the war period, but made a strong comeback in 1947 under the editorship of Konstantin Simonov, the poet and novelist. He was succeeded by Alexander Tvardovsky in 1950 who, soon after Stalin's death, began to publish boldly frank articles critical of the state of Soviet literature. For such "revisionism," Tvardovsky was removed from the editorship and replaced by Simonov, who published Vladimir Dudintsev's novel *Not by Bread Alone* in 1956 and 1957. The publication of this novel was an important milestone in the magazine's history. Tvardovsky returned as editor in 1958, and when *Novy Mir* came under official attack again in the spring of 1963, there were rumors that its editor had again been removed from his position.[10] Tvardovsky maintained dignified silence while Premier Khrushchev's campaign against dissident writing wore itself out. Then he issued a statement, apparently with the regime's sanction, which filled a half-page in *Pravda,* defending most of the Soviet writers under fire but not taking issue with the regime. Tvardovsky, who is a poet in his own right, argued the cause of Alexander Yashin whose poetic sketch "The Vologda Wedding" had been denounced in the press as giving a false picture of Soviet rural life, emphasizing as it did poverty and backwardness. Tvardovsky also came to the defense of Yevgeny Yevtushenko, Andrei Voznesensky, and Ehrenburg himself. Furthermore, he announced his magazine would publish works by other writers who had been denounced by the regime, such as Viktor Nekrasov, Vasily Aksynonov, Vladimir

Tendryakov, and Alexander Solzhenitsin. In 1965 Tvardovsky answered the well-worn argument of the conservatives that exposing the unfavorable sides of Soviet life gave aid and comfort to "our enemies in the bourgeois world." His answer was, "Everything that is talented and truthful in art is beneficial to us. And conversely, any falsity, any lie, any stupidity, is harmful to us, and can most surely be used by our enemies against us." [11]

Oktyabr' Publishes Leading Contemporaries

Oktyabr' (October), a conservative literary-social magazine, has a circulation of more than 170,000. It averages approximately 200 pages in each issue and the type of material published and its distribution are quite similar to that of *Novy Mir.* It shares with *Znamya* the honor of publishing prize-winning fiction and poetry. It keeps its pages open to the works of younger writers. This magazine, too, has published in serial form some of Sholokhov's works, as well as those of Fadeyev. It has published the writings of Feodor Panfeorov (Brussky), Alexei Surkov, Gladkov, Vera Panova, Vladimir Mayakovski, Sergeyev-Tsenski, Mikhail Bubennov, Semyon Babayeosky, and others. The magazine also devotes space to current and pressing problems. A regular section entitled LIFE'S TRIBUNE airs national economic and cultural ills.

Znamya Studies Soviet Society

The leading theme and purpose of *Znamya* (Banner), a magazine which dates back to 1931, is to present a comprehensive study of contemporary Soviet society. This theme is reflected both in the major prose works it publishes, in its short stories and sketches, and its humorous, critical articles. *Znamya* averages approximately 200 pages and since 1957 it has included illustrations in its makeup. Its circulation is approximately 130,000. In comparison with *Novy Mir* and *Oktyabr'*, this journal has been described as "middle-of-the-road." It specializes in publishing new novels and poetry, a policy which has earned the magazine prestige since the war because of its initial publication of wartime poems and stories that have since gained importance as literature, in part because of their unorthodox social themes. Among the best known of these is K. Simonov's *Days and Nights,* a novel about the battle of Stalingrad, and M. Aligher's poem "Zoya" whose protagonist is a young partisan who died at the hands of the German invaders. Panova's *Fellow Travelers* and *Kruzhilikha* also appeared first in *Znamya.* A few other novels appearing in this periodical illustrate the role of the creative arts in the service of the regime. *Happiness,* a novel by P. Pavlenko, treats graphically of the restoration of the Crimea. The setting of A. Chakovsky's book, *It Is Morning,* is a fishing collective on the Don. A collective farm in central Russia provides the locale of *Harvest* by G. Nikolaeva. Emanuel Kazakovich's *Spring on the Oder* and *Star* exalt life under the Communist order.

Leningrad's Star

The three top literary journals discussed above are all published in Moscow. Leningrad's oldest and still leading periodical of this type is *Zvezda* (Star), the organ of the Leningrad Union of Soviet Writers. Dating back to the early 1920s, *Zvezda* follows a plan of organization and prints content similar to that of its Moscow contemporaries. Its character has been changed somewhat and its tone subdued since it was disciplined in 1946 for pro-Western, individualistic "deviation." Though subjected to closer party scrutiny than the others, *Zvezda* has still seen fit to publish such controversial works as B. Lavenyov's *Voice of America,* A. Yakobson's *The Guardian Angel from Nebraska,* and K. Simonov's *Russian Question.*

LITERARY JOURNAL CONTENT AND EFFECT OF CONTROLS

The leading literary journals set the pace for some 80 smaller ones, some of them no more than pamphlets, that serve as the organs of writers' organizations in each republic and region. Some examples are *Nash Sovremennik* (Our Contemporary), the magazine of writers of the Russian Federation; *Druzhba Narodov* (People's Friendship), devoted to the works of writers of the various Soviet republics and the "people's democracies" of East Europe; and *Don,* the journal which specializes in the works of writers of the republics and regions of the North Caucasus (translated into Russian) and of the Don, Kuban, and Stavropol regions. In addition to serving as communications media for the intelligentsia and as outlets for contemporary writings by established authors, these journals with their sponsoring organizations function as workshops for aspiring young writers whose fledgling efforts are subjected to criticism before public exposure.

That the regime is aware of the superior value of magazines over books for propaganda purposes is illustrated by the initial publication in magazines of so many major works of literary merit, when in countries like the United States such works normally appear first in book form. Although the continued publication of novels by Ehrenburg and Panova indicate the regime is permitting treatment of a wider range of subjects, the effectiveness of the controls on periodicals and their literary content was shown in Turkovich's survey of Soviet literature covering fifteen postwar years. She found only a limited number of selected themes that were continuously in use and "woven and rewoven in every literary form." Furthermore, she reports, any deviation from the use of the officially sponsored themes or from the manner of their manipulation is frowned upon or severely censored. "The Party does not want the public's attention distracted from the principal issues by other more novel and less political motifs," [12] she writes. Moreover, Gordey asked Soviet intellectuals to suggest the best novels that had appeared in the country during the years 1949 and 1950. All the novels named were Stalin Prize winners and included such works as Babayevsky's *Knight of the Golden Star,* Ajaev's *Far from Moscow,* and Panova's *The Luminous Shore.* Gordey found the subjects of all three to be strictly in conformance with the general line, though obviously of literary merit. "But I cannot believe that all three authors by themselves would have selected identical themes," he commented. "And if this phenomenon appears altogether normal to Soviet readers, I cannot . . . help seeing in it . . . the positive function of Soviet censorship which dictates when it does not ban." [13]

On the other hand Blake and Hayward take the view that literature need not necessarily suffer from purely negative limitations on the right of publication, pointing out that nineteenth-century Russian literature as well as Soviet literature flourished under censorship. They admit that the way in which "socialist realism" as extraliterary criteria was made binding on Soviet writers adversely affected creative effort. On the whole, they conclude that the Soviet period in Russian literature has by no means been as barren in literary achievement as has often been supposed. Apart from the years 1947 to 1953, these writers conclude that some work is not "unworthy of the great tradition from which it ultimately springs." [14]

These differing interpretations are no doubt close estimates for different periods. From the period known as the Thaw until the middle 1960s the struggle among the younger writers and artists for greater latitude of self-expression and truth seeking has taken on the proportions of an intellectual renaissance, in spite of all the regime can do to discourage it. The new themes they have succeeded in introducing have appeared publicly in the literary journals, in published books, and in the clandestine sheets of the active underground press as well. Although the limits on the range of permissible themes that can be aired in the literary periodicals is still narrow, it is considerably wider than it was, thanks to the Thaw and its aftermath. This significant movement and its implications for public communications will be examined in more detail in the next chapter.

ASSESSMENT OF MEDIA BEHAVIOR AND PERFORMANCE

Assessment of media performance results generally in a broad picture of one-dimensional uniformity. The reviewer of content is struck by its tiresome monotony, heavy-handed approach, tedious repetition, moral preachments, and sterile Puritanism. As a vehicle for conveying information, the media system's presentation of messages and their meaning, with few exceptions, appears to be what it is—cut from the same pattern. If the Soviet reader relies solely on his mass media to present him with a picture of the world that to a reasonable degree corresponds with reality, he is sure to be disappointed. The picture he gets can be described at best as out of focus, without perspective, and foggy. At its worst it is outright false and misleading. Many times there is no picture at all. He is left to fill in startling gaps for himself as best he can, to connect and relate the disconnected fragments. Always he must wade through a language characterized by high-level abstractions, cliches,[15] and jargon—a language overloaded with exaggerated sentimentality, myth, fanciful allusions to the dream world of the future as if such a world really existed, indeed, brought into existence by the Communist regime.

As a vehicle for opinion, the system presents for the most part only one-sided arguments on all questions. Calm, balanced, or unbiased analysis of the several sides of an issue on their merits alone is rarely in evidence and in most cases appears to be impossible to achieve. Instead, the propaganda usually mobilizes an avalanche of bias and launches it in a vigorous frontal attack as if to seize the opposition by surprise and sweep it off its feet. The tone is generally as devoid of subtlety or suggestion as it is of a differing viewpoint. Something akin to the British art of understatement has never been realized. Human interest is still rarely present. The heavy approach is relieved occasionally by flashes of satire, a cartoon, a humorous quip, or live broadcast. Some relief too has been apparent in recent years in the slowly widening range of comment, particularly in the literary criticism that has followed the appearance of strong currents of "deviationist" writing. Press and broadcasting in the 1960s were devoting much more attention to literary criticism.[16] Because criticism of literature is itself a creative work this trend in the media is significant. The public media in the United States and the United Kingdom have been charged at times with overweening sameness of content, an effect attributed to standardizing influences of chain ownership, the growing use of syndicated material, and mass production requirements. Nonetheless, compared with the Soviet media, Western media appear varied, imaginative, and full of spontaneity.

A combination of factors is responsible for this kind of performance. The regime's belief in the principle of direct attack and in the value of repetition as propaganda methods coupled with its eagerness to use the media apparatus as efficiently as possible have contributed to overloading of the media with the same messages. Other contributing factors are associated with the administrative and control machinery. The whole structure, policy, and process of the organization with its attendant bureaucracy breeds and perpetuates a type of enforced uniformity that seems to be a main symptom of a chronic totalitarian syndrome. For example, lack of variety appears to be inevitable in a system which largely ignores audience interests, which strictly delimits the range of subject matter, which requires the dissemination of a large daily volume of standard material dispatched from the capital, and which above all commands the use of and adherence to the current Line as a measure of performance. Other factors are the role of the Central media as models for the whole country, and the growing centralization and nationalization of communications as a part of the centralization of other aspects of the social system. Finally, the education and discipline of the editorial mind has had the effect of developing a voluntary, perhaps subconsciously motivated, decision-making procedure or formula for the selection and rejection of content. Thus editorial judgment contributes to the effect.

Considering the great desire of the Soviet leaders to reach and change huge masses of the population by means of the official public media, it is germane to ask the question, "To what extent does the system defeat itself?" The leaders are aware of the fact that the media fall short of expected results. From time to time performance is reviewed and found to have fallen to such a level that the leaders must whip up new enthusiasm and breathe new life into the operation. This happens when the communication process is deemed to have reached a point of negative returns, of reverse effects—a stage at which it seems to be defeating its avowed purpose—for it appears to be losing instead of gaining audience attention. At this juncture the authorities publicly call attention to the faults and try to do something about the situation.

The next chapter reviews one of the periodic efforts to overhaul the system and examines the broad question of media effect.

8 ★

IMPROVING PERFORMANCE AND ASSESSING EFFECTS

THE QUALITY AND FOCUS of media content and standards of media performance, like most everything else in Soviet Russia, have undergone important changes since the end of the Stalinist era. Although at this writing the process is still in transition, it is not too early to judge it as a new period of general relaxation of controls and of strong professional emphasis in the production of Soviet mass media. To understand fully the impact of the political, social, and literary reforms upon mass communications and public opinion, it is necessary to review first the main currents of the Thaw, including the movements that followed it (the whole period has been called the *New Wave)* and to examine the nature of the communications reforms that seem to be slowly altering the media system in function, structure, and method, but probably not in essential purpose. This will be followed by an examination of some effects of mass communications on society.

THE THAW: STRUGGLE FOR TRUTH AND REALISM

The reforms that have most affected the mass media of communication are the same as those that have affected almost every phase of life in the Communist State. The forces were set in motion by the political changes that followed Stalin's death and culminated in reaction to and attack on all that his regime had symbolized. These were the immediate demolition of the cult of Stalin as the all-wise, omnipotent leader exalted in the absolutist Byzantine fashion; the substitution of this cult for the conception of collective rule; the downgrading of the Security Police; the new emphasis upon production of more consumer goods; and the adoption of other policies designed to make life easier for the average citizen.[1] There were many signs that the new regime was substituting persuasion for coercion in its method of applying controls. According to Lenin the society should be governed by a delicate balance of coercion and persuasion; now the scales were being tipped more on the side of persuasion. The media as the foremost tools of mass persuasion were in addition expected to accomplish ends hitherto gained by force and fear. This was the beginning of the political Thaw, the release from the frozen, rigid straightjacket of orthodoxy. The political situation unleashed an intellectual renaissance, a ferment of daring new thought among the writers and artists that was part of a national wave of self-examination. In this self-analysis the campaign to sharpen mass media effectiveness was started, another of the regime's periodic attempts to improve the communication system in terms of its efficiency as a propaganda weapon. This time the campaign was more vigorous and longer lasting than any that had preceded it.

As an intellectual and literary movement the Thaw was a passionate outburst of individualism coupled with a demand for a wider latitude of freedom of expression and creative thought. It provided a rare opportunity for the mass media not only to engage in a broader range of reporting and comment, but also to join with the writers in the common cause. The movement was characterized by the appearance in literature and art of new themes that attacked Soviet socialism's basic weaknesses, expressed a concern for the individual citizen as a human being instead of as a cog in society's wheel, and made a strong plea for the need to seek and expose the truth for the greater good of communism and the socialist state.[2] The movement derived its name from the title of Ilya Ehrenburg's novelette, *The Thaw,* whose dominant motif satirized the exaggerated overemphasis upon party and social values at the expense of individual human values. In *The Thaw's* underlying philosophy Ehrenburg takes issue with the view expressed by Karl Radek and others (at the first Soviet Writers' Conference in 1934) who rationalized the growing dominance of party-mindedness and exaltation of collective and state values as necessary evils to be tolerated during a transitory period of change and upheaval rather than as ends in themselves. Ehrenburg now feels that the period of compromise has passed, and that literature must be freed of its bonds. Although he does not believe that the ideal society has been born, he recognizes the fact that a new society has evolved with its own norms and systems and believes that this society should be truthfully portrayed. Strict control over content and style of literature therefore can no longer be justified. It is time now, he feels, to take into account the "nonsocialist" personality of Soviet man, his personal opinions, dreams, doubts, ambitions, and aspirations.[3] "We have taken a lot of trouble over one-half of the human being," are the words Ehrenburg puts into the mouth of Koroteyev in *The Thaw,* "but the other half is neglected. The result is that one-half of the house is a slum. I remember that article of Gorky's . . . we need our own Soviet humanism."[4] Following, this idea, the movement was not an anti-regime attack but rather a bold bid for widening the permissive limits of "orthodox" expression as a means of improving society in accordance with its own goals and within the framework of accepted ideology.[5] The intellectual movement was born of the political situation and it raised critical issues of literary politics.[6]

But the spirit of the Thaw was born of the World War II years. Preoccupied with the task of national survival, the regime had suffered a temporary relaxation of its usual vigilance, permitting the people to glimpse what life might be like without eternal party supervision. Hardships, too, had diverted public attention from that mythical, somewhat artificial personality, the ideal "Soviet Socialist man," and had substituted a host of serious new individual problems of personal suffering and sorrow. Moreover as the war drew to a close there was a strong upsurge of pro-Western feeling tinged with patriotic pride in Mother Russia at the expense of Soviet patriotism, all stimulated by military victories. Such were the new themes that found expression, sometimes subtly, not only in the literature but also in other forms of communication. It stemmed from a great eagerness on the part of intellectuals to Westernize Soviet culture and such ideas echoed through the domains of literature, painting, music, history, pure and applied science, and literary and arististic criticism. This new philosophy was viewed as dangerously individualistic or neutral and shockingly pro-Western, and it

Fig. 8.1. **Krokodil** cartoon entitled "The Shave" (of swastika beard) appeared in 1945 during a strong upsurge of pro-Western feeling. This attitude toward the West, and particularly toward the United States, is rarely expressed in the pages of **Krokodil** or other Soviet communication media. Soon after this cartoon was published the Stalin regime in the person of Andrei Zhdanov cracked down on the expression of such "decadent" sentiments.

led to the August 14, 1946, decree on literature, "Resolution on the Journals *Zvezda* and *Leningrad*," which reminded all concerned that any preaching of ideological or political neutrality or of "art for art's sake" was alien to Soviet thinking (Fig. 8.1).

In 1946 and 1947 Andrei Zhdanov, as director of propaganda, inaugurated a succession of purges against this "subservience to the West" and attempted to substitute nationalism in its place. Under Zhdanov's leadership, authorities redoubled their efforts to stamp out proliferation of such ideas and to replace them with more desirable ones. Some writers complied; others kept their silence. Leningrad's literary monthly *Zvezda* published in 1946 a story by the Soviet satirist Mikhail Zoshchenko called "The Adventures of a Monkey," a simple tale about a monkey that had escaped from the zoo, but the analogy was clear. At the same time Leningrad's other, less well-known, magazine *Leningrad* published some poetry by Anna Akhmatova which was found to smack excessively of the old "salon poetry." Zhdanov cracked down on both magazines, taking the occasion to inveigh against nascent Western sympathies on the part of the people. To remedy its oversight, the party suppressed *Leningrad* outright and severely "reoriented" *Zvezda*, dismissing its editor.[7]

The spirit of dissent did not die but went underground. The

end of the old regime and the beginning of the new set the stage for its revival. When latent feelings erupted once again, they were in part a reaction to Zhdanovism. The Thaw reached its peak in the weeks between Nikita Khrushchev's secret attack on Stalin and the "cult of personality," at the Twentieth Party Congress of February, 1956, and that time during the following summer when the regime reasserted the line and launched the counterattack. Official policy was not definitely clarified until Khrushchev's speech a year later during the summer of 1957, when the campaign against the revisionists reached its highest peak. The Thaw officially came to a close at the time of the Writers' and Artists' Conference of 1959. This conference formally acknowledged party discipline and accepted the public confessions of the transgressors. The principle was reestablished: a writer cannot have ideas, only ideologies. But things would never be the same again—a return to the confines of the old dogma was impossible under the new conditions.

What were the principal themes of Thaw literature, the regime's reaction to them, and the issues of freedom and control—in short, the issues of literary politics—that were involved? A brief tracing of the main developments have relevance for mass communications. As for the mass media, the accepted standard for judging all creative expression is its contribution to the advancement of the Communist cause, to *partiinost,* or party spirit. Lenin's 1905 dictum had been, "All literature must become Party literature." Hence the new themes finding expression in 1953 and 1954 conflicted sharply with the well-worn pattern. At least three new ideas[8] that seemed to predominate and to repeat themselves in the literature of these years were especially pronounced in Leonid Zorin's play, *The Guests,* in Vera Panova's *The Seasons of the Year,* and in Ehrenburg's novelette, *The Thaw.* They may be summarized as follows: (1) An Attack on the privileges, hypocrisies, and excesses of a growing bourgeois class oligarchy, the Soviet state bureaucracy; these new privileged classes had been the protagonists of Zorin's play. (2) A substitution of personal things in the popular attention for collective politics and society; human values took the place of party and State values as expressed in Ehrenburg's plea for remedying society's neglect of humanism and individualism. (3) And finally, a new passion for seeking out the truth in order to expose the myths and shams of party dogma that gloss over Soviet reality. This last was a strong appeal for honest writing, an appeal that stressed the critical need to erase fictitious conceptions of the world cultivated so strenuously by the regime for an entire generation.

The state of current literary production was brought under attack in the literary journal *Novy Mir* as early as June, 1953, by Alexander Tvardovsky, poet and editor. Further criticism appeared in his magazine and in *Znamya* during the ensuing months. Ehrenburg in a moderate tone discussed the writer's problems and urged more humanism in belles-lettres. Vladimir Pomerantsev, in *Novy Mir,* more boldly indicted artificiality, didacticism, schematism, and what he called "stereotyped" criticism of "stereotypes." His views and those expressed in *The Thaw* and other works, evoked criticism in *Literaturnaya Gazeta, Komsomolskaya Pravda,* and *Pravda.* The party press generally showed restraint, and it was not until June, 1954, that a *Kommunist* editorial discussed the entire literary situation and advised the Writers' Union not to permit the discussion to drift without guidance in the Union and in the press. The Union's leaders in August officially condemned the material published in *Novy Mir* and sought to outline official policy and perhaps to end the talk. Tvardovsky confessed his mistakes, but lost his job as editor to Konstantin Simonov. Debate did not end, however, and when the Second All-Union Congress of Soviet Writers met in December, 1954, the attitude of the leaders and of the regime, too, was one of compromise between the extremist doctrines of Zhdanovism and the need to adhere more closely to true Leninist dogma.[9]

The Congress did not fully succeed in resolving the argument or in guiding the discussion into the "correct path." There were occasional outbursts of unorthodox writing during the following months and a few sharp reprimands from the guardians of dogma. There were signs of some disorder and confusion in literary circles, and *Kommunist* again attempted to clarify the situation in 1955. This time the periodical probed deeply, defending the restrictions imposed by Communist *partiinost* on artists as an aid in creating a truly popular art and a guide to creative truth without which no really great work of art is possible. Yet *Kommunist,* by its approach and manner, suggested that party policies were being modified. In 1956 some writers became bolder, attacking the basic principle of party guidance, this time in *Voprosy Filosofi.* Khrushchev's denunciation of Stalin and the cult of personality at the Twentieth Party Congress in February, 1956, was used as a reason to reject the idea of guidance of creative work by the party—a Stalinist hallmark. After *Pravda* and *Izvestia* criticized this assault on party controls, *Voprosy Filosofi* promptly repudiated it. The de-Stalinization drive led to other attacks outside the literary field, on the injustices and hardships of life under the old regime. As the relaxation of controls had stimulated writers to express ideas they had long repressed, their challenge to party authority inspired similar challenges in other aspects of the society.[10] Khrushchev's pronouncement was followed by Mao Tse-tung's "hundred flowers" decree, which sounded even more liberal—and which he soon was forced to recant. There were repercussions throughout the Communist world, the most violent of which came in the form of the Hungarian revolution.

Meantime in the Soviet Union the themes of the 1953–1954 period erupted in full force. The literature teemed with bold attacks on rigid controls. Writing reflected an intense idealism, an attachment to humanitarian values, and a struggle to portray reality—a kind of reality uncluttered by notions of "socialist reality." The attack on the new classes assumed a daring political skepticism of the Marxist ideal. Motion pictures and plays presented characters who acted like human beings rather than like artificial Soviet socialist heroes. For example the fictional young man disappointed in love who in former novels had dedicated his life to the glory of the State now found more tangible happiness in the arms of another love. Young poets in a passionate call for honesty urged that "without truth there can be no happiness." The new poetry, the literary magazines (especially *Novy Mir)* as well as the cinema and stage reflected these themes.[11] Vladimir Dudintsev's novel *Not by Bread Alone* stressed the need for intellectual independence and satirized the bureaucracy. The second volume of the almanac *Literaturnaya Moskva* late in 1956 was a literary event of first importance. It contained Alexander Yashin's "Levers" which indicted the party as an evil influence.

In the panic of the Hungarian situation the regime launched a violent counterattack against "revisionism." As in 1954 this offensive by the authorities looked more ominous than it was. The organs of mass communication were brought into full play. *Pravda* labeled as "rotten elements" all who failed to contribute to party unity. Press denunciations referred to such dissidents as "demagogues and malicious fault-finders," who echoed Western attacks on the Soviet Union. *Partinaya Zhizn* on April 28, 1957, served notice that anyone not agreeing with party policy would invite expulsion. The Communist Party is a militant union of persons holding the same views, it declared. It posed the question, "How is it possible to tolerate it if persons with thoughts alien to our views penetrate the union?" The paper warned that recent talk of intraparty democracy must not be interpreted to mean the party now would permit discussion of its main tenets. Elsewhere in the press, writers and artists were accused of distorting Soviet reality, of showing only the gloomier aspects of life, and finally of betraying their responsibility to the State. They were called upon to repudiate their views and apologize publicly.

The party's drive to consolidate the ranks of the writers on the basis of principle included publication by the press of a major document on Soviet policy, a symposium abstract of three former speeches by Chairman Khrushchev.

> The great strength of Soviet society lies in the degree to which the Communist Party and the people are one. The creative worker must have the right attitude. What is this attitude like?
>
> When the struggle for Communist ideals and for his people's happiness is the creative worker's goal in life, when he lives at one with the people's interests, thoughts and sentiments, whatever theme he takes or whatever phenomena of life he depicts, his works will invariably meet the interests of the people, party and state.
>
> The creative worker of this kind chooses the path of devotion to the people freely, without coercion, in response to his own conviction and calling, at the command of his own heart and mind. . . .[12]

For any writer who thus faithfully serves the people the question of whether he is free or not in his creative work simply does not exist, the Chairman declared. Freedom to criticize depends entirely upon "from what position criticism is made and for what purpose." Unfortunately some artists feel that the guidance of the party and the State is oppressive and advocate "freedom of creation."

"We openly declare that such views run counter to Leninist principles of the party's and state's attitude to the question . . . that Soviet literature and art must be inseverably linked with the policy of the Communist Party, which constitutes the vital foundation of the Soviet system. . . ." [13]

Referring to the current situation, Khrushchev took a moderate line, urged unification of forces, and indicated that Tvardovsky and Panfyorov, who had lost their jobs as editors, could be restored to favor. His policy, despite the pyrotechnics, appeared to be one of cautious liberality within the ideological framework—a "middle way" that might be called the new orthodoxy.

Yet the treatment of Boris Pasternak in 1958 demonstrated that the chain of conflicts between party and writers was not at an end. After Pasternak had accepted the Nobel Prize for his novel *Doctor Zhivago,* which had been published outside the country, the regime mounted a campaign that forced him to give up the prize. The campaign was exceedingly bitter, resulting in Pasternak's being accused of treason and in his expulsion from the Writers' Union.[14] *Novy Mir's* editorial board's published reasons why they did not wish to print *Doctor Zhivago* stated that the novel betrayed the author's view that the October Revolution had been a mistake, that the work of the intellectuals who supported it had been in vain, and that the novel was a political sermon using the life and death of Dr. Zhivago to illustrate the life and death of the Russian intellectual.

At the Third Writers' Congress in May, 1959, Tvardovsky attacked those who wanted to guide Soviet literature and urged the writers to "write the way your conscience tells you . . . and don't be frightened in advance of editors and critics." Ehrenburg did not attend the meeting, but wrote for *Novy Mir* an article exhorting writers to "write the truth and nothing but the truth." Konstantin Paustovsky warned in *Literaturnaya Gazeta* that administrative methods could never make literature resemble life. Some speakers demanded literary equality for non-Russian peoples. Khrushchev, conciliatory and eager to come to terms with the writers, urged them to settle matters among themselves, with the aid of the party, thus trying to uphold the ideological position of the party without producing new conflicts. But others of the most prominent writers—Panova, Valentin Ovechkin, Simonov, and Sholokhov—joined Ehrenburg in boycotting the congress, continuing their "conspiracy of silence." [15]

Editorial boards of literary journals were asked to exercise greater vigilance, and the zigzag course of persuasion in literary affairs reached a somewhat uneasy settlement with the party in control, although following a new orthodoxy: the party's policy offered no return to the freedom of 1956, but it did not threaten the repressions of the Zhdanov period. By accommodating their writing to acceptable patterns, Soviet writers were able to find ways to say most of the things they wanted to say on subjects that had been previously forbidden, the new policy permitting a more accurate portrayal of the facts of Soviet life. Discussion and criticism could deal with objectionable, deleterious, or derogatory aspects as long as the favorable was pictured with the unfavorable in a balanced perspective.[16]

THE NEW WAVE DEFIES THE NEW ORTHODOXY

In the early 1960s some writers and artists continued to produce works that went beyond the limits of the new orthodoxy. The spirit of the Thaw continued to be strong, its more liberal elements publishing through clandestine channels, but breaking out in the open from time to time. The revolt against the new orthodoxy reached such proportions in 1962 that in the first months of 1963 the counterattack by the authorities appeared to be a cultural purge evoking memories of the Zhdanov era.[17]

Another crisis in the relationship between the leadership and the liberal intellectuals appeared to be developing when in December, 1962, Premier Khrushchev found serious fault with abstract painting, and his remarks were publicized. This gave the neo-Stalinist group among the writers and artists an opportunity to renew their attacks of alarm at the trends in literature, too, thus triggering an official investigation. The objectionable themes were finding outlets in the public press, on stage and cinema, in the rather large underground press,[18] and even in the manuscript literature. The old themes were more assertive, more persistent, more indicative of a calm self-assurance, and perhaps more fearless than before. Poets and novelists were again concerned with seeking real "truth," as opposed to Marxist truth, with describing Soviet life as they saw it and not as the dogma demands. They were waging a war against stereotypes and for personality and individualism; against crude utilitarianism and for "the necessity of the superfluous"; a yearning simply to live and be let alone, utter disgust after 45 years of worn-out slogans and empty promises; in creative work, a search for variety and uniqueness rather than party uniformity; in private life, anything but the socially necessary, anything but the party compulsory—these were typical of the thoughts and sentiments that seeped through. As before, the movement was reformist rather than revolutionary in concept—the liberal writers not warring against the regime, only against its many abuses. Since the beginning of the Thaw in 1953 they have made a case for the proposition that the society's well-stated objectives cannot be achieved unless more freedom is permitted writers, artists, and journalists. Furthermore they were trying to establish for writers the right *not* to be propagandists, the right to be neutral if they wish. According to the young poet Yevgeny Yevtushenko and his group, the term "thaw" is a misnomer; it is not a thaw but a spring, and the "New Wave" is the more appropriate term to epitomize the entire period. In sum, the movement bears significant implications far beyond their literary milieu. Because in essence it is a struggle for the "democratization" of the whole Soviet system, it may take on the characteristics of a revolution.[19] It extends its ramifications deeply into Soviet social and political orthodoxy, and has important meanings for the mass media.

Chief targets of the official attack were Yevtushenko, Ehrenburg, Alexander Solzhenitsyn, Viktor Nekrasov, Vasily Aksyonov, and a few others. Yevtushenko's *A Precocious Autobiography* clothes in the personal story of his life a strong plea for political change, for the "democratization" of Soviet society. Ehrenburg's memoirs, like Yevtushenko's autobiography, presents an interpretation of Soviet history that conflicts with that of the party. Ehrenburg was criticized for his defense of condemned Soviet writers of the 1920s and 1930s. Solzhenitsyn's prison camp story, *One Day in the Life of Ivan Denisovich,* was the first frank exposé of the brutal facts of life in a Stalinist concentration camp. Aksyonov's popular novel *Ticket to the Stars* was denounced as misrepresenting Soviet young people's attitudes. Nekrasov was attacked because of his favorable descriptions of what he saw during his travels in the United States. Declaring that Coco-Cola is delicious, he had the temerity to suggest that America's virtues as well as her vices should be fairly presented to Soviet readers.[20] Konstantin Simonov's *The Living and the Dead* pictures with realistic savagery the chaos, confusion, and near anarchy that existed at the beginning of the Nazi attack and the war for survival that followed, showing that Russia was not saved by the Communist regime, but rather in spite of it. Yevtushenko's poem "Babiy Yar" indicts Soviet anti-Semitism, and his poem "Stalin's Heirs" warns lest Stalin's ghost slip out of the grave and join the "heirs"—the apostles of orthodoxy. Premier Khrushchev himself instructed *Pravda* to publish "Stalin's Heirs." The words had hardly gone into print before Yevtushenko himself became the chief target of the attack led by dogmatists, an attack in which Khrushchev soon joined.

Press criticism caused Khrushchev's chief deputy on domestic ideological questions, Leonid F. Ilyichev, to dictate an uncompromising line that differed only slightly from that of the Zhdanov period; the party vise tightened over the journals; pressure to conform was urged upon the leadership of the Writers' and Artists' Union; and Aleksei V. Romanov, a party official, was given charge of the film industry. Curbs on travel were placed on liberal writers and editors.[21] In late May the party's Central Committee was summoned to deal with the ideological question. It issued further threats and decided on policy aimed at strengthening control over intellectual life. Pavel C. Romanov, with the rank of cabinet minister, was appointed head of a new State commission created to supervise the output of publishing houses, deciding how many copies of what was to be published. A similar commission was set up to "guide" theatrical producers.[22]

The liberals, instead of bowing to authority and accepting defeat once again, appeared quietly confident. As the press campaign against them died down in the final weeks of 1963, the signs were encouraging for the New Wave. Although a few young writers outwardly recanted, they were not sidetracked, and no action was taken to punish them; no writer was publicly disgraced or ostracized; no editor lost his job.[23] Instead, it appeared that the leaders emerged with new prestige. Speaking before a Leningrad meeting of Leftist West European writers, Ehrenburg reiterated the liberal viewpoint, and the speech was given full play in the *Literary Gazette,* a mark of official approval. After temporary retirement, Yevtushenko came back to read his poems before larger audiences. His new book of poetry, held up during the purge, has been published. Most significant was the action of Tvardovsky—principal sponsor and symbol of the loyal literary opposition, editor of *Novy Mir,* and member of the Central Committee—in defending eloquently most of the writers under attack, and having his defense printed in *Pravda.* It was Tvardovsky who had the courage to call the bureaucrats and petty tyrants—those who have long solidified official Soviet life by obstructing reform and imagination—"the leaders who lead no one and the administrators who administer nothing." It was this same element in Soviet officialdom that Khrushchev had been combating so vigorously. Tvardovsky published his anti-Stalinist satiric poem "Tyorkin in the Netherworld," after it had circulated in manuscript form for two years. It was a sequel to his Lenin prize winning war poem "Vasili Tyorkin." He announced his magazine would continue to publish works by the writers under fire. While not taking issue with Khrushchev's new pronouncement he gave it the broadest interpretation, agreeing with the general points made.[24] By so doing it is possible that he helped Khrushchev to soften his original stand without backing down. Meanwhile the underground literary channels appeared to be operating as before. *Studies in the Soviet Union,* a journal published in Munich, continued to receive from Communist countries revisionist manuscript literature teeming with anonymous poetry on forbidden themes. Copies of the manuscript collection *Phoenix,* reflecting deviationist ideas, were being smuggled out of the Soviet Union.

In summation it appears that the government saw the wisdom of avoiding a last-ditch clash with the liberal intellectuals—a clash which might compel a use of force, and which would not solve the paramout problem now faced: how to preserve and utilize the extensive talents of this group, the elite of the country's creative intellectuals, for achieving the goals of the socialist state? Yet the regime is under pressure from the die-hard dogmatists to do something about unorthodox literature. Hence official policy uses the political expediency of campaigning in the public press against "deviationism" and occasionally tightening the reigns of the control system, even if the results are only a paper war. Western observers agree that out of the zigzags of Soviet literary policy have come important gains in intellectual freedom, the freedom to search for the truth as well as to express it. The liberal leaders dream of the eventual separation of creative expression from the State much as nineteenth-century liberals looked to separation of church from State.

One is reminded that Russian literary figures more than once have been seen in the vanguard of important social and political change. In the reign of Nicholas I, writers produced literature that laid the foundations for education and a kind of public opinion which started the reform movements of the latter half of the century. The slow and painful advances of the post-Stalin era toward greater freedom of literary expression will stimulate critical thinking, rouse public opinion, and present Soviet society with a more realistic image of itself. This last is no doubt a sobering experience. The gains made by literature are being carried over into journalism and the mass media.

EFFORTS TO IMPROVE THE MEDIA

Throughout the ups and downs of the cold war in the field of literary politics, it was clear that the regime was sincere in its desire to encourage innovation, initiative, and within limits, even creative thought. Nowhere was this intention more manifest than in the mass media system. The campaign against dullness in the media began as early as 1953 and it was led by none other than Chairman Khrushchev, speaking to an editors' conference:

"Firmly rooted stereotypes and well-worn methods whereby everything is written according to a single pattern must be vigorously driven from the newspaper pages. . . . Material must be more varied and more thought given to content and form of presentation." [25]

What had been plain to media audiences for a long time—the fact that the media were so boring as to repel readers—was officially noted. The Chairman sought to encourage originality and experimentation with new methods. Criticism was invited.

Asked during his 1955 American visit to explain why Soviet newspapers were so much alike, N. G. Palgunov, former director of Tass, refused to admit to Senator William Benton that similarity of makeup, identical headlines, and other signs of total sameness throughout the press were the result of anything other than pure coincidence.[26] Such a meeting of the minds is beyond the bounds of mathematical probability, Benton thought. Palgunov also refused to admit that Tass dispatches similar material to many newspapers with instructions to editors regarding position and play. "If Tass doesn't send out such instructions, they must come from somewhere," Benton concluded. Konstantin Gubin, former *Pravda* editor, inadvertently provided a plausible, if partial, explanation. "With experience our editors learn how it should be done," he said.

If Palgunov wished to ignore Tass's responsibility for contributing to sameness in media content, other communications officials were more frank. A. E. Lazebnik, deputy director of propaganda for the Central Committee in the Ukraine, bluntly declared, "If one were to conceal the names of newspapers it would be almost impossible to tell which is which." In a similar vein, a high official of the party's Propaganda and Agitation Department in Moscow said, "Before me lie several issues of province and territory newspapers published on the same day. Above all, one is arrested by the papers' striking similarity. Like twins, they can hardly be distinguished from one another. If it were not for the masthead . . . any one of the newspapers could be substituted for another, and neither the reader nor the staff itself would notice!" [27] Referring to editorials on agriculture problems, this official noted that the same approach, the identical pattern of organization and structure, were used by editorials in all of the papers. ". . . As a rule they speak first of the importance of the current agricultural campaign. The outstanding collective farms and districts are mentioned. Then comes the invariable *However:* 'However far from everywhere is genuine concern shown . . .'—and several favorable examples are cited. The conclusion follows: 'Such a situation is intolerable.' At the end a directive is laid down: 'Party and Soviet organizations must . . . .' "[28] Unfortunately, he added, these faults mark not only most local but also many Central newspapers.

Alexsei V. Romanov, one of *Sovetskaya Pechat's* editors, writing in *Partinaya Zhizn,* attacked superficial, routine descriptions which generally leave the reader indifferent because they fail to stir him to thoughts or arouse his desire to share what he has read, to discuss it, or perhaps to dispute it. "In journalism a person who produces an indifferent chronicle, an unthinking record of events, is particularly intolerable when it is a matter of problems that interest many, if not all. . . ."[29]

Turning to press reportage of party matters, Romanov discussed the lack of reader response to press treatment of party subjects. There is nothing strange in this, he said, when one considers how the reports are written. Under the heading PARTY LIFE, many newspapers publish "chiefly dry, monotonous reports of all kinds of meetings . . . plus the lengthiest speeches, sometimes running in identical text in three or four Republic papers." The newspapers were apparently hard put to improve the interest-value of speeches, for the speeches themselves, Romanov claimed, ordinarily repeat worn-out, tired phrases and represent no deeply treated topics, no journalistic sharpness. "We ordinarily write on party topics uninterestingly, in a language that is dull and bureaucratic, so much stereotype and cliche does it contain," he said. It is almost impossible to find under the rubric PARTY LIFE a sketch, a review, live correspondence, a feuilleton, or other creative spark. The critic then urged writers to look for new forms, methods, and personalities in party work to exploit ". . . new ways of educating the public about the functions of elected party groups, the conduct of party meetings, and the moral image of the party member."

Change came slowly. Obviously action was called for, and it came, beginning in 1956, in the form of a succession of Central Committee decrees on press and broadcasting. The decrees were aimed at raising the level of content by eliminating dullness and monotony in style of writing and makeup; at "quotationitis and pedantry that stifles live, creative thought"; and at "revisionist deviations" and "bourgeois vulgarity." A series of measures were taken to raise professional standards and at the same time to exalt the journalist's social role, his position of high moral and political responsibility.

As was discussed earlier in this chapter and in Chapter 2, this was not the first time a general overhaul of the media system had been ordered. The first measure was the creation of a national organization of journalists in April, 1956, an event which placed journalists among the last of the professions to be unionized.[30] The union brought together all creative workers in newspapers, magazines, book publishing, and broadcasting. It admitted all ranks of workers from beginners to top executives. The union was charged with the task of (1) encouraging journalists in mobilizing workers for the victory of Communism, (2) improving the general quality of the press by raising the professional level of presentation (specifically by developing variety in form and style) in order to strengthen the links between the press and the masses, and (3) building professional *esprit* and defending the rights of journalists within the framework of labor legislation. By 1959 the union boasted 17,000 members. By 1963 it was claiming to be the largest journalistic organization in the world with 25,000 members. The magazine *Sovetskaya Pechat* was transferred to the union to serve as its official organ. Besides publishing various reports and compiling statistics on press and broadcasting, *Sovetskaya Pechat* taught lessons in professional techniques. It devoted space to instruction in page makeup, picture cropping, article writing, and so forth. In addition to its professional contributions, the organization of journalists served to raise the status of media workers to the same level as that of workers in literature, art, and music.

A second step taken by the government also elevated the journalist's stature. The highest honor the Soviet state can bestow, the Lenin Prize, was made available to journalists as an added inducement for editors, directors, and their staffs to do superior work in communications.[31]

Third, to show communications experts what they meant by improving media appeal, the Central authorities started a new general circulation Central daily on July 1, 1956 (Fig. 8.2). This paper, *Sovetskaya Rossia* (Soviet Russia) concentrates on Western variety news, lively photographs, reader polls, human interest, and even

СОВЕТСКАЯ РОССИЯ

ЕСТЬ СЕМИЛЕТКА!

ГАРАНТИЯ ОТ ШАБЛОНА

СКОРОСТЬ—ДЕВИЗ ПОКОРИТЕЛЕЙ НЕДР

Румынские гости в Москве

НАГРАДЫ КОЛХОЗНЫМ СТРОИТЕЛЯМ

ПРАЗДНИК ЛИТЕРАТУРЫ В ЧИТЕ

Указ Президиума Верховного Совета СССР

О созыве Верховного Совета СССР

Fig. 8.2. **Sovetskaya Rossia** (Soviet Russia) is a graphic example of how media are created to perform a certain task. This daily was begun July 1, 1956, to provide a model for the regime's new emphasis on the professional techniques of persuasion in the mass media.

display advertising—all presented in a simple, brief style. Within three years this paper was rivaling *Izvestia* in circulation. Another pacesetter in this respect was *Komsomolskaya Pravda,* which ordinarily is a more readable paper than either *Pravda* or *Izvestia.* But under the editorship of Alexsei A. Adzhubei, Khrushchev's son-in-law, this journal blossomed with semisensational features on sex, youth problems, more and livelier pictures, and displayed a lighter, brighter tone. His successful revitalization of this organ of the Young Communist League earned a promotion for Adzhubei in 1959 when he became chief editor of *Izvestia.* Under his expert hand, the once gray, stolid paper began to show similar changes. Cartoons replaced the usual front-page editorial. Three-column pictures of water skiers appeared instead of factory heroes. In 1960 *Izvestia* started a Western-style Sunday supplement *Nedelia* (The Week), a 32-page pictorial tabloid with a party-line comic page and short satires of life outside the USSR.

Even the staid and proper *Pravda* took up the cry in a Press Day editorial, declaring "Soviet newspapers are insipid, lifeless, deadly dull, and difficult to read." This paper's solid expanse of type and austere bearing began to find relief in brighter headlines and more illustrations. This was the signal for other papers to join in the task. Not unlike the pot calling the kettle black, *Pravda* also denounced Radio Moscow for its colorlessness, its dull accounts, and its bad music. In a manner reminiscent of Madison Avenue, *Pravda* also advised announcers to cultivate a "sincere microphone manner so that each [listener] feels that the speaker is addressing him in person."

Trud, the labor union daily, broke into a rash of sensationalism with the kind of passionate human interest that is dear to the heart of the circulation-hungry Western tabloid. An example story: The young, unwed mother, deserted by her lover and threatened with the loss of her job, insists on having her baby. Reporter Vera Trachenko tearfully observes, "I saw with what dignity she bore her . . . position, with what wonderful light and love her face was suffused when she talked about the future of her child."

Yuri Gagarin's flight into space spurred the press into a splurge of excitement. In the days following the event there were red-ink banner headlines, sidebar interviews and intimate photographs of the hero and his family. Reporters for *Komsomolskaya Pravda* went so far as to invade the astronaut's privacy by publishing family photographs inscribed with sentimental expressions, stolen from his apartment. *Pravda* scolded its impulsive younger brother for this breach of ethics. Such violent disregard of Lenin's vow against sensationalism was excused on the grounds that it was designed "to sustain the better things in man," Mikhail Kharlamov, press chief of the Soviet foreign ministry, explained. "We print the account of a man who jumps 23 centimeters, not of one who jumps into the street from the 25th floor," he added.

Although the instances of livelier communications fare marked an important milestone, and measures to brighten the media were productive, the regime still was not satisfied. Six years after the campaign began, Khrushchev again took the press to task. "There is still much dull stuff in our papers," he said. "Sometimes I take a paper, finger it through, and put it aside. And afterwards you cannot even recall what it said." He admitted he tended to read more of "what bourgeois journalists write," than what his own propagandists were saying. He advised communications experts and fellow citizens to study the Western press and learn. "We must be well aware of what is taking place in the capitalist world. We must know what is said and written there about the Soviet Union—what is causing alarm in the capitalist world." [32]

In line with this suggestion, a fourth step was the noticeable effort in the media to transmit straight information about the United States and Western Europe. For the first time, an uncensored policy statement of Secretary of State Christian Herter and the comment of former Secretary of State Dean Acheson were published fully and without comment late in 1959. Did it mark a drastic departure? The answer was clear in the long editorial rebuttals. But at least Soviet readers could learn on occasion directly what the West was actually thinking and doing instead of reading only the official version of these acts.

Articles in the journals reflected a new effort on the part of scholars and specialists to learn the facts about the rest of the world, the United States in particular, to set the record straight, and to bridge gaps created by the nation's long isolation. Foreign news became more topical. Indeed the media showed a real effort to correct some false images of the West that were promulgated during the Stalin era. For example it was possible for the Soviet reader to learn that not all workers in the United States were poorly paid, oppressed serfs—that instead, the average American worker owns his home and possesses an automobile. Resolutions of anti-Communist organizations abroad were reported for the first time as if such views were legitimate subjects for discussion. Comparisons were made between United States and Soviet textile production showing that Soviet production still lagged. Such invidious analogies had never appeared before. There was evidence of heightened interest in investigating United States and British production techniques. With wider access to writings from abroad, Soviet writers showed signs of desiring to correct a few of the more exaggerated historical fabrications projected under Stalin—one, the claim that Alexander F. Mozhaisky, a Russian, and not the Wright Brothers, had made as early as 1882 the first successful flight in heavier-than-air craft.

A fifth aspect of the campaign was to increase both in volume and tempo the forces of persuasion—perhaps as another substitute for coercion. Early in 1960 the press printed a long, abstract and difficult-to-read decree of the Central Committee, "On the Tasks of Party Propaganda in Present-Day Conditions," which dealt with how to make propaganda more effective. It declared that Soviet propaganda is ineffective, formalistic, and abstract, and that it leaves large segments of the society untouched and unhearing. The decree demanded a stepped-up program of propaganda and agitation throughout all media and up and down the party organization. This program resulted the first year in doubling the number of party schools.

The sixth and last step of the program to extend the new propaganda offensive was to increase the number of media units with all possible haste. This phase of the campaign indicated the regime's systematic determination to expand the audience base by building a mass media network that it hopes will touch and influence every individual.

There were other signs of change in the direction of opening up channels of information with other countries. The Iron curtain was no longer impervious. Newsmen were admitted to many previously restricted points in the Soviet Union. There was an increase in the pace and volume of travel, in the number of student exchanges, the number of festivals and exhibits. The use of press conferences by Soviet officials and the discontinuance of formal censorship of outgoing dispatches, in March, 1961, were all signs of a general relaxation of barriers to communication flow. Fear was reported on the decline in most quarters, as economic incentives and persuasion gradually replaced coercion and pressure.[33]

The liberalizing effects of the Thaw and the New Wave transfused into the mass communication system have resulted in substantial change in the direction of making the system better serve its purposes. In some ways the improvements in the mass media work as benefits to the media consumer as well. Notable advances have been seen in the attempts to increase the appeal of broadcasting fare and in the general attractiveness of newspapers and magazines to the public. Still much more needs to be done. There is reason to believe that the mass media are trying to report more factual information and to correct some of the grosser exaggerations and false images they have projected in the past. Alexei Adzhubei, *Izvestia* editor, in 1959 wrote in *Sovetskaya Pechat,* "More and more in our materials is present an observation of mankind, a view of the journalist who is writing. . . . We do not fear to say, 'I thought it out, I observed it, I have encountered it.' There was a period in journalism when this was not encouraged." This kind of realism in news writing like that in literature, presupposes that favorable as well as unfavorable sides will be described by the observing reporter. The clash of opinion that found expression in the mass media during the controversy between the regime and the writers demonstrated, as in the case of other controversies, that there is room within ideological limitations to accommodate differences of viewpoint. From time to time viewpoints directly opposed to those of the established orthodoxy have found their way into the public media. If these trends continue, they will indicate a basic change in policy.

Another encouraging sign is that the regime's efforts to make mass persuasion a more effective weapon of social control, albeit the motive was selfish, has resulted not only in raising the professional standards of the mass media product, but also in developing a body of professionally skilled mass communications workers with higher social and economic standing. Formerly an editor's qualifications depended more on his party loyalty or ideological knowledge than on his knowledge of the techniques of journalism and propaganda; today more emphasis is being placed upon professional qualifications as a communicator, acquired by study of techniques. Adzhubei was attempting to build up the image of the journalist as a man of specialized talent when he said,

> Some opinions hold that anyone with a pen is able to become a journalist. It is important that journalists defend, accentuate, and propagandize the idea that journalism, a creative profession, is a calling. To become a journalist, it is necessary to have mastery of precise talents, it is necessary to cultivate these talents and develop them, it is necessary to work hard and stubbornly . . . it is necessary to have an understanding of the laws of composition and an accuracy with the artistic work. . . . The newspaper art is no less complex or responsible than the art of the belletrist, and no less honorable.[34]

These changes do not mean that anything like the Western doctrine of freedom of the press is gradually coming into use in the Soviet Union. The concept of human freedom still holds. The dictatorship of the party is still supreme. The ends are the same, the means more rational. The gaps in information remain, and the propaganda is often as dull and unappetizing as ever. The philosophy of the sensitive intellectual, and perhaps that of the journalist who has some knowledge of freedom of the press, were epitomized in the outburst of a young Russian novelist in response to an American's question, "How can you create under the prohibitions of the party, under fear of censorship?" The young writer's eyes blazed and he spoke passionately, "The end justifies the means! None of you capitalists will ever understand! . . ." Then he related the idea of his new novel, *The Five-Petaled Lilac.* In the novel the hero sees a lilac tree growing in a courtyard where blood is flowing from the bodies of five executed counter-revolutionists. The lilac was drinking up the blood. The blood-fed plant seemed to the hero a symbol of his country. He took the lilac home to study it, rooted new lilacs from it, naming each one "collective farm lilac," "industrialization lilac," etc. The hero's aspiration was to develop a new breed of lilac, one that would have five petals—a good luck symbol like the four-leaf clover. All of the blood shed, the sacrifice, the suppression and cruelty, the hero learned, were to be justified by the superb new lilac, the symbol of the Soviet State.

SOME INDICATIONS OF COMMUNICATIONS EFFECT

If the Soviet citizen is to have a reasonably accurate, connected account, the performance of Soviet mass media as a mirror of reality reflecting an image of either domestic or foreign affairs still lacks much to be desired. The best body of professionally trained communicators cannot be expected to penetrate the traditional secretiveness of party and government in a closed society, more especially when the communications media are agencies of that government. The scarcity or complete absence of facts in the media about political developments or about the launching of space vehicles forces the discerning Soviet citizen to learn almost as much from what the media do not say as from what they say. The Kremlin's habits of secrecy lend a certain credibility to every rumor; indeed they breed rumor mongering. A whisper from Moscow via Rome in April, 1963, for example, became big news around the world, news without a shred of substance. A Moscow correspondent of Italy's Communist newspaper *L'Unita* described Soviet domestic and foreign troubles and ended with the observation that "Moscow is living through a delicate and interesting political moment." Rome's newspapers headlined this as a prediction of Khrushchev's imminent downfall which did not become fact until October, 1964. The rumor was echoed in New York, London, and Paris headlines. When such rumors burst upon the world's press they give only a hint of what goes on inside the Soviet Union.

Speculation on levels of information among Soviet populations and sub groups raises significant questions that must be answered before any attempt can be made to evaluate the usefulness of the media to the citizen. What are the effects of the communications system, Communist-style, on the average person? What are communications behavior patterns like? The outside world can only rely on insubstantial data to help answer such questions. Effects of communications in any society are difficult to determine and evaluate with scientific precision, and are especially difficult in the case of a communist society. If social science research is being used to any extent in the Soviet Union, its findings are government property and not generally available to the public. Indications of how successfully the media system does the job assigned to it are apparent in the periodic public criticism of media behavior and in the measures taken by the regime to remedy the defects. In regard to how well the mass media of communication operate simply as a conveyer of reliable information, we can draw inferences which may have some validity from pieces of data we have.

Bauer and Inkeles[35] in their extensive studies of socio-political attributes of Soviet refugees have reported on communications behavior and effect, particularly in regard to the dominant news and information media. They found that the Soviet citizen, not unlike the citizen of the democracies, expects his communications system primarily to keep him informed about his world—or in the words of Lasswell, primarily to serve as a means of surveillance of the environment. The Soviet citizen regards information as "what he wants to learn, not that which the regime wants him to know." Yet what he gets most of the time is what the regime wants him to know.

How does he learn about his environment? There exists a difference, which at times may become considerable, between the citizen's sense of reality and logic, and the picture presented to him in the media. The existence of such a gap has fostered the development in the Soviet Union of an extensive use of unofficial channels of communication to supplement those of the official media. The unofficial channels take the form of rumor, listening to foreign radio, and discussions or face-to-face communication with friends. These unofficial sources supplement the official ones to build up the average citizen's stock of information. Their use has increased despite the efforts of officials to discourage "rumor mongering." The citizen uses the unofficial channels in several ways: to correct erroneous impressions gained from the official media system; to discover what the regime suppresses; and to help him interpret the whole so that his picture of the world will correspond reasonably well with his perception of reality, or what his powers of observation and intelligence lead him to perceive. The existence of the extensive informal system of communication, Bauer and Inkeles conclude, suggests the inability of the formal media system to satisfy the basic human need of the individual to identify with his environment, its inability to reflect the world scene to a degree that satisfies the minimum needs of the average person.

How extensively is the unofficial system used? Its frequency of use is exceeded only by that of newspapers. Where nine out of ten refugees interviewed mentioned newspapers as their primary sources of information, about half mentioned radio and word-of-mouth sources as their second most important sources of information. The communist use of agitation as an official medium received mention as a primary source by only about one in five persons. When former Russian citizens were asked to name their most important sources of information, newspapers and word-of-mouth were mentioned most frequently. According to Bauer and Inkeles, the two parallel systems interact to provide a reasonably balanced picture, but different individuals use them in different ways. "For some people the unofficial media serve as a substitute for the official sources and they withdraw almost completely from the use of the latter. Others use the official channels almost exclusively. Most persons, however, use both the official and informal media in a complementary relationship, each utilized as a check on, and as a basis for interpretation of, the other." [36]

Analysis of media exposure patterns in relation to population subgroups revealed a sharp decline in the frequency of exposure from the top to the bottom of the social scale, or from the intelligentsia down to the collective farmers, a decline occurring in the case of both the official as well as the unofficial channels of information. Thus the greatest users of the official media tended to be those most highly educated and in the highest occupational classes. Conversely, those in the lowest educational and occupational ranks tended to use the media least of all. Other less important but revealing independent influences on media behavior—influences correlating positively with the degree of official media exposure—were such factors as the degree of political involvement on the part of the individual, his degree of expressed sympathy toward the regime, and the degree of his ambition to succeed in the social system. The existence of wide differences in the communications behavior patterns of the intelligentsia on the one hand and the peasant on the other was especially notable: the member of the urban intelligentsia has greater access to and can better afford to buy the media, while the peasant is more isolated and indigent; the intelligentsia's background usually whets his appetite for identifying with and participating in the world of affairs, while the peasant's more traditional background tends to make him a nonparticipant in the society, and particularly a nonparticipant in the use of the mass media. He is a follower rather than a leader. Many of the intelligentsia, and particularly those who are government or party officials, find it necessary for occupational survival to keep well informed, but at the same time they happen to move in circles that enable them to receive the most reliable, high-level, word-of-mouth information. The peasant on the contrary tends to withdraw from what little use of the official media is open to him and to utilize rumor and word-of-mouth communication as a substitute for the official media. Yet because of his social position he is least likely to receive reliable information via word-of-mouth channels. While both classes believe that word-of-mouth sources and rumor are more reliable than the official media, nine out of ten among the intelligentsia place greater faith in the accuracy of rumor, but only slightly more than half of the peasants do so.

Lack of confidence in official media sources, however, should not be understood to mean such sources have little impact. The Soviet citizen may cite many examples of media falsification and suppression of information, yet in the same breath prove the success of Soviet propaganda methods by mouthing with conviction the familiar themes to which he has so often been exposed. Not unlike his American counterpart in noting erroneous reports in the press, he accepts what he gets from the media for the most part without much questioning.

The effect of the depiction of such erroneous images and conceptions is summed up by Barghoorn, who examined the acceptance of beliefs, expressed in the propaganda, by Soviet citizens, during the period following the war. The image was anything but realistic, he found.

> . . . in the strange realm of Soviet political mythology, America resembles more closely the horrid fantasy of Orwell's *Nineteen Eighty-Four* than the country we know. The America of Soviet propaganda is ruled by force and fraud. Its handful of rulers pull the strings to which their subjects dance like puppets. Its domestic policy is one of exploitation and oppression, and its foreign policy is characterized by deception and aggression.
>
> . . . Hovering physically and spiritually behind fortress walls, the masters of the Kremlin look out like the prisoners of Plato's cave upon a world of shadows.[37]

The fact that this kind of image could not have changed very much is shown by the examination of the Tass domestic report in late 1959, some ten years later, as depicted in the previous chapter.

Mannes[38] recounts the case of a young married woman of the intelligentsia, who was a regular television fan, watching with her family almost every evening. Her program preferences ran in the category of romantic films and drama, when she was not auditing lessons in the English language. Yet she believed implicitly in the entire news report, often being so impressed by Soviet leaders (and even charmed by Khrushchev's manner) that it never occurred to her to doubt the authenticity of information being transmitted. Her confessed boredom with educational programs was characterized by the same uncritical attitude. Judging by the seriousness with which Soviet intellectuals are addicted to television, one may take her behavior as fairly typical of her class.

Inkeles and Bauer cite examples of rather striking success achieved by communication in shaping the images of the most highly educated and intelligent persons. These individuals adhered to their media-acquired conceptions even in the face of impressive evidence to the contrary from their own life experience.[39] Prominent among the authors' case examples are instances of the regime's ability to sell its own versions of foreign and domestic conditions, and particularly its version of the foreign policies of other countries. The greatest influence in this respect was discovered among the intelligentsia who ". . . whether they accept or reject the regime must, by virtue of their place in society, learn and repeat the official line to a point where it becomes second nature. . . ." [40]

The average Soviet citizen's interpretive devices and other media behavior patterns do not differ substantially from those found among citizens of other countries. But the extent to which the Soviet citizen must be dependent upon reading between the lines appears unusual. In libertarian press countries some speculation takes place about relatively minor currents in the news stream, or about causes and motivations not fully explained by news sources. Media behavior in the Soviet Union differs in the frequency with which the average person must resort to such reading between the lines. Conditions of Soviet society and the function of its official media system tend to encourage the use of unofficial sources, though the regime has attempted to discourage their use, even to the extent of jamming foreign broadcasts. At times, the regime has planted or used rumor to suit its own ends. Yet through it all the citizen in the upper social brackets has developed a certain ingenuity in piecing together from miscellaneous data gathered from all sources to achieve some sort of informational foundation for drawing intelligent conclusions about public affairs. It is difficult to see how his general level of information could be as high as that of his Western counterpart. Moreover, the system of reading between the lines has its disadvantages, for however rewarding in the sense that it provides a degree of perspective to an otherwise one-sided view, it can be misleading and erroneous.

Except for the substantial use of unofficial channels the Soviet pattern of communications behavior resembles in most respects that of the advanced Western cultures. It is a pattern that correlates highly with the advanced stages of industrialization, urbanization, and mass education. The extensive use of all kinds of newspapers in the Soviet Union is mathematically greater than the daily newspaper per capita consumption rates for the United States, but Soviet figures do not report daily use separately from nondaily usage. Straight-line comparison is impossible, but when adjustments are made to account for daily newspaper use, a great weight of the evidence lies on the side of the West. Furthermore the penetration of radio and television is also much greater in Western states.

Perhaps the greatest effect of the Soviet communications system, as indeed of other phases of the indoctrinational program, has been apparent in the shaping of latent or subconscious thought patterns associated with the development of a basic value-system. Such patterns, once acquired, are hard to change. Obviously the constant exposure to a stream of propaganda as persistent as this one—and who in the Soviet Union can escape it?—has a powerful and often subtle influence.

There can be little doubt that mass media contribute heavily to the economic, social, and cultural development of the country. Here Lenin's comparison of the press to the carpenter's scaffolding symbolizes how the mass media function in building the communist state and hopefully the "new kind of socialist man." First, the scaffolding indicates the outline of the building; secondly, it makes contacts between the builders easier; and thirdly, the outlines of the scaffolding make possible a preview of the whole so that the results of organized work may be foreseen.[41] Like the mass media of other countries the Soviet media report developments and progress in attaining the national goals set by the party for every area of the society, albeit through rose-colored lenses. However invidious the overly promotional aspects of media content may appear to Western thought, it should be remembered that a certain degree of nationalistic, parochial bias has been found in news agency or local copy both in the United States and other libertarian democracies. Examples that readily come to mind are the "Chamber of Commerce" type of local or regional "puffing" or boosting to promote economic growth, attract investment, etc. In the development of unsettled regions of the United States during the nineteenth century, local newspapers, pamphlets, handbills, and tracts made wildly exaggerated claims about the virtues of their particular region in order to attract settlers. Conscious or unconscious pronationalistic slanting creeps into news agency copy reporting international conferences or conflicts, hot or cold, the direction depending on what news agency happens to be reporting. The main difference in principle between Soviet and Western practice is what the libertarian media do it by choice. By serving as a catalyst and cohesive agent the mass communication media of both communist and democratic societies are prime instruments of national development and public political participation. Stalin once said that mass media in the Soviet Union, functioning as a "transmission belt" between leaders and people, must share in the credit for national growth speeding the process from a transitional, war- and rebellion-wracked state to a modern, mature society within less than fifty years. This could hardly have been accomplished without the transformation by universal public education, communication, and other factors of a largely backward and illiterate population into a participant society. Besides the presentation in the media of one continuous, year-in and year-out progress report on the building of the whole society, other functions have been to prod and spur the people, to hold out rewards and punishments, to point to the goals, to persuade and drive, and to pose problems. Finally, the function of criticism has revealed corruption, omissions, inefficency, and bungling. Self-criticism has substituted new for outworn methods, exposed fallacies in logic, and caused the abandonment of false premises and overconservative principles. Communications, including mass communications, it seems, have the power under certain conditions and in collaboration with other social forces, to change people and to transform the society in which they live, whether Communist or capitalist. The Communist leaders, however, want to change the society first.

2

CHINA: CONFUCIAN AND COMMUNIST

CHINA (People's Republic of China)

AREA: 3,767,751 sq. mi.
POPULATION: 735,000,000. Largest city: Shanghai. Capital: Peking.
CLIMATE: Northern regions—warm summers, cold winters; moderate summer rainfall, dry winters. Southern regions—warmer winters, heavier rainfall. Western regions—hot summers, cold winters; very dry. Highlands vary from warm to cold, wet to dry.
ALTITUDES: Minya Konka, 24,900 ft.; Peking, 165 ft.

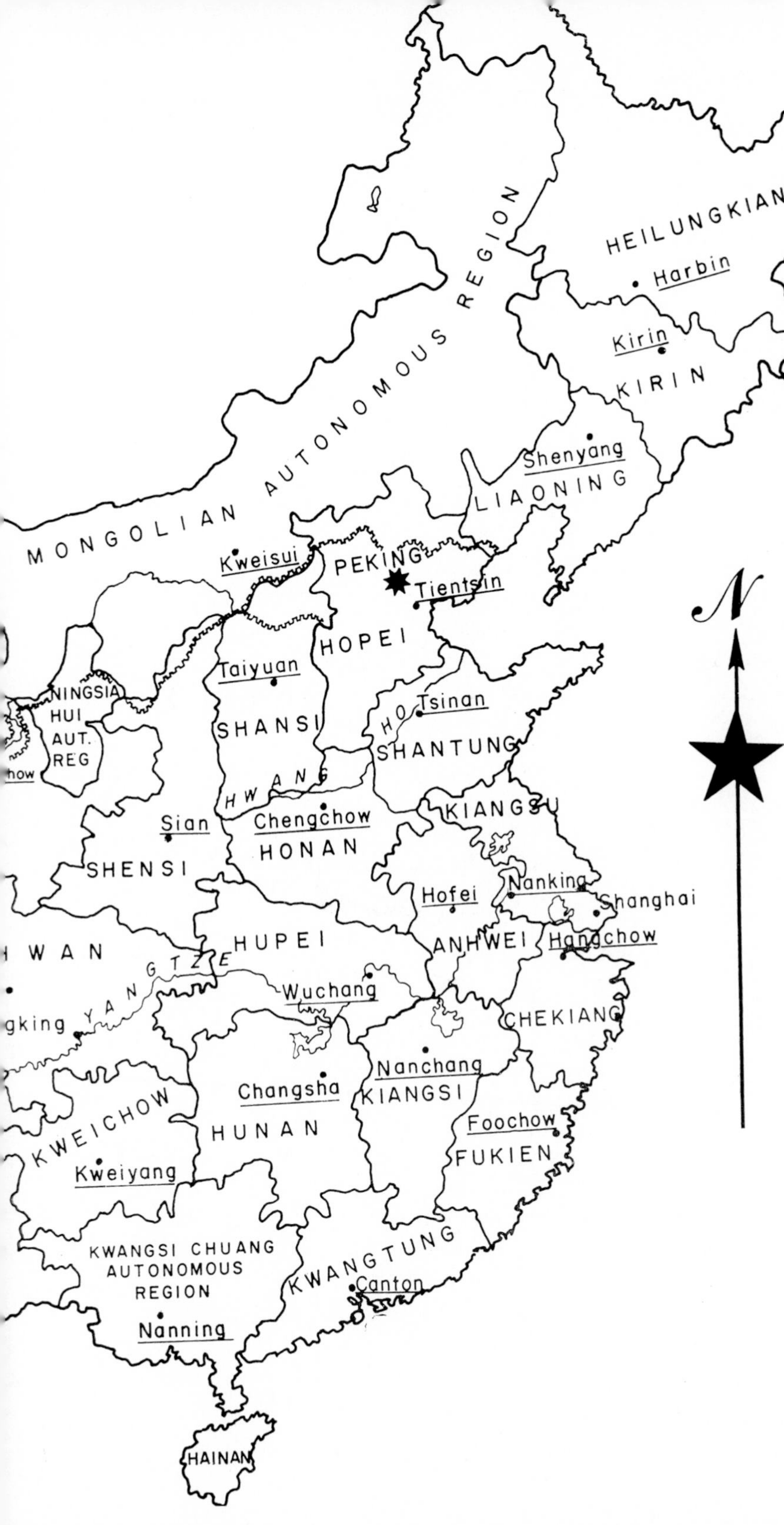
HEILUNGKIANG
Harbin
Kirin
KIRIN
MONGOLIAN AUTONOMOUS REGION
Shenyang
LIAONING
Kweisui
PEKING
Tientsin
HOPEI
Taiyuan
SHANSI
NINGSIA HUI AUT. REG
Tsinan
HO
SHANTUNG
HWANG
Chengchow
HONAN
KIANGSU
Sian
SHENSI
Nanking
Hofei
Shanghai
HUPEI
ANHWEI
Hangchow
YANGTZE
Wuchang
CHEKIANG
Nanchang
KIANGSI
Changsha
HUNAN
KWEICHOW
Kweiyang
Foochow
FUKIEN
KWANGTUNG
Canton
KWANGSI CHUANG AUTONOMOUS REGION
Nanning
HAINAN
N

9

PRESS AND SOCIETY IN TRADITIONAL CHINA: THE CULTURAL SETTING

COMMUNIST CHINA'S LEADERS in the 1960s, in trying to build a modern industrial nation with all speed, are eager to throw off much of China's culture-bound past. But though its apostles of change want to stamp out the influence of history, no civilization can suddenly cast off the heritage of experience, the lessons of existence and survival as a race and as a society. From the highly refined culture of the ancient Chinese to Mao's hyperthyroid superstate runs a thread of evolution that must be analyzed carefully though briefly before the Communist mass communication system of China can be understood. What were the attributes and values of traditional Chinese culture?

THE LAND AND THE PEOPLE

Many concrete facts of geography and sociology combine to make China a potentially powerful nation in world affairs. Sheer size of territory and population are enough to propel it to the forefront among world states. China, with a total land area of 3.66 million acres, is the third largest country in the world, exceeded only by the Soviet Union and Canada.[1] It is more than a half-million square miles larger than continental United States, and about 30 times the size of the United Kingdom. China contains half again as many people as India, almost twice as many as the United States and the Soviet Union combined. Its population in 1961 was estimated at 700 million.[2] This massive superiority in human resources amounts to almost one-fourth of all mankind. At present rates of growth, variously estimated at between 14 and 20 million a year, China's population is expected to reach the billion mark by 1981. The rate of growth, which in 1950 was 2 per cent, was 3.5 per cent in 1959.[3]

Although China's peoples number among them some 38 million who are in some fifty minority groups that do not speak Chinese—and these are widely divided by different dialects, themselves—there are many Chinese not living in mainland China for whom Chinese is the mother tongue. More people speak Chinese than any other language.[4]

China's hungry millions need to cultivate a large proportion of the land they possess, but unfortunately they cannot, for much of the land is unsuitable for crops. It has been estimated that China has less than one-half acre of food-producing land per person. The United States has 2.5 acres under cultivation per person, or five times as much as China, while Europe has one acre, or about twice as much as China.[5] Only 27 per cent of China's total land area is under cultivation.

The ratio of people to land is high in the central eastern area because almost all of the people (more than 95 per cent) are concentrated in 35 per cent of the lowland area of the eastern river plains and areas lying along the southeastern Pacific coast. China's original 18 provinces lie in this area of fertile land. An idea of population density here may be obtained by comparing the population of Honan Province with that of Arkansas in the United States, for their land areas are about equal: Honan has 44 million people—Arkansas has 1.8 million. While in the United States there are about 200 persons to every square mile of arable land, in China there are more than seven times that many.

What are the pluses and minuses of China's human inflation? Obviously it serves as a huge stockpile of cheap manpower for supplying the nation's labor force and for recruiting an army. It is useful for expansionist aims either by slow absorption of alien cultures, as has happened in the past, or by conquest. The advantages of this manpower reservoir are enhanced by Chinese traits of character. The Chinese can be highly productive because they work long hours daily for what Westerners would consider a pittance. They are characteristically industrious, tolerant, and thrifty. The age pyramid shows that China is a land of young people. Maximum life expectancy has been reported at between 30 and 40 years, but 84 per cent of the population in 1959 was estimated to be below the age of 49.[6] The birth rate per 1,000 has fallen slightly, from 37 in 1952 to 32 in 1959. The death rate per 1,000 has declined impressively from 18 in 1952 to 11 in 1959.

On the minus side, the disadvantages of the massive and growing population seem to outweigh the advantages. The population problem has plagued the people for generations, even centuries, defying the efforts of every regime to solve. If most of the labor force is not constantly kept at work, enough food, clothing, and shelter to support the population cannot be produced. China has imported grain since 1721.[7] The production of food is at the mercy of intermittent droughts and floods which have in the past produced famine and epidemics to bring the population down to survival size. Since most able-bodied persons of both sexes must work to produce necessities, the manpower needed for other kinds of production is limited proportionately. Students have been dismissed from the colleges to work in the fields. Standards of living though improving, are low, and poverty, hunger, and disease are common among the masses. China's over-population and its poor land resources pose a Malthusian dilemma that has taxed the ingenuity of its rulers for centuries. It is one that will not be resolved easily or soon.

Seventy-five per cent of the population is engaged in agriculture which in 1957 accounted for 50 per cent of the gross national product.[8] Even with large populations concentrated in cities, urban inhabitants usually make their living from the land. Before the advent of the Communist era, three-fourths of the population lived on small farms averaging about three acres in size, a system that failed to produce enough to support the population due to old and inefficient agricultural methods, lack of modern transportation, and the shortage of arable land. To make more acres productive in times of drought and to harness floods, the Communist government is building a series of great dams along the Yellow River and other streams, a measure that will increase the food production potential and also provide hydroelectric power for industry. Besides water for irrigation, the government is providing fertilizers and improved seeds, and introducing modern farming methods.

Transportation and intercommunication facilities in the pre-Communist era were confined to the larger cities and the eastern seaboard area, but the Communist government now is building highways, bridges, railroad, telephone, and telegraph lines, extending them west toward Tibet, Sinkiang, and Yunnan. Although ancient China had better roads than Europe, modern-day China has fallen far behind, and still must use canals and rivers as a major means of transport. Counting progress that has been made since 1949, the number of miles of modern highways and railroads is small compared with the size of the country. Except for a few overland highways which are penetrating the western provinces, the airways provide the main link with the urban East.

The comparative poverty of China's mineral resources, their location in respect to each other, and their distance both from population centers and from transportation cast doubt on the possibility that China will develop an industrial economy comparable to that of the United States. Yet it could become a leading industrial nation in the Far East.[9] The Communist regime is making slow strides in this direction. As in the Soviet Union, first emphasis was on heavy industry with some expansion of small industries, then on agriculture, and more recently on agriculture-related fertilizer industries. The industrial complex includes cotton, wool, and silk mills, electrical power and appliance manufacturing, tanning, cement production, and other items. The oil produced is less than 1 per cent of United States production. Steel output, often taken as an index of total industrial production, was in 1956 about 4.5 million tons, as compared with a United States production of 115 million tons.[10] The 5-year-plans and the well-publicized "great leap forward" have not met with the success propaganda claims avow. The commune movement in agriculture has not increased production substantially. The local production of steel in backyard furnaces has proved a failure, and a need for capital for industrial expansion is still acute.[11]

THE ECONOMIC AND SOCIAL ORDER

The Family System in the Social Structure

In traditional China the foundation of all economic, political, and social organization—indeed the fundamental philosophy of the culture—rested on that basic social unit, the family. Chinese civilization for centuries and into the modern era revolved around the concept of family and the principles which govern it, as the fountainhead of the Chinese way of life. In contrast, the foundation of socioeconomic organization in Western Europe for several centuries has been provided by industrial, business, and trade organizations. In ancient China the family circle was not limited to just parents and children, it included several generations and counted as members all living kin descending from common ancestors. Organization within the family was hierarchical, with the oldest living male member as head; at his death accession to family headship went to the next surviving oldest son. When there were no male heirs of age, the family council decided the succession. The family hierarchical system places great stock in longevity, respect for elders and males, and even the dead, as evidenced by the cult of ancestor worship. The rigid rules governing position within the family hierarchy dictated a predetermined position for each person born into the family. Social mobility up the scale to prestige and authority depended upon living long enough to survive those above.

But attaining high rank within the family unit was worth the effort. The patriarch head of the family could exercise almost complete sovereignty over the lives and fortunes of other members. He was "the biological, religious, political, economic, and educational head,"[12] whose authority was to be respected and obeyed by other clan members. A family council made up of other senior members advised the head and, if it became necessary, could effectively check him. Since he was conscious of these responsibilities, his rule was rarely arbitrary, dictatorial, or capricious. Confucian teachings stressed the importance of knowing one's position and of living up to the duties of that position.

In ancient times the land was cultivated only to provide food, not for investment, and the family unit was expected to be largely self-sufficient. The land, commercial enterprises, and urban property were all owned by the family unit and could be sold only by the council. All were operated as collectives, with members assigned to work units in either field or shop. When there were several enterprises, a master craftsman supervised the work of the artisans who were members of their respective guilds. Family finances were pooled and controlled by the patriarch with the help of his council of elders, but persons could own a few individual possessions. Families were responsible for the care of the sick, disabled, insane, unemployed, and aged. Since families disciplined the behavior of their members, there was need for police or courts only for regulating interfamily relations.

Standards of morality and behavior enforced in family councils were emphasized in Confucian dictum which taught strict adherence to duty in the proper conduct of the five relationships: (1) between king and subject, (2) between father and son, (3) between husband and wife, (4) between elder brother and younger brother, and (5) between the family group and its outside relationships. Each stressed the propriety of obedience by the weak to the strong, by the young to the old, by the low to the high, and by female to male.[13] In short, every individual was required to adjust to the group will regardless of his own personal desires and feelings. Although such moral discipline was strong, the patriarch's responsibilities were heavy.

As the nation's basic social unit, the family system with its various extensions contributed importantly to the stability and continuity of the society. Under the system, however, the individual as a person and individual values were less important than were the group and its collective values. A man could become important only as a unit in the family, not as an individual person. In the family and other relationships the Chinese was not permitted to be an individualist, or to be independent of these relationships. Yet paradoxically he and the family with other social units to which he belonged were usually relatively independent of the central authority.

Following the familial pattern, villages and towns were organized as collections of families, all self-sustaining, self-governing communities. These autonomous communities banded together to form a province, and provinces combined to form the kingdom. In each of these larger political units the council of elders supervised the educational, religious, economic, and political life of the community, and in times of danger organized in the common defense.

The Empire itself for centuries endured as a federation of autonomous towns, villages, and provinces somewhat loosely strung together, but owing allegiance to a central monarchy, employing a central bureaucracy as its chief instrument of government. The Empire was actually the extension on a national scale of the family idea. Following the analogy, the Emperor was the father-figure and all his subjects were the children. He and his court preserved the established order within whose protected area the family and other social groups functioned. In return the Emperor expected the kind of loyalty, trust, and obedience that a father expects of his children.

An early Chinese writer used this figure: "The Son of Heaven is the parent of the people and rules over the empire . . . the whole universe is but a large family." [14]

Position of the Emperor in the Political Structure

It is hard for Westerners to comprehend the exalted position occupied by the Emperor. It was a position which represented the extension on a larger scale of the family head's position. Like European monarchs of the fifteenth century, he ruled by divine right, the Chinese believing him to be Heaven's representative on earth, exercising Heaven's mandate. In the political sphere he was the absolute sovereign power, not only the executive but also judge and legislator. Still even more than all this, he was the supreme head of the church throughout the kingdom, loosely organized though it was, and of the educational system presiding over the people's spiritual and secular education. In sum, the Emperor was the President, the Congress, the Supreme Court, and the Pope, ruling over a country that had never heard of a constitution, a government of laws, and popular sovereignty. Moreover, since the Emperor owed his commission to Heaven he felt under no obligation to consider the popular will.

Absolutism of such extreme proportions could carry with it equally extreme penalties. When hardship and ill fortune befell the country, the Emperor was to blame. During good times the Emperor was plainly enjoying Heaven's mandate, but a national adversity was proof to the people that their ruler had lost that mandate. During such periods of unrest if adequate reform measures failed, the Emperor was forced to abdicate to be succeeded either by his heir or by an outsider who established a new dynasty. The leader of a new dynasty had to demonstrate by military prowess or otherwise that he was the recipient of Heaven's blessings and could rule more in tune with Heaven's wishes. It did not matter whether he came from the nobility, whether he happened to be a scholar, a peasant, or a rebellion leader with skill in killing, the main test of accession had to be demonstrated powers of leadership. But while the emperor was in favor, his position at the pinnacle of power was secure. To attack or interfere with it was a capital offense.

The image of oriental despotism in the Western mind is one of inhuman cruelty, yet in old China the Emperor's power was tempered and diluted. The instances in Chinese history when tyranny prevailed[15] are rare, for most of the time the emperor-father ruled with a kind of benevolent Confucian-generated morality and paternalism that was relatively liberal in comparison with the worst cases of fifteenth- and sixteenth-century European absolutism, and it appears even more gentle when compared with twentieth-century totalitarianism. In addition, several types of controls, or checks and balances, were in operation such as the institutions of the Board of Censors, the Official Historian, and popular resistance of different kinds. Though the Emperor's power was not thought of as being divided, it was in fact shared by a conservative bureaucracy which, functioning under central authority at the local level, made the Emperor's wishes known locally and advised the Emperor on all local and provincial matters. In the end, of course, though the political system had no provision for peaceful reform, the people, or various powerful groups, could and did on occasion persuade the Emperor to accept reforms or deprive him of his throne.

Social Classes

Traditional China's power elite was the scholar-gentry class, which included the bureaucracy. Though it was intended to be an aristocracy of intellect and not of birth, through the centuries it came to be quite difficult for persons not born in wealthy families to move into this class. Originally it represented the Confucian ideal of rule by superior men possessing the highest educational qualifications, an ideal analogous to Plato's philosopher-king concept. Upward mobility was possible here though rarely attained, for membership could be gained by passing the tests. Appointment to the bureaucracy was on the basis of civil service examinations and promotion was earned on merit. Thus in theory this class was open to any person of learning—which meant those who had mastered the hard task of reading and writing before studying the classics and gaining competence in some fields of knowledge. The Chinese scholar was grounded in Confucian thought, which dealt more with the philosophy of human conduct than with the virtues of practical skills, so that his education was somewhat like that of the nineteenth-century English gentleman—broadly based in liberal but lacking in applied arts. Though a commoner might make the grade, the cost of education restricted membership predominantly to the sons of wealthy families. While the bureaucracy enjoyed the additional prestige associated with its office, all members of the scholar-gentry class received the public respect accorded by tradition to men of intellect.

As a whole the scholar-gentry class provided the principal source of cohesion and stability, thereby contributing substantially to the survival qualities of the society. Cohesion was needed in a kingdom loosely structured from associated, independent, and relatively autonomous units. The bureaucracy afforded continuity in government when dynasties changed. Despite the fact that the bureaucracy received its power from the Emperor, no emperor could remain on the throne without its support; so the bureaucracy remained a power behind the throne. The gentry, made up of landowners, moneylenders, and collectors of rent and taxes, usually worked in common with the bureaucracy as a force against change, as a conservative influence preserving and protecting the social order.

Nonetheless, effective centralization of national political or economic power as a factor in developing a feeling of nationalism was never fully achieved. The average person identified himself only remotely with both the large scale affairs of state and with an amorphous concept of a market place beyond his local environs.

The system, which afforded few useful avenues other than land for capital investment, tended in later centuries to elevate the socioeconomic predominance of the scholar-gentry class and to widen the gap between it and the illiterate masses. The growth of urbanization carried with it a rise in absentee ownership on the one hand and further impoverishment of the peasant class on the other. This process tended to increase the scholar-gentry-class's monopoly of knowledge, power, wealth, and leisure. The more this class gained in such respects the more it valued the cultivation of the virtues. The more it stressed the importance of thinking and other intellectual pursuits, the more it kept itself aloof from occupations associated with profit, physical labor, and commercialism.[16] As a consequence the scholar-gentry class lost interest in civic virtues, and such matters as using science to improve the lands it owned. It is ironic that the class which for hundreds of years constituted the principal bulwark of the society became in the end a principal barrier to progress and a principal force that led to stagnation. The progressive separation of this class from the people, its indifference to their plight, its solidified, static, backward-looking, dogmatic standards of values, coupled with the growing impoverishment of the land and the rising population level, were factors that contributed to the Empire's collapse.

Moreover, the scholar-gentry class managed, with the help of the system, to keep down two other classes which might have arisen to challenge its supremacy: the merchant class and the soldiers. The bureaucracy supervised both classes. The merchants conducted the nation's commerce, mainly distributing products among the various population segments. Distribution was their primary function, for they probably never thought of increasing production at less expense. Commerce remained largely a local matter of many decentralized small businesses; consequently large nationwide industrial concentrations never arose. The economic self-sufficiency of communities precluded the development of foreign trade on any appreciable scale. Besides stifling private business initiative, the bureaucracy organized and the government conducted monopolies in the distribution of basic goods, such as iron, silk, salt, tea, and later opium, matches, and tobacco. Thus large private concerns did not grow on such trade, as they did in Western countries.

Just as state power in the hands of the bureaucracy determined largely the structure and development of economic enterprise, so did it generally control the military leaders and their armies, by virtue of its control of the purse strings. Because of their position as defenders and perpetuators of the order, the military leaders commanded more public esteem than the merchant class, but the common soldier stood at the very bottom of the class hierarchy. On rare occasions a general would rise to the throne on the success of his armies. But if he failed he was executed and his followers were disgraced.

Unlike Occidental societies in modern times, imperial China never produced a strong economic middle class, based either in agriculture or in trade and industry. Since the emperor was the religious head of state, no separate ecclesiastical body arose to contest his monopoly. So the court and the bureaucracy continued their dominance over the illiterate millions down into the twentieth century.

IDEALS AND VALUES

Ideals and values at the roots of traditional Chinese culture stemmed from conceptions of God, of the universe, and of man's relationship to God and the universe. The three great philosophies—Confucianism, Taoism, and Buddhism—have, with the passage of centuries, fused until most Chinese profess them together. Confucianism and Taoism were similar in that they both grew out of ancient beliefs about the forces of nature. While Confucianism taught the principles and ideals of the good society adjusted to and in harmony with physical laws, Taoism stressed the insignificance of mere man in the face of the mystery and majesty of nature as man sees it. Both philosophies regarded man's physical environment and his role in such a setting, as a logical, orderly relationship—one that man should adapt to, rather than try to conquer or change. Buddhism, which seeped into China following the advent of the Christian era, furnished the natural philosophical framework for a blending of the two native faiths. Because Buddhism defined man's place in the physical world, personalizing in a way man's relation with nature, it powerfully influenced Chinese thought. With little loss of substance, all three systems of religious thought merged with each other and were adapted to Chinese culture. Confucianism, modified by Buddhist thought, became the New Confucianism, dedicated to the improvement of human relationships by the application of knowledge. In substance, it can be said with qualification that China has never been essentially a religious country, but more a country ruled by custom, philosophy, and moral and ethical tradition.[17] Of the three philosophies that merged, Taoism was the only one that evolved into a full-fledged church. But the teachings of these combined creeds help explain in the twentieth century much about the Chinese way of life and thought.[18]

Confucianism insisted upon the supremacy of human values. "Wisdom is to know men; virtue is to love men," Confucius wrote.[19] He believed that men should think for themselves and that a man could be happy only through living in a community of free men. The Confucian system fostered the principles of group cooperation and obedience to superiors in the common interest, however, before the highest human values could be realized. Confucianism instilled the importance of knowing one's "position" in the family hierarchy and doing one's "duty" for the sake of the collective good, as the main basis for realistic communal or human relationships. Taoism, on the other hand, preached the cultivation of individual insights, insisted on one's right to call his soul his own, a magnificent assertion of an individual's oneness with nature, of personal autonomy[20] as more to be valued than Confucius' well-ordered system of government. Though Confucian principles were dominant, Taoism contributed to the development in Chinese society of a kind of individualistic philosophy, together with the necessity of compromise in human relationships. Although Taoist individualism was close to it, there was little in the combined teachings of either Confucianism or Taoism that resembled the Judeo-Christian emphasis on the worth of the individual as a being made in God's image, and the necessity of obedience, not to man, but to God. Where the Confucian ethic implied that one had little or no standing apart from his group, the Christian-democratic ethic upheld the sacredness and dignity of the individual personality, out of which sprang ideas of personal rights, individual will, and self-determinism. Although in some ways both Confucianism and Taoism were antidemocratic, together they were responsible for much of the social and political democracy that existed in China at various periods in its history.

Instead of a personal anthropomorphic God, Confucius spoke of the Will of Heaven as expressed in nature. Chinese conceptions of nature were based on observation of the seasons, phases of the moon, and cycles of time as recorded by the calendar. Nature as an expression of Heaven's will was generally good, kind, tranquil, and orderly.[21] Mankind, too, according to Confucius, was basically good and could order his society harmoniously by living in accord with Heaven's will which meant to live in harmony with nature. Mencius, Confucius' disciple, believed that men had the same kind of human nature, which is basically good, but that Heaven might become angry and vengeful; that man could become corrupt and evil. It followed that man must refrain from offending Heaven's will, but should he offend, he must do what he could to make amends. In contrast to the emphasis in Western societies for man to conquer the forces of nature, the emphasis in China has always been to adjust and adapt to nature.

Indeed, this ideal of faith in the innate goodwill of mankind, this trust in men's wisdom in general to think for themselves, made it possible for China to be ruled by a government of men and not of law. There were rules, yes, but varying in accordance with the desires and judgments of the men who administered them, they did not possess the force of law.[22] Chinese political thought was confident that the rules could be trusted to the wisdom of civilized, morally responsible men. Although they were not without grounds for suspicion of betrayal of the public trust, the Chinese people seem never to have come to question central authority as did Western peoples, who learned to place their trust in laws—laws that might check men's passions.

This same exalted trust of human beings carried over into Chinese classical economic theory. Somewhere in between the tenets of capitalism on the one hand—which held ownership of private property to be a personal right—and of Marxian socialism on the other—which held ownership to be a collective state or class right—the Chinese system thought of property (usually land) ownership as a private matter, but not as a personal right. Ownership was rather a joint trust to be exercised morally and responsibly by the family unit. Lands and wealth, Confucius taught, were a gift of Heaven, a gift temporarily placed in the custody of men who were expected to distribute its bounty fairly according to society's needs.[23] In this view natural resources were to be shared by all and not cornered for individual gain or private profit.

According to Confucius, the pursuit of contentment and happiness was more valued than the pursuit of riches. Indeed, accumulation of private wealth as an economic motive tended to be discouraged as morally unjustifiable and reprehensible because it divided members of a society, while sharing brought people together. The ultimate development of this idea led to the belief among the members of the scholar-gentry class that physical labor and training in practical work was as humiliating as the crass display of possessions. In contrast, classical capitalism placed great stock in private accumulation of wealth especially—by efficiency, industry, and labor—as an economic inducement. Marxism taught that all wealth was created by human labor and sought to establish a society in which only those who produce can share. The Marxist, in observing the operation of capitalism, was concerned lest a nation's wealth concentrate in the hands of a minority; therefore it assigned ownership to the state in the name of the people. Similarly the Chinese left it up to the government to regulate the distribution of economic resources and power. Some dynasties saw to this task; others neglected it. As a result throughout the course of 2,000 years, some dynasties followed a laissez-faire policy, others regulated the economy to an extent approaching state socialism. But the tendency toward economic centralization was discouraged, and as a consequence China remained a nation of small independent businesses and shops operating in a pluralistic economy.

In a like manner the political system tended to discourage the development of a strong centralized form of government.[24] Though the emperor's powers and prestige were absolutist in nature, there were few spheres of activity in which the central government needed to engage. The central government then presided over a rather loosely organized federation of small political and family units, saw to their common defense, collected taxes, and provided relief from flood and disaster. As has been seen, China's imperial title and central government, unlike Japan's, could change hands, sometimes drastically, from one ruling house to another. During two periods in history, China was ruled by foreigners, first by Mongol emperors, then by the Manchus. To the Chinese, pragmatically content to accept a ruler even of foreign blood if he could hold Heaven's mandate, continuity of the ruling family was not important—the actual work of governing was usually left in the hands of the bureaucracy. The common people, lacking political identification with their country as a nation, were often accused by Westerners of lacking in patriotism. For a different reason, the scholar class held itself aloof from mundane affairs, giving the impression it too was not concerned about public matters, or lacked political consciousness. But "if the Chinese have often been politically indifferent," Creel writes, "they have always had, for as long as the record runs, a fierce and unquenchable national pride exceeded by that of no other people." [25] It is this pride that has helped unify the people under communism.

The Chinese have sound reasons to be proud of their culture. Among all the nations of the modern world, they alone are the inheritors of a civilization that has endured since well before the beginning of the Christian era—a civilizaton that has endured as a political entity over a longer period of history than any other society known to man and has provided a stable, meaningful social order for hundreds of millions. In many areas of technology, in the arts, in literature, and in philosophy this civilization maintained its lead over the rest of the world. Its cultural achievements spread to neighboring provinces by the power of getting accepted, and to other Asian countries such as Japan and Korea. Although mountains to the south and west, deserts to the north, and the ocean to the east prevented for hundreds of years the spread of ideas both from and to China, many of its inventions, arts, and crafts have been adopted outside of Asia.

Yet this brilliant civilization had its faults. Perhaps the greatest among them in Western eyes was the tradition of authoritarianism inherent in Confucian teachings and in the family structure, because it discouraged the growth of self-expression and self-reliance and favored conformity and obedience. Partly as a result the masses looked to leadership rather than taking initiative or engaging in self-reliant participation. In western Europe a great independent and powerful middle class grew up, demanding a voice in public affairs. A similar class was never fostered in the Chinese system. As the imperial government ceased to be concerned with the people's welfare it became inefficient and corrupt, thus widening the distance between the governing elite and the masses. Natural isolation and overzealous preoccupation with past glories eventually bred reaction and stagnation. Confident in their feelings of superiority, Chinese intellectuals came to look with disdain upon other peoples whom they considered ignorant and barbaric. China's series of ignoble defeats in the nineteenth century by what the Chinese considered upstart, barbaric nations smaller and weaker than their own contributed to the growing sense of wounded pride. The presence of foreigners exercising sovereign rights in Chinese territory, and perhaps most of all the attitude of superiority over the Chinese reflected by foreigners, also contributed to the growing feeling of humiliation and frustration. The Chinese began to realize that however justified their past attitude of superiority over the West had been, the time had come when Western nations had forged ahead, and the old attitude was no longer realistic. European cultures had moved forward on the changes and insights gained from the voyages of discovery, the Renaissance, the age of enlightenment with its Protestant Reformation, the American and French Revolutions, and the industrial revolution. China to them seemed asleep, dreaming of past glories, marking time, and clinging to outmoded ways. Until the beginning of the twentieth century, China's leaders were still unaware that their country had fallen so far behind. After facing almost total collapse under a tottering dynasty, then under inept republicanism, they are struggling now to catch up under a revolutionary Communist government. Though undoubtedly many old revered habits of thought and action will be tossed aside, as they do so, the pattern of the future will be constructed largely upon the values of the past.

THE OFFICIAL GAZETTE

What was communication like during the millenniums of China's history as a civilization? From our knowledge of the rise of early communications in primitive Western societies we could hypothesize that no society as advanced as that just described could have developed without public communication in some form. And our hypothesis would be supported, for we are told that oral communication was a major source of understanding and unity in the councils of family and village. Even long before the Empire was consolidated by Chin Shih Huan Ji, the "spoken press" functioned in China as it did in all countries. As early as 2357 B.C., in Emperor Yao's reign, public narratives in verse rather than prose presaged the medieval ballad singer by 3,000 years.[26] These forms of literary journalism expressed public opinion, mirrored the society, perpetuated fact and legend, engaged in public criticism, and according to one scholar were more important as reflections of public opinion than as conveyors of news.[27]

Origins of the Written Press: the *Ti-pao*

The written press seems to have originated during the Shang and Chou dynasties (1783–247 B.C.). The regular reporting of information, usually on a seasonal or quarterly basis, was required as a duty of the designated court official who made news-gathering trips in the spring and fall of each year. He listened to the ballads and observed conditions throughout the countryside, then made his report to the Emperor on the state of public affairs. The reports were called *Chun Chiu,* or *springs and autumns,* to indicate their semiannual appearance, each covering conditions for the preceding half year.[28] They were kept as an official record for the court's information and were circulated among the feudal lords. Even before imperial unification, China's rulers issued public notices, including proclamations, and posted them in public places. Few could read them, so illustrated notices were issued for the illiterate.[29] If a ceremonial occasion happened to be important enough, it might be commemorated by inscriptions on bronze utensils. The Shang Chinese (1766–1122 B.C.) wrote on wood, bamboo, pottery, and perhaps silk, using a sharp instrument dipped in soot ink. By this time some forms of later Chinese characters, or ideographs, were in use.[30]

Although the seasonal reports and other imperial communications were official in function, what is called the official press is said to date its beginnings during the Han dynasty (206 B.C. to 220 A.D.). It is significant that this was a period of territorial expansion which consolidated the Empire. It was also a period of brilliant cultural achievement, marking the downfall of feudalism. The official press was organized[31] during the reign of the Emperor Han Wu (140–87 B.C.). The central or Middle Kingdom had by conquest brought under its jurisdiction a number of neighboring kingdoms and out of this consolidation had established the Empire. In order to govern its far-flung provinces, the central government created a rather sophisticated system of regular two-way communication. The Emperor and his court wanted to keep up with what was happening in the territories. The princes and generals appointed to govern the territories wanted to stay in touch with what was happening in the capital, as well as in their own and nearby provinces. Out of these practical political needs emerged the *Ti-pao,* or *Metropolitan Gazette.*[32] *Ti* in Chinese means the place where the feudal princes (the provincial governors) lodged when visiting the capital, Ch'ang-an, first located at the present city of Sian in Shensi Province and later at Lohyang, Honan Province. At this lodging place the information from the court was received for transmittal to the provinces and information from the provinces was prepared for transmittal to the court. The *Ti,* as the headquarters of the princes in the capital, served conveniently as as place for exchanging information. After the invention of paper, copies were made at the Ti. The word *pao* is the generic Chinese term meaning gazette, bulletin, report, or newspaper. The *Ti-pao* was the forerunner of a succession of Peking gazettes, published sporadically, but beginning again on a regular basis in the seventh century to become the oldest newspaper of continuous publication, its history covering more than 1,100 years.

At first the *Ti-pao*[33] were essentially a kind of correspondence for provincial viceroys prepared by their agents stationed at the metropolis. It was comparable to today's Washington correspondence sent to newspapers across the land, except that the information sent was for the exclusive consumption of the provincial ruler and his agents who were permitted to see it, and not for the public. The agents also served as convenient means for submitting reports to the court from the provincial governments.

The *Ti-pao* were similar to the transcripts of the *Acta Diurna* of Rome in and after 60 B.C., though the latter were not issued daily. It is probable that the Chinese copyists were serving provincial viceroys at the same time as the Roman scribes and in much the same manner. What they wrote was simple at first, consisting of the emperor's orders, reports of developments or happenings, and some discussion of policy among the emperor, the court officers, and the provincial viceroys. In a narrow sense they were public records. Since they were media for exchanging what would today be called news, they fit the modern day definition of newspaper. The earlier gazettes appeared irregularly, were discontinued for periods of time, then resumed again. Their function and source, however, remained the same. After the invention of paper in China between 89 and 105 A.D.,[34] some ten centuries before it appeared in Europe it was used in copying the gazettes, and thus greatly facilitated communication over distances.

Gazettes of Regular Publication

The first gazettes of regular publication began during the Tang dynasty (619–900 A.D.).[35] From this period until after the fall of the Manchu dynasty in 1911, publication continued with only slight lapses, though various titles were used. During the Tang dynasty the Bureau of Official Reports was organized to perform the transcript service, and the system of roads and relays was expanded.[36] It was also during the Tang dynasty that the first mention of the term *Ti-pao* appeared in scholarly writing, although other terms were used to designate the different types of gazettes which flourished. For example there were the *Pien-pao* (Border Press), *Ch'ao-pao* (Morning Post), *Yi-pao* (Courier Post), or simply *K'aiyuan Tsapao* (periodical published in the K'aiyuan reign, 713–741 A.D.). Because the *Ti-pao* came to be read generally by the end of the eighth century, they had become official bulletins and were no longer private newsletters.

The *Ti-pao's* circulation was enlarged during the Sung dynasty (960–1269 A.D.) as a result of having developed quite a following among the scholar-gentry class. A group of court officers, recognizing the commercial value of certain kinds of information contained in the gazette, published such information in a competitive paper, the *Shiao-pao* (small paper as tabloid, connoting gossip). Although the authorities attempted to prohibit it, the *Ti-pao* and the *Shiao-pao* in various forms are said to have circulated among the literate throughout the empire.[37] Perhaps because of this competition during the Sung dynasty, the *Ti-pao* took on the official responsibility of announcing the news. To accomplish this function more efficiently branch offices were established where copies from Peking

hsin-wen-chih, and either sold on the streets, or posted in prominent places. The third large segment of gazette content consisted of the memorials, or reports, either spoken or written, from officials or commoners, often published together with the emperor's reply. They were always published after having been before the court, and if accompanied by the court's approval, had the effect of an imperial edict.[42]

Circulation of the gazettes in the metropolitan area was by runner; countryside delivery depended upon the uncertain habits of the official post, which were notoriously unreliable. This situation led in the nineteenth century to a rather wide use of private mail services which were faster and more dependable. Some publishing concerns, like those of mid-twentieth-century America, operated their own delivery service. The *hsin-wen-chih* were, of course, hawked in the streets.

The gazettes were duplicated in manuscript form as well as in print, depending upon number of copies needed.[43] Manuscript copies were more expensive than printed ones, and copies could be rented for less than the price of either. They were widely translated by the foreign language press of mid-nineteenth-century China, and collected translations were published, from which studies of Chinese government and society have been made.

How many readers did the imperial press serve? The estimates say between 10 and 20 million.[44] This figure is obtained, not by counting press runs, but by estimating the number of literates at between 3 and 5 per cent of the total population, and multiplying that figure by the estimated average number of readers per copy, which has been variously placed at between 15 and 20. Each copy had a long life, passing from reader to reader until it wore out. Paper and printing were cheap, and the appeal of the press was wide, particularly among the scholars, the government, and merchant classes. Even illiterates were exposed to the main stream of public information through the medium of the professional story teller who knew how to heighten interest with colorful accounts of murders, executions, fires, floods, and battles.

Under a different set of economic and social conditions the gazette press might have advanced from a class to a mass system, as understood in the modern sense of the term. But three principal factors operated to forestall such a development. The complexities of learning the Chinese written language kept the mastery of reading and writing beyond the reach of all unable to afford the years of study such mastery required. The second factor was the relative absence of interest in public affairs among the people. Due to the low level of political consciousness, they scarcely realized their opinion counted for anything in the affairs of community or nation, and did not identify with the news of the day. Except for the bureaucracy and the trades people, few were concerned with the world matters outside their own locality. We have seen how the members of the scholar class tended to avoid involvement in public affairs as beneath their dignity. A nation made up of self-sufficient local political units subject to very little intercommunication could not be expected to develop such broad interests.

In the third place the economy itself tended to restrict the growth of the publishing business more than it did the communication function. Many who could read could not afford the price of newspapers, cheap as they were. Because commercial advertising and political subsidy, as we know it, were undiscovered, the publisher had no sources of revenue beyond the purchase price. Trade was largely in the necessities and operated in a seller's market, a part of a self-sustaining economy. Billboards and signs were common, but space was not sold or rented. In the local markets the better the quality of goods offered, the less need for display and promotion. Some commodities were controlled by the guilds. Advertising was not needed for either one.

Political Attitudes Toward Freedom of Expression

The political system through the centuries was sometimes lenient and sometimes strict in its use of controls on information and opinion, the restraints fluctuating with the regime, or with variant policy within one regime. The Emperor, obligated to Heaven for his mandate, had no desire to give the people either a voice or a hand in government. Confucius rejected any ideas of popular sovereignty. "The people," he said, "may be made to follow a course of action, but can hardly be made to understand the reason for it." [45]

Yet several kinds of checks on the sovereign's prerogative were in operation from dynasty to dynasty and from emperor to emperor. During times of adversity the people had ways of showing their displeasure such as passive resistance, boycott, and even rebellion. Thus one could say that, although there was no legal basis for it, the emperor could rule only as long as he enjoyed his people's confidence—or more accurately, as long as the people thought he enjoyed Heaven's confidence. Moreover, some enlightened absolutist rulers believed in seeking the people's wisdom before determining political policy. Confucius' most learned disciple, Mencius, who lived from 372 to 289 B.C., advanced the principle that the people had the right to alter or abolish a government that stands in the way of life, liberty, or happiness of the common people.[46] "Heaven sees as the people see, Heaven hears as the people hear," was the way he put it. Too, the Chinese familistic tradition, expected an emperor to look after the people's welfare, as a father takes care of his children. Communication from the people was obviously a convenient way for the throne to learn of their needs.

Succeeding dynasties used a board of censure, consisting of officials stationed in different districts throughout the country, whose duty it was to report to the throne on all subjects connected with the public welfare and the conduct of government. The censors were popularly called *Erh Mu Kuan,* or "eyes and ears officials." Sometimes the imperial censors became mere spokesmen of the powerful bureaucracy, thus resembling the reptile press of America and Europe in a later age.[47] To keep his ears attuned to the peoples' voice, Emperor Yao thousands of years ago established the Post of Censure to show that his people might express their disapproval of maladministration. Yao also placed the Drum of Remonstrance outside the palace gate so that his subjects might register complaints by beating the drum. The Official Historian served also as a guardian of the public morality. These were all practices based on a belief in the wisdom both of public criticism and of the peoples' voice.

Two interesting examples from Chinese history illustrate the actual use of democratic principles in government. The Duke of Shau, Emperor Li-Wang's chief minister in 878 B.C., refused to obey the Emperor's order to execute a group of slanderers. After the Emperor had someone else carry out the executions, he asked the Duke, "Well, what has become of your gossipers now?" The Duke retorted, "All you have brought about is a screen which prevents you from learning the real sentiments of the people; but you should know it is more dangerous to shut the people's mouths than to stop the waters of a river. To stop the . . . river means to force it to expand, and thus do more harm than if it had been allowed to take its natural course. Such is the case with your people. If you want to prevent the damage threatening from the inundation of a river, you have to lead it into a proper bed which will hold all its waters; if you want to make an impression on the people, let them have perfect liberty of speech." [48]

The other story concerns Tse Tsan, an able minister of a feudal lord about 554 B.C. (during the Chou dynasty) who was ordered to suppress the "Country Hall," a place where the people gathered to discuss and criticize the conduct of government. Tse Tsan is said to have replied: "Here is a place where our people meet once in the morning and once in the evening, discussing and criticizing my administrative policies. If they resolve that my policy is beneficial, I carry it out; if they consider it harmful, I can improve or even change it. They are in fact my teachers; why should I suppress them?" [49]

Not all rulers agreed, and the people's freedom of expression was suppressed and ignored more frequently than it was allowed or listened to. One of the greatest cases of censorship and suppression on record occurred during the Ch'in dynasty in 212 B.C. To silence the enemies of the state thousands were exiled, and all except medical and agricultural books were burned. People who repeated words from the burned books were beheaded. Charged with having committed sedition, 469 scholars were buried alive. All who discredited the government were put to death and their guilt was held to extend to their family and nearest of kin, who also were executed. Although his political achievements were extensive, the great Ch'in emperor's dynasty was one of the shortest lived, lasting only from 221 to 202 B.C.[50]

Public criticism in ancient China, then, was both official and unofficial. There were the voices of the imperial censors who no doubt exerted considerable influence on public policy because of their prestige and position. On the other hand there were the unofficial forms for the expression of public opinion. The people registered their protests and complaints in various ways such as strikes and "beating the drum." A kind of public criticism that resembled more closely press criticism of modern times, because it reflected popular opinion, was that of the scholar-critics. This criticism took the form of pamphleteering and campaigning in the streets with speeches and placards. During periods of great popular unrest which spearheaded reform movements, scholar-critics submitted memoranda to the emperor over their signatures in a manner not unlike popular petitions of the present day.

In the nineteenth century the ancient principles of absolutism were still operative, although the power of the throne was rapidly dwindling. The gazette press continued as a government instrument under official control, serving its ancient function as a medium of information among the ruling hierarchy. As a source of popular information about government affairs, it served more as a concession to public demand for such information than because of any recognition of the existence of a public need. To this end the court released for general publication large numbers of state documents and papers, requiring that they be printed verbatim. A large portion of the flow of public information of the most important kind thus was controlled not by censorship or subsidy or any other superficial device, but simply by acceding to popular interest. No doubt whetting public appetite were the official censors' reports among such releases, which frequently during this period became lengthy and sensational.[51]

Printed attacks on the throne and the government were, of course, treated as sedition or treason, for which the penalty could be execution. There were no copyright laws and professional copyists flourished. Yet the traditional trappings of authoritarian European monarchs for controlling public expression were absent. There existed no prepublication censorship. There was no official licensing or registration system. Patents and printing monopolies were unheard of. Obscene publications were prohibited, but trafficking in them persisted. Occasionally documents not authorized for publication were smuggled out and released.[52] But even though the usual paraphernalia for control of public communication did not exist, publishing could be hazardous especially for the political reformer, as will be noted in the next chapter.

Contributions of the Gazette Press

The Peking gazettes differed from the *London Gazette,* the *Gazette Officiel* of Paris, and the other European State gazettes in that they did not have the function of government promotion. Because what the Peking gazettes said came directly from the throne and not from the ministers of state, they enjoyed a higher prestige than the European official gazettes. Moreover, since the throne represented more than the political head of government, its utterances were more awesome. In terms of modern day news values, the gazettes were newspapers. Because the news they carried was intended to be information, not propaganda, it was of prime importance to officials throughout the kingdom, to former officials, to the considerable number of graduates awaiting appointment, and to the students seeking to become a part of the official bureaucracy. This group which identified in various ways with the government apparatus provided a consistent, loyal body of readers. Enthusiastic gazette readers were to be found among the gentry who were interested, if not involved in politics. Merchants, too, read the gazettes, often for the amusement they got out of the reports of court gossip and intrigue.

A casual content analysis would reveal that generally there was more space devoted to expression of opinion than report of fact. Imperial edicts gave reasons why they were issued. Memorials and petitions contained arguments in their defense. When the throne commanded viceroys to submit suggestions on important national problems, their responses took on the characteristics of a great national symposium of opinion and debate. Furthermore the official censor's exposure of social evils and his attacks on public abuses were surprisingly vigorous and candid. As Britton said, "The character of the censors quite as much as the character of the sovereign and his executive councillors set the high level of trenchant interest in the Gazette press." [53]

The Chinese gazette press was a communication system of high order, well developed for the function of disseminating official thought and act. It was a product of the culture which shaped it and of the character of the society which made and read it. Because the bureaucracy was closely connected with learning and culture, the gazette system served literary, educational, and political interests. The familial pattern in government structure required the gazettes to cover a wide range of general interest news to the extent that they preempted the field, leaving little room for popular newspapers. It was a unique communication system that had evolved to fulfill the needs of both the court and the scholar-bureaucrats at the same time. It was no doubt an important factor, indeed a strong arm of the government, in unifying and holding together as one empire a people as scattered and divergent as "a sheet of loose sand"—to use the phrase Sun Yat-sen used to describe the common people of his day who seemed never to have experienced the pangs of nationalism. Aside from this unifying effect, it should be noted that in essence the communication system served the Emperor and the ruling oligarchy, but only incidentally the masses of the common people. Therefore when public demand arose, semiofficial and private newspapers were established. In all the press, the promulgation of opinion and of information were equally important functions because the Chinese system admitted in theory the need for responsible criticism of government.

Because of its inherent nature the old gazette communication system clashed with the new Western-style journalism imported from Europe and America during the nineteenth century. The old system—based on a familial society and a manor economy and ethically oriented by scholars steeped in Confucian principles—believed human relationships were to be conducted in complete harmony, and in the absence of conflict and physical distress, an individual's aim in life was to pursue contentment by harmonizing and accommodating his affairs in accordance to the will of nature, not by control of his natural environment. The new journalism of the West, on the contrary, was based on ideals of material progress, of the conquest of nature with the new tools of physical science, of experimental inquiry, and of aggressive industrialism and competitive capitalism.

While the Chinese for eons had been content with simple machines, satisfied with conditioning human aspirations by means of an extremely complex set of ethical principles, the West had found ways of inventing complex machines to liberate man from enslavement by his environment. When Western-type newspapers and magazines appeared in China, they were the products of different social systems, of different values, the work of a new craft. The new indigenous Chinese press that grew up was a correlative development rather than a logical progression from the old—leaning partially on the old imperial communication system but fusing the principles of the new imported press. The period of the official gazette began in the Han dynasty and continued until 1911 A.D., with the fall of the Ching dynasty. Its influence, however, began to decline in the latter half of the nineteenth century. The next chapter will consider other communication systems that arose to challenge its monopoly.

10

THE PRIVATELY OWNED NATIVE PRESS

THE NINETEENTH CENTURY and the first half of the twentieth constituted a period of turbulent change in China—change that proved only a prelude to more radical change. The forces of change were both external and internal. Violent political and economic upheavals were set in motion in part by the communication of ideas from the Western world, whose foreign missionaries and tradesmen had sewn the seeds of the intellectual awakening. Loss of face and loss of territory in several humiliating wars with Japan and the Western powers awakened China to its plight. Internal unrest among impoverished and illiterate masses, bureaucratic corruption, and the monarchy's general debility all generated the demand for reform and eventually for revolution. The press-inspired revolution was followed by inept republican regimes which were actually military dictatorships unable to cope with the pressing problems facing a worn-out country and an unprepared people struggling to modernize. The situation was aggravated by civil war between the Nationalists in power and rising Communist forces, and Japanese aggression in the 1930s, and finally by the second World War.

This period of Chinese history brought successive, interlocking, and simultaneous developments of importance to the communication system. The background will be condensed and related to the several strains of public communication that combined to produce China's Western-type communication system characteristic of the period before the Communists came to power. Subdivisions for this chapter correspond to the various strains of communication that developed and may be outlined as follows: (1) the period of foreign influence, from about 1850 until 1890; (2) the rise of the native, indigenous, private press, from about 1870 to the Chinese Revolution, 1911; (3) the period of modern independent communications, 1912 to 1949. The Communist period, 1949 to the present, will be considered in subsequent chapters.

First, European and American missionaries transplanted to China a press dedicated not only to the conversion of souls to Christianity but also to education in Western knowledge, including what was called the new science. Foreign commercial interests and tradesmen came to "open up" the country to the "benefits" of commerce with the industrial nations. Western businessmen established a press devoted to building trade and geared to a competitive capitalist economy. These two foreign press systems, missionary and commercial, operating within a country in which the old gazette press still held a strong monopoly in publishing official information, demonstrated to the Chinese the need for a popular press of general information and appeal—one that was relatively independent of government. The rise of an indigenous native Chinese press modeled after the Western pattern was soon to follow. Then came the electrifying impact of the reform and revolutionary press, followed by a literary renaissance, and then the full evolution, especially in the urban centers, of a pioneer libertarian capitalist communication system.

IMPACT OF THE WESTERN WORLD

We have seen that the ancient Chinese Empire's official press was a monopoly primarily intended for the use of officialdom to carry on intercourse among the agencies of the government. Although it came to attract a considerable following among the other intelligentsia and the barely literate, this was an incidental function that had little to do with basic purpose and content. The idea of a press that functions mainly for the information and enlightenment of the general public did not take hold in China until it was introduced by alien missionaries and tradespeople.

Missionary Journals in Chinese and English

The introduction of alien institutions, as might be expected, faced opposition; so the first missionary magazines had to be printed outside the country and smuggled into mainland China. The imperial government, as a move to discourage Catholic missionaries who had arrived in China in the eighteenth century, had forbidden all missionary activity, as it had the opium trade. Since it was expensive and dangerous to publish on Chinese territory, Robert Morrison and William Milne, representing the London Missionary Society, decided to establish their press outside Chinese jurisdiction in Malacca. Sponsored by the Anglo-Chinese College for "reciprocal cultivation of Chinese and European literature," [1] the first issue of the magazine *Ch'a-shih-su Mei-yueh T'ung-chi-ch'uan* (Chinese Monthly Magazine, or a monthly record of social manners) appeared in August, 1815. It was not devoted to timely information but consisted mostly of religious articles (Fig. 10.1). Before its death in 1822, it built up a circulation of 2,000 and was widely reprinted.[2] Copies circulated in Canton, South China, and throughout the Malay Peninsula.

Though restrictions against foreign missionary activity had not been lifted, some ten years later a Prussian employed by the Netherlands Missionary Society, Karl Freidrich August Gutzlaff, managed to publish the first periodical on Chinese Soil at Canton in 1833. It too was published in Chinese under the title *Tung Hsi Yang K'ao Ch'a-shih-su Mei-yueh T'ung-chi-ch'uan* (Eastern-Western Monthly Magazine). Gutzlaff succeeded because of his good relations with the Chinese authorities. When he stopped publishing after only 12 issues, it was not because it had been forbidden but because he had too many other duties. Gutzlaff with Morrison's

Fig. 10.1. Four pages from the first Chinese magazine, William Milne's **Chinese Monthly Magazine** published at Malacca. Top right is the title page reading **Ch'a-shih-su Mai-yueh T'ing-chi-ch'uan** of the first issue, August, 1815. Top left is the prefatory article. Below are two pages from the third volume showing the end of an article on comets and the beginning of the first installment of Milne's tract "The Two Friends," which ran in series. Size is about 5 by 7½ inches. (From Roswell S. Britton, **The Chinese Periodical Press 1800–1912,** Shanghai, 1933. Originals in the British Museum.)

嘉慶丙子年全卷

子曰多聞擇其善者而從之

察世俗每月統記傳

博愛者纂

察世俗每月統記傳序

無中生有者乃神也神乃一自然而然當始神創造天地人萬物此乃根本之道理神至大至尊生養我們世人故此善人無非敬畏神但世上論神多說錯了學者不可不察因神在天上而現著其榮所以用一個天字指著神亦有之既然萬處萬人皆由神而原被造化自然學者不可止察一所地方之各物單

的量不定一樣有的大過月又有的小過月也古時人皆說彗星爲喪國崩君破兵磨民饑荒疾疫等災之兆也然未必常是如此彗星之顯隱皆在先神定着如四時之運行然這諸情皆眞神所預定命而宰督也世人多理吉凶之兆所以其心不安定乃如狂濶之海然善人不好理吉凶之兆乃雖見天上地下有奇時不要怕只安心依靠神方着也

張遠兩友相論

第一回

從前有兩個好朋友一名張一名遠他們兩個人同行路間相論古今遠曰我已聽人說尊駕曾經受了耶穌之道理而信從之我看世人論說此事多有不同且我自己不甚明白今有兩端欲求尊駕解之張曰豈敢相公智深才盛如何倒來求於愚弟乎但既是相公自所願則弟應當盡心遵命請相公說那兩

help revived the magazine at Singapore in 1837–1838, and with James Matheson formed the "Society for the Diffusion of Useful Knowledge in China" at Canton. This was a grand scheme for translating and publishing systematically works covering Western science and learning. A 2-volume reprint of the magazine was issued by the society, but the outbreak of the first Anglo-Chinese war brought the society and its plans to an abrupt end.

Two unsuccessful Chinese language monthly periodicals carrying news made their appearance before the Anglo-Chinese War, representing the combined efforts of foreign missionaries and tradesmen. One was published at Malacca in 1828–1829, entitled *T'ien-hsia Hsin-wen* (The Universal Gazette). The other appeared in Canton in 1838 under the title *Ko-kuo Hsiao-hsi* (News of All Nations) shown in Figure 10.2. The former was published from movable type and edited by Samuel Kidd, later first professor of Chinese at University College, London; the latter by Walter Henry Medhurst of the London Missionary Society and Charles Batten Hillier, who became Medhurst's son-in-law and chief magistrate of the Hong Kong Colony.

A notable and widely quoted English language magazine that enjoyed some 20 years of monthly publication was *The Chinese Repository,* founded in 1832 at Canton by the American doctor, Peter Parker. The *Repository's* circulation reached 1,000 at the peak of its popularity, but declined before its demise in 1851. The monthly's goal was to publish "the most authentic" record of China and adjacent lands, and its 20 volumes totaling 12,000 pages presented a comprehensive appraisal of the old Empire in transition. This extraordinary compendium made it a valuable source. Among its contributors were the leading British and American scholars in China. The English *Penny Magazine* gave the *Repository* in 1837 its highest accolade when it said, "This periodical would be considered good even in England." Its press superintendent, contributor of articles on geography and botany, and later its editor was S. Wells Williams, who became a professor of Chinese at Yale University. None of several efforts to replace the *Repository* ever quite matched it.[3]

There was a 15-year period after 1838 when no missionary periodicals in the Chinese language appeared. After the Toleration edict of 1844, the missionaries were so busily engaged in building schools, churches, and hospitals that they had no time for public journalism. It was not until 1853 that another Chinese monthly

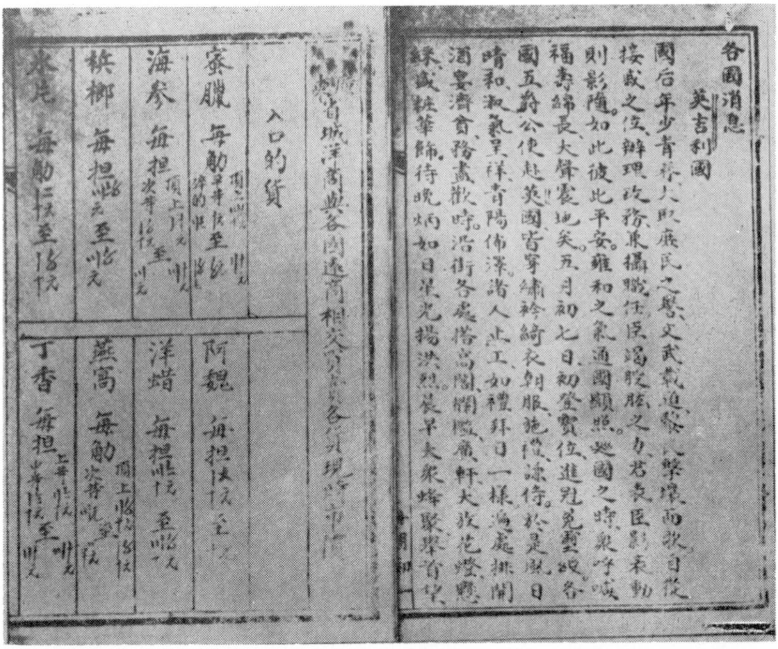

Fig. 10.2. Two pages from the news section of a news monthly published in November, 1838, in Canton by Walter Henry Medhurst and Charles Batten Hillier, of the London Missionary Society. The title was **Ko-kuo Hsiao-hsi** (News of All Nations). On the right the news section begins with news from England, and on the left the "Price Current" with quotations on imported commodities. Size is 5½ by 9 inches. Original in British Museum.

magazine appeared. It was the *Hsia-erh Kuan-chen,* a title signifying "gathered gems from far and near," founded by Medhurst in Hong Kong and edited successively by Hillier and James Legge, a Scottish missionary. This magazine, which continued until 1856, was typographically an improvement over the earlier missionary product, being printed from metal types and well illustrated. The English title, *The Chinese Serial,* together with an English table of contents were later additions. The *Serial* published almost entirely nonreligious matter and it reversed the custom of the earlier missionary publications whose content was often reprinted by others, by using reprint material itself. It carried a sizeable news section, running much information from the official gazettes, and publishing a supplementary market and shipping report.

Shortly after the beginnings of the *Chinese Serial,* an American Baptist physician Daniel Jerome MacGowan edited a monthly magazine in Hong Kong in 1856. The title was *Chung-wai Hsin-pao* (Sino-Foreign News), a journal that had been founded two years earlier at Ning-Po. This periodical, as its title suggests, was primarily devoted to news which it reprinted from the Peking gazettes, departmentalized by localities. The magazine continued until 1860. MacGowan also was associated for a brief time with *Chung-wai Tsa-chih* (Shanghai Miscellany), a magazine begun in 1862 and continued until 1868.[4]

The *Chinese Serial* having ceased publication, the *Shanghai Serial* appeared in Shanghai in 1857, published by Alexander Wylie of the London Mission. It was in Chinese and its official title was *Liu-ho Ts'ung-t'an,* which translates literally as "Compiled Talks of the Six Points." The Chinese idea of points of compass included our four *(e.g.,* north, east, south, and west) plus two additional ones, nadir and zenith. Although the *Shanghai Serial* lasted only about a year, its scholarly presentation of articles and news reports earned for it a good reputation both in China and Japan. Like Medhurst and Williams, however, Wylie came to direct a mission and stayed to become a scholar of Chinese life.

The leading missionary editor of the last half of the century was Young J. Allen, an American from Georgia, who was sent to China by the Southern Methodist Board. For 47 years he founded and conducted Chinese periodicals, served Shanghai authorities as teacher and translator, and ran his mission. Allen established *Chiao-hui Hsin-wen* whose English title was simply *Church News,* a weekly devoted to religion, science, news, and commercial advertising (Fig. 10.3). The first year its 700 copies were read by virtually the entire Protestant missionary group stationed in the port cities and inland. Like the other leading missionary-journalists, Allen was fully as interested in transmitting to the Chinese people the advanced benefits of Western culture and science as he was in propagating the Christian faith. Indeed he changed his weekly paper in 1875 to a weekly magazine that was entirely secular, the *Wan-kuo Kung-pao,* and the *Chinese Globe Magazine* was its English title. This magazine had a long life, interrupted between 1883 and 1889, but resumed in 1889 as a monthly and continued until 1907.[5] Allen enlarged and departmentalized the news section of his new magazine, stating that the paper would be devoted to the "extension of knowledge relating to Geography, History, Civilization, Politics, Science, Art, Industry, and general progress of Western countries," later adding the words ". . . to the awakening of China. . . ." In 1876

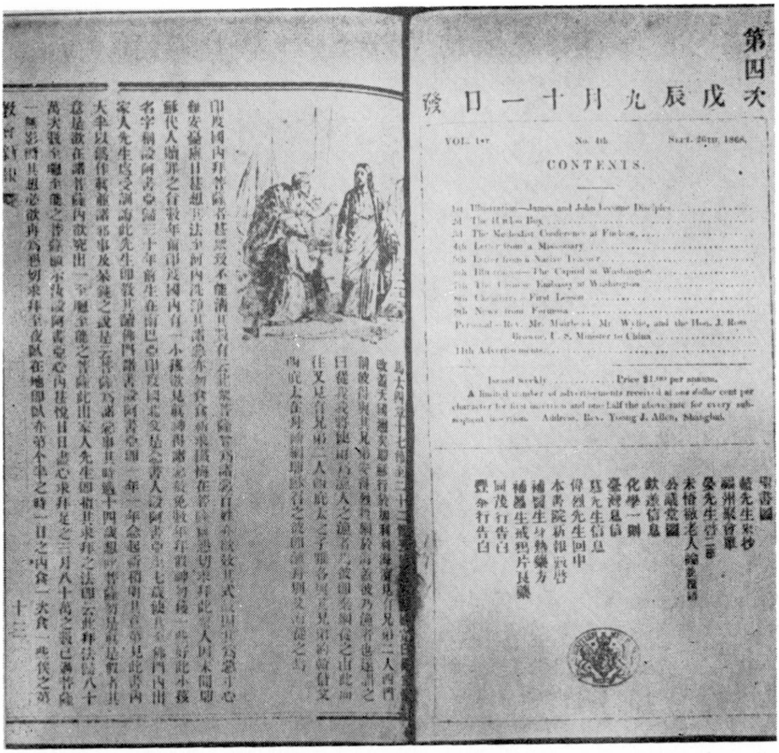
第四次
戊辰九月十一日發

VOL. 1st No. 4th Sept. 26th, 1868.

CONTENTS.

1st Illustration—James and John become Disciples
2d The Hindu Boy
3d The Methodist Conference at Foochow
4th Letter from a Missionary
5th Letter from a Native Teacher
6th Illustration—The Capitol at Washington
7th The Chinese Embassy at Washington
8th Chemistry—First Lesson
9th News from Formosa
Personal—Rev. Mr. Muirhead, Mr. Wylie, and the Hon. J. Ross Browne, U. S. Minister to China
11th Advertisements

Issued weekly .... Price $1.00 per annum.

A limited number of advertisements received at one dollar cent per character for first insertion and one half the above rate for every subsequent insertion. Address, Rev. Young J. Allen, Shanghai.

Fig. 10.3. Sample pages from the fourth (September 26, 1868) issue of a Western missionary periodical published in Chinese by an American, Young J. Allen at Shanghai. The title was **Chiao-hui Hsin-wen** (Church News). Included are a bilingual table of contents; a translation from the Bible text, Matthew iv., 17–22; and an article "The Hindu Boy." Original in British Museum.

the circulation was 1,800, still chiefly among the missionaries. When the Sino-Japanese War (1894–1895) quadrupled the circulation, his objective was to reach the higher official classes. The influence of the *Chinese Globe Magazine* was such that after its death, Chinese journalists established a weekly imitation to take its place.

There were other important church publications in English. One, the *Chinese Recorder,* was a monthly begun in 1867 as an organ of the Protestant missionary body in China. There were also the *Methodist Advocate* and the Presbyterian *Intelligencer,* both weeklies, and other monthlies, such as the *Chinese Churchman.*

Catholic missionaries, the first to come to China, were among the last to establish general periodicals, although they had been among the first to publish textbooks and pamphlets. *I Wen Lu,* the oldest Catholic magazine, was begun by French Jesuits at Zikawei (or Siccawei) near Shanghai in 1878, first as a semimonthly, then weekly and eventually semiweekly. It continued until 1949 with several changes in title and format and a merger in 1898 with a Chinese reform organ devoted to science. In 1912 this paper was reorganized as a monthly church organ, under the title *Sheng-chiao Tsa-chih,* (the Magazine of the Holy Church). *Sheng Hsin Pao,* another Roman Catholic monthly whose English title was *Holy Heart Gazette,* was founded in 1887 at Shanghai. This magazine, edited by Chinese, sold for the now incredible price of ten cents a year. The reputable Catholic daily *Yi-shih-pao* (Social Welfare) was compelled to cease publication by the advent of the Communists in 1949.

Although the general missionary magazines ambitiously covered a wide range of specialized subjects, there were journals that devoted themselves exclusively to specialized fields. One example was *Chung-hsi Wen-chien lu* (The Peking Magazine), published first as a general magazine then as a scientific periodical by another Society for the Diffusion of Knowledge (Fig. 10.4). Indeed, the life of its magazine began and ended with that of the Society, 1872–1875. The magazine was edited by three Protestant missionaries, Joseph Edkins of the London Mission, John Shaw Burdon of the English Church Missionary Society, and W. A. P. Martin, an American Presbyterian missionary.

Articles in the *Peking Magazine* on flood control attracted the attention of the Chinese, and were reprinted in the form of tracts and in other periodicals. Other subjects treated by the magazine were textbook-type treatises on the telegraph, glass and iron making, photography, astronomy, meteorology, and biography. John Fryer, an English ex-missionary, started the *Ko-chih Hui-pien* (Chinese Scientific Magazine) in 1876, the same year the *Peking Magazine* folded, stepping in to take over its readers, an asset the *Peking Magazine* editors donated. It was devoted to popular information ". . . relating to sciences, arts, and manufactures of the West, with which is incorporated the Peking Magazine." Accepting advertisements, it reached a circulation as high as 4,000. It stopped in 1881, but resumed again in 1890.

John Glasgow Kerr, an American Presbyterian medical missionary, in 1880 started a medical journal called the *Hsi-Hsin-pao* (News of Western Medicine) at the Anglo-American Hospital at Canton,

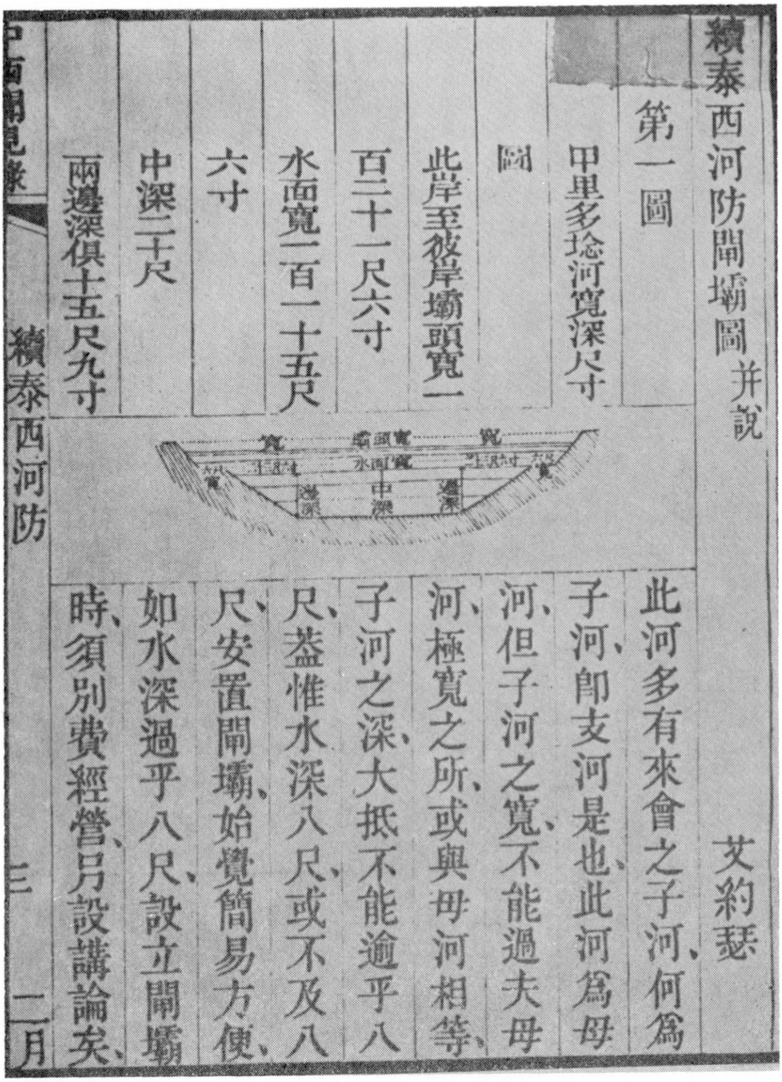

續泰西河防閘壩圖并說　艾約瑟

第一圖

中里多埝河寬深尺寸

圖

此岸至彼岸壩頭寬一百二十一尺六寸

水面寬一百一十五尺六寸

中深二十尺

兩邊深俱十五尺九寸

此河多有來會之子河、何爲子河、即支河是也、此河爲母河、但子河之寬、不能過夫母河、極寬之所、或與母河相等、子河之深、大抵不能逾乎八尺、蓋惟水深八尺、或不及八尺、安置閘壩、始覺簡易方便、如水深過乎八尺、設立閘壩時、須別費經營、另設講論矣、

Fig. 10.4. An article on river flood control by Joseph Edkins in the March, 1873, issue of **Chung-hsi Wen-chien-lu** (Peking Magazine), a periodical devoted to science. Format of this publication was 6 by 10 inches.

where Dr. Sun Yat-sen first became interested in studying medicine. *Ko-chih Hsin-wen* (News of Knowledge and Science), a missionary magazine devoted to natural science, was established in Shanghai in 1898. There were other less-known journals in scientific fields, literature, and philosophy.

The missionaries did not overlook the education of youth, and their juvenile press, beginning in the last quarter of the century, exerted an important influence on China's future leaders. The two first juvenile magazines were launched simultaneously in February, 1874, in different cities. At Foochow, Mrs. N. J. Plumb, wife of the American Methodist missionary, began publishing a monthly illustrated Bible story leaflet in Foochow colloquial; at Canton, the same Kerr who later started the medical monthly mentioned above produced a few numbers of his juvenile magazine before J. M. W. Farnham, an American Presbyterian missionary, took over its publication and moved it to Shanghai. Both of these juvenile publications appeared under the same title: *Hsiao-hai Yueh-pao* (The Child's Paper). Both were successful, and Farnham's paper continued until 1915 when it was publishing 4,500 copies monthly for missionary-taught Sunday school pupils. Farnham also published from 1880 to 1913 a pictorial juvenile entitled *T'u-hua Hsin-pao* (Chinese Illustrated News).

During the last half of the century Farnham and other missionaries made efforts without much success to overcome the barriers imposed by the literary form. They used conversational or spoken language, called *pai-hua* (plain speech), a vernacular disdained by the literati, but occasionally used by the great writers of popular novels and drama. A few adopted a Romanized colloquial for the written form. Several vernacular societies were formed among the missionaries and some papers appeared in colloquials.

The Foreign Language Commercial Press

The first periodical in the English language was a newspaper published at Canton in 1827. W. W. Wood of Philadelphia was the founder, but the paper soon came under the ownership of James Matheson who is often credited with its founding.[6] At first a biweekly and then a weekly, under the title *Canton Register,* the paper reported general news of Canton and the Far East, and news of the local market of which contraband opium was the chief commodity. Matheson's editor was John Slade, and Morrison was a regular contributor. In 1833 it began a market supplement, the

Canton General Prices Current. The *Register* had several rivals in Canton, the most important being the *Canton Press,* started in 1835. Although the *Press* was larger and carried foreign news, it never surpassed the *Register's* prestige. Matheson moved the *Register* to Hong Kong in 1843 after the city was ceded to the British. There it continued as the *Hong Kong Register* until 1859. As Hong Kong and Shanghai gradually replaced Canton as commercial centers, they also became the chief centers for press and publishing. Commerce and trade provided increasing proportions of press revenue, as did subscriptions. In the 1850s the papers had developed regular advertisers, and publications that formerly had been distributed free developed paying subscribers.

The newspaper that became the most famous and widely read English language paper in the Orient was the *China Mail,* started at Hong Kong as a weekly in 1845 by Andrew Shortrede, a Scottish merchant. The *Mail* in 1876 merged with the *Evening Mail and Shipping List* which had been established in 1864, and in the same year started morning daily publication, and continued under a different title as a Chinese daily. Before Shortrede started the *Mail,* another weekly had been founded at Hong Kong called the *Friend of China.* It became semiweekly and moved from Hong Kong to Canton thence to Shanghai before expiring in 1868 after some 26 years of publication.[7] A stronger rival of the *Mail,* however, was the Hong Kong *Daily Press,* founded in 1857 by George N. Ryder, a crusading editor and publisher who opposed corruption in colonial affairs, and thereby earned a high reputation for himself and his paper. The *Daily Press* was British and devoted to general and commercial information. There were other short-lived papers estab lished in Hong Kong during this period.

Meanwhile in Shanghai another English language paper was launched—one that grew to exceed the *Mail's* circulation and financial success. This was the *North China Herald,* a weekly founded in 1850 by a merchant, Henry Shearman. The *Herald* soon introduced its shipping and commercial report as a daily supplement, and in 1864 it was enlarged as the *North China Daily News.* The *Daily News,* independent and British, represented the commercial viewpoint, but it continued the *Herald* as its weekly edition.

Contribution of the Foreign-owned Media

The foreign language press and the Chinese language press owned by foreigners spread to the chief treaty ports and eventually inland to the capital. In addition to English language general papers there was a profusion of Russian and Japanese language periodicals, as well as publications in French, Portuguese, German, Japanese, and Italian. Although there were several French language journals of short life appearing in Shanghai in the 1870s and 1880s, of greater stability was *L'Echo de Chine,* the chief journal of French interests in the Far East,[8] founded in 1895 and continuing publication until the 1920s. The German language paper *Der Ostasiatische Lloyd,* begun in 1886, appeared until 1917 when it was prohibited by China's declaration of war on Germany. By 1926 foreign language dailies in China included 26 English, 16 Japanese, 6 Russian, 3 French, and 1 Korean.[9]

To the causes of the church, of trade and commerce, and the mission of educating the Chinese in Western culture and science—all causes served by the foreign press in China—was later added a wide range of political causes. Foreign governments, with more money than the missionaries and motivated by purposes more temporal than spiritual, employed the native language periodical press in their own interests. The Japanese, already in possession of Formosa, published *Min Pao* (Peoples Gazette) at Foochow in 1898 to help advance their ambitions for more Chinese territory. Japan's modern press system placed her in the same category as the Western powers in relation to China, and Japan produced more papers in China than any other power.[10] Several other governments published Chinese papers, and in the period between the wars subsidized Chinese papers to publish their propaganda. The Allies during World War I produced a handsome propaganda paper at Shanghai called the *Cheng Pao* (Miscellaneous News) edited by John Darroch, a veteran British missionary.

Missionaries and merchants demonstrated the concept of a popular information press operated as an independent profit-making enterprise. Their newspapers and magazines provided models after which the Chinese patterned their own. The missionary magazines introduced the idea of specialized periodicals. Although faulty as models, they had much to do with the general changes in Chinese thinking that led to reform and revolution. Lim Boon-keng wrote in 1900, "The missionaries wield a great influence through a large number of periodicals [that] . . . inspired . . . Chinese with modern, if not revolutionary ideas . . . . The Chinese speak most approvingly of Martin, Timothy Richard, and Allen, as the men who have done most to make the Chinese acquainted with the spirit of Western civilization." [11]

The Chinese language missionary press played an important role in spreading knowledge about the Western world, particularly knowledge of the natural sciences, such as geography, astronomy, physiology, physics, and chemistry. These were areas of human knowledge that could best be demonstrated to the Chinese mind and could least be disputed.[12] Also, this was the kind of thing most interesting to intelligent Chinese readers. Using it as a "trump card" to gain the attention of their readers, the missionary editors also published information about public affairs and reports of new discoveries. Reading the papers helped the Chinese to develop a sense of political awareness.

Foreign-owned, commercially based newspapers perhaps did more than the missionary magazines to help shape the modern Chinese press system. They not only served like the magazines as models but they also served as an important source of news. They were the main source—and for a time the only source—of foreign news and much domestic news as well, for republication in Chinese language papers. In some cases imperial edicts reached the foreign newspapers through foreign diplomats before being released in the Peking gazettes. Foreign editorial criticism of Chinese life and thought helped to engender discontent and dissatisfaction leading to the agitation for reform and demonstrated the use of the press as a means of political change.

The tool was a Western-style press—technically advanced, based on a capitalist economy, politically independent, dedicated to serve the general public, grounded in ideas of freedom of information and opinion, all principles corollary to libertarian systems of the West. Missionary educators used it to teach. Tradesmen with their fleets, supported, if necessary, by armies, reinforced the teaching. Loss of sovereignty, loss of prestige, changing world conditions,[13] and the impact of Western ideas all combined to force Chinese leaders to realize they had been victims of their own complacency and isolated self-sufficiency. They began to see themselves more as a huge faltering nation, humiliated by younger, smaller, and to them less culturally advanced nations—nations they had only yesterday looked upon as scarcely a step away from barbarism. By the end of the nineteenth century the pleasant image of China as the glory of the world was gradually giving way to the desperate conviction that only quick measures could save the country. A disillusioning experience for a proud people.

THE NATIVE PRIVATELY OWNED PRESS, 1844 - 1894

The earliest official Chinese reactions to the alien press were motivated by their desire to learn what the foreigners were doing. In 1839 Commissioner Lin Tse-hsu was empowered to enforce the opium ban in Canton and to look into the activities of foreigners generally. Seeking information from primary sources, he ordered the foreign press translated. One of his aides, Wei Yuan, urged secret surveillance of Macao, where the "barbarians" and the Chinese live side by side, "so that we may learn as quickly as possible what the barbarians are doing and planning." He urged as a major source of government intelligence,[14] the translation and reading of the foreign papers which were then not intended for the Chinese to read. As a result of the efforts of Lin, Wei, and others, a considerable body of literature appeared in Chinese as translated from the early English language press. In 1844 Lin published a collection of translations from Murray's, *Cyclopedia of Geography,* and the 1843–1844 edition of *Hai-kuo T'u-chih* (Illustrated Cyclopedia of the Overseas Nations) contained a substantial amount of material drawn from the Chinese language missionary publications and from the foreign language press too.

But the first Chinese newspapers modeled on Western patterns were translations—the Chinese language editions of the commercial, shipping, and market journals. They came into being because of demand. The Chinese themselves in growing numbers were engaging in the booming business of the port cities and they sought to reach a growing number of native customers.

The earliest modern Chinese daily appeared in Hong Kong in 1858, the *Chung-wai Hsin-pao,* or in Cantonese, *Chung Ngoi San Po,* meaning Sino-Foreign News. It was the Chinese edition of Ryder's *Daily Press*[15] and was first published at the suggestion of Wu Ting-fang, a returned student from England who later became acting premier of the Republic and the first Chinese ambassador to the United States. The *Daily Press* had acquired a font of Chinese type characters to publish a Chinese-English dictionary, and the publication of a Chinese language paper put the idle type to use. Wu was put in charge of the new publication. Although nominally the *Chung-wai Hsin-pao* was the property of the *Daily Press,* all the details of its management were handled by Chinese who received its profits. The arrangement provided for the *Daily Press* to rent the use of its plant and equipment to the new Chinese daily, charging only for the cost of printing. In return *Chung-wai Hsin-pao* published the *Press's* foreign advertisements free of charge. At first the paper appeared every two days then became an evening daily. It prospered and enjoyed a good reputation for a half century, being suspended in 1909.

Some authorities state that the *Chung-wai Hsin-pao* was the Chinese edition of the *China Mail* (erroneously referred to as the *Daily Mail).*[16] But according to Ko, the Chinese edition of the *China Mail* did not appear until 1864 and its title was *Wah Tse Yah Pao* (Chinese Words Daily News). This paper was first edited by Cheng Ah-ting. In 1919 a separate company was formed, the *Wah Tse Yah Pao* severed its relationship with the *China Mail,* and continued until 1941.

Wang T'ao and His Newspapers

The *Wah Tse Yah Pao* and other early Chinese newspapers owe their origins to one Wang T'ao whom Lin Yutang calls the "Chinese pioneer journalist." Wang T'ao, the Franklin of the Chinese native press, was a graduate of the civil examinations and a scholar who had been associated with the missionary James Legge in editing and publishing a 5-volume collection of the Chinese classics. In 1864 Wang collaborated with several Chinese journalists, including Ch'en Ai-tung and Wu Ting-fang, in founding *Wah Tse Yah Pao.* Wu Ting-fang was a foremost advocate of a modern public press for China. Again in 1874 Wang organized another group to establish the more successful *Tsun Wan Yat Po,* or in Mandarin, *Hsun-huan Jih Pao* (Daily Cycle), a general daily (except Sunday) paper. It was commonly called the "Universal Circulating Herald," but this was a loose translation, meaning something like "the mills the gods grind slow but exceeding fine." Wang T'ao's paper soon took the lead over the *Chung-wai Hsin-pao* and the *Chin-shih Pien-lu.* The latter had been established under foreign auspices in 1864, passing into Chinese ownership in 1883. *Tsun Wan Yat Pao* became financially independent because it received steady support from the large class of merchants and tradesmen who took it for its commercial information. But the rest of the paper was of a high quality, containing (as was the general practice throughout the country until the end of the dynasty in 1912) selected material from the Peking gazettes, news from Canton and Kuangtung Province, and foreign news mainly from the foreign press in Hong Kong. Wang's general news section had a literary polish that made it popular and respected among the educated Chinese. But the paper's crowning achievement was the daily editorial article written by Wang himself in a graceful fluid style without the affectations that characterized the writings of early Chinese editors. The editorial articles contained literary and social criticism, and on occasions daring attacks on corrupt Chinese officials. Safe in Hong Kong as long as he did not offend the British, Wang could criticize the imperial government without fear of reprisal. He made recommendations for reform to the Court, thus anticipating by a generation the reform movements of the 1890s. The *Tsun Wan Yat Pao* continued until 1949.

In Shanghai the daily press trailed that of Hong Kong for a while, but soon it captured the leadership in developing the new indigenous Chinese journalism. Modernizing styles in the Far East centered in both cities, but Shanghai at the gateway of the populous Yangtse River valley became the chief metropolis for both new trade and new industry, and grew to epitomize the mainland. While Hong Kong was developing a more cosmopolitan air, looking not only to the mainland but also to the Straits settlements, the Philippines, Japan, and Australia, Shanghai and not Peking became the nation's publishing center, capitalizing upon its intimate link with China's changing life, its size (by 1931 Shanghai had 3 million people), and its expanding commerce that soon supported an independent journalism that eventually preempted the official gazette press.

The *Shun Pao* and the *Sin Wan Pao*

The leading Chinese language daily and the earliest established in Shanghai was the *Shun Pao,* or *Shen Pao* (Shanghai Journal) founded in 1872 (Fig. 10.5). From the first it was essentially a Chinese paper, though it was established and owned by a British merchant named Frederick Major. A businessman who had no personal axe to grind, Major wanted primarily to publish a paper that the Chinese would buy and read, so he left its conduct to Chinese

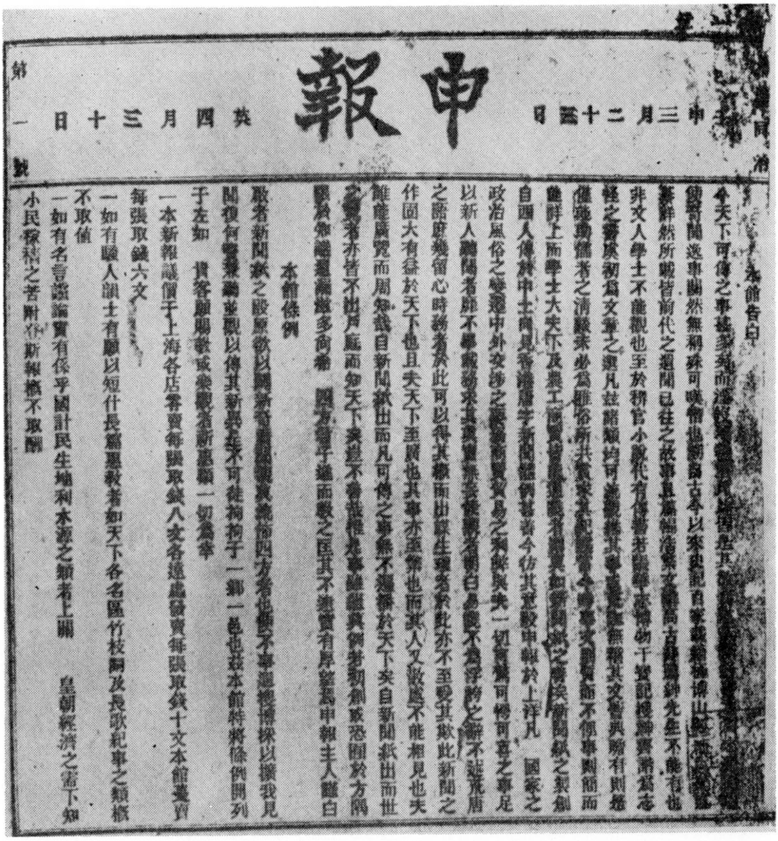
第一號

申報

壬申三月二十三日

英四月三十日

本館告白

本館條例

Fig. 10.5. First page of the first issue of the **Shun Pao** (Shanghai Journal) earliest of the leading Chinese dailies. Format is 10 by 10 inches. The entire page of this April 30, 1872, issue is devoted to a prospectus of the new paper, its reasons for publishing, its cost (6 wen), and advertising rates.

editors, the first of whom had studied under Wang T'ao, resulting in a paper that was native in viewpoint rather than foreign. Yet from the first it employed the Western concept of news, and gained serious attention because of its good news coverage. The Formosan massacre of 1871 and its aftermath that almost led to war with Japan and cost China a loss of face made big news and helped get the new paper on a firm financial footing. With telegraph connections laid to Peking in 1884, Major received wire news from the capital gazettes ahead of local competitors. After Major retired the paper was continued under a joint stock company. Reaching 15,000 circulation in 1895, the *Shun Pao* was the most profitable of the Major enterprises.[17] From this time on the paper was fully Chinese, though a foreign editor's name appeared in the masthead in order to maintain extra-territorial rights, which gave it and other foreign-owned papers greater legal immunity to regulation than the native papers possessed. In 1911 the *Shun Pao* was sold to Sze Liang-zay, who with his son conducted it as a leading metropolitan daily in the leading industrial city until the advent of the Communist regime. Sze's acquisition in 1929 of shares in the *Shun Pao's* leading rival, the *Sin Wan Pao,* made him a foremost publisher of the daily press in the modern era, and earned for him the designation of the Northcliffe of Chinese journalism.

Imitating the format of the contemporary British papers the *Shun Pao* of the earlier period used advertisements on the front and back pages and carried news and editorial matter inside. In the modern period it led in the American custom of putting important news on page one. Its telegraph news, its special correspondence, and its foreign and local news represented the best that was published. In the Kuomintang period it published a special section devoted to poetry, short stories and essays, travel, serial novels, and dramatic criticism. The "common knowledge" section contained nine different departments devoted to law, hygiene, ethics, economics, education, science, religion, markets, and questions and answers. During the 1920s and 1930s the paper published a Sunday supplement, a special weekly supplement, anniversary, and special issues, including a 600-page golden anniversary edition in 1922.

The *Shun Pao's* chief rival for a half-century in Shanghai, the *Sin Wan Pao* or *Hsin Wen Pao* (News Journal), was founded in 1893 by a group of Chinese merchant capitalists and edited at first by Ts'ai Er-k'ang, who had worked on the Chinese edition of the *North China Daily News and Herald.* In spite of financial difficulties which occasioned several changes in ownership during its early period, the paper grew and prospered. The publishing company included foreign as well as Chinese interests, and a British manager was appointed to acquire extraterritorial advantages. Ownership passed to Buchheister & Company and thence in 1900 to an American, John C. Ferguson, who in 1929 sold his controlling shares to a group of Chinese bankers. Ferguson exercised only general direction, leaving the conduct of the paper in the competent hands of Chinese journalists, notably Wang Lung-paio, who was general manager for more than 20 years, and his son P. J. Wang who succeeded him.

Resembling the *Shun Pao* in appearance and content, the *Sin Wan Pao's* policy was to maintain an intelligent public opinion in China, to aid the cause of moral, commercial, and industrial progress, and to discourage extreme measures. Perhaps its two distinguished features were its economic news section and its policy of permitting employees to share in its profits. It was independent, seeking to keep itself free to offer criticism or give praise, but in Ferguson's words, "never . . . to make heroes of those who agreed with its policy, nor traitors of those who disagreed." [18]

A third leading modern popular daily was Shanghai's *Shih Pao,* the journal of the times (or in English, The Eastern Times). Because of its origin, the *Shih Pao* will be discussed below in the section devoted to the press of the revolutionary period. It grew in the twentieth century to rival the other two general newspapers. According to Wang, the *Shun Pao,* the *Sin Wan Pao,* and the *Shih Pao* were the three best examples of modern native daily newspapers in the country.[19] All were popular, rather than quality papers. The *Shun Pao* was conservative, the *Shih Pao,* liberal, and the *Sin Wan Pao* took a position somewhere between the other two. The *Shih Pao* never rivaled the others in circulation however, remaining below 50,000, while the two larger papers reportedly exceeded 150,000 each.

Other Native Journals

A few other native newspapers in Shanghai should be mentioned. The *Huei Pao* (Forum Gazette) was started in 1874 by Yung Wing, a young Chinese who had returned from study in Europe, but it was discontinued the following year. The *Hu Pao* (Shanghai Daily) was established in 1882 as the Chinese edition of the *North China Daily News and Herald.* The founder, Frederick Henry Balfour, employed Chinese editors. The *Hu Pao* reached a circulation of 10,000 by 1895 and continued to be prominent until the eve of the revolution, though it passed from British to Japanese ownership. Most of the other newspaper undertakings, those published daily, weekly, or less frequently, in the prerevolutionary period did not enjoy the same happy combination of Western enterprise and Chinese management that accounted for the progress marking the course of the *Shun Pao,* and the *Sin Wan Pao.* There were other attempts, all short lived. Some sporadic papers were attempted in the form of bilingual publication but these were seldom in the daily field. The bilingual paper being really two papers in one, each with different audiences, was rarely an economical publishing operation. Frederick Major's other popular publication, a pictorial review entitled *Tien-shih Chai Hua-pao* (Illustrated News) begun in 1884 and issued at 10-day intervals, was followed by other pictorial imitators (Fig. 10.6).

There were similar newspaper developments in the other large cities, but the smaller communities and the villages seem to have remained relatively untouched by the literary-journalistic developments of the time. The spread of native newspapers to other metropolitan centers generally followed the pattern of the Shanghai and Hong Kong press, though a few followed that of the missionary magazines. The Hankow *Han Pao,* begun in 1893, perished in a 1900 revolt led to liberate the Emperor Kuang Hsu and to remove the Empress Dowager from power. At Tientsin another daily under the name of *Shih Pao* was published from 1886 to 1891, (to be resumed later) but had influence far beyond the relatively brief span of its life. The Tientsin *Shih Pao* was a class newspaper, appealing to high Chinese officials. The influence of the editorials of the missionary Timothy Richard who edited the paper for a time was great among the rising group of young liberal progressive Chinese. The editorials, having to do with reform, were much reprinted. Besides Wang T'ao's paper the *Tsun Wan Yat Pao* (or in Mandarin, *Hsun-huan Jih-pao)* growth of the Canton press was handicapped by competition from Hong Kong, but a number of short-lived papers appeared there, among them *Kwang Pao,* or *Canton Gazette,* founded in 1886 by Chan Chih-tung, the viceroy. Chao Kwang-chi, a student educated in Europe, was editor and manager. This paper expired after several changes in title.

Incidentally, during the reform and revolutionary agitation from 1896 to 1911, and often under the military juntos after the revolution, change of title was a means of avoiding supervision or punishment by the authorities, just as it was in the early days of the Bolshevik press. Change was so common that it gave an exaggerated and misleading impression of Chinese newspaper proliferation.

On the eve of the Sino-Japanese war of 1894–1895 and the reform movement that followed, there were about 12 native newspapers being published in the chief port cities of China. The

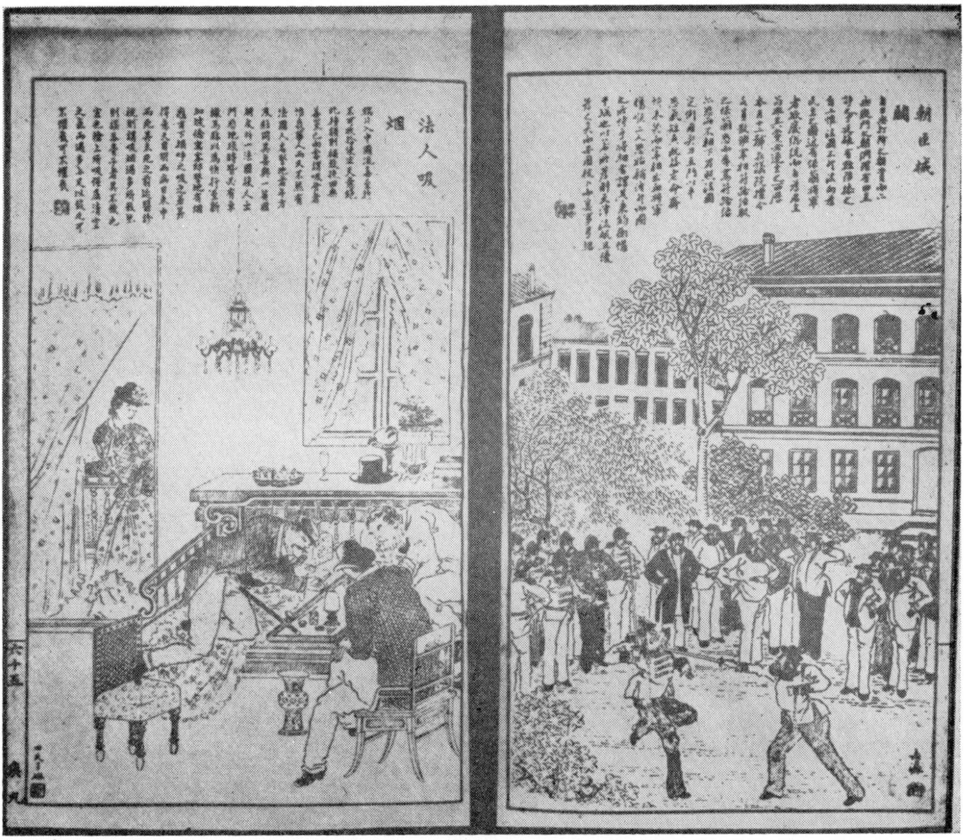

Fig. 10.6. An early Chinese illustrated journal. Two pages from the **Tien-shih Chai Hua-pao** (Illustrated News), founded in 1883 in Shanghai by Frederick Major, publisher of the **Shun Pao**. This pictorial was printed by lithography. At right is a duel between French and English travelers at Singapore. At left the same travelers are taking opium, after which they died. Format is 5½ by 9 inches. Original in British Museum.

dailies, constituting the primary basis for the beginnings of a public press, were published primarily in Shanghai and Hong Kong. The court gazettes still held their monopoly in the capital. The native-owned papers were read and supported at first by populations in the trading centers, and especially the new Chinese class associated with foreign commercial interests. By the middle 1890s these papers were being read by Chinese in the interior. Sharper political and intellectual influences varied the demand and brought into existence magazines and specialized periodicals in the years that immediately followed.

Chinese papers of this period were, as might be expected, primitive when judged by modern standards. Much of their content was gossipy trivia. They were preempted from reporting firsthand the affairs of the empire by the official gazette system, so in this important area they merely copied and transmitted information. Locally reports of provincial examinations, and of crime and disaster were published. The literary columns often served as outlets for the publication of poetry produced by the poetry clubs. The commercial department was filled with news of markets, shipping, and with announcements and advertisements of amusements such as theatre offerings. The papers were often accused by foreigners of being antiforeign and by the Chinese of being proforeign. With the exception of the British-owned *Shun Pao* and Wang T'ao's paper at Hong Kong, the Chinese newspapers avoided criticism of the government, concentrating on operating a businesslike profit-making news organ.

Chinese society was not ready for editorial leadership. Taking little interest in public and world affairs, they regarded their daily papers as foreign-inspired innovations. With a few exceptions, the position of the journalist and editor was not highly regarded. Of scholarly temperament, he sought generally to stay out of trouble. Even competitive rivalries and differences of opinion with other editors were rare. Investigative reporting, which in more aggressive civilizations has its public service appeals, was suspect and resisted, hence it developed slowly. The editor's chief delight was his task of writing the flowery essays which served as his editorial articles. In sum, there was as yet no professional body of communicators.

As the character of the new Chinese press was molded by Western journalistic concepts and methods, so did Western mechanical inventions enable it to adapt advances in lithography, metallic typography, and machine printing. Faster telegraph and cable transmission together with steam navigation and special post office newspaper rates combined to give the large city newspapers a competitive advantage over the local press.

LIANG CH'I-CH'AO AND THE REFORM AND REVOLUTIONARY PRESS, 1895 - 1911

China's defeat in the short war with Japan sharpened dissatisfaction with the Manchu government and set off a rash of reform movements under the leadership of intellectuals, who were either government officials or scholars and writers. Soon the press was enlisted in the effort. (See Fig. 10.7.) The leading reform group was organized in 1895 at Peking as the Association for the Study of National Power, and in August of the same year founded its official organ, a daily entitled *Wan-kuo Kung-pao.* This was the same title as the *Globe Magazine,* which the reformers admired and copied, so it was changed a short time later to *Chung-wai Chi-wen* (Sino-Foreign News). The editor was Liang Ch'i-ch'ao who became a renowned journalist, author, scholar, and educator. Liang had studied at K'ang Yu-wei's school in Canton, and both he and his professor were active in reform organizations. K'ang at first was the reform strategist while Liang was the publicist. With the title change the paper took on new character, dropping its reprint matter and substituting articles on reform doctrine. The paper, financed by the Society, was distributed free to more than 1,000 readers in Peking, but the government censored it and its sponsoring organization and it ended abruptly after only a few months of publication. Liang immediately moved his operation to Shanghai where, aided by his Peking experience, he campaigned more successfully.

Political Communication in Reform

The reform organization kept its title and set up its Shanghai headquarters from which another daily organ was launched in January, 1896. Bearing the title *Ch'iang Hsueh Pao* (meaning to strengthen study), it became a popular generic label for a number of reform periodicals. But the paper under this title appeared only for about three months—the society's chief sponsor was dismissed by imperial decree in March and all reform activities were forced to retrench for a brief time. Liang and his associate Wank Kang-nien formally dissolved the publishing company and organized a new one which soon started a new organ, for all intents and purposes completely dissociated with the former. This publication was a magazine, published at 10-day intervals that first appeared in August, 1896, under the title *Shih Wu Pao* (Current Affairs News), which came to be known in English as *The Chinese Progress.* The new journal found a ready audience among the reform-minded viceroys and governors as well as in the scholar community. By this time the Imperial Court was more favorably inclined toward the cause and withheld censorship. In April, 1898, *Shih Wu Pao* had a circulation of some 10,000 and was known throughout the Empire.

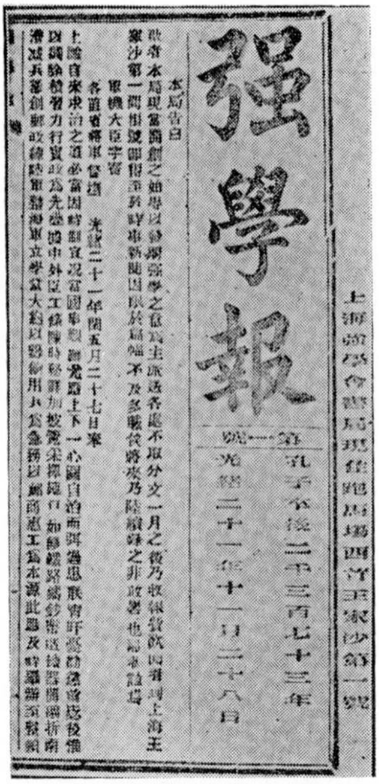
上海強學會書局現在跑馬場西首王家沙第一號

強學報

第一號

孔子卒後二千三百七十三年

光緒二十一年十一月二十八日

本局告白

1

時務報

光緒二十二年七月初一日

第一册

2

蘇報

3

民報

第壹號

4

It carried a considerable amount of news, documents selected from the Peking gazettes, serials drawn from foreign works (for example, a biography of George Washington), essays on British law, etc. Liang wrote much of the original matter himself, and his famous reform essay "Pein-fa T'ung-I" (A General Proposal on Reform) appeared first in the magazine. In May, 1898, the *Shih Wu Pao* management launched *Shih Wu Jih Pao* (Current Affairs Daily), which also enjoyed quick success. This venture, however, was initiated without Liang's help, for he had left Shanghai late in 1897 to take charge of the government's reform projects initiated during the hundred days of 1898.

Meantime, in the more relaxed atmosphere emanating from Peking, reform journalism flourished. The most famous and fearless of the reform dailies was the *Su Pao* (signifying Kiangsu Province Gazette or Revival Gazette). Founded in 1896 by Hu Chang in the comparative safety of the Shanghai International Settlement, this paper eventually went beyond the contemporary reform themes to become a revolutionary propaganda organ.[20] Hu Chang had registered the paper as Japanese owned, under the name of his Japanese wife, but even with these precautions the undertaking became too hazardous. Hu Chang then turned it over to a group which included the three scholars, Wu Chih-huei, Chang T'aiyen, and Ts'ai Yuanp'ei—later known as the "veterans" of the Kuomintang.[21] Tsou Yung, the author of a pamphlet entitled "The Revolu-

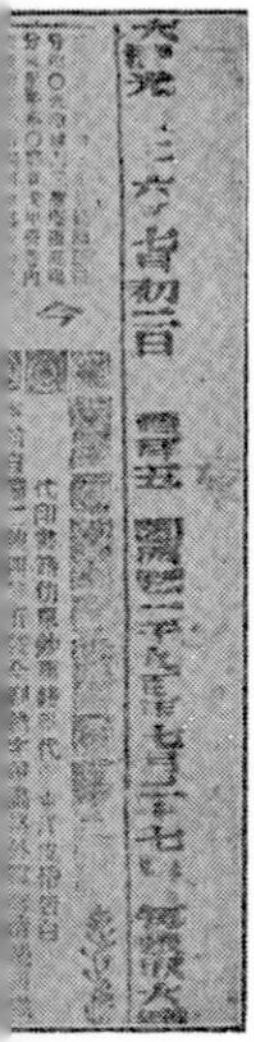

Fig. 10.7. Front pages of Volume 1, Number 1, of four Chinese reform and revolutionary periodicals. (1) **Ch'iang Hsueh-pao** (To Strengthen Knowledge), a daily journal founded by Liang Chi-chao in 1896 in Shanghai. The title became a popular generic label for a number of reform periodicals. Many of the papers of the time bore only the title on the first page, as did this first issue of another Liang periodical (2), founded in August, 1897. Published every 10 days, this paper, **Shi Wu-pao** (Current Affairs News) contained more than 20 pages in each issue and became an official publication of the Constitutional Monarchists, the reform party of Liang and Kang Yu-wei. Liang's group also published **Ching I-pao** from Yokohama, Japan, after the unsuccessful "Hundred Day Reformation," and **Hsin-min Tsung-pao**, a fortnightly, both approximating 40 pages. Front pages of the first issues of two revolutionary party publications of the Sun Yat-sen's group are (3) the **Su Pao**, founded in Shanghai and the most famous and fearless of the reform dailies. (4) **Min Pao** (People's Daily), one of a number of party voices of Sun Yat-sen's Union of Revolutionary Leagues with headquarters in Hong Kong, was published first in Tokyo in 1905.

tionary Army," also joined the editorial staff. After the court's reform efforts stopped with the Empress Dowager's seizure of power the reform movement was driven underground, whereupon *Su Pao* turned radical, advocating force and assassination. This angered the Manchu government which demanded the editors' arrest and the paper's seizure. The inflammatory articles were found to be treason, an offense carrying death. But the editors were given short prison terms because public opinion and the foreign consulates brought pressure to bear on the court. Suppressed, the *Su Pao* promptly resumed under new title, *Kuo-min Jih-jih Pao* (China National Daily, or literally Self-governing People's News).

This earlier reform period, which could not be characterized as revolutionary (the *Su Pao* to the contrary), saw the establishment of a large number of many kinds of periodicals, varying in content and function from mildly educational to militantly propagandistic. From Shanghai they spread to the larger cities. It is difficult to classify and characterize this intellectual outpouring from Chinese presses. Some of the periodicals were general, others specialized. Some were like newspapers in appearance but were filled with the kind of material usually appearing in magazines. Others resembled the magazine in format, but contained current information. Many were high minded in ideals and purposes, devoted to learned textbook style treatises that infringed upon the normal book publishing field.[22] Some were sensational to the point of being pornographic. Although they used different methods to spread the awakening, they all sought the common reform goals. Imperial policy smiled on reform at this time, for between 1896 and 1898 when the reform party was in control, mandate after mandate issued from the throne to inaugurate sweeping changes, mostly in the old political system.[23]

Reform organs similar to Liang Ch'i-ch'ao's papers sprang up in other cities: Liang's party started a paper at Macao in 1897; in Hangchow the same year *Ching Shih Pao* (a journal for setting the age in order) was founded; at Changsha, capital of Hunan Province, and an intellectual center, the paper *Hsiang-hsueh Hsin-pao* (Hunan Province Gazette) was published by Chang T'aiyen in connection with a school devoted to the new learning. Also in Changsha the daily *Hsiang Pao* (Hunan Gazette) appeared, ably edited by the militant scholar T'ang Ts'ai-ch'ang who was martyred at Wuchang in 1900. This paper was considered by K'ang Yu-wei to be among the best of all the reform periodicals. At Chungking was the *Yu Pao* (Chungking Gazette), and at Chengtu the *Shuh Hsuch Pao* (Szechuan Knowledge Gazette). At Tientsin a notable journal, *Kuo Wen Pao* (National News Gazette), made its debut as a daily, with a companion periodical, *Kuo-wen Huei-pao,* appearing at 10-day intervals. Not a crusading paper, it showed courage in attacking the imperial government's refusal to receive a memorial from reformers seeking relief from Russian aggression. This paper was distinguished for its news coverage, including translations from the major foreign language papers. The *Kuo-wen Huei-pao* survived the counter reform period and for long ranked as the best periodical in North China. Yen Fu, a translator of Adam Smith, John Stuart Mill, and Herbert Spencer, was associated with the *Kuo Wen Pao.* As renowned a scholar as Liang Ch'i-ch'ao, Yen appealed for a more open-minded attitude toward Western civilization in his foreword to the paper's first number. He took the position, quite ahead of his times, that it was more important for the people of China to understand foreign than domestic conditions. "For no modern nation can exist by itself to-day, but must take its place with others in the family of nations," [24] he wrote. Since most of the daily papers concentrated on domestic news, giving foreign news second place, Yen Fu sought to correct this imbalance by producing a daily devoted primarily to foreign intelligence.

In Shanghai, *Tungfang Tsachih* (the Eastern Miscellany), probably the oldest surviving magazine, was launched by the Commercial Press first in 1901. Earlier there had been the *T'ung Hsueh Pao* (Journal of General Knowledge) founded in 1897. Its contents ambitiously dealt with geography, history, the physical sciences, and foreign languages. The *Kuot-sui Hsueh-pao* (Journal of National Esprit) was begun in 1904 in Shanghai by another scholar Chang T'ai-yen.

There were a number of popular periodicals published in the vernacular. Of these perhaps typical was *Wusih Paihua-pao* (The Wusih Spoken Language Magazine) an educational journal begun at Wusih, near Shanghai, in1898 by Miss Ch'iu Yu-fang, the first Chinese woman journalist. Also in Shanghai appeared the *Ts-ui Pao* (Select News), a weekly of general world news, first published in 1897, and *Ch'iu Shih Pao* (the Truth Seeker), a magazine devoted to the new learning, publishing material from French sources. A juvenile publication following the pattern of the missionary children's magazines, *Ch'iu Wo Pao* (Ask Me) was begun at Shanghai in 1898.

Prominent among the specialized periodicals were such publications as *Nung Hsueh Pao* (Agriculture Journal) a magazine devoted to agriculture, commerce, and industry. Its agricultural reform propaganda, though doctrinaire and impractical for China, was exceedingly popular, perhaps because of the great need. The *Hsin-hsueh Pao* (New Knowledge Journal), begun in Shanghai in 1897, was the organ of two learned groups. Its first issue, presenting four articles on such broad and diverse subjects as principles of government and medical treatment, was typical of the reform journalist's efforts to handle huge fields of knowledge. The *Kochih Hsinwen* (Science Gazette), begun in 1898, was also like the New Knowledge Journal mainly devoted to physics and mathematics. There were magazines devoted to education like the *Chiaoyu Shihchieh* (Education World), 1901, and the *Chiaoyu Tsachih* (Education Magazine), 1909. There were also magazines dedicated to the feminist cause, to geography, and to law and politics.

Side by side with such scholarly efforts in the guise of popular journalism as the above, Shanghai saw a wave of obscenity which was probably a forerunner of the mosquito press of the 1920s and 1930s. In 1897 and 1898 these journals issued without hindrance from the International Settlement. One, an illustrated monthly, *Ching Lou Pao* (Brothel Gazette) was printed from an establishment adjoining, of all places, the International Settlement's police station. There was also a comic illustrated called *Yu Hsi Pao* (The Sport).

The course of reform was abruptly changed in September, 1898, by the shift of power in Peking. The Empress Dowager seized control of the government, imprisoned the Emperor, and ruled in his name. The policy in Peking which had favored reform now turned to one of reaction and persecution. Six reform leaders, one a brother of K'ang Yu-wei, were promptly executed. K'ang and Liang Ch'i-ch'ao escaped to Japan. Denounced as traitors, they had a price on their heads. Many of the reform periodicals stopped, others became turncoat reactionaries. The press of the port cities and International Settlement continued as before. The leading papers of the reform press returned, but muffled and sobered by persecution. However, the most brilliant and influential reform organs, produced in Japan by the leaders in exile, circulated in China with ease despite the government edict against it. Constitutional monarchists became outright revolutionists. The reaction and counterreform measures of the central government intensified revolutionary feelings and drove loyal reformers into the revolutionary party.

Government and the Official Press

While the older reform press became more revolutionary in tone the position of the government, compelled by the sheer force of reality, became essentially the same as that of the reformers of 1897–1898. The Boxer Rebellion forced the retreat of the Empress Dowager and her court into Shensi Province and demonstrated once again the monarchy's weakness. When she returned in 1902 she began to enact the same kind of measures she had attempted to crush in 1898. During this period a few progressive viceroys who had remained loyal to the dynasty revived the publication of official newspapers, the *kuan-pao,* and with the court's approval, the official communication system spread over the country. Some official organs were founded; some were created merely by arrangement with private publishers of existing papers. The purpose was to improve the government's position with the people and, in part, to use the periodical press to offset the effects of what was the original reform press but had now become the radical revolutionary press. The kuan-pao system essentially realized the journalistic aims of the reform administration of 1898. The ideas it expressed and the causes it fostered were basically the same as those of the reform press's early phases.[25] Although the natural concomitant of the official press system—political subsidy—continued into the post-revolutionary period as the authority's principal method of using the press for its own ends, the kuan-pao movement disappeared into the new private press of the Republic, only to be revived again under the Nationalist government.

While extending the official press, the government engaged in publishing departmental organs from Peking, a practice which proliferated under postrevolutionary regimes. In 1907 a general organ of the imperial government, *Cheng-chih Kuan-pao* (Government Official Gazette), was established. Although it differed in appearance, it carried substantially the same content as the *Peking Gazette;* the difference being that it was printed and published by the government and not by private printers.

But whatever the official press attempted, it could not counteract the spirit of the times. The revolutionary movement, fanned by its press, had gone too far to turn back. Antagonistic feeling against the Manchu government became a rallying point unifying almost all patriotic groups of differing opinions. Anti-governmnt agitation became the dominant theme after 1900, as the crusade to save China changed from reform to revolution.[26]

Anti-government Agitation

While the aims of the original reformers were changing, the characteristics of their movement changed too. The early reformers, it will be remembered, were primarily aristocrats, as were early reform leaders in Russia. They were constitutional monarchists with little antagonistic feeling toward the ruling dynasty. They hoped to improve conditions, and modernize and strengthen the nation within the existing framework of government. The agitators from 1900 to 1911 increased in numbers to cut across class lines and, in political opinion, ranged from reactionary to radical. They agreed generally that the Manchu dynasty must be overthrown. Although the more radical elements wanted to destroy the ancient imperial system as well, the Monarchist Party of K'ang Yu-wei and Liang Ch'i-ch'ao held to the original aristocratic view.[27] The early reformers, addressing themselves primarily to the aristocracy, used as their chief instrument the magazine with a literary flavor. The revolutionaries, on the other hand, directed their appeals to the widest possible audience, publishing newspapers in the common speech, *pai-hua*. The movement, in short, became a popular one, and the means to achieve its purposes was mass communication through a militant political party press. Although a dynamic literary internecine war raged in 1906 in Tokyo between the exiled Republican Party of Sun Yat-sen and his followers and K'ang and Liang, leaders of the Monarchists, the question of internal dispute was not settled by verbal victories, but by the Manchu regime's hopeless situation.[28]

Tokyo was the headquarters of the revolutionary writers and scores of Chinese magazines and newspapers were published there between 1900 and 1911 by Chinese students advocating varying degrees of political and social reform. Sun Yat-sen, the revolutionary chief, was not a journalist, but his political organization employed a large following of able writers and published papers not only in Japan and the coast cities of China but also in overseas Chinese communities as well. The first Sun Yat-sen party organ was *Chung-kuo Jih-pao* (China Daily) established in 1899 at his revolutionary headquarters in Hong Kong, a place that afforded opportunities for smuggling the paper into South China to his largest following among the people. In 1905 a number of party organs were spawned when Sun's organization expanded into a worldwide federation of Chinese associations, supporting the revolution under the name of *Ko-ming Tung-meng Hui* (Union of Revolutionary Leagues). Among the most famous of these were the *Fu Pao* (Reconstruction Gazette) and the *Min Pao* (People's Daily) both dailies[29] published at Tokyo. The former was edited by Liu Shih-p'ei and Chang Ping-lin, both noted revolutionary scholars; the latter, edited by Chang Chi, carried trenchant articles by Wang Ching-wei and Hu Han-min, both of whom became prominent in postrevolutionary governments.

In Shanghai besides the *Su Pao*, whose voice was becoming more persistently subversive, both party organs and privately-published periodicals engaged in the revolutionary crusade. Tseng Ching-i left the turncoat *Chung-wai Jih-pao* to start a revolutionary daily *Pai-hua Pao* (Spoken Language Gazette). Despite the protection to free speech and free press afforded by the International Settlement, the authorities succeeded in suppressing through the agencies of the German consulate *Ching-chung Jih-pao* (Alarming Bell Daily News). The Republican party organs established at Shanghai included the *Hsu-mi Jih-pao* (Sumeru Daily News), founded in 1905, and the famous *Min Pao* series of papers. These were started with the *Min-hu Jih-pao* (The People's Cry Daily News) in 1908, to be followed upon its suppression by the *Min-hsu Jih-pao* (The People's Plight Daily News), and in turn by the *Min Li Pao* (the Democrat).

Two personal private revolutionary dailies which continued to be influential leaders in the postrevolutionary period were founded during this period, which Lin Yutang calls the Golden Age of Chinese Journalism. Both strong voices in the revolutionary outcry, the first was the *Shih Pao* (Eastern Times) of Shanghai, founded in 1904 by T'i Ch'u-ch'ing and ably edited by Ch'en Ling, which introduced the short pungent editorial article in place of the old essay-type articles of greater length and other devices for building lively interest among readers. Its editorial policy introduced a new note in Chinese journalism that indicated a step toward greater stature and maturity. The paper's goals were to make its comments impartial, and to make its news quick, accurate, truthful, and impersonal (or impartial). In carrying out these high aims, T'i

Ch'u-ch'ing infused into the paper "a fine spirit of patriotism, idealism and a truly progressive outlook." [30]

The other private journal was the *Ta Kung Pao* (the Impartial Gazette) founded in 1902 at Tientsin by Ying Lien-chin. Ying's aim was to establish a personal organ to improve the condition of the Chinese people. He was not a Republican, but he found himself on the Republican side. His attacks on the policies of the Empress Dowager were daring enough to align him with the revolutionary cause but contrary to the claims of the paper's title, scarcely impartial. The *Ta Kung Pao* later became a leading financial and economic paper of the Republic and was one of the few older papers that survived the communist conquest.

Contributions of Liang and Revolutionary Communications

While the popular press—party, government, and private—carried the crusade to the people, Liang Ch'i-ch'ao and his group of intellectuals stood among the most powerful literary forces shaping public opinion from 1898 to 1911.[31] Liang, it will be remembered, led the early reform movement among the intellectuals and scholars. After fleeing the 1898 coup d'etat, he fired his literary salvos from Japan against the Empress Dowager and the reactionaries, hoping to reestablish the Emperor Kuang Hsu on the throne, and by this means to continue the interrupted reform program. In this respect, he differed with Sun Yat-sen and the revolutionary party whose goal was the removal of the dynasty. As the prospect dimmed for the Emperor's return, Liang's aims shifted toward those of the revolutionary Republicans, especially his advocacy of a constitution and parliament. Following the overthrow of the Manchus, Liang supported the Republic, holding several offices in the new government and helping defeat President Yuan Shih-kai's abortive effort to make himself emperor in 1915–1916.

Historian and political philosopher, Liang was the first Chinese journalist to exploit the powers of the press for creating and influencing public opinion. He was also a practical thinker who could face change realistically, adopt a constructive, patriotic approach to reform, and when the first reform effort collapsed, accept defeat without bitterness. He made an important contribution to the development of more fluent and simple written style, helping to free the language from the stuffy classical tradition. His editorials and essays were reminiscent of the best of those in the London *Times,* which at the peak of its power was known as "The Thunderer." His life was a fight against bad government and the press was his weapon to make China a democracy and establish universalism and unity among world nations.[32] Liang took up the cry of reform that earlier had been uttered from Hong Kong by Wang Tao, doing for the magazine press what Wang had done in a smaller way for the newspaper press. By fusing scholarship with journalism he made the press a literary and social force that gave it a new purpose beyond mere trade in the news. This elevated the status of the press making it a Chinese institution worthy of the dignity and efforts of the most learned.

In 1898 he established *Ching I Pao* (Clear Discussion Magazine) in Yokohama. It was a 40-page magazine of essays, biography, foreign translations, general news, and opinion on issues of the day issued and circulated widely in China at 10-day intervals. The Empress Dowager's 1900 edict failed to stop the subrosa dispersion of *Ching I Pao,* and was equally ineffectual against other smuggled publications. But the magazine was stopped by a print-shop fire, to be succeeded by the semimonthly *Hsin-min Tsung-pao* (The New People's Journal). The general theme of this magazine, which of all his periodicals came closest to his ideal of an international journal, followed the title's thought, namely the goal of making over or changing the Chinese people. At this time Liang was against sweeping substitution of Chinese institutions for Western, but rather he advocated the practical synthesis of traditional Chinese with the new. This magazine too enjoyed a large circulation on the mainland and continued for almost three years. With his *Hsin Hsiao-shuo Pao* (New Fiction Magazine) established in 1909, Liang employed fiction as a medium for advancing his social causes. In one essay, "The Future of New China," he predicted the formation of the Republic and foresaw accurately the events of the next few years. He continued with *Yung-yen* (Plain Talk) in 1912 at Tientsin, and in 1915 *Ta-Chung-hua* (The Great China) in Shanghai.

During the period from 1896 to 1905 it was estimated that roughly 1,000 publications came into being and disappeared when their objectives had been accomplished. Of the reform and revolutionary journals, only the *Ta Kung Pao,* the *Shih Pao,* and the *Eastern Miscellany* continued their identity into postrevolutionary times.

There was no doubt that the press was one of the most important influences in the forces that brought about the revolution.

Liang remarked that it was a "black blood" instead of a "red blood" revolution.[33] In the face of government opposition, brilliantly conducted without considerations of financial profit, the press was the chief means of agitation for political change, mobilizing public opinion in a cause that grew powerful enough to overthrow the dynasty.[34] The skill and effect with which the thinkers and writers employed the press as a medium of mass communication left its mark on Chinese journalism and literature. The idea of using the periodical press to arouse political consciousness and to achieve political ends remained. The concept of communicating to the masses to achieve concrete political results remained. Partisan, subsidized organs of all kinds multiplied in later decades, to be followed by a Communist mass communication system. Notwithstanding the wide spectrum of political idealism it advocated, the revolutionary press developed a unity of purpose that had never been achieved before and was not duplicated in the press of the Republic, divided as it was by many factions.

In news service and in literary quality the revolutionary journals were superior to the old port city papers, chiefly because of the financial support they received and the high journalistic standards they set for free and unbiased information and expression of opinion.

From its beginning in 1894–1895 the reform movement had as one of its major objectives the establishment of modern public mass press modeled after the Western pattern. In his essay, "The Value of the Periodical Press in National Affairs," Liang in 1896 advocated a public press and outlined his views of how such a public press should function.

> Strength or weakness of nations varies directly with the openness or obstruction of channels of communication. A public press in China should first be a means of communication between the imperial government and the people. By disseminating information, it should be a means of keeping the Chinese people and foreign peoples in mutual touch, to abolish misconceptions and achieve mutual international understanding. A second function should be not only to report the details of government but also to expose and criticize its faults and weaknesses.[35]

Among the proposals for strengthening the Empire in K'ang Yu-wei's petition to the throne against concluding a premature peace with Japan in 1895 was one urging a system of newspapers to perform a new function; namely, that of enlightening the public. Liang's essay, the *Chuan Hsueh Pien* (An Essay Advocating the

Necessity of Studying), urges the people to use the press and sets forth the reform writer's view of the new press. This document exerted an important impact on the new public image of press function.

The reform and revolutionary press succeeded in its mission of political change too fast and too efficiently. The people were not ready for democracy. Traditional bonds were destroyed before political cohesion was achieved. The republic did not work. But the ideal of privately owned independent public press was achieved—and achieved before the development of full public political awakening.

The new Chinese natives press was patterned after the alien periodicals, but was shaped to meet social and economic conditions and the demands of language and reading interests. It was most effective when operated by Chinese who combined Chinese learning and scholarship with the Western viewpoint and method. While foreigners often had a hand in starting the first newspapers, Chinese managers and editors did the work. Before the revolutionary period the new press was a business function confined largely to the commercial port cities. While the imperial gazette press provided the chief domestic news, the foreign language press provided the foreign news. After the revolutionary leaders adopted and used the press so skillfully as a propaganda instrument, the new press had a new purpose and function, for it became identified with the country's awakening and the social causes associated with change.

In the earlier stages the new press depended greatly on the official gazette system but by the end of the dynasty, and with it the end of the old gazettes, the new press had learned to operate independently so the gazettes were hardy missed. The official gazettes of the Republican period, successors to the *kuan-pao,* were not like the old imperial gazettes in either content or function. The new governments were weak and unstable, often paying for their own publicity, which robbed the press of the old authority and prestige, and the managers became increasingly responsive to the voice of the people.

THE INDEPENDENT PRESS OF THE REPUBLIC, 1912 - 1949

Revolutionary ideals set the theme for the new press of the Republic. The established daily newspapers improved and grew under new competitive conditions. New newspapers and magazines spread horizontally as new specialization vertically penetrated the ranks of the population. Publishers of established papers—such as the old *Shun Pao* and *Sin Wan Pao*—who had been in the business for profit, took on new fields of interest opened up by the revolutionary press. Causes became mixed and it was often hard to tell whether a publisher published for the chief purpose of promoting a cause or whether he promoted a cause in order to be able to publish profitably. A publication became popular only when it reflected the spirit of the times.

The press flourished, declined, then flourished again during the decade following the revolution. The provisional constitution guaranteed freedom of speech and of the press, but there was neither definition nor court decision to interpret what freedom meant.

In the first years after the revolution, it was estimated that there were about 500 newspapers throughout the country, about 100 of which were being published in the capital. Total circulation was put at 42 million copies daily,[36] a figure probably representing total press runs for all papers, daily and less frequently, or dailies totaled for one year, but appearing to be erroneous for daily copies alone. But severe restrictions and persecution returned in 1914 when Yuan Shih-kai succeeded Sun Yat-sen in the presidency and sought to revive the monarchy. The press was threatened, intimidated, bribed, suppressed, fined, seized, and closed down until there were only 20 papers left in Peking, 5 in Shanghai, and 2 in Hankow. Total circulation was said to have dropped to 39 million (again apparently total press run figures for all papers).* The period of repression ended with Yuan's death in 1915. The central government was weakened by the subsequent struggle between various factions for the presidency, and as the government power diffused and decentralized, the press revived.

Government controls during the period from 1916 to 1925, being largely in the hands of provincial governors, varied from one part of the country to another. In Canton, for example, Sun Yat-

* One finds it difficult to explain the obviously exaggerated estimates of daily circulation in this paragraph taken from *China Handbook, 1937–1943,* even considering readership, arrived at by multiplying each copy printed by 10 readers. In 1935 Lin Yutang estimated total daily circulation at 3,242,764, a figure which multiplied by 10 would reach over 30 million readers. (See Lin, *op. cit.,* pp. 148–49.) And Lin's estimate at that time compared with post office figures for 10 years earlier gave him a figure of 125 per cent increase for the 10-year period. Since post office counts were reported for the entire year, it seems likely that the 42 and 39 millions are annual totals.

sen's government followed a notably liberal press policy, and in this more temperate atmosphere there was generated the "literary revolution" and the Chinese Renaissance during which the press flourished as never before.

The Chinese Renaissance and Communications Growth

The literary revolution was not entirely literary for it had political motives and overtones. It fostered the development of a political consciousness among Chinese youth and college students by urging their participation in politics. It stimulated a great flood of new periodicals and gave existing ones a new purpose. It set off an intellectual awakening marked by eager interest in Western culture. The renaissance resulted in the student movement of May 4, 1919, and the mass movement of May 30, 1925—two significant youth agitation campaigns in which Chinese students sought to arouse public opinion. Their demands for a share in the determination of national policy brought pressure to bear upon their government. The first student movement resulted from what was considered China's unfair treatment in the Versailles Peace Conference of 1919. Although China had assisted on the side of the allies, decisions at its expense and favorable to its old enemy Japan were made at the conference. In protest the students called nationwide demonstrations and strikes in colleges and schools. The Chinese delegation to the Peace Conference was recalled. Effective public opinion continued to exert its influence during the Washington Conference of 1921. The delegation from China, which included press representatives, hoped to lay before the conference the unsettled issues between their country and Japan. But the conference would not hear this matter and decided that China and Japan should negotiate their own difficulties. The uproar of disappointment and frustration at home almost forced the second withdrawal of a Chinese delegation.[37]

A high point in the expression of Chinese public opinion came in the May 30 Movement of 1925 in Shanghai. This movement was organized and spread by the intelligentsia and the press through labor union membership and to the masses in general. It was touched off by labor agitation at British and Japanese mills in which British police shot several Chinese leaders. Strikes and boycotts against British and Japanese goods spread over the country, British and Japanese prestige suffered, and the British made concessions to the Chinese to repair damaged feelings.

The Kuomintang, at this time working in alliance with the Communist Party, had embarked upon a policy based on the salvation of the country by means of, in Sun Yat-sen's words, "awakening the masses." The mobilization of mass opinion to accomplish goals, as demonstrated by the revolutionary press earlier and exhibited effectively in the student movements, indicated to the Kuomintang leaders that the time was ripe for their popular revolution. The second Nationalist Revolution of 1926–1927 followed closely upon the heels of the youth agitations.[38]

The literary revolution was a magazine movement. The sudden growth, beginning in 1918 and 1919, saw the birth of an estimated 400 new titles,[39] most of them founded by professors and students. *La Jeunesse* (whose Chinese title was *Hsin Chin-nien)* was edited by four Peking University professors who made the magazine, started in 1915 at Shanghai, the main spark of the literary movement. The four, Hu Shih, Ch'en Tu-hsiu, Ch'ien Hsuan-t'ung, and Liu Pan-nung, filled their magazine with brilliant writing about the fusion of Chinese and Western knowledge, together with militant advocacy of social reform, couched in rousing language. With *La Jeunesse* as a beacon, Chinese periodicals proliferated suddenly over the country. Students of the four professors in 1919 started *Hsin Ch'ao* (The Renaissance), which became closely associated with the movement bearing the same name. Sun Yat-sen had founded the monthly *Kuomin* in 1913 and in 1919 he established *Chien Sheh* (The Reconstruction) to lend its voice to the cause.

Earlier periodicals like the *Short Story Magazine* (1910), and the *Eastern Miscellany* (1903) had introduced Western literature through translations sponsored by various literary societies. In 1922 Hu Shih started a weekly political review, *The Endeavor,* with its literary supplement. The *Sinological Quarterly,* published first in 1923 at Peking by the Peking University Sinological Institute, spearheaded a drive for a reevaluation of Chinese history, philosophy, and literature. *Hsiang-tao* (The Guide), a Communist organ, started in 1922 at Canton. Two other important journals founded in the years 1924 and 1925 were *Hsien-tai Ping-lun* (Contemporary Review), and *Yus-se* (Small Talk), both weeklies published at Peking. In the 1930s there was a popular fiction weekly called *Li Pai Liu* (Saturday) and a large number of pictorials, including youth and film magazines. *Shen Huo* (The Life Weekly) which at one time claimed 510,000 circulation, was banned in 1934, charged with encouraging the Fukien revolt. It was followed by two similar weeklies which suffered the same fate.

The popularity of the periodical press was due in part to the spirit of the times when large numbers of the better educated literate public were experiencing a degree of freedom of expression never before enjoyed and in part to the adoption of the spoken Mandarin Chinese language as a standard for written communication. Large numbers of the better educated literate public were for the first time realizing that they could express their views freely, and that such opinions counted. The use of spoken Mandarin in place of the limited powers of expression of the old classical written Chinese made a common medium available to young Chinese writers which freed them from the outmoded cumbersomeness of the classical written language which, like ancient as compared with modern Greek, had limited powers of expression for the general public.

So popular was the periodical press that authors preferred it over books. Short fiction and essay forms were media that lent themselves best to changing events and contemporary emotions. Writers were interested in the short story, free verse, and modern drama. Like those of the entire Renaissance movement, the themes of periodical content were both literary and political. The period was comparable to the outburst of literary journalism in early eighteenth-century England. Even the daily newspapers carried large literary supplements.

The Newspaper Press Proliferates

Recognizing the importance of magazines and the literary movement, one finds that the backbone of the public press was the daily newspaper. Unlike magazines, newspapers grew more in circulation than in numbers of titles. The newspaper press generally improved in quality and professional standards, effectually developing its readership, financial standing, and editorial influence.[40] Independent dailies had long existed in Hong Kong and Shanghai. During the Republican and Kuomintang periods many of these established dailies were already passing through the usual course of capitalistic press evolution, from individual or private undertaking to corporate institution, to investment property. The stimulus of the revolutionary and renaissance periods saved some from decline. Leading dailies like the *Shun Pao,* the *Sin Wan Pao,* the *Shih Pao,* and the *Ta Kung Pao* developed sound modern news services as they ceased to be dependent upon the gazette press and the foreign press for information. In addition to their literary supplements, they developed imposing financial departments and pictorial supplements devoted to education, the arts, and commerce. Indeed the supplement, known as *fu kang,* became a standard part of the Chinese daily newspaper, strictly departmentalized, covering a wide variety of subjects, and appearing with regular weekday issues. As Chinese communities began to observe the Sabbath holiday, port city dailies published large Sunday issues, but the supplements continued to appear with the weekday issues, a distinguishing feature of Chinese daily journalism of this period.

Dailies of the revolutionary period were crusading political journals that provided strong competition for the conservative press establishment. After 1911 some revolutionary organs became progressive-minded independent dailies. Most of the dailies before the revolution were forced to join the popular cause to survive. After the revolution and especially in the 1920s and 1930s newspapers refrained from political criticism in order to stay in business, thus reversing the relation of the independent press to political affairs. Under the shifting militarist regimes, political criticism became as dangerous as it had been under the Empire. Persecution of editors and publishers was frequent. Independent newspapers sought the protection of extraterritorial status or fictitious proprietorships to which foreign missionaries lent their names in the cause of a free press and enlightened leadership.

Silence or deviousness by the large papers in reporting in depth the underlying reasons for the larger political developments encouraged the rise of an extensive tabloid press in the big population centers, numbering into the hundreds between 1928 and 1932. These papers, purporting to give the inside story, supplemented the big dailies as popular reading, and were known as the *mosquito* press. The chief characteristics of the mosquito papers, as defined by Lin, were like their namesakes: ". . . they bite; . . . they swarm about; . . . they are hard to catch; . . . they don't mind little accidents (being less important financial investments); and . . . they try to make an extremely annoying humming noise." [41] Most of the mosquito papers were single sheets published daily or every second or third day, many of them subsisting on blackmail. After the mid-

1930s the mosquito press was replaced by the popular weeklies which gave the news background at a price the consumer could afford, avoiding political controversy.

Decline of the Foreign-owned Media

As the different levels of native-owned press came to meet the public need for information of all kinds, foreign newspaper ownership declined. The *Peking Jih-pao,* founded by German interests in 1904, eventually came under Chinese ownership, as did some other foreign papers. The *Shun Tien Shih Pao,* conducted by the Japanese government from 1902 to 1930, was abandoned as a matter of policy. Existing and new English-language papers continued to circulate in the thousands among foreign nationals as well as Chinese. Three leading American newspapers were begun in the twentieth century. First was *The China Press* founded in Shanghai as a daily in 1911 by Thomas F. Millard, Carl Crow, and B. W. Fleisher, with the help of Dr. Wu Ting-fang and the financial support of Charles R. Crane of Chicago. It soon surpassed its chief rival the British-owned *North China Daily News,* but it was eventually sold to an Englishman. The *Press* was edited for a time by Hollington K. Tong,[42] a graduate of the University of Missouri and the Pulitzer Schools of Journalism and wartime vice minister of information. Fleisher later became editor and publisher of the *Japan Advertiser* in Tokyo. In the early and middle 1930s many young American journalists worked on its staff. Second was Millard's *Review of the Far East,* a weekly, was founded in 1917 in Shanghai by Millard and John B. Powell.[43] The *Review* was a respected independent English-language paper of American news and editorial comment. Powell, a University of Missouri School of Journalism graduate and Missouri newspaperman, edited the *Review* and then became its owner in 1922. After Millard's withdrawal the paper became the *China Weekly Review.*

Third of the American-owned papers was the *Shanghai Evening Post and Mercury,* established in 1930 by C. V. Starr, an American insurance executive. It became a lively medium of the foreign community. Edited for a time by Theodore Thackrey, who became editor of the New York *Evening Post,* the *Shanghai Evening Post and Mercury* built its circulation up to 15,000. Its Chinese language edition *Ta Mei Wan Pao,* however, was said to print as many as

200,000 copies. Its editor of later years, Randall Chase Gould, made it an outspoken voice of thriving business interests and an early critic of the Kuomintang. Rather than submit to the demands of the Communists, Gould suspended publication on June 14, 1949. Its experience was typical of many other foreign papers between 1949 and 1951.

In the middle thirties there were about 30 foreign-owned newspapers in China belonging to American, British, German, Japanese, French, and Russian interests,[44] while in 1926 there had been 52 in this classification. The English-language press, and indeed the press of other foreign languages, gradually died out. The number of titles and circulations shrank; increasing unpopularity of foreign concessions, war, and censorship took their toll. The Communist regime delivered the *coup de grâce*.

The Kuomintang Builds a Communication Network

Sun Yat-sen and his Kuomintang party struggled to overthrow the northern warlord regimes in order to unify the country, an effort which was achieved by Chiang Kai-shek after Sun's death in 1925. These developments placed in power a central government which, like Sun's, was sensitive to the people's needs, but at the same time a government that placed restrictions on the private press and developed a communication system of its own to promote its purposes and programs. The press laws of 1914 were invoked and enforced ostensibly for national security reasons. The government's propaganda department had three arms. The first was the *Central Daily News* (earlier known as the Republican Daily News or *Min-kuo Jih pao),* the central official organ in Nanking. A chain of government-owned official organs of the party numbering some 30 or more spread over the country. The second arm of the government's information apparatus was the Central News Agency of China, the most important and the only national news agency.[45] Founded at Nanking in 1928,[46] this agency soon established branch offices in all of the larger cities and subbranches in important population centers. Its services were made available not only to the domestic press[47] but also to Chinese-language newspapers published elsewhere in the Orient, in the United States, and in Europe. The Central News Agency sent special correspondents abroad to cover the League of Nations in 1931, the Olympic Games of 1936, and began in

1936 to establish offices on foreign soil with the inauguration of its Tokyo bureau. Domestically the agency established a nationwide radio network for news transmission. In 1947 the Central News Agency was transmitting approximately 30,000 words daily from Nanking, in part by means of its radio circuit, in addition to dispatches for foreign consumption from Chungking. It had exclusive distribution in China outside of Shanghai for Reuters and United Press news.

The third arm of the government's communication operation was the Central Broadcasting Station, established by the Kuomintang in 1928.[48] The first Central Broadcasting network station at the capital, Nanking, started as a 500-kilowatt station and was increased four years later to 750 kilowatts. From the first the station was used for newscasts. In 1932 the Central Executive Committee of the Kuomintang organized the Central Broadcasting Administration to make broadcasting policy. The Ministry of Communications was to administer the system.

As government owned and operated stations were founded at other points in China, privately owned stations sprang up, as did government machinery to administer broadcasting. Between 1932 and 1936, 16 new noncommercial stations were established over the country, 3 of which were under the Central Broadcasting Administration, 8 operated by provincial governments, 4 by special municipal governments, and 2 controlled by the Ministry of Communications. Within the same period of time 63 privately owned commercial stations were established in the metropolitan areas. The provisional regulations issued by the Ministry of Communications in 1932 were revised in 1936 to enforce the registration of radio sets, to administer the licensing and assignment of wave lengths to stations, and to improve programming. Government stations were supported out of the public treasury and private stations out of advertising revenues. The Central Broadcasting Administration also had charge of foreign broadcasts, operating short-wave services abroad in Chinese, English, and other languages. The Japanese war and military occupation of Chinese territory dislocated and stopped much broadcasting activity, but by September 1947 there were 41 stations under Central Broadcasting Administration's supervision, 48 privately owned commercial stations, and 4 allied armed forces stations in operation in free China. Broadcasting, however, was still an infant medium in 1949. for there were less than one million radio receiving sets in the whole country, averaging about 0.13 set for every 100 persons, mostly concentrated in the Shanghai-Nanking area.[49]

Communications Development in War and Censorship

Privately owned newspapers and magazines, with the exception of the war period, continued to grow, despite the government-operated communications systems, the flow of government propaganda into private independent communication channels, and the repressive official policy toward the private press. Nationalist programs such as those fostering the development of transportation, the building of railroads and highways, the construction of telegraph, telephone, and radio facilities, improvements in the postal service, and compulsory education acts, all served to help the mass media. On the other hand the Japanese war, the communist threat from within, and World War II were disrupting influences that handicapped mass media development. During the Japanese invasions of the thirties and also during the World War most of the port city papers were driven inland, the government information machinery moving to Chungking. The war and postwar periods brought newsprint shortages and inflation.

Not the least of the factors contributing to media growth was the growth of advertising. For the large dailies, advertising came to provide a substantial proportion of the income; the smaller periodicals continued to depend upon subsidies from private or government sources. In 1924 three-fourths of the *Shun Pao's* space was filled with advertising, much of it advertisements of patent medicine, lotteries, and tobacco.[50] On May 30, 1936, a 28-page copy of the *Shun Pao* contained more than 18 pages of advertising.[51] Booksellers and publishers were also large advertisers. Interesting aspects of the advertising columns were the announcements of divorce cases, runaway employees, formal announcements of marriages and deaths, and denials of political affiliation by party leaders. Newspaper advertising in the native press stressed illustrations in order to appeal to the illiterate. The traditional Chinese respect for the printed word gave impetus to the power of advertising, as it did to print media in general.

Nevertheless from the early 1920s to 1949, growth, spread, and penetration of the mass media showed constant increases. Figures for 1921 report 840 periodicals, both newspapers and magazines, being published in China.[52] Almost 500 of these were daily newspapers. By 1926 the number of Chinese-language daily newspapers was 628. With the addition of nondaily newspapers and magazines of all kinds the total number reached almost 2,000. The large cities were surfeited with daily newspapers, many more, it seems, than the economy could reasonably be expected to support. For example, in 1926, Peking counted 125 dailies; Hankow, 36; Canton, 29; Tientsin, 28; Tsinan, 25; and Shanghai, 23 (not including those of the International Settlement).[53] By 1937 distribution of daily papers among the principal cities was as follows: Nanking, 21; Shanghai, 50; Hankow, 21; Peking, 44; Tientsin, 29; Tsingtao, 16; and Canton, 17.[54]

In the 9 years from 1926 to 1935 the total number of daily newspapers had grown to 910, an increase of almost one-half.[55] If total numbers of periodicals were difficult to estimate accurately, circulation figures were even more so. There were no reliable or certified circulation data. Publishers' estimates, always reported in even thousands, were the best estimates available. On this basis, the total number of copies of daily newspapers published by 910 dailies in 1935 was 3,242,764,[56] or about 7 copies for each 1,000 persons in the total population, estimated at that time at 434,987,000. Literacy was variously placed at between 5 and 20 per cent. Lin Yutang compared data on number of copies of newspapers passing through the post office in the years 1922–1924 with similar data for 1932–1934 and found an increase of approximately 125 per cent over the 10 years.[57] Thus the number of copies of dailies printed more than doubled, while the number of different newspapers increased only one-third. Number of *copies* printed must be distinguished from number of *readers*. Copies went from hand to hand and were often pasted on walls for all passersby to read. Number of readers per copy in print were estimated at from 1 to 25, and 10 was the customary basis for estimates. By this calculation the total number of readers of daily newspapers in 1935 was thought to be in the neighborhood of 32 million, or approximately 5 per cent of the population. Many of the papers were small sheets in size like those of the mosquito press. The number of papers consisting of "one big sheet," or 4 pages and more, each issue was considerably smaller, numbering 315 out of the 910.

War and disaster, though cutting down on number of extant titles, did sell newspapers, and in the next 14 years, from 1935 to 1949, daily circulations soared to all-time highs in spite of difficulties of the immediate postwar period. The larger papers established editions in cities outside their home city. The combined circulation (copies printed) of all daily editions of the *Sin Wan Pao,* the largest daily, reached 200,000, thriving largely on commercial news among merchants, bankers, and brokers. In 1935 both the *Sin Wan Pao* and the *Shun Pao* reported 150,000. The government's *Central Daily News* published editions in Chungking, Nanking, Shanghai, and 17 other centers. *Ta Kung Pao* had a chain of dailies in 5 large cities, publishing 3 daily editions in Shanghai. *Hsin Min Pao,* a chain of 8 popular tabloid dailies published from as many cities, was known for its straightforward news reports. There were smaller chains of specialized papers dealing with military affairs, education, youth organizations, and sports.

Total daily circulation was estimated in 1948 at 4.5 millions of copies per day, or about one copy for every 100 persons—still among the lowest ratios in the world.[58] There were approximately 2,069 registered periodicals, of which 1,372 were daily newspapers.

The spread of the press both led and followed popular education. With a rise in literacy came a corresponding increase in reading; at the same time the availability of periodicals to be read provided a strong incentive for education and a contribution to literacy. Illiteracy had declined to 75 per cent, a decrease of 10 per cent from the 1933 figure.[59] Limited consumer purchasing power continued to be the greatest single factor, however, handicapping newspaper sales and readership. Each printed copy continued to have a large number of readers; families shared single copies, papers were rented, resold, posted on the street for reading, and made available in reading rooms and libraries. These were all devices to solve the cost factor, and gave the better papers a much greater exposure than their press runs indicated, but did not provide commensurate revenue.

Censorship was another handicap. Although freedom of writing and publication was explicitly guaranteed to citizens in the provisional constitution of 1911,[60] and repeated in the Nationalist constitution adopted after the war, real freedom of the press as understood in the West was never realized. The 1911 constitution was never ratified: according to Wang, the provisions had little effect, except to serve as guiding principles in case of interfactional argument, but the political authority in power at the time for the given section of the country was under no obligation to follow them. Court interpretation never came into being, and the legal basis for enforcing them was lacking. Censorship laws, however, were another matter. The press was liable to strict censorship by the ruling party or military junta. The word of military governors and their officers was law, and editors suffered frequently as a result of their whims. Slight criticism of the administration caused the imposition of heavy fines and imprisonment without trial. For example, in September, 1918, six native dailies were promptly suppressed for reporting that money from a Japanese loan for railway construction had been diverted to military uses.[61] Chief censors were the post offices and telegraph stations.

China's unsettled conditions combined with Nationalist government policy and irresponsible segments of the press to keep the censorship laws alive. Their enforcement grew more severe in the 1930s as Communist writing and agitation threatened the regime from the inside and the Japanese threatened from the outside. Censorship laws, adapted by the Nationalists from the earlier law, extended beyond the needs of national security.[62] They were designed to enable the government to regulate and control what it considered unreliable, mercenary, and corrupt elements in the press. The ban applied to (1) military information, (2) unconfirmed, false or premature reports regarding the country's foreign relations, (3) reports creating disturbances or financial panics, (4) reports prejudicial to public morals, and (5) defamatory attacks on government officials.[63] Most of these provisions seem on the surface to be in line with what is usually banned in wartime in libertarian countries. But their broad generalizations left them subject to flexible interpretation to suit the convenience of the enforcing authority, and there was no appeal in the courts. Enforcement was marked by ineptness, inconsistency, discrimination, and abuse. *Current History* reported in 1935 the existence of 2,500 political prisoners, new arrests of intelligentsia, the banning from public circulation of 149 books, and the torture and death of Communist writers. Punishment ranged from proscription of content or whole publications to detention and correction of copy; from suppression of papers to arrest, imprisonment, and death for editors. Although the leading newspapers aided by the news agencies formally appealed to the government to modify these drastic procedures, little was done. There was only a brief period after the Japanese surrender in 1945 when censorship was lifted, and a constitution guaranteeing freedom of speech and the press was finally adopted.

Considering the difficulties under which the communication

system labored, one finds its vigorous proliferation surprising. The great surge of communications in a country still 75 per cent illiterate showed unusual vitality along with signs of increasing maturity and responsibility. Moreover improvement in professional quality during the latter decades of the Nationalist regime was aided by the journalism schools, some of which had been founded with American assistance. Professional standards fostered a tradition of accuracy, objectivity, independence, and public responsibility among the better communication media to a degree that had not been matched in any other Asian nation except Japan. In truth the press which had stimulated the great intellectual awakening was able within less than two generations to make a strong start in bringing Chinese civilization into the twentieth century.

Although the periodical press reached untold millions and these millions influenced untold other millions untouched by print, it is doubtful that its influence penetrated "every corner of society and every walk of life," as Lin Yutang observed. The press never served more than a relatively small proportion of the population still largely centered in the metropolitan area (though even a proportion is a large absolute number), leaving densely populated rural areas without newspapers. The large-circulation papers catered to specialized audiences. None sought, even with multiple editions, to reach the whole literate part of the nation, or to develop circulation on a national scale. Broadcasting brought the possibility of extending media penetration, but its potential had hardly been touched. Notwithstanding the great social ferment of the revolution and subsequent developments including the great proliferation of media, communications failed to penetrate the vast masses of the Chinese people quite as much as the processes of education failed in their attack on illiteracy.

On the eve of the Communist conquest, China was still a confused nation. It had been aroused from its torpor, and had begun to try to build a modern state more in keeping with twentieth-century modernization trends. Democratic forms, Western political ideas, and social institutions, hastily transplanted, had not thrived. They scarcely had a chance to function unhampered by constant crisis conditions. China was economically exhausted by war and politically divided between two regimes: that of the tottering and unimaginative Nationalists and of the Communists—vigorous and optimistic with promises of a brighter existence.

11 ★

THE RED CHINESE COMMUNICATION SYSTEM: FUNCTION, STRUCTURE, CONTROL

WHEN THE COMMUNIST PEASANT ARMIES captured the Chinese mainland in 1949, libertarian communication systems were swept away and their facilities eventually taken over. A Communist press system, which had long operated in the North, expanded as the military moved southward against the crumbling Nationalist opposition. Those who took charge of the country had had many years of experience in using the press as a propaganda and agitation weapon after Leninist-Stalinist methods. They marched into Peking with their own working communications apparatus and the knowledge of how to use it. Unlike the Bolsheviks, who had no model, the Chinese Communists had the Soviet model to emulate, and years of experience in the techniques of mass persuasion in their own territory. Adapting their system to the whole country was a relatively smooth task.

Communist periodicals first appeared in China shortly after the birth of the Chinese Communist Party in 1921. Early party organs were often small, sometimes clandestine sheets that attracted little attention. The chief organs were *Hsiang-tao* (Guide), 1922–1927; *Fen-tou* (Struggle), 1927–1936; *Hsin-hua Jih-pao* (New China Daily), which was renamed in 1941 *Chieh-fang Jih-pao* (Liberation Daily), 1936–1945.[1] These were the predecessors of *Jen-min Jih-pao.* In the early 1930s as many as 34 Communist newspapers were being published in Kiangsi district. Among them was the official organ of the Central Committee, *Hung-se Chung-hua* (Red China) which was said to publish 50,000 copies. After the beginning of the Sino-Japanese War and the subsequent truce between the Nationalist government and the Communist Party, the Reds were permitted to publish in Wuhan, Chungking, and other cities. By 1949 the Communists were operating a press apparatus of approximately 100 newspapers and magazines and a broadcasting network of 16 transmitters, all fed by the central Hsin Hua (NCNA) or New China News Agency. Communist communications served the north and central areas of that part of the country under Communist control and the border regions occupied by Communist guerilla forces and army units.

In 1948 *Jen-min Jih-pao* (the People's Daily) was founded as the supreme organ of the CPC Central Committee.[2] As new territory was occupied, local parties were organized to expropriate and operate existing press facilities. So it was with considerable background of experience and a functioning system capable of expansion that the new regime assumed control of the country's mass media.

The *Central Daily News* and 43 other Kuomintang papers in major cities were the first to be seized and transformed. Although the announced policy was to close without exception all periodicals formerly owned by the Nationalists and to give "all conditions for free development" to the "genuine people's publications," many of the privately owned papers were likewise confiscated.[3] The registration law required all operating papers to furnish information regarding their past and present political creed, qualifications of their executive personnel, capital, source of income, and a file of the previous year's copies. Newspapers judged on the basis of such evidence as politically unacceptable were not permitted to be registered. Since the policy at first was to guarantee all political rights to citizens of accepted segments of society, including the right to own property, some established nonpolitical newspapers were permitted to continue under close surveillance, as were other private businesses. Several hundred papers died outright. Among them were H. H. Kung's *China Press, China Daily Tribune,* the *Peking Chronicle,* and most of the foreign-owned papers. The old *Sin Wan Pao,* which had been reorganized after the war with emphasis on business news and had reportedly the highest circulation of all Shanghai newspapers, was permitted to publish 100,000 copies daily for the "capitalist" class. Its title was slightly changed to *Sin Wan Jih-pao* to permit it to capitalize on its reputation, but its content underwent complete transformation. *Shun Pao,* which had ceased publication after Pearl Harbor and had been forced to resume as a Japanese propaganda organ, was also reestablished after the war. Its building was taken over by the Communists who killed the paper and used the facilities to publish their *Liberation Daily* in Shanghai.[4] *Ta Kung Pao,* the great independent daily, continued with emphasis on finance and economics, its editor, Wang Yun-shen, converted to Communism. Its Shanghai edition was so closely controlled, however, that it differed little from the *Liberation Daily.*

By 1953 the number of privately owned papers had been reduced to five, none of which dealt with political matters. The only United States owned daily paper, the *Shanghai Evening Post and Mercury* was finally forced to close its doors after a campaign of petty sniping both overt and covert, including a severely restricted newsprint allotment. The *Post and Mercury* succumbed when it refused to accede to typographical union demands. Union subversion, together with newsprint control, were favorite methods used by the Communists in eastern European countries to gain control of the press and suppress unfavorable opinion.[5] At its peak the *Post and Mercury* sold 15,000 copies of its English Language edition and 200,000 copies of its Chinese edition, *Ta Mei Wan Pao.* The American-owned weekly the *China Weekly Review* was changed to a party-line monthly by John W. Powell, son of the former owner J. B. Powell. The last foreign-owned paper to be shut down, the *Review* suspended in 1953, after its turncoat voice ceased to be of use to the regime.

The foreign and independent private press having been eliminated or neutralized, and a working communications system of its own having been firmly established, the regime embarked upon a vast drive to encourage and coerce newspaper readership to sharpen the mass communication system as a tool of change. For the first time in its long history a Chinese government was engaged in a full-scale effort to indoctrinate the masses with a standardized political, moral, and economic philosophy cutting across provincial boundaries and ethnic differences.

CHINESE COMMUNIST COMMUNICATION DOCTRINE

The Communist regime in China structured the new national communication system on a foundation of doctrine drawn from Marxist-Leninist philosophy of communication function, and the teachings of Soviet experience adapted to Chinese conditions and shaped to suit its own aims. The essential role of communication became, in the words of *Jen-min Jih-pao,* "the most powerful weapon to educate the population in socialist thought, to propagandize the Communist Party's plans and policies, and to tighten the close relationship between party and the masses." [6] As in the Soviet Union, not only the press but all educational and cultural activities are required to work for the development of socialist consciousness among the people and the construction of the socialist state.[7] Likewise there is no theory of communications separate and apart from the theory of the socialist state. The communications apparatus is considered the instrument of collective propaganda, agitation, and organization—an instrument of all the people to be used as a weapon in the struggle to build the socialist state. The party, representing the people, and eventually becoming synonymous in thought with the people, controls and operates the communication system for the benefit of the people. The word "people" has been substituted here for the word "proletariat" as it appears in Marxist doctrine. The Leninist interpretation of class consciousness is a fundamental precept of the Chinese Communist regime, defined as a large-scale political awakening of the masses. "When the masses are not fully conscious, the duties of the Communists . . . in carrying out any kind of work is to develop their consciousness by every effective and suitable means." [8] The communication system is committed to educate and indoctrinate to develop strong political awareness among all the people.

A second basic precept, the concept of the "mass line," is also a page out of Marxist-Leninist doctrine. In all definitions and interpretations of "mass line" myth, Communist leaders rationalize their actions or their need to act by attributing such action to popular demand. This kind of rationalization, also typical of the Soviet system, does not always mean that the leadership is trying to popularize its measures, but rather that it sincerely strives to crystallize and construe mass sentiment in such a way that, though it appears to be a mass attitude, it is actually in line with party policy. This method is described as follows in the party constitution:

> Whether or not the party leadership is correct depends upon the party's ability to analyze, systematize, summarize, and consolidate the opinions and experiences of the masses, to transform them as the policy of the party and then to return them, through propaganda, agitation, and organization, to the masses as their own guide to thinking and action.[9]

Mao Tse-tung eloquently places his faith in reliance on the people, stating that as long as the foundations of the regime lie firmly rooted in the "creative power" of the people, it will endure and overcome all obstacles. The theoretician Liu Shao-ch'i wrote that the masses of the people were the real makers of history, and on them the Communists depended for everything. Despite these professions of faith in the people as a source of guidance, the regime has shown that it believes, like Lenin, that the masses would never voluntarily participate and therefore must be prodded and guided.[10] It is not clear whether the Communist leaders truly believe in this basic rightness-of-the-people theory or whether they espouse it to further their own ends. Houn suggests that they use it for self-justification.[11] They like to believe their movement draws its mandate from the common people. The formal system of public mass communication and the informal oral person-to-person communication system together become an invaluable two-pronged instrument in the difficult and complicated process of determining public policy from mass aspirations, and in turn selling back to the people that policy as distilled by the leaders.

The third principle, or article of faith, adhered to by the Chinese Communist Party and government is also one that is familiar in Soviet Communist philosophy. This is the principle of unity, not only of thought, but also of action. Unity means in China what it does in the Soviet Union: that the party and the government will not permit the press and other agencies of communication to be controlled or operated by the "enemies of the state." The government, not unlike that of the traditional father-figure power of the Emperor, is the custodian of wisdom, as a representative of all the people, and is morally obligated to conduct the nation's affairs in the interests of all. As the right arm of government and party, then, the mass media, and all manner of communication, must speak with one voice, must be motivated by a singleness of purpose. The media system, like the individual, is not permitted simply to be passive and objective, or neutral. To do so is a serious offense. Thus, it is not enough for the loyal communist citizen to become politically conscious, to mentally accept the mass line. He might do this and still remain silently inactive, or merely give lip service to the dogma with no real acceptance or belief. But he is forced to participate, for it is believed that only by action, by individual and collective experience, can he grasp the universal truths the party is teaching. Unity also means the focusing of all resources on one central task at a time—one public campaign mobilizing all media in the cause at a given time. All revolutions move forward step by step, and each step can be best achieved by one definite, easily grasped goal after the other.

In the light of these precepts, this kind of doctrine, the function of communications in Communist China becomes essentially what it is in the Soviet Union—to disseminate propaganda, to agitate collectively, to organize collectively, and to serve the regime as an instrument of control. This means not only public political control of the country but also control over the minds and hearts of the people. And in the persistence of its efforts to control minds and hearts, the Chinese system of mass communication and mass persuasion far exceeds that of the Soviet system.

THE MASS COMMUNICATION SYSTEM

The structure of the Chinese communication apparatus at first glance appears to be a counterpart of its Soviet prototype. Closer inspection reveals modifications to fit Chinese ideas, Chinese tradition, Chinese social structure, peculiar Chinese conditions, and political expediency. The horizontal structure follows the administrative territorial geographic pattern. Vertically the media are organized to perform various specialized functions. Centralized control is considered fundamental and is vested in the Department of Propaganda of the Chinese Communist Party, the *Hsuen Chuan Pu,* which is under the supervision of the Political Bureau of the Party's

Central Committee.[12] This department determines policy and issues operational directives through three principal means: The first is the party chain of command from the Department of Propaganda to the various regional, provincial, municipal, and local party propaganda departments and committees. The second is the government's hierarchy of agencies, from such Central agencies as the Ministry of Culture, the Ministry of Education, or the Publications Administration, to their regional, provincial, or local subdivisions. Of these the most important for the mass media is the Press Administration which controls all newspapers and radio stations in the country, manages the New China News Agency, and directs foreign propaganda.[13] The department's third avenue through which it functions is the many popular mass organizations such as the unions and the youth pioneers, from the neighborhood groups to the large national organizations dedicated to a specific cause. This is the channel through which the Central Party leadership maintains its contacts with the grass-roots population, for every Chinese belongs to one or more such organizations.

An ingenious combination of interlocking directorates enables the administration to coordinate party, government, and popular avenues of communication. This is done somewhat after the Soviet manner by having the same elite party leaders serve in high positions throughout the hierarchy in party, government, and mass organizations. Graphs of the hierarchies of the press system and the broadcasting system are compared in Figs. 11.2 and 11.3, pages 360 and 362.

The Press

At the peak of the pyramidal press structure is the Central Committee organ and spokesman of the government—a combination of *Pravda* and *Izvestia* wrapped up in one package—*Jen-min Jih-pao* (The People's Daily). Like *Pravda,* it is the official expositer and interpreter of the party line. As the leaders interpret the social role of the *People's Daily,* it is actually a spokesman of the government. Like *Izvestia* it represents the government viewpoint. It reprints in full the speeches of party and government leaders and all government edicts. It reports government business the leaders decide should be matters of public information and instruction. Its editorials are often reprinted in full by other organs throughout the

人民日報
RENMIN RIBAO
庆祝中华人民共和国成立十三周年
高举总路线、大跃进、人民公社三面红旗，奋勇前进
周恩来总理举行盛大国庆招待会
我国人大代表团到达河内
胡志明主席接见我代表团

工人日報
GONGREN RIBAO
人人学习「铁人」 人人争当「铁人」
为无产阶級革命事业奋斗一辈子
讀毛主席的书 听毛主席的話
铁人王进喜在工交工作、工交政治工作扩大会議上作报告
刘主席周总理等领导人
接见工交工作、工交政治工作会议人员
并接見全总等单位的专业会議人員
帶着敌情观念搞生产
——三論王铁人的革命精神

1 2

Fig. 11.1. **Jen-min Jih-pao** (1) is the **Pravda** and **Izvestia** of Communist China's party and government. This special edition of October 1, 1962, celebrates the thirteenth anniversary of the People's Republic of China. Red ink emphasizes the vertical slogans at the left which proclaim: "We march with these three Red Flag goals: 'Be faithful to Mao Tse-tung's teachings,' 'Help the great leap forward,' and 'Participate in the people's communes.'" The story reports that Premier Chou En-lai was host to a great state reception, and the subtitle states that the VIP's of Communist China and leaders from five continents are gathered together for the celebration. Soviet **Trud's** Chinese opposite number is **Kung-jen Jih-pao** (Worker's Daily (2). The Daily prepared for Chinese youth is **Chung-kuo Ching Nien-pao** (3), while **Kuang-ming Jih-pao** (4), Enlightment Daily, ostensibly serves as the organ of the non-Communist parties "assisting" the regime.

country. Other daily organs model their format after the top party paper. (See Fig. 11.1.) Edited and published from Peking, *Jen-min Jih-pao* publishes editions in Shanghai, Sian, Mukden, Chungking, Canton, and Urumchi. Stereotype plates are flown from Peking daily to these centers. The paper's circulation, which was only 30,000 in 1949, has been variously reported 1 and 2 million. It was reported at 810,000 in 1956. Its present circulation is not known but a guess would put it at 1.5 to 2 million. The *People's Daily* publishes six pages except on Sundays and holidays when it is re-

中国青年报
ZHONGGUO QINGNIAN BAO
北方普降瑞雪 仍须预防春旱
活学活用毛主席著作 实现团干部思想革命化
毛泽东思想使她心红眼亮
《人民日报》就刊登卡斯特罗二月六日反华声明发表编者按语
中国一贯忠于无产阶级国际主义从各方面支援古巴人民
卡斯特罗参加反华合唱队没有什么不得了正是自我暴露

3

光明日報
GUANGMING RIBAO
我国政府强烈抗议印度策动反华丑剧
李宗仁先生举行盛大中外記者招待会发表长篇談話
强調爱国必須反对美帝反帝必須反修
各地卫生部門积极行动起来采取革命措施
把重点放到农村为五亿农民服务

4

duced to four. The paper is widely copied and imitated through the press system and is required reading for all party leaders.

In 1957, the last year for which these data are available, there were 19 national Central papers. Central organs, of both general and functional appeals, are *Kung-jen Jih-pao* (Workers' Daily), the trade union federation organ; *Wen-hui Pao,* the teachers' organ; *Kuang-ming Jih-pao* (Enlightenment Daily), a cultural and educational journal which originally served as the organ of the non-Communist parties assisting the regime according to official pronouncement. *Ta Kung Pao,* whose pre-Communist era prestige helped it to retain its name, stresses economics and foreign affairs, and publishes editions at Peking, Tientsin, and Shanghai. There is also the Chinese counterpart of *Komsomolskaya Pravda*—the *Chung-kuo Ching Nien-pao* (Chinese Youth Newspaper).

The next highest level of general newspapers for several years was occupied by the regional papers, but these were abolished when regional administrations were discontinued in 1954.[14] This lifted the provincial press up to the second rung on the hierarchical ladder immediately under the national press. Each province, autonomous region, or city has its own official newspaper which serves the same function for the territorial and political subdivisions as the national papers for the country. They publish national and international information in addition to reports of the affairs and problems of their particular province. They see that Central policy is carried out locally and help guide provincial cadres in matters of doctrine and policy. In 1957 there were about 341 provincial level papers, almost all dailies.

The third and lowest level of the general press apparatus consists of the administrative district papers, including the town and county papers. These devote primary attention to local problems and tasks at hand, leaving to the upper echelon papers matters concerning ideology. One of their major functions is to disseminate information about high-level party decisions. In 1957 there were more than 936 county papers. Supplementing the printed papers on the local level are myriads of mimeographed or handwritten wall or blackboard papers serving farms, factories, construction sites, villages, schools, army units, cooperatives, communes, and industrial sites.

Organization of the press along vertical or functional lines also follows the Soviet pattern. Cutting across the horizontal hierarchy, the functional press is made up of organs created for specialized audiences at every level—national, provincial, and local.[15] These organs serve workers, farmers, young people, the military, and so on. A few such organs at the national level are listed above. Circulations as of 1956 for *Wen-hui Pao* was 180,000; for *Kung-jen Jih-pao,* 150,000, and for *Kuang-ming Jih-pao,* 70,000. Some 352 of these functional papers above the administrative district level were reported in that year, of which 33 were for youth and 24 were published in the languages of minority groups. Estimated growth of dailies is shown in Table 11.1.

Thirty-one newspapers in 10 geographical areas were being published in minority languages in 1957. The largest number (13) being published in Sinkiang Province in the Uighur, Mongolian, Kazakh, Sibo, and Kolkoz languages.

Continental China in the 1952–1954 period reported 776 newspapers with a total single press run newspaper circulation of some 8 million.[16] Daily publication continued to center in the larger cities, but there were no estimates available of the number of copies of daily papers being printed. There were 4 dailies in Peking, 4 in Tientsin, 5 in Harbin, 10 in Shanghai, and 3 in Nanking. By 1955 Chu Hsueh-fan, minister of postal and telecommunications, reported 408 percentage increase over the total number of news-

TABLE 11.1

COMMUNIST CHINESE DAILY NEWSPAPERS*

Year	Number	Single Press Run Circulation	Number Copies Per 100 Persons
		(millions)	
1948........	1,372	4.5	1.0
1952–1954....	260–70	8.0	1.2
1962–1964....	392	12.0	2.0

* Sources: *China Handbook*; Unesco, *World Communications*, 2nd ed., Paris, 1950; 3rd ed., Paris, 1956; 4th ed., New York, 1964.

paper subscriptions in 1950,[17] but did not give the total. A different source reported some 12 million for 1955.[18] By 1958 the total circulation of all newspapers was 15 million copies per issue, or about five times more than the 3 million copies reported for 1951. The 1951 ratio was one copy for every 274 persons, one of the lowest in the world. The 1958 ratio was an estimated 2.0 copies of daily and nondaily papers for every 100 persons.[19] The Union Research Institute Limited, Hong Kong, listed in 1963 a total of 405 Mainland Chinese newspapers which it holds.[20] Not claiming to be exhaustive, this list shows 217 which from internal evidence appeared to be dailies, 184 titles of undetermined periodicity, and 4 carrying the word "weekly" in the title. Copies held by the institute are not always up to date and often go back several years. Since the "Great Leap Forward," which began in 1958, the publishing situation has been quite confused, and the difficulties of gathering reliable information as to numbers and circulations have been compounded by stricter censorship than before. Estimated circulation data are given in Table 11.2.

Monthly and semimonthly magazines in 1952 numbered about half as many as there were newspapers at that time, or between 300 and 400. There were the general popular mass magazines with the largest circulations and, additionally, the more specialized smaller circulation periodicals which address themselves to groups. In 1955 seven magazines with a per issue circulation of 100,000 each or more accounted for approximately two-thirds of the almost 6 million copies total for that year.[21] These were *Shih-shih Shou-tse* (Current Affairs Pocket Magazine), *Hsueh-hsi* (Learning), *Cheng-chi Hsueh-hsi* (Political Study), *Hsin Kuan-cha* (The New Observer), *Shih-chien Chih-shih* (World Affairs), *Jen-min Hua-pao* (The People's Pictorial), and *Lien-hua Hua-pao* (The Popular Illustrated). One-fourth of the total circulation claimed was attributed

TABLE 11.2

NUMBER AND CIRCULATION OF COMMUNIST CHINESE NEWSPAPERS*†

Year	Number	Total Combined Annual Number Copies Published
		(billions)
1948	2,069 (1,372 dailies)	0.045[1]
1950	275	0.079
1951	475	1.11
1952	276	1.60
1953	260	1.68
1954	...	1.71
1955	285	1.95
1956	...	2.55
1957	...	2.44
1958	1,884	3.91
1959	456	2.80
1964	1,577 (392 dailies)	...

* Sources: *China Handbook, 1937–44*; Unesco, *World Communications*, 2nd ed., Paris, 1948; 1951 *Jen-Min Sou-che* (1951 People's Handbook); *Wei-da De Shih-nien* ("The Great Ten Years") Foreign Language Press, Peking, 1960; *Jen-min Sou-che, 1952* (1951 People's Handbook); Bureau of Statistics, *Official Bulletin of 1952; Jen-min Sou-che, 1955;* Bureau of Statistics, *Official Bulletin of 1954;* Bureau of Statistics, *Official Bulletin of 1955;* Bureau of Statistics, *Official Bulletin of 1956; Ta Kung Pao*, Peking, Apr. 27, 1959; *Jen-min Jih-pao*, Apr. 5, 1960.

† Figures obtainable in the Western world on numbers and circulations of newspapers and periodicals in Mainland China are purposely nonspecific, difficult to find, and to verify. The data in this table, admittedly uneven in places, have been patched together from different sources. The data often do not separate daily from nondaily newspapers, and all circulation figures seem to be combined aggregate totals for each year. For example, to understand the astronomical figures in the right-hand column, we assume that the *People's Daily* has a one-time press run of 1 million daily, then we must multiply by 365 to arrive at a figure which is included along with the aggregate annual totals similarly calculated for all newspapers published in the country to reach 2.8 billion given for the year 1959. Since it is not known in every case how many papers are daily and nondaily (even some of those counted as dailies may not publish more than 4 issues weekly), it is impossible to arrive at any estimate of single-issue press runs for each paper. The nature of such data, though of some interest, prohibits comparisons with data for Soviet newspapers given in Table 3.2. It is likely that the figures showing number of different newspaper titles in publication given for the years 1950–1953, 1955, and 1959 are total number of daily newspapers and that the nondailies are not reported. By the same token, the figure of 1,884 given for the year 1958 probably includes dailies and all other newspaper and periodical titles.

[1] The 4.5 million for 1948 represents single-issue press run totals, combined, not aggregate combined number of copies annually.

to two youth publications, *Chung-kuo Ching-nien Pao* (Chinese Youth), a semimonthly with 62,500 each issue (in 1957), and *Chung Hsueh Sheng* (The High School Student). *Wen Yi Yueh Pao* (Literature and Art Monthly) published 178,000 copies each issue in 1957; *Wen Yi Pao* (Literature and Art), a semimonthly, published only about one-twentieth as many. Some others are *I Wen* (Translation), a monthly; *Ta Chung Tien Ying* (Popular Motion Picture), a semimonthly; and *Chung Kuo Kung Jen* (Chinese Workers), a semimonthly. There were other publications for such groups as women, children, theatrical workers, the arts, etc.

Data for the year 1957 indicate a total of 600 periodicals (separate titles), of which 197 were classified as major periodicals. (See

TABLE 11.3

NUMBER AND CIRCULATION OF COMMUNIST CHINESE PERIODICALS*

Year	Number	Total Combined Annual Number Copies Published
		(millions)
1950	274	35
1952	356	204
1954	304	204
1955	370	288
1957	600	315
1958	818	530
1959	859	510
1962–1964	1,908†	600

* Sources: *1951 Jen-min Sou-che* (1951 People's Handbook); *Wei-da De Shih-nien* ("The Great Ten Years"), Foreign Language Press, Peking, (1960); Bureau of Statistics, *Official Bulletin of 1952; Jen-min Jih-pao,* Sept. 23, 1952; Bureau of Statistics, *Official Bulletin of 1954;* Bureau of Statistics, *Official Bulletin of 1955;* Franklin Houn, *To change a Nation,* Glencoe, 1961; *Ta Kung Pao,* Peking, Apr. 27, 1959; *Jen-min Jih-pao,* Apr. 5, 1960; Unesco, *World Communications,* 4th ed., New York, 1964.

† This figure from Unesco data seems extraordinarily high in view of the reversals suffered by press and publishing after 1958. Actual Mainland Chinese holdings of the Union Research Institute, Hong Kong, in 1963, admittedly incomplete, showed only 397 titles. Another source—a confidential one—indicated by count 1,450 titles as of 1964.

Table 11.3.) The 600 total includes 130 titles in social science, 230 devoted to natural science, 110 to literature and the arts, and 130 to minority and foreign languages. The 197 major periodicals include 35 titles each to economics and finance and applied technology; 27 each to medicine and hygiene and to literature and the arts; 24 to culture and education; 20 to natural science; 12 to social science; 10 to workers, women, youth, and children; and 5 to current international events.

In 1958 a group of theoretical magazines appeared, the first of which was the fortnightly journal *Hung-chi* (Red Flag), with one of the leading theoreticians, Chen Po-ta as its editor. Mao Tse-tung and other party members have contributed to this magazine, whose first-issue circulation reportedly numbered almost 2 million copies. Provincial counterparts of *Red Flag* were begun by the various provincial party committees. Since it is almost mandatory for those who wish to rise in party circles to understand such matters as established doctrine and its latest interpretation, reading of such journals is routine for leading officials.

Since the capital is the communications center of the country all of the major magazines are published there, though some have branch offices and publishing plants in Shanghai, Tientsin, and Nanking.

Mainland Chinese magazine holdings of the Union Research

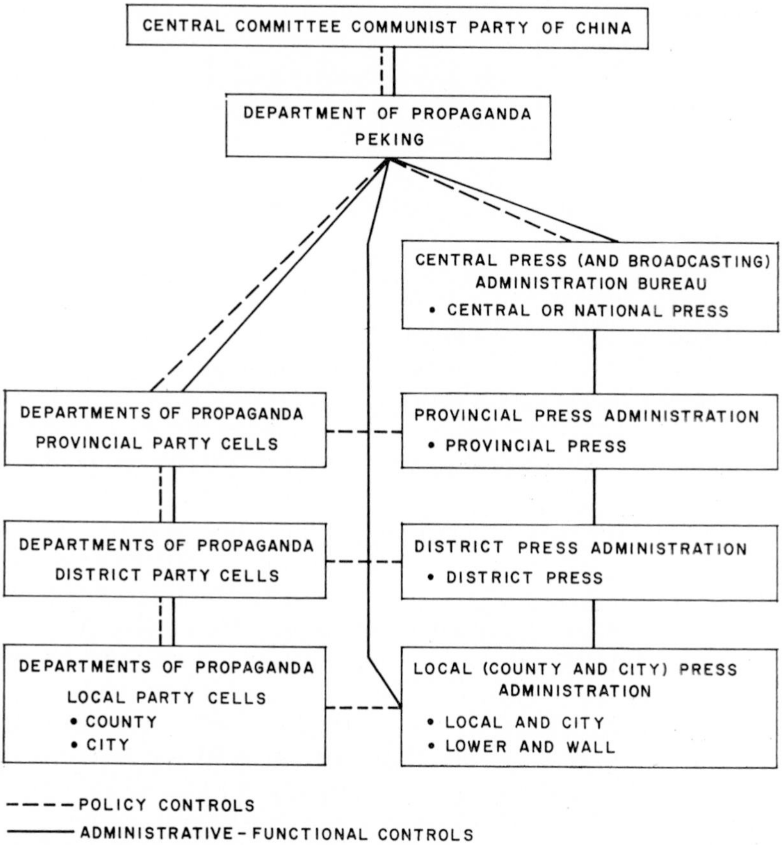

Fig. 11.2. Administrative and Functional Structure of the Mainland Chinese Press System. At the top and at the left is the party mechanism with lines of control indicated by dotted lines. At the right is the government bureaucratic hierarchy.

Institute in 1963 showed a total of 397 magazines. The largest number of these, 171, were monthly, but there were 93 semimonthlies, 40 quarterlies, 33 bimonthlies, 31 unclassified as to periodicity, 9 weeklies, and 9 semiannuals. These data are subject to the same limitations as those enumerated above for newspapers.

Broadcasting

The wide pattern of the Communist broadcasting structure in China resembles that of the press and both, in the main, resemble the chief attributes and characteristics of Soviet systems.

When the Chinese Communists seized power in 1949 they were

operating a network of 16 radio stations. Their first station at Yenan went on the air four years earlier (Sept. 5, 1945) for just two hours daily.[22] From its studios in a temple, this tiny station beamed on its 300-watt transmitter propaganda messages for the consumption of the Kuomintang leaders. In the next three years, programming was slightly improved, time on the air was slightly increased, and stations were opened in Manchuria, Kalgan, Southern Hopei, and Northern Kiangsu.

Broadcasting is under the governmental supervision of the Broadcasting Administration Bureau, which is in turn supervised by the party's Central Committee through its Propaganda Department. These agencies determine the nature, scope, policy, and operation of the broadcasting network. In 1950 the Communist party's network was virtually a monopoly which, in addition to the former Nationalist stations and some 33 privately owned stations, numbered 83 stations in all. As in the case of the press, the privately owned and operated stations were rigidly controlled and eventually either were absorbed by the state or became joint state and private enterprises.

The hierarchy of the broadcasting organization and network apparatus, like that of the press system, operates on three levels. (See Fig. 11.3, p. 362). At the national level is the Central People's Broadcasting Station in Peking which, like Central Broadcasting in Moscow and like *Jen-min Jih-pao* for the press, has jurisdiction over all broadcasting. This station, with 24 studios and a 300-kilowatt transmitter, was joined in 1954 by an educational station, and in 1958 by a central television station. The provincial station network, the second level, consists of at least one station in each of the provincial capitals. The third-level municipal stations serve the larger cities. Generally the provincial and city stations relay official programs from Peking, and add local information, propaganda, and indoctrination. They are supervised by provincial and local bureaus of broadcasting affairs, and by the stations operating at the next highest levels. Control remains with the party and government agencies at the corresponding level, with all performance subject to regulation and scrutiny from above.

Growth in the wireless broadcasting structure since 1949 has not been impressive. Emphasis has been placed upon increasing the power and channels of existing units rather than upon multiplying the number of units. A number of factors have contributed to this trend: shortage of equipment, shortage of electronic manu-

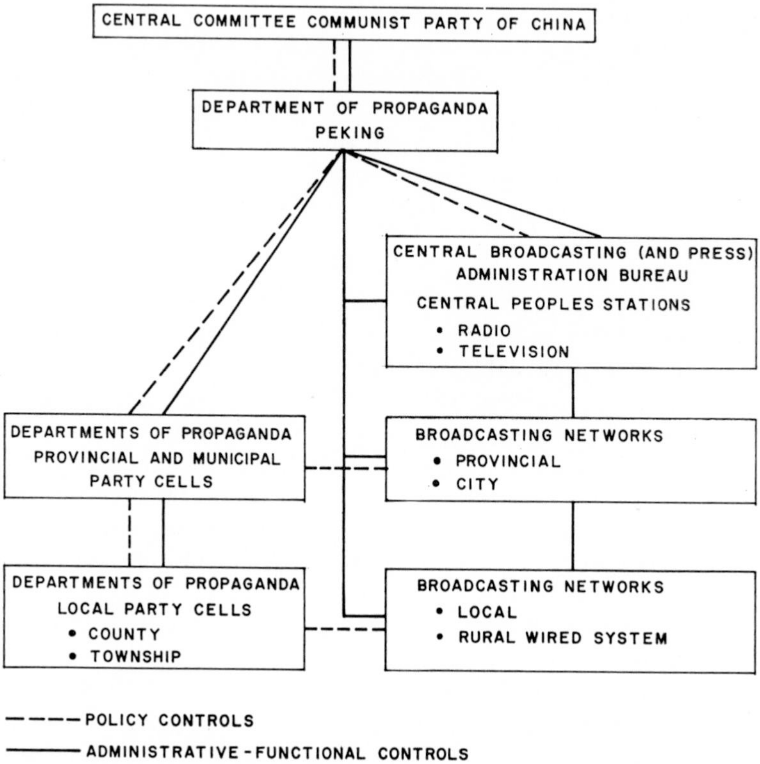

Fig. 11.3. The administration and control of Communist Chinese Broadcasting. Government administration, operations, and functional departments are at the right while the party organizations in control are at the top and left.

facturing plants, shortage of trained and trustworthy Communist personnel, the language barrier, and the obvious advantages in centralized control. Various measures have been taken to extend the penetration of broadcasting as has been done in all media. Between 1950 and 1957, only 15 stations were added, making the total 98.[23] By 1957 the total combined strength was scheduled to be increased by 460 per cent of the 1954 figure.[24]

Broadcast messages are received by individual sets and by wired diffusion network speakers wherever the people congregate and work. The estimated 1.5 million individual receiving sets of the early 1950s were concentrated among the more affluent urban families living along the eastern seaboard. The number of sets has increased slowly, reportedly reaching 4.5 million in 1960, but the stress has been on extension of the wired-speaker systems and facilities for relaying messages to them. By the end of 1958, wired stations were in operation in some 1,800 counties and cities and 5,800 people's communes. The regime has attempted to distribute the expansion of access to radio more evenly over the country and to make it available in areas that formerly lacked it. In 1951 there were only about 2,000 wired-speaker exchanges in the urban areas; by the end of the Second Five-Year-Plan in 1962, the number was to have been increased to 5,400 exchanges with some 6,700,000 speakers. This was to provide one speaker for every three peasant homes and for most of the collective farms and to establish radio-diffusion as the dominant broadcasting method in the country.[25] In addition to being less expensive than individual sets, the wired networks are more adaptable to control, more effective for emergency messages, less susceptible to enemy monitoring, and they cannot be jammed, thus serving better the purposes of Communist social and political persuasion. A declassified US Department of State report, "World Wide Distribution of Radio Receiver Sets," dated February, 1962, estimated that Communist China had 9,070,000 sets, 4,500,000 of which were individual sets, the rest being wired speakers. Unesco in 1964 estimated China had one radio receiver for every 100 persons.[26] These data, for no later than 1962, also report 233 wireless transmitters, and almost 7 million receivers in use. (See Table 11.4.)

To develop the collective listening habit and to extend the reach of broadcasting, the regime has organized radio monitoring teams whose purpose is to use every means possible to expand the audience reached by the radio message. Some monitoring teams are equipped with headphone sets and loudspeakers. Working with local party units, they organize collective listening, abstract and transmit important broadcasts, or redisseminate by word of mouth, by wall newspapers, or by posted notices. In 1956 more than 50,000 monitoring teams were said to be at work.

Visitors returning from China in the early 1960s report the unceasing ubiquitous blare of the loud speaker in public places and its blatant invasion of privacy. Such reports to the contrary and despite the gains made in extending the reach of broadcasting such as the monitoring program, much remains to be done to make the system available to the rank and file Chinese. Unless he is motivated to attend a broadcast at a community auditorium—and there has been little to attract him—he is likely to remain un-

TABLE 11.4

RADIO BROADCASTING IN COMMUNIST CHINA *

Year	Wireless Broadcasting		Wired		Total	
	Transmitters	Receivers	Transmitters	Speaker Outlets	Transmitters	Receivers
		(*millions*)		(*millions*)		(*millions*)
1949	83	1.1	8	.0005	91	
1950	49	1.1	51	.0022	100	1.1
1951	54	1.1	183	.0061	237	1.1+
1952	71		327	.0162	398	
1953	73		541	.0318	614	
1958	97	3.0	6,772	2.98	6,879	5.98
1959	122	3.5	11,124	4.57	11,246	8.07
1961	138	4.5			5,633	
1962	233	7.0	5,400	6.7		
1963	233	7.0		4.5		11.5

* Sources: Alan P. L. Liu, *Radio Broadcasting in Communist China*, Cambridge, M.I.T., 1964; Unesco, *World Communications*, 2nd, 3rd, and 4th eds.; Franklin Houn, *To Change a Nation*, Glencoe, 1961; some 1950–1958 figures from *Wei-da De Shih-nien* ("The Great Ten Years"), Foreign Language Press, Peking, 1960.

touched by radio. Aware of this kind of difficulty, the government makes listening to some programs obligatory for certain classes, and sometimes for all within reach.

Besides direct-to-the-public networks, radio is used extensively as a news and information transmission vehicle much as it is in the Soviet Union. Dictation-speed news is transmitted to print media by means of the airwaves, with messages being transmitted in both voice and code.

If radio sets are too expensive for most Chinese to afford, television sets are still farther beyond their reach. Nevertheless, television broadcasting began in Peking in May, 1958, and regular telecasts went on the air in September of that year. The following December a station opened in Shanghai. A station established at Harbin in late 1958, however, did not go on the air until 1960, to be followed by other stations in Shenyang, Changchun, and Canton. By the middle of 1961 there were reported to be 29 stations and relay centers combined in the country and 16 stations still in the experimental stage.[27] Collective watching is the main pattern of television, as it is for radio, because of the regime's aims and the economic condition of the average communications consumer. Nearly all of the 12,700 sets in use in 1960 were for public use, set up in railroad stations, parks, hotels, schools and other places where crowds of watchers might collect. Estimated numbers of television receivers for each 100 of the population in 1964 was 0.003.[28] As in the case of radio, the Chinese have been quick to employ television for educational purposes. A television "university" was established in 1960 by the Peking station. Courses in Chinese literature, mathematics, physics, and chemistry were offered, and by the end of the first year nearly 9,000 students had taken the courses. By 1964 the Peking station had 23,000 regular students, and other television "universities" had gone on the air in Shanghai, Canton, Tientsin, and Harbin.

Making allowances for technical deficiencies, low consumer buying power, vast audience potential, and geographic barriers (among other problems), growth since 1950 has been considerable, though still small in relation to population size. Estimates of audience size must take into account the devices used to multiply exposure, including captive audiences, and therefore must be reckoned at many times the number of receiving sets in existence at a given period. Yet in 1965, it could not be said that broadcasting was reaching remote rural areas with any regularity.[29] Moreover, the medium, like the press, has not measured up to the regime's sanguine expectations either as a weapon of political indoctrination or as an instrument for transmitting the culture. The need for compulsory attention makes this apparent. Complaints have indicated that radio is as devoid of interest as the press, broadcasting fare being described as monotonous, abstract, couched in nonpopular dialects, or unintelligible to the uneducated mind. Steps to overcome these weaknesses, as in the Soviet Union, have met with only partial success. Yet the Central People's Broadcasting Station in Peking moved in late 1958 into an 11-story modern building fully equipped for broadcasting and telecasting. The building has facilities for transmitting simultaneously 17 different programs from its 24 broadcasting studios, the largest of which accommodates 250 performers and 650 spectators. The building foreshadows the regime's intentions regarding broadcasting.

ADMINISTRATION AND CONTROL

Freedom of speech and of the press guaranteed in the Constitution of the Chinese People's Republic and other legal instruments governing communications policy indicate on the surface that the regime wishes to encourage the free expression of ideas.

Article 87 of the Constitution, adopted in 1954, upholds the principle of freedom in these two areas as a right of the citizen. Yet Article 19 of the same document avers that these rights and other civil liberties are denied those whose views are not in accord with the system, or those who are against it. Analysis of such provisions, together with the lessons of experience, leads to the conclusion that neither true freedom of expression as it is understood in the West nor independent use of the media by others than the party-government leaders is possible. Hence the regime monopolizes the media and operates them like the Soviet regime, so that they speak with one voice and express one view. The party makes policy and the government agencies administer and execute policy. Under this dual system the regime is able to plan, guide, instruct, supervise, control, finance, and criticize the mass media by the now familiar Communist methods.[30]

Since the media are a part of the government, direct censorship plays a minor role as a control mechanism, just as in the Soviet Union. Moreover, since censorship is ordinarily a means of prohibiting or negating certain action or conduct, it is not very useful to the Communists who seek to stimulate positive action toward a desired goal.

Instruments of Control

The chief instruments of control may be summarized as follows:

The power to create or dissolve media. The Central authority makes the decisions which establish media, define their function, designate their audiences, and eventually decree their demise.

Regulations and directives. Communications editors and directors are guided by a set of standing rules based on fundamental policy. Some are found in the constitution of the party, some are standing party rules, and others are government statutes. For example, rules state that news is to be reported from a Marxist-Leninist point of view, that the journalist must resist the tendency toward objectivity or idealism. The constitution requires that newspapers conduct themselves as good party members. That is, the media must believe in, support, and defend party goals, and avoid premature expression of opinion relating to policy. Expression of views on any party policy either in the absence of instructions or counter to such instructions is forbidden the media, as it is loyal party members. A rule governing content requires it stay within the framework of the party line and its goals. Laws providing for the punishment of counterrevolutionaries and for the protection of state secrets set forth in detail the kinds of information that media cannot disseminate. Among these prohibitions are material reflecting on government prestige, counterrevolutionary propaganda, material fostering the disobedience of laws or decrees, or disseminating knowledge of state secrets. Violation of such regulations relating to loyalty to the state is criminal, punishable by penalties ranging from three years in prison to death.

Standing regulations are general and may not anticipate unforeseen situations that arise. Under such circumstances the authorities issue specific directives when needed to cover changes in policy, new policy, new interpretations of old policy, or to correct errors and inadequacies, or fill in gaps in the propaganda stream. Current and timely directives help media executives adapt to change.

Planning. Editors and program directors must make rather detailed plans on a monthly and quarterly basis of major news and feature material they expect to develop for future dissemination. Such plans are regularly submitted for approval to the party bureaus having jurisdiction. Copy prepared for dissemination must be submitted for examination before publication by the appropriate official responsible for the information contained in the copy so that its complete accuracy can be assured. Media are prohibited from gathering news from sources other than the official ones. Planning hardly interferes with the timely quality of content because timeliness from the standpoint of recency is not as important in the news as is political and ideological timing. Alhough editors are theoretically free and are even encouraged to initiate ideas, they know in advance what will be approved, so the use of originality and initiative is restricted accordingly.

Personnel control. The power of appointment, promotion, dismissal, and assignment of duty for media personnel is exercised by party-government officials of a given level and subject to approval by the next highest party committee. For example, local district appointees must be confirmed by provincial party committees. This kind of control over the careers of professional personnel in the media system is one of the most effective, as party loyalty and ideology reliability are foremost among the criteria for appointment.

The expansion of party and party-supervised communication services following the accession to power of the Communist regime placed a strain on the number of available qualified media personnel. The proper training of journalists and communications workers was speeded by means of short courses in cadre, party, and journalism schools. Courses stressed indoctrination above professional skills and included such subjects as "the thought of Mao Tse-tung," "history of the Chinese Communist Party," "dialectical materialism," "theory of the state and the revolution," and "USSR Communist Party history." Schools of journalism now train cadres and communications workers stressing doctrinal as well as professional curricula. But it is still more important for a communications professional to know Communism than it is to know how to write.

Finance. Although at the outset communications depended upon subsidy from party and government funds, it was not long before it appeared that a state-supported communication system of the proportions needed by the new regime would prove economically burdensome. Full support might also deprive editors of incentives for making their media appealing and for improving their sales quality. Consequently early in 1950 newspapers, magazines, and broadcasting stations were told they were expected to operate on a budget aiming at eventual self-sufficiency. Media were encouraged to seek outside sources of revenue first by increasing subscription charges to cover at least newsprint costs and, secondly, by actively soliciting sources of revenue from commercial and government printing as well as from advertising. Purely product advertising was restricted to specified commercial and industrial establishments, publishing houses, and cultural organizations. Advertising policy dictates that no product advertising is to be carried except as a final measure to make the medium self-supporting, but recognizes as legitimate the advertising of state services, coming events, entertainment, and classified advertising of goods and services. Rank profit-motive commercial advertising must not occupy an undue proportion of space so that it restricts or hampers the medium's basic purpose as an organ of propaganda.[31] The national papers and magazines under this new policy have reportedly made progress in paying their own way and some have shown a profit. In addition to the new policy permitting the inflow of revenue, policy was adopted at the same time to save on internal expenditures. Cost accounting, budgeting, and auditing practices were introduced; economy was affected by cutting personnel services, eliminating waste, caring for equipment, and providing employee incentives toward greater productivity.

Criticism. Regular examination and criticism is imposed upon the final printed product and broadcast production. The lowest media in the pyramid may receive criticism not only from party officials of their own level but also from each level above it. Postpublication review serves as a final check on editorial faults and ideological deviations both of content and performance. Criticisms of the media are both private and public. They may be sent only to the media concerned or published and widely disseminated. They may also furnish the basis for a new regulation, or for calling a conference of professionals to help improve the product. Self-criticism from correspondents and letter writers is also an important phase of the critical function, as in the Soviet Union.

Controlling the flow of information. The amount and quality of information and propaganda to which the average Chinese is exposed is selected and regulated by the regime. Indeed the rigidity with which this measure is enforced resembles that of the Stalin era in the Soviet Union. Control of this nature is both negative and positive, and here censorship and suppression operate incisively. One of the earliest steps was to eradicate the sources of deviationist ideas and thoughts by ordering the destruction of books. All titles of books in stock held by publishing concerns deemed "objectionable" or "pernicious" were suppressed and made into pulp. The Commercial Press, largest publishing company in China before 1949, was permitted to retain only 1,354 of its 15,000 titles.[32] Books in libraries and private collections were also destroyed.

THE NEW CHINA NEWS AGENCY

Prime instrument for the control of media content is the New China News Agency. Both print and broadcast media rely on this monopoly, together with *Jen-min Jih-pao* and the Central People's Broadcasting Station, for all information not from local sources. *Jen-min Jih-pao* supplies editorials and party-line pronouncements which are often carried on the news agency's daily broadcasts to clients. Media are required to use in full all important news stories, articles, and pictures distributed by the agency.[33] Since editors and program directors do not have other sources of national and international information, and enjoy little range of choice from the agency's offerings, the New China News Agency report determines largely what goes into print, what goes on the air, and thus what the world's largest potential national audience reads or hears.

The Chinese Communists organized their own news agency as early as 1929 in Juichin, Kiangsi Soviet Province. It was then known as the Red China News Agency. In 1937 with headquarters at Yenan, in Northern Shensi Province, it was renamed the New China News Agency. With two small receiving sets and one 100-watt transmitter, the agency intercepted messages from Domei, Havas, Tass, and Central News Agency and transmitted 1,500 words daily to the underground Communist organs, party leaders, and front organizations. This was increased to 5,000 words daily and the dispatches aimed at promoting the Communist cause. In 1942 the agency became a full-fledged propaganda medium with regular voice broadcasts in English, and the following year for the domestic audience. After 1946 its main purpose was to attack and undermine the Kuomintang administration. By this time it was carrying 8,000 to 12,000 words of domestic and foreign information daily. Under the new regime in 1949 the agency received the exclusive franchise for the country for gathering and disseminating national and international news. It annexed and merged an estimated 659 Chinese news agencies that were in operation at the time.[34]

With headquarters in Peking, the New China News Agency is supervised by several units of the administrative hierarchy. It operates immediately under the authority of the State Council or cabinet but its work is supervised by the Culture-Education Office. Policy on content and business operations is controlled by the Department of Propaganda of the Central Committee of the party.

The agency has three spheres of operation; its domestic news function, its foreign news function, and its publishing function, which includes a *Top-secret Pamphlet* similar to Tass's confidential file.[35]

In its domestic news operation, NCNA in 1963 was organized into seven area branches located in strategic cities and covering territory largely corresponding to administrative districts; a number of general branches in lesser municipalities, and less populated areas; more than 40 rural subbranches; and a correspondence system. There were some 1,500 suboffices and 70,000 part-time correspondents of NCNA within the country. The largest service goes to the national level newspapers and all broadcasting stations. This service consists of approximately 30,000 words each of national and international information. The photograph department transmits a score or more of pictures daily. The report for provincial and local papers is about half the volume of that for the nationals, and the smaller papers receive about 10,000 words daily.

The foreign organization consisted in 1963 of branches in those 41 foreign countries diplomatically recognized by the Peking regime and 18 branches in countries not having diplomatic relations with the regime. The branches abroad not only gather and transmit public information but also serve as intelligence sources. The Havana office of NCNA was established in 1959, and by 1963, operations had been extended from there to five other Latin American countries.[36] Formerly the Tass Agency supplied the New China News Agency with a considerable proportion of its foreign news report, but as the Red Chinese agency has expanded its operations, it has relied less on Tass.

The NCNA also operates a daily English broadcast to the world and a daily Russian broadcast to Tass. The agency's publishing arm prints three kinds of newsletters: one called *Reference Materials* includes a backgrounding report of foreign news not available to the general public, but for the use of party members and the agency's personnel; another is called *Top-secret Pamphlet,* for the exclusive use of high-ranking party members and government officials; the third, *Today's News,* reports party news, both domestic and international.

The only other news agency permitted to exist in China does not compete with the New China News Agency. It is the China News Agency, a private business organization founded in 1950 whose function is to provide news to overseas Chinese periodicals. This private agency's existence is a tacit admission that news from a private source is more acceptable to the overseas Chinese than from NCNA.[37]

The purpose of the NCNA as set forth to its employees are the same as those of an army engaged in the ideological struggle, "This Army should be well trained, and strengthened in order to help the people to defeat the enemies."

EXTENDING THE REACH OF COMMUNICATIONS

In their unprecedented drive to develop a centralized national system that will enable them to communicate with a whole nation of 650 million people scattered over a large land area, the Chinese Communists are engaged in a mammoth struggle to overcome stupendous odds. They face a task somewhat similar to that which the Bolsheviks faced in the 1920s. Yet the problems for the Chinese are in almost every sphere multiplied many times over because of a combination of factors stemming from demographic, geographic, economic, social, and cultural conditions. They are multiplied by the need for speed. The pressure of nationalism enhanced by pride in its ancient heritage is a force that makes China ambitious and eager to forge a new modern industrial nation with the greatest possible haste. Early Soviet editors rarely encountered pressures and problems of such magnitude or character. Faced with different problems arising from different culture patterns, attitudes, and pressures, the mass media system has employed different methods and more prodigious efforts to reach essentially the same goals as those of the Russian Communists.

For example several large-scale programs were launched in the early 1950s: (1) to increase the geographic penetration and per capita exposure of the mass media, (2) to offset the related problem of high illiteracy, and (3) to break down language barriers. The last two would in time contribute enormously to the first objective.

Dealing with the problem of increasing exposure and penetration called for multiplying the media network and expanding the reach of existing media as rapidly as circumstances warranted. Since relatively few new media have been created, the latter problem received primary attention from the first. The main attack was aimed at the masses of workers and peasants who had never used newspapers and magazines or listened to radio with regularity, many of whom lived in inland rural areas. In 1950 the national post office was assigned responsibility for handling the administration of all periodical circulation.[38] Newspaper and magazine circulation personnel were transferred to the post office department and the postal service became a giant, sprawling, nationwide circulation department. The local postman became at the same time delivery agent and salesman of new subscriptions and renewals. This plan, however ingenious, did not provide either the coverage or the service wanted, for nearly one-fourth of native administrative village groups were not reached by the postal service. Even when a regular service was organized, established post offices could reach rural subscribers only slowly, infrequently, and with considerable difficulty because of inadequate transportation facilities and poor roads. Forcing people to buy subscriptions encountered some resistance. When post offices sent postmen to collect subscription fees, people were reported to remark, "Here they come again to force us to pay the 'newspaper tax.'"[39] Post offices were charged with being too slow with deliveries and with losing subscribers' papers. Such inefficiency, the authorities said, helped to alienate potential subscribers, impeding the drive for more circulation.

To assist the post office with its problems, special agencies for the distribution and sale of print media were ordered established in 1954, but it was two years later before a corps of 15,000 newspaper sales agents was appointed for the population of the large cities.[40] The press system then organized a national distribution service employing 300,000 persons. In the meantime, periodicals were offered for sale at cooperatives and retail outlets. The party's direct aid was enlisted in the campaign, and *Jen-min Jih-pao* remarked that for a loyal party worker, to help swell the circulation volume of the party's organs must be regarded as a political assignment.[41]

Other practical steps were taken to achieve the 2-pronged objective of obtaining maximum traffic, or usage, for each copy in print and of reaching larger and larger numbers of illiterates. The first of these was the organization of reading circles by the local party units working with the post offices. By 1952 it was estimated that 23,000 such groups with 320,000 members were functioning in Shensi Province. Shanghai had 904 reading circles and every block in Peking had its group.[42] Figures are not available to show the nationwide extent of this program. The reading groups are under the supervision of some 5 million propaganda officers, members of the party assigned by blocks to facilitate the communication of the party line, thus supplementing and reinforcing the media with personal contact communication.[43] Presumably block reading circles meet at least once a day, but information is lacking as to the frequency and length of such meetings. Literate persons are expected to help lead the reading circles and thus cannot escape the pressures to read newspapers regularly because they are sought out for information. Illiterates have the papers read to them. The party propaganda officer in charge aids in the selection of the most effective and appropriate content for oral reading, thereby influencing what newspapers are to be used most and what content is to receive exposure. Thus the party has one more valuable means of checking on loyalty and performance. The newspaper-reading groups are just one of many kinds of "cultural" organizations that interlace the society of a typical commune, all useful for varied propaganda activities.[44]

For the first seven years thousands of party members, government employees, teachers, students, and military personnel received periodicals free of charge to themselves, but paid for out of their organization's funds. Doubtless these group-supported subscriptions were counted in the 408 per cent increase in newspaper subscriptions between 1949 and 1955, as reported by official government data. This policy was changed by directive in 1956 calling upon all members of such groups to finance their own subscriptions. Since by this time these groups of workers were salaried, it was felt that they could afford to buy their own papers. To require them to do so might foster closer reading and greater appreciation of media services it was said. How this measure affected total circulations was not revealed, but it was followed by a nationwide reduction in subscription rates, ranging from 16 to 30 per cent.[45] Such a reduction was probably made to counteract a drop in circulations that doubtless followed abandonment of the free subscription policy. The concurrent step to extend broadcasting's reach was the organization of radio monitoring teams together with the development of the networks as already described. According to information available up to 1957, no taxation or fee of any kind was imposed on radio sets. Owners were required to register with security authorities radio sets capable of receiving shortwave signals. Special permission was also required to buy tubes used in transmitting or receiving.

Political censorship of information and restrictions on exports of publications since 1959 have severely limited the data available in the Western world for assessing changes in Chinese media growth patterns. Evidence tends to indicate there was a rapid growth until 1959, and that 1958 was the peak year from the standpoint of number of titles extant. The year 1959 was presumably the most critical one in Communist Chinese publishing history, marking a sudden decline. The large number of mergers, title changes, and titles ceasing publication was the greatest registered in any year.[46] The number of publishing houses in operation decreased. Information is still inadequate for estimating the condition of publishing in the years since 1959. There was a drop in circulations in the early 1960s with a slow recovery until by 1965 circulation totals of the 1958–1959 period were being again matched. A comparison of data for the Communist period with those of the 1930s shows that periodical publishing activity levels were greater under the old Republic than at present. Another notable change under the Communists was the centralization of publishing and broadcasting activity in Peking, whereas formerly the publishing industry was concentrated in Shanghai, the chief industrial center and port.

Some progress has been made in overcoming geographical barriers. The improvement of highways, railroads, and canals; the gradual replacement of ancient modes of transportation with modern machines; and use of the airplane are all factors that are slowly affecting media use and media impact. Increase in the manufacture of receiving sets and transmitters, the use of transistors and the building of dams for hydroelectric power to operate them are among the many items on the gigantic national agenda that are receiving attention as resources permit.

LANGUAGE REFORM AND ILLITERACY

Any nation aiming to institute large-scale fundamental reform leading to modernization must solve the illiteracy problem, for literacy is a critical component of communication—and indeed, of the whole modernizing process.[47] The fact that Communist regimes stress the importance of communication, coupled with the fact that China's age-old language barriers are particularly formidable, illiteracy and language problems are especially acute and complex in China, as they are in India. In the Soviet Union, language is still a problem in the communication system but illiteracy has presumably been overcome. An analysis of the language problem in China will indicate why the achievement of literacy is so difficult here.

The Chinese language is one of the world's oldest living languages. Nobody knows how old the spoken language forms are, but written language forms date back nearly 4,000 years.[48] Intercommunication in speech through the centuries has been complicated by the inevitable development of dialects. Speech in one dialect may become unintelligible to one who speaks a different dialect. Thus the sounds of the spoken language over the country came to vary from province to province, even from city to city. Along with the growth of dialects, the conquest by the Empire of subject peoples of different ethnic and linguistic backgrounds introduced entirely new languages into the situation.

In modern times the most important of dialects is the North Chinese, a slight variation of which is known to foreigners as Mandarin and to the Chinese as *kuo yu,* or "national language." Yet Mandarin itself is by no means uniform. For example North Chinese varies slightly from Peking Mandarin, and both vary from Cantonese, the language of the Southeast. "Cabbage" in Peking Mandarin is pronounced *bai tsai;* in Cantonese, *bak choi.* The various forms of Mandarin then are spoken and understood by an estimated two-thirds of the population in the heartland of the nation. Dialectical differences are much greater to the point of becoming real barriers to intelligible communication in the mountain regions of the South and West.[49] Dialectical gaps in conversation are to some extent bridged by writing and by the fact that many urban Chinese speak in more than one dialect. Nevertheless the handicaps barring the prospect of a common tongue for the entire nation are formidable. Western leaders have been able to speak to great audiences at once by radio since that medium became generally available. But broadcasting, the medium that partly transcends illiteracy, has its limitations where dialectical and language differences stand in the way. This lesson was painfully apparent when Mao Tse-tung addressed the overseas Chinese over shortwave radio, speaking naturally in his native provincial dialect. But it happened to be one that could not be understood by the majority of his listeners, either overseas or at home. What he said was a mystery for most until the interpreter translated each sentence.

If the spoken language impedes communication, the written language poses its problems too. The written language is a picture language with symbols representing whole words and ideas rather than phonetic sounds such as those the letters of the Greek alphabet represent. Though recognizable as pictures today, pictographs or ideographs as drawn are known as characters.

Because the ideograph is relatively independent of sound, the written language could bridge over the differing spoken vernaculars, but even this advantage disappeared through the centuries. Though the written language acted as a cohesive force to bind the Empire together, it did not keep step with the evolution of the spoken language used by the common people. In time the difference between the two became so great that the rank-and-file person could not understand the written tongue, even if he could read it. It was known as the classical style and could be understood only by the scholar class. Since most documents, histories, laws and the literature were written in the classical style, popular education for common people became virtually impossible. Because simply becoming literate was so hard and time consuming—the written classical being so far removed from common speech, there grew up a scholar class among the nation's wealthiest sons—the only ones who could afford to take the time to become literate and devote the lifetime required to become knowledgeable in the classics.

The complicated task of language reform was attacked systematically after World War I by scholars led by Hu Shih. The Renaissance movement encouraged writing in the vernacular, and contemporary writers of much popular literature used it. So did the press. Eventually this "plain talk" was taught in the schools, and soon Mandarin-speaking children could learn to read and write in their mother tongue and other children learned the standard dialect. Efforts to simplify and shorten the size of the vocabulary needed for ordinary intercourse were not very successful. Moreover, the Chinese could not benefit from the use of print because so many different characters were necessary. When modern typecasting machines and typewriters were invented, minimum Chinese needs were beyond the limits of ordinary machines. Typesetting of books, magazines, and newspapers was a complicated and intricate process. Typewriters had several hundred keys and therefore were not much in use. Nevertheless, through the work of Hu Shih and others, the literary revolution and the mass education movement made a significant beginning in the hard task of bringing literacy within the grasp of the common man.

Benefiting from the work of their predecessors, the Chinese Red regime recognized the pressing need for a common language for both speech and writing, as had the Sun Yat-sen and Chiang-kai-shek governments. The language problem is especially painful to the Communists seeking, as they are, to change the nation's way of life by gigantic national reorientation. The earlier governments had attempted to devise a phonetic alphabet based on Roman symbols, but many Chinese syllables were incapable of reproduction by this means. Shortly after coming to power the regime created a committee to reform the written language and assigned to it the task of (1) simplifying the written characters, (2) encouraging greater use of *pu tong hua*, the plain speech, and (3) devising and adapting to general use a plan for a Chinese phonetic alphabet annotating the characters by sound symbols. After much experimentation an alphabet of 30 letters—a simplified version of the earlier Roman adaptations and based on the spoken Mandarin as the universal language of the country—was adopted in February, 1956.[50] This is taught in schools, stressed and used in the mass media, and required for transcribing spoken Mandarin. The program has required the preparation of teachers for many of whom the language was new.

Contrary to impressions in the West, the plan does not call for abandoning the vernacular written language and starting from scratch.[51] The Latinized alphabet makes the language easier to learn by converting it to the common speech and indicating its standard pronunciation by phonetic symbols. To simplify the writing process, 544 of the most commonly used characters have been redesigned for greater ease of transcription. The average number of strokes required to write these 544 characters was 16; now the number is half that many.

When the new alphabet and the new pronunciations become standardized, the task of cutting down on illiteracy will be less difficult. The regime is interested in overcoming the illiteracy barrier as rapidly as possible not only to increase the use of print in education and mass communication, but also to aid progress toward industrialization and the other hallmarks of modernization. General estimates in the 1940s put China's literacy at only about 20 per cent of the total population. The Nationalist Government at the end of 1945 reported an estimated 53.1 per cent of China's 373,905,966 persons of or above school age who were defined as literate, but this included all who had been enrolled in the schools regardless of length of time spent. Estimates in 1956 put the over-all literacy level at 30 per cent.[52] About 45 million peasants and 65 per cent of the nation's industrial workers, all adults, were said to have gained some degree of literacy. Because population increases absorb any gains made, literacy levels had risen but little by 1964, at which time Liu estimated the illiteracy level for the entire population at about 78 to 80 per cent.[53] Plans are in effect to achieve the difficult goal of almost complete adult literacy by 1970, but the probability of reaching this goal is low.

The pace of growth under communism in the media apparatus has not been rapid but the extent to which mass communications reach into the population is impressive. They make it easier for the regime to mobilize and regiment mass thought and action. But the barriers have not yielded completely to the onslaughts against them. Many stubborn problems remain and new problems, often unpredictable, appear.

12 ★

HOW THE CHINESE MEDIA PERFORM

FROM EXAMINATION in Chapters 4 and 5 of Soviet Communist professional concepts and policies undergirding the mass communication system, the nature of the social role, goals, and functions of the mass media system as they theoretically apply in China are apparent. The foregoing chapters also discussed how Communist communications systems define and treat news, opinion, criticism and self-criticism, advertising, and feature or human interest material. This section will examine the content of a number of randomly selected issues of various Chinese newspapers and magazines and the offerings of radio and television. The purpose shall be to describe in a general way what the media are saying to look for significant differences in the way Chinese media perform as compared with the way Soviet media perform, and to formulate conclusions from the analysis.

THE NATIONAL DAILIES:
Jen-min Jih-pao, Ta Kung Pao, Kuang-ming Jih-pao

Nowhere in the world's press can be found more revealing evidence of the benumbing effect of rigid political totalism than in examining even cursorily the pages of the Communist Chinese publications, and comparing them with the best of the port city press of pre-Communist days.

Before 1956 all national dailies published only four pages, seven days a week, with occasional supplements devoted to literary reviews, sports, illustrations, education, and other subjects. After 1956, *Jen-min Jih-pao* expanded to eight pages on a regular basis, but after 1962 cut back to six pages. A comparative analysis of three of the leading national dailies of January 3, 1954, made by Wu[1] gives a fair sampling of the typical results of party-government selection and treatment. The front pages of all three, as the student of the communist press has learned to expect, exhibit the greatest similarity, for they customarily display matters deemed of primary importance by the regime. The last pages devoted to international news are also quite similar. One must look to the inside pages to find whatever diversity may exist. These cover national news, feature articles, editorial comment of less than front-page urgency, and the supplements. Like the Soviet *Pravda,* the front pages usually carry the day's editorial. *Jen-min Jih-pao's* front page of this date is no exception. The editorial is copied from *Pravda* of the previous day and it calls for further relaxation of the tense international situation. The other major item on the page reports Soviet Premier Georgi Malenkov's replies to questions asked him by the American news agency, International News Service. The same two items were front-paged by the other two papers examined, *Kuang-ming Jih-pao* (Enlightenment Daily), devoted to education and cultural affairs and *Ta Kung Pao* (The Impartial Gazette), concentrating on economics and finance. Both items, though originating in the Soviet Union, were considered of more importance to the people of China than the day's developments at home. The second page in all of the papers turned to practical, though colored, examples of the working out of general party production goals. AGRICULTURAL PRODUCTION INCREASED THROUGH PROPAGATION OF THE GENERAL LINE, the headline from *Jen-min Jih-pao,* is typical. Though underlying party slant is ever present, the third pages reflect greater differences, appropriate to the differing functions of the three papers. *Jen-min Jih-pao* deals with party matters, such as the elections, "counterrevolutionary" activities, and short cultural items. *Kuang-ming Jih-pao,* a Chinese version of *Literaturnaya Gazeta,* offered reports in the activities of literary circles, a few book reviews, and items covering agricultural cooperatives. *Ta Kung*

Pao's third page was concerned principally with the reorganization of private businesses to permit government "participation." It was headlined As THE HAPPY DAY APPROACHES. This page also presented price quotations, advertisements, and public notices. The fourth page in all three papers reported international news, in this case almost exclusively matters dealing with developments in the Soviet Union and those among foreign Communist groups.

JEN-MIN JIH-PAO, *The People's Daily*. The 8-page editions of *Jen-min Jih-pao* offered no striking variation from this pattern,[2] the additional space given to more of the same. Here one finds more articles of an ideological-philosophical nature, more letters from "readers," and abstracts from periodicals. The arrangement of the 8-page paper follows these general lines: the front page is reserved for the top-level documents, speeches in full text, important reports, and the usual editorial. Second and third pages present items on industry, agriculture, commerce, construction, transportation, and communications. The fourth page covers domestic political and party matters in capital and country. The fifth and sixth pages report international news, with the fifth page often given over to Communist world matters consisting of items from the Soviet Union and other Communist countries. The sixth page presents the non-Communist world. Page seven concentrates on education and culture. Since this page attracts the top literary and artistic figures in the country who are in position to recommunicate by means of their art, doctrinal arguments and dogma are frequently presented here. The final page carries short stories, poems, essays, plays and other literary efforts bearing ideological themes and classified advertisements.

This pattern of content had changed only slightly eight years later, in October, 1962, though front page news and editorials were no longer Soviet in origin (Fig. 12.1). China by this time was in an undeclared war with India and the United States-Cuban situation was developing. Furthermore, the ideological split between China and the Soviet Union had cooled relations between the two countries perceptibly, and the Communist Chinese line was to show that China could stand on its own feet, to the point of repudiating Soviet leadership of the Communist world. Within the same general format and pattern of organization described for 1954, what

人民日報
REN MIN RI BAO

我国防部发言人正式宣告

印度政府越过所謂麦克馬洪綫发动大規模进攻最后破坏了这条綫的約束
为防止印軍卷土重来,我在自卫战斗中沒有必要再受非法麦克馬洪綫約束

印軍向"麦克馬洪綫"东端猛攻遭我反击
我軍在边境东段收复吉普等地

譴責印度拒絕中印边界談判

尼赫魯叫嚷要长期打下去

美帝国主义野心毕露
公然支持印度政府进攻中国

印度陆軍征召退休軍官

社论
积极做好秋季农副产品的收购工作

Fig. 12.1. Unlike the usual stolid display typical of its counterparts **Pravda** and **Izvestia, Jen-min Jih-pao** can wax sensational. Front page news of October 23, 1962, reflects China's undeclared war with India. The headline declares that the Chinese Government will not be bound by the illegal MacMahon Line since Indian troops have crossed it. Other items include a roundup of world opinion blaming India's refusal to talk peace with China, reports of the success of the Chinese army in recovering "disputed" territory, and American "Imperialism's" open support of India's "invasion" of Chinese territory.

does the paper say in 1962? Across the front page of the October 23, 1962, issue headlines declare that the Chinese government will not be bound by the "illegal" MacMahon Line since Indian troops have crossed it. The story under these sensational headlines is displayed in two double-column spreads. Various related items report (1) condensed opinion from Indonesian, Swedish, Burmese, and Canadian newspapers blaming India's refusal to talk peace with China, (2) successes of the Chinese army in "recovering" disputed territory, (3) Prime Minister Nehru's preparation for a long period of fighting, and (4) open support by ambitious American "imperialism" of India's "invasion" of China. The editorial talks about agricultural production. On page two, reporters for the New China News Agency present an essay on Lhasa, the Tibetan capital, containing several songs from the people of Tibet praising the better life they are now enjoying under Communist rule. Foreign news on pages three and four concentrates on Asia and Latin America respectively. News of demonstrations at US military bases in Japan stress the "Go Home, Yankee" slogans. A report on Vietnam extravagantly praises North Vietnamese achievements and attributes the Cambodian embassy in China with a charge that South Vietnamese soldiers have invaded North Vietnam territory. Argentineans and Puerto Ricans are pictured as supporting the Cuban government against invasion by the United States. A Communist Party analysis from Equador concludes that American Imperialism is the main enemy of mankind. A cartoon depicts the "real aim" of the Kennedy administration, under its slogan "to acquire mutual progress" (referring to the Alliance for Progress), is to filch Latin-American people out of their resources. Under the cartoon and the heading FIGURES AND FACTS, data show how much the United States has squeezed capital and resources from Latin-American countries.

The October 24th issue blossoms with the full reaction to the Cuban crisis. The New China News Agency's report from Cuba states that Castro, shouting "we will win," is ready to fight US imperialism. The front-page editorial demands that US imperialism and its threat to the peace be stopped. The US quarantine against shipping offensive weapons to Cuba is regarded as dangerous interference with Cuban independence and international rights on the high seas. On October 25, 8-column spreads in large characters report the Communist Chinese government's official statement in support of Cuba which protests "United States imperialism's actions of piracy." The news reports from Latin America, Japan, the east European countries, and the Soviet Union depict uniform actions of Communist parties in these countries rallying to Cuba's support. Nowhere in these papers is mention made of the discovery and presence of Russian missile bases in Cuba. The report covering the United Nations Security Council's action cites the Cuban ambassador's statement declaring that the only foreign base on Cuban soil is under US control (referring to Guantanamo Naval Base). United States charges against Russia in the United Nations—a part of the official record that might have had the effect of neutralizing somewhat the Chinese version of the episode—are, of course, not reported. The coverage of the affair in this issue and in other issues of this week of world crisis leave the reader with the unmistakable impression that US imperialism is a dangerous threat to the Cuban revolution.

Since publication of NCNA foreign news together with the regime's pronouncements and preachments is required, there is little opportunity for individual variation among the newspapers except for the coverage of matters below the national level, and even

人民日报

REN MIN RI BAO

我外交部强烈抗议印军最近连续侵犯我领土

严正警告印度必须承担侵略后果

依靠农民修好管好用好水利

热烈祝贺朝鲜民主主义人民共和国成立十七周年

刘少奇主席接见巴基斯坦大使罗查

号召陆海空军歼灭印度侵略者

陈副总理由大马士革到阿尔及尔

首都各界集会庆祝朝鲜人民的伟大节日

祝贺保加利亚社会主义革命二十一周年

朱德委员长接见法议员代表团

Fig. 12.2. Page one of the September 9, 1965, issue of **Jen-min Jih-pao** (The People's Daily) is an attractive combination of horizontal and vertical display. Conspicuously absent are the characteristic editorial, news of the Vietnamese war, and pictures of Mao Tse-tung and other party dignitaries. The two major stories are concerned with the India-Pakistan war. As in many Chinese periodicals the title line carries the phonetic sounds of the title words transliterated in the English language alphabet —thus the classic **Jen-min Jih-pao** becomes **Ren Min Ri Bao.** Reformed Chinese writing may read horizontally from left to right (top left-hand story) or vertically from right to left as shown by the top right-hand story.

this material offers little variation from the standard theme, though fresh information is to be found.[2]

Scanning the pages of a sample issue of *Jen-min Jih-pao* for September 9, 1965, one finds no report indicating any other source than that of the New China News Agency (Fig. 12.2). The page is fully devoted to both foreign and domestic information. There is no editorial either on page one or inside, and nothing about the Vietnamese war on page one of this issue. The India-Pakistan war is the focus of two major items, one stating that China's foreign ministry has sent a note to the Indian government demanding the immediate withdrawal of Indian troops from Chinese territory and warning India of the consequences of aggression against China; the other quoting the Pakistani commander-in-chief exhorting his troops to ". . . annihilate the enemy invading our land. This is not only a time of test, but also a time of glory," he declares. Party matters occupy other space on the page. Chinese Communist party and government leaders have sent a telegram of congratulations to the North Korean heads of state on the occasion of the seventeenth anniversary of the founding of the People's Democratic Republic of North Korea, the full text of the telegram appearing in the story. Moreover Peking is celebrating North Korea's birthday, another story says. News of government includes a report of Liu Shao-chi's conference with the Pakistani ambassador in Peking on the "invasion of Pakistan's territory by the Indian army."

Page two of this issue is given over to national news and letters to the editor. The main group of stories deals with the first Tibetan People's Congress of the Tibetan Autonomous Region; thirty delegates, the reports say, have elected a chairman, a vice chairman, and members of a "People's Committee." They are determined, the story avers, that Tibetans, once oppressed for generations, are now to become their own masters. One item reports a discussion of plans for the Second National Athletic Meet to be held in Peking and another makes much of the defection of a Republic of China diplomat, who receives a warm welcome in Peking. The three letters on this page are written by village electricians and they tell how to do a better job of wiring a village.

Page three and four are devoted to foreign news, the war in Vietnam prominent on page three. The reports say that North Vietnam has shot down six United States planes, and the Viet Cong have killed nearly 2,000 enemy soldiers in 20 days. There are short items about the heroism of the Viet Cong, one about a guerilla killing eight US Marines with nine bullets, with a photograph showing him using a mortar. Other matters on this page return to the India-Pakistan conflict. London newspaper opinion criticizing the Indian "invasion" is quoted, there is a background brief about the Kashmir issue, and a report says that Pakistanis are determined to unite and defeat the Indian "aggressors." A dispatch from Japan on page four reports that Japan's Communist party members of Parliament have protested against the suppression by the military of "the people's struggle for justice." The item refers to forceful suppression of demonstrations in Japan. Another informs the reader that South Korean students have taken action to oppose the "cruelty" of President Chung Hee Park's regime. There are a number of other brief news items on this page.

Page five is what American journalists describe as a feature page. This particular one is devoted to interpretation, with the expected propaganda and ideological slant, on Tibet. There is an account by a Lhasa electrical power plant worker giving testimony as to how bad the old days were and in contrast how good it is now, and (not incidentally) how much he devotes himself to his work.

There is a similar account by an automobile factory worker describing how much he suffered under the serfdom of the pre-Communist regime and how he, after the Communists came into power, became his own master. A general roundup under the heading OLD TIBET CHANGES ITS WAY, advances the theme that under the party's guidance, Tibetans are abolishing serfdom and building a better life for themselves.

Page six is assigned to literary and cultural items and advertising. There are essays, poems, art criticism, notices of book publications and magazines, musical and theatre performances, and motion picture productions. The commercial advertisements are small and include theatre and movie announcements, and such product advertisements as tools, sports equipment, and electric light bulbs.

Unlike *Pravda* and *Izvestia* which miss few chances to run editorials in every issue, *The People's Daily* throughout the month of September, 1965, carried no editorials at all in ten, or about one-third of its issues for the month. Four issues, however, carried two editorials each, and the September 11 issue carried two editorials on page one. Out of a total of 24 editorials that appeared during the month, here is a sampling. On the front page for September 2 under a 1-line banner reading, U.S. IMPERIALISM CAN BE DEFEATED, JUST AS JAPANESE IMPERIALISM WAS DEFEATED is a subdeck: ON THE OCCASION OF THE 20TH ANNIVERSARY OF THE VICTORY IN WAR OVER JAPAN. In its body the editorial unblushingly ignores a fact of history, saying ". . . in the struggle against the Japanese aggressors, the Chinese people received support from the Soviet people, Asian peoples, and peoples of the whole world." The United States is not mentioned specifically. The editorial advances the argument that "U.S. imperialism," though it seems on the surface to be a monster, is actually weaker because of its vulnerability than Japanese imperialism was. For evidence the editorial writer compares the morale of US troops with that of the wartime Japanese soldiers and finds that the morale and combat ability of US fighting men is far below that of the former Japanese army. "Although U.S. imperialism has nearly three million troops, it occupies so many places in the world that it cannot use its full strength to invade a single nation. On the contrary, the nation invaded can mobilize its full strength to repel United States aggression," so the argument goes.

A page one editorial on September 11, 1965, written on the occasion of the forthcoming second annual Athletic Meet in Peking, interestingly associates athletics, civil defense, and skill in communications. According to the writer Chinese athletes have broken more than 100 world records and set more than 5,700 new national records in the past 16 years. The editorial states that thousands of workers, farmers, soldiers, and young students, responding to Comrade Mao's slogan "To Develop Athletics, To Strengthen the People's Physical Fitness," participate in swimming, mountain climbing, communication and correspondence, shooting, and other activities. They have decided to make themselves physically sound, mentally determined persons with rifle and pen. "When the enemy invades our country," the editorial concludes, "we can join the armed forces at once and become fighters who shoot sharply, communicate well, climb when mountains appear, and swim when water crosses our path."

An analysis of *Jen-min Jih-pao* issues from Sunday, September 5, through Saturday, September 11, indicates a continuity in following up news developments but shows little departure from the traditional format we have learned to expect of the communist newspaper.

TA KUNG PAO, *The Impartial Gazette.* In *Ta Kung Pao* for September 21, 1965, the regime's concern with the Vietnam conflict is apparent on the front page where the headline tells the story: A U.S. JET DOWNED OVER HAINAN; FLYING THIEF CAPTURED. Hainan is a Red Chinese island in the Gulf of Tonkin. Pilot of the US Jet F-104 is a Captain Philip Smith, whose pictures and identification materials are shown. A second story reports the concern for national defense: a working session of the Mainland Militia will approve the "social education campaign" to build a better and stronger national defense program. "The United States imperialists, if they have the guts to invade, will be flooded in the ocean of a people's war," the story threatens. China's protest to India's military "provocation and invasion of Chinese territory" is the subject of another item on this page. *Ta Kung Pao's* editorial appears in left-hand columns of the front page under this title, TO PUNISH SEVERELY U.S. AGGRESSORS. Its central purpose is to accuse the United States "imperialists" of seeking to widen the war in Asia. It does not accuse the US people, only those they call the imperialists (meaning the USA government). "The Chinese People," the editorial observed, "are fully aware of the U.S. plot and are prepared for it."

Page two this day also carries an editorial, mainly devoted to developments in agriculture, industry, and commerce. The editorial calls on the masses to unite to do a good job of harvesting the cotton crop. The general theme is a familiar one—a faith in the opinions of the masses—and it urges readers to listen more to what the people have to say. Another editorial is a directive to those in charge of the cotton harvest, reminding them to communicate to the masses the party's and country's need for gathering and processing the cotton crop. This should be done so that the masses will understand the meaning of the party's policy, for as Mao has said, "Our policy must be made known not only to the leaders, but also to the masses." The editorial concludes with the reminder that all must listen to mass opinion. News items concern: a Kiangsu cotton mill that has adopted a new labor technique and thereby raised its production levels; a new wholesale business area that has been set up in Tientsin; and a contribution of articles from factory workers and managers, all advancing the idea that business and industry need to be infused with the revolutionary spirit.

Medical science and sports are the subjects treated on page three. There is a dispatch from a Shanghai hospital reporting a complete operation to repair a women's heart after a heart attack; a studio photographer and his assistant give first-hand accounts of their travels through mountain villages to take pictures of the inhabitants, some of whom have never in their lives faced a camera; in another is the personal account of two weight lifters who, inspired by Mao's books and teachings, have set world records. "Persevere and fear naught," they counsel.

The fourth and final page carries international news. A chapter in the Vietnam struggle is reported from the North Vietnamese viewpoint. The India-Pakistan cease-fire ordered by the UN Security Council is the lead story. Other items make the point that Soviet leaders have supported India in opposing China, and that while Albania has backed China's stand, the United States and the Soviet Union have supported India. It is interesting that no issue of *Ta Kung Pao,* the business, economic, and financial journal, ever carries a commercial advertisement!

KUANG-MING JIH-PAO, *the Enlightenment Daily.* Next to be examined is the so-called organ and spokesman of the non-Communist "democratic" parties, one of the five papers the regime labels as "private" newspapers. This is *Kuang-ming Jih-pao* (Enlightenment

Daily) of Peking, whose September 27, 1965, issue leads off with a 6-column headline to introduce an extensive press conference held by Lee Tsung-jen, former vice president of the Republic of China, who the story says defected from the United States to Mainland China. In his news conference Lee is quoted as saying, ". . . if we want to love our country, we must fight U.S. imperialism; to insure the victory against imperialism, we must fight to end Khrushchev's revisionism." Following the Line, Lee goes on to state that Taiwan is a part of the undivided territory of China, charging that the United States is to blame for the absence of peaceful relations with the Chinese People's Republic. This is because the United States has "occupied" Taiwan, he explained. Lee got around also to praising China's achievements under the Communist party as "a miracle" rarely to be seen in the world. The report is illustrated with two photographs of the news conference. Lee also held a cold-plate dinner for the newsmen who had attended the conference.

Elsewhere on the page appears a government item stating that the Foreign Ministry has sent the Indian embassy a note of protest against the anti-Chinese "clown comedy" staged by the Indian government. The "clown comedy" refers to a demonstration by Indians in front of the Chinese embassy in New Delhi, after China had accused Indian soldiers of crossing the Chinese border, kidnaping residents, and stealing livestock. Making a joke at the expense of the Chinese, the Indian "reactionaries" (as they were called by the *People's Daily*) while demonstrating brought along several sheep to repay China for the alleged thefts.

The principal information on page two is a full text of Lee's prepared remarks at the press conference reported on page one. The rest of the page is devoted primarily to two medical articles, one reporting a new electronic device for medical diagnostic work being manufactured in a Shanghai factory, and the other is a similar story about cooperation between a small factory and the Nanking Medical College to produce a small instrument for stimulating the heart to make it beat properly. The rest of the page is devoted to three short news items from Tibet, Inner Mongolia, and Manchuria.

Page three of the *Enlightenment Daily* presents editorials and international news. In the international section the reader finds the following items of information and enlightement: China's Foreign Ministry and the Red Cross of China together issue a protest against the International Red Cross's invitation to the Nationalist Chinese delegation to attend its twentieth international conference—an egregious slip for which China has decided to sever all relations with the International Red Cross. The Viet Cong has accused the USA of authorizing its military forces to use gas in the Vietnam war. Pakistani Foreign Minister Butto has told an Algerian reporter at the United Nations that unless the problem of Kashmir's plebescite is solved, Pakistan would withdraw from the United Nations. Pakistan has accused Indian troops of violating the cease-fire agreement by bombing Pakistani outposts. India is insisting on the seizure of Kashmir. Finally the reader can expose himself to three short items on this page covering the Vietnam war. There are also two editorials on page three, one welcoming the visit to Peking of the "Indonesian Delegation of Friendship," and a short comment reprinted from the *People's Daily,* "New Delhi's Anti-Chinese Clown Comedy," explained above.

Two articles on economic problems comprise the entire content of page four of this issue: one discusses the problems arising from developing agricultural by-products, and the other raises questions about problems resulting from the exploitation of pre-Communist China by capitalist interests.

As in the other Chinese newspapers, all the news stories in this issue are supplied by the New China News Agency. There is no advertising. There seems to be little in the *Enlightenment Daily* to differentiate it from party and government dailies, the regime's claims for its role and function to the contrary notwithstanding. The regime's adherence to the principle of private ownership and with it the implications of the existence of competitive voices outside the single-party monopoly control are sheer myth.

MAGAZINES:

Min-tsu Hua-pao, the National Picture Magazine

Turning to the magazines, we first pick up *Min-tsu Hua-pao* (Nationalities Pictorial). This large 10-by-14½-inch popular illustrated monthly magazine appeals to the minority races of China and depicts their activities. Begun in 1956 as a bimonthly, it has editions in Chinese and six minority languages including Korean, Mongolian, Tibetan, and Uighur. The issue for December, 1964, has 40 pages, including the covers (Fig. 12.3). It is a quality magazine, attractively printed, the photography is excellent (two interior pages and the covers are in color), there is good definition in the reproductions, and the pictures with type are skillfully arranged, some on double-page spreads. The method of reproduction by US standards is now technically outmoded. The front cover shows a young Korean and an older, grey-bearded Chinese with pleased expressions on their faces as they examine the full heads in a field of golden rice, ripe for harvesting. The colors are soft blues, golds, and greens. Approximately 44 of the 99 pictures used in this issue with their texts tell stories about developments in agriculture and industry. One full-page photograph shows mountains of threshed wheat piled high on a Mongolian plain. Another two-page spread shows acres of sacked grain arranged in rows of piles awaiting transportation. The captions say that Mongolian and Tibetan farmers have reaped a large harvest, and that dairy production by minority peoples is increasing. Other displays show people working the fields picking cotton, digging sweet potatoes, driving tractors, or cultivating rice paddies. In one photograph a young girl holds a large armload of shucked ears of corn. One interesting full-page picture shows a number of horse-drawn wagons loaded with cotton from the fields waiting outside a cotton gin. Although agriculture occupies most of the space in this issue, a few picture-stories feature industrial achievements. One covers a new Tungsin dam and hydroelectric power station; another shows the inside of a community workshop where irrigation pumps are installed; and a third presents eight pictures about mine workers in Sinkiang and their newly constructed dormitory.

Eleven pictures, five of them in color, concern the activities of a special class in drama at the Central College of Drama—a class made up of members of non-Chinese minority races. Students are shown practicing dancing and attending anti-US demonstrations.

This being a time of crisis in the Congo, *Nationalities Pictorial* presents 16 pictures showing rallies and demonstrations in Peking and other Chinese cities in support of the Congolese people against "U.S. aggression." The demonstrators carry a long banner which reads: "U.S. Imperialists, get out of the Congo! Get out of Taiwan! Get out of Africa! Get out of Asia! and get out of Latin America!" There are also a few "news" events presented in photographic form, one showing Mao Tse-tung receiving members of a Japanese ballet troupe, and another showing Liu Shao-chi posing with members of the Cuban National Ballet. A few other short items show the members of a whole family who the story line says have devoted their hearts to the party; describe the tremendous changes in the mountain area that have taken place where the Red Army passed in 1934 during its Long March; another shows how a machine selects seeds; tells the story of a young Korean who has dedicated his youth and knowledge to the betterment of his agricultural village. Here and there the reader is urged to become a laborer or farmer or is reminded that having tasted the bitterness of the past, he should sense the sweetness of the present (under the Communists). Some magazines are published in both the Chinese and English languages (Figs. 12.4 and 12.5).

Shih-chieh Chi-shih, World Affairs Monthly

Shih-chieh Chi-shih (World Affairs) is a semimonthly magazine of smaller size (7¼ by 10¼) than the *Nationalities Pictorial* and is less attractive. It is one of the seven popular magazines that in 1955 reported a per issue circulation of over 100,000. This periodical has a cover in one color and its complete inside pages are

Fig. 12.3. **Min-tsu Hua-pao** (Nationalities Pictorial) is one of the most attractive of China's magazines, although its color reproductions are by a method now technologically outmoded. Published about the minority nationalities of Mainland China, the illustrated monthly resembles the American **Life** in format. Cover and pages on this and the opposite page are taken from an issue featuring the harvest. The inside back cover (below) shows a cotton gin near Peking in Hopei Province. The headline on the spread opposite reads: "Minority Peoples Celebrate Abundant Harvest." The lower picture in the spread was taken in Inner Mongolia. The upper picture shows a scene in Tibet.

printed on poor quality newsprint. In the issue of January 10, 1964, the magazine has taken the opportunity offered at the beginning of a new year to survey 1963 developments in global politics and the international scene. On the basis of the survey, it appraises the situation and offers predictions for 1964. The conclusions are that during 1963, United States imperialism was in trouble from inside and out, and that it (imperialism) now finds itself in increasingly deteriorating straits. Therefore, in the year 1964 United States global strategy and actions will suffer further deterioration due to the opposition of peoples from all over the world. In fact, the magazine says, the over-all world situation in 1963 confirmed Mao's scientific conclusion: "The East Wind prevails over the West Wind."

Another article pointing to the fifth anniversary of the Cuban revolution lauds the success of the second Cuban land reform and Cuba's anti-US line. Still another describes the growing food shortage in India and expresses the opinion that the dumping of United States food and agricultural products has caused many serious consequences, one of which is the destruction of India's

少数民族地区欢庆农牧业丰收

Fig. 12.4. Two of China's magazines are published in both Chinese- and English-language editions. **Jen-min Hua-pao** and **China Pictorial** (left) for January, 1966, are identical page-for-page, picture-for-picture, except for the language difference. **Chung-kuo Fü-nü** and **Women of China** (below), on the other hand differ considerably. The English edition uses finer paper and better printing and focuses on material of international interest. The Chinese edition is planned to have more domestic appeal. The articles are larded with the usual indoctrinal dogma. This issue for January, 1966, has an article advocating birth control.

basic agricultural structure. There is an article translated from a Cuban newspaper reporting on the activities of "the valiant Venezuelan guerillas"; an article about a Sudan city, El Obeid; and another about an African country, WHAT I SAW IN MALI. Another entitled, IS THE WORLD ENTERING A NEW YEAR GEARED TO THE SAME TIME? describes time reckoning systems. There is discussion of trends in Western films. In a section called SMALL KNOWLEDGE there is a report on the nations that have diplomatic relations with China; and an item entitled U.S. SEIZES STRATEGIC MATERIALS IN AFRICA. Three short "humorous" items and an article called MAN IN THE NEWS: THANOM KITTIKACHORN OF THAILAND complete the offerings. There are only a few illustrations in this issue. The front cover has a photograph of Chou En-lai and Foreign Minister Chen Yi posing with President Gamel Abdel Nasser of the United Arab Republic; inside of this cover are four pictures showing views from Ghana. On the back cover appear five pictures about Guinea and inside this cover are four pictures from Mali. Inside the magazine there is a map of Africa illustrating those states that have won independence, and those under white "domination." There are a few cartoons and dim halftones illustrating the text material.

Chung-kuo Ching-nien, Periodical for Youth

Chung-kuo Ching-nien, or *Chinese Youth* is the principal youth magazine (Fig. 12.6). Also a semimonthly, its size and format resemble that of *World Affairs.* This periodical and *Chung-hsueh Sheng* (High School Student) together in 1955 accounted for almost one million per issue circulation. The magazine deals principally with the activities of the millions of younger people, not neglecting their ideological "education." Examination of the July 1, 1965, issue reveals the now-familar theme: The editorial headed CHINESE PEOPLE MUST LIBERATE TAIWAN—U.S. BANDITS, GET OUT OF TAIWAN! which devotes most of its 28 pages to the proposition that the United States is occupying Taiwan. In a related article the writer states that China will not excuse the atrocious crimes the "U.S. imperialists" are committing in Taiwan. The article says the United States has established a military base in Taiwan and is aiding Chiang's clique to invade the mainland. Four other articles, totaling 12 pages, are devoted to a campaign to promote the study of Mao's books, a campaign launched by a production brigade in Kansu commune. There is an installment of a serial novel entitled *Blood Dyes Three Stones,* which describes how the capitalists exploited young apprentices. This fiction serial is to be used for "class struggle education," the overline states. There is the regular semimonthly talk on ideology, the essence of which is the importance of helping those comrades who fall out of the marching columns to catch up. The talk also suggests helping those who make mistakes.

The front cover of this issue has a many-colored photograph of a happy group—men and women delegates representing minority nationalities meeting at a conference in Chinghai Province all dressed in colorful native costumes. The back cover is a line drawing poster in color showing a strong young farmer scooping up a handful of golden grain. The caption says "Work Hard for a Big Harvest Yield." The inside covers include a layout of pictures illustrating the campaign to study Mao's books and a song with its musical notes on the same campaign theme. The song starts with this line: "For the Revolution you have to start with Mao's books!"

The pages are illustrated with small drawings, but the editors of this publication have been wise enough not to try zinc etchings or halftones on poor grade newsprint. There are no commercial advertisements.

Fig. 12.5. Article from the January, 1966, English-language edition of **China Pictorial** shows how US anti-Vietnamese war demonstrations were handled by the Communist press. Lead-off picture is of "thousands of Americans from 40 states in a march of protest at the White House November 27, 1965, carrying flags of the National Front for Liberation (left) and the Vietnam Democratic Republic (right)." The spread (opposite) shows 50,000 Americans at the Washington Monument to protest "the aggressive policy of the Johnson government in Vietnam." Other pictures show marchers in a New York parade, draft-card burners, Stanford University students signing up to send blood to North Vietnam, and demonstrators stopping a troop train and picketing Gen. Maxwell Taylor, "'ambassador' to the South Vietnam puppet regime."

Specialized cultural magazines (Fig. 12.7) cover a wide variety of subjects from art to physical education—all promoting Chinese superiority in these fields.

Hung-chi (Red Flag), the Party Theoretical Journal

The leading theoretical magazine *Hung-chi* (Red Flag) is a monthly launched by the Central Committee of the Chinese Communist party in 1958 (Fig. 12.8). The regime claims that 1,980,000 subscriptions to this magazine had been received by the time the first issue came out. It is the same size as *Chinese Youth,* but printed on better quality paper with no illustrations. Except for lettering in red on the covers, the 54-page magazine is entirely in black and white. The lead article of the October, 1965, issue is written by Defense Minister Lin Piao and is published to commemorate the twentieth anniversary of Japan's defeat in World War II. The heading says LONG LIVE THE PEOPLE'S WAR OVER JAPAN. The writer reveals and explains the reasons why the Communists could win the war over Japan in this manner: The anti-Japanese war was a people's war directed by the party and Mao; the Marxist-Leninist political objectives were carried out; and the Com-

The American People Are Speaking Out!

Fig. 12.6. Two magazines devoted to Communist education of youth are (left) **Zhongguo Quingnian** (Chinese Youth) and **Shiao Peng You** (Little Friend). **Zhongguo Quingnian** (earlier phonetic spelling was **Chung-kuo Ching-nien)** carries only line drawings and text, although the covers often carry photographs and are in color. Detail from a back cover (above) is a typical campaign poster and slogan "Prepare and struggle for a big harvest." **Shiao Peng You** is for a younger reader and is filled with instructive illustrations and text that carries a heavy load of Communist dogma indoctrination.

munist troops were the people's soldiers who executed the strategy and tactics of a people's war planned by Mao. In closing, the article urges the waging of a people's war against American imperialism and labels Khrushchev's revisionism a "rebel" in this people's war.

A second article discusses somewhat vaguely the abstract uses of dialectical materialism in technical renovation by a factory worker. Things he should know: smallness and bigness are not absolute qualities; smallness can become bigness, and bigness can become small; to know and not to know—through Mao's teachings, working persistently, and experimentation one can proceed from not knowing to knowing; difficulty and easiness—difficulty draws attention, for it is so hard to solve, but easiness, being easy, does not draw attention; failure and success—success comes from failure. A third item is a philosophic, scientific discussion of how the universe (the cosmos) is evolving. A performance by an armed propaganda team is related in another item which tells how a female team member located in a Japanese occupation area during the war was able to convince the squad leader of quisling troops to lead his men to defect to the Red Army. *Red Flag* carries no commercial advertising. Some of its issues carry poetry.

There is little in the basic themes of Communist Chinese newspaper and magazine content that differs markedly from that of the now-familiar Soviet Communist press. While both appear to function on the assumption that any means is justified by the ends to be achieved, it is apparent that the Chinese press is in some respects more dogmatic in its extremes, more militant, more sensational, more obsessed with hatred for the United States, perhaps more biased, heavy-handed, and one-sided in its depiction of facts, events, and their context. Although here and there is evidence of a lighter and more artistic touch in the Chinese media than in the Soviet media to relieve the dullness of trite themes and repetition, this hardly makes it more palatable. There is some indication that Communist definitions have not entirely erased traces of the Western concept of news as the reporting of events, a heritage of the Chinese press's period of Western influence. There is also present in most of the content, particularly that of the magazines, an incredible naïveté, reminiscent of the sterile, ascetic morality of the Soviet media, as if the media were talking to children. Through it all the Western reader perceives a mysticism in the exaggerated exaltation of Mao's personality, exceeded only perhaps by the opposite extreme of hatred toward the United States.

1 2

Fig. 12.8. The bimonthly **Shih-chieh Chi-shih** (World Affairs) (1) features on its cover a photograph of Foreign Minister Chou En-lai with United Arab Republic President Gamal Abdel Nasser during his African visit. A major story in this issue is a "survey" of the world scene for 1963 with predictions for 1964. The predictions conclude that US imperialism around the world is in trouble from within and without and is in a rapidly deteriorating condition. **Hung-chi** (Red Flag) (2) is the major theoretical journal of the Chinese Communist Party. The September, 1965, issue features a lead article by Defense Minister Lin Piao commemorating the twentieth anniversary of the defeat of Japan. Lin reveals why the "Communists could win this war over Japan: It was a 'people's war' directed by the party and Mao Tse-tung." The article urges waging a similar "people's war" against American imperialism and labels Khrushchev's revisionism a "rebel" in this kind of war. The table of contents and the first page of the lead article are shown on the opposite page (3) and (4).

> . . . broadcasting should promote the propaganda of the Great Leap Forward. Radio broadcasting must carry out propaganda for agriculture and industry . . . . Broadcasting is allowed to criticize but its primary function is to encourage. . . . Broadcasting should put more stress on . . . the popularization of science and technology . . . [stations should] . . . also broadcast dialectical method, current affairs, and logic. . . . We should adopt three levels of broadcasting programs dealing with literature and art. First, good traditional, local drama. Second, good modern drama, songs, and literature. Third, programs which relate literature and art to the ongoing task of the nation. Though it may be difficult to have high quality in the third program, it is necessary to do so.[4]

This appears, as it emerges in the form of radio programming, to be a 3-dimensional design in programming aimed at dif-

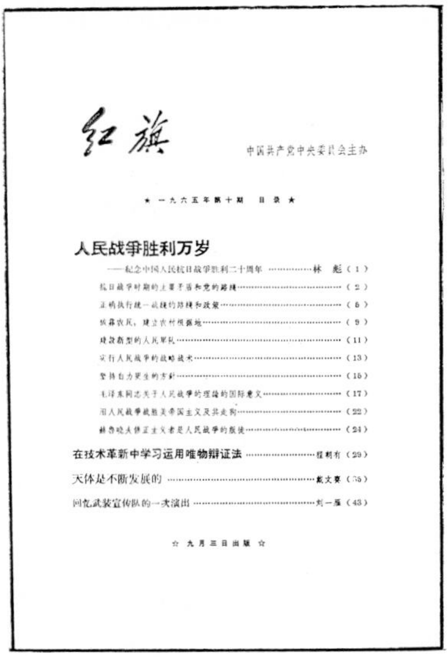

红旗

中国共产党中央委員会主办

★ 一九六五年第十期　目录 ★

☆ 九月三日出版 ☆

3

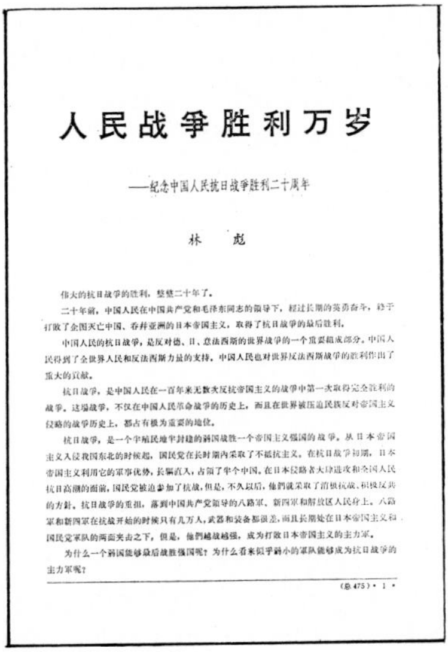

人民战争胜利万岁

——纪念中国人民抗日战争胜利二十周年

林　彪

偉大的抗日战争的胜利，整整二十年了。

二十年前，中国人民在中国共产党和毛泽东同志的領导下，經过長期的英勇奋斗，終于打败了企图灭亡中国、吞并亚洲的日本帝国主义，取得了抗日战争的最后胜利。

中国人民的抗日战争，是反对德、日、意法西斯的世界战争的一个重要組成部分。中国人民得到了全世界人民和反法西斯力量的支持，中国人民也对世界反法西斯战争的胜利作出了重大的貢献。

抗日战争，是中国人民在一百年来无数次反抗帝国主义的战争中第一次取得完全胜利的战争。这場战争，不仅在中国人民革命战争的历史上，而且在世界被压迫民族反对帝国主义侵略的战争历史上，都占有极为重要的地位。

抗日战争，是一个半殖民地半封建的弱国战胜一个帝国主义强国的战争。从日本帝国主义入侵我国东北的时候起，国民党在長时期內采取了不抵抗主义。在抗日战争初期，日本帝国主义利用它的軍事优势，長驅直入，占領了半个中国。在日本侵略者大肆进攻和全国人民抗日高潮的面前，国民党被迫参加了抗战，但是，不久以后，他們就采取了消极抗战、积极反共的方針。抗日战争的重担，落到中国共产党領导的八路軍、新四軍和解放区人民身上。八路軍和新四軍在抗战开始的时候只有几万人，武器和装备都很差，而且長期处在日本帝国主义和国民党軍队的两面夹击之下，但是，他們越战越强，成为打败日本帝国主义的主力軍。

为什么一个弱国能够最后战胜强国呢？为什么看来似乎弱小的軍队能够成为抗日战争的主力軍呢？

（总475）· 1 ·

4

ferent intellectual levels and cultural tastes of the population, similar to the British Broadcasting Corporation's three programs. The first group of programs is designed for the masses, having a large entertainment base, but also carrying the heaviest political propaganda loading of the three. The second program series, for audiences with middle levels of taste, schedules greater amounts of classical music, lectures, and so-called educational programs. The third level differs little from the second in structure, but carries more of the same.

A Central People's Broadcasting Station schedule reported by Liu for September 2, 1963, showed approximately 30 per cent of air time out of a 20-hour daily schedule devoted to news and current affairs, 25 per cent to cultural, scientific, and educational programs, and 45 per cent to musical programs, primarily folk music, dancing, and opera. A schedule of the same station for December 1, 1965, showed approximately the same kind of distribution. But analysis of the daily programs of the Central People's Television Broadcasting Station in Peking for the six days from Tuesday, December 7, to Sunday, December 12, 1965, indicated considerable variation from day to day and some general labeling, as if specific program content had not been finally decided on when the program was released for print. The television station goes on the air each weekday evening at 6:30 and signs off between

10 and 10:30 or slightly earlier. On the Sunday evening, December 12, 1965, telecasting began at 7 o'clock. There are 10-minute telecasts of foreign news, 10-minutes of domestic news, documentary films, movies, and live shows staged in Peking or in Sian, Shanghai, Shantung, and other cities. There are children's programs and occasional political talks. Adjustments made since 1957 reflect some deference to audience appeal and the lengthening broadcasting day. It must not be supposed that the segments of air time assigned to nonpolitical content are devoid of political and ideological implications. On the contrary, cultural content is carefully selected to drive home the desired socialist lessons, though perhaps in a more subtle, indirect way than that of the news. In recent years changes in programming have been characterized by increasing stress on folk music and other popular art forms.

News programs cover the Central Government's plans, utterances, and achievements, but ignore the failures, both at home and in international relations. The nation's economic growth is reported in every category from farming to industrial output to transportation and distribution. Domestic shortcomings are aired when the blame can be attributed to other than the top party brass. The lower echelon officials, the bureaucracy, and the amorphous general public come in for a share of the faultfinding. Natural causes such as drought or mythical "flies in the ointment of socialist realism" such as the "imperialistic warmongers" are also held up for retribution when these causes can be exploited. Except on special occasions foreign coverage is limited largely to news of the Communist world with stress on eastern Europe and the Soviet Union. Africa and the uncommitted countries of Asia and Latin America receive some attention. The United States and the Western democracies are sparsely covered, and when they are treated the emphasis is highly selective in order to present only facts, half-truths, or outright fictions which support the Communist interpretation of events or reveal the worst side of life in non-Communist countries. Science broadcasting stresses such practical matters as the need to apply scientific knowledge in crop production; in socialist industrialization, manufacturing and distribution; in conservation of natural resources; and in transportation. Discussions, lectures, and readings characterize the literary programs. Material selected for its philosophical and political themes may range from ancient classical to modern Chinese writings, both poetry and prose. Literary presentations are for a special audience of artists and writers and therefore are especially designed to instruct them not only in the proper political principles and doctrines but also in how to produce works that will meet the regime's approval. Noted authors lecture on literary style and form, the selection of the proper themes for works, and criticize current production, drawing lessons from the "mistakes" authors make. Music over the air is likewise selected for its ideological themes and drama consists mostly of live performances on stage and screen. Like the Soviet broadcast drama, Chinese radio and television drama is not thus far usually created especially for presentation on the media. Children's programs are perhaps more entertaining and less propagandistic than anything else on the air, yet they have their didactic purposes, teaching lessons in patriotism drawn from folklore, historical tradition, and accomplishments in science, engineering, and other fields. Literary selections must be slanted in the correct socialist direction and music must carry revolutionary themes. Even humorous repartee is loaded with slogans. In short, broadcasting is scarcely utilized at all as an entertainment medium—at least not consciously or purposely so.

The Central People's Broadcasting Station makes simultaneous broadcasts for domestic and foreign audiences. Foreign shortwave broadcasts emanate in Indonesian, Vietnamese, Thai, Burmese, English, Korean, Japanese, Cantonese, Mandarin and three other Chinese dialects. The station conducts regular program exchanges with the Soviet Union, Poland, Rumania, Hungary, the German Democratic Republic, Bulgaria, and Czechoslovakia.[5]

CHARACTERISTIC COMMUNICATION THEMES AND BEHAVIOR

In general the dominant mass media themes—indeed the themes for art, music, and literature—are ideological, the always obvious purpose that of indoctrination rather than information. The goals are the achievement of the ideal socialist state and the ultimate development of the ideal socialist man. The press does not hesitate to publish abstract dogma. *Jen-min Jih-pao* has published the complete texts of Mao Tse-tung's theoretical works, such as *On People's Democratic Dictatorship, On Practice,* and *On Contradiction.* It has published verbatim Stalin's *Economic Problems of Socialism in the USSR,* and *Marxism and Linguistics.*[6]

Philosophy is accompanied by its application to the current plan, policy, campaign, or problem of the day.

Basic themes in the international news stress differences with the Soviet Union, but still the need for Communist countries to stick together to resist "encirclement" by the "capitalist enemy." Favorable attributions from the capitalist enemy reflecting credit on the Communist regime in China are sought and widely quoted. Brash flattery of the uncommitted countries replete in the foreign coverage from that part of the world seeks to leave the impression with readers that China is growing in world esteem, especially among "neutral" neighbors of Southeast Asia and Africa.

Domestically the effort is channeled toward the constant application of the regime's policies. In one respect, the formal communication system is utilized somewhat like it was in the days of the Empire to keep fully instructed those members of officialdom and bureaucracy who are located beyond the immediate reach of informal methods. The chief purpose, however, is to achieve a maximum degree of public support of the regime and participation in its program.

Edelstein and Liu analyzed anti-American propaganda in the *People's Daily* during the year 1959 and found that the functional purpose was to promote acceptance of the regime's domestic policy internally and its foreign policy externally. Anti-Americanism was found to be woven deeply into the fabric of the ideology itself, for internally it was needed as a persuasive instrument for social control, and externally it was basic to the long-range strategy of ideological leadership of the Communist bloc and among the new nations.[7] Thus, the anti-United States theme provided a useful device for reaffirmation of the ideology, for a reassessment of the regime's position within the communist world, for stressing constant vigilance, for concentrating on domestic goals, for coping with Soviet policies, for justifying conditions of deprivation at home, and supporting antirightist campaigns, the authors write. An illustration of how the "hate United States" syndrome dominates the behavior of the entire Communist mass media system is illustrated in the history and content of the English-language weekly, *Peking Review,* founded on March 4, 1958. The first issue explained that the *Review* was to be a magazine of Chinese news and views designed to satisfy the "growing interest abroad both in what is happening in China and in the views of New China." The purpose, it said, would be "to promote better understanding and friendship between China and the other countries of the world." [8] The impression was fostered that the magazine would give English-speaking people throughout the world a knowledge of events in China and friendly feelings for the Communist Chinese regime.* Oliphant, after examining earlier issues and comparing them with a sample of 1963 issues, five years later could find little evidence of effort by the editors to advance understanding or to win many friends among the community of nations, least of all the Western democracies. From his study of the *Review's* consistent use of distortions, half-truths, misrepresentations, outright falsehoods, and quotations out of context in reference to the American people and the United States, this researcher drew fifteen themes which together form a composite image. The image is being projected not only to Mainland Chinese but to the English-reading international community in Asia, Latin America, and Africa. In the repetition of symbols, according to Oliphant's analysis, the word "imperialism" stands out as the central focus of Communist Chinese thinking about us. The foregoing analyses of 1964 and 1965 newspapers and magazines in the Chinese language bears out this finding. "This is the picture they see of the United States," Oliphant wrote.

> (1) It is an imperialist nation bent on world conquest. (2) It interferes constantly in the internal affairs of other nations. (3) It is a nation with few friends in the world. (4) It is a nation on the decline in prestige and economic strength. (5) It is a nation seeking to subvert and control the newly emerging states of Africa, Asia, and Latin America. (6) It is an advocate of colonialism. (7) It is inferior to the Soviet Union in scientific achievement. (8) It desires to hold a nuclear monopoly in the Western world. (9) It is engaged in a deadly struggle with its allies for "spheres of influence." (10) It is the enemy of the people of underdeveloped nations. (11) It is a nation whose capital city is so filled with crime that its streets are not safe. (12) It is filled with racial strife and oppression of the Negro. (13) It is a hypocritical nation. (14) It is more interested in profit than in the welfare of its friends. (15) It is a nation of exploiters, even [to the exploitation] of its own children.[9]

The themes are a well-known Communist mass communication technique, a favorite one of the Communist Chinese—arousing mass hatred, righteous indignation, and sympathy for oppressed and deprived classes at home and everywhere. This in turn in-

* The *Peking Review* is being published in French and Spanish, and no doubt will appear in other languages.

spires mass hatred for their alleged oppressors, and lays the psychological groundwork for the people's war.

Campaigns

The usual mass media device for public exhortation is the campaign—one after another to stimulate the continuous series of mass movements. These campaigns are typical of the mass media scene in China from top to bottom. They are a primary force in the succession of reform drives that characterizes Communist society. When the aim is to transform a backward, illiterate, impoverished people into a model of a modern nation, there is so much to be done and the people must ever be spurred to greater achievement. Campaigns have been conducted to collectivize agriculture; to institute a system of communes; to promote the practice of austerity in the use of resources; to increase production in each and every sphere of the economy; to make steel in backyard furnaces; to persuade more intellectuals to join the party; to teach the value of "thought reform"; to encourage experimentation with "new ideas" in literature and the arts; to attack "deviationists" from and "revisionists" of orthodox Leninism-Stalinism; and to promote many similar endeavors. Notable for its vilification was the pure fantasy poured out in the campaign charging the United States with the use of germ warfare in Korea.

A practical illustration of how fast the word filters down from the top to spread out through the nationwide communications network was the campaign to increase pork production started in the fall of 1956. The State Council issued an instruction calling for an increase in pig breeding. This was displayed prominently with an account of how one cooperative had done unusually well with pigs, earning the commendation of Chairman Mao himself. This and other material relating to raising pork almost filled *Jenmin Jih-pao's* first page. The other newspapers and the radio network throughout the country carried the identical messages, and in due time there was an increase in pig production.[10] Most concrete aspects of communist life can be manipulated in the same manner by the leaders through the media. In explaining matters of abstract dogma or in gaining sincere acceptance of complex ideas, the results are neither as productive nor as easily measured.

Propaganda campaigns are decided on and planned carefully in some cases as much as a year before the first publicity starts to flow. Party leaders and professional communication workers at all levels are instructed in advance. During the campaign's progress each step is reviewed, and after its completion the results are weighed, the performance criticized. Press activity is officially censured in *People's Daily* under the heading SURVEY AND COMMENTS ON THE PRESS.

Since propaganda themes at all times must adhere strictly to party Line and since that fickle Line, like its Soviet counterpart, has been known to shift abruptly, the uses of inconsistency are served best by the authoritative weather vane, the *People's Daily*. Newspapers of lesser authority are constrained to await the official word before venturing to relay political matter when change in the Line may be involved. Even after the change has been interpreted, the provincial and local media are slow to express their own views.

Concepts of News, Truth, and Criticism

As the preceding analysis indicates, the Chinese Communists define news very much as the Soviet Communists define it. Communist-style news is a continuing report of the social process instead of a cumulative record of current history or a timely, objective, accurate, and truthful account of an event of public interest. Accidents, disasters, and crimes, for example, are not systematically reported unless they can be used to teach a lesson. Factual information plays its part but the facts must add up to the "correct" viewpoint. News communication considered worthy of dissemination must have a viewpoint. If a news report happens to display qualities of objectivity, accuracy, or timeliness, it possesses them because they help serve the purpose, or at least do not interfere with it. Such Western-style attributes of news are incidental to the primary purpose of the mass media. News communication, in sum, is whatever is believable or can be made believable which at the same time is calculated to serve the best interests of party and people. The phrase "bests interests of the people" in actual practice means "best interests of the regime." Truth, of course, is Marxist truth as interpreted by the party in terms of "Socialist realism." Viewed in this light, the unnamed leading Chinese newspaper executive was perhaps not entirely insincere when he told Hitoshi Wada of the *Asahi Shimbun,* Osaka, Japan, that "Reporting of truth is guaranteed in Communist China. The reporters enjoy full freedom to report what they believe is right in view of the interests of the people and world peace." [11]

Western concepts of freedom and truth are as spurious in analyzing Communist media behavior in the areas of opinion and criticism as they are in news and information. The range of permissible opinion or independent thought that can be expressed in the media is confined within the limits of the orthodox line and to matters which, in the editor's judgment, cannot chance to be construed as deviating. To stray from the narrow spectrum of permissive comment is denounced as ideological looseness which at worst becomes a crime. In such a situation the reticence of editors to comment at all is understandable. The mass media therefore usually behave in the following manner when it comes to the opinion function: (1) refrain from venturing their own opinion, particularly on ideological and political matters; (2) broadcast or reprint *Jen-min Jih-pao's* editorials expressing party and government views; (3) choose safe nonpolitical topics for original editorial treatment; or (4) publish no editorial at all. The wide extent to which the *People's Daily* is parroted was indicated by a 168-day survey of *Kuang-ming Jih-pao* covering the first six months of 1954.[12] During this period 19 editorials from *Jen-min Jih-pao* and 7 from *Pravda* were reprinted, as compared with 31 original editorials and 111 days of no editorial comment. This was the performance of a large national daily. Since the period chosen for examination was one during which the National Constitution was being written and discussed, this national daily's reluctance to comment is unusually significant. *Ta Kung Pao,* whose editorial leadership made it respected during pre-Communist days, published no editorials on 70 of the 168 days, used 23 of *Jen-min Jih-pao's* editorials, 8 of *Pravda's,* and 75 of its own. The national dailies do better in this respect than the provincials. The Chekiang Province daily published only 12 editorials of all kinds during the 6-months period. The Central organs complained about such a poor showing on the part of the lesser organs, but the complaints had little effect in stimulating a greater volume of comment. During September, 1956, *Kuang-ming Jih-pao* published only one editorial on domestic politics, an editorial with the soul-stirring title of UNITY AND PROGRESS, ONE AND ALL, UNDER THE LEADERSHIP OF THE CHINESE COMMUNIST PARTY. Of the other 20 published during the month, 9 dealt with education, 8 with international affairs, and 3 with relief work. It appears that the narrow limits of permissible comment, together with such factors discussed below as regimented fear and lack of professional skill, combine to impede the editorial writing art.[13]

Another form of comment, popular self-criticism in the media stream, appears in the form of letters ostensibly from the rank and file of the people, from a huge corps of worker-peasant correspondents, and from the top leaders. On the surface the existence of such an elaborate mechanism for encouraging grass-roots criticism gives the impression that all and sundry may freely speak and that national policy and program are always open to popular review. The opposite is nearer the truth: criticism from outside the party is not tolerated, and, of course, those with alien views have no channels open to them. To permit the publication of this kind of criticism runs against the rigid belief that it would undermine the common cause. Criticism from below, from all except the Central Government and party officials, is implicitly confined to trivial or innocuous subjects, or subjects which aid the execution of policy such as exposure of corruption, inefficiency, or waste in the bureaucracy. Self-criticism then, like editorial comment, must never be directed at leaders, party, policy, or basic doctrine. The most severe criticism that appears in the public media originates with the leaders themselves, the makers and administrators of policy, and there is no higher authority to hold them to task. When a journalist companion of Robert Guillain (of Paris' *Le Monde*) asked Chinese writers why they never criticized members of the government, they simply replied, "Oh, because their policy is always correct." [14] These writers naïvely told Guillain, as if it were the normal state of affairs, about how books were censored. Manuscripts are always submitted to a committee of writers, two-thirds of whom are Communist, they explained. After "thorough" discussion, which in this case was so thorough it lasted four days, the book had to be rewritten completely.

Correspondence and reader letters serve the regime as they do in the Soviet Union in ways other than criticism. Chinese Communist leaders like to have it appear that all mass movements arise spontaneously from the ranks of the people and to create this illusion, nonprofessional correspondents and readers' letters are used after the manner of their Soviet prototypes. The correspondents may report the widespread upsurge of voluntary mass meetings in support of a cause; then volumes of reader letters endorse the drive. This makes it appear that the government is merely acceding to the people's wishes, the pressure of public sentiment. Afterwards, the regime takes the action it wanted to take all along, but such action then can, without facetiousness, claim to have been precipitated by public demand.

The correspondence and letters columns also serve another role valuable to the government—the escape-valve function for the irritations and frustrations of the people. Though this kind of material is carefully supervised and circumscribed, the man in the street can air his difficulties, and occasionally as a result of publicity something is done to remedy the situation. At the same time a degree of relief is afforded simply by the act of airing the complaint. The columns are filled with the outpourings of a people whose every move is dictated by a faceless bureaucracy. The newspapers, besides supervising, censoring, and in some cases originating such letters, investigate complaints, and if they are found not to be concerned with interdicted subjects, attempt to assuage feelings and do what they can to relieve tensions.

In general, it must be said that Chinese media performance, much like that of the Soviet Union, is monotonous, repetitious, and dull because it must be heavily stamped with the Communist party's ideological imprint. Although the presses pour forth a glut of messages and the media are different and varied, what they say is essentially monolithic. In most of those segments of the media system the propaganda is as obvious, heavy-handed, and direct in approach as is Soviet media content—and virtually as unrelieved by subtle or suggestive touches. Comics, light feature material, or advertising are not permitted to infringe upon the serious demands of the business at hand. Allowing for some exceptions in both countries, it seems that Chinese media have perhaps been more successful than their Communist Soviet counterparts in injecting mass appeal techniques into their communication products. Schramm noted the emphasis on human interest.[15] This slightly lighter tone, though seldom without its moral preachments, may be attributed to Chinese native artistry in expression and perhaps to traces of Western press influence. But so uniform is the communications message, it would seem that the simplest method in both countries would be to publish one big newspaper for all—one that because of its official content but not its ideological slant and propagandistic purpose—would resemble the old Peking gazettes. But such a plan would negate the well-nourished image of a "public" media system the regime seeks to perpetuate;

namely, that the system is really a people's press designed specifically to serve all aspects of society. Such a system must needs consist of many kinds of specialized media and of general appeal media as well. At any rate media saturation with economic and political material to the virtual exclusion of other things assures that the average consumer of media content can find little else to which he can give attention. He looks to subject matter for variety, not to the cast or the slant.

Professional Communicators

The creative barrenness and generally poor literary quality that has characterized media content in the past may be a reflection in part of the critical shortage of skilled personnel to man the media. The early and immediate demand for the expansion of Communist media placed a strain on the supply of professionally qualified workers who at the same time could be loyal cadres and teachers. The sharp reduction in 1949 in the number of non-Communist media no doubt increased the number of available journalists who might have helped supply the demand, but these did not qualify as Communists. The regime's early alienation of the intellectuals and its subsequent Pavlovian policy toward the intellectuals of alternate periods of obsequious cultivation and intimidation has further deprived the mass media of talent. Thus the regime has failed largely to stimulate the enthusiasm and cooperation of many among the very group of educated elite[16] it must rely on most for the specialized skills that are as sorely needed to build a professionally competent corps of communication workers as they are to build a modern nation.

In their attempt to supply the communication system with well-trained professionals, the Communists have concocted a mixture of purely technical training with proper ideological conditioning. A few of the great Chinese universities of the pre-Communist era with their strong liberal traditions of emphasis on philosophy and broad fields of knowledge turned out broadly trained journalists. But the university system was reorganized by the Communists with a view toward more effective political control. Different professional areas of specialization were assigned to each institution, and there now are colleges devoted to comprehensive education, polytechnical education, agriculture and forestry, the arts, medicine, finance and economics, political science and law, etc. Curricula and texts were revised at the same time, with stress on principles of dialectical and historical determinism, the writings of Marx, Lenin, Stalin, and Mao, and training designed to teach political orientation, to inculcate social consciousness, and to substitute new values for old. One aspect of the value reorientation program, for example, was the requirement that teachers and students must spend a third of their time at manual labor; the purpose was to drive home the lesson that the intellectual under the Communist regime is no longer a member of the highly respected privileged class for which it was undignified to waste time engaging in physical work. The new higher education for professional communicators, in sum, is designed to produce workers who are first thoroughly grounded in the political ideology and secondly trained in specialized persuasive communication techniques, but lacking in broad, general education.

13 ★

ELEMENTS IN COMMUNICATIONS EFFECT

THE MASSIVE COMMUNICATION EFFORT, both formal and informal, is totalitarian from concept to execution, from organization to tactic and technique, from inspiration to goal. Besides print and air waves, every possible channel or tool is employed. The message is all-pervasive everywhere except in the least populous sections. "The word" blares from loudspeakers wherever captive audiences may be harangued—on trains, buses, boats, and planes in transit; in factory, mill, mine, shop, and school. Slogans seep into songs schoolgirls sing, wave from banners on buildings, and restaurant calendars display dogma as if it is to be consumed along with food. The Line appears in poster art, painting, sculpture, poetry, and prose. Commercial displays in store windows and exhibits, and even the traditional tales village storytellers relate have their propaganda slant. Diaries are printed with quotations from the magic words of Marx and Mao. Slogans have been knitted into women's garters.[1]

CAPTURING MINDS AND HEARTS

These represent the outward signs of the gigantic revolutionary struggle that is being waged with fervor to remold the thinking and reorient the values of almost a quarter of the human race. This struggle for the minds and hearts of a whole nation extends to the grass-roots village level on a scale unprecedented and is the most ambitious of its kind in history.[2] Because the Communist Chinese aims and techniques of mass persuasion and conversion are in some respects unique as aspects of a State communication system, and may well exceed Soviet mass persuasion achievements, they should be examined in some detail. Indeed so single-minded is its purpose and its directed effort that the success or failure of the whole communications system may well be judged in terms of the success or failure of thought-control methods.

Thought Control

The Chinese have developed thought-reform techniques beyond the scale of any other country. "Other Communist countries have, to be sure, used elaborate propaganda techniques and various psychological pressures," observed Lifton, "but never with thought reform's meticulous organization, its depth of psychological probing, or its national scale. Nowhere else has there been such a mass output of energy directed toward changing people.[3] Sources and origins of Chinese thought reform are complex, stemming from a synthesis of Russian Communist indoctrination, with its confession and purge techniques, and certain Confucian precepts of traditional Chinese culture.[4] As brought out in Chapter 1, thought control was attempted in the Iron Code of Admiral Shishkov as early as 1826, long before the advent of Communism. Communist dichotomous concepts of morality are combined with Confucian concepts of self-cultivation, personal sincerity, modesty, obedience, and acceptance of social position. Thought reform also draws upon the traditional Chinese art of human relationships practiced for centuries in the family circle. As modern thought-reform theory and method are descended from both Western Communism and traditional China, they also inherited from both cultures the worst aspects of rigid dogmatism and absolutist tyranny in human manipulation. Communists in China, however, in their urgent program for the here and now, needed to nullify the traditional Chinese practice of restraint and dispassionate dignity with its belief in the quiet cultivation of individual tranquility and social harmony—concepts alien to Communist goals. In place of the cult of restraint, the Communists have imported and substituted the cult of enthusiasm, which perhaps as a reaction to centuries of restraint has flourished extensively in China. Lifton writes, ". . . in breaking out of its traditional cult of restraint, while retaining its old penchant for the reordering of human emotions, China has created a cult of enthusiasm of such proportions that it must startle even the most immoderate Christian or Communist visionary." [5]

The power of motivation in thought-reform strategy relies partly on negative police-enforced, suppression-fear psychology, and partly on positive persuasion-indoctrination techniques. The police control methods used fit the familiar Stalinist Soviet and Nazi patterns, but the Chinese Communists go deeper into the social strata to invade private lives and personal thoughts more insidiously and more persistently—and in some ways more mentally and emotionally destructive—but perhaps less physically brutal than the worst Soviet or Nazi practices. The positive organization of the population into minute subgroups for study and work makes it simpler for negative police controls to enforce conformity, suppress or assuage explosive tensions, discover and punish deviation, and bring group pressure to bear on the expression of unpopular or undesirable attitudes. In cities, for example, every 15 to 40 households are grouped into residents' teams under local police supervision.

The Surveillance System

Residents' teams, operating under the guise of security regulations, keep the people of their neighborhood under watchful surveillance, scrutinizing all activities. They are authorized and empowered to investigate and report not only behavior but also attitudes. The organized surveillance system stretches from Peking to remote villages to remind the people that their government is omnipresent, probably omniscient, and usually omnipotent. The village leader is the lowest, but perhaps the most important official in the hierarchical chain of coercive control over the country. A person is chosen who, because of his community standing, is already naturally influential. After being appointed by the party he becomes the constant eyes and ears of the Peking regime and the symbol of its authority in his area. Reuters correspondent David Chipp has portrayed this strategic symbol in the person of Aitik, the veterinary surgeon of a nomad cooperative a day's ride from Urumchi, Sinkiang Province, Northwestern China.[6] Aitik's qualifications for party responsibility include his literacy, his wealth (which in his community is judged by the number of livestock he owns), his profession which brings him into contact with most of the native herdsmen, and his ethnic origin (he is a Kazakh, a small minority group) which makes him more influential with his group than a native Chinese in the same position could be. Aitik is the only Communist party member in his community. His tent is the nerve center of communication and the end of the propaganda transmission belt from Peking. His tent possesses the only radio receiver in the area. There are no telephone or telegraph lines. The nearest party headquarters is in Urumchi, a day's ride away. Urumchi, itself is two days by air from Peking. A railroad had been constructed by 1962,[7] but before that time the land route from Peking was traveled by automobile or caravan. Mail arrives in Aitik's tent twice a week in good weather, and he distributes newspapers to those who can read and reads them to the many who can't. Aitik's wife serves the community as nurse, first-aid attendant, and midwife. Aitik and his wife can diagnose psychological disaffection and ideological aberration while ministering to the physical ills of cattle and people. At the same time they make known the regime's wishes and policies.

In addition to Aitik and thousands like him who openly wear the garments of authority, there are thousands of other more covert informers on whom the Communists have bestowed the honorable label "patriotic and vigilant citizens." These people have been taught that it is laudable behavior in the new society to spy and report "wrongdoing" and "wrongthinking" on the part of friend, neighbor, or even kin. In mutual criticism sessions at group meetings children have been known to denounce parents for trading in the black market or for other small digressions from socially accepted and approved norms of behavior. Brother may secretly report to the police such minor malefactions in the conduct of brother or sister, and thus avoid indentification as an informer. These are the amateur vultures who prey upon freedom of thought and privacy. Their work supplements the work of key party men like Aitik and that of a third power, the secret police who back them up and lurk mysteriously in the background.

Communication by and to Subgroups

With its threads for surveillance, reporting, and coercion woven throughout the society's fabric, the regime applies the positive techniques of persuasion to the goals of mind conditioning and social change. Here again the fragmentation of the population into thousands of groups serves the purpose. The *hsueh hsi* subgroups, the units in the nationwide group system for organized study and work, have become an established feature of Communist Chinese society.[8] Yu reports that the Shih Chi Commune of Tsao Hsien, consisting of 21,000 persons in more than 5,000 families, had 1,688 cultural organizations. These groups range across the spectrum of community interest from basketball and playground groups to night schools, to kiddie dancing teams, to art and literary circles, to newspaper reading groups, to people's "fun" centers.[9] The study group movement extends to the workers in every factory, office, and store, to soldiers and to students. They attempt to sweep into their membership every person within reach. Under party leadership groups study approved materials, discuss and debate, and engage in party assigned tasks. In their meetings they seek to be "liberated" from all ideas and ideologies deemed to be "reactionary," "hostile," or "erroneous." A basic enforcement weapon in the group process of ideological transformation is physical labor. With this tool the individual is taught by experience the "wisdom and dignity" of productive work through physical exertion.

Except in the remote, sparsely populated areas, almost every one belongs to one or more of these subgroups which purposely cut across occupation, age, hobby, and recreation categories. All groups are units of the centrally directed nationwide federations organized by interest classifications. Through subgroup study and work units the regime dispenses its indoctrination and propaganda. Through them active supporters are chosen as leaders or put to work to set examples, while others are subjected to systematic, organized group pressure to conform.

In the 1950s specific segments of the population from time to time became the objects of specially directed mass campaigns which have followed one another with short lulls between, ever since the Communists took control. Each campaign has taken on the characteristics of a gigantic emotional binge in which heavy propaganda guns amassed by the regime aim at the particular minority group and fire relentlessly, all the while mobilizing through the mass media opinion to support the cause. The campaign of denunciation closes with the public confessions of the transgressors sometimes after undergoing periods of ideological rectification. In the two most important campaigns against landlords, capitalists, and "counter-revolutionaries" there were executions, estimated variously into the hundreds of thousands and perhaps millions.[10] Though some executions were secretly carried out, others were public, done after public trials at which mass regime-organized demonstrations reinforced the findings of guilt. Thus the regime publicly stressed what it called "education of the masses." Since the earlier violence, the process of thought control has been directed at obtaining public conversion, or at least submission. An example of this kind of "ideological remolding" campaign was the campaign directed against university professors and other intellectuals, including journalists in 1951–1952. During this period China witnessed the spectacle of its venerated professors of leading universities engaging in debasing self-criticism, mutual recrimination, and character assassination. These orgies were climaxed by the publication of lengthy confessions from the most famous and nationally respected among them. Typical was the confession of Peking University's Law College dean who apologized for the "serious mistake of holding on to my views." [11] Cruel and degrading treatment for the scholar class of a nation that for centuries has been taught to value and honor men of intellect and things of the mind! This incident illustrates the way a sense of guilt and a feeling of shame are used to coerce.[12] In subsequent years the Communists have conducted similar campaigns against other social classes with deviant ideologies, such as the bourgeois, the merchants and industrialists, and others.

Problems in Thought Reform

A crucial problem of thought reform characteristic of any totalitarian political order—a problem that has been faced from time to time but not solved satisfactorily either by the Soviet or the Chinese Communist regimes—is the one of maintaining orthodoxy without stifling creative thinking, of making maximum utilization of the country's intellectual resources without generating explosive tensions, of stimulating productive participation in place of passive neutrality. In China many intellectuals had assisted the regime in the revolution and in establishing the people's government, only to be told less than two years later by Chou En-lai that they should remold themselves to fit the needs of the State.[13] After the ideological reform campaign, intellectuals who wanted to survive had no choice but to outwardly conform and follow the party leadership. Inward hostility and frustration led to apathy. By early 1956 Chou apologized personally for the regime's treatment of the intellectuals,[14] noted how in the early days of the Republican revolution intellectuals and Communists shared ideals, and now the cooperation of the intellectual was acknowledged as essential for the social and technical development of the nation. Nonconformist thought on the part of intellectuals would be treated more tolerantly in the future, Chou promised, provided it did not militate against the people's interests. Life became a bit easier for intellectuals. They were granted free work time away from political meetings and other nonprofessional activities. Research scientists and professors received more generous food allowances, more freedom of choice in their work assignments, and other privileges.

Chou's relaxed policy toward intellectuals appeared to be underscored a few months later by Mao's promulgation of his now famous slogan, "Let a hundred flowers bloom (or blossom); let a hundred schools (of thought) contend"[15] in a speech on May 2, 1956, before the Supreme State Conference. Mao's thesis was repeated a short time later by the director of the Propaganda Department, Lu Ting-yi, in an official speech to scientists, journalists, and writers meeting in Peking. Lu urged all engaged in intellectual endeavors to raise professional standards by actively participating in productive work that would contribute to advancing the cause. Lu explained that the "hundred flowers" campaign was an effort to draw intellectuals out of their apathy by stimulating a new competitive spirit among them, and even among the general public, but all within the framework of the existing ideological controls. Lu differentiated at length between the kind of freedom intended by the new policy and that enjoyed in China's classical age, or even that advocated in capitalist countries. Classical freedoms do not apply to today's conditions, he said, and besides the thinkers of the earlier age were not aware of the class struggle. Freedom permitted in capitalist countries is not the kind of freedom we mean, either, he said. Freedom in capitalist countries is limited to the minority group. We do not permit freedom to the counterrevolutionary elements. We have democracy and freedom for the people. But the new kind of freedom applies only to certain points of difference between the people themselves. No difference of opinion, for example, can exist on such questions as "love of the fatherland or support of socialism. . . . But ideological differences between materialism and idealism . . . might be openly discussed . . . ," he said.[16]

Lu continued, "In announcing the new policy . . . the Communists had not for a moment relinquished the ideological supremacy of Marxism-Leninism, . . . they were proposing a new method of struggle . . . forced to this by a realization that the old methods of thought reform had not been successful." As Lu candidly admitted, the counterrevolutionary elements "could be suppressed . . . but ideological questions cannot be settled by administrative orders. . . . Only through open debate can materialism overcome idealism step by step." [17]

Although Lu had made it plain that the new freedom was a new tactic in the general strategy and not a reversal of policy, there were some who thought the slogan literally meant what it said, an invitation to engage in free and frank expression, Western-style. After Chairman Mao's February 27, 1957, speech restating the policy and urging public criticism of the regime, those advocating the literal interpretation gained ground. Although few noticed the stipulation, Mao did qualify his statement to provide that no criticsm should be in violation of the Constitution.[18] While the Constitution set forth certain criteria for distinguishing permissible from forbidden criticism, no specific guidelines were enunciated until June 18, 1957, after the short period of freedom had begun to get out of hand.

The Chinese Thaw and Public Criticism

Main developments of the Chinese Thaw, as they affected the mass media, began when Chairman Mao early in 1956 admonished periodical editors to do something about the drab uniformity and dull stolidity of their products. "Many articles are overloaded with party jargons," he warned. They are "unvivid, unimaginative, and unreadable," and editors should strive to do away with such a state of affairs as soon as possible.[19] The *People's Daily* and other organs quickly conceded that the situation, if continued, would seriously impede the media. On July 1, 1956, *Jen-min Jih-pao* announced that it planned to encourage a wider latitude of discussion in its columns, thus leading the movement to make the press more attractive to readers. Its pages became more interesting and readable; satire, an almost nonexistent literary form in Communist China, was introduced into discussions of contemporary affairs; readers were treated to discussions of previously forbidden subjects; and the paper which had built its image as a paragon that could do no wrong published letters criticising it for inaccuracies.[20] Three months later the

People's Daily expressed the opinion that free discussion should take place within the ranks of the party only and not be aired outside.[21]

Notwithstanding the paper's reluctance to see internal party differences bared to the general public, the period of freedom produced a flood of fundamental criticism in the mass media. Criticism was also rife in public speeches and discussions by nonparty intellectuals seeking to break the Communist one-party monopoly, and even within the ranks of loyal Communists themselves. Recurrent themes running through the criticism may be summed up as follows: (1) the Communist party is degenerating into a new privileged, ruling-class oligarchy, exercising a tyranny comparable to that of the Mongols or the Manchus; (2) the regime has done relatively little to improve the people's living conditions, especially the lot of the peasants—indeed, cases were cited in which official blunders had worsened conditions; (3) foreign policy has shown an extreme pro-Soviet alignment when Soviet policy in Asia has been against Chinese interests;[22] (4) certain inherent defects exist in the Communist leadership, including "bureaucracy, sectarianism, and subjectivism"; and (5) the masses of the people who once supported communism are now disenchanted with and do not want it.

The Chinese Thaw began to flourish in the early months of 1957 and reached its peak in the last days of May and the first week of June.[23] The Hungarian uprising and its aftermath had frightened the Communist leadership so that it sought to assuage the discontented elements and release pent-up emotions by further encouraging their "blossoming and contending" policy. Concrete steps were taken in the form of (1) measures to improve living conditions and (2) a rectification campaign within the party to correct abuses; those outside the party were soon invited to join. Mao's February speech admitted that the regime had made certain mistakes and had indulged in certain excesses, mistakes which were now to be corrected not by crude coercive methods but by "painstaking reasoning." Chen writes that the new policy was dictated by hard realism and not moved by any sentimental ideas about freedom and democracy. The objective was "democracy under centralized guidance," within the bounds of "socialist discipline." There were limits to the blooming of the hundred flowers and to areas of contention: Well-disciplined Communists would distinguish carefully between fragrant flowers and poisonous weeds. Those who move beyond the bounds, who abuse their freedom, are counterrevolutionaries and will simply be deprived of their freedom of speech.[24]

But such limitations went unheeded in opposition quarters. Early in May journalists meeting in Shanghai raised loud complaints against party restrictions and interference, and demanded more freedom to comment and criticize. Taking formal action, they asked for the establishment of regular press conferences after the manner of those held in the United States, conferences in which there would be the opportunity for the free play of questions and answers between press representatives and public officials. There were complaints against "pseudo-journalists" holding executive positions on newspapers but working as official censors. There were charges that the Communist press received official information denied non-Communist papers.[25]

Within the next few weeks public criticism became more daring. Ch'u An-p'ing, editor of *Kuang-ming Jih-pao,* attacked Mao Tse-tung himself and Premier Chou En-lai, accusing them and other top party leaders of betraying their promise—pledges given earlier that non-Communist parties would be permitted to take part in the government. The Communist concept of party rule, the "party kingdom," is the reason, the paper said, for "worsening relations between the party and the masses." Lung Yun, vice chairman of the National Defense Council, sharply assailed the Soviet Union. Equally unorthodox criticism, some of it directed at basic ideology, appeared in other organs. Caught up on the orgy of self-examination, the chief Central party organ, *Jen-min Jih-pao,* found itself among the papers that reported a lecture by Professor Ko Pai-chi of the Chinese People's University in Peking, an institution established by the Communists to produce a "new type" of intelligentsia thoroughly grounded in proletarian ideology. Professor Ko's sharp attack included the following statement:

> . . . This country does not belong to the Communist Party alone. . . . If you Communists are working for the general good, all is in order. If not, the masses will kill you and overthrow the regime. This will not be considered as an anti-patriotic act since you will no longer be able to claim to be serving the people. And the downfall of the Communist Party will be far from implying the end of China.[26]

Intellectual leaders of non-Communist parties voiced broad criticisms of the political order—criticisms that appealed to all intellectuals, including journalists and writers, college professors and teachers. Chen summarizes the most frequent themes widely discussed during what he calls "one month of floral splendour," as follows: (1) The role of the "democratic parties" is too subservient and powerless—they are prevented from recruiting members and from advancing their own program; (2) the nonparty members holding government positions were always "assisted" by party members who exercised the real power, making nonparty officials mere figureheads and preserving a facade of nonparty participation in government; (3) there exists wide discrimination in all levels of society between Communists and non-Communists, the latter being treated in all cases as outsiders and denied privileges enjoyed by members; (4) the Communist party is so closely identified with the State that the two are essentially one, the party often exercising State functions usually delegated to State agencies; (5) there is a great need for a system of law to guide leaders and people alike; and (6) abuses resulting from transferring educational administration from the hands of the faculties and skilled educators to unlearned party members should be corrected.[27]

Such outbursts from trenchant critics not only among the nonparty ranks but also from intellectuals within the party's institutions demonstrated how widespread and bitter dissatisfaction with the regime had become. The leadership had not foreseen and was not prepared to tolerate this kind of reaction. The party began its "antirightist" (meaning anti-intellectual) campaign which steadily intensified in the public media. The campaign was followed by the application of party discipline. Premier Chou En-lai, in a report to the National People's Congress on June 26, warned that "right-wing" elements were trying to "drive our country from the path of socialism to the path of capitalism," and "to get our State power away from the vanguard of the working class—away from the leadership of the Communist Party." He noted that "remnants of counterrevolutionaries" are still trying to engage in wrecking activities.[28] The Central Committee condemned *Kuang-ming Jih-pao* and the teachers' journal *Wen-hui Pao* for their bourgeois views and called for a fight against deviationism in the press. Nimbly executing a quick about-face, the *People's Daily* in a vigorous editorial on June 14 did the same. By the end of June *Kuang-ming Jih-pao's* administrative board, its editor,[29] and Chang Po-chun, minister of communications, were fired. Ch'u An-p'ing publicly confessed in July, accusing himself of publishing lies fabricated by non-Communist ex-ministers, of reproducing tendentious news and attempting to instigate disorder. The purge spread to include prominent names in literature and members of the staff of the New China News Agency. Critics were denounced and dismissed from their positions, and pressured to recant. In selected universities more than half of the students were dismissed and sent out to work in the countryside. The non-Communist parties which had enabled the government to claim it was a coalition, were told that in the future they must completely accept Communist leadership, and actively support its causes. Several thousand officials were assigned to "strengthen" the guiding role of the party in educational, cultural, and communications spheres.

Too late to stem the tide, what was purportedly the full text of Mao's February 27th speech was first published on June 18 with "certain additions," according to the New China News Agency's release. The text contained six criteria delimiting the scope of political criticism, and specifying substantially the same conditions as the Constitutional proviso, criteria distinguishing "fragrant flowers from poisonous weeds." These criteria are as follows: (1) Criticism must help unite the people of the various nationalities, not divide them; (2) it must be beneficial, not harmful, to socialist transformation and socialist construction; (3) it must help consolidate, not undermine or weaken, the people's dictatorship; (4) it must help consolidate, not undermine or weaken, democratic centralism; (5) it must tend to strengthen, not cast off or weaken, the leadership of the Communist party; and (6) it must be beneficial, not harmful, to international socialist solidarity and the solidarity of the peace-loving peoples of the world.[30]

Mao doubtless had in mind these standards when he originally uttered his "hundred flowers" statement, and it is probable that he used the phrase as a figure of speech rather than as a serious enunciation of policy. But it was interpreted literally. Nevertheless the six criteria should have clarified, though belatedly, the permissible limits of criticism for even the dullest mentality.

As in other Communist-ruled countries, the Chinese regime in the reaction against Stalinism sought to liberalize the rules somewhat after his death. By the end of 1956, the Chinese Communists seemed to be moving further from Stalinism than the Russians had. The Chinese regime had supported Gomulka in Poland, and at first the press had commented favorably on the Hungarian revolt, but it suddenly changed its line after it learned the Russian viewpoint. Internally the liberalization continued and in the first half of 1957 a surprising degree of free criticism was allowed—even encouraged. There is some evidence that opinions were divided within the high party councils as to the wisdom of this policy. Mao Tse-tung's views in favor of it prevailed over those of the party secretary Liu Shao-chi and his sympathizers. Perhaps Mao misjudged the situation in the belief that greater latitude of criticism of the right sort would have a cathartic effect, perhaps in the hope that he could have a Communist regime confirmed and validated by real popular support. But criticism went too far, indicating to the leaders that their regime must either remain Stalinist or accept far-reaching revisionism; that given a little freedom, the "noxious weeds" remaining from the old society or introduced by foreign contacts would grow faster than the "flowers" of Communist doctrine. The decision was made to swing Chinese policy back to Stalinism.[31] The denunciation of Tito and all forms of revisionism followed in 1958, and by 1961 the Sino-Soviet schism in world communism was evident. After the "rectification program designed to correct erring party members" and purge "rightists" from their ranks, the minor parties and other fringe elements, acting under pressure, launched a "dedication of hearts" campaign in March, 1958—a campaign in which each person eternally surrendered his heart to the party and to socialism. Intellectuals were told that in the future it was not enough merely to contribute their specialized talents. They must now be "both Red and expert." [32]

Thus the pall of enforced silence closed in on the brief period of relaxation that characterized the Chinese Thaw. But not before opposition to the Chinese Communists broke out among nonintellectual groups as well. Organized riots and rebellions which flared up among peasants and students in different parts of the country in 1957 and 1958 had to be forcibly put down.[33]

The Chinese Thaw differed from the Soviet Thaw in a number of ways. It appeared at first to permit and invite a much wider degree of public expression and criticism. The themes expressed were more violently unorthodox, reflected deeper resentment against the regime. Because de facto opposition parties existed in China and not in the Soviet Union, the Chinese movement was on the surface more of an extra-party matter than was the Soviet. Just as the outspoken and subversive criticism was more violent in China, so was the regime's reaction. In no other country except Hungary were the voices of dissent more brutally silenced. And likewise in no other country except Hungary did organized rebellion appear. These differences reflect the less mature, less stable, less successful

Chinese Communist order, its soaring ambitions, its short timetable, the prodigious problems it faces, and the greater discontent among the people.

Since the Thaw; the Personnel Officer

Since the Thaw the effort to capture minds and hearts has been quickened. More than ever the role of study groups in the process of persuasion and conversion has been emphasized. Under skillful guidance they afford a surprising opportunity for the regime in the play of criticism and self-criticism to exploit extensively a sense of personal guilt and fear. Chipp, for example, cites the case of a group of topflight scientists who spent four afternoons a week discussing each other's philosophy of life to make sure all understood the "correct" attitude. "One of them said . . . : 'You see, it is not like ______ (here he mentioned a well-known American university where he had been educated). At ______ our social life was a mixture of dancing and drinking and going to the movies. Here in our social life we criticize one another.' "[34] By nature the Chinese are garrulous and enjoy social interaction, so this kind of group pressure is more insidiously effective than it might be among peoples of more stolid habits. The intellectual of scholarly ways especially finds it very difficult to keep silent when he is urged to be frank in expressing opinion. Group leaders usually find it easy to loosen him up, but if he proves obstinate, group ridicule or ostracism brings him around. Among people like the Chinese, and among other peoples around the world where group acceptance and approval are highly valued, this cunning treatment can be a terribly effective weapon.[35]

No group of intellectuals in the country is more vitally indispensable to the regime than scientists. In such situations their political beliefs should normally be of relatively minor importance, but the society provides the greatest incentives and rewards for those of proven political reliability. While the regime has made it plain that one must be both Red and expert, being Red comes first. Those who place their political loyalties above everything else are the ones who qualify for group leadership, to serve in the role of catalyst in the thought-reform process. The leader, not chosen by the group itself but by the party, may be a well-known scholar who serves as a party official, an outstanding teacher, a member of the Youth League (for youth groups), a trade union organizer, a bright student in a class, or a personnel officer.

The personnel officer, by virtue of the records he keeps, occupies a strategic position of influence in any unit whether he be the appointed leader or not. His judgement may be final in determining the future of each person in the group. He keeps elaborate records on each person, such a dossier being known as the personnel file. The contents of this file are secret to all except party brass—most of all it is kept secret to the individual concerned. Nevertheless the file is used as a basis for party decisions concerning the individual's assignment to duty, promotions, working conditions, food rations, etc. The file is updated periodically by adding long forms calling for the citizen to report detailed information about himself, his personal (even intimate) relations with his family, friends, and coworkers, about his political viewpoints, and his opinions concerning public and international affairs. The personnel officer has the power to invite an individual to come to him for a private talk about certain inconsistencies or questionable ideas revealed in his questionnaire. Whether or not he happens to be the personnel officer, the group leader usually is a party member, though nonparty members of tested reliability are appointed.

The surveillance system described earlier in this chapter, whether conducted by amateurs or professionals, adds to the file all personal information it obtains by observation, and the street committee may follow up by checking into matters concerning the kind of people one entertains in one's home, the strangers who may visit, or newcomers who move in. In this kind of jungle society the individual has a constant feeling of being watched, of having his inner thoughts bared to the public.[36] With this feeling would normally go the fear of being victimized, and case after documented case reported in the West reinforces the lesson that such fear is not without foundation. Even loyal party members may not live immune from this kind of total overlordship of minds and hearts.

At the close of the Thaw period, it was relatively easy to cut off debate, but this measure has not solved the problem of maintaining morale and high levels of productive achievement among intellectuals. Apathy and frustration were inevitable, and the regime has not met the problem satisfactorily. Communist policy in China, as in the Soviet Union, has alternated between long periods of rigid orthodoxy and short periods of slight accommodation to changing conditions.[37] The period of accommodation is aimed at improving levels of production and performance, and, in the case of China, reflects little real basic change in attitude either toward greater recognition of individual freedoms or toward old line dogma.

Developments that followed the hundred flowers period have

seen the reinforcement of thought-control policy and method. Silence and outward conformity for all expert intellectuals—including journalists and communications workers—are in themselves inadequate and not acceptable. Positivism by everyone is called for. It is often necessary to be enthusiastic about showing support for the new order. An old Chinese maxim says, "Submission by mouth is not nearly as desirable as submission by heart." The role of the journalist in modern China, then, is now one of devoted, if blind, service to party and regime. His standing is no higher than that of workers in other less vital lines of endeavor. In traditional China the scholar helped run the government, provided the leadership in most other areas of national life, and enjoyed a post of high esteem. His position has changed; he now takes orders. While some intellectuals have been disenchanted,[38] the regime has succeeded in mobilizing large numbers in the service of its cause. It treats them as a functional group with equivalent national prestige and rewards accorded similar groups.[39]

But the intellectuals are not the only dissident group. The whole question of whether the Communist party—under Mao Tse-tung—is capable of maintaining a unified political structure seems in doubt. The "great proletarian cultural revolution" which the so-called Red Guards staged throughout China in 1966 and 1967 was officially described by Peking as a power struggle in which left-wing revolutionaries opposed right-wing revisionists. The events supported this kind of explanation, for it seemed that the revolution was less concerned with ideology than with dismissing from leading posts of authority those who were said to be taking the capitalist road. Mao's revolutionaries, by letting loose the Red Guard movement and purging the dissident elements in party leadership, apparently hoped to recapture party and government control. These chaotic developments demonstrated (for the second time in 17 years) that the Communist regime was facing a crisis. Personal jealousies and deep divisions on policy lay behind the struggle. For the first time a substantial number of the party elite who had spent most of their lives following Mao now seemed to view his thoughts as dangerous and his plans as an unworkable blueprint for running the nation. In the eight years since the Chinese Thaw had been silenced, the pace of national development had slowed. Industry had not moved forward, agricultural production had not made the advances expected, and living conditions had not improved perceptibly. There was thus reason to believe that the revisionists within the party's rank holding important posts in the government were obstructing development. Hence Mao and Lin Piao, Defense Minister and Chairman of the Military Commission of the Central Committee, set out to rally effective control by purging uncooperative officials and replacing them with those more in tune with Mao's thought.

The steps in this "revolution from above" may be outlined as follows: Marshal Lin Piao, who became Defense Minister in 1959, began to enforce his policy of "politics in command" first within the army. Then, after many abortive attempts, he was able gradually to extend his control into various segments of the economy, the unions, industry, and transportation. Ultimately, when disputes erupted among the party ranks, Lin, with his guerilla generals and politcommissars, prevailed over a faction of party leaders who had begun their careers in the 1930s as agitators and who now controlled the party organizations. Lin's coup radically changed the structure of the power alignment between urban masses led by party intellectuals and peasant armies led by guerilla generals—a structure upon which had rested the Communist movement under Mao.

Once Lin (with Mao's approval) had succeeded in contesting the established party mechanism, he began to gain control of the party's media of mass communication in order to silence his opponents. From November, 1965, onward, a campaign continued against "bourgeois and revisionist elements" among the party intellectuals. In April, 1966, the army paper *Chieh-fang Chun-pao* proclaimed the "great socialist cultural revolution," to cover up the fact that Lin was slowly gaining possession of the most important propaganda media, for he immediately launched through the army paper a violent attack on the chief party paper *Jen-min Jih-pao,* which by the end of May he turned into virtually a branch of the army paper. While the prestigious *People's Daily* was forced to undergo the indignity of reprinting army newspaper editorials, its editor Wu Leng-hsi, who was also director of *Hsin-hua,* the New China News Agency, was replaced early in June by Tang Ping-chu, the army newspaper's managing editor. The papers published by the Peking City Committee after its reorganization, stopped appearing in September, 1966. The Communist youth organization paper, *Chung-kuo Ching-nien Pao,* vanished without advance notice on August 20. *Ta Kung Pao,* the commercial paper, changed its name to *Chien Chin Pao* (Progressive Daily) but later it reappeared under its old title. Some provincial papers have been replaced by the Red

Guard's *Hung-wei Pao* group. The purges also placed the Mao-Lin branch of the party in control of Radio Peking and other broadcasting units, post offices, and editorial offices. Lu Ting-zi was replaced by Tao Chu as head of the party propaganda department. The reorganized *Jen-min Jih-pao,* along with the theoretical journal *Hung-chi,* continued their roles as official voices of the pro-Mao forces. *Hung-chi,* edited by Mao's friend Chen Po-ta, did not suffer a purge.

In Shanghai, where economic sabotage by opposition elements of Liu Shao-chi, head of state, and Teng Hsiao-ping, the party's secretary general, was reported, the two main papers *Wen-hui Pao* and *Chieh-fang Pao* announced their "rebirth" after Mao-Lin supporters "wrested leadership" from their former executives. *Chieh-fang Pao* was described as "a voice that spread the poison of those within the party who are in authority and are taking the capitalist road." Thus throughout the struggle, the Mao-Lin faction moved swiftly to seize control of the mass communication media.

As a result of the turmoil, factual information in China, seldom prevalent under the Communist regime, became still more elusive. Wall posters, called *tatze-pao,* have long been a favorite form of communication. Now, as newspapers have ceased publication or have not been delivered, and as wireless radio has remained silent for fear of informing the outside world, they have become important sources of information. *Hung-chi* editorialized, "The enemy . . . cunningly takes over revolutionary slogans raised by the party's Central Committee and Chairman Mao and distorts them to serve his counterrevolutionary political purposes." It appeared that no one, not even the Mao-Lin faction, could be sure of allegiance—either of the communication media or of their friends and enemies.

INDICATIONS OF EFFECT AND ACCOMPLISHMENT

To what extent has the Chinese Communist regime succeeded? What is the end product like of this vast total weapon of organization, propaganda, indoctrination, and personal thought control of millions of lives? The aims have been stated: (1) to produce a new kind of ideal socialist society at some vague time in the future (according to Mao Tse-tung, "Twenty years of tremendous effort and then a thousand years of happiness"), and (2) to produce the new "socialist man." For the present this means a regimented society in which men live who accept the dogma, and who support wholly the program; who place party will ahead of personal desire or aspiration; who are willing to sacrifice to live austerely; who are eager to struggle for the cause; who agree with communist-type "either-or" thinking; who are committed to communist concepts of morality and truth; and who resist all those people defined by party as enemies and all ideas and influences indentified by party as neutral, divisionist, capitalist, imperialist, or bourgeois. The future Chinese citizen—the product of this kind of social conditioning—will live in a literate, industrial society which has transformed China into a strong modern power, which has sought to rebuild at great cost in human suffering and humanistic principles the lost image of China and Chinese culture as the glory of the world, thus satisfying present-day nationalistic passions. In the light of the overwhelming odds yet to be reckoned with, these are clearly ambitious goals.

In the attainment of goals, mass communication is expected to play a fundamental role—a role which because of the heavy obstacles to overcome is probably relied upon more as a strategic weapon in the process of causing social change than it is in other communist countries. In spite of such barriers as illiteracy, poverty of natural and man-made resources, and the lethargic pull of traditional motivations and value-systems, the Chinese Communists have developed a specialized communications apparatus which, though diversified in order to reach and influence all segments of the population, is at the same time heavily centralized. To an extent greater than that of any other communist society, the formal public mass media system is supplemented by informal, face-to-face methods—methods that invade the individual's personal thought patterns. Such informal methods merge so subtly with and at the same time extend the power of the formal media system so effectively that it is difficult to distinguish between them. Therefore in considering both operation and effect, the two must be dealt with as one. In order to attack their own peculiar problems of demography and geography, the Chinese have been adept in developing their own adaptation of Soviet Communist methods and in improvising new ones. While these innovations in communication have arisen to meet the pressure of conditions, they reflect a feeling of independence from Moscow. In general, they have forged a politically reliable communication system sensitive to push-button control from Peking.

Without more information than is available in the Western

World it is impossible to judge with much precision what may have been the over-all effects on the Chinese people. From the regime's standpoint, of course, the ends justify any workable means, and theoretically total means should bring total results. A whole series of colossal failures in many areas of the Communist program in China has been reported in the West. The commune plan in agriculture was hardly a roaring success. The grass-roots iron-smelting project with everyone operating a crude backyard furnace not only failed to provide more iron for the nation but it also took away valuable time from the harvest work.[40] The "great leap forward" has in fact slid backward. Among the apparently successful achievements reported in the West have been the compulsory public school program which has cut down perceptibly on the number of illiterates; the extension of railroads, airways, and highways into the interior; the development of flood-control, irrigation, and hydroelectric projects; increases in production in such vital areas of the national economy as steel, petroleum and minerals, chemical fertilizers, paper, cement, textiles, etc.[41] Concrete evidence of success or failure, gain or loss, such as this can be be seen and reported. However, the subtle changes wrought in the minds, attitudes, and values of the people by the constant din of the communications machine do not lend themselves so readily to measurement, observation, or report.

On such seemingly tangible matters as living conditions and the regime's popularity, authoritative opinion is not in accord. Chiao in 1962 classified recently published trends analyses according to value judgements expressed by the authorities on these questions. Eight sources were of the opinion that the Chinese Communist regime is "working wonders" in transforming living conditions for the average Chinese and that it has the decisive and unwavering support of the people. Six sources were less sanguine, generally expressing admiration for what material progress has admittedly been made and finding that some support exists for the government and its policies. Yet these sources are critical of the coercive methods used. Chiao found eight other sources which categorically reject the idea that the Communists have done, or mean to do, anything to improve conditions. In the opinion of these writers, the regime has no basis of popular support and exists today only because of its use of force and suppression.[42] Force, repression, and fear in the process of persuasion have yielded impressionistic evidence of startling transformation, in attitudes and reactions. How much this indicates deep, beneath-the-surface change cannot be determined. The surface manifestations were so rapid and complete they must have surprised the Communists themselves. Within the first few years visitors reported that the Chinese masses had become a nation of "yes-men" reciting party line slogans mechanically without understanding, much as an amalgam of automatons might. Barnett reported factory workers in Mukden industrial plant dormitories declaiming Marxist dogma; a Lanchow professor preaching dialectical materialism; the shopkeepers of Canton uttering the clichés of the class struggle; Shanghai's clever businessmen, famous for their competitive vigor, dancing in the streets to celebrate the socialization of their companies; while peasants in Hunan, who in common with their ancestors had longed to own a plot of land, singing lip-service praises to the virtues of collectivization.[43]

The stolid uniformity of ideas expressed publicly was described as unbelievable by Sripati Chandra-sekhar, social scientist, director of the Indian Institute for Population Studies in Madras, and editor of *Population Review,* a journal of Asian demography. Chandra-sekhar returned from a 1958–1959 visit to China disenchanted, disillusioned, and profoundly disturbed by what he saw as a nation displaying the "peace of the graveyard." Traveling from Canton to Harbin and from Lanchow to Shanghai, Chandra-sekhar reported he did not find a "single person who talked freely to me as man to man, and all the courtesies that were extended to me resulted from the directives of the people in power. . . I found I could almost guess what the next person was going to say, for it would be the same song, merely sung from a different platform." [44]

It is no wonder that the people are afraid to stray from the well-worn paths of the official propaganda line when they speak publicly. The extensiveness and pervasiveness of the organized surveillance system creates an atmosphere of mutual suspicion in which people feel they are being spied upon not only by government officials but also by their neighbors or friends. Almost anything one does or says under such conditions has "ideological implications," a Hong Kong refugee reported. Her neighbors saw her return from shopping and subjected her to criticism for indulging her "bourgeois" appetite, she said. A refugee bank clerk testified his residents' group pressed him to cut down on smoking because spending too much money on tobacco was unprogressive.[45] While freedom of behavior and expression are thus circumscribed, the freedom of silence is also denied. Chandra-sekhar reported, "The second thing that no one can escape [the first being the dull uniformity on every hand] is the ubiquitous loudspeaker. I first heard it at the frontier station of Shum Chun. . . . The radio haunted all my waking and many of my sleeping hours. . . . Even in the most backward and traditional villages I saw the loudspeakers hidden in the treetops. One can escape the sun and the moon—but not the loudspeaker." [46]

With this kind of mass media saturation, increasingly greater numbers of people are being reached perhaps more efficiently and effectively than ever before. The people are learning the new ideology, substituting new for old values and expressing their verbal acquiescence. Some no doubt believe genuinely and behave accordingly. Others are torn between doubt and conviction. Some perhaps have tried to stop thinking, closing their minds and deafening their ears to the persistent message stimuli. Others give lip service to the new ways, but at heart doggedly resist giving up cherished values. In the near unanimous clamor of willing voices, who can separate the believers from the nonbelievers, the changed and the changing from the unchanged?

Gauging Effect on Population Subgroups, Classes

With two population subgroups, representing small minorities, indoctrination has been more successful, perhaps, than with others. One is the middle-aged intellectual whose disillusionment with the Nationalist regime proved fruitful soil for the growth of the new faith. Typical explanation for this group by a refugee editor was, "You can't think clearly while taking part in intensive 'study.' You instinctively know that your real thoughts will some day pop out. . . therefore to be safe you either have to change your real thoughts or not think at all." While the intellectuals generally are not as involved socially and economically as are the peasants or the propertied class, most of them are highly patriotic. More than other classes, they take great pride in the regime's accomplishments in enhancing the national image. Yet what has been said of the middle-aged intellectual must not be taken to apply to all intellectuals. Many have been disillusioned and apathetic, made to feel insecure in the face of their treatment and above all the rigid policies of thought control.

The other minority group with which indoctrination has been

most successful is the youth. Youth are impressionable;—they have never known anything else;—and they are more easily captivated by the dreams of the utopian society; they are more easily swayed by the revolutionary, crusading spirit. A young girl university graduate reported that most students begin to change after undergoing "study." This does not mean the change was really a "conversion," she explained. For most youth there was not much to convert, only a vacuum. They had no developed ideological convictions, so the change consisted of acceptance of new ideas in place of the blank that formerly existed.[47] Yet youthful enthusiasms have been quenched. Many students who enthusiastically endorsed the new order at its inception have become disenchanted. Student unrest and dissatisfaction resulting in riots have been widely reported from the Chinese mainland.

There appears to be some evidence, too, that other population subgroups in part are convinced and converted. This is especially true of the party members, government officials, and bureaucracy. The latter includes a few intellectual leaders, the policy and decision makers, who seem to believe to a considerable extent in the dogma taught by their own propaganda, and in the picture of the world portrayed by their media. These, of course, stand to be rewarded for their commitment, more so than less directly involved classes.

With other classes, indoctrination has been less successful. Generally speaking, relatively well-to-do classes which stood to lose most are more resistant to the new ideology. So are the older groups in the society who are more inclined to adhere to older values and less willing to adapt to change. The peasantry—materialistically minded, conservative, and highly property conscious—has found its interests and aspirations at variance with Communist aims. The regime has admitted that after fifteen years of propaganda promises and intensive efforts to "educate" him, the peasant has not done as well economically as other groups. Although he mouths a few slogans, he has not yet developed the degree of political awareness his government seeks. The younger groups of peasants, however, have been more responsive, some of them organizing and leading rural programs. Among industrial workers, the attitudes toward the regime vary according to economic status. Their lot has been hard; and as with others their degree of acceptance of the regime depends perhaps on their willingness to sacrifice and endure hardships today for the evanescent glories of tomorrow. Businessmen and industrialists experience a situation in which restrictions become tighter, much as extending controls envelop and stifle intellectual freedom.

Changing Values and Belief Patterns

The mass media and other propaganda instrumentalities have also been less successful in changing centuries-old value-systems, traditional behavior patterns and ways. Although some of these time-honored attributes of Confucian society fit the orthodox Communist requisites, many conflict seriously. In their drive against Western influence, which they labeled imperialist, semifeudal, and reactionary, the Communists sought not only to erase the objectionable features of the recent past but also those of China's ancient cultural heritage. They took the dichotomous view that the old and the new were locked in a death struggle and that one must die so that the other could live,[48] rather than attempting to fuse the better features of the two.

Nonetheless there existed certain personal and social characteristics that identify with Marxist methods and aims and therefore lend themselves to Communist exploitation. Confucian ideas of morality have been relatively easy for the Communists to adapt with little change. The Confucian and Mencian belief that man was essentially good and did not behave in a socially harmful manner unless he lacked guidance has been slightly modified to fit the Communist desire to provide guidance and to divert good behavior in the good society into the development of a kind of selfless altruistic type of citizen. The highest development of Communist morality is the devotion and sacrifice of the individual for the society. The Confucian belief that the individual is a product primarily of his environment also finds a sympathetic echo in the Marxist teaching that man is molded by his class. To achieve qualities of good behavior and to condition his character after ideal models, the Chinese Communist like his Confucian ancestor seeks to improve by self-study, self-analysis, and self-criticism. Foremost among those attributes of the old society that play into Communist hands is the highly valued tradition of cultivating *chien yang,* that is humility, tolerance, patience, docility, self-effacement, obedience, and yielding to others in human relations. The entire pattern of authority from the father to family head to village patriarch to emperor tended to discipline the ordinary individual to obedience to rules of conduct enforced upon him from above and to limit his freedom of choice. These traditional attitudes toward authority the Communists have directed into channels that suit their needs, and at the same time have appealed to those rebelling against the tyrannies of the old authority by the argument that they have freed them from family loyalties so that they will have time to cultivate self interests. Nevertheless, because in the traditional Chinese pattern true belief and true discipline come from inside rather than outside, the Communists have sought to inject indoctrination by such methods which make it seem to come from the inside. Finally, the collective political and economic organization of ancient Chinese society into a hierarchy of units based on the family, the collective ownership of common property, and other collective values would seem to have much in common with modern Communist ideas of organization.

On the other hand there are some values and ways of thinking deeply rooted in the Chinese heritage that seem to conflict with Communist ideas. Among them are conservativism stemming from ancestor worship, respect for history and tradition, respect for the aged and the scholar, provincialism arising from family and village self-sufficiency and solidarity, private or individual ownership of land and other property, the intellectual's disdain for manual labor, the people's contentment and lack of aggressiveness, their contempt for the military class, the more recently acquired concepts especially among the intellectuals of democracy and civil liberty, and the pure individualism of the traditional Chinese—his "live and let live" philosophy, his reluctance to interfere with another's affairs, which make him work well individually but not as a team, his concepts of work and leisure, his notion of "face," and his concept of the Central Government as benevolently paternalistic. The regime has sought to channel the strong traditions of paternal domination of the emperor to the father-image of Mao and the top party leadership.[49] The other political pattern of traditional Chinese life, the brotherhood relationship of equals, has been channeled into the "comradeship" of the mass organizations.

The regime's assault on such solid institutions as the family unit has met with resistance.[50] There have been several efforts to break up family-oriented society, each one followed by concessions to the culture values of centuries. First was the reversal of the class system among the millions of peasants, the wealthier deprived, and the "have nots" given plots. Then women were given equal rights with men. Control of parents over the upbringing and education of their children was shifted to the State. Newly landed peasants, however, enjoyed their status only briefly for they were soon forced to pool their small plots into collective farms. Village and family living soon were swallowed up in the commune. These were all measures aimed at substituting loyalty to State in place of loyalty to family and clan. After the "great leap forward" began to falter, collectivization became an admitted failure, and the commune became little more than a work unit operated by teams in place of the family, but operated much in the same self-sufficient way as the family system. Small family life with custody of children has been resumed.[51]

Even so the large family unit as a basis for the society has been broken up and its smaller modern counterpart has been weakened, as has the authority of man over women, and of parents over children. The urgency, the tempo, the pressures have quickened pulses, prodded the slothful, and left little time for leisure or contemplation. There is much more civic and social consciousness.

Indeed, in this area, perhaps more than in others, the regime has been successful in capitalizing upon the people's fierce ethnical pride, which after the humiliations of the past hundred years, has emerged in a new fervent nationalism. This sudden surge of extreme nationalism is a transfer of traditional family loyalty to the State coupled with the dire need for a strong central government to help man survive the natural ravages of flood and famine as well as resist foreign aggression.[52] The Chinese character is both ambivalent and dualistic: On the one hand he has been traditionally an unselfish, easily satisfied, socially unambitious and politically indifferent individualist; on the other he was a self-made serf, ready to accept obedience, even subservience, to a leader in absolute authority at any necessary time and at high personal sacrifice. Under the Communists more than ever before, the common people have frequent and direct contact with their central government, and that government has developed in them a definite sense of political identity and national mission.[53]

Hu and his associates conclude that on the whole the people's reaction is one of acquiescence.

> They are pleased to find themselves members of a nation which, for the first time in over a century, can demand and expect international recognition of its power and importance in world affairs. They have been constantly reminded that their country can meet and exceed the requirements for modernization and industrialization in the foresee-

able future. They are told, and some are willing to believe, that they have a mission in the new world: to help other Asian countries to "throw off the colonial yoke" and to join the "free and united democratic nations" of the Communist bloc. By fanning the fire of anti-imperialism and by using saturation in its propaganda tactics, the Communist regime has succeeded, at least partially, in satisfying the nationalist aspirations of the population. But there is a price to pay for these gains and no doubt many people, aside from the devoted party and government workers, hold at least some serious though secret reservations about the new regime.[54]

In summary, the Red Chinese communications system resembles its Soviet prototype in most respects. It serves the regime as well and as completely as a totally regimented mass media system can. It serves the people only insofar as their collective interests and welfare coincide with those of the regime. It suffers from many of the same kind of weaknesses just as it has mobilized many of the same kind of strengths exhibited by Soviet Communism. In its short period of existence, the Chinese mass media system has done more with less than the early Soviet system had achieved in a comparable period of time. But the regime had more to accomplish and, it thought, less time in which to establish itself. Compared with the stupendous problems faced by Lenin and the early Soviet regime, the Chinese Communists are beset with problems of a different kind and dimension. Where the Soviet leaders were presented with problems related to the consolidation of political and economic power, the Chinese leaders have been presented with overwhelming demographic odds and inadequate resources to meet the need. Still the political regime, despite its seizure of total power, has not felt itself stable, and each step in the extension of public communications facilities has been accompanied by closer centralization and more rigid control. The regime's feelings of insecurity at home and sullen inferiority in international affairs, the tensions and pressures it suffers from time to time, and the dimensions of the task it has set itself to accomplish in the face of difficulties probably unparalleled anywhere else—these are some of the factors which combine to make the Chinese mass communication effort more rapidly paced, more frenetic and intensive than that of other communist societies. All has led to the extension of thought-reform methods, to the ultimate party supervision of intimate details of personal life to an extent beyond anything known elsewhere. The Chinese system has not yet developed as highly trained a body of professional communications workers as has the more mature Soviet system. Similarly aided by face-to-face methods, the media apparently have been surprisingly successful in transforming the face of the nation within a relatively short period of time. Yet underneath the facade of apparently radical change, the external flow of superficial verbalization, the extent and nature of the real transformation in basic ways of life and thought cannot be determined. Quite obviously words cannot alter conditions. In the hands of a total system words can deceive, can produce a dangerous myopia, a disorientation to reality. The map cannot be the territory, yet the communication system appears to predicate its assumptions on the belief that it is.

3

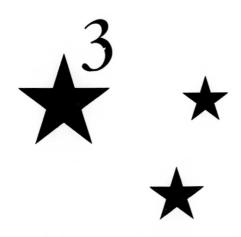

COMMUNIST REGIMES, THE MASS MEDIA, AND SOCIETY

14 ★

SYNTHESIS AND SUMMARY

BY WAY OF A CONCLUDING NOTE, certain generalizations based on the foregoing analysis may be advanced. In regard to theory and method the Communist communication system as a social institution was born of Hegelian-Marxist doctrine. It was shaped and interpreted by the Russian revolutionaries whose rigid, extremist, 2-valued orientation philosophy left a strong imprint. It borrowed from the experience of both the private and government-owned press under tsarist absolutism. It learned secrecy and intolerance of opposition from its own successes and failures in its struggle against the imperial government and likewise from the government's effort to control and contain nonconformist, revolutionary thought. It was tested and refined as a political institution and party weapon in the experience of the revolutionary press both at home and in exile. It developed to a considerable extent by trial and error in the early years of the new Soviet state.

Though nourished in Russia, Communist ideology was a foreign transplant in Russia as well as in China. Contrary to Marx's formula, it took roots in traditional-agrarian rather than advanced-industrial societies, among a large class of illiterate peasants. But both countries had long-established authoritarian traditions, the Russian perhaps in some ways being more absolutist than the Chinese. Both oriental despotisms experienced revolutionary upheavals brought on by the communication of Western ideas. The course of events in China differed from that in Russia, however, for in China the influence of John Stuart Mill for a time triumphed over that of Marx. But just as the ideology was a transplant, so was the concept of a newspaper or journal as a public information medium strictly a Western import. Western press systems, when introduced into Russia and China, were used first by religious institutions as organs to propagate the faith, then by business interests in the marketplace. The press thrived whereever trade and commerce flourished. Western experience has shown that modern mass communication systems attain their highest degree of influence and prestige as economically independent institutions in libertarian capitalist societies; that they attain their highest degree of structural development, capability, and mass penetration in modern, industrial, technologically advanced societies. The evidence of Western experience also tends to show that modern mass communication systems are also products of urban communities of people with relatively high literacy and high economic and education levels.

When a Western-type press system was introduced in both countries it clashed with an environment quite alien to that which had given it birth and nourishment. Both Russian and Chinese societies were largely traditional agrarian-based societies made up of self-sufficient families and villages as the basic political units of the larger territorial subdivisions. At the base of both societies were the millions of illiterate, poverty-ridden peasants and at the top a comparatively small ruling oligarchy and bureaucracy; in between was a relatively small middle class. The masses in both countries had never heard of the Magna Charta, the rights of man, government by the consent of the governed, or a government of laws and not of men. The liberating influences of the Renaissance, the Reformation, the Industrial Revolution and the rise of the common man—forces that resulted in the concepts of individual and political liberty—were among the factors of modernization that profoundly changed Europe and America; but aside from a thin layer of wealthy intelligentsia, all these ideas never existed as far as the bulk of Russian and Chinese people were concerned. These groups of intelligentsia in both countries sought to bring about changes in their societies conducive to modernization after the

Western model, first by peaceful reform, then later by revolution. Both used the press as a major instrument to promote reform and revolution—revolution that eventually toppled centuries-old dynasties. But the libertarian concept of the press's role as both mediator between the government and the governed and as a critic of government separate from and independent of both society and government hardly had a chance to take root.

But there were reasons for hope that the libertarian tradition might gain strength. In Russia centuries of Christianity under the State church had left its mark on the culture. In China the humane concepts of Confucian philosophy, imbedded deeply in Chinese tradition and civilization, offered a promising environment in which these Western ideals might grow. China differed from Russia in that she experienced for almost 100 years a period of foreign occupation in the form of territorial trade concessions to the Western powers. The Chinese could see a libertarian capitalist press operating in their own front yard. China, also unlike Russia, experienced a brief period of Republican rule in which a native Western-type press system flourished—a system in which almost all of the attributes of a libertarian press were apparent. The advent of the Communist regime abruptly halted this development and today the Communist communication system is a major link in a chain of communication and persuasion that has been successful at least in bringing to the Chinese people a rebirth of nationalism and pride in achievement. In Russia the long history of censorship and suppression was the primary heritage. It was not until the last half of the nineteenth century that the Russian press began to perceive its role as one of mass information. Since the privately owned press shared with the government-owned press responsibility for publishing, conditions did not foster the development of independent responsibility. As a consequence the Western sense of responsibility and independence of government control for mass communications was seldom envisaged and hardly ever put into practice. When the Bolsheviks came to power they were greatly impressed with the success of their propaganda methods and fully versed in the devious ways of control by the authoritarian state over mass communication and over the minds of men. They used this knowledge to consolidate political power, and to forge a stable regime based on force and fear.

Although there are important differences, the Russian and the Chinese mass communication systems today are cut from the same cloth. Both appear to represent different stages of development relating generally to each country's stage of social and economic development. The Soviet Communist media system mirrors the maturity and success the country has achieved as a first-rate world power. Still the ideal state has not been built, nor has the ephemeral socialist superman emerged. So the work of socialism must go on. On the other hand, Chinese communications reflect the tensions of a nation driving its people relentlessly in the struggle to catch up—a proud nation of extravagant ambitions and flaming nationalism, but a nation still behind in the modernizing process, still in a stage of painful transition. The Chinese system has profited from the Soviet experience and, like the Russian brand of communism, has proved to be enormously adaptive. Yet it still has much farther to go before it catches up with the other Communist giant. Moreover, it faces different and greater odds in the form of traditional values, geography, and demography. The situation has forced the Chinese regime to take extreme measures such as mass organized thought control at a time when the Soviet Union is relaxing its use of force.

Because the philosophy calls for using the media system alongside the political system to effect changes in the character of the people, both Russian and Chinese Communists have stressed the agitation function as a device for crystallizing propaganda into action. They also stress the media as focal points for party organizational work. Therefore the importance of communication systems to Communist regimes lies quite as much in the social as in the mass communications function of the media institutions. The mass media institutions, for example, provide a hierarchical base from which political organizations are built and manipulated—a system of control through which all aspects of the entire society are systematically governed from a central location. The Communists have learned that the ability to use and control information to shape and change attitudes not alone by messages in the mass media but also by face-to-face contact is fundamental to political power. Hence the Communists judge total formal and informal media performance by the extent of their combined contribution to organized action by social groups in the approved direction. From this standpoint they are concerned that the messages conform to the line quite as much because of their probable influence on the communicator of the message as because of any probable influence on the audience. Audiences, however, are playing a greater role than before in the mass communication process.

Judged by Communist standards, the mass media appear to be accomplishing their task and fulfilling their purpose, though perhaps not to the fullest extent the regimes desire. If expansion of the mass communication system is to be taken as an indication of the regime's satisfaction with it, then the Soviet regime is apparently well satisfied. Although the Soviet media have been developed rapidly, full penetration at all social levels has not been achieved. Still, the press is available on a fairly uniform basis. In China the print media have not expanded as rapidly as they are needed. In both countries the electronic media have expanded rapidly, yet because of linguistic and other barriers they still do not—in Pulitzer's phrase—"speak to a whole nation rather than a select group." The media systems are technically adequate, however, for transmitting the regime's messages to the people. Communist communication systems have demonstrated a high capability to change people and society. They do this by using mass communication to create a strong feeling of "nation-ness" and loyalty to the country, by helping prepare people to participate and to play their new roles in the new society, by promulgating and popularizing national plans and goals, by helping develop the necessary skills, and eventually by preparing the people for their country's role as a member of the family of nations—in short, to modify society and human behavior.

However rigid the dogma, Communist mass communication systems—as the Soviet system since Stalin has demonstrated—are amazingly flexible and adaptable to change. Any means, according to the ideology, is justified by the ends to be achieved. While the ends today remain the same the means have become more versatile and less rigidly bound, to meet what are rationally perceived as changing conditions. Whether the regime was in full command all the time and deliberately led, or whether it was forced by pressures to innovate, the changes of the past decade are impressive. Today's Soviet society and its mass communication system are more open, more inquiring, less motivated by terror, than they were under Stalin. The Socialist parties of Western Europe have abandoned the Marxist conception of the class struggle, and there is reason to believe that in the Soviet Union Marxism-Leninism is giving way to the modern idea of the affluent welfare state. Yet the Soviet Union remains a tightly controlled totalitarian dictatorship with its ideological and organizational foundations intact. The single party is more powerful than ever. The doctrine is revitalized and made more relevant to the needs of the times. In China the changes have not been so profound, although the Chinese at first showed ingenuity in adapting Russian methods to Chinese society. In both countries change has been reflected in the mass media, but media behavior has shown little basic change.

Since persuasion is replacing coercion and terror as a manipulative instrument in the Soviet Union, it seems that public opinion in the future will play a larger role in the communications process than it has in the past. Indeed, the very fact that persuasion is receiving greater emphasis is in itself tacit recognition that public opinion is a factor in the decisions made by the top leadership. Traditionally in Communist countries public opinion has not been considered the sovereign power. It was assumed that public opinion was completely unanimous on all important issues and revealed itself through the party and its leaders. Therefore the communications system hitherto has not been expected to reflect or necessarily to provide a basis for the development of opinion among the general public. The prevailing "public" opinion—the kind that finds expression—is either the opinion of the leaders or those opinions of others which are approved by the leaders. The channels of information are almost exclusively used by the leaders, and the information crystallized by the party provides the basis for the formulation of national policy, just as it provides the basis for the bias of the official communication line. Thus is distilled the collective wisdom of the leaders, who until the State withers away, must paternalistically see after the people's needs. The formal communication system then has the responsibility of "selling" the regime's ideas—of molding and unifying public opinion in the direction the regime wants it to go, so that in the end the regime's opinion and that of the public will be one and the same.

To maintain uniformity, Communist regimes tolerate neither oppositional media nor oppositional thought. The corollary of this situation is that mass communication serves the regimes and not necessarily the people. The function of the media becomes one that primarily concerns the processes of persuasion through monopolistic manipulation by the authorities. Under libertarian capitalistic systems, many channels and many voices competing for attention sometimes tend to drown each other out unless synchronized. In the Soviet Union and Communist China there is only one voice speaking through many channels. The messages conveyed are unwavering, positive, clear, and almost uniformly the same. These mediated messages are supplemented skillfully and reinforced by face-to-face communication and agitation leading to action. With such apparently favorable conditions for effective communication and persuasion, the potential power of Communist communications to condition, change, or contain public opinion seems to be greater than in less regimented societies. The evidence tends to show that the systems have been successful in changing attitudes.

Still, despite the traditional attitude toward the function of public opinion, there is mounting evidence to indicate that what the Soviet citizen thinks—the direction of public opinion as a thing apart from the official viewpoint—is of considerable concern to the regime. The regime is paying more attention to public opinion mainly because it wishes to maintain control of the society and to continue to guide the course of popular thought. Another reason is that the regime is beginning to suspect that the public may have a real contribution to make. Behavior that indicates sincere deference to public opinion or reaction was seen in the handling of news of the Soviet resumption of nuclear tests. The news was broken to the Soviet public slowly and gradually. The full story of the tests' extent was not reported at all to the people. In the Berlin situation the Kremlin has been careful to avoid the impression among Soviet citizens that the door has been finally closed on negotiations with the United States. In matters of civil defense the regime, quite wary of frightening the Soviet public, has limited public display of defense measures against the possibility of nuclear war. This does not mean, of course, that under present conditions the expression of a genuine public opinion contrary to the regime's will be permitted in the media. Nor does it mean that public opinion will make itself felt directly in political action. But it does mean that public opinion will work indirectly as a force influencing the regime's policies and programs, both in Russia, and perhaps to a lesser extent in China, and in this way it will make itself felt indirectly in the decision and policy making processes. This development, if it is one, is a helpful improvement, but it does not substitute adequately for the failure of the mass media to serve as vehicles for the expression of individual opinion and a broad cross-section of different shades of opinion. The chief means of developing and crystallizing intelligent public opinion—that of free and open discussion on all important questions—so prevalent in the Western democracies is denied the Soviet and Chinese people. One of the most serious limitations of Communist communication systems, then, is the absence of the clash of opinions, an open marketplace for ideas—the citizen's exposure to a wide range of ferment and thought on a variety of subjects.

In fairness, exceptions to the limitation stated in the preceding paragraph must be stressed. There may exist quite a wide range of discernible views among the Soviet people which do not run counter to established orthodoxy on certain social and economic questions (rarely on political questions) about which the regime has no particular position or simply does not care either way. There also may arise some controversial matters about which the regime, for policy reasons, hesitates to take a stand and make its wishes known until it can whip up at least a semblance of public support for its view; after which it is in a position to take action and make it appear that such action was the *result* of public demand. The leaders may have more confidence in the views of the masses than before. In any event, admittedly the press and the other mass media can enjoy relatively wide lattitude of public discussion and debate through letters, editorials, and signed articles. As we have seen, such discussions may at times get out of control. Thus, if one has in mind these areas where the regime sees fit to permit the expression of public opinion—whether genuine or "planted" by the party—one could argue as did Mikhail Igitkhanyan, researcher in the Institute of Philosophy, in the July, 1965, issue of *Soviet Life,* that "A highly important function of the [Soviet] press . . . [is] to reflect all the essential shades of public opinion, to reach the truth on vital problems through discussion." One could further state with conviction, as Igitkhanyan did, that Soviet ". . . newspapers shape Soviet public opinion, not by imposing a certain viewpoint on the population, but by freely presenting different viewpoints for argument." Such interpretations are valid only when applied to those areas of public opinion the regime chooses to leave to the mass communications media and to the people.

The introduction of public-opinion polling in recent years is a significant indication of a departure from the old assumption that official policy and public attitudes were completely congruent—an assumption that made it superfluous to sample public opinion on certain questions. More important, it may represent a real desire of the leadership to develop more scientific methods of assessing and understanding the society it governs. The more captive people are, the less likely they are to speak their minds even when invited to do so. Hence it becomes correspondingly more difficult to know what they are thinking. For a totalitarian regime then, the nagging problem of "engineering consent" can be somewhat eased by the regular sampling of public opinion even on a limited scale. The information received may be useful as an index of public thought, and the people are impressed that their opinions are considered important enough to be sought. Still, as Paul Hollander concludes (in "The Dilemma of Soviet Sociology," *Problems of Communism*, Vol. XIV, No. 6, Nov.-Dec., 1965, pp. 43–44), this new concern with public opinion has "a paradoxical quality" in that assertions of unanimity persist while at the same time public opinion is not seen as "an autonomous force relatively independent of the institutions of society, but rather as an integral part of them, as a resource to be manipulated even while it is being gauged and assessed." However, official sanction of public opinion polling on approved nondeviant or innocuous topics together with other developments in public discussion indicate a degree of tolerance of conflicting opinion and a growing belief on the part of the leadership that differences of opinion in areas outside strict ideological lines may be beneficial to the public and useful to the regime.

In theory the Communist communication system was intended to function primarily as a channel or a transmission belt to carry the message from party and government leaders down to the masses of the people. But communication was not expected to flow only in one direction. Theory envisioned a two-way flow in which the structure would provide the means by which communication could flow just as well from the bottom to the top of the hierarchy through the channels of self-criticism—both party interpersonal and media related. Experience, however, in both Russia and China indicates that the downward flow of communication literally overwhelms the feedback. Communication from the top downward has a number of advantages over communication from below. It lacks dissonance in that it speaks with one voice—consistently, systematically, and with deliberate planned purpose; the downward flow far exceeds the upward in volume and intensity; and finally, the voices from the top speak with far greater authority and credibility than the disorganized, dissonant voices from below. Thus in practice, the communication system operates for all intents and purposes as a unidirectional channel. More stress on public-opinion polling in the Soviet Union, therefore, may serve to provide more feedback and may eventually help make communication work reciprocally. China appears to be as far from instituting openly this kind of feedback channel as the Soviet Union was forty years ago.

Turning to the information function it is germane then to ask how well do the mass media, with the aid of informal communications, serve to build an informed public to provide the basis for a viable public opinion. In other words, how adequately do mass communications provide a realistic surveillance of the environment? How well do they convey reality? It seems fair to put Communist mass communications to this kind of test and to judge their performance on this kind of standard, because the average Soviet and Chinese citizen expects his media to present him with a reasonably accurate picture of his immediate environment and of the outside world. Yet, arguments of Soviet journalists to the contrary, this function is not a recognized or practiced principle of Communist systems. It seems clear that the media do reflect fairly faithfully the Soviet and Chinese governments' Promethean ambitions, plans, and goals—the struggle to reshape all facets of life in the Communist state. They reflect many of the problems encountered, and the difficulties involved. Faults are aired with the aim of providing corrections, so that the communication stream is full of the sting of unidimensional criticism. Referring to the Soviet media, Gruliow concluded they exist for one purpose, to serve the State as an instrument for containing public thought on a mass scale. If they "chance to serve the reader, that is purely coincidental," he wrote. Schramm, also speaking of the Soviet media, said they are intended to be "efficient pipelines, efficient instruments of the controlling hierarchy. And," he added, "they are held to this assignment by a strictly enforced responsibility." Obviously the adequacy of one's stock of information is essential to a realistic appraisal of and adjustment to one's environment. Just as obviously, it seems, the Communist leaders would want the people to adjust to real-life conditions. If these assumptions are correct, the communication systems should be expected to present within limited bounds a certain amount of accurate, unbiased information. Yet they are not neutral reporters of fact, except insofar as the fact may have social relevance. The extraordinary degree of reliance by the society on unofficial information sources testifies to the existence of a real need for a kind of information not being supplied. Lack of confidence in the official media is partly indicative of attitude toward the regimes and partly the result of unsatisfactory experience with the media. But if he relied solely on the official media, the average citizen would get a picture of many aspects of the environment that differs sharply from reality. Although he seldom is aware of this unless he has the opportunity to check what the media say against his own observations, he can read between the lines. He can deduce much from what the media do not say. He finds that communications picture not so much the society as it is but more as its planners want it to become.

In essence the picture the reader gets of the world, both domestic and foreign, is often one that Western readers would scarcely recognize. There is much that is not reported. Values are pictured as either right or wrong, good or bad—a world of dichotomy and of extremes. The Communist order and its goals are associated with the good, the true, and the beautiful. Enemies of the Communist state are associated with the sordid, the evil, the corrupt, the dangerous, the deceitful, and the reprehensible. Such dissident elements either at home or abroad are demonstrated to be the sole obstructionists, the only barriers to the achievement of true socialist unity and harmony. Contrary to the teachings of human experience elsewhere, Soviet and Chinese decisions as to what is right or wrong are seldom a difficult matter to determine. The slant, the position, or the Line is never depicted as uncertain, foggy, or wavering. Though perplexity may occasionally befuddle the minds of the all-powerful leaders in Moscow and Peking, the admission of such bourgeois capitalistic weaknesses almost never creeps into the stream of official communications. The general atmosphere is one of optimism; the future of socialism is bright. The communist world is getting better and more powerful every day. If it isn't, then it is the fault of capitalist warmongers, the enemies of socialism, and never the responsibility of the planners. The picture the average citizen gets from his media is one that must frequently conflict with his sense of perspective. It must be supplemented with information from other sources, if he is to have a balanced and not fragmentary view. Moreover, he cannot even expect his media to present a consistent picture over time. Emphasis may shift, frowns of displeasure may change to smiles of blandishment, from one day to the next or from one month to the next. Men, institutions, parties, and nations may be reindexed from a favored category to an unfavored or neutral one, or vice versa. This is the kind of confused, fragmentary, disconnected, biased, and distorted mirror of the outside world that is Communist communications. A second limitation of Communist communication systems, therefore, is the inadequacy of the surveillance function—the failure of mass communications to convey reality. However, this is not to imply that the world picture the Western reader gets from his media is perfect by any means.

Furthermore the negative effects of heavy propaganda contribute also to the state of ignorance on the part of the Communist citizen. Most well-educated citizens grow immune to government propaganda and agitation somewhat in the manner of an American listening to detergent advertising: he simply doesn't hear it; he may scoff at the slogans or joke at the exaggerations, but listlessly or subconsciously he buys the advertised brand. Often the Soviet or Chinese intellectual appears outwardly to accept the official view, not because he is convinced, but because it has become so much a part of his ingrained system of values, because it is useful to him if he wishes to do well and get ahead in the society, because group pressures are exerted, or because he is afraid for other reasons to behave differently.

The growing resistance to and immunity against propaganda is one of the built-in limitations of Communist communication systems. Among the others are apathy and indifference on the part of communications personnel and other intellectuals. The problem is essentially one of stimulating and maintaining high levels of initiative and creativity in a controlled, stifling atmosphere. Another is the chronic dullness and tediousness of media content which from time to time reaches the point of repelling readers, thus defeating its own purpose.

Though somewhat tempered by the effect of unofficial communication channels, the mass communication system suffering from such limitations can hardly be expected to produce an enlightened public. Rather, the media audience is more likely to be one that is filled with ignorance and misconception, and lacking a context of meaning that creates understanding. In a democracy where public opinion provides the basis for policy, such misrepresentations, half-truths, gaps, and distortions in the public information stream, we believe, unless challenged and corrected, would dangerously impair the opinion processes and functions. In Communist countries the effect may not prove disastrous, but it would seem that over time such myopia and naïvete as mass communication messages foster among the people cannot help but work self-defeating handicaps, preventing the achievement of the very goals the Communists themselves have set. Traditional fear and suspicion of the mass public by both Soviet and Chinese regimes explains in part why they must control what the public is told and why they are not particularly interested in broadening the latitude of public information and knowledge. The Soviet experience seems to indicate that as a Communist regime finds itself in a position of greater strength and stability it will have less need to control the content of communications, to promulgate falsehoods, and distort reality. As stability increases a regime will have less need to use force and coercion and will turn more to persuasion to accomplish what coercion has accomplished before. Whether it also widens the spectrum of permissible expression depends upon the extent to which it believes such a widening will increase the effects of persuasion, and thus enable the media to perform their tasks more efficiently.

The crux of the problem lies in the approach which reflects the fundamental notion of the role of communications in modern society. The dilemma for Communist regimes will not be resolved—and the resulting faults in the communication system corrected—until more attention is given to the uses of mass communication for people instead of the uses of people for mass communication. The traditional attitude can be expressed in the question, "What does mass communication do *to* people?" The question represents only part of the multidimensional role of communication in society. More stress needs to be placed on another dimension: "What do people do *with* mass communication?"

NOTES

Chapter 1. RUSSIAN SOCIETY AND PRESS: THE CULTURAL SETTING

1. Chauncey D. Harris, "Industrial and Agricultural Resources," in Alex Inkeles and Kent Geiger, eds., *Soviet Society, A Book of Readings,* Boston, 1961, pp. 5, 16.
2. *Statesman's Year-Book,* London, 1963, p. 1513.
3. John Gunther, *Inside Russia Today,* rev. ed., New York, 1962, p. 4.
4. Unesco, *World Communications,* 4th ed., Amsterdam, 1964, p. 364. Other populations given here are also from this source.
5. United Nations Food and Agricultural Organization, *1960 Production Year Book,* Rome, 1961, p. 3. This estimate was calculated by dividing 221,366,000 hectares of land in cultivation by the total population, and converting to acres.
6. John F. Kantner, "A Comparison of the Current Population in the U.S.S.R. and U.S.A.," in Inkeles and Geiger, pp. 22–25.
7. Frank Lorimer, "Trends in Soviet Population History," in Inkeles and Geiger, p. 15.
8. *Demographic Year Book of the United Nations,* 1961, p. 640.
9. Harris, pp. 6–7. These estimates indicate that the United States and the Soviet Union together have more than half the energy resources of the entire world.
10. Hugh Seton-Watson, *The Decline of Imperial Russia, 1855–1914,* New York, 1952, p. 4.

11. See: Daniel Lerner, *The Passing of Traditional Society,* New York, 1958, pp. 1–14, 43–75; W. W. Rostow, *The Stages of Economic Growth,* Cambridge, 1960, pp. 4–35; and Lucien Pye, ed., *Communications and Political Development,* Princeton, 1964, pp. 3–57, 234–53, and 327–50.
12. Vera Micheles Dean, *The Nature of the Non-Western World,* New York, 1957, pp. 17–23.
13. An estimate given by Seton-Watson, p. 5.
14. Anatole G. Mazour, *Russia, Past and Present,* New York, 1951, pp. 85–90.
15. Seton-Watson, pp. 13–14.
16. Robert H. McNeal, "Introduction," in Sergei Pushkarev, *The Emergence of Modern Russia, 1801–1917,* New York, 1963, pp. xix–xxiii.
17. Pushkarev, p. 412.
18. In 1730 the Supreme Privy Council met to deal with the problem of succession and drew a document designed to limit the sovereign's power, but this failed. (See Mazour, pp. 92–93.) The reorganization of the cabinet and the establishment of ministries by Alexander I in 1811 did not create a legislative body to whom the ministries were to be responsible. So the crown's power was not altered, but the new cabinet was a step forward. Mazour, pp. 100–101.
19. Michael T. Florinsky, *Russia, a History and an Interpretation,* New York, 1953, Vol. II, pp. 768–69.
20. *Ibid.,* pp. 771–72. According to this authority the melancholy task of prying into men's hearts and thoughts had been pursued in the Russian past by the *oprichina* of Ivan IV (the Terrible) and by a long line of police agencies since Peter I.
21. Seton-Watson, p. 17.
22. Pushkarev, p. 27.
23. Seton-Watson, p. 17.
24. *Ibid.,* pp. 16–18; Pushkarev, p. 412.
25. Gabriel de Wesselitsky, *Russia and Democracy,* London, 1915, p. 4. Wesselitsky states that the Mongols first introduced into Russia the concept of the all-powerful potentate.
26. For example, P. N. Krekshin, a contemporary admirer of Peter the Great, composed the following tribute to him: "Our Father, Peter the Great! You have led us from nonexistence into existence . . . you have enlightened us and glorified us. . . . The drops of sweat of your labors was our aromatic myrrh which perfumed the glory of Russia to the ends of the world." From Michael Cherniavsky, *Tsar and People,* New Haven, 1961, p. 85.
27. Donald McKenzie Wallace, *Russia,* New York, 1905, p. 260.
28. *Cf.* Stuart Ramsay Tompkins, *The Russian Intelligentsia, Makers of the Revolutionary State,* Norman, Okla., 1957, pp. 227–50.
29. E. H. Carr, "Historical Background of the Russian Revolution," in Inkeles and Geiger, p. 31.
30. Stuart Ramsay Tompkins, *The Russian Mind from Peter the Great through the Enlightenment,* Norman, Okla., 1953, p. 23.
31. See: Pushkarev, pp. 24–27; also Tompkins, *The Russian Mind,* pp. 14–16.
32. *Cf.* Seton-Watson, p. 6; Pushkarev, p. 28; Geroid Tanquary Robinson, *Rural Russia under the Old Regime,* London and New York, 1932, pp. 62–63.

33. Pushkarev, pp. 30–31.
34. *Ibid.,* pp. 38–43; Seton-Watson, pp. 7, 10.
35. Seton-Watson, pp. 18–21.
36. Mazour, p. 313.
37. Tompkins, *The Russian Intelligentsia,* p. vii.
38. Seton-Watson, p. 24.
39. Thomas Fitzsimmons, Peter Malof, and John C. Fiske, *U.S.S.R., Its People, Its Society, Its Culture,* New Haven, 1960, p. 3.
40. Wesselitsky, p. 4.
41. As quoted in Warren B. Walsh, *Readings in Russian History,* New York, 1948, pp. 276–77.
42. Fitzsimmons and others, pp. 405–14.
43. Seton-Watson, pp. 22–23.
44. Tompkins, *The Russian Mind,* pp. 240–43, develops this idea.
45. Nikolai Alexandrovich Berdyaev, *Origin of Russian Communism,* London, 1937, p. 18, notes that the Russian intelligentsia's habit of evaluating in extremes led them to derive dogma from scientific hypotheses.
46. Tompkins, p. 235.
47. *Ibid.,* p. 263.
48. *Ibid.*
49. See Tompkins, *loc. cit.,* for development of this point.
50. *Ibid.,* p. 240.
51. *Ibid.*
52. Fitzsimmons, and others, p. 405.
53. *Ibid.,* pp. 413–14.
54. *Ibid.*
55. *Ibid.*
56. George Vernadsky, *A History of Russia,* New Haven, 1929, pp. 34–35.
57. *Ibid.,* p. 65.
58. *Ibid.*
59. Tompkins, p. 98.
60. *McGraw-Hill Encyclopedia of Russia and the Soviet Union,* Michael T. Florinsky, ed., New York, 1961, p. 450. For a brief account see: Jay Jenson and Richard Bayley, "Highlights of the Development of Russian Journalism, 1553–1917," *Journalism Quarterly,* Vol. XLI, No. 3 (Summer 1964), pp. 403–15.
61. *McGraw-Hill Encyclopedia, loc. cit.*
62. Jenson and Bayley, p. 405. Tompkins, p. 99, states that the *Peterburgski Vedomosti* began on January 1, 1728. *McGraw-Hill Encyclopedia, loc. cit.,* indiciates the paper was a continuation of the *Vedomosti.*
63. *Ibid.*
64. Alfred Rambaud, *A Popular History of Russia, From Earliest Times to 1880,* Boston, 1880, Vol. II, p. 170.
65. Jenson and Bayley, *loc. cit.*
66. Tompkins, pp. 100–101.
67. N. A. Dobrolyubov, *Selected Philosophical Essays,* Moscow, 1948, Vol. I, pp. 108–202.
68. Hans Rogger, *National Consciousness in Eighteenth Century Russia,* Cambridge, 1960, p. 70.
69. These were *Vechernaya Zarya* (The Evening Dawn), *Ekonomicheskii Magazin, Pokoyuschiisya Trudolyubets* (The Resting Laborers), and *Moskovskaya Memetskaya Gazeta* (The Moscow German Gazette).

70. Charles Raymond Beazley, Nevill Forbes, and G. A. Birkett, *Russia,* London, 1918, p. 298.
71. Tompkins, pp. 103–5.
72. *Ibid.,* p. 107.
73. *Ibid.*
74. *Ibid.,* p. 174. The *McGraw-Hill Encyclopedia,* p. 450, dates the founding of this journal two years earlier.
75. *Ibid.,* p. 171.
76. M. V. Nechkina, *Russia in the Nineteenth Century,* Ann Arbor, Mich., 1953, pp. 444–45.
77. Tompkins, p. 185.
78. *Ibid.,* pp. 124–27, 141n; Florinsky, pp. 812–13.
79. Florinsky, p. 813.
80. *Ibid.,* pp. 811–12; Tompkins, p. 138.
81. Tompkins, pp. 133–35.
82. Bernard Pares, *A History of Russia,* New York, 1953, p. 350.
83. Florinsky, pp. 815–20.
84. As quoted in Tompkins, p. 182.
85. *Ibid.,* p. 185.

Chapter 2. THE PRESS GENERATES CHANGE, 1855–1917

1. Bernard Pares, *A History of Russia,* New York, 1953, p. 383; Stuart Ramsey Tompkins, *The Russian Intelligentsia, Makers of the Revolutionary State,* Norman, 1957, p. 68.
2. *McGraw-Hill Encyclopedia of Russia and the Soviet Union,* Michael T. Florinsky, ed., New York, 1961, p. 451.
3. Alfred Rambaud, *A Popular History of Russia From Earliest Times to 1880,* Boston, 1880, Vol. III, p. 272.
4. *McGraw-Hill Encyclopedia,* p. 451.
5. Rambaud, *loc. cit.*
6. Sources do not always differentiate periodicals by periodicity. The ones listed as daily here have been so designated, but this list makes no claim to completeness.
7. Rambaud, p. 274.
8. Tompkins, p. 100.
9. A list of the émigré or expatriate papers appears in E. E. Kluge, *Die Russische Revolutinäre Presse in der Zweiten Halfte der Neunzehnten Jahrhunderts, 1855–1905,* Zurich, 1948.
10. Nikolai Popov, *Outline History of the Communist Party of the Soviet Union,* A. Fineberg, ed., New York, 1934, Part I, p. 7.
11. Thomas G. Masaryk, *The Spirit of Russia,* London, 1919, Vol. II, p. 52.
12. See: Tompkins, pp. 73–80; Michael T. Florinsky, *Russia, A History and an Interpretation,* New York, 1953, Vol. II, pp. 1054–56; and Sergei Mikhailovich Kravchinsky (Stepniak) *Russia Under the Tsars,* New York, 1885, pp. 317–21.
13. Kravchinsky, p. 333.
14. Hugh Seton-Watson, *The Decline of Imperial Russia, 1855–1914,* London and New York, 1952, pp. 116–23.
15. *McGraw-Hill Encyclopedia,* p. 1099.
16. *Ibid.,* p. 214.
17. *Cf.* DeWitt Reddick, "Development of the Press in Nineteenth Century Russia," *Journalism Quarterly,* Vol. XXI, No. 1, Mar. 1944, p. 48.

18. Tompkins, p. 95.
19. Alexander Kornilov, *Modern Russian History,* New York, 1917, Vol. II, pp. 56–57.
20. George Plekhanov, *Selected Philosophical Works,* Moscow, 1960, p. 827.
21. Seton-Watson, p. 63–64.
22. Masaryk, p. 92.
23. Florinsky, p. 1123. See also: Tompkins, p. 148.
24. Popov, p. 27.
25. Florinsky, p. 1149.
26. Tompkins, pp. 158–59.
27. Popov, p. 97.
28. V. I. Lenin, *Collected Works,* New York, 1929, Vol. II, p. 240.
29. Florinsky, p. 1149.
30. Lenin, Vol. I, pp. 18–19.
31. *Ibid.,* Vol. II, p. 219. The editors also published a theoretical journal called *Zarya* (The Dawn).
32. Lenin, as quoted in Popov, pp. 115–16.
33. See Tompkins' account, pp. 162–74; also Pares, pp. 447–56.
34. Florinsky, p. 1188.
35. Tompkins, pp. 175–85, 209–26.
36. *Ibid.;* see also Seton-Watson, London and New York, 1952, p. 146; and Pares, p. 425.
37. Tompkins, especially pp. 215–26.
38. This interpretation is largely that of Tompkins who attributes the revolution to a considerable extent to the uncompromising extremist positions the various factions worked themselves into. Florinsky, pp. 1188–1201, also supports this view. Pares, however, does not.
39. Popov, p. 141.
40. Andrew Rothstein, ed., *History of the Communist Party of the Soviet Union,* Moscow, 1960, p. 116.
41. Popov, pp. 211–12.
42. *Ibid.,* p. 165n.
43. Rothstein, pp. 123–31; Pares, p. 452.
44. Rothstein, p. 122. Leon D. Trotsky, chairman of the St. Petersburg Soviet of Workers' Deputies, introduced a resolution to cease publication of *Proletary,* and it was approved by the central committee.
45. For accounts of these developments see: Rothstein, pp. 141–45; Popov, pp. 233–49; and Pares, p. 464.
46. Popov, pp. 250–76.
47. Whitman Bassow, "The Pre-Revolutionary *Pravda* and Tsarist Censorship," *The American Slavic and East European Review,* Vol. XIII, 1954, p. 65.
48. *Ibid.,* p. 59.
49. Rothstein, p. 172; Bassow, p. 63.
50. Bassow, p. 50.
51. Lenin, p. 407.
52. Rothstein, p. 172. The number of workers had grown. In 1913 there were about 3.5 million workers in industry, more than half in factories employing 500 or more.
53. *Ibid.,* p. 175.
54. Bassow, p. 57.
55. Popov, pp. 276–89, Rothstein, p. 171.
56. Rothstein, p. 171.

57. Popov, pp. 336–38.
58. Seton-Watson, p. 363.
59. Maurice Friedberg, "Keeping Up With the Censor," *Problems of Communism,* Vol. XIII, No. 6, Nov.-Dec. 1964, p. 23.
60. *Bolshaia Sovetskaia Entsiklopediia,* Moscow, 1945, Vol. XVII, p. 366.
61. Jenson and Bayley, p. 414.
62. Tompkins, pp. 90–91.
63. W. J. Nagradow, *Moderne Russiche Zensur and Presse vor und Hinter den Coulissen,* Berlin, 1894, p. 58, as quoted in Tompkins, p. 91.
64. As quoted in Florinsky, p. 1112–13.
65. Tompkins, pp. 91–92.
66. Nagradow, p. 146, as cited in Tompkins, p. 92.
67. Tompkins, p. 96.

Chapter 3. SOVIET MASS COMMUNICATIONS: GROWTH AND DEVELOPMENT

1. Bernard Pares, *A History of Russia,* New York, 1953, pp. 500–503.
2. *Bolshaia Sovetskaia Entsiklopediia,* Vol. L, pp. 412–16.
3. V. I. Lenin, *Collected Works.* Vol. XXIII, pp. 225–27; see also: Alex Inkeles, *Public Opinion in Soviet Russia, A Study in Mass Persuasion,* Cambridge, 1950, pp. 161–62.
4. Inkeles, p. 163.
5. Theodore E. Kruglak, *The Two Faces of TASS,* Minneapolis, 1962, pp. 14–21.
6. *Ibid.*
7. These and other data on Soviet periodicals are from *Bolshaia Sovetskaia Entsiklopediia,* Vol. VIII, pp. 411–14; Vol. X, pp. 3–9; Vol. XVI, pp. 248–51; Vol. XLIII, p. 325. Supplement, pp. 1656–60. Also from *Encyclopaedia Britannica,* Vol. XVI, pp. 346–47; *Current Digest of the Soviet Press,* Vols. I–XV, 1949–1963, *passim;* Unesco, *World Communications,* 3rd ed., Paris, 1956, and 4th ed., New York, 1964; Unesco, *Statistics on Newspapers and Other Periodicals,* Paris, 1959; and press reports.
8. This was the revival of an earlier periodical of the same name edited by A. Lunacharskii from 1918 to 1920.
9. See: Inkeles, pp. 184–85; Maurice Friedberg, "Keeping up with the Censor," *Problems of Communism,* Vol. XIII, Nov.-Dec. 1964, pp. 23, 24.
10. V. Gsovski, *Soviet Civil Law,* Ann Arbor, 1948, Vol. I, pp. 65–66.
11. *Bolshaia Sovetskaia Entsiklopediia,* Vol. XL, p. 597.
12. See Inkeles, pp. 226–33.
13. Kenneth Durant, "Russia," *Journalism Quarterly,* Vol. XIV, March 1937, pp. 83–85.
14. These are one-time press run circulation figures and should not be construed as daily aggregates. See: Inkeles, pp. 144–46; also Tables 3.2, 3.3, and 4.1.
15. *Bolshaia Sovetskaia Entsiklopediia,* Vol. XVI, pp. 250–51.
16. Figures for 1964 are from *Sovetskaya Pechat,* May 1965; also *Current Digest of the Soviet Press,* Vol. XVII, No. 19, June 2, 1965, p. 11.
17. Unesco sources also count as dailies those papers that publish four times a week or more.
18. Unesco, *World Communications,* 3rd ed., pp. 243–45.
19. *Bolshaia Sovetskaia Entsiklopediia,* Vol. X, p. 4; Inkeles, pp. 22, 135.

20. See Fred S. Siebert, Theodore Peterson, and Wilbur Schramm, *Four Theories of the Press,* Urbana, 1956, pp. 128, 140.
21. See: Marshall I. Goldman, "Marketing Lessons for Marx," *Harvard Business Review,* Vol. XXVIII, Jan.-Feb. 1960, pp. 78–86; Peter Bart, "Advertising: Soviets Turn to Salesmanship," *New York Times,* June 12, 1962, p. 48; also Marshall I. Goldman, "New Perspective of Product Differentiation and Advertising, The Soviet View," *Boston University Business Review,* Vol. VIII, Spring 1962, pp. 3–12.
22. Edward Crankshaw, "Installment Buying and Advertising," London *Observer* Service as published in the Harrisburg, Pa., *Patriot-News,* Apr. 17, 1960, p. 24.
23. Elizabeth Swayne, "Soviet Advertising: Communism Imitates Capitalism," in C. H. Sandage and Vernon Fryburger, *The Role of Advertising,* Homewood, Ill., 1960, p. 100.
24. "Advertising in the Communist Press," *East Europe,* Vol. VIII, Sept. 1959, p. 31.
25. "Admen Infiltrate the Kremlin," *Business Week,* June 11, 1960, pp. 129–30.
26. See: James W. Markham, "Is Advertising Necessary in the Soviet Economy?" *Journal of Marketing,* Vol. XXVIII, No. 2, Apr. 1964, pp. 32–33; also "Outdoor and Newspaper Advertising Grows," *New York Times,* Nov. 28, 1948, p. 15.
27. Harrison E. Salisbury, "Advertising in the Soviet Union," *New York Times,* Apr. 17, 1949, p. 10.
28. *New York Times,* June 6, 1956, p. 52.
29. Swayne, p. 95.
30. Theodore Shabad, "Soviet May Adopt Profit Incentive to Spur Output," *New York Times,* Oct. 14, 1962, p. 1.
31. "Russians Copying Madison Avenue," *New York Times,* Oct. 2, 1960, p. 13.
32. "Russia Thinks About Advertising," *The Times* of London, Feb. 24, 1961, p. 13.
33. Leo Gruliow, "Advertising—USSR," *Collier's Encyclopedia,* Vol. I, New York, 1962, pp. 152–53; Peter Bart, "Soviet Copy is Mostly Solemn," *New York Times,* Feb. 21, 1962, p. 74.
34. "It's Hard, but a Company Can Advertise in Russia," *New York Times,* June 10, 1960, p. 40.
35. Goldman, as quoted by Bart, "Soviets Turn to Salesmanship," *New York Times,* June 12, 1962, p. 48.
36. Robert W. Campbell, "Economics: Roads and Inroads," *Problems of Communism,* Vol. XIV, No. 6 (Nov.-Dec. 1965), pp. 32–33.
37. Mark W. Hopkins, "Soviet Press Prodded to Improve and Grow," *Editor & Publisher,* Nov. 12, 1960, p. 40; and Hopkins, "Newspapers Sprout All Over Russia," *Editor & Publisher,* Jan. 30, 1960, p. 14.

Chapter 4. SOVIET MASS COMMUNICATIONS: FUNCTION STRUCTURE, CONTROL

1. See Fred S. Siebert, Theodore Peterson, and Wilbur Schramm, *Four Theories of the Press,* Urbana, 1956, p. 19.
2. *Ibid.,* pp. 43–56.
3. *Ibid.,* pp. 105–46; see also Alex Inkeles, *Public Opinion in Soviet Russia, A Study in Mass Persuasion,* Cambridge, 1950, pp. 135–286;

Wilbur Schramm, *Responsibility in Mass Communication,* New York, 1957, pp. 61–99.

4. Siebert, and others, p. 116. "In the Soviet system there is not a theory of the state and a theory of communication: there is only one theory."
5. Vladimir Ilyich Lenin, *Collected Works,* New York, 1927, Vol. IV, p. 114.
6. IPI Report, *The Press in Authoritarian Countries,* Zurich, 1959, p. 15.
7. *Bolshaia Sovetskaia Entsiklopediia,* Moscow, 1949, 2nd ed., Vol. X, pp. 8–9.
8. Nikita S. Khrushchev, "Khrushchev Lays Down the Line on the Arts," *New York Times Magazine,* Sept. 29, 1957, pp. 18ff; also *The Press in Authoritarian Countries,* p. 27.
9. Maurice Friedberg, "Keeping up with the Censor," *Problems of Communism,* Vol. XIII, No. 6 (Nov.-Dec. 1965), p. 22.
10. *Ibid.,* p. 23.
11. As quoted in *Encyclopaedia Britannica, Chicago,* 1960, Vol. XVI, p. 345.
12. As cited from a 1921 pamphlet on the press by Lenin in *The Press in Authoritarian Countries,* p. 13.
13. *Konstituts iya (Oznovnoy Zakon) USSR* [The Constitution (Basic Laws) of the U.S.S.R.] 1947 ed., Moscow, p. 34.
14. Andrei Vyshinsky, *The Law of the Soviet State,* New York, 1948, p. 617.
15. Serge L. Levitsky, "Soviet Law and the Press," *Journalism Quarterly,* Vol. XXXIV, No. 1 (Winter 1957), p.51.
16. V. Gsovski, *Soviet Civil Law,* Ann Arbor, 1948, Vol. I, pp. 64–65.
17. Inkeles, pp. 135–42, lucidly discusses the Soviet versus Anglo-American conceptions of the press.
18. Lenin, pp. 32, 108.
19. *Bolshaia Sovetskaia Entsiklopediia,* Vol. X, p. 4.
20. Mark Arkodyev, "Soviet Newspapers," *USSR,* Apr. 5, 1959.
21. Constitution of the USSR, Article 25; see also, Andrei Vyshinsky, *The Law of the Soviet State,* New York, 1948, pp. 539–617, for development of this and other points.
22. *Ugolovny Kodeks* (The Criminal Code of the R.S.F.S.R.), Moscow, 1953, p. 103.
23. Levitsky, p. 55.
24. Siebert, and others, p. 130.
25. Because Soviet data report combined totals for all papers of daily and less frequent publication, circulation figures must be understood as single press run totals without regard for periodicity.
26. Based on figures found in *Unclassified Intelligence Report,* No. 8099, Sept. 11, 1959, Bureau of Intelligence and Research, U.S. Department of State.
27. Leo Gruliow, "How the Soviet Newspaper Operates," *Problems of Communism,* Vol. V, Mar.-Apr. 1956, pp. 5, 6.
28. For an account of broadcasting in the Soviet Union, see: Inkeles, pp. 225–33.
29. E. W. Ziebarth, "Electronic Media in the Soviet Union," *Quarterly Journal of Speech,* Vol. XLIV, Oct. 1959, p. 279.
30. M. Andreev, "Television in the USSR," *Bulletin: Institute for the Study of the USSR,* Vol. VII, No. 1, Jan. 1960, pp. 31–32. See also:

Richard Tuber, "A Survey of Programming on the Central Studios of Television, Moscow, USSR, Jan.–June, 1960," *Journal of Broadcasting,* Vol. IV, No. 4 (Fall 1960), p. 317.

31. Anniversaries and holidays are important dates in editorial "futures books," for they provide occasions for propaganda tie-ins. For example, Maxim Gorky's birth date anniversary is the signal for printing Gorky's criticisms of American life, more applicable to another day and age. But the dates are ignored and the articles made to sound as if they applied to contemporary conditions. Gruliow, p. 10.
32. A declaration of the Central Committee, as quoted in Inkeles, p. 176.
33. See Inkeles, p. 178. During the late 1950s greater stress was placed upon education in technical skills.
34. Khrushchev, *loc. cit.*
35. Broadcasting's directors are "chief editors of programming."
36. *Pravda* has been criticized in *Izvestia* by its editor, Alexei Adzhubei.
37. Quoted from Gruliow, p. 11.
38. See: Inkeles, pp. 184–88; also Merle Fainsod, "Censorship in the USSR—A Documented Record," *Problems of Communism,* Vol. V, No. 2, Mar.-Apr. 1956, p. 12.
39. Not including foreign correspondence prepared in the Soviet Union for dissemination through the media of other countries. Glavlit, as indicated above, formerly had charge of this work, which was discontinued in Mar. 1961.
40. Inkeles, p. 136; Gruliow, p. 8.
41. Antony Buzek, *How the Communist Press Works,* New York, 1964, pp. 185–98, gives a good account of Tass operations; for examples of domestic censorship by Tass, see pp. 136–37.
42. Gruliow relates an amusing story of a self-reflexive discourse that was quoted and requoted widely in the Soviet media. A. Y. Vyshinsky, former Soviet Ambassador to the United Nations, often cited quotations from foreign periodicals in his U.N. speeches to show that world opinion (at least a portion of it) supported the Russian view. These same quotations were republished in Tass's and *Pravda's* reports of the Vyshinsky addresses.
43. *Cf.* Theodore E. Kruglak, *The Two Faces of TASS, An Analysis of the Soviet News Agency,* Minneapolis, 1962, pp. 7–37, for a historical account.
44. *Ibid.,* p. 214.
45. *Ibid.,* pp. 219–20; *Sovetskaya Pechat,* July 1961, pp. 28, 29. (As translated by Daniel Baumann in *The Soviet Press in Translation,* Vol. II, No. 1, Oct. 1961.)
46. "TASS Monopoly on News Raises Questions for East-West Understanding," *IPI Report,* Vol. II, No. 2, May 1953, p. 6.
47. The Smolensk Archive, at Army Records Center, Alexandria, Va., includes among a collection of party, government, and police files, secret orders to the district censorship arm of Glavlit, copies of central censorship directives, a 1934 issue of the *Bulletin of the Glavlit,* and lists of proscribed books and authors.
48. Absolute figures, and even percentages were forbidden unless projected from a 1933 index. Deliveries could be described as "good" or "bad."
49. On the contrary, Inkeles, p. 106, stresses that Glavlit never played more than a secondary role in censorship of the press.

50. In the process some relatively harmless works were proscribed, including books and poems deemed to possess a "counter-revolutionary character."
51. The Western world has no knowledge of whether such prosecutions actually took place, but there seems to be no reason for believing they did not.
52. For example, in Moscow area only 20 of the 23 *raions* had full-time censors who had been thoroughly checked for political reliability. Censors were found to be "illiterate." See: Fainsod, pp. 14, 15.
53. *Ibid.*, pp. 17–19. In addition to the censorship operation reported in the *Bulletin,* the Archive also contains data picturing the dramatic book burnings of the mid-1930s.
54. Fainsod, p. 17.
55. Notably Boris Kampov-Polevoi, head of a delegation of Soviet journalists visiting in the United States in 1955, and N. G. Palgunov, former director of the Tass Agency.
56. Gruliow, pp. 4, 5.
57. Quotes are mine. An adequate definition of "on time," of course, would necessarily take into consideration how late or how soon after date appearing on the periodical does it reach the subscriber. The question of the practice of postdating has not been explained.
58. Inkeles, p. 229.

Chapter 5. PROFESSIONAL CONCEPTS AND POLICIES

1. Alex Inkeles, *Public Opinion in Soviet Russia, A Study in Mass Persuasion,* Cambridge, 1950, p. 135n. Inkeles noted only two references under the various Russian words for "news," found in alphabetical indexes of two basic collections of party decisions on the press.
2. IPI Report, *The Press in Authoritarian Countries,* Zurich, 1959, p. 23.
3. *Ibid.* See also: N. G. Palgunov, *Osnovii Informatzii v Gazetta: Tass i evo Rol* (Principles of Newspaper Information: Tass and Its Role), Moscow, 1955, p. 34; William Benton, *This Is The Challenge,* New York, 1958, pp. 49–51, 202–12; and Theodore E. Kruglak, *The Two Faces of TASS,* Minneapolis, 1962, pp. 78–80.
4. Some exceptions to this rule have been made in cases involving foreign nationals and more recently in the efforts to popularize the media. In the former instance, a departure was seen on the back page of *Pravda,* Aug. 8, 1955, where a small item inserted by the "Anti-Fascist Committee of Soviet Women" announced with deep sorrow the death in a plane crash of 10 members of a visiting Norwegian delegation. No mention was made of the 15 Russians who lost their lives in the accident.
5. Marc Jaryc, *Press and Publishing in the Soviet Union,* London: School of Slavonic and East European Studies in the University of London, 1935, pp. 9–10.
6. Among them are: *Voprosi Ekonomiki* (Problems of Economics), a monthly published by the Institute of Economics and the Academy of Sciences; *Planovoye Khozyiastvo* (Planned Economy), a monthly periodical published by the Gosplan; *Vneshnaya Torgovlya* (Foreign Trade), published by the Ministry of Foreign Trade; *Financy USSR* (Finance of USSR) published by the Ministry of Finance; and *Dengi i Kredit* (Money and Credit), published by the State Bank.
7. *Current Digest of the Soviet Press,* May 24, 1961, p. 10.

8. *Ibid.*
9. Harrison Salisbury, "Red China Against Russia?" *The Saturday Evening Post,* Mar. 19, 1960, p. 91.
10. Inkeles, pp. 140–41.
11. Wilbur Schramm in Fred S. Siebert, Theodore Peterson, and Wilbur Schramm, *Four Theories of the Press,* Urbana, 1956, p. 119.
12. Stefan T. Possony, *Wordmanship, Semantics as a Communist Weapon,* Committee on the Judiciary. U.S. Senate, 87th Congress, 2nd Session, Washington, 1961, pp. 1–2.
13. Inkeles, pp. 138–39.
14. D. Kuzmichev, *Problemy Gazetovedeniya,* as cited in Marc Jaryc, p. 3.
15. Inkeles, pp. 203–7.
16. Leo Gruliow, "How the Soviet Newspaper Operates," *Problems of Communism,* Vol. V, Mar.–Apr. 1956, p. 9; Inkeles, p. 208.
17. *Cf.* Alex Inkeles and Kent Geiger, "Critical Letters to the Editors of the Soviet Press," *Sociological Review,* Vol. XVII, 1952, pp. 694–703, and Vol. XVIII, 1953, pp. 12–22.
18. See Inkeles, *Public Opinion in Soviet Russia,* pp. 215–22, for an evaluation of the function of self-criticism. See also: Gruliow, p. 10.
19. *Time,* July 30, 1965, p. 32.
20. Irving R. Levine, *Main Street, U. S. S. R.,* New York, 1959, p. 174.
21. *Ibid.,* p. 176.
22. *Ibid.,* p. 184.
23. Excerpted from the quotation cited by Gruliow, pp. 6–7.
24. Inkeles, pp. 175–76.
25. The nonprofessional specialist is discussed by Inkeles, pp. 178–81. This authority does not mention the instructor, whose function is not clearly delineated but is described in *The Press in Authoritarian Countries,* pp. 31–32.
26. UNESCO, *The Training of Journalists,* Paris, 1958, p. 197.
27. *Ibid.*
28. *Ibid.,* p. 198.
29. *Sovetskaya Pechat,* 1962, No. 1, pp. 36–42.
30. Inkeles, pp. 181–83.
31. *New York Times,* Jan. 20, 1957.
32. One editor was said to have had only ten days of work a month on his paper, the rest of the time he was busy with various assignments for his district committee. See: Gruliow, p. 11; and *The Press in Authoritarian Countries,* pp. 30–31.
33. As quoted in *The Press in Authoritarian Countries,* pp. 16–17.
34. *Ibid.*

Chapter 6. HOW THE MEDIA PERFORM: NEWS, ADVERTISING, BROADCASTING

1. John Gunther, *Inside Russia Today,* New York, 1958, p. 303.
2. William J. Eaton, "Red Editor: Alexei Adzhubei," *Nieman Reports,* Vol. XVI, No. 2, June 1963, p. 12.
3. Theodore E. Kruglak, *The Two Faces of TASS,* Minneapolis, 1962, pp. 103–25.
4. *Ibid.,* pp. 126–46.
5. Leo Gruliow, "What the Soviet Reader Never Knew," *IPI Report,* Vol. XI, No. 8, Dec. 1962, p. 3.
6. *Ibid.,* p. 4.

7. Kruglak, p. 170.
8. *Ibid.*, pp. 185–86.
9. *Ibid.*, p. 147.
10. Leo Gruliow, "Advertising–USSR," *Collier's Encyclopedia,* Vol. I, New York, 1962, pp. 152–53.
11. "Soviet Now Calls for Artistic Ads," *New York Times,* Oct. 8, 1955, p. 10.
12. Elizabeth Swayne, "Soviet Advertising: Communism Imitates Capitalism," in C. H. Sandage and Vernon Fryburger, *The Role of Advertising,* Homewood, Ill., 1960, p. 97.
13. Peter Hart, "Soviet Copy is Mostly Solemn," *New York Times,* Feb. 21, 1962, p. 74.
14. Tobia Frankel, "Matchbox Messages," *New York Times Magazine,* March 8, 1959, pp. 66–67; anon., "Postal Persuaders," *New York Times Magazine,* March 15, 1959, p. 70.
15. E. W. Ziebarth, "Electronic Media in the Soviet Union," *Quarterly Journal of Speech,* Vol. XLIV, Oct. 1959, pp. 275–81.
16. *Parade,* February 8, 1959, p. 8.
17. Swayne, p. 94.
18. Peter Bart, "Advertising Ban on Cut-Rate Subscriptions," *New York Times,* April 5, 1962, p. 52.
19. Swayne, p. 94.
20. As quoted from *Sovetskaya Kultura* by *Parade,* Feb. 8, 1959, p. 8.
21. Alex Inkeles, *Public Opinion in Soviet Russia,* Cambridge, 1950, 1958, pp. 224–25. See also: Frederick Williams, "The Soviet Philosophy of Broadcasting," *Journal of Broadcasting,* Vol. VI, No. 1 (Winter 1961–62), pp. 3–10.
22. Marya Mannes, "A Word from Our Sponsor–The Kremlin," *New York Times Magazine,* March 5, 1961, pp. 41, *passim.*
23. A. Barinov, "On the Blue Screen of Volgagrad," *Sovetskaya Pechat,* No. 7, July 1962, (as translated by Olga S. Zingale in *The Soviet Press in Transition,* Vol. III, No. 3, Jan. 1963, p. 4.)
24. Ziebarth, p. 280.
25. Mannes, p. 49.
26. Williams, pp. 6–7; The First Program service is seen on the full facilities of the Central CST network, while the second is limited to Moscow and environs.
27. "You think you have free television," Sakontikov told Mannes, "but does not business dictate what the people will see in your country? We will never use the air for business. We will never interrupt our programs with selling toothpaste, as you do. It is a terrible thing." The American reporter refrained from reminding him that the difference between the American and the Soviet systems of broadcasting is that while the former sells many products for many sponsors, the latter sells only one product, dogma, for one sponsor, the State.
28. As quoted in *Newsweek,* Mar. 8, 1965, p. 83.

Chapter 7. HOW THE MEDIA PERFORM: THE SPECIALIZED JOURNALS

1. See: Allen Kassof, "Now the Angry Young Ivans," *New York Times Magazine,* Nov. 19, 1961, pp. 22ff.
2. Emilia Wilder, "Opinion Polls," *Survey, A Journal of Soviet and East European Studies No. 48,* July 1963, pp. 125–27.

3. Ludmilla B. Turkevich, "Soviet Literary Periodicals," *Books Abroad,* Vol. XXXII, No. 4 (Autumn 1958), p. 370. I am indebted to this work for many of the facts reported here about a number of the periodicals discussed in this chapter.
4. William Nelson, ed., *Out of the Crocodile's Mouth,* Washington, D.C., 1949, p. 54.
5. As quoted from David Shub, *Lenin, A Biography,* Garden City, N.Y., 1948, pp. 45–46.
6. Tobia Frankel, "Sovietski Ekran," *New York Times Magazine,* March 15, 1959, pp. 52, 54.
7. Turkevich, pp. 369–73.
8. Deming Brown, "Muffled Voice of Russian Liberalism," *New York Times Magazine,* December 18, 1965, p. 11.
9. *Ibid.,* p. 10.
10. Harry Schwartz in the *New York Times,* May 19, 1963, p. 6. See also: Marc Slonim, "Some Russians Want to Write," *New York Times Book Review,* October 27, 1963, p. 5; and Patricia Blake and Max Hayward, eds., *Dissonant Voices in Soviet Literature,* New York, 1963, especially pp. vii–xlii.
11. As quoted in Brown, p. 32.
12. Turkevich, p. 369.
13. Michel Gordey, "What You Can Read in Russia," *Harper's Magazine,* Apr. 1952, p. 82.
14. Blake and Hayward, pp. vii, xix.
15. Max Oppenheimer, Jr., "Some Linguistic Aspects of Mind Conditioning by the Soviet Press," *Journal of Human Relations,* Vol. X, No. 1, 1962, pp. 29, 30.
16. Mikhail Kuznetsov, "The Work, the Writer, and the Public," *Sovetskaya Pechat,* No. 7, July 1962.

Chapter 8. IMPROVING PERFORMANCE AND ASSESSING EFFECT

1. Edward Crankshaw, *Russia Without Stalin: The Emerging Pattern.* New York, 1956, pp. 119–20.
2. *Ibid.,* pp. 121–30, traces the Thaw's early phases.
3. See: Jeri Labor, "The Soviet Writer's Search for New Values," *Problems of Communism,* Vol. V, No. 1, Jan.-Feb. 1956, pp. 14–20.
4. Ilya Ehrenburg, *The Thaw,* Chicago, 1955, p. 153.
5. Patricia Blake and Max Hayward, eds., *Dissonant Voices in Soviet Literature,* New York, 1962, pp. xxix–xxxiii.
6. Harold Swayze, *Political Control of Literature in the USSR, 1946–1959,* Cambridge, 1962, pp. 83–85.
7. For a detailed account of the literary controversy period which now bears Zhdanov's name, see Swayze, pp. 26–82.
8. Merle Fainsod, Address at the Pennsylvania State University, May 4, 1961. For a discussion of divergent views in the press, see: IPI Report, *The Press in Authoritarian Countries,* Zurich, 1959, pp. 41–43; and James W. Markham, "Effects of 'The Thaw' on the Soviet Press," *Journalism Quarterly,* XXXVIII, No. 4 (Autumn 1961), pp. 511–18.
9. Swayze, pp. 107–42; Crankshaw, pp. 122–23; and Blake and Hayward, pp. 84–115.
10. *Ibid.,* 145–86.

11. Blake and Hayward, p. xxii; Fainsod, *loc. cit.; Current Digest of the Soviet Press,* Vols. VIII–IX, Feb. 15, 1956–Aug. 28, 1957, *passim.*
12. Nikita S. Khrushchev, "Khrushchev Lays Down the Line on the Arts," *New York Times Magazine,* Sept. 29, 1957, pp. 18ff.
13. *Ibid.*
14. See: Swayze, pp. 200–203; also Wolfgang Leonhard, *The Kremlin Since Stalin,* New York, 1962 (German Edition, Cologne, 1959), pp. 296–99, for an account of the Pasternak case.
15. Leonhard, pp. 340–41.
16. Swayze, pp. 201–24.
17. Mark Frankland, "Khrushchev Faces a Khrushchevian Dilemma," *New York Times Magazine,* May 12, 1963, pp. 21, *passim.*
18. Audun Rigov, "Evgeny Evtushenko–Opposition with Permission," *Studies on the Soviet Union,* New Ser., Vol. II, No. 2, 1962, p. 122.
19. See: Harrison E. Salisbury, "The Poets Versus the Commissars," *New York Times Book Review,* Aug. 11, 1963, pp. 1ff; and Marc Slonim, "In Russia, at Long Last, It's Spring," *New York Times Book Review,* Apr. 15, 1962, pp. 1ff.
20. Frankland, pp. 76–78.
21. Seymour Topping, "Khrushchev's Culture," *New York Times,* Apr. 14, 1963, p. 4E.
22. Henry Tanner, "Eased Line on Arts in Soviet Is Hinted by Two New Works," *New York Times,* Aug. 18, 1963, p. 1.
23. Marc Slonim, "Some Russians Want to Write as They Please," *New York Times Book Review,* Oct. 27, 1963, pp. 5, 48.
24. Harry Schwartz, "Editor in Soviet Defends Writers," *New York Times,* May 19, 1963, p. 6. By this time, Tvardovsky had been restored to his old job as *Novy Mir* editor.
25. *Pravda,* Dec. 4, 1953.
26. *Editor & Publisher,* Dec. 17, 1955, p. 65.
27. Leo Gruliow, "How the Soviet Newspaper Operates," *Problems of Communism,* Vol. V, No. 2, Mar.-Apr. 1956, p. 5.
28. *Ibid.*
29. "Journalism—A Most Important Province of Party and Public Activity," *Partinaya Zhizn,* May 9, 1961, pp. 17–24.
30. For example, the Writers' and Artists' Union was first organized in 1933.
31. Mark W. Hopkins, "Soviet Press Prodded to Improve and Grow," *Editor & Publisher,* Nov. 12, 1960, p. 40, and Hopkins, "Newspapers Sprout All Over Russia," *Editor & Publisher,* Jan. 30, 1960, p. 14.
32. As cited by Osgood Caruthers in the *New York Times,* Nov. 29, 1959.
33. Marshall D. Schulman, "Since Stalin: Have Things Changed?" *New York Times Magazine,* Mar. 19, 1961, pp. 23ff; Philip E. Mosely, "How the Kremlin Keeps Ivan in Line," *New York Times Magazine,* Feb. 19, 1961, pp. 16, 67–68; and Richard Pipes, "The Public Mood," in "The Mood of the Russian People," *Harper's Magazine,* May 1961, pp. 107–12.
34. Alexei I. Adzhubei, "Journalism Is a Calling," *Sovetskaya Pechat,* No. 12, Dec. 1959, pp. 43–45 (translated by Daniel Baumann and printed in *The Soviet Press in Translation,* Vol. II, No. 3, Dec. 1961).
35. See: Alex Inkeles and Raymond A. Bauer, *The Soviet Citizen, Daily Life in a Totalitarian Society,* Cambridge, 1959, pp. 159–88.
36. *Ibid.,* p. 165.
37. Frederick C. Barghoorn, *The Soviet Image of the United States,* New York, 1950, p. 277.

38. Marya Mannes, "A Word from Our Sponsor--The Kremlin," *New York Times Magazine,* Mar. 5, 1961, p. 50.
39. See: Inkeles and Bauer, especially pp. 178, 179.
40. *Ibid.,* p. 186.
41. Cited by Alexander Vichnevski, assistant director general, Tass, in "A Soviet Point of View," a panel discussion on the general topic *The Responsibility of Journalists in International Understanding* at the VIIIth International Session of the International Centre for Advanced Training in Journalism, University of Strassbourg, Oct. 5–10, 1964. Reported in *Journalism Quarterly Review,* No. 22, pp. 29–32.

Chapter 9. PRESS AND SOCIETY IN TRADITIONAL CHINA: THE CULTURAL SETTING

1. S. H. Steinberg, ed., *The Statesman's Year-Book,* London and New York, 1961, p. 895; H. T. F. Rhodes and C. J. Smith, eds., *The International Year Book and Statesman's Who's Who,* London, 1961, p. 171.
2. *Ibid.* The 1953 Census, which according to the Communist regime in Peking, is the only relatively complete census ever taken of China's millions, reported the population as 601.9 million in 1953. This figure included 574.2 million Mainland Chinese; 7.6 million living on Taiwan; 11.7 million Chinese residents studying abroad; and 8.4 million Chinese in remote border regions. Urban populations totaled 77.3 million, and those classified as rural totaled 505.3 million. In percentages the urban population was 13.3 per cent, as compared with 86.7 per cent counted as rural. The estimate of 700 million was made by the *Statesman's Year-Book* and was for July 1, 1961.
3. Sripati Chandra-sekhar, "The Human Inflation of Red China," *New York Times Magazine,* Dec. 6, 1959, p. 24.
4. Helmut G. Callis, *China, Confucian, and Communist,* New York, 1959, p. 3, and map, p. 376.
5. *Ibid.,* p. 18.
6. Sripati Chandra-sekhar, *Red China, An Asian View,* New York, 1961, p. 127. The author reports 36.7 per cent of the population as below 14 years of age, and 47.2 per cent between 15 and 49 years. See also: Chang-tu Hu and others, *China, Its People, Its Society, Its Culture,* New Haven, 1960, p. 57.
7. Chandra-sekhar, *Red China, An Asian View,* p. 29.
8. Hu and others, p. 334.
9. Callis, p. 14. See also: Hu, pp. 367–69, and *The Christian Science Monitor,* Feb. 8, 1964, 2nd section, p. 1. Recent visitors to China tend to disagree with this view.
10. Callis, pp. 360–61; steel production had increased to 18,400,000 tons in 1960. See: John Scott, *Crisis in Communist China,* New York, 1962, pp. 120, 126–27; also Felix Greene, *Awakened China,* New York, 1961, pp. 95–109, presents a more optimistic view of China's industrial potential.
11. Hu and others, pp. 368–69.
12. Callis, p. 45.
13. Subordination of women to men was an established and unquestioned custom. The dominance of the male lies deep in Chinese tradition and goes back to earliest times, when the concept was

represented by the symbols *Yin* and *Yang*. *Yin* stood for all things female, weak, dark, and passive; while *Yang* was symbolical of all things male, strong, light, and active. See: *Encyclopedia Sinica,* London, 1917, p. 615.

14. As quoted in Callis, p. 48.
15. As during the reign of Chin Shih Huang Ti (221–206 B.C.), the Emperor who built the Great Wall.
16. Vera Micheles Dean, *The Nature of the Non-Western World,* New York, 1957, pp. 92–95.
17. Edgar Snow, *The Other Side of the River, Red China Today,* New York, 1961, pp. 34, 558.
18. *Cf.* Callis, p. 41.
19. H. G. Creel, *Chinese Thought from Confucius to Mao Tse-tung,* Chicago, 1953, Mentor Books Edition, New York, 1960, p. 44.
20. *Ibid.,* pp. 96–97.
21. Callis, pp. 38, 39.
22. *Ibid.,* p. 51.
23. *Ibid.,* p. 56.
24. Dean, pp. 94, 95.
25. Creel, p. 12.
26. See: Y. P. Wang, *The Rise of the Native Press in China,* New York, 1924, p. 11. This was a period roughly contemporary with the building of the pyramids in Egypt. Confucius immortalized Yao and his heirs as great rulers of the Middle Kingdom. Their period, 2356 to 2205 B.C., is known as the Golden Age of Chinese history. Also Callis, pp. 101–2.
27. Yutang Lin, *A History of the Press and Public Opinion in China,* Chicago, 1936, p. 12.
28. See: *Encyclopedia Sinica,* p. 115. The title suggests that the records for the four seasons were kept but that two copies or issues were used to report the four. Also, Lin, p. 14.
29. Roswell S. Britton, *The Chinese Periodical Press, 1800–1912,* Shanghai, 1933, p. 1.
30. Callis, p. 104.
31. Kung-chen Ko, *Chung-kuo Pao-hsüeh Shih* (The History of Chinese Journalism), Shanghai, 1927, Chap. 2, p. 1. This and subsequent references are to the first edition, whose page numbering was by chapters. Later editions numbered their pages continuously.
32. This translation is Lin's, p. 14.
33. Lin, p. 15, finds no direct mention of *Ti-pao* during the Han dynasty. The term seems to have been used first by scholars and historians in a later period. Regardless of what it was called at the time, the official press existed, for *Ti* was definitely a Han institution where private newsletters were transmitted and circulated by means of the extensive system of imperial couriers and post relays.
34. Authorities credit Ts'ai Lun, a Chinese, with inventing the art of papermaking and place the date of his report to the Emperor about this achievement at 105 A.D. However, *Encyclopaedia Britannica* does not mention him but states that different writers have traced papermaking back to the second century B.C. The Chinese knew how to make felt from animal hair, and making paper from vegetable fiber was a parallel step. In the eighth century A.D. the Arabs at Samarkand learned how to make paper from Chinese they captured. The craft was introduced into Europe by the Moors in twelfth-century Spain.

35. Wang, p. 13. Lin, p. 11, states that " . . . at least beginning from the tenth century onwards, they [the Gazettes] were published at regular periodical intervals. . . ."
36. There were 1,297 horse relay stations ten *li* (one third of a mile) apart on the imperial highways, 260 stations along waterways, and some 86 stations that served the purposes of both. On land the speed for sending such messages was 300 *li* or 100 miles a day. Emergency messages got faster service. Lin, p. 15.
37. *Ibid.,* p. 16.
38. Identity of the inventor of block printing, said by several authorities to have been one Feng Tao, is apparently unknown. Feng Tao was a scholar who died in 954 A.D. Reliable historians, however, assert that this method of printing can be traced to the Sui dynasty (589–618 A.D.). Chan Lee, in his book, *Shih Chieh Hsin Hwen Hsieh (History of World Journalism),* Vol. III, Taipei, Taiwan, 1963, pp. 1, 4, definitely states that block printing was in use during the Tang dynasty and at some time between 713 and 755 A.D. The earliest block printed book in existence, the *Diamond Sutra,* bears the date 868 A.D. Feng Tao must have been one of several to use block printing, but was not its originator. As early as 175 A.D., Wang *(op. cit.,* p. 12), reports, knowledge of making inked impressions from carved forms was employed. Emperor Ling of the Han dynasty ordered the classics cut on stone tablets placed in front of the palace so that scholars might rub impressions from them.
39. S. Wells Williams in *The Middle Kingdom,* p. 603, gives credit to Pi Shing, who lived about 1000 A.D., for the invention of movable type.
40. Lee, pp. 1, 4. However, Ko, Chap. 2, pp. 11, 12, says that before 1638 the *Ti-pao* were handwritten.
41. *Ibid.* Although Ko dates the first use of movable type in printing the *Ti-pao* at 1638, Britton reports that even into the nineteenth century the *Ti-pao* were both printed and handwritten. Book printing in movable type was started in the Sung dynasty (960–1279 A.D.), Ko states, citing as evidence an idea in a book of the time which was set in reverse.
42. Britton, pp. 11–12.
43. *Ibid.,* p. 5.
44. Britton, p. 2, believes this estimate, which is his own, is perhaps a bit too high.
45. From "The Evolution of Li," as quoted by Callis, p. 51.
46. *Ibid.,* p. 119.
47. Lin, p. 6.
48. Friederich Hirth, *The Ancient History of China,* New York, 1908, p. 155, as quoted from *Kuo Yu* (State speeches), a work compiled during the Ch'ou dynasty.
49. Wang, p. 36.
50. For accounts of the Ch'in censorship, see: Callis, p. 122 and Wang, p. 36. For an account of public criticism during the Han dynasty, see Lin, pp. 28–39.
51. Britton, p. 4.
52. *Ibid.,* p. 11. An 1836 case of leakage caused the Emperor to issue a decree affirming the principle of publicity for government acts in general, but stressing the need to keep confidential certain matters for state reasons.
53. *Ibid.,* p. 13.

Chapter 10. THE PRIVATELY OWNED NATIVE PRESS

1. Roswell S. Britton, *The Chinese Periodical Press, 1800–1912,* Hong Kong and Singapore, 1933, p.17.
2. Y. P. Wang, *The Rise of the Native Press in China,* New York, 1924, p. 16; Britton, p. 18.
3. Britton, p. 28.
4. Lin Yutang, *A History of the Press and Public Opinion in China,* Chicago, 1936, p. 92; Britton, p. 52.
5. This follows Britton's version, as given on p. 54. Lin, however, p. 92, shows the *Globe Magazine* as a monthly beginning in 1875 and continuing without interruption until 1904.
6. This follows Britton's account. The *Encyclopedia Sinica,* p. 459, states that the first English language newspaper in China was founded by Matheson. Since, according to Britton, Matheson owned it almost from the start, the difference is perhaps negligible.
7. *Encyclopedia Sinica,* p. 459.
8. *Ibid.,* p. 460.
9. Lin, p. 124.
10. Britton, p. 62.
11. As cited in Britton, p. 61.
12. Lin, p. 84.
13. Werner Levi, *Modern China's Foreign Policy,* Minneapolis, 1953, p. 34.
14. Kung-chen Ko, *Chung-kuo Pao-hsüeh Shih* (The History of Chinese Journalism), Shanghai, 1927, Chap. 3, p. 31.
15. *Ibid.,* Chap. 3, pp. 10–11. This account is also given in Chang-chao Yuan, *Chung-kuo Pao Yeh Hsiao* (A Brief History of Chinese Journalism), Hong Kong, 1957, p. 25.
16. Lin, p. 88, and *Encyclopedia Sinica,* p. 397, connect China's first daily with the *China Mail.* Britton associates it with the *Daily Press,* but denies that Wu Ting-fang had anything to do with it (pp. 45–46). Britton dates the *Wah Tse Yah Pao* some ten years later than Ko's date of 1864, a date which Lin borrows and adds a question mark.
17. Britton, p. 68.
18. Wang, p. 30.
19. *Ibid.,* p. 33.
20. Lin, p. 102; Britton, p. 94.
21. Lin, *loc. cit.*
22. Britton, pp. 94–101; Lin, pp. 101–2.
23. Helmut G. Callis, *China, Confucian and Communist,* New York, 1959, pp. 214–15.
24. As quoted in Lin, pp. 99–100.
25. Britton, pp. 108–9.
26. The 1904–1905 Russo-Japanese War, fought on and for Chinese territory, intensified the revolutionary movement because of dissatisfaction with the Chinese government which was powerless to do anything about it.
27. James C. Y. Shen, *Liang Chi-chao and His Times,* Columbia, Mo., Unpublished Dissertation, 1953, pp. 218–29.
28. *Cf.* Lin, pp. 103–4.
29. Lin lists them both as dailies, but Britton, p. 113, reports that *Fu Pao* was monthly.

30. Ko, Chap. 6, p. 171; also Lin, p. 106.
31. Britton, p. 118. Also see the evaluation made by Shen, pp. 222–27.
32. Shen, pp. 5–13.
33. Wang, p. 21; Shen, p. 248.
34. *Cf.* Lin, p. 94.
35. Britton, pp. 86–90; Shen, p. 348.
36. *China Handbook, 1937–1943,* New York, 1943, p. 697.
37. For the historical developments, see Callis, pp. 229–33.
38. See: Lin Yutang's discussion, pp. 119–24.
39. *China Handbook, 1937–1943,* p. 697.
40. Britton, p. 123.
41. Lin, pp. 140–41.
42. Hollington K. Tong, *China and the World Press,* Nanking, 1948, p. 9.
43. John B. Powell, *My Twenty-five Years in China,* New York, 1945, pp. 10, 11, 90, 91.
44. Robert W. Desmond, *The Press and World Affairs,* New York and London, 1937, p. 347.
45. Among a profusion of private agencies scattered throughout China in the late 1930s. For example, a Unesco report of 1947 counted 30 agencies in Canton and 14 in Peking.
46. The agency had seen daylight at Canton in 1924 as a Kuomintang Party news bureau. *China Handbook, 1937–1943,* p. 702.
47. The services, looked upon as party propaganda, had difficulty getting into print, though distributed free.
48. This was neither the first public radio broadcasting in China nor the first government-owned station. Radio broadcasting was introduced into China in 1922 by a small field station, which was set up in the Wing Oil Company building in Shanghai. Two years later an American firm, the Kellogg Radio Company, started to operate a station. By 1926–1928 the station was supported by the China Broadcasting Association, which had 600 listeners. The first government-owned stations were established at Peking and Tientsin in 1927, *China Handbook, 1937–1943,* p. 278.
49. *Ibid.*
50. Wang, pp. 44–45.
51. Lin, pp. 141–42.
52. This estimate is conservative. It comes from *The China Year Book,* which lists only papers registered by the post office for special rates. There were many papers not distributed through the post office, but by carriers and street sales. In comparison, the *Shun Pao* counted 1,134 periodicals for the same year.
53. Ko, Chap. 6, p. 175.
54. *China Handbook, 1937–1943,* p. 697.
55. Lin, pp. 143–44.
56. *Ibid.,* pp. 147–48.
57. *Ibid.*
58. Unesco, *World Communications,* 2nd ed., Paris, 1950, pp. 82–83. The 3,000 periodicals listed here include papers not registered by the post office.
59. *Ibid.*
60. Wang, p. 36.
61. *Ibid.,* pp. 36–37.
62. See: Lin, pp. 167–79; *Encyclopaedia Britannica,* Vol. XVI, p. 357.

63. See *China Handbook, 1937–1943,* pp. 707–11 for laws regulating the press, and pp. 278–81 for the Ministry of Communication's broadcasting regulations.

Chapter 11. THE RED CHINESE COMMUNICATION SYSTEM: FUNCTION, STRUCTURE, CONTROL

1. The title *Liberation Daily,* being popular with the Chinese Communists, did not end in 1945, but was continued and repeated for various newspapers. For a list of Chinese Communist papers see Yuan-li Wu, "Press Regulations in Mao's China," *Problems of Communism,* Vol. VI, No. 4 (July-Aug. 1957), p. 33n; also Franklin Houn, *To Change a Nation,* New York, 1961, p. 28.
2. See Frederick T. C. Yu, *Mass Persuasion in Communist China,* New York and London, 1964, Appendix, pp. 161–69, for a party view of *Jen-min Jih-pao* and its function.
3. Doak Barnett, *China on the Eve of the Communist Takeover,* New York, 1963, pp. 351–52.
4. Chang-chao Yuan, *Chung-kuo Pao Yeh Hsiao Shih* (Newspaper History of China), Hong Kong, 1957, pp. 88–89.
5. Milton Shieh, "Red China Patterns Controls of Press on Russian Model," *Journalism Quarterly,* Vol. XXVIII, No. 1 (Winter 1951), p. 79; also: Franklin Houn, "The Press in Communist China: Its Structure and Operation," *Journalism Quarterly,* Vol. XXXIII, No. 4 (Fall 1956), p. 509. Houn noted a significant change in official policy toward privately owned periodicals occurring in 1952, which resulted in closing, merging, or drastically reorienting them.
6. As quoted in Wu, p. 33.
7. *Cf.* Shieh, pp. 74, 75; I am indebted also to Frederick T. C. Yu, "Communications and Politics in Communist China," (ms. prepared for the Seminar on Communications and Political Development, Dobbs Ferry, New York, 1961, and especially to Yu, "Communications and Politics in Communist China," Chap. 16 in *Communications and Political Development,* Lucien W. Pye, ed., Princeton, 1964, pp. 259–97, for the interpretations of this section.
8. See Yu, "Communications and Politics . . . ," pp. 261–62. The quotation is from Liu Shao-chi, *On the Party,* Peking, 1950, p. 2.
9. As cited by Yu, *ibid.,* p. 264, from the *Constitution of the Chinese Communist Party.*
10. Houn, *To Change a Nation,* pp. 9–10.
11. *Ibid.*
12. Shieh, pp. 75–77.
13. Frederick T. C. Yu, "How the Chinese Reds Transfer Mass Grievances to Power," *Journalism Quarterly,* Vol. XXX, No. 3 (Summer 1953), p. 357; Shieh, pp. 74–76.
14. Houn, *To Change a Nation,* pp. 105–6.
15. Houn, "The Press in Communist China . . . ," pp. 506–11.
16. Unesco, *World Communications,* 3rd ed., 1956, p. 147.
17. Houn, *To Change a Nation,* p. 123.
18. IPI Report, *The Press in Authoritarian Countries,* Zurich, 1959, p. 49.
19. Raymond B. Nixon, "Freedom of the World's Press: An Appraisal with New Data," *Journalism Quarterly,* Vol. XLII, No. 1 (Winter 1965), p. 12.

20. Union Research Institute, Ltd., *Catalogue of Mainland Chinese Magazines and Newspapers Held by the Union Research Institute,* 2nd ed., Hong Kong, 1963.
21. Houn, *To Change a Nation,* pp. 117–18.
22. See Houn's description of radio in "Radio Broadcasting and Propaganda in Communist China," *Journalism Quarterly,* Vol. XXXIV, No. 3 (Summer 1957), pp. 366–77.
23. Chang-tu Hu and others, *China, Its People, Its Society, Its Culture,* New Haven, 1960, p. 252.
24. Houn, *To Change a Nation,* p. 156. See Yu, *Mass Persuasion in Communist China,* pp. 123–24, for an account of the development of the broadcasting system.
25. The probability is that this goal was not reached; see Houn, *To Change a Nation,* pp. 163–64.
26. Unesco, *World Communications,* 4th ed., New York, 1964, p. 209.
27. Felix Greene, *Awakened China, The Country Americans Don't Know,* 1961, pp. 419–20.
28. Nixon, *loc. cit.*
29. See an illustration of how radio reaches a remote village in: David Chipp, "How 650 Million Chinese Are Controlled," *New York Times Magazine,* Sept. 14, 1958, pp. 21, 76. Judging by this, radio directly contacts these people only infrequently, or at least not regularly. See also: Alan P. L. Liu, *Radio Broadcasting in Communist China,* Cambridge, 1964, for a report on rural radio and the wired speaker network.
30. The major sources for the basic information about structure and organization of the press and radio are Houn, *To Change a Nation,* pp. 92–144, 155–66; the other works of Houn cited above; and Wu, pp. 34–35.
31. Houn, *To Change a Nation,* p. 147n.
32. *Ibid.,* pp. 112–13.
33. See: Wu, p. 35; and Ignatius Peng Yao, "The New China News Agency," *Journalism Quarterly,* Vol. XL, No. 1 (Winter 1963), p. 83.
34. Yao, p. 86; Houn, *To Change a Nation,* pp. 97–100.
35. *Ibid.,* p. 84.
36. *Ibid.,* p. 85.
37. *Ibid.,* p. 86.
38. Wu, p. 34.
39. Houn, *To Change a Nation,* pp. 150, 67n.
40. *Ibid.,* p. 121. Houn dates the change of policy augmenting the postal service in April, 1956, whereas *The Press in Authoritarian Countries,* p. 36, states that the change was ordered in 1954. The two sources do not necessarily conflict.
41. Wu, p. 35.
42. *Ibid.,* p. 34.
43. Wilbur Schramm, *One Day in the World's Press,* Stanford, 1959, p. 96.
44. See Yu, "Communications and Politics . . . ," pp. 266–69, for an illuminating description of "Communications in a Commune." Yu lists 1,446 different unit organizations, in a commune of 21,000 people, that are engaged in "cultural work."
45. Houn, *To Change a Nation,* p. 122.
46. *Cf.* G. Raymond Nunn, *Publishing in Mainland China,* Cambridge: MIT Report No. 4, 1966, pp. 30–35, 44.

47. Lucien Pye, pp. 24–29, 86–95.
48. Helmut G. Callis, *China, Confucian and Communist,* New York, 1959, pp. 31–34.
49. *Ibid.*
50. *Statesman's Year-Book,* London, 1963, p. 894.
51. Greene, p. 394.
52. Houn, "The Press in Communist China . . . ," p. 508.
53. Liu, p. 1.

Chapter 12. HOW THE CHINESE MEDIA PERFORM

1. I am indebted to Yuan-li Wu, "Press Regulation in Mao's China," *Problems of Communism,* Vol. VI, No. 4 (July-Aug. 1957), pp. 35–36, for this analysis.
2. See: Frederick T. C. Yu, *Mass Persuasion in Communist China,* New York and London, 1964, pp. 111–16; and Wilbur Schramm, *One Day in the World's Press,* Stanford, 1959, pp. 97–104 for literal translations of the *Jen-min Jih-pao* of other dates.
3. *Cf.* Franklin Houn, *To Change a Nation,* New York, 1961, pp. 132–36, for complete daily broadcast schedules for one day in 1950, again in 1952, and in 1959.
4. *Hsin-hua Pan-zu Kan* (New China Fortnightly), No. 11, 1958, pp. 118–19.
5. Unesco, *World Communications,* 3rd ed., 1956, p. 147.
6. Houn, pp. 104–5.
7. Alex Edelstein and Alan P. L. Liu, "Anti-Americanism in Red China's *People's Daily:* A Functional Analysis," *Journalism Quarterly,* Vol. XL, No. 2 (Spring 1963), p. 195.
8. C. A. Oliphant, "The Image of the United States Projected by *Peking Review,*" *Journalism Quarterly,* Vol. XLI, No. 3 (Summer 1964), p. 416.
9. *Ibid.,* p. 420.
10. David Chipp, "How 650 Million Chinese Are Controlled," *New York Times Magazine,* Sept. 14, 1958, p. 78.
11. IPI Report, *The News from Asia,* Zurich, 1956, p. 54.
12. IPI Report, *The Press in Authoritarian Countries,* Zurich, 1959, p. 58. The original source of the survey data is Wu, p. 37.
13. Houn, pp. 129–44.
14. IPI Report, *The News from Asia,* p. 59; also Robert Guillain, *600 Million Chinese,* New York, 1957, p. 115.
15. Schramm, p. 96.
16. Houn, pp. 129, 236–37. This point is also documented in Theodore H. E. Chen, *Thought Reform of the Chinese Intellectuals,* Hong Kong and Oxford, 1960, especially pp. 177–201.

Chapter 13. ELEMENTS IN COMMUNICATIONS EFFECTS

1. A. Doak Barnett, "Mao's Aim: To Capture 600 Million Minds," *New York Times Magazine,* Sept. 9, 1956, p. 12.
2. Frederick T. C. Yu, "Communications and Politics in Communist China," in *Communications and Political Development,* Lucien Pye, ed., Princeton, 1964, p. 290.
3. Robert Jay Lifton, *Thought Reform and the Psychology of Totalism,* New York, 1961, pp. 389–90.

4. *Ibid.,* pp. 388–98 for an analysis of the origins of thought control.
5. *Ibid.,* p. 398.
6. David Chipp, "How 650 Million Chinese Are Controlled," *New York Times Magazine,* p. 21.
7. John Scott, *Crisis in Communist China,* New York, 1962, p. 152.
8. T. H. E. Chen, *Thought Reform of the Chinese Intellectuals,* Hong Kong and Oxford, pp. 12–13, 33.
9. Yu, pp. 266–69.
10. Chipp, p. 72.
11. Barnett, p. 72.
12. Lifton, p. 247.
13. Fu-sheng Mu, *The Wilting of the Hundred Flowers,* New York, 1962, pp. 210–11.
14. Franklin Houn, *To Change a Nation,* New York, 1961, pp. 55–63.
15. The rendition of the slogan varies in different sources. Chen, p. 117, adds the word "together" after "blossom," and again after "contend." Houn, p. 6, transcribes it thusly: "Let One Hundred Schools of Thought Contend and One Hundred Flowers Bloom." Houn notes that the saying was not original with Mao, but a classical phrase used originally to describe a period in Chinese history following civil war when new reforms became popular and new ideas emerged. See: Edgar Snow, *The Other Side of the River,* New York, 1961, p. 391.
16. Chen, p. 119.
17. *Ibid.,* pp. 119–20.
18. Houn, pp. 6, 5n.
19. Franklin Houn, "The Press in Communist China: Its Structure and Operation," *Journalism Quarterly,* Vol. XXXIII, No. 4 (Fall 1956), p. 511.
20. IPI Report, *The Press in Authoritarian Countries,* p. 59.
21. Wu, Yuan-li, "Press Regulations in Mao's China," *Problems of Communism,* Vol. VI, No. 4 (July-Aug. 1957), p. 39.
22. Michael Lindsay, "Chinese Puzzle: Mao's Foreign Policy," *New York Times Magazine,* Oct. 12, 1958, p. 79.
23. Chen, p. 164.
24. *Ibid.,* pp. 139–40.
25. *The Press in Authoritarian Countries,* p. 59.
26. *Ibid.,* p. 60; also Chen, pp. 164–65.
27. Chen, pp. 156–57.
28. Wu, p. 40.
29. According to *The Press in Authoritarian Countries,* the decision was made by the committee of the non-Communist parties to which the editor belonged and of which the paper was the organ.
30. See: Houn, *To Change a Nation,* p. 33, 5n; also Chen, p. 140.
31. See: Lifton, pp. 431–32, for an analysis of the psychology of what he calls the primacy of doctrine over personal and human experience.
32. Houn, *To Change a Nation,* p. 7; Chipp, p. 76.
33. *Cf.* Chen, pp. 199–200.
34. Chipp, p. 78.
35. See Lifton's analysis of the psychological steps employed, pp. 65–85.
36. Barnett, p. 76.
37. Houn, p. 62–63.
38. *Ibid.*
39. Chang-tu Hu and others, *China, Its People, Its Society, Its Culture,* New Haven, 1960, pp. 482–83.

GENERAL SOURCES

Books, Articles, and Periodicals

Basic Facts and Figures. Paris: Unesco, 1961.

Buzek, Antony, *How the Communist Press Works.* New York and London: Frederick A. Praeger, 1964.

Codding, George A., Jr., *Broadcasting without Barriers.* Paris: Unesco, 1959.

Dean, Vera Micheles, *The Nature of the Non-Western World.* New York: The New American Library, 1957.

———, and Harry Harootunian, *West and Non-West: New Perspectives.* New York: Holt, Rinehart and Winston, Inc., 1963.

De Fleur, Melvin L., *Theories of Mass Communication.* New York: David McKay Company, Inc., 1966.

Demographic Year Book. New York: United Nations, 1961.

Desmond, Robert W., *The Press and World Affairs.* New York and London: D. Appleton-Century, 1937.

Editor & Publisher, Weekly, 1952–1964.

Encyclopaedia Britannica, Chicago: 1960. 24 vols.

Gerald, J. Edward, *The Social Responsibility of the Press.* Minneapolis: Univ. of Minn. Press, 1963.

IPI Survey, *Government Pressures on the Press.* Zurich: International Press Institute, 1956.

———, *The Press in Authoritarian Countries,* Zurich: International Press Institute, 1959.

The International Year Book and Statesman's Who's Who. H. T. F. Rhodes and C. J. Smith, eds. London: Burke's Peerage, Ltd., 1963, 1964. Annual.

Kayser, Jacques, *One Week's News.* Paris: Unesco, 1953.

Lerner, Daniel, *The Passing of Traditional Society.* Glencoe: The Free Press, 1958.

Lopez, Salvador P., *Freedom of Information.* Paris: Unesco, 1953.

Merrill, John C., *Handbook of the Foreign Press.* Baton Rouge: La. State Univ. Press, 1958.

———, and others, *The Foreign Press.* Baton Rouge: La. State Univ. Press, 1964.

Nafziger, Ralph O., *International News and the Press: Communications, Organization of News Gathering, International Affairs and the Foreign Press—An Annotated Bibliography.* New York: H. W. Wilson Co., 1940.

The *New York Times,* 1954–1964.

New York Times Magazine, Weekly, 1952–1964.

News in Asia. Zurich: International Press Institute, 1956.

Nixon, Raymond B., "Factors Related to Freedom in National Press Systems," *Journalism Quarterly,* Vol. XXXVII, No. 1, Winter 1960.

———, "Freedom of the World's Press: An Appraisal with New Data," *Journalism Quarterly,* Vol. XLI, No. 3, Summer 1964.

Price, Warren C., *The Literature of Journalism, An Annotated Bibliography.* Minneapolis: Univ. of Minn. Press, 1959.

Production Year Book, 1960. Rome: FAO, 1961.

Pye, Lucien W., ed., *Communications and Political Development.* Princeton: Princeton Univ. Press, 1964.

Rostow, Walt Whitman, *The Stages of Economic Growth: A Non-Communist Manifesto.* Cambridge: Harvard Univ. Press, 1960.

Schramm, Wilbur, ed., *Mass Communications.* Urbana: Univ. of Ill. Press, 1960.
———, *One Day in the World's Press.* Stanford: Stanford Univ. Press, 1960.
Siebert, Fred S., and others, *Four Theories of the Press.* Urbana: Univ. of Ill. Press, 1956.
Smith, Bruce Lannes, and Chitra M. Smith, *International Communication and Public Opinion.* Princeton: Princeton Univ. Press, 1956.
———, and others, *Propaganda Communication, and Public Opinion: A Comprehensive Reference Guide.* Princeton: Princeton Univ. Press, 1946.
The Statesman's Year-Book. S. H. Steinberg, ed. London: Macmillan & Co., Ltd., 1963. Annual.
Terrou, Fernand, and Lucien Solal, *Legislation for Press, Film, and Radio.* Paris: Unesco, 1951.
Ulrich's Periodicals Directory; A Classified Guide to a Selected List of Current Periodicals, Foreign and Domestic. New York: R. R. Bowker Co., 1932–1947.
World Communications: Press, Radio, Television, Film. 3rd Ed. Paris: Unesco, 1956.
World Communications: Press, Radio, Television, Film. 4th Ed. Amsterdam and New York: Unesco, 1964.
Wright, Charles R., *Mass Communication: A Sociological Perspective.* New York: Random House, 1959.

RUSSIA AND THE SOVIET UNION

Books, Articles, and Periodicals

"Admen Infiltrate the Kremlin," *Business Week,* June 11, 1960.
"Advertising in the Communist Press," *East Europe,* Vol. VIII, Sept. 1959.
Adzhubei, Alexei I., "Journalism Is a Calling," *Sovetskaya Pechat,* No. 12, Dec. 1959.
Andreev, M., "Television in the USSR," *Bulletin of the Institute for the Study of the USSR,* Vol. VII, No. 1, Jan. 1960.
Arkodyev, Mark, "Soviet Newspapers," *USSR,* Apr. 5, 1959.
Bardens, Dennis, *A Press in Chains.* London: Batchworth Press, 1953.
Barghoorn, Frederick C., *The Soviet Image of the United States: A Study in Distortion.* New York: Harcourt, Brace and Company, 1950.
Bart, Peter, "Advertising: Soviets Turn to Salesmanship," *New York Times,* June 12, 1962.
———, "Advertising Ban on Cut-Rate Subscriptions," *New York Times,* Apr. 5, 1962.
———, "Soviet Copy is Mostly Solemn," *New York Times,* Feb. 21, 1962.
Bassow, Whitman, "The Pre-Revolutionary *Pravda* and Tsarist Censorship," *The American Slavic and East European Review,* Vol. XIII, 1954.
Bauer, Raymond A., and others, *How the Soviet System Works.* New York: Vintage Books, 1960.
Beazley, Charles Raymond, and others, *Russia from the Varangians to the Bolsheviks.* Oxford: Clarendon Press, 1918.
Benton, William, *This Is the Challenge.* Edward W. Barrett, ed. New York: Associated College Presses, 1958.
Berdyaev, Nikolai Alexandrovich, *Origin of Russian Communism.* London: G. Bles, The Centenary Press, 1937.

Blake, Patricia, and Max Hayward, eds., *Dissonant Voices in Soviet Literature*. New York: Pantheon Books, 1962.

Bolshaia Sovetskaia Entsiklopediia. Moscow: 1950–1958. 51 vols.

Brown, Deming, "Muffled Voice of Russian Liberalism," *New York Times Magazine,* Dec. 18, 1965.

Campbell, Robert W., "Economics: Roads and Inroads," *Problems of Communism,* Vol. XIV, No. 6, Nov.-Dec. 1965.

Cantril, Hadley, *Soviet Leaders and Mastery Over Man*. New Brunswick: Rutgers Univ. Press, 1960.

Carr, E. H., "Historical Background of the Russian Revolution," in Alex Inkeles and Kent Geiger, eds., *Soviet Society*. Boston: Houghton Mifflin Co., 1961.

Cherniavsky, Michael, *Tsar and People: Studies in Russian Myths*. New Haven and London: Yale Univ. Press, 1961.

Clarkson, Jesse D., *A History of Russia*. New York: Random House, 1961.

Current Digest of the Soviet Press. Washington: Joint Committee of Slavic Studies, 1949–1963, *passim*. 15 vols.

Dallin, David, *The Changing World of Soviet Russia*. New Haven: Yale Univ. Press, 1956.

Dizard, Wilson P., "Television in the USSR," *Problems of Communism,* Vol. XII, No. 6, Nov.-Dec. 1963.

Crankshaw, Edward, "Installment Buying and Advertising," London *Observer* Service as published in the Harrisburg, Pa., *Patriot-News,* Apr. 17, 1960.

———, *Russia Without Stalin: The Emerging Pattern*. New York: The Viking Press, 1956.

Dobrolyubov, N. A., *Selected Philosophical Essays*. Moscow: Foreign Languages Publishing House, 1948. Vol. I.

Durant, Kenneth, "Russia," *Journalism Quarterly,* Vol. XIV, No. 1, Mar. 1937.

Durham, F. Gayle, *Radio and Television in the Soviet Union*. Cambridge: The Center for International Studies, M.I.T., 1965.

Eaton, William J., "Red Editor: Alexei Adzhubei," *Nieman Reports,* Vol. XVI, No. 2, June 1963.

Ehrenburg, Ilya, *The Thaw*. Chicago: Henry Regnery Company, 1955.

Fainsod, Merle, "Censorship in the USSR—A Documented Record," *Problems of Communism,* Vol. V, No. 2, Mar.-Apr. 1956.

———, *How Russia Is Ruled*. Cambridge: Harvard Univ. Press, 1953.

Fitzsimmons, Thomas, and others, *USSR: Its People, Its Society, Its Culture*. New Haven: HRAF Press, 1960.

Florinsky, Michael T., *Russia: A History and an Interpretation*. New York: The MacMillan Co., 1953. 2 vols.

Frankel, Max, "Russia, Revisited, Is Still a Mystery," *New York Times Magazine,* Sept. 15, 1963.

Frankel, Tobia, "Matchbox Messages," *New York Times Magazine,* Mar. 8, 1959.

———, "Sovietski Ekran," *New York Times Magazine,* Mar. 15, 1959.

Frankland, Mark, "Khrushchev Faces a Khrushchevian Dilemma," *New York Times Magazine,* May 12, 1963.

Friedberg, Maurice, "Keeping Up with the Censor," *Problems of Communism,* Vol. XIII, No. 6, Nov.-Dec. 1964.

Goldman, Marshall I., "Marketing Lessons for Marx," *Harvard Business Review,* Vol. XXVIII, Jan.-Feb. 1960.

———, "New Perspective of Product Differentiation and Advertising, the Soviet View," *Boston University Business Review,* Vol. VIII, Spring 1962.

Gordey, Michel, "What You Can Read in Russia," *Harper's Magazine,* April, 1952.

Gorokhoff, Boris I., *Publishing in the U.S.S.R.* Bloomington: Ind. State Univ. Research Center in Anthropology, Folklore, and Linguistics, 1959.

Gruliow, Leo, "Advertising—USSR," in *Collier's Encyclopedia.* New York, 1962, Vol. I.

———, "How the Soviet Newspaper Operates," *Problems of Communism,* Vol. V, No. 2, Mar.-Apr. 1956.

———, "What the Soviet Reader Never Knew," *IPI Report,* Vol. XI, No. 8, Dec. 1962.

———, ed., *Current Soviet Policies II, The Documentary Record of the 20th Communist Party Congress and Its Aftermath.* New York: Frederick A. Praeger, Inc., 1957.

Gsovski, V., *Soviet Civil Law.* Ann Arbor, 1948, Vol. I.

Gunther, John, *Inside Russia Today.* Rev. Ed. New York: Harper and Row, 1962.

Harris, Chauncey D., "Industrial and Agricultural Resources," in Alex Inkeles and Kent Geiger, eds., *Soviet Society: A Book of Readings.* Boston: Houghton Mifflin Co., 1961.

Herzen, Alexander, *My Past and Thoughts: The Memoirs of Alexander Herzen.* London: Chatto & Windus, Ltd., 1924–1927.

Hopkins, Mark W., "Newspapers Sprout All Over Russia," *Editor & Publisher,* Jan. 30, 1960.

———, "Soviet Press Prodded to Improve and Grow," *Editor & Publisher,* Nov. 12, 1960.

Inkeles, Alex, *Public Opinion in Soviet Russia: A Study in Mass Persuasion.* Cambridge: Harvard Univ. Press, 1950, 1958.

———, and Raymond A. Bauer, *The Soviet Citizen.* Cambridge: Harvard Univ. Press, 1959.

———, and Kent Geiger, "Critical Letters to the Editors of the Soviet Press," *Sociological Review,* Vol. XVII, Dec. 1952, and Vol. XVIII, Feb. 1953.

———, eds., *Soviet Society: A Book of Readings.* Boston: Houghton Mifflin Co., 1961.

IPI Survey, *The News from Russia.* Zurich: International Press Institute, 1952.

"It's Hard, but a Company Can Advertise in Russia," *New York Times,* June 10, 1960.

Jaryc, Marc, *The Press and Publishing in the Soviet Union.* London: School of Slavonic and East European Studies in the Univ. of London, 1935.

Jorden, William J., " 'Fit to Print'—Moscow's Formula," *New York Times Magazine,* Dec. 29, 1957.

Kalb, Marvin, "Now Russia's 'Angry Young Poets,' " *New York Times Magazine,* Dec. 31, 1961.

Kantner, John F., "A Comparison of the Current Population in the U.S.S.R. and U.S.A.," in Alex Inkeles and Kent Geiger, eds., *Soviet Society: A Book of Readings.* Boston: Houghton Mifflin Co., 1961.

Kassof, Allen, "Now the Angry Young Ivans," *New York Times Magazine,* Nov. 19, 1961.

Kennan, George F., *Russia and the West Under Lenin and Stalin.* Boston: Atlantic-Little, Brown, 1961.

Khrushchev, Nikita S., "Khrushchev Lays Down the Line on the Arts" (A Summary from Recent Speeches), *New York Times Magazine,* Sept. 29, 1957.

Kluge, Ernfried Eduard, *Die Russiche Revolutionäre Presse in der Zweiten Halfte der Neunzehnten Jahrhunderts, 1855–1905.* Zurich: Artemis-Verlag, 1948.

Kornilov, Alexander, *Modern Russian History.* New York: The Borzoi, A. A. Knopf, 1917.

Kosa, John, *Two Generations of Soviet Man: A Study in the Psychology of Communism.* Chapel Hill: Univ. of N.C. Press, 1962.

Kravchinskii, Sergei Mikhailovich (Stepniak), *Russia Under the Tsars.* New York: Charles Scribner's Sons, 1885.

Kruglak, Theodore E., *The Two Faces of TASS.* Minneapolis: Univ. of Minn. Press, 1962.

Kuznetsov, Mikhail, "The Work, the Writer, and the Public," *Sovetskaya Pechat,* No. 7, July 1962.

Labor, Jeri, "The Soviet Writer's Search for New Values," *Problems of Communism,* Vol. V, No. 1, Jan.-Feb. 1956.

Lenin, V. I., *Collected Works.* New York: International Publishers, 1927.

———, *On the International Working-Class and Communist Movement.* Moscow: Foreign Languages Publishing House, 1960.

Leonhard, Wolfgang, *The Kremlin Since Stalin.* New York: Frederick A. Praeger, Inc., 1962. German Edition, Cologne: Verlag fur Politik und Wirtschaft, 1959.

Levine, Irving R., *Main Street U.S.S.R.* Garden City, N.Y.: Doubleday, 1959.

Levitsky, Serge L. "Soviet Law and the Press," *Journalism Quarterly,* Vol. XXXIV, No. 1, Winter 1957.

Lorimer, Frank, "Trends in Soviet Population History," in Alex Inkeles and Kent Geiger, eds., *Soviet Society: A Book of Readings.* Boston: Houghton Mifflin Co., 1961.

Mannes, Marya, "A Word from Our Sponsor—The Kremlin," *New York Times Magazine,* Mar. 5, 1961.

Markham, James W., "Effects of the *Thaw* on the Soviet Press," *Journalism Quarterly,* Vol. XXXVIII, No. 4, Autumn 1961.

———, "Is Advertising Important in the Soviet Economy?" *Journal of Marketing,* Vol. XXVIII, No. 2, Apr. 1964.

Masaryk, Tomas G., *The Spirit of Russia.* London: G. Allen & Unwin, Ltd., 1919. 2 vols.

Mazour, Anatole G., *Russia Past and Present.* New York: D. Van Nostrand Company, Inc., 1951.

McGraw-Hill Encyclopedia of Russia and the Soviet Union. Michael T. Florinsky, ed. New York: McGraw-Hill Book Co., Inc., 1961.

McNeal, Robert H., "Introduction," in Sergei Pushkarev, *The Emergence of Modern Russia, 1801–1917.* New York: Rhinehart and Winston, 1963.

Mead, Margaret, *Soviet Attitudes toward Authority.* New York: The Rand Corporation, 1951.

Meissner, Boris, *The Communist Party of the Soviet Union* (with a chapter on the Twentieth Party Congress by John S. Reshetar, Jr.). New York: Frederick A. Praeger, Inc., 1956.

Miliukov, Paul, *Outlines of Russian Culture.* Philadelphia: Univ. of Pa. Press, 1948.

Mosely, Philip E., "How the Kremlin Keeps Ivan in Line," *New York Times Magazine,* Feb. 19, 1961.

Nechkina, M. V., *Russia in the Nineteenth Century.* Ann Arbor: Univ. of Mich. Press, 1953.

Nelson, William, ed., *Out of the Crocodile's Mouth: Russian Cartoons about the U.S. from "Krokodil," Moscow's Humor Magazine.* Washington: Public Affairs Press, 1949.

Olson, Kenneth E., *The History Makers: The Press of Europe From Its Beginnings Through 1965.* Baton Rouge: La. State Univ. Press, 1966.

"Opiate of the Masses," *Newsweek,* Mar. 8, 1965.

Oppenheimer, Max, Jr., "Some Linguistic Aspects of Mind Conditioning by the Soviet Press," *Journal of Human Relations,* Vol. X, No. 1, 1962.

"Outdoor and Newspaper Advertising Grows," *New York Times,* Nov. 28, 1948.

Palgunov, N. G., *Osnovii Informatzii v Gazetta: Tass i evo Rol.* Moscow: Moscow State Univ., 1955.

Pares, Bernard, *A History of Russia.* New York: Alfred A. Knopf, 1953.

Periodicals of the USSR. Moscow: V/O "Mezhdunarodnaya Kniga," 1962.

Pipes, Richard, ed., *The Russian Intelligentsia.* New York: Columbia Univ. Press, 1961.

Plekhanov, George, *Selected Philosophical Works.* Moscow: Foreign Languages Publishing House, 1960. 5 vols.

Popov, Nikolai, *Outline History of the Communist Party of the Soviet Union.* New York: International Publishers, 1934. 2 vols.

Possony, Stefan T., *Wordmanship, Semantics as a Communist Weapon.* Committee on The Judiciary, U.S. Senate, 87th Cong., 2nd Sess., Washington, 1961.

Pushkarev, Sergei, *The Emergence of Modern Russia 1801–1917.* New York: Holt, Rinehart and Winston, 1963.

Rambaud, Alfred, *A Popular History of Russia, from the Earliest Times to 1880.* Boston: Dana Estes and Charles E. Lauriat, 1880. 3 vols.

Reddick, DeWitt, "Development of the Press in Nineteenth Century Russia," *Journalism Quarterly,* Vol. XXI, No. 1, Mar. 1944.

Rigov, Audun, "Evgeny Evtushenko—Opposition with Permission," *Studies on the Soviet Union,* New Series, Vol. II, No. 2, 1962.

Robinson, Geroid Tanquary, *Rural Russia Under the Old Regime.* New York: The Macmillan Co., 1949.

Rogger, Hans, *National Consciousness in Eighteenth-Century Russia.* Cambridge: Harvard Univ. Press, 1960.

Rostow, Walt Whitman, and others, *The Dynamics of Soviet Society.* New York: New American Library, 1954.

Rothstein, Andrew, ed., *History of the Communist Party of the Soviet Union.* Moscow: Foreign Languages Publishing House, 1960.

"Russia Thinks About Advertising," *The Times,* London, Feb. 24, 1961.

"Russians Copying Madison Avenue," *New York Times,* Oct. 2, 1960.

Salisbury, Harrison E., *American in Russia.* New York: Harper & Brothers, 1955.

———, *A New Russia?* New York: Harper & Brothers, 1962.

———, "The Poets Versus the Commissars," *New York Times Book Review,* Apr. 15, 1962.

———, "Red China Against Russia?" *The Saturday Evening Post,* Mar. 19, 1960.

Schwartz, Harry, "Editor in Soviet Defends Writers," *New York Times,* May 19, 1963.

Seton-Watson, Hugh, *The Decline of Imperial Russia, 1855–1914*. London: Methuen & Co., Ltd., and New York: Frederick A. Praeger, Inc., 1952.
Shabad, Theodore, "Behind the Smile on Krokodil," *New York Times Magazine,* June 7, 1964.
———, "Soviet May Adopt Profit Incentive to Spur Output," *New York Times,* Oct. 14, 1962.
Shub, David, *Lenin: A Biography*. Garden City, N.Y.: Doubleday, 1948.
Shulman, Marshall D., "Since Stalin: Have Things Changed?" *New York Times Magazine,* Mar. 19, 1961.
Slonim, Marc, "Some Russians Want to Write as They Please," *New York Times Book Review,* Oct. 27, 1963.
The Soviet Press, Vol. V, No. 1, Spring 1966.
The Soviet Press in Translation. Madison: Univ. of Wis., 1959–1963.
Swayne, Elizabeth, "Soviet Advertising: Communism Imitates Capitalism," in C. H. Sandage and Vernon Fryburger, eds., *The Role of Advertising*. Homewood, Ill.: Richard D. Irwin, Inc., 1960.
Swayze, Harold, *Political Control of Literature in the U.S.S.R., 1946–59*. Cambridge: Harvard Univ. Press, 1962.
Tanner, Henry, "Eased Line on Arts in Soviet Is Hinted by Two New Works," *New York Times,* Aug. 18, 1963.
Tompkins, Stuart Ramsay, *The Russian Intelligentsia: Makers of the Revolutionary State*. Norman: Univ. of Okla. Press, 1957.
———, *The Russian Mind: From Peter the Great Through the Enlightenment*. Norman: Univ. of Okla. Press, 1953.
Topping, Seymour, "Khrushchev's Culture," *New York Times,* Apr. 14, 1963.
The Training of Journalists. Paris: Unesco, 1958.
Tuber, Richard, "A Survey of Programming on the Central Studios of Television, Moscow, U.S.S.R. Jan.–June, 1960," *Journal of Broadcasting,* Vol. IV, No. 4, Fall 1960.
Turkevich, Ludmilla B., "Soviet Literary Periodicals," *Books Abroad,* Vol. XXXII, No. 4, Autumn 1958.
Ugolovny Kodeks RSFSR (The Criminal Code of the R. S. F. S. R.). Moscow: 1953.
Ulam, Adam B., *The New Face of Soviet Totalitarianism*. Cambridge: Harvard Univ. Press, 1963.
Venturi, Franco, *Roots of Revolution: A History of the Populist and Socialist Movements in Nineteenth Century Russia*. London: Weidenfeld and Nicolson, 1952.
Vernadsky, George, *A History of Russia*. New Haven: Yale Univ. Press, 1929.
Vichnevski, Alexander, "A Soviet Point of View," in *The Responsibility of Journalists in International Understanding, Journalism Quarterly Review,* No. 22.
Vyshinsky, Andrei, *The Law of the Soviet State,* New York: The Macmillan Co., 1948.
Wallace, Donald McKenzie, *Russia*. New York: Henry Holt & Co., 1905.
Walsh, Warren B., *Readings in Russian History*. Syracuse: Syracuse Univ. Press, 1948.
Wesselitsky, Gabriel de, *Russia and Democracy*. London: W. Heineman, 1915.
Whiteside, Duncan, "Visit to a Russian Village," *New York Times Magazine,* Dec. 8, 1963.
Wilder, Emilia, "Opinion Polls," *Survey, A Journal of Soviet and East European Studies,* No. 48, July 1963.

Williams, Frederick, "The Soviet Philosophy of Broadcasting," *Journal of Broadcasting,* Vol. VI, No. 1, Winter 1961–1962.
Zeibarth, E. W., "Electronic Media in the Soviet Union," *Quarterly Journal of Speech,* Vol. XLIV, Oct. 1959.

CHINA, ANCIENT AND MODERN

Books, Articles, and Periodicals

Barnett, A. Doak, "Mao's Aim: To Capture 600 Million Minds," *New York Times Magazine,* Sept. 9, 1956.
Britton, Roswell S., *The Chinese Periodical Press, 1800–1912.* Shanghai: Kelly & Walsh, Ltd., 1933.
Callis, Helmut G., *China, Confucian and Communist.* New York: Henry Holt and Company, 1959.
Catalogue of Mainland Chinese Magazines and Newspapers Held by the Union Research Institute. 2nd Ed. Hong Kong: Union Research Institute, 1963.
Chandra-sekhar, Sripati, "The Human Inflation of Red China," *New York Times Magazine,* Dec. 6, 1959.
———, *Red China, An Asian View.* New York: Frederick A. Praeger, 1961.
Chao, Chung, *The Communist Program for Literature and Art in China.* Hong Kong: Union Research Institute, 1955.
Chen, James C. Y., *Liang Chi-chao and His Times.* Columbia: Unpublished Dissertation, Univ. of Mo., 1953.
Chen, Theodore H. E., *Thought Reform of the Chinese Intellectuals.* Hong Kong: Hong Kong Univ. Press, 1960.
China Handbook, 1937–43. New York: The Macmillan Company, 1943.
Chiao, Theodore Tse-Hou, *The Value Constellations of the Red Chinese People: A Study of Audience Characteristics in International Communications.* Minneapolis: Unpublished Thesis, Univ. of Minn., 1962.
Chinese People's Republic, Bureau of Statistics, *Official Bulletins* for 1952, 1954, 1955, and 1956.
Chipp, David, "How 650 Million Chinese Are Controlled," *New York Times Magazine,* Sept. 14, 1958.
Chu, Valentin, *Ta Ta, Tan Tan.* New York: W. W. Norton and Co., 1963.
Clark, Gerald, *The Impatient Giant.* New York: D. McKay Co., 1959.
Creel, H. G., *Chinese Thought from Confucius to Mao Tse-Tung.* Chicago: Univ. of Chicago Press, 1953. New York: Mentor Books Edition, 1960.
Durdin, Peggy, "Chinese Village: Then and Now," *New York Times Magazine,* Oct. 22, 1961.
Edelstein, Alex, and Alan P. L. Liu, "Anti-Americanism in Red China's *People's Daily:* A Functional Analysis," *Journalism Quarterly,* Vol. XL, No. 2, Spring 1963, pp. 194–95.
Encyclopedia Sinica, Samuel Goulding, ed., London: Oxford Univ. Press, 1917.
Fairbank, John K., *The United States and China.* Cambridge: Harvard Univ. Press, 1958.
Greene, Felix, *Awakened China: The Country Americans Don't Know.* Garden City, N. Y.: Doubleday, 1961.
Guillain, Robert, *600 Million Chinese.* New York: Criterion Books, Inc., 1957.
Hirth, Friederich, *The Ancient History of China; to the End of the Chou Dynasty.* New York: Columbia Univ. Press, 1908.
Houn, Franklin W., "The Press in Communist China: Its Structure and Operation," *Journalism Quarterly,* Vol. XXXIII, No. 4, Fall 1956.

———, "Radio Broadcasting and Propaganda in Communist China," *Journalism Quarterly,* Vol. XXXIV, No. 3, Summer 1957.

———, *To Change A Nation: Propaganda and Indoctrination in Communist China.* New York: Crowell-Collier Publishing Co., 1961.

Hu, Chang-tu, and others, *China, Its People, Its Society, Its Culture.* New Haven: HRAF Press, 1960.

Hughes, Richard, "China Makes a Bitter Retreat," *New York Times Magazine,* July 15, 1962.

———, "What 'Dateline Peiping,' Means," *New York Times Magazine,* June 23, 1957.

Jen-min Sou-che (The People's Handbook), 1951, 1955.

Ko, Kung-chen, *Chung-kuo Pao-hsüeh Shih* (The History of Chinese Journalism). Shanghai: The Commercial Press, 1927.

Lee, Chan, *Shih Chieh Hsin Hwen Hsieh* (History of World Journalism). Taipei: n. pub., 1963. 3 vols.

Levenson, Joseph R., *Confucian China and Its Modern Fate.* Berkeley and Los Angeles: Univ. of Calif. Press, 1958.

Levi, Werner, *Modern China's Foreign Policy.* Minneapolis: Univ. of Minn. Press, 1953.

Lifton, Robert Jay, *Thought Reform and the Psychology of Totalism.* New York: W. W. Norton Co., 1961.

Lin Yutang, *A History of the Press and Public Opinion in China.* Chicago: Univ. of Chicago Press, 1936.

Lindsay, Michael, "Chinese Puzzle: Mao's Foreign Policy," *New York Times Magazine,* Oct. 12, 1958.

Liu, Alan P. L., *Radio Broadcasting in Communist China.* Cambridge: The Center for International Studies, M.I.T., 1964.

Mende, Tibor, *China and Her Shadow.* London: Thames & Hudson, 1960.

Mu, Fu-sheng, *The Wilting of the Hundred Flowers: The Chinese Intelligentsia under Mao.* New York: Frederick A. Praeger, 1962.

Nunn, G. Raymond, *Publishing in Mainland China.* Cambridge: M.I.T. Rept. No. 4, 1966.

Oliphant, C. A., "The Image of the United States Projected by *Peking Review,*" *Journalism Quarterly,* Vol. XLI, No. 3, Summer 1964.

Patterson, Don D., *The Journalism of China.* Columbia: Univ. of Mo. Journalism Series, No. 26, 1922.

Powell, John B., *My Twenty-five Years in China.* New York: The Macmillan Co., 1945.

Scott, John, *Crisis in Communist China.* New York: Time, Inc., 1962.

Shieh, Milton, "Red China Patterns Controls of Press on Russian Model," *Journalism Quarterly,* Vol. XXVIII, No. 1, Winter 1951.

Snow, Edgar, *The Other Side of the River: Red China Today.* New York: Random House, 1961.

Tang, Peter S. H., *Communist China Today.* New York: Frederick A. Praeger, 1957.

Tong, Hollington K., *China and the World Press.* Nanking: n.pub., 1948.

Walker, Richard L., *China Under Communism: The First Five Years.* New Haven: Yale Univ. Press, 1955.

Wang, Y. P., *The Rise of the Native Press in China.* New York: Columbia Univ. Press, 1924.

Wei-da De Shih-nien (The Great Ten Years). Peking: Foreign Language Press, 1960.

Williams, S. Wells, *The Middle Kingdom.* Rev. Ed. London: Allen & Unwin, 1883.

Wu, Yuan-li, "Press Regulation in Mao's China," *Problems of Communism,* Vol. VI, No. 4, July-Aug. 1957.

Yao, Ignatius Peng, "The New China News Agency: How It Serves the Party," *Journalism Quarterly,* Vol. XL, No. 1, Winter 1963.

Yu, Frederick T. C., "How the Chinese Reds Transfer Mass Grievances into Power," *Journalism Quarterly,* Vol. XXX, No. 2, Summer 1953.

———, *Mass Persuasion in Communist China.* New York: Frederick A. Praeger, 1964.

Yuan, Chang-chao, *Chung-kuo Pao Yeh Hsiao Shih* (A Brief History of Chinese Journalism). Hong Kong. Hsin Wen Tien ti She, 1957.

INDEX

F

G

H

I

J

M

N

O

P

R

S

T

U

V

W

Y

Z